FLORIDA AND FEDERAL EVIDENCE RULES

WITH COMMENTARY

2012-2013

FLORIDA AND FEDERAL EVIDENCE RULES
WITH COMMENTARY
2012-2013

Peter Nicolas

Jeffrey & Susan Brotman Professor of Law

University of Washington School of Law

Wolters Kluwer

Law & Business

Published by Wolters Kluwer Law & Business in New York.

Wolters Kluwer Law & Business serves customers worldwide with CCH, Aspen Publishers, and Kluwer Law International products. (www.wolterskluwerlb.com)

To contact Customer Service, e-mail customer.service@wolterskluwer.com, call 1-800-234-1660, fax 1-800-901-9075, or mail correspondence to:

Wolters Kluwer Law & Business Attn: Order Department PO Box 990 Frederick, MD 21705

Printed in the United States of America.

1234567890

ISBN 978-1-4548-3078-8

About Wolters Kluwer Law & Business

Wolters Kluwer Law & Business is a leading provider of research information and workflow solutions in key specialty areas. The strengths of the individual brands of Aspen Publishers, CCH, Kluwer Law International and Loislaw are aligned within Wolters Kluwer Law & Business to provide comprehensive, in-depth solutions and expert-authored content for the legal, professional and education markets.

CCH was founded in 1913 and has served more than four generations of business professionals and their clients. The CCH products in the Wolters Kluwer Law & Business group are highly regarded electronic and print resources for legal, securities, antitrust and trade regulation, government contracting, banking, pension, payroll, employment and labor, and healthcare reimbursement and compliance professionals.

Aspen Publishers is a leading information provider for attorneys, business professionals and law students. Written by preeminent authorities, Aspen products offer analytical and practical information in a range of specialty practice areas from securities law and intellectual property to mergers and acquisitions and pension/benefits. Aspen's trusted legal education resources provide professors and students with high-quality, up-to-date and effective resources for successful instruction and study in all areas of the law.

Kluwer Law International supplies the global business community with comprehensive English-language international legal information. Legal practitioners, corporate counsel and business executives around the world rely on the Kluwer Law International journals, loose-leafs, books and electronic products for authoritative information in many areas of international legal practice.

Loislaw is a premier provider of digitized legal content to small law firm practitioners of various specializations. Loislaw provides attorneys with the ability to quickly and efficiently find the necessary legal information they need, when and where they need it, by facilitating access to primary law as well as state-specific law, records, forms and treatises.

Wolters Kluwer Law & Business, a unit of Wolters Kluwer, is headquartered in New York and Riverwoods, Illinois. Wolters Kluwer is a leading multinational publisher and information services company.

To my brother, Alex

PREFACE

Florida and Federal Evidence Rules, With Commentary, is designed to help both students and practitioners learn the differences between the Federal Rules of Evidence and the Florida Evidence Code.

The book is organized in the same order as are the Federal Rules of Evidence. The full text of each Federal Rule of Evidence is followed by its legislative history, which in turn is followed by the corresponding provision in the Florida Evidence Code and its legislative history. Following each federal and Florida rule pairing is detailed commentary explaining the similarities and differences between the federal rule and its Florida law counterpart, with citations to key federal and Florida case law. Whenever possible, citations to Eleventh Circuit decisions—which are binding on federal courts in Florida—are included in the commentary.

The book is divided into eleven sections that correspond to the eleven articles of the Federal Rules of Evidence. At the beginning of each section is a correlation table that makes it easy for you to find the corresponding provision of the Florida Evidence Code if you know the federal rule number, and vice versa.

This edition of the book includes the restyled text of the Federal Rules of Evidence, which took effect on December 1, 2011. It also includes the 2011 amendment to Section 90.404 of the Florida Evidence Code (addressing the admissibility of evidence of prior sex offenses), as well as newly enacted Section 90.5021 of the Florida Evidence Code (codifying the fiduciary lawyer-client privilege).

My goal is that you will find this book well-suited to your purpose whether you are using it in a law school course in evidence, as an aid in studying for the Florida bar examination, or as a practicing lawyer litigating cases in both federal and state courts in Florida. Should you have any comments or suggestions for future editions of this book, I invite you to contact me via e-mail at pnicolas@uw.edu.

I wish to thank the following individuals for providing me with valuable assistance in preparing this book:

Aspen Publishers Personnel: Jen Armstrong, Lynn Churchill, Carolyn Czick, Taylor Kearns, Roberta O'Meara, and Barbara Roth.

Florida State Archives Personnel: Boyd Murphree.

Library Personnel: Judy Davis and Mary Whisner of the University of Washington Gallagher Law Library, and Yvonne Parks and Patricia Simonds of the Florida State University College of Law Library.

Secretarial Assistant: Wendy Condiotty.

Student Assistants (prior editions): La Rond Baker, Alexander Casey, Blythe Chandler, Scott I. Fitzgerald, Sarah R. Kermgard, Jenny Houghton McAuliffe, and John M. Peterson.

Student Assistants (2012-2013 edition): Chris Olah, Walter Smith.

Peter Nicolas
Jeffrey & Susan Brotman Professor of Law
University of Washington School of Law
January 2012

CONTENTS

ARTICLE I. GENERAL PROVISIONS

Federal Rule	Florida Stat. §	Description
101	90.103	Scope; Definitions
102	90.102	Purpose
103	90.104	Rulings on Evidence
104	90.105	Preliminary Questions
105	90.107	Limiting Evidence That Is Not Admissible Against Other Parties or for Other Purposes
106	90.108	Remainder of or Related Writings or Recorded Statements
—	90.106	Summing Up and Comment by Judge

Federal Rule 101. Scope; Definitions

(a) Scope. These rules apply to proceedings in United States courts. The specific courts and proceedings to which the rules apply, along with exceptions, are set out in Rule 1101.

(b) Definitions. In these rules:

(1) "civil case" means a civil action or proceeding;

(2) "criminal case" includes a criminal proceeding;

(3) "public office" includes a public agency;

(4) "record" includes a memorandum, report, or data compilation;

(5) a "rule prescribed by the Supreme Court" means a rule adopted by the Supreme Court under statutory authority; and

(6) a reference to any kind of written material or any other medium includes electronically stored information.

ADVISORY COMMITTEE'S NOTE

Rule 1101 specifies in detail the courts, proceedings, questions, and stages of proceedings to which the rules apply in whole or in part.

ADVISORY COMMITTEE'S NOTE (2011 AMENDMENT)

The language of Rule 101 has been amended, and definitions have been added, as part of the general restyling of the Evidence Rules to make them more easily understood and to make style and terminology consistent throughout the rules. These changes are intended to be stylistic only. There is no intent to change any result in any ruling on evidence admissibility.

The reference to electronically stored information is intended to track the language of Fed. R.Civ. P. 34.

The Style Project

The Evidence Rules are the fourth set of national procedural rules to be restyled. The restyled Rules of Appellate Procedure took effect in 1998. The restyled Rules of Criminal Procedure took effect in 2002. The restyled Rules of Civil Procedure took effect in 2007. The restyled Rules of Evidence apply the same general drafting guidelines and principles used in restyling the Appellate, Criminal, and Civil Rules.

1. General Guidelines

Guidance in drafting, usage, and style was provided by Bryan Garner, *Guidelines for Drafting and Editing Court Rules,* Administrative Office of the United States Courts (1969) and Bryan Garner, *Dictionary of Modern Legal Usage* (2d ed. 1995). *See also* Joseph Kimble, *Guiding Principles for Restyling the Civil Rules,* in *Preliminary Draft of Proposed Style Revision of the Federal Rules of Civil Procedure,* at page x (Feb. 2005) (available at
http://www.uscourts.gov/uscourts/RulesAndPolicies/rules/Prelim_draft_proposed_pt1.pdf);   Joseph Kimble, *Lessons in Drafting from the New Federal Rules of Civil Procedure,* 12 Scribes J. Legal Writing

25 (2008-2009). For specific commentary on the Evidence restyling project, see Joseph Kimble, *Drafting Examples from the Proposed New Federal Rules of Evidence*, 88 Mich. B.J. 52 (Aug. 2009); 88 Mich. B.J. 46 (Sept. 2009); 88 Mich. B.J. 54 (Oct. 2009); 88 Mich. B.J. 50 (Nov. 2009).

2. Formatting Changes

Many of the changes in the restyled Evidence Rules result from using format to achieve clearer presentations. The rules are broken down into constituent parts, using progressively indented subparagraphs with headings and substituting vertical for horizontal lists. "Hanging indents" are used throughout. These formatting changes make the structure of the rules graphic and make the restyled rules easier to read and understand even when the words are not changed. Rules 103, 404(b), 606(b), and 612 illustrate the benefits of formatting changes.

3. Changes to Reduce Inconsistent, Ambiguous, Redundant, Repetitive, or Archaic Words

The restyled rules reduce the use of inconsistent terms that say the same thing in different ways. Because different words are presumed to have different meanings, such inconsistencies can result in confusion. The restyled rules reduce inconsistencies by using the same words to express the same meaning. For example, consistent expression is achieved by not switching between "accused" and "defendant" or between "party opponent" and "opposing party" or between the various formulations of civil and criminal action/case/proceeding.

The restyled rules minimize the use of inherently ambiguous words. For example, the word "shall" can mean "must," "may," or something else, depending on context. The potential for confusion is exacerbated by the fact the word "shall" is no longer generally used in spoken or clearly written English. The restyled rules replace "shall" with "must," "may," or "should," depending on which one the context and established interpretation make correct in each rule.

The restyled rules minimize the use of redundant "intensifiers." These are expressions that attempt to add emphasis, but instead state the obvious and create negative implications for other rules. The absence of intensifiers in the restyled rules does not change their substantive meaning. *See, e.g.,* Rule 104(c) (omitting "in all cases"); Rule 602 (omitting "but need not"); Rule 611(b) (omitting "in the exercise of discretion").

The restyled rules also remove words and concepts that are outdated or redundant.

4. Rule Numbers

The restyled rules keep the same numbers to minimize the effect on research. Subdivisions have been rearranged within some rules to achieve greater clarity and simplicity.

5. No Substantive Change

The Committee made special efforts to reject any purported style improvement that might result in a substantive change in the application of a rule. The Committee considered a change to be "substantive" if any of the following conditions were met:

a. Under the existing practice in any circuit, the change could lead to a different result on a question of admissibility (e.g., a change that requires a court to provide either a less or more stringent standard in evaluating the admissibility of particular evidence);

b. Under the existing practice in any circuit, it could lead to a change in the procedure by which an admissibility decision is made (e.g., a change in the time in which an objection must be made, or a change in whether a court must hold a hearing on an admissibility question);

c. The change would restructure a rule in a way that would alter the approach that courts and litigants have used to think about, and argue about, questions of admissibility (e.g., merging Rules 104(a) and 104(b) into a single subdivision); or

d. The amendment would change a "sacred phrase" — one that has become so familiar in practice that to alter it would be unduly disruptive to practice and expectations. Examples in the Evidence Rules include "unfair prejudice" and "truth of the matter asserted."

Florida Stat. § 90.103. Scope; Applicability

(1) Unless otherwise provided by statute, this code applies to the same proceedings that the general law of evidence applied to before the effective date of this code.

(2) This act shall apply to criminal proceedings related to crimes committed after the effective date of this code and to civil actions and all other proceedings pending on or brought after October 1, 1981.

(3) Nothing in this act shall operate to repeal or modify the parol evidence rule.

COMMENTARY ON FEDERAL AND FLORIDA RULE DIFFERENCES

Florida Stat. § 90.103 and its federal counterpart, Federal Rule 101, delineate in general terms the types of proceedings to which the Florida Evidence Code and the Federal Rules of Evidence, respectively, are applicable. In addition, Federal Rule 101 sets forth definitions of common phrases used throughout the Federal Rules of Evidence.

Federal Rule 101 provides that the rules are applicable in proceedings taking place in federal court, subject to exceptions set forth in Federal Rule 1101. The latter rule, examined below, sets forth in detail those types of proceedings in which the federal rules (save for those governing privileges) are inapplicable and those types in which they are applicable only in part. In addition, some Federal Rules of Evidence are, by their terms, applicable only in certain types of proceedings, or provide for different rules in different types of proceedings. See, e.g., FED. R. EVID. 803(8)(A)(ii)-(iii).

Unlike Federal Rule 101 (with its cross-reference to Federal Rule 1101), the Florida Code does not delineate the types of proceedings to which it does and does not apply. Rather, Florida Stat. § 90.103(1) merely states that (unless otherwise provided by law) the Florida Evidence Code applies to those proceedings to which it applied before the date when the Code was enacted. Thus, when engaged in specialized types of proceedings in Florida state courts—such as family law or probate—one must look to the statutory provisions or specific rules governing those types of proceedings, or to judicial precedent, to determine whether and the extent to which the Florida Evidence Code governs. See, e.g., FLA. FAM. L. R. P. 12.010(a)(2) ("All actions governed by these [family law] rules shall also be governed by the Florida Evidence Code, which shall govern in cases where a conflict with these rules may occur."); Eaton Corp. v. Votour, 895 So. 2d 466, 468 (Fla. 1st DCA 2005) (holding Florida Evidence Code applies in workers' compensation proceedings); Fleitas v. State, 835 So. 2d 376, 377 (Fla. 3d DCA 2003) ("A probation violation hearing is subject to the same Florida Evidence Code as any other hearing with the exception that hearsay is admissible."). Moreover, certain provisions of the Florida Evidence Code are, by their terms, applicable only in civil cases. See, e.g., FLA. STAT. § 90.301(4).

Pursuant to § 90.103(2) of the Florida Evidence Code, the provisions of the Florida Evidence Code apply to all non-criminal proceedings pending on or brought after October 1, 1981. However, for criminal proceedings, the Florida Evidence Code is applicable only if the crime itself was committed after the effective date of the Code, July 1, 1979. See, e.g., Mangram v. State, 392 So. 2d 596, 597 (Fla. 1st DCA 1981). By contrast, the effective date of the Federal Rules of Evidence was July 1, 1975, and the Federal Rules are made applicable to cases brought subsequent to that date as well as to further proceedings in those cases then pending unless doing so "would not be feasible or would work injustice." Pub. L. No. 93-595, 88 Stat. 1926 (1975). Thus, in federal court— even in criminal cases—the date on which the underlying crime was committed is not relevant in determining the applicability of the Federal Rules.

Finally, § 90.103(3) of the Florida Evidence Code makes clear that the parol evidence rule is a rule of substantive law and not in any way repealed, modified, or governed by the Evidence Code. While Federal Rule 101 makes no reference to the parol evidence rule, federal case law likewise treats the parol evidence rule as a substantive rule of law and not an evidentiary rule. *See, e.g., MCC-Marble Ceramic Ctr., Inc. v. Ceramica Nuova d'Agostino, S.p.A.*, 144 F.3d 1384, 1388-89 (11th Cir. 1998); *Southern Stone Co. v. Singer*, 665 F.2d 698, 701 (5th Cir. 1982).

Federal Rule 102. Purpose

These rules should be construed so as to administer every proceeding fairly, eliminate unjustifiable expense and delay, and promote the development of evidence law, to the end of ascertaining the truth and securing a just determination.

ADVISORY COMMITTEE'S NOTE

For similar provisions see Rule 2 of the Federal Rules of Criminal Procedure, Rule 1 of the Federal Rules of Civil Procedure, California Evidence Code § 2, and New Jersey Evidence Rule 5.

ADVISORY COMMITTEE'S NOTE (2011 AMENDMENT)

The language of Rule 102 has been amended as part of the restyling of the Evidence Rules to make them more easily understood and to make style and terminology consistent throughout the rules. These changes are intended to be stylistic only. There is no intent to change any result in any ruling on evidence admissibility.

Florida Stat. § 90.102. Construction

This chapter shall replace and supersede existing statutory or common law in conflict with its provisions.

COMMENTARY ON FEDERAL AND FLORIDA RULE DIFFERENCES

Federal Rule 102 sets forth as a principle for interpreting the federal rules of evidence that they should be construed so as to ensure that proceedings are fairly yet efficiently administered and in a manner that will promote the ascertainment of the truth. When construing an ambiguous provision of the federal rules, federal courts will on occasion cite Rule 102 as support for an interpretation of the provision that the court believes will either promote the ascertainment of the truth or fairness in the administration of justice. *See, e.g., Holbrook v. Lykes Bros. S.S. Co.*, 80 F.3d 777, 782-783 & n.1 (3d Cir. 1996) (Rule 702's requirement that experts be qualified should not be interpreted in an unduly restrictive manner as doing so would unjustly increase litigation costs by requiring litigants to hire multiple experts to hedge their bets); *U.S. v. Panzardi-Lespier*, 918 F.2d 313, 317-18 (1st Cir. 1990) (holding that notice requirement for offering evidence under catchall exception to hearsay rule should not be interpreted so as to call for automatic exclusion of otherwise reliable evidence when not given in advance of trial but instead in a flexible manner that is consistent with the underlying goal of preventing surprise); *U.S. v. Licavoli*, 604 F.2d 613, 622-23 (9th Cir. 1979) (declining to adopt an "inflexible rule" that business records containing expert opinion are admissible only if the proponent establishes the expert's qualifications under Rule 702 in favor of a flexible approach that gives trial court discretion to exclude such records under the trustworthiness proviso of Rule 803(6) in cases in which expert's qualifications are in serious doubt).

Although the Florida Evidence Code contains no language analogous to that of Federal Rule 102, Florida case law likewise recognizes that the purpose underlying the Florida Evidence Code is the ascertainment of the truth. *See* Michael P. Dickey, *The Florida Evidence Code and the Separation of Powers Doctrine: How to Distinguish Substance and Procedure Now That it Matters*, 34 STETSON L. REV. 109, 141 & n.162 (2004).

Florida Stat. § 90.102 also provides that the Florida Evidence Code supersedes earlier statutory or common law in conflict with its provisions. However, because the Florida Evidence Code in large part represents a codification of the pre-existing common law, such decisions will often serve as useful aids in construing the meaning of provisions of the Florida Evidence Code. *See, e.g., Dean v. Dean*, 607 So. 2d 494, 497 (Fla. 4th DCA 1992). Secondary authority suggests that the Florida Evidence Code does not occupy the entire field of evidence law, and thus that if the Code does not address a matter, it is deemed not to have repealed pre-existing common law on that matter. *See* 1 CHARLES W. EHRHARDT, FLORIDA PRACTICE: EVIDENCE § 102.1 (2005). The Federal Rules of Evidence do not in terms address this issue. Like the Florida Evidence Code, the federal rules of evidence largely codify the pre-existing common law and thus such decisions serve as useful aids in construing their meaning, although to the extent the rules conflict with the pre-existing common law the former controls. Moreover, the federal rules of evidence are viewed as occupying the field of federal evidence law. *See Daubert v. Merrell Dow Pharm., Inc.*, 509 U.S. 579, 587-88 (1993) ("the Rules occupy the field, but...the common law nevertheless could serve as an aid to their application."); *U.S. v. Abel*, 469 U.S. 45, 51-52 (1984).

Federal Rule 103. Rulings on Evidence

(a) Preserving a Claim of Error. A party may claim error in a ruling to admit or exclude evidence only if the error affects a substantial right of the party and:

> **(1)** if the ruling admits evidence, a party, on the record:
>
>> **(A)** timely objects or moves to strike; and
>>
>> **(B)** states the specific ground, unless it was apparent from the context; or
>
> **(2)** if the ruling excludes evidence, a party informs the court of its substance by an offer of proof, unless the substance was apparent from the context.

(b) Not Needing to Renew an Objection or Offer of Proof. Once the court rules definitively on the record — either before or at trial — a party need not renew an objection or offer of proof to preserve a claim of error for appeal.

(c) Court's Statement About the Ruling; Directing an Offer of Proof. The court may make any statement about the character or form of the evidence, the objection made, and the ruling. The court may direct that an offer of proof be made in question-and-answer form.

(d) Preventing the Jury from Hearing Inadmissible Evidence. To the extent practicable, the court must conduct a jury trial so that inadmissible evidence is not suggested to the jury by any means.

(e) Taking Notice of Plain Error. A court may take notice of a plain error affecting a substantial right, even if the claim of error was not properly preserved.

ADVISORY COMMITTEE'S NOTE

Subdivision (a) states the law as generally accepted today. Rulings on evidence cannot be assigned as error unless (1) a substantial right is affected, and (2) the nature of the error was called to the attention of the judge, so as to alert him to the proper course of action and enable opposing counsel to take proper corrective measures. The objection and the offer of proof are the techniques for accomplishing these objectives. For similar provisions see Uniform Rules 4 and 5; California Evidence Code §§ 353 and 354; Kansas Code of Civil Procedure §§ 60-404 and 60-405. The rule does not purport to change the law with respect to harmless error. See 28 USC § 2111, F.R.Civ.P. 61, F.R.Crim.P. 52, and decisions construing them. The status of constitutional error as harmless or not is treated in Chapman v. California, 386 U.S. 18 (1967), reh. denied *id.* 987.

Subdivision ([c][1]). The first sentence is the third sentence of Rule 43(c) of the Federal Rules of Civil Procedure virtually verbatim. Its purpose is to reproduce for an appellate court, insofar as possible, a true reflection of what occurred in the trial court. The second sentence is in part derived from the final sentence of Rule 43(c). It is designed to resolve doubts as to what testimony the witness would have in fact given, and, in nonjury cases, to provide the appellate court with material for a possible final disposition of the case in the event of reversal of a ruling which excluded evidence. See 5 Moore's Federal Practice § 43.11 (2d ed. 1968). Application is made discretionary in view of the practical impossibility of formulating a satisfactory rule in mandatory terms.

Subdivision ([d]). This subdivision proceeds on the supposition that a ruling which excludes evidence in a jury case is likely to be a pointless procedure if the excluded evidence nevertheless comes to the attention of the jury. Bruton v. United States, 389 U.S. 818 (1968). Rule 43(c) of the Federal Rules of Civil Procedure provides: "The court may require the offer to be made out of the hearing of the jury." In re McConnell, 370 U.S. 230 (1962), left some doubt whether questions on which an offer is based must first be asked in the presence of the jury. The subdivision answers in the negative. The judge can foreclose a particular line of testimony and counsel can protect his record without a series of questions before the jury, designed at best to waste time and at worst "to waft into the jury box" the very matter sought to be excluded.

Subdivision ([e]). This wording of the plain error principle is from Rule 52(b) of the Federal Rules of Criminal Procedure. While judicial unwillingness to be constricted by mechanical breakdowns of the adversary system has been more pronounced in criminal cases, there is no scarcity of decisions to the same effect in civil cases. In general, see Campbell, Extent to Which Courts of Review Will Consider Questions Not Properly Raised and Preserved, 7 Wis.L.Rev. 91, 160 (1932); Vestal, Sua Sponte Consideration in Appellate Review, 27 Fordham L.Rev. 477 (1958–59); 64 Harv.L.Rev. 652 (1951). In the nature of things the application of the plain error rule will be more likely with respect to the admission of evidence than to exclusion, since failure to comply with normal requirements of offers of proof is likely to produce a record which simply does not disclose the error.

CONFERENCE REPORT

The House bill contains the word "judge". The Senate amendment substitutes the word "court" in order to conform with usage elsewhere in the House bill.

---

[1] Editor's Note: When the Federal Rules of Evidence were restyled in 2011, the subdivisions of many rules were re-numbered or re-lettered. Throughout this book, where reference is made to rule subdivisions in the Advisory Committee Notes or the legislative history using the previous numbering or lettering system, the current subdivision lettering or numbering has been inserted in brackets.

FLORIDA AND FEDERAL EVIDENCE RULES

The Conference adopts the Senate amendment.

ADVISORY COMMITTEE'S NOTE (2000 AMENDMENT)

[Subdivision (b).] The amendment applies to all rulings on evidence whether they occur at or before trial, including so-called "*in limine*" rulings. One of the most difficult questions arising from *in limine* and other evidentiary rulings is whether a losing party must renew an objection or offer of proof when the evidence is or would be offered at trial, in order to preserve a claim of error on appeal. Courts have taken differing approaches to this question. Some courts have held that a renewal at the time the evidence is to be offered at trial is always required. *See, e.g., Collins v. Wayne Corp.*, 621 F.2d 777 (5th Cir. 1980). Some courts have taken a more flexible approach, holding that renewal is not required if the issue decided is one that (1) was fairly presented to the trial court for an initial ruling, (2) may be decided as a final matter before the evidence is actually offered, and (3) was ruled on definitively by the trial judge, *See, e.g., Rosenfeld v. Basquiat*, 78 F.3d 84 (2d Cir. 1996) (admissibility of former testimony under the Dead Man's Statute; renewal not required). Other courts have distinguished between objections to evidence, which must be renewed when evidence is offered, and offers of proof, which need not be renewed after a definitive determination is made that the evidence is inadmissible. *See, e.g., Fusco v. General Motors Corp.*, 11 F.3d 259 (1st Cir. 1993). Another court, aware of this Committee's proposed amendment, has adopted its approach. *Wilson v. Williams*, 182 F. 3d 562 (7th Cir. 1999) (en banc). Differing views on this question create uncertainty for litigants and unnecessary work for the appellate courts.

The amendment provides that a claim of error with respect to a definitive ruling is preserved for review when the party has otherwise satisfied the objection or offer of proof requirements of Rule 103(a). When the ruling is definitive, a renewed objection or offer of proof at the time the evidence is to be offered is more a formalism than a necessity. *See* Fed.R.Civ.P. 46 (formal exceptions unnecessary); Fed.R.Cr.P. 51 (same); *United States v. Mejia-Alarcon*, 995 F.2d 982, 986 (10th Cir. 1993) ("Requiring a party to renew an objection when the district court has issued a definitive ruling on a matter that can be fairly decided before trial would be in the nature of a formal exception and therefore unnecessary."). On the other hand, when the trial court appears to have reserved its ruling or to have indicated that the ruling is provisional, it makes sense to require the party to bring the issue to the court's attention subsequently. *See, e.g., United States v. Vest*, 116 F.3d 1179, 1188 (7th Cir. 1997) (where the trial court ruled *in limine* that testimony from defense witnesses could not be admitted, but allowed the defendant to seek leave at trial to call the witnesses should their testimony turn out to be relevant, the defendant's failure to seek such leave at trial meant that it was "too late to reopen the issue now on appeal"); *United States v. Valenti*, 60 F.3d 941 (2d Cir. 1995) (failure to proffer evidence at trial waives any claim of error where the trial judge had stated that he would reserve judgment on the *in limine* motion until he had heard the trial evidence).

The amendment imposes the obligation on counsel to clarify whether an *in limine* or other evidentiary ruling is definitive when there is doubt on that point. *See, e.g., Walden v. Georgia-Pacific Corp.*, 126 F.3d 506, 520 (3d Cir. 1997) (although "the district court told plaintiffs' counsel not to reargue every ruling, it did not countermand its clear opening statement that all of its rulings were tentative, and counsel never requested clarification, as he might have done.").

Even where the court's ruling is definitive, nothing in the amendment prohibits the court from revisiting its decision when the evidence is to be offered. If the court changes its initial ruling, or if the opposing party violates the terms of the initial ruling, objection must be made when the evidence is offered to preserve the claim of error for appeal. The error, if any, in such a situation occurs only when the evidence is offered and admitted. *United States Aviation Underwriters, Inc. v. Olympia Wings, Inc.*, 896 F.2d 949, 956 (5th Cir. 1990) ("objection is required to preserve error when an opponent, or the court itself, violates a motion *in limine* that was granted"); *United States v. Roenigk*, 810 F.2d 809 (8th Cir. 1987)

8

(claim of error was not preserved where the defendant failed to object at trial to secure the benefit of a favorable advance ruling).

A definitive advance ruling is reviewed in light of the facts and circumstances before the trial court at the time of the ruling. If the relevant facts and circumstances change materially after the advance ruling has been made, those facts and circumstances cannot be relied upon on appeal unless they have been brought to the attention of the trial court by way of a renewed, and timely, objection, offer of proof, or motion to strike. *See Old Chief v. United States*, 519 U.S. 172, 182, n.6 (1997) ("It is important that a reviewing court evaluate the trial court's decision from its perspective when it had to rule and not indulge in review by hindsight."). Similarly, if the court decides in an advance ruling that proffered evidence is admissible subject to the eventual introduction by the proponent of a foundation for the evidence, and that foundation is never provided, the opponent cannot claim error based on the failure to establish the foundation unless the opponent calls that failure to the court's attention by a timely motion to strike or other suitable motion. *See Huddleston v. United States*, 485 U.S. 681, 690, n.7 (1988) ("It is, of course, not the responsibility of the judge *sua sponte* to ensure that the foundation evidence is offered; the objector must move to strike the evidence if at the close of the trial the offeror has failed to satisfy the condition.").

Nothing in the amendment is intended to affect the provisions of Fed.R.Civ.P. 72(a) or 28 U.S.C. § 636(b)(1) pertaining to nondispositive pretrial rulings by magistrate judges in proceedings that are not before a magistrate judge by consent of the parties. Fed.R.Civ.P. 72(a) provides that a party who fails to file a written objection to a magistrate judge's nondispositive order within ten days of receiving a copy "may not thereafter assign as error a defect" in the order. 28 U.S.C. § 636(b)(1) provides that any party "may serve and file written objections to such proposed findings and recommendations as provided by rules of court" within ten days of receiving a copy of the order. Several courts have held that a party must comply with this statutory provision in order to preserve a claim of error. *See, e.g., Wells v. Shriners Hospital*, 109 F.3d 198, 200 (4th Cir. 1997) ("[i]n this circuit, as in others, a party 'may' file objections within ten days or he may not, as he chooses, but he 'shall' do so if he wishes further consideration."). When Fed.R.Civ.P. 72(a) or 28 U.S.C. § 636(b)(1) is operative, its requirement must be satisfied in order for a party to preserve a claim of error on appeal, even where Evidence Rule 103([b]) would not require a subsequent objection or offer of proof.

Nothing in the amendment is intended to affect the rule set forth in *Luce v. United States*, 469 U.S. 38 (1984), and its progeny. The amendment provides that an objection or offer of proof need not be renewed to preserve a claim of error with respect to a definitive pretrial ruling. *Luce* answers affirmatively a separate question: whether a criminal defendant must testify at trial in order to preserve a claim of error predicated upon a trial court's decision to admit the defendant's prior convictions for impeachment. The *Luce* principle has been extended by many lower courts to other situations. *See United States v. DiMatteo*, 759 F.2d 831 (11th Cir. 1985) (applying *Luce* where the defendant's witness would be impeached with evidence offered under Rule 608). *See also United States v. Goldman*, 41 F.3d 785, 788 (1st Cir. 1994) ("Although *Luce* involved impeachment by conviction under Rule 609, the reasons given by the Supreme Court for requiring the defendant to testify apply with full force to the kind of Rule 403 and 404 objections that are advanced by Goldman in this case"); *Palmieri v. DeFaria*, 88 F.3d 136 (2d Cir. 1996) (where the plaintiff decided to take an adverse judgment rather than challenge an advance ruling by putting on evidence at trial, the *in limine* ruling would not be reviewed on appeal); *United States v. Ortiz*, 857 F.2d 900 (2d Cir. 1988) (where uncharged misconduct is ruled admissible if the defendant pursues a certain defense, the defendant must actually pursue that defense at trial in order to preserve a claim of error on appeal); *United States v. Bond*, 87 F.3d 695 (5th Cir. 1996) (where the trial court rules *in limine* that the defendant would waive his fifth amendment privilege were he to testify, the defendant must take the stand and testify in order to challenge that ruling on appeal).

The amendment does not purport to answer whether a party who objects to evidence that the court finds admissible in a definitive ruling, and who then offers the evidence to "remove the sting" of its anticipated prejudicial effect, thereby waives the right to appeal the trial court's ruling. *See, e.g., United States v. Fisher*, 106 F.3d 622 (5th Cir. 1997) (where the trial judge ruled in limine that the government could use a prior conviction to impeach the defendant if he testified, the defendant did not waive his right to appeal by introducing the conviction on direct examination); *Judd v. Rodman*, 105 F.3d 1339 (11th Cir. 1997) (an objection made *in limine* is sufficient to preserve a claim of error when the movant, as a matter of trial strategy, presents the objectionable evidence herself on direct examination to minimize its prejudicial effect); *Gill v. Thomas*, 83 F.3d 537, 540 (1st Cir. 1996) ("by offering the misdemeanor evidence himself, Gill waived his opportunity to object and thus did not preserve the issue for appeal"); *United States v. Williams*, 939 F.2d 721 (9th Cir. 1991) (objection to impeachment evidence was waived where the defendant was impeached on direct examination).

ADVISORY COMMITTEE'S NOTE (2011 AMENDMENT)

The language of Rule 103 has been amended as part of the restyling of the Evidence Rules to make them more easily understood and to make style and terminology consistent throughout the rules. These changes are intended to be stylistic only. There is no intent to change any result in any ruling on evidence admissibility.

Florida Stat. § 90.104. Rulings on Evidence

(1) A court may predicate error, set aside or reverse a judgment, or grant a new trial on the basis of admitted or excluded evidence when a substantial right of the party is adversely affected and:

(a) When the ruling is one admitting evidence, a timely objection or motion to strike appears on the record, stating the specific ground of objection if the specific ground was not apparent from the context; or

(b) When the ruling is one excluding evidence, the substance of the evidence was made known to the court by offer of proof or was apparent from the context within which the questions were asked.

If the court has made a definitive ruling on the record admitting or excluding evidence, either at or before trial, a party need not renew an objection or offer of proof to preserve a claim of error for appeal.

(2) In cases tried by a jury, a court shall conduct proceedings, to the maximum extent practicable, in such a manner as to prevent inadmissible evidence from being suggested to the jury by any means.

(3) Nothing in this section shall preclude a court from taking notice of fundamental errors affecting substantial rights, even though such errors were not brought to the attention of the trial judge.

SPONSORS' NOTE (1976 ENACTMENT)

Subsection (1) This section amplifies § 59.041 of the Florida Statutes in stating the "harmless error" rule as it applies to evidentiary rulings by the court. In addition to the requirement that a substantial right of a party be affected, the nature of the error must be called to the attention of the court so that proper remedial measures by judge and counsel may be taken. The objection and the offer of proof are the means to accomplish that goal. The Florida cases have long followed this rule. In Butler v. State, 94 Fla. 163, 113 So. 699 (1927) the court said:

Technical error, committed by a trial court in the reception or rejection of evidence, does not necessarily constitute harmful error. It is injury resulting from error that warrants an appellate court in reversing a judgment of the trial court.

The provisions of § 59.041 regarding other alleged errors are not affected. The question of harmless constitutional error is not covered by this section but is examined in <u>Chapman v. California</u>, 386 U.S. 18 (1967).

Existing Florida law also requires that a timely specific objection be made to preserve the point on appeal; see <u>Nat Harrison Associates, Inc. v. Byrd</u>, 256 So. 2d 50 (Fla. 4th Dist. 1971); <u>Hanis[c]h v. Wilde[r]</u>, 210 So. 2d 491 (Fla. 3rd Dist. 1968), and that an offer of proof be made when the evidence is excluded unless the answer is apparent from the question asked, see <u>Browder v. Da Costa</u>, 91 Fla. 1, 109 So. 448 (1926). Fla. R. Civ. Pro. 1.450(b) provides that the court may add to the offer that shows the character of the evidence, the form in which it was offered, the objection made and the ruling thereon in order to reproduce for higher tribunals, as exactly as possible, a reproduction of the events in the trial court. Rule 1.450(b) also allows the court to exercise its discretion to produce on the record, in both jury and non-jury cases, what the witness's testimony would have been if the question had been answered.

Similar provisions are contained in Fed. Rule Evid. 103, Calif. Evid. Code §§ 353-54, Kansas Code of Civ. Pro. §§ 60-404, 60-405 and Uniform Rules 4 and 5.

<u>Subsection (2)</u> A ruling which excludes evidence is a pointlessly formal and ritualistic procedure if the excluded evidence nevertheless comes to the attention of the jury. B[ru]ton v. United States, 389 U.S. 818 (1968). Both Fed. R. Civ. Pro. 43(c) and Fla. R. Civ. Pro. 1.450(b) provide that "[t]he court may require the offer to be made out of the hearing of the jury." Additionally, this section provides that preliminary questions upon which the offer is based do not have to first be asked in the jury's presence. A similar provision is contained in Fed. Rule Evid. 103.

<u>Subsection (3)</u> The purpose of this subsection, which is in accord with Fed. R. Crim. Pro. 2(b), is to allow appellate courts to raise issues <u>sua sponte</u>. Under Fla. R. Civ. Pro. 1.530, the judge may order a new trial or rehearing and under Fla. R. Crim. Pro. 3.580 order a new trial or arrest the judgment.

The subsection is applicable to both criminal and civil cases although it is traditional that only in criminal cases have appellate courts displayed unwillingness to be bound by breakdowns in the adversary system, although, numerous examples exist with the same effects in civil cases. See Campbell, <u>Extent to Which Courts of Review will Consider Questions Not Properly Raised and Preserved</u>, 7 Wis. L. Rev. 91 (1932); Vestal, <u>Sua Sponte Consideration in Appellate Review</u>, 27 Fordham L. Rev. 477 (1958-59). Generally, this section will be applied more often when evidence is erroneously admitted since the failure to comply with the requirements of offer of proof will result in an absence of material in the record to disclose the error.

A similar provision is contained in Fed. Rule Evid. 103. See McCormick, <u>Evidence</u> § 52 (2nd ed. 1972).

COMMENTARY ON FEDERAL AND FLORIDA RULE DIFFERENCES

Florida Stat. § 90.104 and its federal counterpart, Federal Rule 103, delineate the circumstances under which a trial court's erroneous admission or exclusion of evidence can serve as the basis for setting aside or reversing a judgment or granting a new trial.

As a general rule, under both Florida and federal practice, an error in admitting evidence can only serve as the basis for setting aside or reversing a judgment or granting a new trial if the error was preserved by a timely objection, meaning that it was made as soon as the basis for objection was known or reasonably should have been known (usually after a question is asked but before the witness answers). *See U.S. v. Meserve*, 271 F.3d 314, 324 (1st Cir. 2001); *Crumbley v. State*, 876 So. 2d 599, 601 (Fla. 5th DCA 2004). Moreover, under both Florida and federal practice, neither a general objection nor a specific objection on other grounds will preserve an issue for review; only those specific grounds objected to at trial are preserved. *See U.S. v. Wynn*, 845 F.2d 1439, 1442 (7th Cir.

FLORIDA AND FEDERAL EVIDENCE RULES

1988); *Johnson v. State*, 969 So. 2d 938, 954 (Fla. 2008); *Marshall v. State*, 915 So. 2d 264, 268-69 (Fla. 4th DCA 2005); *Couzo v. State*, 830 So. 2d 177, 179 (Fla. 4th DCA 2002).

Under both Florida and federal practice, a party can lodge a "continuing objection," which, if granted by the trial court, serves as an objection to all the questions in a given line of questioning on specific grounds, obviating the need to repeatedly object. *See U.S. v. Gomez-Norena*, 908 F.2d 497, 500 n.2 (9th Cir. 1990); *Viglione v. State*, 861 So. 2d 511, 512-13 (Fla. 5th DCA 2003). Moreover, in cases involving multiple parties in either system, such as a criminal prosecution with multiple defendants, an objection by one defendant does not preserve that claim for his co-defendants unless the trial court agrees on the record that an objection from one will be considered an objection for all. *See U.S. v. Leon-Delfis*, 203 F.3d 103, 113 (1st Cir. 2000); *Johnson v. State*, 726 So. 2d 359, 360 (Fla. 1st DCA 1999).

An error in excluding evidence can only serve as the basis for setting aside or reversing a judgment or granting a new trial under Florida and federal practice if the error was preserved by a timely offer of proof, meaning one that was made at the time the evidence was excluded. *See International Land Acquisitions, Inc. v. Fausto*, 39 Fed. Appx. 751, 755-56 (3d Cir. 2002); *Johnson v. State*, 494 So. 2d 311, 313 (Fla. 1st DCA 1986). Under federal practice, an offer of proof preserves for review only those specific grounds for admissibility raised at trial, *see Fausto*, 39 Fed. Appx. at 755-56, while under Florida practice there are no precedents on point.

If the excluded evidence is testimony, the offer of proof should indicate how the witness would have testified if permitted. *See U.S. v. Adams*, 271 F.3d 1236, 1241-42 (10th Cir. 2001); *Morrison v. State*, 818 So. 2d 432, 448 (Fla. 2002). In the case of documentary evidence, the documents should be marked for identification and included in the record. *See Brantley v. Snapper Power Equip.*, 665 So. 2d 241, 243 (Fla. 3d DCA 1996); *Adams*, 271 F.3d at 1242. In both the federal and Florida systems, the trial court has discretion to determine the method by which a party makes an offer of proof. *Adams*, 271 F.3d at 1241; *Porro v. State*, 656 So. 2d 587, 587 & n.* (Fla. 3d DCA 1995). And in both systems, a failure to make a proffer will not preclude review if the trial court judge refused to let a party make such an offer. *Moss v. Ole South Real Estate, Inc.*, 933 F.2d 1300, 1310-11 & n.10 (5th Cir. 1994); *Porro*, 656 So. 2d at 587. Moreover, under Florida law, a failure to make a proffer will not preclude appellate review "where the offer would be a useless ceremony, or the evidence is rejected as a class, or where the court indicates such an offer would be unavailing." *O'Shea v. O'Shea*, 585 So. 2d 405, 407 (Fla. 1st DCA 1991); *Reaves v. State*, 531 So. 2d 401, 403 (Fla. 5th DCA 1988).

In both the federal and Florida systems, an appellate court can affirm a trial court's decision to admit or exclude evidence on any ground that finds support in the record, even if the trial court reached its conclusion from a different (even erroneous) course of reasoning. *Abuan v. Level 3 Communications, Inc.*, 353 F.3d 1158, 1171 n.3 (10th Cir. 2003); *Robertson v. State*, 829 So. 2d 901, 906 (Fla. 2002).

Language was added to Federal Rule 103 in 2000 to provide that once the court has made a definitive ruling admitting or excluding evidence at or before trial (such as in response to a motion *in limine*), a party need not renew an objection or offer of proof to preserve a claim of error for appeal. *See* FED. R. EVID. 103(b). Similar language was added to Florida Stat. § 90.104(1) in 2003, which has been described by the Florida Supreme Court as "consistent with [the] changes made to Federal Rule of Evidence 103[(b)] in 2000." *In re Amendments to the Florida Evidence Code–Section 90.104*, 914 So. 2d 940, 941 (Fla. 2005). Under both provisions, however, a party is excused from renewing an objection or offer of proof only if the earlier ruling is "definitive"; if it is not, the party must renew the objection or offer of proof in order to preserve a claim of error. *See Crowe v. Bolduc*, 334 F.3d 124, 133-34 (1st Cir. 2003); *Tolbert v. State*, 922 So. 2d 1013, 1016-18 (Fla. 5th DCA 2006). Some Florida precedent suggests that this amendment effectively creates an automatic continuing objection to all the questions in a given line of questioning on a specific ground that has been objected to and definitively ruled upon. *See Stokes v. State*, 914 So. 2d 514, 516 n.2 (Fla. 4th DCA 2005).

In the federal courts, to preserve a claim that the trial court erred in holding that a witness could be impeached with his prior convictions, uncharged misconduct, or other evidence if he testifies, a party must actually call the person as a witness and the impeaching evidence must be introduced. *See Luce v. U.S.*, 469 U.S. 38 (1984); Advisory Committee's Note to 2000 Amendment to FED. R. EVID. 103. Moreover, in the federal courts, if such a ruling is made, and the party opposing the introduction of the evidence brings it up himself in order to remove its sting, he is deemed to have waived the right to challenge the ruling. *See Ohler v. U.S.*, 529 U.S. 753 (2000). Florida practice is in accord. *See State v. Raydo*, 713 So. 2d 996, 1000 (Fla. 1998) (following *Luce*); *Rivers v. State*, 792 So.2d 564, 566-67 (Fla. 1st DCA 2001) (following *Ohler*).

Even if a claim of error is properly preserved, and even if the appellate court concludes that the trial court did err, that will not serve as the basis for setting aside or reversing a judgment or granting a new trial if the error is deemed to be harmless in that it would not have affected the outcome. While the harmless error doctrine exists in both the federal and Florida systems, there are important differences. First, in criminal cases in the federal system, a constitutional error will be excused only if the appellate court finds beyond a reasonable doubt that the error did not affect the outcome, *U.S. v. Nielsen*, 371 F.3d 574, 581 (9th Cir. 2004), while a non-constitutional error—such as an error in applying the rules of evidence—will be excused on a lower showing, albeit one that varies by federal circuit. *Compare U.S. v. Malol*, 476 F.3d 1283, 1291 (11th Cir. 2007) ("nonconstitutional evidentiary errors are not grounds for reversal absent a reasonable likelihood that the defendant's substantial rights were affected."), *with U.S. v. Marshall*, 432 F.3d 1157, 1162 (10th Cir. 2005) ("In non-constitutional harmless error cases, the government bears the burden of demonstrating, by a preponderance of the evidence, that the substantial rights of the defendant were not affected."), *and U.S. v. Piper*, 298 F.3d 47, 56-57 (1st Cir. 2002) ("A non-constitutional evidentiary error is harmless...so long as it is highly probable that the error did not influence the verdict"). By contrast, in criminal cases in the Florida system, no distinction is made between constitutional and non-constitutional errors: for both types of errors, the appellate court must find beyond a reasonable doubt that the error did not affect the outcome. *Goodwin v. State*, 751 So. 2d 537, 538-46 (Fla. 2000). Second, in the federal system, errors in civil cases are subject to the same harmless error standard as is used for non-constitutional errors in criminal cases. *See Obrey v. Johnson*, 400 F.3d 691, 701 (9th Cir. 2005). In Florida, it is unclear exactly what standard applies in civil actions, *see Florida Patient's Comp. Fund v. Von Stetina*, 474 So. 2d 783, 793-94 (1985) (Overton, J., concurring in part and dissenting in part) ("This Court has never expressly set forth a harmless error test for the appellate courts of this state to apply in civil cases."), although most courts hold that in such cases the error is harmful where there is a reasonable probability that a different result would have been reached but for the error, *see Florida Inst. for Neurologic Rehab., Inc. v. Marshall*, 943 So. 2d 976, 978-79 (Fla. 2d DCA 2006); *Chrysler v. Department of Prof'l Regulation*, 627 So. 2d 31, 34-35 (Fla. 1st DCA 1993).

Under both federal and Florida practice, the appeals court has discretion to review unpreserved errors under narrow circumstances. *Compare* FED. R. EVID. 103(e) (plain error), *with* FLA. STAT. § 90.104(3) (fundamental error). In the federal system, this discretion is to be exercised only where the error is clear or obvious, affected the outcome of the proceedings, and "seriously affect[s] the fairness, integrity or public reputation of judicial proceedings." *U.S. v. Cotton*, 535 U.S. 625, 631 (2002); *Johnson v. U.S.*, 520 U.S. 461, 466-67 (1997); *U.S. v. Olano*, 507 U.S. 725, 732 (1993). Under both the federal and Florida standards, that the error is "harmful" in that it affected the outcome of the proceedings is a necessary but not a sufficient prerequisite for reviewing an unpreserved error. *See Johnson*, 520 U.S. at 469-70; *Reed v. State*, 837 So. 2d 366, 370 (Fla. 2002) ("[A]ll fundamental error is harmful error. However...not all harmful error is fundamental."). Moreover, under both systems, the standard applies only to errors that undermine the fairness and integrity of the proceedings. *Compare Olano*, 507 U.S. at 736 (describing plain errors as those that seriously affect the fairness, integrity or public reputation of judicial proceedings), *with Grau v. Branham*, 761 So. 2d 375, 378 (Fla. 4th DCA 2000) (describing a fundamental error as one "which go[es] to the heart of a trial and vitiate[s] its fairness," and that is "so extreme that it could not be corrected by an instruction if an objection had been lodged, and that it so damaged the fairness of the trial that the public's interest in our system of justice justifies a new trial.") Unlike the federal standard, however, the Florida standard does not appear to be concerned with the clearness or obviousness of the error. In any event, it is rare that the plain error standard under federal law or the fundamental error standard under Florida law will be satisfied. *See, e.g., State v. Osvath*, 661 So. 2d 1252, 1254 (Fla. 3d DCA 1995) (noting that fundamental error has not "ever been invoked to cure an unpreserved evidentiary error at trial, whether the error be one of constitutional dimensions or not.")

Federal Rule 104. Preliminary Questions

(a) In General. The court must decide any preliminary question about whether a witness is qualified, a privilege exists, or evidence is admissible. In so deciding, the court is not bound by evidence rules, except those on privilege.

(b) Relevance That Depends on a Fact. When the relevance of evidence depends on whether a fact exists, proof must be introduced sufficient to support a finding that the fact does exist. The court may admit the proposed evidence on the condition that the proof be introduced later.

(c) Conducting a Hearing So That the Jury Cannot Hear It. The court must conduct any hearing on a preliminary question so that the jury cannot hear it if:

  (1) the hearing involves the admissibility of a confession;

  (2) a defendant in a criminal case is a witness and so requests; or

  (3) justice so requires.

(d) Cross-Examining a Defendant in a Criminal Case. By testifying on a preliminary question, a defendant in a criminal case does not become subject to cross-examination on other issues in the case.

(e) Evidence Relevant to Weight and Credibility. This rule does not limit a party's right to introduce before the jury evidence that is relevant to the weight or credibility of other evidence.

ADVISORY COMMITTEE'S NOTE

Subdivision (a). The applicability of a particular rule of evidence often depends upon the existence of a condition. Is the alleged expert a qualified physician? Is a witness whose former testimony is offered unavailable? Was a stranger present during a conversation between attorney and client? In each instance the admissibility of evidence will turn upon the answer to the question of the existence of the condition. Accepted practice, incorporated in the rule, places on the judge the responsibility for these determinations. McCormick § 53; Morgan, Basic Problems of Evidence 45–50 (1962).

To the extent that these inquiries are factual, the judge acts as a trier of fact. Often, however, rulings on evidence call for an evaluation in terms of a legally set standard. Thus when a hearsay statement is offered as a declaration against interest, a decision must be made whether it possesses the required against-interest characteristics. These decisions, too, are made by the judge.

In view of these considerations, this subdivision refers to preliminary requirements generally by the broad term "questions," without attempt at specification.

This subdivision is of general application. It must, however, be read as subject to the special provisions for "conditional relevancy" in subdivision (b) and those for confessions in subdivision ([c]).

If the question is factual in nature, the judge will of necessity receive evidence pro and con on the issue.

The rule provides that the rules of evidence in general do not apply to this process. McCormick § 53, p. 123, n. 8, points out that the authorities are "scattered and inconclusive," and observes:

"Should the exclusionary law of evidence, 'the child of the jury system' in Thayer's phrase, be applied to this hearing before the judge? Sound sense backs the view that it should not, and that the judge should be empowered to hear any relevant evidence, such as affidavits or other reliable hearsay."

This view is reinforced by practical necessity in certain situations. An item, offered and objected to, may itself be considered in ruling on admissibility, though not yet admitted in evidence. Thus the content of an asserted declaration against interest must be considered in ruling whether it is against interest. Again, common practice calls for considering the testimony of a witness, particularly a child, in determining competency. Another example is the requirement of Rule 602 dealing with personal knowledge. In the case of hearsay, it is enough, if the declarant "so far as appears [has] had an opportunity to observe the fact declared." McCormick, § 10, p. 19.

If concern is felt over the use of affidavits by the judge in preliminary hearings on admissibility, attention is directed to the many important judicial determinations made on the basis of affidavits. Rule 47 of the Federal Rules of Criminal Procedure provides:

"An application to the court for an order shall be by motion. . . . It may be supported by affidavit."

The Rules of Civil Procedure are more detailed. Rule 43(e), dealing with motions generally, provides:

"When a motion is based on facts not appearing of record the court may hear the matter on affidavits presented by the respective parties, but the court may direct that the matter be heard wholly or partly on oral testimony or depositions."

Rule 4(g) provides for proof of service by affidavit. Rule 56 provides in detail for the entry of summary judgment based on affidavits. Affidavits may supply the foundation for temporary restraining orders under Rule 65(b).

The study made for the California Law Revision Commission recommended an amendment to Uniform Rule 2 as follows:

"In the determination of the issue aforesaid [preliminary determination], exclusionary rules shall not apply, subject, however, to Rule 45 and any valid claim of privilege." Tentative Recommendation and a Study Relating to the Uniform Rules of Evidence (Article VIII, Hearsay), Cal.Law Revision Comm'n, Rep., Rec. & Studies, 470 (1962). The proposal was not adopted in the California Evidence Code. The Uniform Rules are likewise silent on the subject. However, New Jersey Evidence Rule 8(1), dealing with preliminary inquiry by the judge, provides:

"In his determination the rules of evidence shall not apply except for Rule 4 [exclusion on grounds of confusion, etc.] or a valid claim of privilege."

Subdivision (b). In some situations, the relevancy of an item of evidence, in the large sense, depends upon the existence of a particular preliminary fact. Thus when a spoken statement is relied upon to prove notice to X, it is without probative value unless X heard it. Or if a letter purporting to be from Y is relied upon to establish an admission by him, it has no probative value unless Y wrote or authorized it. Relevance in this sense has been labelled "conditional relevancy." Morgan, Basic Problems of Evidence 45–46 (1962). Problems arising in connection with it are to be distinguished from problems of logical relevancy, e.g., evidence in a murder case that accused on the day before purchased a weapon of the kind used in the killing, treated in Rule 401.

If preliminary questions of conditional relevancy were determined solely by the judge, as provided in subdivision (a), the functioning of the jury as a trier of fact would be greatly restricted and in some cases virtually destroyed. These are appropriate questions for juries. Accepted treatment, as provided in the rule, is consistent with that given fact questions generally. The judge makes a preliminary determination whether the foundation evidence is sufficient to support a finding of fulfillment of the condition. If so, the item is admitted. If after all the evidence on the issue is in, pro and con, the jury could reasonably conclude that fulfillment of the condition is not established, the issue is for them. If the evidence is not such as to allow a finding, the judge withdraws the matter from their consideration. Morgan, *supra*; California Evidence Code § 403; New Jersey Rule 8(2). See also Uniform Rules 19 and 67.

The order of proof here, as generally, is subject to the control of the judge.

Subdivision (c). Preliminary hearings on the admissibility of confessions must be conducted outside the hearing of the jury. See Jackson v. Denno, 378 U.S. 368 (1964). Otherwise, detailed treatment of when preliminary matters should be heard outside the hearing of the jury is not feasible. The procedure is time consuming. Not infrequently the same evidence which is relevant to the issue of establishment of fulfillment of a condition precedent to admissibility is also relevant to weight or credibility, and time is saved by taking foundation proof in the presence of the jury. Much evidence on preliminary questions, though not relevant to jury issues, may be heard by the jury with no adverse effect. A great deal must be left to the discretion of the judge who will act as the interests of justice require.

Subdivision (d). The limitation upon cross-examination is designed to encourage participation by the accused in the determination of preliminary matters. He may testify concerning them without exposing himself to cross-examination generally. The provision is necessary because of the breadth of cross-examination under Rule 611(b).

The rule does not address itself to questions of the subsequent use of testimony given by an accused at a hearing on a preliminary matter. See Walder v. United States, 347 U.S. 62 (1954); Simmons v. United States, 390 U.S. 377 (1968); Harris v. New York, 401 U.S. 222 (1971).

Subdivision (e). For similar provisions see Uniform Rule 8; California Evidence Code § 406; Kansas Code of Civil Procedure § 60-408; New Jersey Evidence Rule 8(1).

REPORT OF HOUSE COMMITTEE ON THE JUDICIARY

Rule 104(c) as submitted to the Congress provided that hearings on the admissibility of confessions shall be conducted outside the presence of the jury and hearings on all other preliminary matters should be so conducted when the interests of justice require. The Committee amended the Rule to provide that where an accused is a witness as to a preliminary matter, he has the right, upon his request, to be heard outside the jury's presence. Although recognizing that in some cases duplication of evidence would occur and that the procedure could be subject to abuse, the Committee believed that a proper regard for the right of an accused not to testify generally in the case dictates that he be given an option to testify out of the presence of the jury on preliminary matters.

The Committee construes the second sentence of subdivision (c)[2] as applying to civil actions and proceedings as well as to criminal cases, and on this assumption has left the sentence unamended.

REPORT OF SENATE COMMITTEE ON THE JUDICIARY

Under rule 104(c) the hearing on a preliminary matter may at times be conducted in front of the jury. Should an accused testify in such a hearing, waiving his privilege against self-incrimination as to the

---

[2] Editor's Note: This refers to subsections (c)(2) and (c)(3) of the restyled version of the rule.

preliminary issue, rule 104(d) provides that he will not generally be subject to cross-examination as to any other issue. This rule is not, however, intended to immunize the accused from cross-examination where, in testifying about a preliminary issue, he injects other issues into the hearing. If he could not be cross-examined about any issues gratuitously raised by him beyond the scope of the preliminary matters, injustice might result. Accordingly, in order to prevent any such unjust result, the committee intends the rule to be construed to provide that the accused may subject himself to cross-examination as to issues raised by his own testimony upon a preliminary matter before a jury.

ADVISORY COMMITTEE'S NOTE (2011 AMENDMENT)

The language of Rule 104 has been amended as part of the restyling of the Evidence Rules to make them more easily understood and to make style and terminology consistent throughout the rules. These changes are intended to be stylistic only. There is no intent to change any result in any ruling on evidence admissibility.

Florida Stat. § 90.105. Preliminary Questions

(1) Except as provided in subsection (2), the court shall determine preliminary questions concerning the qualification of a person to be a witness, the existence of a privilege, or the admissibility of evidence.

(2) When the relevancy of evidence depends upon the existence of a preliminary fact, the court shall admit the proffered evidence when there is prima facie evidence sufficient to support a finding of the preliminary fact. If prima facie evidence is not introduced to support a finding of the preliminary fact, the court may admit the proffered evidence subject to the subsequent introduction of prima facie evidence of the preliminary fact.

(3) Hearings on the admissibility of confessions shall be conducted out of the hearing of the jury. Hearings on other preliminary matters shall be similarly conducted when the interests of justice require or when an accused is a witness, if he or she so requests.

SPONSORS' NOTE (1976 ENACTMENT)

Subsection (1) When a party objects to the introduction of proffered evidence on the basis of an exclusionary rule, the applicability of the rule and the admission or exclusion of the evidence often turn upon the existence of a condition. This section makes preliminary questions the responsibility of the judge, e.g., whether the witness is competent to testify, whether the alleged medical expert is a currently licensed physician, and whether the witness whose former testimony is offered is unavailable. See Bell v. Kendrick, 25 Fla. 778, 6 So. 868 (1889); Perma Spray Mfg. Co. v. La France Indus., Inc., 161 So. 2d 13 (Fla. 3rd Dist. 1964). To the extent that these inquiries are factual, the judge acts as a trier of fact. Of necessity, he will receive evidence, both pro and con, on the issue in dispute.

Similar provisions are contained in Fed. Rule Evid. 104, and New Jersey Evid. Rule 8(1).

Subsection (2) This subsection concerns conditional relevancy, i.e., the relevancy of one fact depending upon the existence of another fact. For example, if an oral statement is relied upon as notice to the defendant, it has no probative value unless the defendant heard it. Under this subsection, the court makes a preliminary determination whether the foundation evidence is sufficient. If so, the item is admitted. If, upon the close of all the evidence submitted, pro and con, the jury could reasonably conclude that the preliminary fact is established, the issue is for their determination. If the evidence will not permit such a finding, the court withdraws the matter from their consideration. For example, if a letter from A is relied upon to establish an admission by him, and after all the evidence is heard, it is reasonable to conclude that A did not write or authorize the letter, the jury will determine whether A has made the admission relied upon. If, however, it appears that the evidence will not allow the jury to conclude whether A is responsible for the letter, consideration of the admission will be removed by the judge from their deliberations.

Similar provisions are contained in Calif. Evid. Code § 403, New Jersey Evid. Rule 8(2) and Uniform Rules of Evid. 19 and 67.

Subsection (3) Pursuant to the Supreme Court decision in Jackson v. Denno, 378 U.S. 368 (1964), hearings on the admissibility of confessions must be conducted outside the hearing of the jury. Detailed classification and categorization of other situations when similar treatment of preliminary matters is desirable are difficult to formulate. A great deal of evidence on preliminary questions, although not relevant to jury issues, may be heard by the jury with no adverse effect, avoiding time consuming delay and repetition. This is particularly true where the same evidence used to establish fulfillment of a condition precedent to admission is also relevant to weight or credibility. See Fed. Rule Evid. 104.

COMMENTARY ON FEDERAL AND FLORIDA RULE DIFFERENCES

Florida Stat. § 90.105 and its federal counterpart, Federal Rule 104, govern the method by which trial court judges determine preliminary questions in applying the rules of evidence. As a general rule, these two provisions are similar. *Tucker v. State*, 884 So. 2d 168, 173-74 (Fla. 2d DCA 2004) (noting that 90.105(1) is modeled after Federal Rule 104(a)); *First Union Nat'l Bank v. Turney*, 824 So. 2d 172, 184 n.10 (Fla. 1st DCA 2001) ("The United States Supreme Court's interpretation of [Federal] Rule 104(a) is persuasive authority as to the proper interpretation of [Florida] section 90.105(1).").

Under both the federal and Florida rules, the trial judge alone decides most preliminary questions in applying the rules of evidence. To the extent that these inquiries are factual in nature, the trial judge acts as factfinder. *See* Advisory Committee's Note to FED. R. EVID. 104(a); Sponsors' Note to FLA. STAT. § 90.105(1). Thus, for example, it is for the trial judge alone to determine whether a witness is qualified, *see Anderson v. State*, 863 So. 2d 169, 178-79 (Fla. 2003); *Daubert v. Merrell Dow Pharm., Inc.*, 509 U.S. 579, 592 & n.10 (1993), or whether the predicate factual requirements for invoking a privilege have been satisfied, *see Turney*, 824 So. 2d at 183-84; *U.S. v. Zolin*, 491 U.S. 554, 565-66 (1989), or whether the predicate factual requirements for invoking an exception to the hearsay rule have been satisfied, *see Mariano v. State*, 933 So. 2d 111, 115-16 (Fla. 4th DCA 2006); *Tucker v. State*, 884 So. 2d 168, 173-74 (Fla. 2d DCA 2004); *Bourjaily v. U.S.*, 483 U.S. 171, 175 (1987). Moreover, under both the Florida and federal rules, in criminal and civil cases alike the judge need only find by a preponderance of the evidence that these factual prerequisites have been satisfied. *See Romani v. State*, 542 So. 2d 984, 985 n.3 (Fla. 1989); *Turney*, 824 So. 2d at 184 n.10; *Bourjaily*, 483 U.S. at 175-76.

In certain instances, whether an item of evidence is relevant, and thus admissible, depends upon the existence of a particular preliminary fact or set of facts. Thus, for example, when a spoken statement is relied upon to prove notice to a particular person, evidence of that spoken statement is relevant only if there is evidence that the person actually heard the statement. However, under both the federal and Florida rules, the trial court plays a different role where such questions of conditional relevance are involved. Unlike with most preliminary questions, in which the trial judge alone determines whether the factual prerequisites for admissibility have been satisfied, here the trial court asks only whether a reasonable trier of fact *could* find the conditional fact by a preponderance of the evidence. *See* Advisory Committee's Note to FED. R. EVID. 104(b); Sponsors' Note to FLA. STAT. § 90.105(2). The most common form of conditional relevance is the determination whether evidence is authentic or not: the trial court does not determine whether or not proffered evidence is in fact authentic, but admits it so long as sufficient evidence of its authenticity is introduced such that a reasonable jury could so find. *See Van Den Borre v. State*, 596 So. 2d 687, 691 (Fla. 4th DCA 1992); *Ricketts v. City of Hartford*, 74 F.3d 1397, 1409-11 (2d Cir. 1996).

There is one major difference between the federal and Florida rules: Federal Rule 104(a) provides that in determining preliminary questions concerning admissibility, the court is not bound by the rules of evidence except those with respect to privilege, while there is no similar language in the Florida counterpart. Thus, in making preliminary determinations regarding admissibility, a Florida trial court cannot rely on otherwise inadmissible evidence but a federal trial court can. *See generally* 21A CHARLES ALAN WRIGHT & KENNETH W. GRAHAM, JR., FEDERAL PRACTICE AND PROCEDURE: EVIDENCE § 5055 & n.17 (2d ed. 2005). Thus, for example, in determining whether a statement qualifies as a co-conspirator admission, a federal court can use the disputed statements themselves to find that a conspiracy existed while a Florida court cannot. *Compare Romani v. State*, 542 So. 2d 984, 985-86 (Fla. 1989), *with Bourjaily v. United States*, 483 U.S. 171, 178-79 (1987). Or in deciding whether or not the crime-fraud exception to the attorney-client privilege applies, a Florida court cannot rely on the disputed communications themselves while a federal court can. *Compare Turney*, 824 So. 2d at 183, *with Zolin*, 491 U.S. at 565-68.

Federal Rule 105. Limiting Evidence That Is Not Admissible Against Other Parties or for Other Purposes

If the court admits evidence that is admissible against a party or for a purpose — but not against another party or for another purpose — the court, on timely request, must restrict the evidence to its proper scope and instruct the jury accordingly.

ADVISORY COMMITTEE'S NOTE

A close relationship exists between this rule and Rule 403 which requires exclusion when "probative value is substantially outweighed by the danger of unfair prejudice, confusion of the issues, or misleading the jury." The present rule recognizes the practice of admitting evidence for a limited purpose and instructing the jury accordingly. The availability and effectiveness of this practice must be taken into consideration in reaching a decision whether to exclude for unfair prejudice under Rule 403. In Bruton v. United States, 389 U.S. 818 (1968), the Court ruled that a limiting instruction did not effectively protect the accused against the prejudicial effect of admitting in evidence the confession of a codefendant which implicated him. The decision does not, however, bar the use of limited admissibility with an instruction where the risk of prejudice is less serious.

Similar provisions are found in Uniform Rule 6; California Evidence Code § 355; Kansas Code of Civil Procedure § 60-406; New Jersey Evidence Rule 6. The wording of the present rule differs, however, in repelling any implication that limiting or curative instructions are sufficient in all situations.

REPORT OF HOUSE COMMITTEE ON THE JUDICIARY

Rule 106 as submitted by the Supreme Court (now Rule 105 in the bill) dealt with the subject of evidence which is admissible as to one party or for one purpose but is not admissible against another party or for another purpose. The Committee adopted this Rule without change on the understanding that it does not affect the authority of a court to order a severance in a multi-defendant case.

ADVISORY COMMITTEE'S NOTE (2011 AMENDMENT)

The language of Rule 105 has been amended as part of the restyling of the Evidence Rules to make them more easily understood and to make style and terminology consistent throughout the rules. These changes are intended to be stylistic only. There is no intent to change any result in any ruling on evidence admissibility.

Florida Stat. § 90.107. Limited Admissibility

When evidence that is admissible as to one party or for one purpose, but inadmissible as to another party or for another purpose, is admitted, the court, upon request, shall restrict such evidence to its proper scope and so inform the jury at the time it is admitted.

SPONSORS' NOTE (1976 ENACTMENT)

This section allows evidence which is incompetent as to one party or issue, but admissible as to another, to be offered and received by the court for only the specific purpose for which it is competent. The section also requires the court to inform the jury of the limited purpose for which the evidence may be considered when counsel so requests. Under Section 90.403, the court can exclude such evidence if it deems it to be so prejudicial that a limiting instruction would not adequately protect a party.

In <u>Barnett v. Butler</u>, 112 So. 2d 907, 910 (Fla. 2nd Dist. 1959), a case involving the ownership of a negligently operated automobile, the court recognized that evidence could be admissible for a limited purpose and said:

> the court can, by appropriate charge, impress upon the jury the importance of considering the evidence of insurance only to the extent of shedding light on the issue of ownership.

This section follows the rule expressed in <u>Sprinkle v. Davis</u>, 111 F.2d 925 (4th Cir. 1940), and recognized in most jurisdictions. Calif. Evid. Code § 355 and Fed. Rule Evid. 105 contain similar provisions. New Jersey Evid. Rule 6 also contains a similar rule, with the exception that a request for a limiting instruction need not be made.

COMMENTARY ON FEDERAL AND FLORIDA RULE DIFFERENCES

Florida Stat. § 90.107 and its federal counterpart, Federal Rule 105, provide that when evidence is admissible against some parties but not others, or is admissible for some purposes but not others, the trial court may admit the evidence for the limited purpose and so instruct the jury.

A critical difference between the federal and state rules is when such an instruction is given to the jury. Under Federal Rule 105, the trial court has discretion to decide whether to give the instruction contemporaneously with the admission of the evidence or during closing jury instructions, or at both times. See *U.S. v. Chance*, 306 F.3d 356, 387-89 (6th Cir. 2002); *U.S. v. Peterson*, 244 F.3d 385, 394 (5th Cir. 2001); *U.S. v. Youts*, 229 F.3d 1312, 1319 (10th Cir. 2000). By contrast, under Florida Stat. § 90.107, the instruction, if requested, can *only* be given at the time the evidence is admitted, not at the close of trial; thus, a request for such an instruction made at a point in time after the evidence has already been admitted, such as at the close of the evidence, will be untimely. See *Johnson v. State*, 747 So. 2d 436, 438 (Fla. 4th DCA 1999); *Lopez v. State*, 716 So. 2d 301, 303-04 (Fla. 3d DCA 1998); *Standard Jury Instruction in Criminal Cases (95-1)*, 657 So. 2d 1152, 1153 (Fla. 1995) (noting that limiting instruction that prior convictions can be used only for impeachment purposes is to be given "at the time the evidence is admitted"); *Lightfoot v. State*, 591 So. 2d 305, 307 (Fla. 1st DCA 1991) ("There is no authority for requiring a trial court to give such an instruction at the close of trial."). Moreover, if a proper request is made to have the instruction given at the time the evidence is admitted, it is error for the trial court to delay giving such an instruction until the close of the evidence, although likely one that will be deemed harmless. See *Varnadore v. State*, 626 So. 2d 1386 (Fla. 5th DCA 1993).

Federal Rule 106. Remainder of or Related Writings or Recorded Statements

If a party introduces all or part of a writing or recorded statement, an adverse party may require the introduction, at that time, of any other part — or any other writing or recorded statement — that in fairness ought to be considered at the same time.

ADVISORY COMMITTEE'S NOTE

The rule is an expression of the rule of completeness. McCormick § 56. It is manifested as to depositions in Rule 32(a)(4) of the Federal Rules of Civil Procedure, of which the proposed rule is substantially a restatement.

The rule is based on two considerations. The first is the misleading impression created by taking matters out of context. The second is the inadequacy of repair work when delayed to a point later in the trial. See McCormick § 56; California Evidence Code § 356. The rule does not in any way circumscribe the right of the adversary to develop the matter on cross-examination or as part of his own case.

For practical reasons, the rule is limited to writings and recorded statements and does not apply to conversations.

ADVISORY COMMITTEE'S NOTE (2011 AMENDMENT)

The language of Rule 106 has been amended as part of the restyling of the Evidence Rules to make them more easily understood and to make style and terminology consistent throughout the rules. These changes are intended to be stylistic only. There is no intent to change any result in any ruling on evidence admissibility.

Florida Stat. § 90.108. Introduction of Related Writings or Recorded Statements

(1) When a writing or recorded statement or part thereof is introduced by a party, an adverse party may require him or her at that time to introduce any other part or any other writing or recorded statement that in fairness ought to be considered contemporaneously. An adverse party is not bound by evidence introduced under this section.

(2) The report of a court reporter, when certified to by the court reporter as being a correct transcript of the testimony and proceedings in the case, is prima facie a correct statement of such testimony and proceedings.

SPONSORS' NOTE (1976 ENACTMENT)

Generally, when a party introduces only a part of a writing or document, the adverse party may prove the contents of the remainder of the instrument or require his adversary to do so. See Crawford v. United States, 212 U.S. 183, 53 L.Ed. 465, 29 S.Ct. 260 (1909). The remainder of the document or writing can only be admitted in so far as it relates to the same subject matter and tends to explain and shed light on the meaning of the part already received. McCormick, Evidence § 56 (2nd ed. 1970).

This section allows an adverse party to have his opponent introduce the remainder of a writing at the same time that a portion of it is introduced, and also have contemporaneously introduced any other writing or recorded statement which in fairness ought to be considered contemporaneously. The reasoning of this section is twofold. First, it avoids the danger of mistaken first impressions when matters are taken out of context. Second, it avoids the inadequate remedy of requiring the adverse party to wait until a later point in the trial to repair his case.

This section is in addition to Fla. Rules of Civ. Pro. 1.330(b) and 1.340(b) which provide that when portions of depositions and interrogatories are not offered by a party, an adverse party may require the introduction of any other part that in fairness ought to be considered with the part introduced, and any party may introduce any other parts.

This section does not apply to conversations but is limited to writings and recorded statements because of the practical problem involved in determining the contents of a conversation and whether the remainder of it is on the same subject matter. These questions are often not readily answered without undue consumption of time. Therefore, remaining portions of conversations are best left to be developed on cross-examination or as a part of a party's own case.

This treatment of conversations is in accord with Morey v. State, 72 Fla. 45, 72 So. 490 (1916), where in a criminal prosecution, when the state offered evidence of inculpatory statements made by the defendant, the court found that the defendant had the right to have placed before the jury, by means of cross-examination, the entire conversation or all statements made by the defendant at the same time and relating to the same subject matter, whether such other statements or the remainder of the conversation are exculpatory in nature.

See Fed. Rule Evid. 106[.] Calif. Evid. Code § 356 allows the admission of remaining portions of acts, declarations, writings, and conversations that have been received in part.

COMMENTARY ON FEDERAL AND FLORIDA RULE DIFFERENCES

Florida Stat. § 90.108 and its federal counterpart, Federal Rule 106, codify the "rule of completeness." Both the Florida provision and its federal counterpart provide that when a writing or recorded statement or some part thereof is introduced by one party, an adverse party may require the introduction at that time of any other part of the writing or any related writings or recorded statements that in fairness ought to be considered contemporaneously with it. The rationales for the rule are to guard against the risk of a misleading impression when a statement is taken out of context and a belief that requiring an adverse party to wait until a later point in the trial to repair his case by bringing up the context is an inadequate remedy. See Advisory Committee's Note to FED. R. EVID. 106; Sponsors' Note to FLA. STAT. § 90.108.

Neither the Florida rule nor its federal counterpart create an absolute right to introduce the remainder of a writing or recorded statement; rather, the standard is whether fairness requires that it be introduced at that time. See Ramirez v. State, 739 So. 2d 568, 580 (Fla. 1999); U.S. v. Simms, 385 F.3d 1347, 1359 (11th Cir. 2004). The trial judge decides whether fairness so requires, and her determination is reviewed deferentially on appellate review. See Mendoza v. State, 700 So. 2d 670, 673 (Fla. 1997); U.S. v. Ramos-Caraballo, 375 F.3d 797, 802 (8th Cir. 2004). However, a determination that fairness does not require that the context be introduced at that time does not prevent an adverse party from bringing up that context at a later point in the trial. Vazquez v. State, 700 So. 2d 5, 8-9 (Fla. 4th DCA 1997).

In terms, both the Florida and federal rules apply only to *written or recorded* statements and not to conversations. See Advisory Committee's Note to FED. R. EVID. 106; Sponsors' Note to FLA. STAT. § 90.108. Nonetheless, both federal and Florida decisions, while conceding that testimony about conversations is not covered by the plain text of the rule, extend the principle underlying the rule to testimony about conversations. *See U.S. v. Baker*, 432 F.3d 1189, 1223 (11th Cir. 2005) (relying on FED. R. EVID. 611(a)); *Ramirez*, 739 So. 2d at 580; *Johnson v. State*, 608 So. 2d 4, 9-10 (Fla. 1992).

One source of confusion under both Federal and Florida practice is whether or not the rule of completeness can be invoked to introduce the contextual parts of a writing or recording even if they are otherwise inadmissible because, say, they are hearsay not falling within a hearsay exception. The federal courts are split on this issue, with some holding that Rule 106 merely alters the order of proof and is limited to evidence that is otherwise admissible, and others holding that it allows for the admission of otherwise inadmissible evidence. *Compare U.S. v. Collicott*, 92 F.3d 973, 983 (9th Cir. 1996) (Rule 106 alters the order of proof only), with *U.S. v. Sutton*, 801 F.2d 1346, 1368 (D.C. Cir. 1986) ("Rule 106 can adequately fulfill its function only by permitting the admission of some otherwise inadmissible evidence when the court finds in fairness that the proffered evidence should be considered contemporaneously."). *See also U.S. v. LeFevour*, 798 F.2d 977, 981 (7th Cir. 1986) ("If otherwise inadmissible evidence is necessary to correct a misleading impression, then either it is admissible for this limited purpose by force of Rule 106...or, if it is inadmissible...the misleading evidence must be excluded too [under Rule 403]"). By contrast, it seems relatively clear that the Florida rule of completeness allows for the admission of otherwise inadmissible evidence, even if it is hearsay, provided that it is relevant and sheds light on the parts of the statement already admitted. *See Whitfield v. State*, 933 So. 2d 1245, 1248-49 (Fla. 1st DCA 2006); *Vazquez*, 700 So. 2d at 8-9; *Johnson v. State*, 653 So. 2d 1074, 1075 (Fla. 3d DCA 1995). *See also Ramirez*, 739 So. 2d at 579-80 (explaining that the rule of completeness falls within the more general evidentiary principle of "opening the door," which allows for the admission of otherwise inadmissible testimony to "qualify, explain, or limit" testimony or evidence previously admitted). *But see Schreiber v. State*, 973 So. 2d 1265, 1269 & n.2 (Fla. 2d DCA 2008) (indicating that it is an open question whether § 90.108 can be invoked to introduce otherwise inadmissible hearsay). However, that the otherwise inadmissible remainder of a writing or recording is unreliable is a factor that Florida trial courts may take into account in determining whether fairness requires its admission. *Jordan v. State*, 694 So. 2d 708, 712 (Fla. 1997)

Two other minor differences exist between the federal and Florida rules. First, there is an additional sentence at the end of Florida Stat. § 90.108(1) indicating that "[a]n adverse party is not bound by evidence introduced under this section." While the federal rule contains no analogous language, the elimination in the federal rules of evidence of the common law rule that a party vouches for and thus is bound by the testimony of his witnesses makes federal and Florida practice identical in this regard. *See* FED. R. EVID. 607; Advisory Committee's Note to FED. R. EVID. 611(b).

The second minor difference between the federal and Florida rules is that the latter contains an additional provision, Florida Stat. § 90.108(2), which provides that "[t]he report of a court reporter, when certified to by the court reporter as being a correct transcript of the testimony and proceedings in the case, is prima facie a correct statement of such testimony and proceedings." Although Federal Rule 106 contains no such language, a separate federal statute contains language analogous to that of Florida Stat. § 90.108(2). *See* 28 U.S.C. § 753(b).

Florida Stat. § 90.106. Summing Up and Comment by Judge

A judge may not sum up the evidence or comment to the jury upon the weight of the evidence, the credibility of the witnesses, or the guilt of the accused.

SPONSORS' NOTE (1976 ENACTMENT)

This section codifies the existing Florida law that a judge may not comment on the weight of the evidence, the credibility of a witness or the guilt of the accused. See <u>Seward v. State</u>, 59 So. 2d 529 (Fla.

1952); Hamilton v. State, 261 So. 2d 184 (Fla. 3rd Dist. 1972); Lister v. State, 226 So. 2d 238 (Fla. 4th Dist. 1969).

The basis for this section was expressed in Hamilton v. State, 109 So. 2d 422, 424 (Fla. 3rd Dist. 1959):

> The dominant position occupied by a judge in the trial of a cause before a jury is such that his remarks or comments...overshadow those of the litigants, witnesses and other court officers. Where such comment expresses or tends to express the judge's view as to the weight of the evidence, the credibility of a witness, or the guilt of the accused, it thereby destroys the impartiality of the trial....

Under existing Florida law, remarks made by a judge in a jury trial which constitute forbidden comment, to which no objection is made, do not require a reversal unless they constitute fundamental error. Worthington v. State, 183 So. 2d 728 (Fla. 3rd Dist. 1966). It is envisioned that under this section such Florida law will remain unchanged.

COMMENTARY ON FEDERAL AND FLORIDA RULE DIFFERENCES

Florida Stat. § 90.106—which codifies the preexisting common law rule in Florida—bars a trial court judge from summing up the evidence or commenting to the jury on the weight of the evidence, the credibility of witnesses, or the accused's guilt. The scope of the rule is broad, barring not only direct comments by the trial judge that a witness is or is not believable or about the trial court's view of the weight of the evidence, but also statements that indirectly do the same. See *Leavine v. State*, 147 So. 897, 902-03 (Fla. 1933) ("[A] trial court should avoid making any remark within the hearing of the jury that is capable directly or indirectly, expressly, inferentially, or by innuendo of conveying any intimation as to what view he takes of the case or that intimates his opinion as to the weight, character, or credibility of any evidence adduced.").

Thus, for example, it violates the Florida rule for the trial judge to declare before the jury that a witness qualifies as an expert, *Whitaker v. State*, 742 So. 2d 530 (Fla. 1st DCA 1999), to interrupt a party's closing argument or questioning and say before the jury that the party is mischaracterizing the evidence, *Vaughn v. Progressive Cas. Ins. Co.*, 907 So. 2d 1248, 1253-54 (Fla. 5th DCA 2005); *Jacques v. State*, 883 So. 2d 902, 904-06 (Fla. 4th DCA 2004); *Brown v. State*, 678 So. 2d 910, 911-12 (Fla. 4th DCA 1996), or to say to an expert witness before the jury that she is acting more as an advocate than a witness, *Fogelman v. State*, 648 So. 2d 214, 218-19 (Fla. 4th DCA 1995).

Moreover, the Florida rule bars trial judges from inviting jurors to infer conclusions from certain types of evidence. Thus, under the Florida rule, a trial court judge is barred from instructing jurors that they may infer guilt from evidence of a defendant's flight, his refusal to submit to fingerprinting, or the fact that he has made inconsistent exculpatory statements. See *Fenelon v. State*, 594 So. 2d 292, 294-95 (Fla. 1992) (flight); *Whitfield v. State*, 452 So. 2d 548, 549 (Fla. 1984) (refusal to be fingerprinted); *In re Instructions in Criminal Cases*, 652 So. 2d 814, 815 (Fla. 1995) (inconsistent exculpatory statements). In a recent decision, however, the Florida Supreme Court distinguished this line of cases, holding that the rule does not bar a trial court from instructing jurors in theft or burglary cases that proof of possession by an accused of recently stolen property, if unexplained, gives rise to an inference that the person knew or should have known the property was stolen. *Walker v. State*, 896 So. 2d 712, 719-20 (Fla. 2005). The court distinguished the prior line of cases on the ground that they involved matters that were extrinsic to the charged crime, while the instruction at issue in the case was "inextricably intertwined" with the crime charged. *Id.* at 719. A perhaps more compelling reason for distinguishing the case, alluded to in the opinion, is that the instructions at issue were derived directly from the theft and burglary statutes themselves, and can thus be construed as a more specific statutory provision creating an exception to Florida Stat. § 90.106's general rule. *Id.* at 714 & n.2, 719-20 & n.3.

There is no specific federal rule of evidence governing the ability of a judge to sum up and comment on evidence. A proposed federal rule of evidence would have provided as follows:

> After the close of the evidence and arguments of counsel, the judge may fairly and impartially sum up the evidence and comment to the jury upon the weight of the evidence and the credibility of the witnesses, if he also instructs the jury that they are to determine for themselves the weight of the evidence and the credit to be given to the witnesses and that they are not bound by the judge's summation or comment.

Proposed FED. R. EVID. 105. The proposed rule restated the common law rule governing in the federal courts. *See* Advisory Committee's Note to Proposed FED. R. EVID. 105. Congress opted not to let the proposed rule take effect, although its failure to do so was understood not to disturb the preexisting federal practice that was in accord with the proposed rule. *See* Report of Senate Committee on the Judiciary, Proposed FED. R. EVID. 105. That preexisting federal practice, which prevails in the federal courts today, is as follows:

> In charging the jury, the trial judge is not limited to instructions of an abstract sort. It is within his province, whenever he thinks it necessary, to assist the jury in arriving at a just conclusion by explaining and commenting upon the evidence, by drawing their attention to the parts of it which he thinks important, and he may express his opinions upon the facts, provided he makes it clear to the jury that all matters of fact are submitted to their determination.

Quercia v. U.S., 289 U.S. 466, 469 (1933). Thus, for example, trial judges are free to instruct jurors that they may infer guilt from evidence of flight. *See, e.g., U.S. v. Dillon*, 870 F.2d 1125, 1126 (6th Cir. 1989). The only significant restrictions on a federal judge's ability to sum up or comment upon the evidence is that he must make clear to the jury that they are the sole judge of the facts and are not bound by his comments, that he not distort or add to the evidence, and that he exercise care in giving his opinion so as not to mislead or appear to be one-sided. *Quercia,* 289 U.S. at 470; *U.S. v. Jenkins*, 901 F.2d 1075, 1082-83 (11th Cir. 1990). Accordingly, the Federal and Florida rules are nearly the mirror-image of one another. *See Moton v. State*, 659 So. 2d 1269, 1270 (Fla. 4th DCA 1995) ("Unlike the rule in our federal courts...in Florida state courts it is improper for a trial judge to comment on the weight of the evidence, i.e. to suggest that some evidence may be more important than other evidence."); Report of House Committee on the Judiciary, Proposed FED. R. EVID. 105 (noting that the "authority of a judge to comment on the weight of the evidence and the credibility of witnesses [is] an authority not granted to judges in most State courts").

ARTICLE II. JUDICIAL NOTICE

Federal Rule	Florida Stat. §	Description
201	90.201-90.207	Judicial Notice of Adjudicative Facts

Federal Rule 201. Judicial Notice of Adjudicative Facts

(a) Scope. This rule governs judicial notice of an adjudicative fact only, not a legislative fact.

(b) Kinds of Facts That May Be Judicially Noticed. The court may judicially notice a fact that is not subject to reasonable dispute because it:

    (1) is generally known within the trial court's territorial jurisdiction; or

    (2) can be accurately and readily determined from sources whose accuracy cannot reasonably be questioned.

(c) Taking Notice. The court:

    (1) may take judicial notice on its own; or

    (2) must take judicial notice if a party requests it and the court is supplied with the necessary information.

(d) Timing. The court may take judicial notice at any stage of the proceeding.

(e) Opportunity to Be Heard. On timely request, a party is entitled to be heard on the propriety of taking judicial notice and the nature of the fact to be noticed. If the court takes judicial notice before notifying a party, the party, on request, is still entitled to be heard.

(f) Instructing the Jury. In a civil case, the court must instruct the jury to accept the noticed fact as conclusive. In a criminal case, the court must instruct the jury that it may or may not accept the noticed fact as conclusive.

ADVISORY COMMITTEE'S NOTE

Subdivision (a). This is the only evidence rule on the subject of judicial notice. It deals only with judicial notice of "adjudicative" facts. No rule deals with judicial notice of "legislative" facts. Judicial notice of matters of foreign law is treated in Rule 44.1 of the Federal Rules of Civil Procedure and Rule 26.1 of the Federal Rules of Criminal Procedure.

The omission of any treatment of legislative facts results from fundamental differences between adjudicative facts and legislative facts. Adjudicative facts are simply the facts of the particular case. Legislative facts, on the other hand, are those which have relevance to legal reasoning and the lawmaking process, whether in the formulation of a legal principle or ruling by a judge or court or in the enactment of a legislative body. The terminology was coined by Professor Kenneth Davis in his article An Approach to Problems of Evidence in the Administrative Process, 55 Harv.L.Rev. 364, 404–407 (1942). The following discussion draws extensively upon his writings. In addition, see the same author's Judicial Notice, 55 Colum.L.Rev. 945 (1955); Administrative Law Treatise, ch. 15 (1958); A System of Judicial Notice Based on Fairness and Convenience, in Perspectives of Law 69 (1964).

The usual method of establishing adjudicative facts is through the introduction of evidence, ordinarily consisting of the testimony of witnesses. If particular facts are outside the area of reasonable controversy, this process is dispensed with as unnecessary. A high degree of indisputability is the essential prerequisite.

Legislative facts are quite different. As Professor Davis says:

"My opinion is that judge-made law would stop growing if judges, in thinking about questions of law and policy, were forbidden to take into account the facts they believe, as distinguished from facts which are 'clearly . . . within the domain of the indisputable.' Facts most needed in thinking about difficult problems of law and policy have a way of being outside the domain of the clearly indisputable." A System of Judicial Notice Based on Fairness and Convenience, *supra*, at 82.

An illustration is Hawkins v. United States, 358 U.S. 74 (1958), in which the Court refused to discard the common law rule that one spouse could not testify against the other, saying, "Adverse testimony given in criminal proceedings would, we think, be likely to destroy almost any marriage." This conclusion has a large intermixture of fact, but the factual aspect is scarcely "indisputable." See Hutchins and Slesinger, Some Observations on the Law of Evidence — Family Relations, 13 Minn.L.Rev. 675 (1929). If the destructive effect of the giving of adverse testimony by a spouse is not indisputable, should the Court have refrained from considering it in the absence of supporting evidence?

"If the Model Code or the Uniform Rules had been applicable, the Court would have been barred from thinking about the essential factual ingredient of the problems before it, and such a result would be obviously intolerable. What the law needs at its growing points is more, not less, judicial thinking about the factual ingredients of problems of what the law ought to be, and the needed facts are seldom 'clearly' indisputable." Davis, supra, at 83.

Professor Morgan gave the following description of the methodology of determining domestic law:

"In determining the content or applicability of a rule of domestic law, the judge is unrestricted in his investigation and conclusion. He may reject the propositions of either party or of both parties. He may consult the sources of pertinent data to which they refer, or he may refuse to do so. He may make an independent search for persuasive data or rest content with what he has or what the parties present. . . . [T]he parties do no more than to assist; they control no part of the process." Morgan, Judicial Notice, 57 Harv.L.Rev. 269, 270–271 (1944).

This is the view which should govern judicial access to legislative facts. It renders inappropriate any limitation in the form of indisputability, any formal requirements of notice other than those already inherent in affording opportunity to hear and be heard and exchanging briefs, and any requirement of formal findings at any level. It should, however leave open the possibility of introducing evidence through regular channels in appropriate situations. See Borden's Farm Products Co. v. Baldwin, 293 U.S. 194 (1934), where the cause was remanded for the taking of evidence as to the economic conditions and trade practices underlying the New York Milk Control Law.

Similar considerations govern the judicial use of non-adjudicative facts in ways other than formulating laws and rules. Thayer described them as a part of the judicial reasoning process.

"In conducting a process of judicial reasoning, as of other reasoning, not a step can be taken without assuming something which has not been proved; and the capacity to do this with competent judgment and efficiency, is imputed to judges and juries as part of their necessary mental outfit." Thayer, Preliminary Treatise on Evidence 279–280 (1898).

As Professor Davis points out, A System of Judicial Notice Based on Fairness and Convenience, in Perspectives of Law 69, 73 (1964), every case involves the use of hundreds or thousands of non-evidence facts. When a witness in an automobile accident case says "car," everyone, judge and jury included, furnishes, from non-evidence sources within himself, the supplementing information that the "car" is an automobile, not a railroad car, that it is self-propelled, probably by an internal combustion engine, that it may be assumed to have four wheels with pneumatic rubber tires, and so on. The judicial process cannot construct every case from scratch, like Descartes creating a world based on the postulate *Cogito, ergo sum*. These items could not possibly be introduced into evidence, and no one suggests that they be. Nor are they appropriate subjects for any formalized treatment of judicial notice of facts. See Levin and Levy, Persuading the Jury with Facts Not in Evidence: The Fiction-Science Spectrum, 105 U.Pa.L.Rev. 139

(1956).

Another aspect of what Thayer had in mind is the use of non-evidence facts to appraise or assess the adjudicative facts of the case. Pairs of cases from two jurisdictions illustrate this use and also the difference between non-evidence facts thus used and adjudicative facts. In People v. Strook, 347 Ill. 460 (1932), venue in Cook County had been held not established by testimony that the crime was committed at 7956 South Chicago Avenue, since judicial notice would not be taken that the address was in Chicago. However, the same court subsequently ruled that venue in Cook County was established by testimony that a crime occurred at 8900 South Anthony Avenue, since notice would be taken of the common practice of omitting the name of the city when speaking of local addresses, and the witness was testifying in Chicago. People v. Pride, 16 Ill.2d 82 (1951). And in Hughes v. Vestal, 264 N.C. 500 (1965), the Supreme Court of North Carolina disapproved the trial judge's admission in evidence of a state-published table of automobile stopping distances on the basis of judicial notice, though the court itself had referred to the same table in an earlier case in a "rhetorical and illustrative" way in determining that the defendant could not have stopped her car in time to avoid striking a child who suddenly appeared in the highway and that a nonsuit was properly granted. Ennis v. Dupree, 262 N.C. 224 (1964). See also Brown v. Hale, 263 N.C. 176 (1964); Clayton v. Rimmer, 262 N.C. 302 (1964). It is apparent that this use of non-evidence facts in evaluating the adjudicative facts of the case is not an appropriate subject for a formalized judicial notice treatment.

In view of these considerations, the regulation of judicial notice of facts by the present rule extends only to adjudicative facts.

What, then, are "adjudicative" facts? Davis refers to them as those "which relate to the parties," or more fully:

"When a court or an agency finds facts concerning the immediate parties — who did what, where, when, how, and with what motive or intent — the court or agency is performing an adjudicative function, and the facts are conveniently called adjudicative facts. . . ." Stated in other terms, the adjudicative facts are those to which the law is applied in the process of adjudication. They are the facts that normally go to the jury in a jury case. They relate to the parties, their activities, their properties, their businesses." 2 Administrative Law Treatise 353.

Subdivision (b). With respect to judicial notice of adjudicative facts, the tradition has been one of caution in requiring that the matter be beyond reasonable controversy. This tradition of circumspection appears to be soundly based, and no reason to depart from it is apparent. As Professor Davis says:

"The reason we use trial-type procedure, I think, is that we make the practical judgment, on the basis of experience, that taking evidence, subject to cross-examination and rebuttal, is the best way to resolve controversies involving disputes of adjudicative facts, that is, facts pertaining to the parties. The reason we require a determination on the record is that we think fair procedure in resolving disputes of adjudicative facts calls for giving each party a chance to meet in the appropriate fashion the facts that come to the tribunal's attention, and the appropriate fashion for meeting disputed adjudicative facts includes rebuttal evidence, cross-examination, usually confrontation, and argument (either written or oral or both). The key to a fair trial is opportunity to use the appropriate weapons (rebuttal evidence, cross-examination, and argument) to meet adverse materials that come to the tribunal's attention." A System of Judicial Notice Based on Fairness and Convenience, in Perspectives of Law 69, 93 (1964).

The rule proceeds upon the theory that these considerations call for dispensing with traditional methods of proof only in clear cases. Compare Professor Davis' conclusion that judicial notice should be a matter of convenience, subject to requirements of procedural fairness. Id., 94.

This rule is consistent with Uniform Rule 9(1) and (2) which limit judicial notice of facts to those "so universally known that they cannot reasonably be the subject of dispute," those "so generally known or of such common notoriety within the territorial jurisdiction of the court that they cannot reasonably be the subject of dispute," and those "capable of immediate and accurate determination by resort to easily accessible sources of indisputable accuracy." The traditional textbook treatment has included these general categories (matters of common knowledge, facts capable of verification), McCormick §§ 324, 325, and then has passed on into detailed treatment of such specific topics as facts relating to the personnel and records of the court, *id.* § 327, and other governmental facts, *id.* § 328. The California draftsmen, with a background of detailed statutory regulation of judicial notice, followed a somewhat similar pattern. California Evidence Code §§ 451, 452. The Uniform Rules, however, were drafted on the theory that these particular matters are included within the general categories and need no specific mention. This approach is followed in the present rule.

The phrase "propositions of generalized knowledge," found in Uniform Rule 9(1) and (2) is not included in the present rule. It was, it is believed, originally included in Model Code Rules 801 and 802 primarily in order to afford some minimum recognition to the right of the judge in his "legislative" capacity (not acting as the trier of fact) to take judicial notice of very limited categories of generalized knowledge. The limitations thus imposed have been discarded herein as undesirable, unworkable, and contrary to existing practice. What is left, then, to be considered, is the status of a "proposition of generalized knowledge" as an "adjudicative" fact to be noticed judicially and communicated by the judge to the jury. Thus viewed, it is considered to be lacking practical significance. While judges use judicial notice of "propositions of generalized knowledge" in a variety of situations: determining the validity and meaning of statutes, formulating common law rules, deciding whether evidence should be admitted, assessing the sufficiency and effect of evidence, all are essentially nonadjudicative in nature. When judicial notice is seen as a significant vehicle for progress in the law, these are the areas involved, particularly in developing fields of scientific knowledge. See McCormick 712. It is not believed that judges now instruct juries as to "propositions of generalized knowledge" derived from encyclopedias or other sources, or that they are likely to do so, or, indeed, that it is desirable that they do so. There is a vast difference between ruling on the basis of judicial notice that radar evidence of speed is admissible and explaining to the jury its principles and degree of accuracy, or between using a table of stopping distances of automobiles at various speeds in a judicial evaluation of testimony and telling the jury its precise application in the case. For cases raising doubt as to the propriety of the use of medical texts by lay triers of fact in passing on disability claims in administrative proceedings, see Sayers v. Gardner, 380 F.2d 940 (6th Cir. 1967); Ross v. Gardner, 365 F.2d 554 (6th Cir. 1966); Sosna v. Celebrezze, 234 F.Supp. 289 (E.D.Pa. 1964); Glendenning v. Ribicoff, 213 F.Supp. 301 (W.D.Mo. 1962).

Subdivision [(c)]. Under subdivision (c)[(1)] the judge has a discretionary authority to take judicial notice, regardless of whether he is so requested by a party. The taking of judicial notice is mandatory, under subdivision [(c)(2)], only when a party requests it and the necessary information is supplied. This scheme is believed to reflect existing practice. It is simple and workable. It avoids troublesome distinctions in the many situations in which the process of taking judicial notice is not recognized as such.

Compare Uniform Rule 9 making judicial notice of facts universally known mandatory without request, and making judicial notice of facts generally known in the jurisdiction or capable of determination by resort to accurate sources discretionary in the absence of request but mandatory if request is made and the information furnished. But see Uniform Rule 10(3), which directs the judge to decline to take judicial notice if available information fails to convince him that the matter falls clearly within Uniform Rule 9 or is insufficient to enable him to notice it judicially. Substantially the same approach is found in California Evidence Code §§ 451–453 and in New Jersey Evidence Rule 9. In contrast, the present rule treats alike all adjudicative facts which are subject to judicial notice.

Subdivision (e). Basic considerations of procedural fairness demand an opportunity to be heard on the propriety of taking judicial notice and the tenor of the matter noticed. The rule requires the granting of that opportunity upon request. No formal scheme of giving notice is provided. An adversely affected party may learn in advance that judicial notice is in contemplation, either by virtue of being served with a copy of a request by another party under subdivision [(c)(2)] that judicial notice be taken, or through an advance indication by the judge. Or he may have no advance notice at all. The likelihood of the latter is enhanced by the frequent failure to recognize judicial notice as such. And in the absence of advance notice, a request made after the fact could not in fairness be considered untimely. See the provision for hearing on timely request in the Administrative Procedure Act, 5 U.S.C. § 556(e). See also Revised Model State Administrative Procedure Act (1961), 9C U.L.A. § 10(4) (Supp.1967).

Subdivision ([d]). In accord with the usual view, judicial notice may be taken at any stage of the proceedings, whether in the trial court or on appeal. Uniform Rule 12; California Evidence Code § 459; Kansas Rules of Evidence § 60-412; New Jersey Evidence Rule 12; McCormick § 330, p. 712.

Subdivision ([f]). Much of the controversy about judicial notice has centered upon the question whether evidence should be admitted in disproof of facts of which judicial notice is taken.

The writers have been divided. Favoring admissibility are Thayer, Preliminary Treatise on Evidence 308 (1898); 9 Wigmore § 2567; Davis, A System of Judicial Notice Based on Fairness and Convenience, in Perspectives of Law, 69, 76–77 (1964). Opposing admissibility are Keeffe, Landis and Shaad, Sense and Nonsense about Judicial Notice, 2 Stan.L.Rev. 664, 668 (1950); McNaughton, Judicial Notice — Excerpts Relating to the Morgan-Whitmore Controversy, 14 Vand.L.Rev. 779 (1961); Morgan, Judicial Notice, 57 Harv.L.Rev. 269, 279 (1944); McCormick 710–711. The Model Code and the Uniform Rules are predicated upon indisputability of judicially noticed facts.

The proponents of admitting evidence in disproof have concentrated largely upon legislative facts. Since the present rule deals only with judicial notice of adjudicative facts, arguments directed to legislative facts lose their relevancy.

Within its relatively narrow area of adjudicative facts, the rule contemplates there is to be no evidence before the jury in disproof. The judge instructs the jury to take judicially noticed facts as established. This position is justified by the undesirable effects of the opposite rule in limiting the rebutting party, though not his opponent, to admissible evidence, in defeating the reasons for judicial notice, and in affecting the substantive law to an extent and in ways largely unforeseeable. Ample protection and flexibility are afforded by the broad provision for opportunity to be heard on request, set forth in subdivision (e).

Authority upon the propriety of taking judicial notice against an accused in a criminal case with respect to matters other than venue is relatively meager. Proceeding upon the theory that the right of jury trial does not extend to matters which are beyond reasonable dispute, the rule does not distinguish between criminal and civil cases. People v. Mayes, 113 Cal. 618 (1896); Ross v. United States, 374 F.2d 97 (8th Cir. 1967). Cf. State v. Main, 94 R.I. 338 (1962); State v. Lawrence, 120 Utah 323 (1951).

ADVISORY COMMITTEE'S NOTE ON JUDICIAL NOTICE OF LAW

By rules effective July 1, 1966, the method of invoking the law of a foreign country is covered elsewhere. Rule 44.1 of the Federal Rules of Civil Procedure; Rule 26.1 of the Federal Rules of Criminal Procedure. These two new admirably designed rules are founded upon the assumption that the manner in which law is fed into the judicial process is never a proper concern of the rules of evidence but rather of the rules of procedure. The Advisory Committee on Evidence, believing that this assumption is entirely correct, proposes no evidence rule with respect to judicial notice of law, and suggests that those matters of law which, in addition to foreign-country law, have traditionally been treated as requiring pleading and proof and more recently as the subject of judicial notice be left to the Rules of Civil and Criminal Procedure.

REPORT OF HOUSE COMMITTEE ON THE JUDICIARY

Rule 201([f]) as received from the Supreme Court provided that when judicial notice of a fact is taken, the court shall instruct the jury to accept that fact as established. Being of the view that mandatory instruction to a jury in a criminal case to accept as conclusive any fact judicially noticed is inappropriate because contrary to the spirit of the Sixth Amendment right to a jury trial, the Committee adopted the 1969 Advisory Committee draft of this subsection, allowing a mandatory instruction in civil actions and proceedings and a discretionary instruction in criminal cases.

ADVISORY COMMITTEE'S NOTE (2011 AMENDMENT)

The language of Rule 201 has been amended as part of the restyling of the Evidence Rules to make them more easily understood and to make style and terminology consistent throughout the rules. These changes are intended to be stylistic only. There is no intent to change any result in any ruling on evidence admissibility.

Florida Stat. § 90.201. Matters Which Must Be Judicially Noticed

A court shall take judicial notice of:

(1) Decisional, constitutional, and public statutory law and resolutions of the Florida Legislature and the Congress of the United States.

(2) Florida rules of court that have statewide application, its own rules, and the rules of United States courts adopted by the United States Supreme Court.

(3) Rules of court of the United States Supreme Court and of the United States Courts of Appeal.

SPONSORS' NOTE (1976 ENACTMENT)

Judicial notice of the matters included in Section 90.201 is mandatory even though the matter may likewise be included in the discretionary provisions of Section 90.202. For example, public statutory law of this state is a subject for mandatory notice under Section 90.201, even though it would also be included under the official acts of the legislature under Section 90.202(5).

Subsection (1) The need to judicially notice the decisional, constitutional and public statutory law of the United States and of this state is apparent. Generally domestic law is mandatorily judicially noticed; therefore state courts will notice the federal law that is controlling in each state. McCormick, Evidence § 335 (2nd ed.1972). Florida law is in accord. The constitution and public acts of the legislature of Florida will be judicially noticed, without the necessity of their being specially plead. Atlantic Coast Line R.R. v. State, 73 Fla. 609, 74 So. 595 (1917). The constitution and statutes are judicially noticed by state courts, and such judicial notice includes authoritative decisions construing them and settling questions of law. State ex rel. Landis v. Prevatt, 110 Fla. 29, 148 So. 578 (1933). See Calif. Evid. Code § 451 for a similar provision.

This section also combines portions of existing Sections 92.01-92.03 of the Florida Statutes, which provide for the admission of printed copies of all acts of the Florida legislature and of the United States which are published under the authority of the government, as sufficient evidence of such statutes, acts and resolutions.

Subsection (2)[3] This subsection provides for the mandatory judicial notice of ordinances and municipal and county charters when their enforcement is within the jurisdiction of the court. Existing Florida law recognizes the discretion of a court to take judicial notice of those municipal ordinances that it is charged with enforcing. See Holmes v. State, 273 So.2d 753 (Fla. 1972). Thus, appellate courts as well as trial courts are able to notice the ordinance. This section makes the existing judicial notice mandatory rather than discretionary. See Comment, Judicial Notice: Florida's New Look at Municipal Ordinances, 25 U. Fla. L. Rev. 811 (1973).

Subsection (3) [Renumbered as Subsection (2) in 1978] This subsection provides for the mandatory judicial notice of rules of court having statewide application in Florida. The Florida Rules of Civil or Criminal Procedure would be judicially noticed by a court without the necessity of giving timely written notice pursuant to Section 90.203. A Florida court must also take judicial notice of Federal Rules of Procedure as well as the local court's own rules. However, this subsection does not provide for the mandatory judicial notice of local rules of a circuit court by another court, the provisions of 90.202(7) are applicable.

Subsection (4) [Renumbered as Subsection (3) in 1978] This subsection provides for the mandatory judicial notice of the rules of the various United States Courts of Appeal and of the United States Supreme Court.

Florida Stat. § 90.202. Matters Which May Be Judicially Noticed

A court may take judicial notice of the following matters, to the extent that they are not embraced within s. 90.201:

(1) Special, local, and private acts and resolutions of the Congress of the United States and of the Florida Legislature.

(2) Decisional, constitutional, and public statutory law of every other state, territory, and jurisdiction of the United States.

(3) Contents of the Federal Register.

(4) Laws of foreign nations and of an organization of nations.

(5) Official actions of the legislative, executive, and judicial departments of the United States and of any state, territory, or jurisdiction of the United States.

(6) Records of any court of this state or of any court of record of the United States or of any state, territory, or jurisdiction of the United States.

(7) Rules of court of any court of this state or of any court of record of the United States or of any other state, territory, or jurisdiction of the United States.

(8) Provisions of all municipal and county charters and charter amendments of this state, provided they are available in printed copies or as certified copies.

(9) Rules promulgated by governmental agencies of this state which are published in the Florida Administrative Code or in bound written copies.

(10) Duly enacted ordinances and resolutions of municipalities and counties located in Florida, provided such ordinances and resolutions are available in printed copies or as certified copies.

---

[3] Editor's Note: This refers to a subsection that was deleted in 1978.

(11) Facts that are not subject to dispute because they are generally known within the territorial jurisdiction of the court.

(12) Facts that are not subject to dispute because they are capable of accurate and ready determination by resort to sources whose accuracy cannot be questioned.

(13) Official seals of governmental agencies and departments of the United States and of any state, territory, or jurisdiction of the United States.

SPONSORS' NOTE (1976 ENACTMENT)

Judicial notice of the matters listed in Section 90.202 is discretionary. The court may take judicial notice of these matters, whether or not it is requested by a party to do so. However, if a party requests that judicial notice be taken and satisfies the requirements of Section 90.203, then judicial notice of these matters is mandatory. The purpose behind making judicial notice discretionary unless the requirements of Section 90.203 are met, is that of basic fairness. Since these matters are usually less "known" and "available" (than the mandatory items in Section 90.201), there is a requirement of notice to adverse parties before judicial notice is compulsory. Thus, adverse parties will be alerted to reliance on judicial notice to prove one of the particular matters and can prepare to meet the request. Also since the matters included in Section 90.202 may neither be known to the court nor easily discoverable, judicial notice is not mandatory unless the party requesting it supplies the court with sufficient information for it to take judicial notice and gives the requisite notice to adverse parties.

Although this section allows judicial notice of some matters not judicially noticed by the courts of this state under existing law, this wider scope of notice is balanced by the assurance that the matter need not be judicially noticed unless sufficient information to support its truth is furnished to the court. The burden of supplying the information is upon the party requesting that judicial notice be taken. It is also envisioned that when the court feels that judicial notice of a matter is necessary to the disposition of the case, the court may call upon counsel to obtain information as to the matter. The parties are afforded, under Section 90.204, an opportunity to be heard as to the propriety of taking judicial notice and as to the tenor of the matter to be noticed.

Subsection (1) This subsection allows judicial notice of special, local, and private acts and resolutions of the Congress of the United States and of the Florida legislature. Existing Florida law allows judicial notice of all public statutes, see City of Lakeland v. Select Tenures, Inc., 129 Fla. 338, 176 So. 274 (1937), as well as special or local laws, Howarth v. City of DeLand, 117 Fla. 692, 158 So. 294 (1934), Charlotte Harbor & N.R.R. v. Welles, 78 Fla. 227, 82 So. 770, aff'd, 260 U.S. 8, 43 S.Ct. 3, 67 L.Ed. 100 (1922), and private acts, Section 92.01 of the Florida Statutes, but see Gard, Florida Evidence p. 106 (1967). Regardless of the number of people affected by a legislative act, it is capable of accurate and ready determination by sources which cannot reasonably be disputed since it is a written pronouncement by the Congress of the United States or the legislature of this state.

Subsection (2) This subsection allows the decisional, constitutional and public statutory law in force in every other state, territory and jurisdiction of the United States to be judicially noticed. Subsection (2) is in accord with existing law since Florida presently does judicially notice the common law and statutes of every other state, territory and jurisdiction of the United States under its Uniform Judicial Notice of Foreign Law Act, Fla. Stat. § 92.031. The manner of bringing the foreign law to the court's attention is discussed in Section 90.203.

Subsection (3) This subsection allows the courts to take judicial notice of documents which are published in the Federal Register. Although the Federal Register Act, 44 U.S.C. § 1507, provides that the "contents of the Federal Register shall be judicially noticed," it has not been made clear that the Act requires state courts to take such notice.

This subsection, which provides for judicial notice of all portions of the Federal Register, follows the modern trend of including matters for judicial notice that are capable of accurate and ready determination by access to sources of indisputable accuracy.

<u>Subsection (4)</u> This subsection authorizes that judicial notice be taken of the laws of foreign countries and of organizations of nations. The majority of jurisdictions, including Florida, disagree and require that a foreign country's law be plead and proved by the party relying on it. The usual reasons advanced for this requirement of pleading and proof are that foreign countries' law is difficult to prove and sources are not easily accessible. See <u>Courtlandt Corp. v. Whitmer</u>, 121 So. 2d 57 (Fla. 2nd Dist. 1960); cf. <u>Hieber v. Hieber</u>, 151 So. 2d 646 (Fla. 3rd Dist. 1963) (law of foreign state). Calif. Evid. Code § 451 is similar.

The existing Florida Uniform Judicial Notice of Foreign Law Act, Fla. Stat. § 92.031 provides for judicial notice to be taken of the "common law and statutes of every state, territory and other jurisdiction of the United States," and that the law "of a jurisdiction other than those referred to," i.e., a foreign nation, is "an issue for the court." Thus, laws of foreign nations are treated as a fact to be plead and proved by the party relying thereon and a determination of the existence of that foreign law is for the court. In the absence of such an allegation the court will presume that the foreign law is the same as that of the forum. Cf. <u>United Mercantile Agencies v. Bissonette</u>, 155 Fla. 22, 19 So. 2d 466 (1944); <u>Movielab, Inc. v. Davis</u>, 217 So. 2d 890 (Fla. 3rd Dist. 1969) (law of foreign state).

Rule 44.1 of the Federal Rules of Civil Procedure provides that:

> A party who intends to raise an issue concerning the law of a foreign country shall give notice in his pleadings or other reasonable written notice. The court, in determining foreign law, may consider any relevant material or source, including testimony, whether or not submitted by a party or admissible under Rule 43. The court's determination shall be treated as <u>a ruling on a question of law</u>. (Emphasis added.)

Rule 26.1 of the Federal Rules of Criminal Procedure is substantially the same.

Thus, federal courts handle foreign law as a matter of procedure, and make the foreign law "a ruling on a question of law."

Although this subsection treats the issue as one of evidence and a matter of judicial notice, the court, in complying with Section 90.204, makes a determination similar to that made under the Federal Rules. Uniform Rule 9 similarly provides for judicial notice of the laws of foreign countries.

While foreign nations' law and that of organizations of nations can be difficult to ascertain, it is felt that they should be discretionary subjects for judicial notice for if the court has not been provided "sufficient information" then it is not required to take judicial notice. In that situation, the court would resort to the presumption that the law is the same as that of the forum.

<u>Subsection (5)</u> This subsection provides for judicial notice of the official actions of the legislative, executive and judicial departments of the United States and any state, territory or jurisdiction of the United States. Florida courts have judicially noticed executive orders, signed by the governor and attested by the Secretary of State under the seal of the state, <u>Johns v. State</u>, 144 Fla. 256, 197 So. 791 (1940), official reports and records filed with the Secretary of State's office, <u>Cherry Lake Farms, Inc. v. Love</u>, 176 So. 486 (Fla. 1937), <u>Amos v. Gunn</u>, 84 Fla. 285, 94 So. 615 (1922); and legislative journals, <u>Amos v. Moseley</u>, 74 Fla. 555, 77 So. 619 (1917). Cf. <u>State ex rel. Adams v. Lee</u>, 122 Fla. 639, 166 So. 249, 259, <u>rehearing denied</u>, 166 So. 574 (1936).

However, if such an official act falls within the matters set out in Section 90.201, judicial notice is mandatory.

Neither Section 92.031 of the Florida Statutes nor the Florida courts provide for the judicial notice of the official acts of sister states as provided in this subsection. However pursuant to this subsection, when there is compliance with the provisions of Section 90.204, which place the burden on counsel to provide sufficient information upon which the court can make its determination, foreign state official acts are proper subjects for judicial notice. These matters are capable of ready and accurate determination by access to sources of indisputable accuracy.

See Calif. Evid. Code § 452(b).

Subsection (6) This subsection allows the records of any court of this state or of any court of record of the United States or of any state, territory or jurisdiction of the United States to be judicially noticed. These matters are appropriate subjects for judicial notice because they are capable of determination by access to sources of indisputable accuracy.

Florida's present position on judicial notice of court records is that a court will take judicial notice of all its own records in a pending case and of orders and proceedings relating thereto. Kelley v. Kelley, 75 So. 2d 191 (Fla. 1954). See also Bayview Homes Co. v. Sanders, 102 Fla. 516, 136 So. 234 (1931). However, a Florida court will not judicially notice the contents of the records of another distinct case, unless it is proved or in some way directly brought into and made a part of the record of the pending case. Kelley v. Kelley, supra; Atlas Land Corp. v. Norman, 116 Fla. 800, 156 So. 885 (1934). Making the record of another case a part of the record of the pending case can be accomplished by an appropriate order of the court referring to and adopting the record of the other case and can include the outside record as a part of the pending case's record. Kelley v. Kelley, supra.

The effect of subsection (6) is similar to the existing law. If counsel relies upon a court record, under Section 90.203 he must give notice and supply the court with sufficient information.

Calif. Evid. Code § 452(d) and New Jersey Evid. Rule 9(2)(b) are similar.

Subsection (7) This subsection provides for the taking of judicial notice of the rules of court of any court of this state or of any court of record of the United States or any other state, territory or jurisdiction of the United States. Including the judicial notice of these court rules is in keeping with the modern trend since they are matters which are capable of accurate and ready determination by access to sources which cannot reasonably be disputed. Calif. Evid. Code § 452(e) is similar.

Subsection (8) This subsection expands existing law in providing for judicial notice of Florida municipal and county charters which are available in printed copies or as certified copies. Sections 166.12 and 166.13 of the Florida Statutes, which allow judicial notice to be taken of the provisions of all municipal charters and charter amendments adopted and recorded as provided therein, are broadened. Section 166.13 states that the courts "shall take judicial notice," while in this Act these items fall under the discretionary section.

Subsection (9) This subsection provides that the courts may take judicial notice of rules and regulations of Florida governmental agencies when they are available in their official compilation, the Florida Administrative Code, or in bound printed copies.

Florida's position on judicially noticing such matters is unclear. The Florida Supreme Court has taken judicial notice of officially published administrative rules of the Florida Industrial Commission. Daoud v. Matz, 73 So. 2d 51 (Fla. 1954). However, when the Second District Court of Appeals took judicial notice of rules and regulations promulgated by the Florida Game and Fresh Water Fish Commission, in State v. Mobley, 133 So. 2d 334 (Fla. 2nd Dist. 1961), the Florida Supreme Court quashed the decision saying that the court could judicially notice such a rule only when it has been made a part of the record of the trial court. Mobley v. State, 143 So. 2d 821 (Fla. 1962). Section 475.05 of the Florida Statutes requires that judicial notice be taken of the rules and regulations of the Florida Real Estate Commission if such rules are printed or, if written, under the seal of the commission.

The trend is toward allowing judicial notice of administrative rules and regulations. See Ladd & Carlson, Cases and Materials on Evidence, p. 92 (1972); Uniform Rule 9(2); Calif. Evid. Code § 452(b). In the past the hesitancy to take judicial notice of administrative rules has been based on the inaccessibility of a source of indisputable evidence since often there was no regular publication of the rules.

Since the publication of the Florida Administrative Code, which includes all effective administrative rules and regulations, the problem no longer exists in Florida. This subsection also provides that judicial notice may be taken when the rules and regulations are available in bound printed copies.

Subsection (10) This subsection permits judicial notice of resolutions and ordinances of Florida counties and municipalities. Recently, the Florida Supreme Court recognized that judicial notice could be taken of municipal ordinances. See Holmes v. State, 273 So. 2d 753 (Fla. 1973). These matters are capable of exact ascertainment when the proper source is present and there is no ground for reasonable dispute. Under this subsection, all courts are permitted to take judicial notice of the ordinance. See Comment, Judicial Notice: Florida's New Look at Municipal Ordinances, 25 U. Fla. L. Rev. 811 (1973).

See New Jersey Evid. Rule 9(2)(a) and Model Code of Evid. Rule 802(a) for similar provisions.

Subsection (11) provides for judicial notice of matters generally known within the territorial jurisdiction of the court which are not subject to reasonable dispute. The Florida courts have spoken of judicial notice of facts which are "open and notorious," Voelker v. Combined Ins. Co., 73 So.2d 403, 407 (Fla. 1954); involve "common notoriety," Amos v. Moseley, 74 Fla. 555, 77 So. 619, 622 (1917); and are "'commonly' known," Amos v. Moseley, supra at 623; City of Miami Beach v. Seacoast Towers – Miami Beach, Inc., 156 So. 2d 528 (Fla. 3rd Dist. 1963). This subsection is similar to Fed. Rule Evid. 201(b)(1), Uniform Rule 9, Calif. Evid. Code §§ 451, 452.

Subsection (12) provides for judicial notice of facts that are not subject to reasonable dispute in that they are capable of accurate determination by resort to sources whose accuracy cannot be questioned. In other words the facts need not be actually known by the judge if they are "capable of accurate and ready determination." Sources upon which this determination is based include treatises, encyclopedia, as well as persons learned in the subject matter. The use of these sources would be limited to consultation by the judge and the parties for the purposes of determining whether or not to take judicial notice and determining the nature of the matter to be noticed. For example, the distance between two cities is a fact capable of accurate and ready determination, of which judicial notice should be taken. See Fed. Rule Evid. 201(b)(2); Calif. Evid. Code § 452(h). McCormick, Evidence § 330 (2nd ed. 1972).

Subsection (13) Presently there are several Florida statutes which authorize a state agency to adopt an official seal and require the courts to take judicial notice of such seals.

These statutes are:

1. Fla. Stat. § 947.05 – Parole and Probation Commission.

2. Fla. Stat. § 582.20(10) – Soil Conservation Districts.

3. Fla. Stat. § 440.44(6) – Florida Industrial Commission.

4. Fla. Stat. § 471.10 – Florida State Board of Engineer Examiners.

5. Fla. Stat. § 92.17 – Board of Trustees of the Internal Improvement Trust Fund (statute provides that seal of the board upon a contract entitles same to be received in evidence).

Since the Florida legislature has determined that some governmental seals should be judicially noticed, there is no reason to restrict this kind of notice to only those five seals. Therefore, all seals of governmental departments in Florida will be judicially noticed under this section. In addition, similar seals from other jurisdictions may be noticed.

Florida Stat. § 90.203. Compulsory Judicial Notice Upon Request

A court shall take judicial notice of any matter in s. 90.202 when a party requests it and:

(1) Gives each adverse party timely written notice of the request, proof of which is filed with the court, to enable the adverse party to prepare to meet the request.

(2) Furnishes the court with sufficient information to enable it to take judicial notice of the matter.

SPONSORS' NOTE (1976 ENACTMENT)

This section provides that the court must take judicial notice of any matter which is listed in Section 90.202, if a party requests that judicial notice be taken, gives each adverse party timely written notice of the request in order to prepare to meet it, files proof of the notice with the court, and furnishes the court with sufficient information to enable it to take judicial notice of the matter.

This section is not intended to be a limitation on the court's discretionary power to take judicial notice of matters listed in Section 90.202 when it feels such notice is appropriate. Therefore, if a party requests judicial notice of a matter and fails to give the requisite notice to adverse parties or sufficient information to the court, the court may judicially notice the matter despite the failure to satisfy the requirements of this section. In this situation, the adverse parties are protected, in that, they have the right under Section 90.204 to be heard and to present information as to the propriety of taking judicial notice and as to the nature of the matter to be noticed. When the notice and information requirements of section 90.203 are not met, judicial notice of the matter is not mandatory.

See Calif. Evid. Code § 453. New Jersey Evid. Rule 9(3) requires that notice be given in the pleadings or at least 20 days before the trial.

This notice requirement is not intended to work as the Florida courts have interpreted the notice requirement of Florida's Uniform Judicial Notice of Foreign Law Act. The Act requires courts to take judicial notice of certain matters and imposes upon any party requesting that judicial notice be taken, the giving of reasonable notice "to the adverse parties either in the pleadings or otherwise." In interpreting the Act, the Florida courts have said that it does not work automatically and have required a party intending to take advantage of it to give reasonable notice to the adverse parties. Kingston v. Quimby, 80 So. 2d 455 (Fla. 1955). Several cases have said that this reasonable notice can only be by the pleadings and have required foreign (sister-state) law to be "plead" in order for the court to take judicial notice of it. Movielab, Inc. v. Davis, 217 So. 2d 890 (Fla. 3rd Dist. 1969). See Aboandandolo v. Vonella, 88 So. 2d 282 (Fla. 1956); Lanigan v. Lanigan, 78 So. 2d 92 (Fla. 1955). The notice requirement of this section is not to be read as requiring that notice be given in the pleadings; the statute only requires that the notice be timely and written and that proof of it be filed with the court.

Even though a party requested judicial notice be taken under this section and gave proper notice to each adverse party, a decision by a judge not to take judicial notice will be upheld on appeal unless the reviewing court determines that the party furnished information to the judge that was so persuasive that no reasonable judge would have refused to take judicial notice of the matter.

Calif. Evid. Code § 453 and Uniform Rule of Evidence 9 are similar.

Florida Stat. § 90.204. Determination of Propriety of Judicial Notice and Nature of Matter Noticed

(1) When a court determines upon its own motion that judicial notice of a matter should be taken or when a party requests such notice and shows good cause for not complying with s. 90.203(1), the court shall afford each party reasonable opportunity to present information relevant to the propriety of taking judicial notice and to the nature of the matter noticed.

(2) In determining the propriety of taking judicial notice of a matter or the nature thereof, a court may use any source of pertinent and reliable information, whether or not furnished by a party, without regard to any exclusionary rule except a valid claim of privilege and except for the exclusions provided in s. 90.403.

(3) If a court resorts to any documentary source of information not received in open court, the court shall make the information and its source a part of the record in the action and shall afford each party reasonable opportunity to challenge such information, and to offer additional information, before judicial notice of the matter is taken.

SPONSORS' NOTE (1976 ENACTMENT)

Subsection (1) provides the procedure when a court on its own motion determines that judicial notice should be taken, or when a party shows good cause for not filing a timely written request, and provides procedural safeguards which are designed to afford the parties reasonable opportunity to be heard as to the propriety of taking judicial notice of certain matters and as to the tenor of certain matters to be noticed.

A "reasonable opportunity" to present information on the propriety of taking judicial notice and on the tenor of the matter to be noticed will depend on the complexity of the matter and its importance to the case. For example, in a case where there is no dispute as to the existence and validity of a regulation of the Florida Real Estate Commission, no formal hearing would be necessary to determine the propriety of taking judicial notice of the regulation and of its nature. However, where there is a complex question as to the nature of a foreign nation's law applicable to the case, the granting of a hearing under subsection (1) would be mandatory.

The opportunity to be heard as to the propriety of taking judicial notice means that the party can argue whether the item the court is considering falls under the specified matters, e.g., whether a document is a rule or regulation of a governmental agency of the state, whether the agency has the authority to issue such rule, and whether it is in the Florida Administrative Code or in a bound printed copy.

The opportunity to be heard as to the nature of a matter listed means that a party can present information to show that although the item is a proper one for judicial notice the contents of the matter is in some way not correct, and, thus, should not be judicially noticed in the form presented to the court.

Subsection (2) is based on the policy that since one of the purposes of judicial notice is to simplify the process of proofmaking, the judge should be given latitude in deciding what sources are trustworthy. Thus, this section allows the court to use any source of pertinent and reliable information, and this includes the advice of persons learned in the subject matter.

This section probably is in accord with present Florida law, since Section 92.031(2) of the Florida Statutes grants the court the right to inform itself on the matters listed for judicial notice therein, in any manner it deems proper.

Subsection (2) of this section preserves a limitation on the form of the information. It must meet the relevancy test of Section 90.403 and cannot violate valid claims of privilege, which are specified in Sections 90.501 through 90.508. Calif. Evid. Code § 454 and Uniform Rule 10 have similar provisions.

Subsection (3) requires that when the court resorts to sources of information not previously known to the parties, upon request, such information and its source will be made a part of the record. This requirement will assure the availability of such information and sources for examination by the parties and a reviewing court. The subsection also guarantees the parties a reasonable opportunity to meet such additional information before judicial notice of a matter may be taken. Calif. Evid. Code § 455 is substantially the same

Florida Stat. § 90.205. Denial of a Request for Judicial Notice

Upon request of counsel, when a court denies a request to take judicial notice of any matter, the court shall inform the parties at the earliest practicable time and shall indicate for the record that it has denied the request.

SPONSORS' NOTE (1976 ENACTMENT)

This section simply requires the judge, upon counsel's request, to advise parties and indicate for the record at the earliest practicable time any denial of a request to take judicial notice of a matter. The purpose of this requirement is to provide the parties with an adequate opportunity to submit evidence on matters that judicial notice was anticipated but not taken. Calif. Evid. Code § 456 is the same.

Florida Stat. § 90.206. Instructing Jury on Judicial Notice

The court may instruct the jury during the trial to accept as a fact a matter judicially noticed.

SPONSORS' NOTE (1976 ENACTMENT)

This section makes matters which are judicially noticed binding on the jury and thereby eliminates any possibility of presenting to the jury, evidence disputing or rebutting the matter as noticed by the judge. The section is limited to instruction on a matter which would, had it not been judicially noticed, have been a matter for determination by a jury. This is because the instruction of juries on matters of law is not a matter of evidence, but is covered by the general provisions of law governing instruction of juries. Calif. Evid. Code § 457 and Uniform Rule 11 are substantially the same. See McCormick, Evidence § 332 (2nd ed. 1972).

The indisputability of judicially noticed facts is contrary to the existing general rule in Florida. In Makos v. Prince, 64 So. 2d 670, 673 (Fla. 1953), the Supreme Court stated:

> The rule is that the fact that a matter is judicially noticed means merely that it is taken as true without the necessity of offering evidence by the party who should ordinarily have done so. This is because the court assumes that the matter is so notorious that the matter will not be disputed. But the rule does not prevent an opponent's disputing the matter by evidence if he believes it disputable. (Emphasis by court.)

This Florida rule seems to give a judicially noticed fact the status of only a presumption. Thus, when rebuttal evidence raises a genuine issue of material fact, the matter is given to the jury for determination. Nielson v. Carney Groves, Inc., 159 So. 2d 489 (Fla. 2nd Dist. 1964).

The policy supporting judicial notice is that parties should not be permitted to dispute by proof what the judge has found to be a moot or sham issue, not susceptible of reasonable dispute. McCormick, Evidence § 332 (2nd ed. 1972). The effect of judicial notice is to dispense with introducing proof of matters that need none. The existing Florida rule is contrary thereto, in that, the party who has a fact judicially noticed, also has to present his proof as to the truth of the matter in order to rebut the evidence offered by the adverse party. The proper time for objection and controversy is before, and not after, judicial notice is properly taken. Section 90.204 provides adequate means to dispute the propriety of taking judicial notice of a particular fact.

Florida Stat. § 90.207. Judicial Notice by Trial Court in Subsequent Proceedings

The failure or refusal of a court to take judicial notice of a matter does not preclude a court from taking judicial notice of the matter in subsequent proceedings, in accordance with the procedure specified in ss. 90.201-90.206.

SPONSORS' NOTE (1976 ENACTMENT)

This section provides that the failure or even the refusal of the trial court judge to take judicial notice of a matter, does not bar the trial judge or another trial judge from taking judicial notice of that matter in a subsequent proceeding such as a hearing on a motion for a new trial. Although no Florida case on point could be found, it would seem that the trial judge should have the power to judicially notice a matter in a subsequent proceeding, since appellate courts in Florida are permitted to judicially notice many things that the trial court could, and in some cases, are required to judicially notice an item if it is overlooked by the trial court. See Peterson v. Paoli, 44 So. 2d 639 (Fla. 1950). Calif. Evid. Code § 458 and Uniform Rule 12 are substantially the same.

This section does not change the power of an appellate court to judicially notice matters when a lower court has not done so. See Storch v. Allgood, 184 So. 2d 170 (Fla. 1966); Peterson v. Paoli, 44 So. 2d 639 (Fla. 1950); Ramsey v. City of Kissimmee, 111 Fla. 387, 149 So. 553 (1933).

COMMENTARY ON FEDERAL AND FLORIDA RULE DIFFERENCES

Florida Stat. §§ 90.201-90.207 and their federal counterpart, Federal Rule 201, set forth the rules governing the taking of judicial notice.

The scope of the federal and Florida rules differ substantially from one another. Federal Rule 201 governs only judicial notice of adjudicative facts (facts germane to what happened in the case, or "who did what, where, when, how, and with what motive or intent"); it does not govern judicial notice of legislative facts (facts considered by a court in formulating common law policy or interpreting a statute) or so-called basic or evaluative facts (basic concepts that jurors and judges are assumed to know and that are necessary to reasoning, such as the fact that a witness is related to a party might cause them to be biased), nor does it govern judicial notice of law. See FED. R. EVID. 201(a); Advisory Committee's Note to FED. R. EVID. 201(a). In the federal system, judicial notice of legislative and evaluative facts are not subject to regulation by Rule 201 or any rule, see U.S. v. Bowers, 660 F.2d 527, 530-31 (11th Cir. 1981) (legislative facts); U.S. v. Amado-Núñez, 357 F.3d 119, 121-22 (1st Cir. 2004) (evaluative facts), while judicial notice of domestic law is governed by federal common law, see Lamar v. Micou, 114 U.S. 218, 223 (1885) (federal courts obligated to take judicial notice of state statutory or decisional law), and judicial notice of foreign law is governed by rules of civil and criminal procedure, see FED. R. CIV. P. 44.1; FED. R. CRIM. P. 26.1.

By contrast, the provisions of the Florida Evidence Code address not only judicial notice of adjudicative facts, but also extensively regulate judicial notice of law. *See* FLA. STAT. §§ 90.201-90.202. Indeed, most of the matters listed as appropriate for taking judicial notice in the Florida Evidence Code involve international, foreign, federal, state, and local law in some format. *See id.; Turner v. City of Clearwater*, 789 So. 2d 273, 281 (Fla. 2001). While there is virtually no authority on the issue, judicial notice of evaluative and legislative facts, as with the federal rule, appears to be unregulated by the Florida Evidence Code. *See, e.g., Green v. State*, 765 So. 2d 910, 912-13 (Fla. 2nd DCA 2000).

Under Federal Rule 201, to take judicial notice of an adjudicative fact, it must be a fact that is "not subject to *reasonable* dispute," which can be established by showing that it is either "generally known within the trial court's territorial jurisdiction" or "can be accurately and readily determined from sources whose accuracy cannot reasonably be questioned." *See* FED. R. EVID. 201(b) (emphasis added). The provisions of the Florida Evidence Code that apply in general terms to judicial notice of adjudicative facts track (and indeed cite) the language of Federal Rule 201(b), save for the omission of the word "reasonable," although there is no indication in the legislative history or the case law that this is of significance. *See* FLA. STAT. § 90.202(11)-(12). Under both the Florida and federal rules, for a fact to qualify as "generally known" it must be one of common knowledge within the jurisdiction. *See Maradie v. Maradie*, 680 So. 2d 538, 542 (Fla. 1st DCA 1996) (defining it to include facts that are "open and notorious", involve "common notoriety" or are "commonly known"); *U.S. v. Bello*, 194 F.3d 18, 23 (1st Cir. 1998) (defining it to include facts that exist in the unaided memory of reasonable people in the jurisdiction). And under both the Florida and federal rules, the sorts of sources whose accuracy cannot reasonably be questioned include such things as treatises, encyclopedias, almanacs, and the like, and the sorts of facts judicially noticed include such things as population statistics, geographic facts, and historical events. *See* Sponsors' Note to FLA. STAT. § 90.202(12); *Cordova v. State*, 675 So. 2d 632, 636 (Fla. 3d DCA 1996); 1 JACK B. WEINSTEIN, FEDERAL EVIDENCE § 201.12 (Joseph M. McLaughlin ed., 2d ed. 1997). Under both the Florida and federal rules, it is error for a judge to take judicial notice based on his *personal* knowledge. *See McKinney v. State*, 640 So. 2d 1183, 1184 (Fla. 2d DCA 1994); *U.S. v. Lewis*, 833 F.2d 1380, 1385-86 (9th Cir. 1987).

Both the Florida and federal rules empower a judge to take judicial notice *sua sponte. See* FED. R. EVID. 201(c)(1); *Elmore v. Florida Power & Light Co.*, 895 So. 2d 475, 478 (Fla. 4th DCA 2005); Sponsors' Note to FLA. STAT. §§ 90.202, 90.203. However, under certain circumstances, a judge must take judicial notice. Under the federal rule, a judge is obligated to take judicial notice if a party requests it and supplies the court with the necessary information to enable it to take judicial notice. *See* FED. R. EVID. 201(c)(2). Under the Florida rule, a judge is obligated to take judicial notice of federal and Florida decisional, statutory, and constitutional law and rules of court, *see* FLA. STAT. § 90.201; they are also obligated to take judicial notice of any other matters falling within the scope of the provisions of the Florida Evidence Code when a party requests it, gives timely written notice to adverse parties, and provides the court with sufficient information to enable it to take judicial notice. *See* FLA. STAT. § 90.203. Under both Florida and federal law, a party is entitled to an opportunity to be heard on the propriety of taking judicial notice. *See* FED. R. EVID. 201(e); FLA. STAT. § 90.204. Florida law provides that in making the determination whether to take judicial notice, the court may use any source of information without regard to any exclusionary rules of evidence save for a valid claim of privilege and Florida Stat. § 90.403. *See* FLA. STAT. § 90.204(2). Under federal practice, the rules of evidence (other than those respecting privileges) do not apply when a trial court decides whether to take judicial notice, *see* FED. R. EVID. 104(a); 1 MICHAEL H. GRAHAM, HANDBOOK OF FEDERAL EVIDENCE § 201:1 (6th ed. 2006). Florida law also requires that when a court resorts to any documentary source of information not received in open court, it should make such materials a part of the record, *see* FLA. STAT. § 90.204(3), and that if the court denies a request to take judicial notice, it shall inform the parties at the earliest practicable time and so indicate on the record, *see* FLA. STAT. § 90.205. The federal rule contains no comparable provisions.

Under federal practice, judicial notice can be taken at any stage of the proceedings, and may even be done for the first time on appeal. *See* FED. R. EVID. 201(d); Advisory Committee's Note to FED. R. EVID. 201(d); *Denius v. Dunlap*, 330 F.3d 919, 926-27 (7th Cir. 2003). However, in light of the fact that in criminal cases the instruction to jurors on matters judicially noticed is permissive (as explained below), the federal courts have held that in a criminal case tried before a jury, judicial notice cannot be taken for the first time on appellate review. *See Government of Canal Zone v. Burjan V.*, 596 F.2d 690, 694 (3d Cir. 1979); *U.S. v. Jones*, 580 F.2d 219, 222-24 (6th Cir. 1978). Florida authority likewise holds that judicial notice may be taken at any stage, including for the first time on appeal. *See* FLA. STAT. § 90.207; Sponsors' Note to FLA. STAT. § 90.207; *City of Miami v. F.O.P. Miami Lodge 20*, 571 So. 2d 1309, 1318-19 n.10 (Fla. 3d DCA 1989). No Florida authority considers the propriety of taking it for the first time on appeal in criminal cases.

Under federal practice, in civil proceedings, the trial court must instruct the jury to accept as conclusive any fact judicially noticed, while in criminal cases, the court must instruct the jury that it may, but is not required to, accept as conclusive any fact judicially noticed. *See* FED. R. EVID. 201(f). In civil cases, once judicial notice is taken, the party opposing the taking of judicial notice cannot introduce counterproof before the jury on the point judicially noticed, *see* Advisory Committee's Note to FED. R. EVID. 201(f), while in criminal cases it appears that they can. *See U.S. v. Horn*, 185 F. Supp. 2d 530, 549 n.34 (D.Md. 2002). Under Florida law, the rule is worded so as to give the trial court discretion to decide whether to give the jury a conclusive or a permissive instruction and accordingly whether to permit evidence in counterproof of the fact judicially noticed, yet precedent establishes that in a criminal case, the trial court must give the jury a permissive instruction and permit the defendant to introduce evidence in counterproof. *See* FLA. STAT. § 90.206; *Cordova*, 675 So. 2d at 635.

ARTICLE III. PRESUMPTIONS IN CIVIL CASES

Federal Rule	Florida Stat. §	Description
301	90.301-90.304	Presumptions in Civil Cases Generally
302	—	Applying State Law to Presumptions in Civil Cases

Federal Rule 301. Presumptions in Civil Cases Generally

In a civil case, unless a federal statute or these rules provide otherwise, the party against whom a presumption is directed has the burden of producing evidence to rebut the presumption. But this rule does not shift the burden of persuasion, which remains on the party who had it originally.

ADVISORY COMMITTEE'S NOTE

This rule governs presumptions generally. See Rule 302 for presumptions controlled by state law and Rule 303 [deleted] for those against an accused in a criminal case.

Presumptions governed by this rule are given the effect of placing upon the opposing party the burden of establishing the nonexistence of the presumed fact, once the party invoking the presumption establishes the basic facts giving rise to it. The same considerations of fairness, policy, and probability which dictate the allocation of the burden of the various elements of a case as between the prima facie case of a plaintiff and affirmative defenses also underlie the creation of presumptions. These considerations are not satisfied by giving a lesser effect to presumptions. Morgan and Maguire, Looking Backward and Forward at Evidence, 50 Harv.L.Rev. 909, 913 (1937); Morgan, Instructing the Jury upon Presumptions and Burden of Proof, 47 Harv.L.Rev. 59, 82 (1933); Cleary, Presuming and Pleading: An Essay on Juristic Immaturity, 12 Stan.L.Rev. 5 (1959).

The so-called "bursting bubble" theory, under which a presumption vanishes upon the introduction of evidence which would support a finding of the nonexistence of the presumed fact, even though not believed, is rejected as according presumptions too "slight and evanescent" an effect. Morgan and Maguire, *supra*, at p. 913.

In the opinion of the Advisory Committee, no constitutional infirmity attends this view of presumptions. In Mobile, J. & K. C. R. Co. v. Turnipseed, 219 U.S. 35 (1910), the Court upheld a Mississippi statute which provided that in actions against railroads proof of injury inflicted by the running of trains should be prima facie evidence of negligence by the railroad. The injury in the case had resulted from a derailment. The opinion made the points (1) that the only effect of the statute was to impose on the railroad the duty of producing some evidence to the contrary, (2) that an inference may be supplied by law if there is a rational connection between the fact proved and the fact presumed, as long as the opposite party is not precluded from presenting his evidence to the contrary, and (3) that considerations of public policy arising from the character of the business justified the application in question. Nineteen years later, in Western & Atlantic R. Co. v. Henderson, 279 U.S. 639 (1929), the Court overturned a Georgia statute making railroads liable for damages done by trains, unless the railroad made it appear that reasonable care had been used, the presumption being against the railroad. The declaration alleged the death of plaintiff 's husband from a grade crossing collision, due to specified acts of negligence by defendant. The jury were instructed that proof of the injury raised a presumption of negligence; the burden shifted to the railroad to prove ordinary care; and unless it did so, they should find for plaintiff. The instruction was held erroneous in an opinion stating (1) that there was no rational connection between the mere fact of collision and negligence on the part of anyone, and (2) that the statute was different from that in *Turnipseed* in imposing a burden upon the railroad. The reader is left in a state of some confusion. Is the difference between a derailment and a grade crossing collision of no significance? Would the *Turnipseed* presumption have been bad if it had imposed a burden of persuasion on defendant, although that would in nowise have impaired its "rational connection"? If *Henderson* forbids imposing a burden of persuasion on defendants, what happens to affirmative defenses?

Two factors serve to explain *Henderson*. The first was that it was common ground that negligence was indispensable to liability. Plaintiff thought so, drafted her complaint accordingly, and relied upon the presumption. But how in logic could the same presumption establish her alternative grounds of negligence that the engineer was so blind he could not see decedent's truck and that he failed to stop after he saw it? Second, take away the basic assumption of no liability without fault, as *Turnipseed* intimated might be done ("considerations of public policy arising out of the character of the business"), and the structure of the decision in *Henderson* fails. No question of logic would have arisen if the statute had simply said: a prima facie case of liability is made by proof of injury by a train; lack of negligence is an affirmative defense, to be pleaded and proved as other affirmative defenses. The problem would be one of economic due process only. While it seems likely that the Supreme Court of 1929 would have voted that due process was denied, that result today would be unlikely. See, for example, the shift in the direction of absolute liability in the consumer cases. Prosser, The Assault upon the Citadel (Strict Liability to the Consumer), 69 Yale L.J. 1099 (1960).

Any doubt as to the constitutional permissibility of a presumption imposing a burden of persuasion of the nonexistence of the presumed fact in civil cases is laid at rest by Dick v. New York Life Ins. Co., 359 U.S. 437 (1959). The Court unhesitatingly applied the North Dakota rule that the presumption against suicide imposed on defendant the burden of proving that the death of insured, under an accidental death clause, was due to suicide.

"Proof of coverage and of death by gunshot wound shifts the burden to the insurer to establish that the death of the insured was due to his suicide." 359 U.S. at 443.

"In a case like this one, North Dakota presumes that death was accidental and places on the insurer the burden of proving that death resulted from suicide." *Id.* at 446.

The rational connection requirement survives in criminal cases, Tot v. United States, 319 U.S. 463 (1943), because the Court has been unwilling to extend into that area the greater-includes-the-lesser theory of Ferry v. Ramsey, 277 U.S. 88 (1928). In that case the Court sustained a Kansas statute under which bank directors were personally liable for deposits made with their assent and with knowledge of insolvency, and the fact of insolvency was prima facie evidence of assent and knowledge of insolvency. Mr. Justice Holmes pointed out that the state legislature could have made the directors personally liable to depositors in every case. Since the statute imposed a less stringent liability, "the thing to be considered is the result reached, not the possibly inartificial or clumsy way of reaching it." *Id.* at 94. Mr. Justice Sutherland dissented: though the state could have created an absolute liability, it did not purport to do so; a rational connection was necessary, but lacking, between the liability created and the prima facie evidence of it; the result might be different if the basis of the presumption were being open for business.

The Sutherland view has prevailed in criminal cases by virtue of the higher standard of notice there required. The fiction that everyone is presumed to know the law is applied to the substantive law of crimes as an alternative to complete unenforceability. But the need does not extend to criminal evidence and procedure, and the fiction does not encompass them. "Rational connection" is not fictional or artificial, and so it is reasonable to suppose that Gainey should have known that his presence at the site of an illicit still could convict him of being connected with (carrying on) the business, United States v. Gainey, 380 U.S. 63 (1965), but not that Romano should have known that his presence at a still could convict him of possessing it, United States v. Romano, 382 U.S. 136 (1965).

In his dissent in Gainey, Mr. Justice Black put it more artistically:

"It might be argued, although the Court does not so argue or hold, that Congress if it wished could make presence at a still a crime in itself, and so Congress should be free to create crimes which are called 'possession' and 'carrying on an illegal distillery business' but which are defined in such a way that unexplained presence is sufficient and indisputable evidence in all cases to support conviction for those offenses. See Ferry v. Ramsey, 277 U.S. 88. Assuming for the sake of argument that Congress could make unexplained presence a criminal act, and ignoring also the refusal of this Court in other cases to uphold a statutory presumption on such a theory, see Heiner v. Donnan, 285 U.S. 312, there is no indication here that Congress intended to adopt such a misleading method of draftsmanship, nor in my judgment could the statutory provisions if so construed escape condemnation for vagueness, under the principles applied in Lanzetta v. New Jersey, 306 U.S. 451, and many other cases." 380 U.S. at 84, n. 12.

FLORIDA AND FEDERAL EVIDENCE RULES

And the majority opinion in *Romano* agreed with him:

"It may be, of course, that Congress has the power to make presence at an illegal still a punishable crime, but we find no clear indication that it intended to so exercise this power. The crime remains possession, not presence, and with all due deference to the judgment of Congress, the former may not constitutionally be inferred from the latter." 382 U.S. at 144.

The rule does not spell out the procedural aspects of its application. Questions as to when the evidence warrants submission of a presumption and what instructions are proper under varying states of fact are believed to present no particular difficulties.

REPORT OF HOUSE COMMITTEE ON THE JUDICIARY

Rule 301 as submitted by the Supreme Court provided that in all cases a presumption imposes on the party against whom it is directed the burden of proving that the nonexistence of the presumed fact is more probable than its existence. The Committee limited the scope of Rule 301 to "civil actions and proceedings" to effectuate its decision not to deal with the question of presumptions in criminal cases. (See note on Rule 303 in discussion of Rules deleted.) With respect to the weight to be given a presumption in a civil case, the Committee agreed with the judgment implicit in the Court's version that the so-called "bursting bubble" theory of presumptions, whereby a presumption vanishes upon the appearance of any contradicting evidence by the other party, gives to presumptions too slight an effect. On the other hand, the Committee believed that the Rule proposed by the Court, whereby a presumption permanently alters the burden of persuasion, no matter how much contradicting evidence is introduced — a view shared by only a few courts — lends too great a force to presumptions. Accordingly, the Committee amended the Rule to adopt an intermediate position under which a presumption does not vanish upon the introduction of contradicting evidence, and does not change the burden of persuasion; instead it is merely deemed sufficient evidence of the fact presumed, to be considered by the jury or other finder of fact.

REPORT OF SENATE COMMITTEE ON THE JUDICIARY

The rule governs presumptions in civil cases generally. Rule 302 provides for presumptions in cases controlled by State law.

As submitted by the Supreme Court, presumptions governed by this rule were given the effect of placing upon the opposing party the burden of establishing the nonexistence of the presumed fact, once the party invoking the presumption established the basic facts giving rise to it.

Instead of imposing a burden of persuasion on the party against whom the presumption is directed, the House adopted a provision which shifted the burden of going forward with the evidence. They further provided that "even though met with contradicting evidence, a presumption is sufficient evidence of the fact presumed, to be considered by the trier of fact." The effect of the amendment is that presumptions are to be treated as evidence.

The committee feels the House amendment is ill-advised. As the joint committees (the Standing Committee on Practice and Procedure of the Judicial Conference and the Advisory Committee on the Rules of Evidence) stated: "Presumptions are not evidence, but ways of dealing with evidence." This treatment requires juries to perform the task of considering "as evidence" facts upon which they have no direct evidence and which may confuse them in performance of their duties. California had a rule much like that contained in the House amendment. It was sharply criticized by Justice Traynor in *Speck* v. *Sarver*[4] and was repealed after 93 troublesome years.[5]

Professor McCormick gives a concise and compelling critique of the presumption as evidence rule:

"Another solution, formerly more popular than now, is to instruct the jury that the presumption is 'evidence', to be weighed and considered with the testimony in the case. This avoids the danger that the jury may infer that the presumption is conclusive, but it probably means little to the jury, and certainly runs counter to accepted theories of the nature of evidence."[6]

For these reasons the committee has deleted that provision of the House-passed rule that treats presumptions as evidence. The effect of the rule as adopted by the committee is to make clear that while evidence of facts giving rise to a presumption shifts the burden of coming forward with evidence to rebut or meet the presumption, it does not shift the burden of persuasion on the existence of the presumed facts. The burden of persuasion remains on the party to whom it is allocated under the rules governing the allocation in the first instance.

The court may instruct the jury that they may infer the existence of the presumed fact from proof of the basic facts giving rise to the presumption. However, it would be inappropriate under this rule to instruct the jury that the inference they are to draw is conclusive.

CONFERENCE REPORT

The House bill provides that a presumption in civil actions and proceedings shifts to the party against whom it is directed the burden of going forward with evidence to meet or rebut it. Even though evidence contradicting the presumption is offered, a presumption is considered sufficient evidence of the presumed fact to be considered by the jury. The Senate amendment provides that a presumption shifts to the party against whom it is directed the burden of going forward with evidence to meet or rebut the presumption, but it does not shift to that party the burden of persuasion on the existence of the presumed fact.

Under the Senate amendment, a presumption is sufficient to get a party past an adverse party's motion to dismiss made at the end of his case-in-chief. If the adverse party offers no evidence contradicting the presumed fact, the court will instruct the jury that if it finds the basic facts, it may presume the existence of the presumed fact. If the adverse party does offer evidence contradicting the presumed fact, the court cannot instruct the jury that it may *presume* the existence of the presumed fact from proof of the basic facts. The court may, however, instruct the jury that it may infer the existence of the presumed fact from proof of the basic facts.

The conference adopts the Senate amendment.

ADVISORY COMMITTEE'S NOTE (2011 AMENDMENT)

The language of Rule 301 has been amended as part of the restyling of the Evidence Rules to make them more easily understood and to make style and terminology consistent throughout the rules. These changes are intended to be stylistic only. There is no intent to change any result in any ruling on evidence admissibility.

Florida Stat. § 90.301. Presumption Defined; Inferences

---

[4] 20 Cal.2d 585, 594 (1942).
[5] Cal.Ev.Code 1965 § 600.
[6] McCormick, Evidence, 669 (1954); id. 825 (2d ed. 1972).

(1) For the purposes of this chapter, a presumption is an assumption of fact which the law makes from the existence of another fact or group of facts found or otherwise established.

(2) Except for presumptions that are conclusive under the law from which they arise, a presumption is rebuttable.

(3) Nothing in this chapter shall prevent the drawing of an inference that is appropriate.

(4) Sections 90.301-90.304 are applicable only in civil actions or proceedings.

SPONSORS' NOTE (1976 ENACTMENT)

This section recognizes that presumptions are either conclusive or rebuttable. Conclusive presumptions preclude the opposing party from showing by evidence that the presumed fact does not exist. See 9 Wigmore, Evidence § 2492 (3rd ed. 1940). For example Section 794.05 of the Florida Statutes conclusively presumes that a child under the age of eighteen years is incapable of consenting to sexual intercourse, and Section 736.05 provides that when two persons die simultaneously, each will be presumed to have survived the other for the purpose of title and devolution of property.

"Inference," "prima facie case" and the doctrine of res ipsa loquitur are closely associated with the concept of a presumption, and many writers have tended to use the terms interchangeably or blur the distinctions. Presumptions differ in that when the basic fact giving rise to the presumed fact is established and there is an absence of contradictory testimony, the presumed fact must be found to exist.

An inference is a deduction of fact that the fact-finder, in his discretion, may logically draw from another fact or group of facts that are found to exist or are otherwise established in the action.

The res ipsa loquitur doctrine constitutes a sufficient basis for the submission of the issue of negligence to the jury in that it permits the jury to draw an inference of negligence. See American Dist. Elec. Protective Co. v. Seaboard Air Line R.R., 129 Fla. 518, 177 So. 294 (1937).

A prima facie case arises any time enough evidence is introduced to sustain a verdict for the plaintiff.

This definition of presumption is similar to Calif. Evid. Code § 600 and Uniform Rule of Evid. 13.

Florida Stat. § 90.302. Classification of Rebuttable Presumptions

Every rebuttable presumption is either:

(1) A presumption affecting the burden of producing evidence and requiring the trier of fact to assume the existence of the presumed fact, unless credible evidence sufficient to sustain a finding of the nonexistence of the presumed fact is introduced, in which event, the existence or nonexistence of the presumed fact shall be determined from the evidence without regard to the presumption; or

(2) A presumption affecting the burden of proof that imposes upon the party against whom it operates the burden of proof concerning the nonexistence of the presumed fact.

SPONSORS' NOTE (1976 ENACTMENT)

All presumptions that are not conclusive are rebuttable presumptions. For several decades, courts and legal scholars have wrangled over the purpose and function of these presumptions. The view espoused by Professor Thayer (Thayer, Preliminary Treatise on Evidence 313-352 (1898)) and Wigmore (9 Wigmore, Evidence §§ 2485-2493 (3rd ed. 1940)), accepted by most courts (see Morgan, Presumptions, 10 Rutgers L. Rev. 512, 516 (1956)), and adopted by the American Law Institute's Model Code of Evidence, is that a presumption is a preliminary assumption of fact that disappears from the case upon the introduction of evidence sufficient to sustain a finding of the nonexistence of the presumed fact.

Professors Morgan and McCormick argue that a presumption should shift the burden of proof to the adverse party. Morgan, Some Problems of Proof 81 (1956); McCormick, Evidence § 317 (1945). They believe that presumptions are created for reasons of policy and argue that, if the policy underlying a presumption is of sufficient weight to require a finding of the presumed fact when there is no contrary evidence, it should be of sufficient weight to require a finding when the mind of the trier of fact is in equilibrium or if he does not believe the contrary evidence.

Under Fed. Rule Evid. 301, in civil cases all presumptions are of the "bursting bubble" type.

This Code recognizes that presumptions have been created for different purposes. While the effect of presumptions and the weight of evidence required to rebut various presumptions cannot be allowed to widely differ, the policies behind the creation of each presumption are not well served by a single uniform rule. This section, as does existing Florida law, provides an alternative and classifies rebuttable presumptions into two groups: those affecting the burden of producing evidence and those affecting the burden of proof. Whether a presumption affects the burden of producing evidence or affects the burden of proof is set forth in Sections 90.303 and 90.304.

A presumption affecting the burden of producing evidence is a procedural device which raises the assumption that a fact exists and shifts the burden of producing evidence. When evidence is introduced by the other party, the presumption disappears and the jury will not be told of it. However, an inference of the presumed fact may be found by the jury if one may logically be drawn. A presumption that affects the burden of proof is one which imposes on the other party the burden of proving the nonexistence of the presumed fact. See McCormick, Evidence § 345 (2nd ed. 1972).

In a recent case, In re Estate of Carpenter, 253 So. 2d 697, 703 (Fla. 1971), the Florida Supreme Court, in reversing a lower court ruling that evidence sufficient to raise a presumption of undue influence over a testator shifted the burden of proof to the proponent, reaffirmed the general rule and quoted Leonetti v. Boone, 74 So. 2d 551, 552 (Fla.1954):

> A presumption of law which arises upon the pleading or during the course of the trial after the introduction of evidence may aid a party in the discharge of the burden of proof cast upon him and shift to his adversary the burden of explanation or of going on with the case, but does not, as a general rule, shift the burden of proof; a presumption simply changes the order of proof to the extent that one upon whom it bears must meet or explain it away....

However, in a few situations the Florida courts hold that a presumption shifts the burden of proof. In Eldridge v. Eldridge, 153 Fla. 873, 16 So. 2d 163 (1944), the court stated that "[w]here the legitimacy of a child born in wedlock is questioned by the husband and reputed father, one of the strongest rebuttable presumptions known to the law is required to be overcome before the child can be bastardized....The better rule is that the husband is not required to prove his contention beyond all reasonable doubt, yet his proof must be sufficiently strong to clearly remove the presumption of legitimacy." In a case where the existence of common-law marriage was in dispute, In re Estate of Alcala, 188 So. 2d 903, 907 (Fla. 2nd Dist. 1966), the court stated that "[t]he appellant's evidence, properly weighed, presents a prima facie case of marital consent and raises the strong presumption of marriage. The burden then shifted to the appellee, who asserted the illegality of the marriage, to rebut the presumption."

For a similar provision, see Calif. Evid. Code §§ 601, 604, 606.

Florida Stat. § 90.303. Presumption Affecting the Burden of Producing Evidence Defined

In a civil action or proceeding, unless otherwise provided by statute, a presumption established primarily to facilitate the determination of the particular action in which the presumption is applied, rather than to implement public policy, is a presumption affecting the burden of producing evidence.

Florida Stat. § 90.304. Presumption Affecting the Burden of Proof Defined

In civil actions, all rebuttable presumptions which are not defined in s. 90.303 are presumptions affecting the burden of proof.

SPONSORS' NOTE (1976 ENACTMENT)

Sections 90.303 and 90.304 define the two types of rebuttable presumptions. Section 90.302 sets forth the manner in which each presumption in a civil case affects the proceeding.

Presumptions affecting the burden of producing evidence, as defined in Section 90.303, are established primarily to facilitate the determination of the action, rather than to implement public policy. A presumption affecting the burden of producing evidence is a procedural device designed to dispense with unnecessary proof of facts that are likely to be true if not disputed.

The presumptions described in Section 90.303 are not expressions of policy; they are expressions of experience. They are intended solely to eliminate the need for the trier of fact to reason from the proven or established fact to the presumed fact and to forestall argument over the existence of the presumed fact when there is no evidence tending to prove the nonexistence of the presumed fact. These presumptions are typically those that are so likely to be true that the law requires a fact to be assumed in the absence of contrary evidence, e.g., the presumption that a member of the family of the owner of an automobile was driving with the consent of the owner. In other situations, such as the presumption of due care of a decedent in an accident when there are no eyewitnesses, there may be no direct evidence of the existence or nonexistence of the presumed fact, but, because the case must be decided, a presumption is created as a procedural convenience. Other presumptions of the type defined in Section 90.303 are: a letter correctly addressed is presumed to have been received in the ordinary course of mail, see Brown v. Giffen Indus., Inc., 281 So. 2d 897 (Fla. 1973); Snell v. Mayo, 84 So. 2d 581 (1956); the things which a person possesses are presumed to be owned by him, see Boynton Beach State Bank v. J.I. Case Co., 99 So. 2d 633 (Fla. 2nd Dist. 1957).

When a party relies on a presumption affecting the burden of producing evidence, the basic fact must be proved before the presumption becomes operative. If the adversary offers evidence going only to the existence of the basic facts giving rise to the presumption and not to the presumed fact, the jury will be instructed that if they find the existence of the basic fact, they must also find the presumed fact. If the existence of the basic fact is not subject to dispute, i.e., it has been established by the pleadings or by judicial notice, so that it is not a question of fact for the jury, unless sufficient evidence has been presented to sustain a finding of the nonexistence of the presumed fact, the court should instruct the jury that it must also find the presumed fact.

The court must make a determination of whether sufficient evidence has been presented to sustain a finding of the nonexistence of the presumed fact. If such evidence has not been presented, the court should instruct the jury that if it finds the basic fact, it must also find the presumed fact. If sufficient evidence to sustain the finding of the nonexistence of the presumed fact has been presented, the presumption disappears and the court should say nothing about the presumption in his instructions.

Even though a judge does not instruct the jury concerning a Section 90.303 presumption because sufficient evidence is presented to sustain a finding of the nonexistence of the presumed fact, any logical inferences that may be drawn from the basic fact may still be argued to the jury by counsel.

The presumptions affecting the burden of proof, which are defined in Section 90.304, place a greater burden on the one asserting the nonexistence of the presumed fact because of the greater harm to the individual or to societal stability that would ensue, should the presumed fact be disproved. Examples of this type of presumption are as follows:

1. Legitimacy

Eldridge v. Eldridge, 153 Fla. 873, 875, 16 So. 2d 163, 164 (1944). ("[P]roof must be sufficiently strong to clearly remove the presumption of legitimacy.")

2. Validity of marriage

McMichael v. McMichael, 158 Fla. 413, 415, 28 So. 2d 692, 693 (1947). ("[T]he law would presume a marriage to be legal until otherwise shown")

3. Acts of public officials

Hillsborough County Aviation Authority v. Taller & Cooper, Inc., 245 So. 2d 100 (Fla. 2nd Dist. 1971). (Presumption exists that public officials properly performed their duties in accordance with the law. It is incumbent upon those challenging such performance to overcome presumption.)

4. Sanity

Alexander v. Estate of Callahan, 132 So. 2d 42, 43 (Fla. 3rd Dist. 1961). ("In order to overturn the presumption of sanity...there must be proof showing that insanity...existed."); Schaefer v. Voyle, 88 Fla. 170, 102 So. 7 (1924). (Every person is presumed sane. Generally, in civil actions the burden of proof of insanity rests upon the party who alleges it.)

When a party relies on a presumption affecting the burden of proof, the court must determine whether sufficient evidence has been presented to sustain a finding of the nonexistence of the presumed fact. If the court determines that sufficient evidence has not been presented, the jury should be instructed that if the basic fact is found, it must also find the presumed fact. However, if sufficient evidence has been presented to sustain a finding of the nonexistence of the presumed fact, the court should instruct the jury on the manner in which the presumption affects the fact-finding process. The basic facts must, of course, be proved before the presumption becomes operative. If the basic fact from which the presumption arises is so established that the existence of the basic fact is not a question of fact for the jury, the court should instruct the jury that the existence of the presumed fact is to be assumed unless the jury is persuaded to the contrary by the requisite degree of proof (preponderance of the evidence, clear and convincing, etc.). If the basic fact may be found by the jury, the court should instruct the jury that if it finds that the basic fact exists, it must also find the presumed fact unless persuaded of the nonexistence of the presumed fact by the requisite degree of the evidence.

Sections 90.303 and 90.304 recognize that situations which would be included in the definition of that presumption may be given a different effect by statute. Even if they would be included within the definition of a presumption, an existing Florida statute providing that one fact or set of facts is prima facie evidence of another fact is not affected.

See Calif. Evid. Code §§ 603, 605.

COMMENTARY ON FEDERAL AND FLORIDA RULE DIFFERENCES

Florida Stat. §§ 90.301-90.304 and their federal counterpart, Federal Rule 301, set forth the rules governing the use of presumptions and inferences.

Florida and federal law distinguish among three different types of presumptions. With a presumption, the establishment of certain basic facts (e.g., that a letter was properly addressed and placed in the mail), gives rise to a presumed fact (e.g., that the letter was received by the addressee), and in the absence of counterproof, the trier of fact is instructed that it *must* find the presumed fact to exist (if the basic facts are subject to dispute, the jury will be given a contingent instruction that if it finds the basic facts, it must also find the presumed fact). There are three types of presumptions: conclusive presumptions, rebuttable presumptions that shift the burden of production, and rebuttable presumptions that shift the burden of proof (or persuasion). With a conclusive presumption, once the basic facts are established, the trier of fact *must* find the presumed fact to exist, and the party against whom the presumption is directed is not permitted to introduce evidence to show that the presumed fact does not exist. With a rebuttable presumption that shifts the burden of *production*, once the basic facts are established, then *unless* the party against whom the presumption is directed produces some evidence to rebut the presumed fact, the trier of fact is instructed that it *must* find the presumed fact. By contrast, with a rebuttable presumption that shifts the burden of *proof (or persuasion)*, once the basic facts are established, the trier of fact is instructed that it *must* find the presumed fact *unless* the party against whom the presumption is directed proves the nonexistence of the presumed fact. *See* FLA. STAT. §§ 90.301-90.302; Sponsors' Note to FLA. STAT. §§ 90.301-90.304; *Sandstrom v. Montana*, 442 U.S. 510 (1979).

Under Federal Rule 301, as a general rule, presumptions shift to the party against whom they are directed only the burden of *producing* evidence that rebuts the presumption, *not* the burden of *persuading* the trier of fact of the nonexistence of the presumed fact. *See* FED. R. EVID. 301. Under this rule, once the party against whom the presumption is directed produces some evidence to counter the presumed fact, the presumption disappears from the case and the court *cannot* instruct the jury that it *must* find the presumed fact. *See In re Yoder Co.*, 758 F.2d 1114 (6th Cir. 1985); *Legille v. Dann*, 544 F.2d 1 (D.C. Cir. 1976); Conference Report to FED. R. EVID. 301. However, to the extent there is a logical connection between the basic facts and the presumed fact, the trial court is free to instruct the jury that it *may infer* the existence of the presumed fact upon proof of the basic facts. *See In re Yoder Co.*, 758 F.2d at 1119-20 n.13; Conference Report to FED. R. EVID. 301. However, this default principle notwithstanding, a presumption in federal court on a federal claim will sometimes be deemed to be conclusive or to shift the burden of *persuasion* to the party against whom it is directed, for Federal Rule 301 contains a proviso indicating that it applies unless otherwise provided for by Act of Congress or by these rules. *See* FED. R. EVID. 301; *Alabama By-Products Corp. v. Killingsworth*, 733 F.2d 1511, 1517 & n.7 (11th Cir. 1984).

Florida law, by contrast, has several default principles for determining the effect of a presumption. First, as a general principle, all presumptions are deemed rebuttable unless made conclusive under the law from which they arise, *see* FLA. STAT. § 90.301(2), which has been interpreted to mean that a presumption is rebuttable unless the legislature specifically designates it as conclusive. *See Don King Prods., Inc. v. Chavez*, 717 So. 2d 1094, 1095 (Fla. 4th DCA 1998). Within the category of rebuttable presumptions, whether a presumption shifts the burden of production or the burden of persuasion under Florida law turns on the *purpose* that the presumption is designed to serve. If the presumption is created primarily as a procedural convenience and grounded in experience, and not to further some public policy, then it shifts only the burden of production. *See* FLA. STAT. § 90.303. The presumptions in this category include those things that are so likely to be true as a statistical matter that they are presumed to be true in the absence of counterproof as a matter of convenience, and include such things as the mailed-letter presumption. *See* Sponsors' Note to FLA. STAT. § 90.303. As with the federal rule, once the party against whom this sort of presumption is directed produces evidence to counter the presumed fact (which Florida law requires to be "credible evidence sufficient to sustain a finding of the nonexistence of the presumed fact"), the presumption disappears from the case and the court *cannot* instruct the jury that it *must* find the presumed fact. *See* FLA. STAT. § 90.302(1); Sponsors' Note to FLA. STAT. §§ 90.302-90.304. Moreover, unlike the federal rule, the court *cannot* give the jury a permissive inference instruction, *see* FLA. STAT. § 90.106, although logical inferences that may be drawn from the basic fact may be argued by counsel to the jury or may be drawn by the jury on its own. *See* FLA. STAT. § 90.301(3); Sponsors' Note to FLA. STAT. §§ 90.301-90.304. As under federal practice, even if a presumption is created primarily as a procedural convenience, it will be deemed to shift the burden of persuasion if the legislature so provides. *See* FLA. STAT. § 90.303.

Under Florida law, all other rebuttable presumptions shift the burden of persuasion to the party against whom they are directed. *See* FLA. STAT. § 90.304. The presumptions in this category include those situations in which the effect of disproving the presumed fact is thought to result in greater harm to the individual or to societal stability—thus making it appropriate to force the party who seeks to overcome the presumption to bear the burden of disproving its truth—and include such things as the presumptions of legitimacy, validity of marriage, official regularity, and sanity. *See* Sponsors' Note to FLA. STAT. §§ 90.303-90.304. To be sure, it is not always easy to determine whether a presumption is designed to further a public policy or merely as a matter of procedural convenience. In some cases, the legislature will direct by statute that a particular presumption is designed to implement public policy, in which case it is easy to make that determination. *See, e.g., Hack v. Janes*, 878 So. 2d 440, 441-44 (Fla. 5th DCA 2004); *Mallardi v. Jenne*, 721 So. 2d 380, 383-84 (Fla. 4th DCA 1998). *See also Warfel v. Universal Ins. Co. of North America*, 36 So. 3d 136, 138-399 (Fla. 2nd DCA 2010) (holding that the legislature's *failure* to declare a presumption either public policy-related or burden-shifting implies an intent not to shift the burden of persuasion). Other times, particularly when what is involved is a presumption created by the courts as a matter of common law, the court will state (with little analysis) that something is or is not designed to implement public policy. *See, e.g., Insurance Co. of Pa. v. Estate of Guzman*, 421 So. 2d 597, 602 (Fla. 1982) (holding that common law bailed goods presumption is only for procedural convenience).

Both the Florida and federal rules apply only in civil cases, *see* FED. R. EVID. 301; FLA. STAT. § 90.301(4), with the use of presumptions and inferences in criminal cases governed by limitations imposed by federal due process principles. *See County Ct. of Ulster v. Allen*, 442 U.S. 140 (1979); *Sandstrom*, 442 U.S. at 510.

Federal Rule 302. Applying State Law to Presumptions in Civil Cases

In a civil case, state law governs the effect of a presumption regarding a claim or defense for which state law supplies the rule of decision.

ADVISORY COMMITTEE'S NOTE

A series of Supreme Court decisions in diversity cases leaves no doubt of the relevance of Erie Railroad Co. v. Tompkins, 304 U.S. 64 (1938), to questions of burden of proof. These decisions are Cities Service Oil Co. v. Dunlap, 308 U.S. 208 (1939), Palmer v. Hoffman, 318 U.S. 109 (1943), and Dick v. New York Life Ins. Co., 359 U.S. 437 (1959). They involved burden of proof, respectively, as to status as bona fide purchaser, contributory negligence, and nonaccidental death (suicide) of an insured. In each instance the state rule was held to be applicable. It does not follow, however, that all presumptions in diversity cases are governed by state law. In each case cited, the burden of proof question had to do with a substantive element of the claim or defense. Application of the state law is called for only when the presumption operates upon such an element. Accordingly the rule does not apply state law when the presumption operates upon a lesser aspect of the case, i.e. "tactical" presumptions.

The situations in which the state law is applied have been tagged for convenience in the preceding discussion as "diversity cases." The designation is not a completely accurate one since *Erie* applies to any claim or issue having its source in state law, regardless of the basis of federal jurisdiction, and does not apply to a federal claim or issue, even though jurisdiction is based on diversity. Vestal, Erie R.R. v. Tompkins: A Projection, 48 Iowa L.Rev. 248, 257 (1963); Hart and Wechsler, The Federal Courts and the Federal System, 697 (1953); 1A Moore, Federal Practice ¶ 0.305 [3] (2d ed. 1965); Wright, Federal Courts, 217–218 (1963). Hence the rule employs, as appropriately descriptive, the phrase "as to which state law supplies the rule of decision." See A.L.I. Study of the Division of Jurisdiction Between State and Federal Courts, § 2344(c), p. 40, P.F.D. No. 1 (1965).

ADVISORY COMMITTEE'S NOTE (2011 AMENDMENT)

The language of Rule 302 has been amended as part of the restyling of the Evidence Rules to make them more easily understood and to make style and terminology consistent throughout the rules. These changes are intended to be stylistic only. There is no intent to change any result in any ruling on evidence admissibility.

COMMENTARY ON FEDERAL AND FLORIDA RULE DIFFERENCES

Federal Rule 302 governs the application of presumptions in civil cases in which state law provides the rule of decision. Under this rule, the federal court is required to look to state law to determine the content of presumptions as well as their effect (i.e., whether they shift the burden of production or the burden of persuasion).

Florida has no comparable rule directing it to apply federal law when adjudicating a federal claim. However, the "reverse *Erie*" doctrine might compel the application of federal law in those circumstances to determine the content and effect of any presumptions. *See* 1 PAUL C. GIANNELLI & BARBARA ROOK SNYDER, BALDWIN'S OHIO PRACTICE: EVIDENCE § 301.14 (2004).

ARTICLE IV. RELEVANCE AND ITS LIMITS

Federal Rule	Florida Stat. §	Description
401	90.401	Test for Relevant Evidence
402	90.402	General Admissibility of Relevant Evidence
—	90.4025	Admissibility of Paternity Determination in Certain Criminal Prosecutions
—	90.4026	Statements Expressing Sympathy; Admissibility; Definitions
403	90.403	Excluding Relevant Evidence for Prejudice, Confusion, Waste of Time, or Other Reasons
404	90.404	Character Evidence; Crimes or Other Acts
405	90.405	Methods of Proving Character
406	90.406	Habit; Routine Practice
407	90.407	Subsequent Remedial Measures
408	90.408	Compromise Offers and Negotiations
409	90.409	Offers to Pay Medical and Similar Expenses
410	90.410	Pleas, Plea Discussions, and Related Statements
411	—	Liability Insurance
412	794.022	Sex-Offense Cases: The Victim's Sexual Behavior or Predisposition
413	90.404	Similar Crimes in Sexual-Assault Cases
414	90.404	Similar Crimes in Child-Molestation Cases
415	—	Similar Acts in Civil Cases Involving Sexual Assault or Child Molestation

Federal Rule 401. Test for Relevant Evidence

Evidence is relevant if:

(a) it has any tendency to make a fact more or less probable than it would be without the evidence; and

(b) the fact is of consequence in determining the action.

ADVISORY COMMITTEE'S NOTE

Problems of relevancy call for an answer to the question whether an item of evidence, when tested by the processes of legal reasoning, possesses sufficient probative value to justify receiving it in evidence. Thus, assessment of the probative value of evidence that a person purchased a revolver shortly prior to a fatal shooting with which he is charged is a matter of analysis and reasoning.

The variety of relevancy problems is coextensive with the ingenuity of counsel in using circumstantial evidence as a means of proof. An enormous number of cases fall in no set pattern, and this rule is designed as a guide for handling them. On the other hand, some situations recur with sufficient frequency to create patterns susceptible of treatment by specific rules. Rule 404 and those following it are of that variety; they also serve as illustrations of the application of the present rule as limited by the exclusionary principles of Rule 403.

Passing mention should be made of so-called "conditional" relevancy. Morgan, Basic Problems of Evidence 45–46 (1962). In this situation, probative value depends not only upon satisfying the basic requirement of relevancy as described above but also upon the existence of some matter of fact. For example, if evidence of a spoken statement is relied upon to prove notice, probative value is lacking unless the person sought to be charged heard the statement. The problem is one of fact, and the only rules needed are for the purpose of determining the respective functions of judge and jury. See Rules 104(b) and 901. The discussion which follows in the present note is concerned with relevancy generally, not with any particular problem of conditional relevancy.

Relevancy is not an inherent characteristic of any item of evidence but exists only as a relation between an item of evidence and a matter properly provable in the case. Does the item of evidence tend to prove the matter sought to be proved? Whether the relationship exists depends upon principles evolved by experience or science, applied logically to the situation at hand. James, Relevancy, Probability and the Law, 29 Calif.L.Rev. 689, 696, n. 15 (1941), in Selected Writings on Evidence and Trial 610, 615, n. 15 (Fryer ed. 1957). The rule summarizes this relationship as a "tendency to make the existence" of the fact to be proved "more probable or less probable." Compare Uniform Rule 1(2) which states the crux of relevancy as "a tendency in reason," thus perhaps emphasizing unduly the logical process and ignoring the need to draw upon experience or science to validate the general principle upon which relevancy in a particular situation depends.

The standard of probability under the rule is "more...probable than it would be without the evidence." Any more stringent requirement is unworkable and unrealistic. As McCormick § 152, p. 317, says, "A brick is not a wall," or, as Falknor, Extrinsic Policies Affecting Admissibility, 10 Rutgers L.Rev. 574, 576 (1956), quotes Professor McBaine, " . . . [I]t is not to be supposed that every witness can make a home run." Dealing with probability in the language of the rule has the added virtue of avoiding confusion between questions of admissibility and questions of the sufficiency of the evidence.

The rule uses the phrase "fact that is of consequence to the determination of the action" to describe the kind of fact to which proof may properly be directed. The language is that of California Evidence Code § 210; it has the advantage of avoiding the loosely used and ambiguous word "material." Tentative Recommendation and a Study Relating to the Uniform Rules of Evidence (Art. I. General Provisions),

Cal.Law Revision Comm'n, Rep., Rec. & Studies, 10–11 (1964). The fact to be proved may be ultimate, intermediate, or evidentiary; it matters not, so long as it is of consequence in the determination of the action. Cf. Uniform Rule 1(2) which requires that the evidence relate to a "material" fact.

The fact to which the evidence is directed need not be in dispute. While situations will arise which call for the exclusion of evidence offered to prove a point conceded by the opponent, the ruling should be made on the basis of such considerations as waste of time and undue prejudice (see Rule 403), rather than under any general requirement that evidence is admissible only if directed to matters in dispute. Evidence which is essentially background in nature can scarcely be said to involve disputed matter, yet it is universally offered and admitted as an aid to understanding. Charts, photographs, views of real estate, murder weapons, and many other items of evidence fall in this category. A rule limiting admissibility to evidence directed to a controversial point would invite the exclusion of this helpful evidence, or at least the raising of endless questions over its admission. Cf. California Evidence Code § 210, defining relevant evidence in terms of tendency to prove a disputed fact.

ADVISORY COMMITTEE'S NOTE (2011 AMENDMENT)

The language of Rule 401 has been amended as part of the restyling of the Evidence Rules to make them more easily understood and to make style and terminology consistent throughout the rules. These changes are intended to be stylistic only. There is no intent to change any result in any ruling on evidence admissibility.

Florida Stat. § 90.401. Definition of Relevant Evidence

Relevant evidence is evidence tending to prove or disprove a material fact.

SPONSORS' NOTE (1976 ENACTMENT)

Relevancy is the result of a relationship between an item of evidence and a matter properly provable in the case. Whether the relationship exists, depends upon principles evolved by experience or science, applied logically to the situation at hand. The Florida courts have said that "relevancy describes evidence that has a legitimate tendency to prove or disprove a given proposition that is material as shown by the pleadings. [It is] a tendency to establish a fact in controversy or to render a proposition more or less probable." Zabner v. Howard Johnson's Inc., 227 So. 2d 543, 545 (Fla. 4th Dist. 1969). Uniform Rule 1(2) defines relevant evidence as "evidence having any tendency in reason to prove any material fact." The A.L.I. Model Code of Evidence Rule 1(12) defines relevant evidence as "evidence having any tendency in reason to prove any material matter."

COMMENTARY ON FEDERAL AND FLORIDA RULE DIFFERENCES

Florida Stat. § 90.401 and its federal counterpart, Federal Rule 401, define the phrase "[r]elevant evidence" as it is used in Florida Stat. § 90.402 and its federal counterpart, Federal Rule 402.

The two rules, although using slightly different language, define relevancy in the same way. The phrase "fact [] of consequence in determining the action" as used in the federal rule is synonymous with the phrase "material fact" as used in the Florida rule. See U.S. v. Shomo, 786 F.2d 981, 985 (10th Cir. 1986). A fact is "material" (or "of consequence") if its existence would provide the trier of fact with a basis for making some inference, or chain of inferences, about an issue that is necessary to a verdict. See U.S. v. McVeigh, 153 F.3d 1166, 1190 (10th Cir. 1998), abrogated on other grounds, Hooks v. Ward, 184 F.3d 1206 (10th Cir. 1999). The word "tending" as used in the Florida rule is interpreted to mean "any tendency" as used in the federal rule. See, e.g., State v. Taylor, 648 So. 2d 701, 704 (Fla. 1995).

The definition under both rules thus encompasses two requirements: a materiality requirement and a probative worth requirement, both of which must be satisfied for evidence to be deemed relevant. *See Ramirez v. State*, 810 So. 2d 836, 842 (Fla. 2001); *McVeigh*, 153 F.3d at 1190. For evidence to be relevant under either rule, it must have some tendency, however slight, to prove or disprove a fact that would provide the trier of fact with a basis for making some inference, or chain of inferences, about an issue that is necessary to a verdict.

Federal Rule 402. General Admissibility of Relevant Evidence

Relevant evidence is admissible unless any of the following provides otherwise:

- the United States Constitution;

- a federal statute;

- these rules; or

- other rules prescribed by the Supreme Court.

Irrelevant evidence is not admissible.

ADVISORY COMMITTEE'S NOTE

The provisions that all relevant evidence is admissible, with certain exceptions, and that evidence which is not relevant is not admissible are "a presupposition involved in the very conception of a rational system of evidence." Thayer, Preliminary Treatise on Evidence 264 (1898). They constitute the foundation upon which the structure of admission and exclusion rests. For similar provisions see California Evidence Code §§ 350, 351. Provisions that all relevant evidence is admissible are found in Uniform Rule 7(f); Kansas Code of Civil Procedure § 60-407(f); and New Jersey Evidence Rule 7(f); but the exclusion of evidence which is not relevant is left to implication.

Not all relevant evidence is admissible. The exclusion of relevant evidence occurs in a variety of situations and may be called for by these rules, by the Rules of Civil and Criminal Procedure, by Bankruptcy Rules, by Act of Congress, or by constitutional considerations.

Succeeding rules in the present article, in response to the demands of particular policies, require the exclusion of evidence despite its relevancy. In addition, Article V recognizes a number of privileges; Article VI imposes limitations upon witnesses and the manner of dealing with them; Article VII specifies requirements with respect to opinions and expert testimony; Article VIII excludes hearsay not falling within an exception; Article IX spells out the handling of authentication and identification; and Article X restricts the manner of proving the contents of writings and recordings.

The Rules of Civil and Criminal Procedure in some instances require the exclusion of relevant evidence. For example, Rules 30(b) and 32(a)(3) of the Rules of Civil Procedure, by imposing requirements of notice and unavailability of the deponent, place limits on the use of relevant depositions. Similarly, Rule 15 of the Rules of Criminal Procedure restricts the use of depositions in criminal cases, even though relevant. And the effective enforcement of the command, originally statutory and now found in Rule 5(a) of the Rules of Criminal Procedure, that an arrested person be taken without unnecessary delay before a commissioner or other similar officer is held to require the exclusion of statements elicited during detention in violation thereof. Mallory v. United States, 354 U.S. 449 (1957); 18 U.S.C. § 3501(c).

While congressional enactments in the field of evidence have generally tended to expand admissibility beyond the scope of the common law rules, in some particular situations they have restricted the admissibility of relevant evidence. Most of this legislation has consisted of the formulation of a privilege or of a prohibition against disclosure. 8 U.S.C. § 1202(f), records of refusal of visas or permits to enter United States confidential, subject to discretion of Secretary of State to make available to court upon certification of need; 10 U.S.C. § 3693, replacement certificate of honorable discharge from Army not admissible in evidence; 10 U.S.C. § 8693, same as to Air Force; 11 U.S.C. § 25(a)(10), testimony given by bankrupt on his examination not admissible in criminal proceedings against him, except that given in hearing upon objection to discharge; 11 U.S.C. § 205(a), railroad reorganization petition, if dismissed, not admissible in evidence; 11 U.S.C. § 403(a), list of creditors filed with municipal composition plan not an admission; 13 U.S.C. § 9(a), census information confidential, retained copies of reports privileged; 47 U.S.C. § 605, interception and divulgence of wire or radio communications prohibited unless authorized by sender. These statutory provisions would remain undisturbed by the rules.

The rule recognizes but makes no attempt to spell out the constitutional considerations which impose basic limitations upon the admissibility of relevant evidence. Examples are evidence obtained by unlawful search and seizure, Weeks v. United States, 232 U.S. 383 (1914); Katz v. United States, 389 U.S. 347 (1967); incriminating statement elicited from an accused in violation of right to counsel, Massiah v. United States, 377 U.S. 201 (1964).

REPORT OF HOUSE COMMITTEE ON THE JUDICIARY

Rule 402 as submitted to the Congress contained the phrase "or by other rules adopted by the Supreme Court". To accommodate the view that the Congress should not appear to acquiesce in the Court's judgment that it has authority under the existing Rules Enabling Acts to promulgate Rules of Evidence, the Committee amended the above phrase to read "or by other rules prescribed by the Supreme Court pursuant to statutory authority" in this and other Rules where the reference appears.

ADVISORY COMMITTEE'S NOTE (2011 AMENDMENT)

The language of Rule 402 has been amended as part of the restyling of the Evidence Rules to make them more easily understood and to make style and terminology consistent throughout the rules. These changes are intended to be stylistic only. There is no intent to change any result in any ruling on evidence admissibility.

Florida Stat. § 90.402. Admissibility of Relevant Evidence

All relevant evidence is admissible, except as provided by law.

SPONSORS' NOTE (1976 ENACTMENT)

This section is a restatement of existing Florida law. See Williams v. State, 110 So. 2d 654, 660 (Fla. 1959), cert. denied, 361 U.S. 847. For similar provisions see Calif. Evid. Code §§ 350, 351. Provisions that all relevant evidence is admissible are found in Fed. Rule Evid. 402; Uniform Rule of Evid. 7(f); Kansas Code of Civ. Pro. § 60-407(f); and New Jersey Evid. Rule 7(f); the exclusion of evidence which is not relevant is left to implication.

Not all relevant evidence is admissible. Relevant evidence may be excluded by this Code, by the Rules of Civil and Criminal Procedure, by other acts of the United States Congress or the Florida Legislature, or by constitutional considerations. Succeeding sections in this chapter, in response to the demands of particular policies, require the exclusion of evidence despite its relevancy. In addition, §§ 90.501-.508

recognize a number of privileges; §§ 90.601-.615 impose limitations upon witnesses and the manner of dealing with them; §§ 90.701-.705 specify requirements with respect to opinion and expert testimony; §§ 90.801-.806 exclude hearsay not falling within an exception; §§ 90.901-.903 spell out the handling of authentication and identification; and §§ 90.[951-.958] restrict the manner of proving the contents of writing and recordings.

The Rules of Civil and Criminal Procedure in some instances require the exclusion of relevant evidence. For example, Rules 1.280(d) and 1.290(a)(4) of the Florida Rules of Civil Procedure, by imposing requirements of notice and unavailability of the deponent, place limits on the use of relevant depositions.

Examples of constitutional limitations on the admissibility of evidence are found in Weeks v. United States, 232 U.S. 383, 34 S.Ct. 341, 58 L.Ed. 652 (1914) and Katz v. United States, 389 U.S. 347, 88 S.Ct. 507, 19 L.Ed. 2d 576 (1967), excluding evidence obtained by unlawful search and seizure; and in Massiah v. United States, 377 U.S. 201, 84 S.Ct. 1199, 12 L.Ed. 2d 246 (1964), excluding incriminating statements elicited from an accused in violation of his right to counsel.

COMMENTARY ON FEDERAL AND FLORIDA RULE DIFFERENCES

Florida Stat. § 90.402 and its federal counterpart, Federal Rule 402, set forth the basic rule governing the admissibility of relevant evidence.

The two rules, although using slightly different language, in fact state the same principle. The first sentence of the federal rule provides that all relevant evidence is admissible, except as otherwise provided by various sources of federal law, including federal statutes, other federal rules of evidence and procedure, and the U.S. Constitution. *See* FED. R. EVID. 401. The Florida rule provides that all relevant evidence is admissible "except as provided by law," *See* FLA. STAT. § 90.402, which is understood to include other provisions of the Florida Evidence Code, rules of procedure, federal and state statutes, and the U.S. Constitution. *See* Sponsors' Note to FLA. STAT. § 90.402.

Unlike the Florida rule, the federal rule has a second sentence that provides that irrelevant evidence is not admissible. However, the inadmissibility of irrelevant evidence is understood to be implicit in the Florida rule. *See Shaw v. Jain*, 914 So. 2d 458, 460 (Fla. 1st DCA 2005); Sponsors' Note to FLA. STAT. § 90.402.

Florida Stat. § 90.4025. Admissibility of Paternity Determination in Certain Criminal Prosecutions

If a person less than 18 years of age gives birth to a child and the paternity of that child is established under chapter 742, such evidence of paternity is admissible in a criminal prosecution under ss. 794.011, 794.05, 800.04, and 827.04(3).

COMMENTARY ON FEDERAL AND FLORIDA RULE DIFFERENCES

Florida Stat. § 90.4025 provides that, in a criminal prosecution (under various statutes) for engaging in unlawful sexual activity with a minor, evidence regarding the paternity of a child that the minor gave birth to is admissible. It appears that the rule could be invoked by the prosecution (offering evidence that the defendant is the father to prove that he engaged in sexual activity with the minor) or by the defense (offering evidence that someone else is the father). There are no published decisions to date applying or interpreting this provision.

There is no comparable provision in the federal rules of evidence, although such evidence would be probative of whether the defendant engaged in sexual activity with the minor and thus would be presumptively admissible under Federal Rule 402, unless excluded for some other reason. *See U.S. v. Johnson*, 54 Fed. Appx. 453, 454 (8th Cir. 2002); *Daniels v. Delaware*, 2002 WL 31716422 (3d Cir. 2002).

Florida Stat. § 90.4026. Statements Expressing Sympathy; Admissibility; Definitions

(1) As used in this section:

(a) "Accident" means an occurrence resulting in injury or death to one or more persons which is not the result of willful action by a party.

(b) "Benevolent gestures" means actions that convey a sense of compassion or commiseration emanating from human impulses.

(c) "Family" means the spouse, parent, grandparent, stepmother, stepfather, child, grandchild, brother, sister, half-brother, half-sister, adopted child of parent, or spouse's parent of an injured party.

(2) The portion of statements, writings, or benevolent gestures expressing sympathy or a general sense of benevolence relating to the pain, suffering, or death of a person involved in an accident and made to that person or to the family of that person shall be inadmissible as evidence in a civil action. A statement of fault, however, which is part of, or in addition to, any of the above shall be admissible pursuant to this section.

COMMENTARY ON FEDERAL AND FLORIDA RULE DIFFERENCES

Florida Stat. § 90.4026 provides that evidence of statements or "benevolent gestures" expressing sympathy relating to a person's pain, suffering, or death as a result of an accident, and made to that person or a member of his family is inadmissible in civil actions. The goal, as with many of the categorical rules of exclusion, is to encourage (or at least not to discourage) the statements or conduct covered by the rule. *See* Fla. S. Comm. on Com., CS for SB 1066 (2001), Staff Analysis (rev. Mar. 20, 2001). Absent this provision, such statements would likely be deemed relevant and, although hearsay, admissible as a party admission or statement against interest. *See id.*

The scope of the rule is narrow, however, and it makes clear that statements of *fault* are admissible. *See* Fla. Stat. § 90.4026(2). Thus, if an accident occurs and the driver says, "I'm sorry you were hurt. The accident was all my fault," the first sentence would be barred by the rule but the second sentence would not be. *See* Fla. S. Comm. on Com., CS for SB 1066 (2001), Staff Analysis (rev. Mar. 20, 2001).

There is no comparable provision in the federal rules of evidence, and such evidence is probative of fault and thus likely admissible in federal court. *See generally* Aviva Orenstein, *Apology Excepted: Incorporating a Feminist Analysis Into Evidence Policy Where You Would Least Expect It*, 28 Sw. U. L. Rev. 221 (1999).

Federal Rule 403. Excluding Relevant Evidence for Prejudice, Confusion, Waste of Time, or Other Reasons

FLORIDA AND FEDERAL EVIDENCE RULES

The court may exclude relevant evidence if its probative value is substantially outweighed by a danger of one or more of the following: unfair prejudice, confusing the issues, misleading the jury, undue delay, wasting time, or needlessly presenting cumulative evidence.

ADVISORY COMMITTEE'S NOTE

The case law recognizes that certain circumstances call for the exclusion of evidence which is of unquestioned relevance. These circumstances entail risks which range all the way from inducing decision on a purely emotional basis, at one extreme, to nothing more harmful than merely wasting time, at the other extreme. Situations in this area call for balancing the probative value of and need for the evidence against the harm likely to result from its admission. Slough, Relevancy Unraveled, 5 Kan.L.Rev. 1, 12–15 (1956); Trautman, Logical or Legal Relevancy — A Conflict in Theory, 5 Van.L.Rev. 385, 392 (1952); McCormick § 152, pp. 319–321. The rules which follow in this Article are concrete applications evolved for particular situations. However, they reflect the policies underlying the present rule, which is designed as a guide for the handling of situations for which no specific rules have been formulated.

Exclusion for risk of unfair prejudice, confusion of issues, misleading the jury, or waste of time, all find ample support in the authorities. "Unfair prejudice" within its context means an undue tendency to suggest decision on an improper basis, commonly, though not necessarily, an emotional one.

The rule does not enumerate surprise as a ground for exclusion, in this respect following Wigmore's view of the common law. 6 Wigmore § 1849. Cf. McCormick § 152, p. 320, n. 29, listing unfair surprise as a ground for exclusion but stating that it is usually "coupled with the danger of prejudice and confusion of issues." While Uniform Rule 45 incorporates surprise as a ground and is followed in Kansas Code of Civil Procedure § 60-445, surprise is not included in California Evidence Code § 352 or New Jersey Rule 4, though both the latter otherwise substantially embody Uniform Rule 45. While it can scarcely be doubted that claims of unfair surprise may still be justified despite procedural requirements of notice and instrumentalities of discovery, the granting of a continuance is a more appropriate remedy than exclusion of the evidence. Tentative Recommendation and a Study Relating to the Uniform Rules of Evidence (Art. VI. Extrinsic Policies Affecting Admissibility), Cal.Law Revision Comm'n, Rep., Rec. & Studies, 612 (1964). Moreover, the impact of a rule excluding evidence on the ground of surprise would be difficult to estimate.

In reaching a decision whether to exclude on grounds of unfair prejudice, consideration should be given to the probable effectiveness or lack of effectiveness of a limiting instruction. See Rule [105] and Advisory Committee's Note thereunder. The availability of other means of proof may also be an appropriate factor.

ADVISORY COMMITTEE'S NOTE (2011 AMENDMENT)

The language of Rule 403 has been amended as part of the restyling of the Evidence Rules to make them more easily understood and to make style and terminology consistent throughout the rules. These changes are intended to be stylistic only. There is no intent to change any result in any ruling on evidence admissibility.

Florida Stat. § 90.403. Exclusion on Grounds of Prejudice or Confusion

Relevant evidence is inadmissible if its probative value is substantially outweighed by the danger of unfair prejudice, confusion of issues, misleading the jury, or needless presentation of cumulative evidence. This section shall not be construed to mean that evidence of the existence of available third-party benefits is inadmissible.

SPONSORS' NOTE (1976 ENACTMENT)

At trial, nothing that fails to meet the tests of Sections 90.401 and 90.403 may be admitted. The offered evidence is excluded if the stated reasons are found to outweigh the probative value of the offered evidence. See Weinstein & Berger, Basic Rules of Relevancy in the Proposed Federal Rules of Evidence, 4 Ga. L. Rev. 43 (1969).

While the Florida courts speak in somewhat different terms, they achieve a similar result. The courts have not made certain exclusions mandatory, but have exercised judicial "discretion" in reaching that end. In Young v. State, 234 So.2d 341, 348 (Fla. 1970), the Supreme Court found an abuse of the trial court's discretion in its admission of large numbers of gruesome photographs:

"[W]here there is an element of relevancy to support admissibility then the trial judge in the first instance and this Court on appeal must determine whether the gruesomeness of the portrayal is so inflammatory as to create an undue prejudice in the minds of the jury and detract them from a fair and unimpassioned consideration of the evidence."

In Perper v. Edell, 44 So. 2d 78, 80 (Fla. 1949) the Supreme Court stated that:

We conceive the rule to be that, if the introduction of the evidence tends in actual operation to produce a confusion in the minds of the jurors in excess of the legitimate probative effect of such evidence – if it tends to obscure rather than illuminate the true issues before the jury – then such evidence should be excluded.

Language from a recent Florida case supports the trial judge's power to exclude merely cumulative evidence. In Coral Plaza Corp. v. Hersman, 220 So. 2d 672 (Fla. 3rd Dist. 1969), the appellant claimed that the refusal by the trial court to permit three letters offered by the plaintiff into evidence during the trial was error. The court ruled that:

[T]he record reveals that there was oral testimony presented to the jury which contained the same evidence which would have been presented had the letters themselves been introduced into evidence. We do not find, under the circumstances, that the plaintiff was prejudiced by the refusal of the trial court to permit the introduction of the three letters into evidence.

The existing Florida law does not generally recognize surprise as a ground for excluding evidence, but as a ground for a continuance in a proper case. See Seaboard Airline R.R. v. Cain, 175 So. 2d 561 (Fla. 3rd Dist. 1965); Bowen v. Manuel, 144 So. 2d 341 (Fla. 2nd Dist. 1962). See also 6 Wigmore, Evidence § 1849 (3rd ed. 1940). While Uniform Rule 45 incorporates surprise as a ground and is followed in Kansas Code of Civ. Pro. § 60-445, surprise is not included in Calif. Evid. Code § 352 or New Jersey Evid. Rule 4, though both the latter otherwise substantially embody Uniform Rule 45. See Fed. Rule Evid. 403. While claims of unfair surprise may be justified, the granting of a continuance is a more appropriate remedy than exclusion of the evidence.

COMMENTARY ON FEDERAL AND FLORIDA RULE DIFFERENCES

Florida Stat. § 90.403 and its federal counterpart, Federal Rule 403, provide for the exclusion of relevant evidence when its probative value is substantially outweighed by unfair prejudice and other dangers.

In many respects, the two rules are identical. First, both rules are weighted heavily in favor of admitting relevant evidence, permitting it to be excluded only if its probative worth is *substantially* outweighed by the identified dangers. *See Lebron v. State*, 894 So. 2d 849, 853 (Fla. 2005); *U.S. v. Tinoco*, 304 F.3d 1088, 1120 (11th Cir. 2002). Second, under both the federal and Florida rules, great deference is given to the trial court's balancing of probative worth against unfair prejudice and other dangers, with reviewing courts finding error only if it can be said that the trial court abused its discretion. *See Floyd v. State*, 913 So. 2d 564, 574-75 (Fla. 2005); *U.S. v. Matthews*, 431 F.3d 1296, 1308 (11th Cir. 2005). Third, both rules define the phrase "unfair prejudice" in the same way, namely, as an undue tendency to suggest decision on an improper basis, commonly an emotional one. *See Old Chief v. U.S.*, 519 U.S. 172, 180 (1997); *McDuffie v. State*, 970 So. 2d 312, 327 (Fla. 2007); *State v. McClain*, 525 So. 2d 420, 422 (Fla. 1988). Fourth, under both Florida and federal law, the availability of other means of proof is a pertinent consideration; to the extent that a party can prove its point with equally probative but less prejudicial evidence, the trial court can apply Federal Rule 403 (or Florida Stat. § 90.403) to exclude evidence that has greater prejudicial effect. *See Old Chief*, 519 U.S. at 183-84 (holding that "the discretionary judgment [in applying Federal Rule 403] may be informed not only by assessing an evidentiary item's twin tendencies, but by placing the result of that assessment alongside similar assessments of evidentiary alternatives."); *Brown v. State*, 719 So. 2d 882, 884-89 (Fla. 1998). Fifth, under both Florida and federal law, the probable effectiveness of a limiting instruction (pursuant to Federal Rule 105 or Florida Stat. § 90.107) should be considered as an alternative to outright exclusion under Federal Rule 403 or Florida Stat. § 90.403. *See Huggins v. State*, 889 So. 2d 743, 756-57 (Fla. 2004); *McClain*, 525 So. 2d at 422; *U.S. v. Beechum*, 582 F.2d 898, 917 n.23 (5th Cir. 1978); Advisory Committee's Note to FED. R. EVID. 403. Finally, under both Florida and federal practice (subject to one exception in Federal Rule 609), Rule 403 must be applied to all evidence, even if it survives scrutiny under other exclusionary rules. *See Ramirez v. State*, 810 So. 2d 836, 842 (Fla. 2001); *Forrest v. Beloit Corp.*, 424 F.3d 344, 355 (3d Cir. 2005) ("Rule 403 is an 'umbrella rule' spanning the whole of the Federal Rules of Evidence," and as such trial judges must apply Rule 403 'in tandem with other Federal Rules under which evidence would be admissible.'").

One difference between the federal and Florida rules is that the list of dangers set forth in each, while similar to one another, are not identical. Both rules provide for the exclusion of relevant evidence when its probative worth is outweighed by the danger of unfair prejudice, confusion of the issues, misleading the jury, or needless presentation of cumulative evidence; however, the federal rule also includes in its list of dangers "undue delay" and "wasting of time," while the Florida rule does not. *See* FLA. STAT. § 90.403; FED. R. EVID. 403. Indeed, although wasting time was included in the initial version of the Florida rule, it was amended by the legislature in 1978 to remove it as a ground for exclusion. *See Tobin v. Leland*, 804 So. 2d 390, 397 (Fla. 4th DCA 2001) (Farmer, J., dissenting). Nonetheless, some Florida precedent holds that evidence that has minimal probative value can be excluded under Florida Stat. § 90.612(1)(b) on the ground that it is a waste of time, even though it cannot be excluded on that ground under Florida Stat. § 90.403. *See Tobin v. Leland*, 804 So. 2d 390, 395 n.3 (Fla. 4th DCA 2001).

A second difference between the federal and Florida rules is that the latter includes an additional sentence that provides that "[t]his section shall not be construed to mean that evidence of the existence of available third-party benefits is inadmissible." The significance of this language is examined in the commentary to Federal Rule 411 ("Liability Insurance.").

Federal Rule 404. Character Evidence; Crimes or Other Acts

(a) **Character Evidence.**

(1) *Prohibited Uses.* Evidence of a person's character or character trait is not admissible to prove that on a particular occasion the person acted in accordance with the character or trait.

(2) *Exceptions for a Defendant or Victim in a Criminal Case.* The following exceptions apply in a criminal case:

(A) a defendant may offer evidence of the defendant's pertinent trait, and if the evidence is admitted, the prosecutor may offer evidence to rebut it;

(B) subject to the limitations in Rule 412, a defendant may offer evidence of an alleged victim's pertinent trait, and if the evidence is admitted, the prosecutor may:

    (i) offer evidence to rebut it; and

    (ii) offer evidence of the defendant's same trait; and

(C) in a homicide case, the prosecutor may offer evidence of the alleged victim's trait of peacefulness to rebut evidence that the victim was the first aggressor.

  (3) Exceptions for a Witness. Evidence of a witness's character may be admitted under Rules 607, 608, and 609.

(b) Crimes, Wrongs, or Other Acts.

  (1) *Prohibited Uses.* Evidence of a crime, wrong, or other act is not admissible to prove a person's character in order to show that on a particular occasion the person acted in accordance with the character.

  (2) Permitted Uses; Notice in a Criminal Case. This evidence may be admissible for another purpose, such as proving motive, opportunity, intent, preparation, plan, knowledge, identity, absence of mistake, or lack of accident. On request by a defendant in a criminal case, the prosecutor must:

    (A) provide reasonable notice of the general nature of any such evidence that the prosecutor intends to offer at trial; and

    (B) do so before trial — or during trial if the court, for good cause, excuses lack of pretrial notice.

ADVISORY COMMITTEE'S NOTE

Subdivision (a). This subdivision deals with the basic question whether character evidence should be admitted. Once the admissibility of character evidence in some form is established under this rule, reference must then be made to Rule 405, which follows, in order to determine the appropriate method of proof. If the character is that of a witness, see Rules 608 and 609 for methods of proof.

Character questions arise in two fundamentally different ways. (1) Character may itself be an element of a crime, claim, or defense. A situation of this kind is commonly referred to as "character in issue." Illustrations are: the chastity of the victim under a statute specifying her chastity as an element of the crime of seduction, or the competency of the driver in an action for negligently entrusting a motor vehicle to an incompetent driver. No problem of the general relevancy of character evidence is involved, and the present rule therefore has no provision on the subject. The only question relates to allowable methods of proof, as to which see Rule 405, immediately following. (2) Character evidence is susceptible of being used for the purpose of suggesting an inference that the person acted on the occasion in question consistently with his character. This use of character is often described as "circumstantial." Illustrations are: evidence of a violent disposition to prove that the person was the aggressor in an affray, or evidence of honesty in disproof of a charge of theft. This circumstantial use of character evidence raises questions of relevancy as well as questions of allowable methods of proof.

In most jurisdictions today, the circumstantial use of character is rejected but with important exceptions: (1) an accused may introduce pertinent evidence of good character (often misleadingly described as "putting his character in issue"), in which event the prosecution may rebut with evidence of bad character; (2) an accused may introduce pertinent evidence of the character of the victim, as in support of a claim of self-defense to a charge of homicide or consent in a case of rape, and the prosecution may introduce similar evidence in rebuttal of the character evidence, or, in a homicide case, to rebut a claim that deceased was the first aggressor, however proved; and (3) the character of a witness may be gone into as bearing on his credibility. McCormick §§ 155–161. This pattern is incorporated in the rule. While its basis lies more in history and experience than in logic an underlying justification can fairly be found in terms of the relative presence and absence of prejudice in the various situations. Falknor, Extrinsic Policies Affecting Admissibility, 10 Rutgers L.Rev. 574, 584 (1956); McCormick § 157. In any event, the criminal rule is so deeply imbedded in our jurisprudence as to assume almost constitutional proportions and to override doubts of the basic relevancy of the evidence.

The limitation to pertinent traits of character, rather than character generally, in paragraphs [(2)(A)] and [(2)(B)] is in accordance with the prevailing view. McCormick § 158, p. 334. A similar provision in Rule 608, to which reference is made in paragraph (3), limits character evidence respecting witnesses to the trait of truthfulness or untruthfulness.

The argument is made that circumstantial use of character ought to be allowed in civil cases to the same extent as in criminal cases, i.e. evidence of good (nonprejudicial) character would be admissible in the first instance, subject to rebuttal by evidence of bad character. Falknor, Extrinsic Policies Affecting Admissibility, 10 Rutgers L.Rev. 574, 581–583 (1956); Tentative Recommendation and a Study Relating to the Uniform Rules of Evidence (Art. VI. Extrinsic Policies Affecting Admissibility), Cal.Law Revision Comm'n, Rep., Rec. & Studies, 657–658 (1964). Uniform Rule 47 goes farther, in that it assumes that character evidence in general satisfies the conditions of relevancy, except as provided in Uniform Rule 48. The difficulty with expanding the use of character evidence in civil cases is set forth by the California Law Revision Commission in its ultimate rejection of Uniform Rule 47, id., 615:

"Character evidence is of slight probative value and may be very prejudicial. It tends to distract the trier of fact from the main question of what actually happened on the particular occasion. It subtly permits the trier of fact to reward the good man and to punish the bad man because of their respective characters despite what the evidence in the case shows actually happened."

Much of the force of the position of those favoring greater use of character evidence in civil cases is dissipated by their support of Uniform Rule 48 which excludes the evidence in negligence cases, where it could be expected to achieve its maximum usefulness. Moreover, expanding concepts of "character," which seem of necessity to extend into such areas as psychiatric evaluation and psychological testing, coupled with expanded admissibility, would open up such vistas of mental examinations as caused the Court concern in Schlagenhauf v. Holder, 379 U.S. 104 (1964). It is believed that those espousing change have not met the burden of persuasion.

Subdivision (b) deals with a specialized but important application of the general rule excluding circumstantial use of character evidence. Consistently with that rule, evidence of other crimes, wrongs, or acts is not admissible to prove character as a basis for suggesting the inference that conduct on a particular occasion was in conformity with it. However, the evidence may be offered for another purpose, such as proof of motive, opportunity, and so on, which does not fall within the prohibition. In this situation the rule does not require that the evidence be excluded. No mechanical solution is offered. The determination must be made whether the danger of undue prejudice outweighs the probative value of the evidence in view of the availability of other means of proof and other facts appropriate for making decisions of this kind under Rule 403. Slough and Knightly, Other Vices, Other Crimes, 41 Iowa L.Rev. 325 (1956).

REPORT OF HOUSE COMMITTEE ON THE JUDICIARY

The second sentence of Rule 404(b)[7] as submitted to the Congress began with the words "This subdivision does not exclude the evidence when offered". The Committee amended this language to read "It may, however, be admissible", the words used in the 1971 Advisory Committee draft, on the ground that this formulation properly placed greater emphasis on admissibility than did the final Court version.

REPORT OF SENATE COMMITTEE ON THE JUDICIARY

This rule provides that evidence of other crimes, wrongs, or acts is not admissible to prove character but may be admissible for other specified purposes such as proof of motive.

Although your committee sees no necessity in amending the rule itself, it anticipates that the use of the discretionary word "may" with respect to the admissibility of evidence of crimes, wrongs, or acts is not intended to confer any arbitrary discretion on the trial judge. Rather, it is anticipated that with respect to permissible uses for such evidence, the trial judge may exclude it only on the basis of those considerations set forth in Rule 403, *i.e.* prejudice, confusion or waste of time.

ADVISORY COMMITTEE'S NOTE (1991 AMENDMENT)

Rule 404(b) has emerged as one of the most cited Rules in the Rules of Evidence. And in many criminal cases evidence of an accused's extrinsic acts is viewed as an important asset in the prosecution's case against an accused. Although there are a few reported decisions on use of such evidence by the defense, *see, e.g., United States v. McClure*, 546 F.2d 670 (5th Cir. 1990) (acts of informant offered in entrapment defense), the overwhelming number of cases involve introduction of that evidence by the prosecution.

The amendment to Rule 404(b) adds a pretrial notice requirement in criminal cases and is intended to reduce surprise and promote early resolution on the issue of admissibility. The notice requirement thus places Rule 404(b) in the mainstream with notice and disclosure provisions in other rules of evidence. *See, e.g.,* Rule 412 (written motion of intent to offer evidence under rule), Rule 609 (written notice of intent to offer conviction older than 10 years), Rule 803(24) and 804(b)(5) (notice of intent to use residual hearsay exceptions).

The Rule expects that counsel for both the defense and the prosecution will submit the necessary request and information in a reasonable and timely fashion. Other than requiring pretrial notice, no specific time limits are stated in recognition that what constitutes a reasonable request or disclosure will depend largely on the circumstances of each case. *Compare* Fla.Stat.Ann. § 90.404(2)(b) (notice must be given at least 10 days before trial) *with* Tex.R.Evid. 404(b) (no time limit).

Likewise, no specific form of notice is required. The Committee considered and rejected a requirement that the notice satisfy the particularity requirements normally required of language used in a charging instrument. *Cf.* Fla.Stat.Ann. § 90.404(2)(b) (written disclosure must describe uncharged misconduct with particularity required of an indictment or information). Instead, the Committee opted for a generalized notice provision which requires the prosecution to apprise the defense of the general nature of the evidence of extrinsic acts. The Committee does not intend that the amendment will supercede other rules of admissibility or disclosure, such as the Jencks Act, 18 U.S.C. § 3500, *et. seq.* nor require the prosecution to disclose directly or indirectly the names and addresses of its witnesses, something it is currently not required to do under Federal Rule of Criminal Procedure 16.

---

[7] Editor's Note: This refers to the first sentence of Rule 404(b)(2) in the restyled version of the rule.

The amendment requires the prosecution to provide notice, regardless of how it intends to use the extrinsic act evidence at trial, i.e., during its case-in-chief, for impeachment, or for possible rebuttal. The court in its discretion may, under the facts, decide that the particular request or notice was not reasonable, either because of the lack of timeliness or completeness. Because the notice requirement serves as condition precedent to admissibility of 404(b) evidence, the offered evidence is inadmissible if the court decides that the notice requirement has not been met.

Nothing in the amendment precludes the court from requiring the government to provide it with an opportunity to rule *in limine* on 404(b) evidence before it is offered or even mentioned during trial. When ruling *in limine*, the court may require the government to disclose to it the specifics of such evidence which the court must consider in determining admissibility.

The amendment does not extend to evidence of acts which are "intrinsic" to the charged offense, *see United States v. Williams*, 900 F.2d 823 (5th Cir. 1990) (noting distinction between 404(b) evidence and intrinsic offense evidence). Nor is the amendment intended to redefine what evidence would otherwise be admissible under Rule 404(b). Finally, the Committee does not intend through the amendment to affect the role of the court and the jury in considering such evidence. See *United States v. Huddleston*, 485 U.S. 681 (1988).

ADVISORY COMMITTEE'S NOTE (2000 AMENDMENT)

Rule [404(a)(2)(B)(ii)] has been amended to provide that when the accused attacks the character of an alleged victim under subdivision [(a)(2)(B)] of this Rule, the door is opened to an attack on the same character trait of the accused. Current law does not allow the government to introduce negative character evidence as to the accused unless the accused introduces evidence of good character. *See, e.g., United States v. Fountain*, 768 F.2d 790 (7th Cir. 1985) (when the accused offers proof of self-defense, this permits proof of the alleged victim's character trait for peacefulness, but it does not permit proof of the accused's character trait for violence).

The amendment makes clear that the accused cannot attack the alleged victim's character and yet remain shielded from the disclosure of equally relevant evidence concerning the same character trait of the accused. For example, in a murder case with a claim of self-defense, the accused, to bolster this defense, might offer evidence of the alleged victim's violent disposition. If the government has evidence that the accused has a violent character, but is not allowed to offer this evidence as part of its rebuttal, the jury has only part of the information it needs for an informed assessment of the probabilities as to who was the initial aggressor. This may be the case even if evidence of the accused's prior violent acts is admitted under Rule 404(b), because such evidence can be admitted only for limited purposes and not to show action in conformity with the accused's character on a specific occasion. Thus, the amendment is designed to permit a more balanced presentation of character evidence when an accused chooses to attack the character of the alleged victim.

The amendment does not affect the admissibility of evidence of specific acts of uncharged misconduct offered for a purpose other than proving character under Rule 404(b). Nor does it affect the standards for proof of character by evidence of other sexual behavior or sexual offenses under Rules 412–415. By its placement in Rule 404(a)[(2)(B)], the amendment covers only proof of character by way of reputation or opinion.

The amendment does not permit proof of the accused's character if the accused merely uses character evidence for a purpose other than to prove the alleged victim's propensity to act in a certain way. *See United States v. Burks*, 470 F.2d 432, 434–5 (D.C.Cir. 1972) (evidence of the alleged victim's violent character, when known by the accused, was admissible "on the issue of whether or not the defendant reasonably feared he was in danger of imminent great bodily harm"). Finally, the amendment does not permit proof of the accused's character when the accused attacks the alleged victim's character as a witness under Rule 608 or 609.

The term "alleged" is inserted before each reference to "victim" in the Rule, in order to provide consistency with Evidence Rule 412.

ADVISORY COMMITTEE'S NOTE (2006 AMENDMENT)

The Rule has been amended to clarify that in a civil case evidence of a person's character is never admissible to prove that the person acted in conformity with the character trait. The amendment resolves the dispute in the case law over whether the exceptions in subdivisions [(a)(2)(A)] and [(a)(2)(B)] permit the circumstantial use of character evidence in civil cases. *Compare Carson v. Polley*, 689 F.2d 562, 576 (5th Cir. 1982) ("when a central issue in a case is close to one of a criminal nature, the exceptions to the Rule 404(a) ban on character evidence may be invoked"), *with SEC v. Towers Financial Corp.*, 966 F.Supp. 203 (S.D.N.Y. 1997) (relying on the terms "accused" and "prosecution" in Rule 404(a) to conclude that the exceptions in subdivisions [(a)(2)(A)] and [(a)(2)(B)] are inapplicable in civil cases). The amendment is consistent with the original intent of the Rule, which was to prohibit the circumstantial use of character evidence in civil cases, even where closely related to criminal charges. *See Ginter v. Northwestern Mut. Life Ins. Co.*, 576 F.Supp. 627, 629–30 (D. Ky. 1984) ("It seems beyond peradventure of doubt that the drafters of F.R.Evi. 404(a) explicitly intended that all character evidence, except where 'character is at issue' was to be excluded" in civil cases).

The circumstantial use of character evidence is generally discouraged because it carries serious risks of prejudice, confusion and delay. *See Michelson v. United States*, 335 U.S. 469, 476 (1948) ("The overriding policy of excluding such evidence, despite its admitted probative value, is the practical experience that its disallowance tends to prevent confusion of issues, unfair surprise and undue prejudice."). In criminal cases, the so-called "mercy rule" permits a criminal defendant to introduce evidence of pertinent character traits of the defendant and the victim. But that is because the accused, whose liberty is at stake, may need "a counterweight against the strong investigative and prosecutorial resources of the government." C. Mueller & L. Kirkpatrick, *Evidence: Practice Under the Rules*, pp. 264–5 (2d ed. 1999). See also Richard Uviller, *Evidence of Character to Prove Conduct: Illusion, Illogic, and Injustice in the Courtroom*, 130 U.Pa.L.Rev. 845, 855 (1982) (the rule prohibiting circumstantial use of character evidence "was relaxed to allow the criminal defendant with so much at stake and so little available in the way of conventional proof to have special dispensation to tell the factfinder just what sort of person he really is"). Those concerns do not apply to parties in civil cases.

The amendment also clarifies that evidence otherwise admissible under Rule [404(a)(2)(B)] may nonetheless be excluded in a criminal case involving sexual misconduct. In such a case, the admissibility of evidence of the victim's sexual behavior and predisposition is governed by the more stringent provisions of Rule 412.

Nothing in the amendment is intended to affect the scope of Rule 404(b). While Rule 404(b) refers to the "accused", the "prosecution" and a "criminal case", it does so only in the context of a notice requirement. The admissibility standards of Rule 404(b) remain fully applicable to both civil and criminal cases.

ADVISORY COMMITTEE'S NOTE (2011 AMENDMENT)

The language of Rule 404 has been amended as part of the restyling of the Evidence Rules to make them more easily understood and to make style and terminology consistent throughout the rules. These changes are intended to be stylistic only. There is no intent to change any result in any ruling on evidence admissibility.

Florida Stat. § 90.404. Character Evidence; When Admissible

(1) Character evidence generally. Evidence of a person's character or a trait of character is inadmissible to prove action in conformity with it on a particular occasion, except:

(a) *Character of accused.* Evidence of a pertinent trait of character offered by an accused, or by the prosecution to rebut the trait.

(b) *Character of victim.*

1. Except as provided in s. 794.022, evidence of a pertinent trait of character of the victim of the crime offered by an accused, or by the prosecution to rebut the trait; or

2. evidence of a character trait of peacefulness of the victim offered by the prosecution in a homicide case to rebut evidence that the victim was the aggressor.

(c) *Character of witness.* Evidence of the character of a witness, as provided in ss. 90.608-90.610.

(2) Other crimes, wrongs, or acts.

(a) Similar fact evidence of other crimes, wrongs, or acts is admissible when relevant to prove a material fact in issue, including, but not limited to, proof of motive, opportunity, intent, preparation, plan, knowledge, identity, or absence of mistake or accident, but it is inadmissible when the evidence is relevant solely to prove bad character or propensity.

(b) 1. In a criminal case in which the defendant is charged with a crime involving child molestation, evidence of the defendant's commission of other crimes, wrongs, or acts of child molestation is admissible, and may be considered for its bearing on any matter to which it is relevant.

2. For the purposes of this paragraph, the term "child molestation" means conduct proscribed by s. 787.025(2)(c), s. 794.011, excluding s. 794.011(10), s. 794.05, s. 796.03, s. 796.035, s. 796.045, s. 800.04, s. 827.071, s. 847.0135(5), s. 847.0145, or s. 985.701(1) when committed against a person 16 years of age or younger.

(c) 1. In a criminal case in which the defendant is charged with a sexual offense, evidence of the defendant's commission of other crimes, wrongs, or acts involving a sexual offense is admissible and may be considered for its bearing on any matter to which it is relevant.

2. For the purposes of this paragraph, the term "sexual offense" means conduct proscribed by s. 787.025(2)(c), s. 794.011, excluding s. 794.011(10), s. 794.05, s. 796.03, s. 796.035, s. 796.045, s. 825.1025(2)(b), s. 827.071, s. 847.0135(5), s. 847.0145, or s. 985.701(1).

(d) 1. When the state in a criminal action intends to offer evidence of other criminal offenses under paragraph (a), paragraph (b), or paragraph (c), no fewer than 10 days before trial, the state shall furnish to the defendant or to the defendant's counsel a written statement of the acts or offenses it intends to offer, describing them with the particularity required of an indictment or information. No notice is required for evidence of offenses used for impeachment or on rebuttal.

2. When the evidence is admitted, the court shall, if requested, charge the jury on the limited purpose for which the evidence is received and is to be considered. After the close of the evidence, the jury shall be instructed on the limited purpose for which the evidence was received and that the defendant cannot be convicted for a charge not included in the indictment or information.

(3) Nothing in this section affects the admissibility of evidence under s. 90.610.

SPONSORS' NOTE (1976 ENACTMENT)

Character questions arise in two fundamentally different ways. When the character of a person is an issue in the litigation because it is an element of a crime, claim, or defense, evidence concerning the person's character is admissible. For example, the reputation of a plaintiff in a libel action, the chastity of the victim under a statute specifying her chastity as an element of the crime of seduction, and the competency of the driver in an action for negligently entrusting a motor vehicle to an incompetent driver are situations in which the character of the person is an issue in the litigation and is admissible. There is no provision specifically limiting the admissibility of this evidence. The allowable methods of proof are set forth in Section 90.405.

When character evidence is offered for the purpose of inferring that the person acted in conformity with his character during the occasion in question, this section limits the use of character evidence for this purpose and is basically a codification of existing Florida case law. The Florida Supreme Court has upheld the rejection of "certain proffered evidence and testimony which tended to show the plaintiff to be of bad moral character," when the moral character of the plaintiff was not at issue. Pandula v. Fonseca, 145 Fla. 395, 199 So. 358, 360 (1940). However, the court has recognized the subsection (1)(a) exception in Norman v. State, 156 So. 2d 186, 189 (Fla. 3rd Dist. 1963), where it was stated that:

> The general rule, and the one recognized in Florida is that the accused in a criminal prosecution may introduce evidence of his good character and reputation where such evidence has reference to the trait involved in the offense with which the defendant is charged. (Emphasis added.)

In Young v. State, 141 Fla. 529, 142 Fla. 361, 195 So. 569 (1939) it was further explained that:

> the doctrine has been established beyond question that a defendant's character may not be assailed by the State in a criminal prosecution unless good character of the accused has first been introduced.

See Williams v. State, 110 So. 2d 654 (Fla. 1959).

In Nickels v. State, 90 Fla. 659, 106 So. 479, 481 (1925) the Court recognized the Section 90.404(1)(b) exception when it stated that:

> Where...the defense [to a charge of rape] rests upon the fact of consent, evidence of the general reputation of the prosecutrix for unchastity, within recognized limits, is competent evidence as bearing upon the probability of her consent to the act with which the defendant is charged.

The admissibility of character evidence concerning a witness is explained in detail in Sections 90.608-90.610.

Section 90.404(2) [closely paraphrases] Williams v. State, 110 So. 2d 654, 663 (Fla. 1959), where the court, in finding admissible evidence relating to the commission by the defendant of another crime, stated:

> Evidence of any facts relevant to a material fact in issue except where the sole relevancy is character or propensity of the accused is admissible unless precluded by some specific exception or rule of exclusion. This rule we hold applies to relevant similar fact evidence...even though it points to the commission of another crime.

This decision has been interpreted in <u>Green v. State</u>, 190 So. 2d 42, 46 (Fla. 2nd Dist. 1966) to mean that evidence of other offenses is admissible if:

(1) it is relevant and has probative value in proof of the instant case or some material fact or facts in issue; and
(2) its sole purpose is not to show the bad character of the accused; and
(3) its sole purpose is not to show the propensity of the accused to commit the instant crime charged; and
(4) its admission is not precluded by some other specific exception or rule of exclusion.

The other crimes, etc., may be both prior and subsequent to the crime at issue. <u>Talley v. State</u>, 36 So. 2d 201 (Fla. 1948); <u>Andrews v. State</u>, 172 So. 2d 505 (Fla. 1st Dist. 1965). Whether evidence of a crime on which there has been an acquittal is admissible under this section is not settled. Compare <u>Wingate v. Wainwright</u>, 464 F.2d 209 (5th Cir. 1972) (evidence inadmissible) with <u>Davis v. State</u>, 277 So. 2d 311 (Fla. 4th Dist. 1973) and <u>Blackburn v. State</u>, 208 So. 2d 625 (Fla. 3rd Dist. 1968) (evidence admissible).

In order to insure that the use of testimony of prior crimes is not abused, the use of proof of other crimes by the State in a criminal prosecution is limited to instances in which the State makes the preliminary showing required by subsection (2)(b).

COMMENTARY ON FEDERAL AND FLORIDA RULE DIFFERENCES

Florida Stat. § 90.404 and its federal counterpart, Federal Rule 404, govern the admissibility of character evidence. In general, both rules ban evidence of a person's character when offered to prove action in conformity therewith on a particular occasion. See FLA. STAT. § 90.404(1); FED. R. EVID. 404(a)(1). There are, however, a number of exceptions to both rules.

First, under the Florida rule, evidence of a pertinent trait of the accused's character can be offered by the accused to prove action in conformity therewith on a particular occasion, and if the accused chooses to do so, by the prosecution to rebut the same. See FLA. STAT. § 90.404(1)(a). Thus, as a general rule, the prosecution cannot initiate the use of evidence of the accused's character, but may introduce such evidence only if the accused first introduces evidence of his own character. See Von Carter v. State, 468 So. 2d 276, 278 (Fla. 1st DCA 1985). The federal rule contains a similar exception, but it is broader in that it permits such evidence not only when offered by the accused or by the prosecution to rebut the same, but also provides that if the defendant introduces evidence of a trait of the victim's character under Federal Rule 404(a)(2)(B) (examined below), the prosecution is then allowed to introduce evidence of the same trait of character of the accused. See FED. R. EVID. 404(a)(2)(A), 404(a)(2)(B)(ii). Thus, under the federal rule, the prosecution is permitted to introduce evidence of the accused's character if the accused either introduces evidence of his own character or that of the victim. See Advisory Committee's Note to 2000 Amendment to FED. R. EVID. 404.

Second, under both the Florida and federal rules, evidence of a pertinent trait of the victim's character can be offered by the accused to prove action in conformity therewith on a particular occasion, and if the accused chooses to do so, by the prosecution to rebut the same. See FLA. STAT. § 90.404(1)(b)(1); FED. R. EVID. 404(a)(2)(B). The Florida exception is explicitly subject to the limitations set forth in Florida Stat. § 794.022 (Florida's rape-shield statute), and Federal Rule 412 (the federal rape-shield rule) likewise limits the scope of Federal Rule 404(a)(2)(B)'s exception. In addition, under both rules, in homicide cases, the prosecution can offer evidence of the victim's character trait of peacefulness to rebut any evidence that the victim was the aggressor. See FLA. STAT. § 90.404(1)(b)(2); FED. R. EVID. 404(a)(2)(C); Advisory Committee's Note to FED. R. EVID. 404(a).

Federal Rule 404(a)(2) was amended effective December 1, 2006, to make clear that the exceptions set forth therein can be invoked only in criminal, not civil, cases. See Advisory Committee's Note to 2006 Amendment to FED. R. EVID. 404. This is consistent with Florida case law, which holds that the use of the words "accused" and "prosecution" in the exceptions set forth in

Florida Stat. § 90.404(1)(a)-(b) means that those exceptions can be invoked only in criminal, not civil, cases. *See Smith v. Hooligan's Pub & Oyster Bar, Ltd.*, 753 So. 2d 596, 599 (Fla. 3d DCA 2000).

Third, under both the Florida and federal rules, an exception to the general ban on character evidence offered to prove action in conformity therewith on a particular occasion applies when the evidence is of the character of a witness, offered to impeach his credibility. *See* FLA. STAT. § 90.404(1)(c); FED. R. EVID. 404(a)(3). The exceptions cross-reference Federal Rules 607-609 and Florida Stat. §§ 90.608-90.610, and the scope of the exception is examined in the commentary to those provisions.

In those rare instances in which character is actually an *element* of a crime, claim, or offense, evidence of such character is admissible, and neither Federal Rule 404 nor Florida Stat. § 90.404 serve as a bar to admissibility, since in those instances the evidence of character is not being offered to prove action in conformity therewith and thus falls outside the scope of the rules. *See* Advisory Committee's Note to FED. R. EVID. 404; Sponsors' Note to FLA. STAT. § 90.404.

The permissible methods of proving character, assuming that such evidence falls within one of the exceptions set forth in Florida Stat. § 90.404 or Federal Rule 404 (or falls outside the scope of those rules because not offered to prove action in conformity therewith), are set forth in Florida Stat. § 90.405 and Federal Rule 405, examined below.

Both the Florida and federal rules make clear that the ban on character evidence extends to indirect evidence of a person's character by way of offering evidence of other crimes, wrongs or acts to prove the character of a person and, in turn, action in conformity therewith on a particular occasion. *See* FLA. STAT. § 90.404(2)(a); FED. R. EVID. 404(b)(1). However, both rules also make clear that evidence of other crimes, wrongs, or acts may be admissible when offered for some purpose *other than* to prove the character of a person in order to show action in conformity therewith, such as when offered to prove motive, opportunity, intent, preparation, plan, knowledge, identity, or absence of mistake or accident. *See* FLA. STAT. § 90.404(2)(a); FED. R. EVID. 404(b)(2).

When offered for such other purposes, the evidence may consist not only of evidence of other crimes, wrongs or acts for which a person was convicted, but also evidence of uncharged misconduct. For such evidence to be admitted under the federal rule, the trial court need only determine that there is sufficient evidence that the jury could find by a preponderance of the evidence that the incident occurred, thus treating it as a question of conditional relevancy. *See Huddleston v. U.S.*, 485 U.S. 681, 689-91 (1988). By contrast, evidence of uncharged acts is admissible under the Florida rule only if the trial court finds by clear and convincing evidence that the person committed the prior act, thus *not* treating it as a question of conditional relevancy and setting a higher standard of proof. *Henrion v. State*, 895 So. 2d 1213, 1216 (Fla. 2nd DCA 2005); *Acevedo v. State*, 787 So. 2d 127, 129-30 (Fla. 3d DCA 2001).

Although evidence offered under these rules typically consists of the accused's prior bad acts offered by the prosecution in a criminal case, it is not so limited. Under both the Florida and federal rules, the accused in a criminal case can offer evidence of a third person's other crimes, wrongs or acts in an effort to convince the jury that the third person committed the crime. *See U.S. v. South*, 295 Fed. Appx. 959, 969-70 (11th Cir. 2008); *U.S. v. Della Rose*, 403 F.3d 891, 901-02 (7th Cir. 2005); *Simpson v. State*, 3 So. 3d 1135, 1145 n.6 (Fla. 2009); *State v. Storer*, 920 So. 2d 754, 755-57 (Fla. 2d DCA 2006). *See also McDuffie v. State*, 970 So. 2d 312, 323-24 & n.2 (Fla. 2007) (holding that such evidence is admissible only if it would be admissible if the third person were on trial for the present offense). Such evidence may be offered not only in criminal cases, but in civil cases as well. *See Ansell v. Green Acres Contracting Co., Inc.*, 347 F.3d 515, 520 (3d Cir. 2003); *Storer*, 920 So. 2d at 757. Moreover, the other acts need not be unlawful or bad; a party can offer evidence of a person's lawful or good acts when offered for some reason other than to prove action in conformity therewith. *See Ansell*, 347 F.3d at 520; *Bogren v. State*, 611 So. 2d 547, 549-50 (Fla. 5th DCA 1992). Furthermore, the other crimes, wrongs, or acts need not have occurred *prior* to the crime or act at issue in the case, but may also have occurred subsequent to it. *See U.S. v. Jernigan*, 341 F.3d 1273,

1283 (11th Cir. 2003); *Smith v. State*, 464 So. 2d 1340, 1341 (Fla. 1st DCA 1985); Sponsors' Note to FLA. STAT. § 90.404.

Under both Florida and federal law, evidence of other crimes, wrongs, or acts—even if offered for some reason other to prove character—remains subject to exclusion under Federal Rule 403 or Florida Stat. § 90.403. *See Huddleston*, 485 U.S. at 691; *White v. State*, 817 So. 2d 799, 805-06 (Fla. 2002). When such evidence is admitted, both Florida and federal law entitle the party against whom it is offered, upon request, to have the jury instructed on the limited purpose for which the evidence may be used. *See* FLA. STAT. § 90.404(2)(c)(2); *Huddleston*, 485 U.S. at 691-92.

Under Florida law, the government in a criminal action must give written notice to the defendant of its intent to offer evidence of "other criminal offenses" no fewer than ten days in advance of trial. *See* FLA. STAT. § 90.404(2)(c)(1). No notice is necessary if the offenses are to be used for impeachment or on rebuttal. *See id.* The federal rule likewise requires that the government in a criminal case give the accused notice, upon request, of its intent to offer evidence of other crimes, wrongs or acts, but unlike the Florida rule, there is no specific timeframe; the federal rule requires only that "reasonable notice" in advance of trial be given or, if excused for good cause shown, during trial. *See* FED. R. EVID. 404(b)(2). Whether notice is "reasonable" turns on when the government learned or reasonably should have learned of the evidence, the extent to which the defendant would suffer from abbreviated notice, and the importance of the evidence to the government's case. *See U.S. v. Perez-Tostra*, 36 F.3d 1552, 1561-62 (11th Cir. 1994). Unlike the Florida rule, the federal rule requires notice regardless of whether the government intends to use the evidence in its case-in-chief, on rebuttal, or for impeachment purposes. *See U.S. v. Carrasco*, 381 F.3d 1237, 1240 (11th Cir. 2004).

Both federal and Florida law hold that acts that are inseperable from or "inextricably intertwined" with the charged offense fall outside the scope of Federal and Florida Rules 404 and are thus admissible so long as they are relevant and not otherwise inadmissible. *See U.S. v. Baker*, 432 F.3d 1189, 1205 n.9 (11th Cir. 2005); *Sliney v. State*, 944 So. 2d 270, 287 (Fla. 2006).

In criminal prosecutions for child molestation and sexual assault (and, under the federal rule, in civil actions predicated on an act of sexual assault or child molestation), evidence of prior acts *is* admissible to prove action in conformity therewith. *See* FLA. STAT. § 90.404(2)(b)-(c); FED. R. EVID. 413-415. The admissibility of such evidence is addressed in the Commentary to Federal Rules 413 through 415.

Federal Rule 405. Methods of Proving Character

(a) **By Reputation or Opinion.** When evidence of a person's character or character trait is admissible, it may be proved by testimony about the person's reputation or by testimony in the form of an opinion. On cross-examination of the character witness, the court may allow an inquiry into relevant specific instances of the person's conduct.

(b) **By Specific Instances of Conduct.** When a person's character or character trait is an essential element of a charge, claim, or defense, the character or trait may also be proved by relevant specific instances of the person's conduct.

ADVISORY COMMITTEE'S NOTE

The rule deals only with allowable methods of proving character, not with the admissibility of character evidence, which is covered in Rule 404.

Of the three methods of proving character provided by the rule, evidence of specific instances of conduct is the most convincing. At the same time it possesses the greatest capacity to arouse prejudice, to confuse, to surprise, and to consume time. Consequently the rule confines the use of evidence of this kind to cases in which character is, in the strict sense, in issue and hence deserving of a searching inquiry. When character is used circumstantially and hence occupies a lesser status in the case, proof may be only by reputation and opinion. These latter methods are also available when character is in issue. This treatment is, with respect to specific instances of conduct and reputation, conventional contemporary common law doctrine. McCormick § 153.

In recognizing opinion as a means of proving character, the rule departs from usual contemporary practice in favor of that of an earlier day. See 7 Wigmore § 1986, pointing out that the earlier practice permitted opinion and arguing strongly for evidence based on personal knowledge and belief as contrasted with "the secondhand, irresponsible product of multiplied guesses and gossip which we term 'reputation'." It seems likely that the persistence of reputation evidence is due to its largely being opinion in disguise. Traditionally character has been regarded primarily in moral overtones of good and bad: chaste, peaceable, truthful, honest. Nevertheless, on occasion nonmoral considerations crop up, as in the case of the incompetent driver, and this seems bound to happen increasingly. If character is defined as the kind of person one is, then account must be taken of varying ways of arriving at the estimate. These may range from the opinion of the employer who has found the man honest to the opinion of the psychiatrist based upon examination and testing. No effective dividing line exists between character and mental capacity, and the latter traditionally has been provable by opinion.

According to the great majority of cases, on cross-examination inquiry is allowable as to whether the reputation witness has heard of particular instances of conduct pertinent to the trait in question. Michelson v. United States, 335 U.S. 469 (1948); Annot., 47 A.L.R.2d 1258. The theory is that, since the reputation witness relates what he has heard, the inquiry tends to shed light on the accuracy of his hearing and reporting. Accordingly, the opinion witness would be asked whether he knew, as well as whether he had heard. The fact is, of course, that these distinctions are of slight if any practical significance, and the second sentence of subdivision (a) eliminates them as a factor in formulating questions. This recognition of the propriety of inquiring into specific instances of conduct does not circumscribe inquiry otherwise into the bases of opinion and reputation testimony.

The express allowance of inquiry into specific instances of conduct on cross-examination in subdivision (a) and the express allowance of it as part of a case in chief when character is actually in issue in subdivision (b) contemplate that testimony of specific instances is not generally permissible on the direct examination of an ordinary opinion witness to character. Similarly as to witnesses to the character of witnesses under Rule 608(b). Opinion testimony on direct in these situations ought in general to correspond to reputation testimony as now given, *i.e.*, be confined to the nature and extent of observation and acquaintance upon which the opinion is based. See Rule 701.

REPORT OF HOUSE COMMITTEE ON THE JUDICIARY

Rule 405(a) as submitted proposed to change existing law by allowing evidence of character in the form of opinion as well as reputation testimony. Fearing, among other reasons, that wholesale allowance of opinion testimony might tend to turn a trial into a swearing contest between conflicting character witnesses, the Committee decided to delete from this Rule, as well as from Rule 608(a) which involves a related problem, reference to opinion testimony.

CONFERENCE REPORT

The Senate makes two language changes in the nature of conforming amendments. The Conference adopts the Senate amendments.

ADVISORY COMMITTEE'S NOTE (2011 AMENDMENT)

The language of Rule 405 has been amended as part of the restyling of the Evidence Rules to make them more easily understood and to make style and terminology consistent throughout the rules. These changes are intended to be stylistic only. There is no intent to change any result in any ruling on evidence admissibility.

Florida Stat. § 90.405. Methods of Proving Character

(1) Reputation. When evidence of the character of a person or of a trait of that person's character is admissible, proof may be made by testimony about that person's reputation.

(2) Specific instances of conduct. When character or a trait of character of a person is an essential element of a charge, claim, or defense, proof may be made of specific instances of that person's conduct.

SPONSORS' NOTE (1976 ENACTMENT)

This section deals only with allowable methods of proving character, not with the admissibility of character evidence, which is covered in Section 90.404.

[In recognizing opinion as a means of proving character, the rule departs from the usual contemporary practice which is followed in Florida, which limits the testimony to reputation. Maloy v. State, 52 Fla. 101, 41 So. 791 (1906); Fla. Stat. § 90.08. Dean Wigmore points out that the earlier practice permitted opinion and argued strongly for evidence based on personal knowledge and belief as contrasted with "the secondhand, irresponsible product of multiplied guesses and gossip which we term 'reputation.'" 7 Wigmore[, Evidence] § 1986 (3rd ed. 1940). If character is defined as the kind of person one is, then account must be taken of varying methods of arriving at the estimate. These may range from the opinion of the employer who has found the man honest to the opinion of the psychiatrist based upon examination and testing. No effective dividing line exists between character and mental capacity, and the latter traditionally has been provable by opinion. Opinion is recognized as being generally as reliable as reputation.

Both the Model Code of Evidence, Rules 305 and 306, and Uniform Rules 46 and 47 recognize the use of opinion to prove character. Recently enacted evidence codes in California, Kansas, and New Jersey all recognize the use of opinion evidence in proving character (Calif. Evid. Code § 1100, Kans. Code of Civil Procedure § 60-446 and New Jersey Rule 46). See Federal Rule Evid. 405.][8]

The section confines the use of specific instances of conduct to cases in which character is in issue; that is, when character is one of the facts necessary to establish a liability or defense or is a factor in the measurement of damages. When character is used circumstantially and hence occupies a lesser status in the case, proof may be only by reputation and opinion. Of the three methods of proving character provided by this section, evidence of specific instances of conduct is the most convincing. At the same time it possesses the greatest capacity to arouse prejudice, confuse, surprise, or consume time. Consequently, the use of evidence of this kind is confined to cases in which character is, in the strict sense, in issue, and hence deserving of a searching inquiry. This treatment of specific instances of conduct, as well as the treatment of reputation, follows conventional contemporary common-law doctrine.

---

[8] Editor's Note: The bracketed language refers to the original version of the rule, which was subsequently amended by the legislature to eliminate the use of opinion testimony.

The following language from <u>Nickels v. State</u>, 90 Fla. 659, 687, 106 So. 479, 489 (1925) illustrates the conventional doctrine in a situation where character is in issue:

> Where, however, the defense rests upon the fact of consent, evidence of the general reputation of the prosecutrix for unchastity, within recognized limits, is competent evidence as bearing upon the probability of her consent to the act with which the defendant is charged. Such evidence, however, must be confined to the general reputation of the prosecutrix for chastity, except that she may be interrogated as to her previous intercourse with the defendant or as to promiscuous intercourse with other men, or common prostitution.

However, if the defendant only places in issue his general reputation for being a peaceful and law-abiding citizen, it is error to allow the prosecution to introduce rebuttal evidence of specific acts of violence or turbulence. See <u>Cornelius v. State</u>, 49 So. 2d 332 (Fla. 1950).

Where character is only circumstantially relevant, inquiry is allowable on cross-examination as to whether the reputation witness has heard of particular instances of conduct pertinent to the trait in question. The theory is that, since the reputation witness relates what he has heard, the inquiry tends to shed light on the accuracy of his hearing and reporting. As stated in <u>Cornelius v. State</u>, 49 So. 2d 332, 335 (Fla. 1950):

> We hold that a witness who has testified as to general reputation or character may on cross examination be interrogated as to whether he had ever known or heard of specific acts of violence committed by the accused because the true purpose of such cross examination is to enlighten the jury as to whether the witness actually—as a matter of fact—knows the general reputation of the defendant and to place the jury in a better position to pass upon the credibility of the witness' testimony.

COMMENTARY ON FEDERAL AND FLORIDA RULE DIFFERENCES

Once evidence of a person's character is determined to be admissible under Florida Stat. § 90.404 or its federal counterpart, Federal Rule 404, Florida Stat. § 90.405 and Federal Rule 405, respectively, delineate the permissible methods of proving character. Under both the federal and Florida rules, testimony as to reputation is always a permissible means of proving character, while evidence of specific instances of a person's conduct can be offered to prove character only in those instances in which character is an essential element of a charge, claim, or defense.

However, a significant distinction between the two provisions is that under Federal Rule 405, testimony in the form of an opinion is *always* a permissible means of proving character, while under Florida Stat. § 90.405, it is *never* a permissible means of doing so. *See, e.g., Wyatt v. State,* 578 So. 2d 811, 813 (Fla. 3d DCA 1991). While the original version of the Florida rule permitted proof of character by way of testimony in the form of an opinion, it was amended in 1978 to eliminate opinion testimony as a method of proving character. In this regard, Florida law differs not only from the federal rule, but also finds itself in the minority nationwide. *See* Josephine Ross, *"He Looks Guilty": Reforming Good Character Evidence to Undercut the Presumption of Guilt,* 65 U. PITT. L. REV. 227, 239 & n.46 (2004) (noting that only 11 states, including Florida, do not permit opinion testimony to prove character).

On their face, the Florida and federal rules appear to differ from one another in a second way: while the federal rule explicitly permits inquiry on cross-examination of a character witness into specific instances of conduct, the Florida rule does not. Indeed, while the original version of the Florida rule contained similar language, that language was struck out by the 1978 amendment. Somewhat paradoxically, however, some Florida authority suggests that striking this language does not prevent inquiry on cross-examination into whether the witness has heard that the defendant committed certain acts. *See, e.g., Robinson v. State,* 393 So. 2d 33, 34-35 (Fla. 1st DCA

1981). *See also Ivester v. State*, 429 So. 2d 1271, 1275 (Fla 1st DCA 1983) (Ervin, J., dissenting). As under federal practice, *see, e.g., U.S. v. Adair*, 951 F.2d 316, 319 (11th Cir. 1992), before asking such questions on cross-examination, the questioner must demonstrate to the court that a good faith factual basis exists for asking the question. *See Rhodes v. State*, 547 So. 2d 1201, 1205 (Fla. 1989).

Under both federal and Florida law, before admitting reputation testimony regarding a person's character, it must be established that the witness is familiar with the person and the community in which the person's reputation has been formed, and that the testimony is based on discussions among a broad group of people rather than rumor or conversations with a narrow group of people. *See Blackburn v. United Parcel Service, Inc.*, 179 F.3d 81, 100-01 (3d Cir. 1999); *Rigterink v. State*, 66 So. 3d 866, 895 (Fla. 2011); *Ibar v. State*, 938 So. 2d 451, 469 (Fla. 2006). Moreover, under both federal and Florida law, a person's community need not be a residential community, but could instead be a work or school community. *See U.S. v. Oliver*, 492 F.2d 943, 945-46 (8th Cir. 1974); *Webster v. State*, 500 So. 2d 285, 287 (Fla. 1st DCA 1986). However, under Florida practice, some authority holds that one can offer evidence of a person's reputation in a non-residential community only if no character witnesses from the person's residential community are available. *See Webster*, 500 So. 2d at 287.

As with the federal rule, *see, e.g., Schafer v. Time, Inc.*, 142 F.3d 1361, 1371-72 (11th Cir. 1998), only rarely will character be determined to be an "essential element" of a charge, claim, or defense within the meaning of Florida Stat. § 90.405 so as to open the door to using evidence of specific instances of a person's conduct to prove her character. *See Pantoja v. State*, 59 So. 3d 1092, 1098 (Fla. 2011). Under both the federal and Florida rules, where evidence of prior specific instances of conduct of a person is offered for some reason other than to prove that person's character, the restrictions of Florida Stat. § 90.405 and Federal Rule 405 do not apply. See *Government of Virgin Islands v. Carino*, 631 F.2d 226, 229-30 (3d Cir. 1980); *State v. Smith*, 573 So. 2d 306, 318 (Fla. 1990).

Federal Rule 406. Habit; Routine Practice

Evidence of a person's habit or an organization's routine practice may be admitted to prove that on a particular occasion the person or organization acted in accordance with the habit or routine practice. The court may admit this evidence regardless of whether it is corroborated or whether there was an eyewitness.

ADVISORY COMMITTEE'S NOTE

An oft-quoted paragraph, McCormick, § 162, p. 340, describes habit in terms effectively contrasting it with character:

"Character and habit are close akin. Character is a generalized description of one's disposition, or of one's disposition in respect to a general trait, such as honesty, temperance, or peacefulness. 'Habit,' in modern usage, both lay and psychological, is more specific. It describes one's regular response to a repeated specific situation. If we speak of character for care, we think of the person's tendency to act prudently in all the varying situations of life, in business, family life, in handling automobiles and in walking across the street. A habit, on the other hand, is the person's regular practice of meeting a particular kind of situation with a specific type of conduct, such as the habit of going down a particular stairway two stairs at a time, or of giving the hand-signal for a left turn, or of alighting from railway cars while they are moving. The doing of the habitual acts may become semi-automatic."

Equivalent behavior on the part of a group is designated "routine practice of an organization" in the rule.

Agreement is general that habit evidence is highly persuasive as proof of conduct on a particular occasion. Again quoting McCormick § 162, p. 341:

"Character may be thought of as the sum of one's habits though doubtless it is more than this. But unquestionably the uniformity of one's response to habit is far greater than the consistency with which one's conduct conforms to character or disposition. Even though character comes in only exceptionally as evidence of an act, surely any sensible man in investigating whether X did a particular act would be greatly helped in his inquiry by evidence as to whether he was in the habit of doing it."

When disagreement has appeared, its focus has been upon the question what constitutes habit, and the reason for this is readily apparent. The extent to which instances must be multiplied and consistency of behavior maintained in order to rise to the status of habit inevitably gives rise to differences of opinion. Lewan, Rationale of Habit Evidence, 16 Syracuse L.Rev. 39, 49 (1964). While adequacy of sampling and uniformity of response are key factors, precise standards for measuring their sufficiency for evidence purposes cannot be formulated.

The rule is consistent with prevailing views. Much evidence is excluded simply because of failure to achieve the status of habit. Thus, evidence of intemperate "habits" is generally excluded when offered as proof of drunkenness in accident cases, Annot., 46 A.L.R.2d 103, and evidence of other assaults is inadmissible to prove the instant one in a civil assault action, Annot., 66 A.L.R.2d 806. In Levin v. United States, 338 F.2d 265 (1964), testimony as to the religious "habits" of the accused, offered as tending to prove that he was at home observing the Sabbath rather than out obtaining money through larceny by trick, was held properly excluded:

"It seems apparent to us that an individual's religious practices would not be the type of activities which would lend themselves to the characterization of 'invariable regularity.'[9] Certainly the very volitional basis of the activity raises serious questions as to its invariable nature, and hence its probative value." *Id.* at 272.

These rulings are not inconsistent with the trend towards admitting evidence of business transactions between one of the parties and a third person as tending to prove that he made the same bargain or proposal in the litigated situation. Slough, Relevancy Unraveled, 6 Kan.L.Rev. 38-41 (1957). Nor are they inconsistent with such cases as Whittemore v. Lockheed Aircraft Corp., 65 Cal.App.2d 737 (1944), upholding the admission of evidence that plaintiff's intestate had on four other occasions flown planes from defendant's factory for delivery to his employer airline, offered to prove that he was piloting rather than a guest on a plane which crashed and killed all on board while en route for delivery.

A considerable body of authority has required that evidence of the routine practice of an organization be corroborated as a condition precedent to its admission in evidence. Slough, Relevancy Unraveled, 5 Kan.L.Rev. 404, 449 (1957). This requirement is specifically rejected by the rule on the ground that it relates to the sufficiency of the evidence rather than admissibility. A similar position is taken in New Jersey Rule 49. The rule also rejects the requirement of the absence of eyewitnesses, sometimes encountered with respect to admitting habit evidence to prove freedom from contributory negligence in wrongful death cases. For comment critical of the requirements see Frank, J., in Cereste v. New York, N.H. & H.R. Co., 231 F.2d 50 (2d Cir. 1956), cert. denied 351 U.S. 951, 10 Vand.L.Rev. 447 (1957); McCormick § 162, p. 342. The omission of the requirement from the California Evidence Code is said to have effected its elimination. Comment, Cal.Ev.Code § 1105.

REPORT OF HOUSE COMMITTEE ON THE JUDICIARY

Rule 406 as submitted to Congress contained a subdivision (b) providing that the method of proof of habit or routine practice could be "in the form of an opinion or by specific instances of conduct sufficient in number to warrant a finding that the habit existed or that the practice was routine." The Committee deleted this subdivision believing that the method of proof of habit and routine practice should be left to

---

[9] 1 Wigmore 520.

the courts to deal with on a case-by-case basis. At the same time, the Committee does not intend that its action be construed as sanctioning a general authorization of opinion evidence in this area.

ADVISORY COMMITTEE'S NOTE (2011 AMENDMENT)

The language of Rule 406 has been amended as part of the restyling of the Evidence Rules to make them more easily understood and to make style and terminology consistent throughout the rules. These changes are intended to be stylistic only. There is no intent to change any result in any ruling on evidence admissibility.

Florida Stat. § 90.406. Routine Practice

Evidence of the routine practice of an organization, whether corroborated or not and regardless of the presence of eyewitnesses, is admissible to prove that the conduct of the organization on a particular occasion was in conformity with the routine practice.

SPONSORS' NOTE (1976 ENACTMENT)

Under this section, the routine practice of an organization is admissible to prove that the organization, whether a private business or governmental agency, acted in conformity with that routine practice on the instance in controversy. Unless this evidence is admissible, it might be impossible for a large business to prove that a particular letter was mailed.

Despite some earlier cases which required corroborating evidence that the custom of the business was followed on the occasion in controversy, the most recent Florida decisions apparently are in accord with this section. See Brown v. Giffen Industries, Inc., 281 So. 2d 897 (Fla. 1973) (presumption that the ordinary course of business has been followed in a particular case, absent a contrary showing); Milros-San Souci, Inc. v. Dade County, 296 So. 2d 545 (3rd D.C.A. 1974) (where mail has been properly addressed, stamped, and mailed pursuant to normal office procedures of the County Tax Assessor, there is a presumption that the mail was received by the addressee.)

This section is not applicable to the habit of an individual.

For similar rules, see Calif. Evid. Code § 1105, New Jersey Evid. Rule 49, and Kansas Code of Civ. Pro. § 60-450, Fed. Rule Evid. 406.

COMMENTARY ON FEDERAL AND FLORIDA RULE DIFFERENCES

Both Florida Stat. § 90.406 and its federal counterpart, Federal Rule 406, provide that evidence of the routine practice of an organization is admissible to prove that the organization acted in conformity with that routine practice on a particular occasion. The purpose of both the Florida and federal provisions is to make clear that such evidence is different from "character" evidence and thus is not subject to exclusion under Florida Stat. § 90.404 or its federal counterpart, Federal Rule 404.

Both the Florida rule and its federal counterpart reject the common law requirements prevalent in some jurisdictions that such evidence was admissible only if there was some corroborating evidence that the organization acted in conformity with its routine practice on the particular occasion at issue in the suit, and that such evidence was admissible only when eyewitness testimony about what happened on the occasion in question was not available.

The most significant difference between Florida Stat. § 90.406 and its federal counterpart is that the latter also applies to evidence of the routine practice, or habit, of an *individual*, while the former does not. However, Florida authority holds that Florida Stat. § 90.406 does not *exclude* evidence of the habit of an individual, and thus the trial court can admit such evidence so long as it determines it to be probative and not otherwise excludable. *See McKeithan ex. rel. McKeithan v. HCA Health Servs. of Fla., Inc.*, 879 So. 2d 47, 49 (Fla. 4th DCA 2004); 23 Charles Alan Wright & Kenneth W. Graham, Jr., Federal Practice & Procedure: Evidence § 5275 n.10 (1980 & Supp. 2005); 1 Charles W. Ehrhardt, Florida Practice: Evidence § 406.1 (2005). However, because evidence of the habit of an individual does not fall within the scope of Florida Stat. § 90.406, it appears as though it remains subject to the common law requirement that it is admissible only if corroborated. *See Duffell v. South Walton Emergency Servs., Inc.*, 501 So. 2d 1352, 1356 (Fla. 1st DCA 1987) (Ervin, J., concurring in part and dissenting in part).

Note that although the Sponsors' Note to Florida Stat. § 90.406 cites several cases involving presumptions, Florida Stat. 90.406 does *not* provide that introducing evidence of an organization's routine practice creates a presumption that the organization acted in conformity with that routine practice, but only supports an inference that the practice was followed. *See Tabb ex. rel. Tabb v. Florida Birth-Related Neurological Injury Comp. Ass'n*, 880 So. 2d 1253, 1259 (Fla. 1st DCA 2004).

Federal Rule 407. Subsequent Remedial Measures

When measures are taken that would have made an earlier injury or harm less likely to occur, evidence of the subsequent measures is not admissible to prove:

- negligence;

- culpable conduct;

- a defect in a product or its design; or

- a need for a warning or instruction.

But the court may admit this evidence for another purpose, such as impeachment or — if disputed — proving ownership, control, or the feasibility of precautionary measures.

ADVISORY COMMITTEE'S NOTE

The rule incorporates conventional doctrine which excludes evidence of subsequent remedial measures as proof of an admission of fault. The rule rests on two grounds. (1) The conduct is not in fact an admission, since the conduct is equally consistent with injury by mere accident or through contributory negligence. Or, as Baron Bramwell put it, the rule rejects the notion that "because the world gets wiser as it gets older, therefore it was foolish before." Hart v. Lancashire & Yorkshire Ry. Co., 21 L.T.R. N.S. 261, 263 (1869). Under a liberal theory of relevancy this ground alone would not support exclusion as the inference is still a possible one. (2) The other, and more impressive, ground for exclusion rests on a social policy of encouraging people to take, or at least not discouraging them from taking, steps in furtherance of added safety. The courts have applied this principle to exclude evidence of subsequent repairs, installation of safety devices, changes in company rules, and discharge of employees, and the language of the present rule is broad enough to encompass all of them. See Falknor, Extrinsic Policies Affecting Admissibility, 10 Rutgers L.Rev. 574, 590 (1956).

The second sentence of the rule directs attention to the limitations of the rule. Exclusion is called for only when the evidence of subsequent remedial measures is offered as proof of negligence or culpable conduct. In effect it rejects the suggested inference that fault is admitted. Other purposes are, however, allowable, including ownership or control, existence of duty, and feasibility of precautionary measures, if controverted, and impeachment. 2 Wigmore § 283; Annot., 64 A.L.R.2d 1296. Two recent federal cases are illustrative. Boeing Airplane Co. v. Brown, 291 F.2d 310 (9th Cir. 1961), an action against an airplane manufacturer for using an allegedly defectively designed alternator shaft which caused a plane crash, upheld the admission of evidence of subsequent design modification for the purpose of showing that design changes and safeguards were feasible. And Powers v. J.B. Michael & Co., 329 F.2d 674 (6th Cir. 1964), an action against a road contractor for negligent failure to put out warning signs, sustained the admission of evidence that defendant subsequently put out signs to show that the portion of the road in question was under defendant's control. The requirement that the other purpose be controverted calls for automatic exclusion unless a genuine issue be present and allows the opposing party to lay the groundwork for exclusion by making an admission. Otherwise the factors of undue prejudice, confusion of issues, misleading the jury, and waste of time remain for consideration under Rule 403.

For comparable rules, see Uniform Rule 51; California Evidence Code § 1151; Kansas Code of Civil Procedure § 60-451; New Jersey Evidence Rule 51.

ADVISORY COMMITTEE'S NOTE (1997 AMENDMENT)

The amendment to Rule 407 makes two changes in the rule. First, the words "an injury or harm allegedly caused by" were added to clarify that the rule applies only to changes made after the occurrence that produced the damages giving rise to the action. Evidence of measures taken by the defendant prior to the "event" causing "injury or harm" do not fall within the exclusionary scope of Rule 407 even if they occurred after the manufacture or design of the product. See *Chase v. General Motors Corp.*, 856 F.2d 17, 21–22 (4th Cir. 1988).

Second, Rule 407 has been amended to provide that evidence of subsequent remedial measures may not be used to prove "a defect in a product or its design, or that a warning or instruction should have accompanied a product." This amendment adopts the view of a majority of the circuits that have interpreted Rule 407 to apply to products liability actions. See *Raymond v. Raymond Corp.*, 938 F.2d 1518, 1522 (1st Cir. 1991); *In re Joint Eastern District and Southern District Asbestos Litigation v. Armstrong World Industries, Inc.*, 995 F.2d 343 (2d Cir. 1993); *Cann v. Ford Motor Co.*, 658 F.2d 54, 60 (2d Cir. 1981), *cert. denied*, 456 U.S. 960 (1982); *Kelly v. Crown Equipment Co.*, 970 F.2d 1273, 1275 (3d Cir. 1992); *Werner v. Upjohn, Inc.*, 628 F.2d 848 (4th Cir. 1980), *cert. denied*, 449 U.S. 1080 (1981); *Grenada Steel Industries, Inc. v. Alabama Oxygen Co., Inc.*, 695 F.2d 883 (5th Cir. 1983); *Bauman v. Volkswagenwerk Aktiengesellschaft*, 621 F.2d 230, 232 (6th Cir. 1980); *Flaminio v. Honda Motor Company, Ltd.*, 733 F.2d 463, 469 (7th Cir. 1984); *Gauthier v. AMF, Inc.*, 788 F.2d 634, 636–37 (9th Cir. 1986).

Although this amendment adopts a uniform federal rule, it should be noted that evidence of subsequent remedial measures may be admissible pursuant to the second sentence of Rule 407. Evidence of subsequent measures that is not barred by Rule 407 may still be subject to exclusion on Rule 403 grounds when the dangers of prejudice or confusion substantially outweigh the probative value of the evidence.

ADVISORY COMMITTEE'S NOTE (2011 AMENDMENT)

The language of Rule 407 has been amended as part of the general restyling of the Evidence Rules to make them more easily understood and to make style and terminology consistent throughout the rules. These changes are intended to be stylistic only. There is no intent to change any result in any ruling on evidence admissibility.

Rule 407 previously provided that evidence was not excluded if offered for a purpose not explicitly prohibited by the Rule. To improve the language of the Rule, it now provides that the court may admit evidence if offered for a permissible purpose. There is no intent to change the process for admitting evidence covered by the Rule. It remains the case that if offered for an impermissible purpose, it must be excluded, and if offered for a purpose not barred by the Rule, its admissibility remains governed by the general principles of Rules 402, 403, 801, etc.

Florida Stat. § 90.407. Subsequent Remedial Measures

Evidence of measures taken after an injury or harm caused by an event, which measures if taken before the event would have made injury or harm less likely to occur, is not admissible to prove negligence, the existence of a product defect, or culpable conduct in connection with the event. This rule does not require the exclusion of evidence of subsequent remedial measures when offered for another purpose, such as proving ownership, control, or the feasibility of precautionary measures, if controverted, or impeachment.

SPONSORS' NOTE (1976 ENACTMENT)

As quoted in Seaboard Air Line R.R. v. Parks, 89 Fla. 405, 410, 104 So. 587, 588 (1925):

> The rule laid down by Mr. Wigmore is: "Accordingly, it is conceded by almost all courts, that no act in the nature of repairs, improvements, substitutions, or the like done after the occurrence of an injury, is receivable as evidence of a consciousness, on the part of the owner, of negligence, connivance, or other culpability in causing the injury," 1 Wigmore on Evidence (2d Ed.) p. 582.

This general rule is followed in subsequent Florida cases. See City of Miami Beach v. Wolfe, 83 So. 2d 774 (Fla. 1955). City of Niceville v. Hardy, 160 So. 2d 535 (Fla. 1st Dist. 1964). The social policy for the rule, that if such evidence could be received against a defendant he would be penalized for an attempt to prevent injuries to others, has been approved in Florida. See City of Miami Beach v. Wolfe, supra at 776; Seaboard Air Line R.R. v. Parks, supra at 589.

The allowance of exceptions to the general rule, is based upon Federal Rule of Evidence 407. The rule in California is similar. See the Comment to Calif. Evid. Code § 1151. No Florida cases were found which specifically reject or approve any exceptions to the general rule. However, in City of Niceville v. Hardy, supra at 539, the Court noted that:

> Some courts have recognized exceptions to this general rule, but those exceptions are not pertinent in our present consideration. The decisions recognizing the general rule and its exceptions are collated in comprehensive annotations in 170 A.L.R. 7 and 64 A.L.R.2d 1296.

COMMENTARY ON FEDERAL AND FLORIDA RULE DIFFERENCES

Both Florida Stat. § 90.407 and its federal counterpart, Federal Rule 407, regulate the admissibility of evidence of remedial measures taken subsequent to an event causing injury or harm.

The Florida rule, like its federal counterpart, excludes evidence when offered as proof that the defendant, by not having taken that measure before the event causing injury or harm, acted negligently. Moreover, the Florida rule, like its federal counterpart (although using slightly different language), extends the exclusionary rule to strict product liability actions as well (in which the defendant's negligence need not be shown). See Alderman v. Wysong & Miles Co., 486 So. 2d 673, 679 (Fla. 1st DCA 1986); Voynar v. Butler Mfg. Co., 463 So. 2d 409, 411-12 (Fla. 4th DCA 1985).

Under both the federal and Florida rules, evidence that such measures were taken are not excluded when offered for other purposes, such as proving ownership, control, or the feasibility of precautionary measures (if controverted), or when offered for impeachment purposes. However, under both rules, even if the evidence is offered for such other purposes, it may nonetheless be excluded by Florida Stat. § 90.403 (or its counterpart, Federal Rule 403), when there is a risk that the evidence might be misused by the jury for one of the purposes forbidden by the first sentence of Florida Stat. § 90.407 (or its federal counterpart). *See Stecyk v. Bell Helicopter Textron, Inc.*, 295 F.3d 408, 415-16 (3d Cir. 2002); *Watson v. Builders Square, Inc.*, 563 So. 2d 721, 723 (Fla. 4th DCA 1990).

Under both the Florida rule and its federal counterpart, the pivotal date for determining whether or not the rule applies is the date on which the accident causing the injury or harm occurred, not the date when a product that caused the injury or harm was manufactured, designed, or sold. Accordingly, measures taken before the date when the accident that precipitated the suit occurred, but after the date when the product was manufactured, designed, or sold, are not excluded by the rule. *See Keller Indus. v. Volk*, 657 So. 2d 1200, 1204 (Fla. 4th DCA 1995).

A significant difference between the Florida rule and its federal counterpart, however, is their applicability to remedial measures taken by someone who is not a party to the suit. The federal courts have held that the exclusionary principle of Federal Rule 407 does not extend to subsequent remedial measures taken by those not party to the action. *See Millennium Partners, L.P. v. Colmar Storage, LLC*, 494 F.3d 1293, 1302-03 (11th Cir. 2007). Under the Florida rule, by contrast, whether evidence of subsequent remedial measures taken by those not party to the action is subject to exclusion depends on the purpose for which such evidence is offered. If offered to prove negligence, culpable conduct, or the like *on the part of a party to the action*, it is inadmissible. *See Thursby v. Reynolds Metals Co.*, 466 So. 2d 245, 247-48 (Fla. 1st DCA 1984). However, if it is offered by a party to the action in an effort to shift the blame to someone not a party to the action, it is not subject to exclusion. *See id.* at 248 (distinguishing *Hartman v. Opelika Machine & Welding Co.*, 414 So. 2d 1105, 1110 (Fla. 1st DCA 1982).

Federal Rule 408. Compromise Offers and Negotiations

(a) **Prohibited Uses.** Evidence of the following is not admissible — on behalf of any party — either to prove or disprove the validity or amount of a disputed claim or to impeach by a prior inconsistent statement or a contradiction:

   (1) furnishing, promising, or offering — or accepting, promising to accept, or offering to accept — a valuable consideration in compromising or attempting to compromise the claim; and

   (2) conduct or a statement made during compromise negotiations about the claim — except when offered in a criminal case and when the negotiations related to a claim by a public office in the exercise of its regulatory, investigative, or enforcement authority.

(b) **Exceptions.** The court may admit this evidence for another purpose, such as proving a witness's bias or prejudice, negating a contention of undue delay, or proving an effort to obstruct a criminal investigation or prosecution.

ADVISORY COMMITTEE'S NOTE

As a matter of general agreement, evidence of an offer to compromise a claim is not receivable in evidence as an admission of, as the case may be, the validity or invalidity of the claim. As with evidence of subsequent remedial measures, dealt with in Rule 407, exclusion may be based on two grounds. (1) The evidence is irrelevant, since the offer may be motivated by a desire for peace rather than from any concession of weakness of position. The validity of this position will vary as the amount of the offer varies in relation to the size of the claim and may also be influenced by other circumstances. (2) A more consistently impressive ground is promotion of the public policy favoring the compromise and settlement of disputes. McCormick §§ 76, 251. While the rule is ordinarily phrased in terms of offers of compromise, it is apparent that a similar attitude must be taken with respect to completed compromises when offered against a party thereto. This latter situation will not, of course, ordinarily occur except when a party to the present litigation has compromised with a third person.

The same policy underlies the provision of Rule 68 of the Federal Rules of Civil Procedure that evidence of an unaccepted offer of judgment is not admissible except in a proceeding to determine costs.

The practical value of the common law rule has been greatly diminished by its inapplicability to admissions of fact, even though made in the course of compromise negotiations, unless hypothetical, stated to be "without prejudice," or so connected with the offer as to be inseparable from it. McCormick § 251, pp. 540–541. An inevitable effect is to inhibit freedom of communication with respect to compromise, even among lawyers. Another effect is the generation of controversy over whether a given statement falls within or without the protected area. These considerations account for the expansion of the rule herewith to include evidence of conduct or statements made in compromise negotiations, as well as the offer or completed compromise itself. For similar provisions see California Evidence Code §§ 1152, 1154.

The policy considerations which underlie the rule do not come into play when the effort is to induce a creditor to settle an admittedly due amount for a lesser sum. McCormick § 251, p. 540. Hence the rule requires that the claim be disputed as to either validity or amount.

The final sentence of the rule[10] serves to point out some limitations upon its applicability. Since the rule excludes only when the purpose is proving the validity or invalidity of the claim or its amount, an offer for another purpose is not within the rule. The illustrative situations mentioned in the rule are supported by the authorities. As to proving bias or prejudice of a witness, see Annot., 161 A.L.R. 395, *contra*, Fenberg v. Rosenthal, 348 Ill.App. 510 (1952), and negativing a contention of lack of due diligence in presenting a claim, 4 Wigmore § 1061. An effort to "buy off" the prosecution or a prosecuting witness in a criminal case is not within the policy of the rule of exclusion. McCormick § 251, p. 542.

For other rules of similar import, see Uniform Rules 52 and 53; California Evidence Code §§ 1152, 1154; Kansas Code of Civil Procedure §§ 60-452, 60-453; New Jersey Evidence Rules 52 and 53.

REPORT OF HOUSE COMMITTEE ON THE JUDICIARY

Under existing federal law evidence of conduct and statements made in compromise negotiations is admissible in subsequent litigation between the parties. The second sentence of Rule 408[11] as submitted by the Supreme Court proposed to reverse that doctrine in the interest of further promoting non-judicial settlement of disputes. Some agencies of government expressed the view that the Court formulation was likely to impede rather than assist efforts to achieve settlement of disputes. For one thing, it is not always easy to tell when compromise negotiations begin, and informal dealings end. Also, parties dealing with government agencies would be reluctant to furnish factual information at preliminary meetings; they would wait until "compromise negotiations" began and thus hopefully effect an immunity for themselves with respect to the evidence supplied. In light of these considerations, the Committee recast the Rule so that admissions of liability or opinions given during compromise negotiations continue inadmissible, but evidence of unqualified factual assertions is admissible. The latter aspect of the Rule is drafted, however, so as to preserve other possible objections to the introduction of such evidence. The Committee intends no modification of current law whereby a party may protect himself from future use of his statements by couching them in hypothetical conditional form.

---

[10] Editor's Note: This refers to subsection (b) of the restyled version of the rule.
[11] Editor's Note: This refers to subsection (a)(2) of the restyled version of the rule.

REPORT OF SENATE COMMITTEE ON THE JUDICIARY

This rule as reported makes evidence of settlement or attempted settlement of a disputed claim inadmissible when offered as an admission of liability or the amount of liability. The purpose of this rule is to encourage settlements which would be discouraged if such evidence were admissible.

Under present law, in most jurisdictions, statements of fact made during settlement negotiations, however, are excepted from this ban and are admissible. The only escape from admissibility of statements of fact made in a settlement negotiation is if the declarant or his representative expressly states that the statement is hypothetical in nature or is made without prejudice. Rule 408 as submitted by the Court reversed the traditional rule. It would have brought statements of fact within the ban and made them, as well as an offer of settlement, inadmissible.

The House amended the rule and would continue to make evidence of facts disclosed during compromise negotiations admissible. It thus reverted to the traditional rule. The House committee report states that the committee intends to preserve current law under which a party may protect himself by couching his statements in hypothetical form.[12] The real impact of this amendment, however, is to deprive the rule of much of its salutary effect. The exception for factual admissions was believed by the Advisory Committee to hamper free communication between parties and thus to constitute an unjustifiable restraint upon efforts to negotiate settlements—the encouragement of which is the purpose of the rule. Further, by protecting hypothetically phrased statements, it constituted a preference for the sophisticated, and a trap for the unwary.

Three States which had adopted rules of evidence patterned after the proposed rules prescribed by the Supreme Court opted for versions of rule 408 identical with the Supreme Court draft with respect to the inadmissibility of conduct or statements made in compromise negotiations.[13]

For these reasons, the committee has deleted the House amendment and restored the rule to the version submitted by the Supreme Court with one additional amendment. This amendment adds a sentence to insure that evidence, such as documents, is not rendered inadmissible merely because it is presented in the course of compromise negotiations if the evidence is otherwise discoverable. A party should not be able to immunize from admissibility documents otherwise discoverable merely by offering them in a compromise negotiation.

CONFERENCE REPORT

The House bill provides that evidence of admissions of liability or opinions given during compromise negotiations is not admissible, but that evidence of facts disclosed during compromise negotiations is not inadmissible by virtue of having been first disclosed in the compromise negotiations. The Senate amendment provides that evidence of conduct or statements made in compromise negotiations is not admissible. The Senate amendment also provides that the rule does not require the exclusion of any evidence otherwise discoverable merely because it is presented in the course of compromise negotiations.

The House bill was drafted to meet the objection of executive agencies that under the rule as proposed by the Supreme Court, a party could present a fact during compromise negotiations and thereby prevent an opposing party from offering evidence of that fact at trial even though such evidence was obtained from independent sources. The Senate amendment expressly precludes this result.

---

[12] See Report No. 93-650, dated November 15, 1973.
[13] Nev.Rev.Stats. § 48.105; N.Mex.Stats.Anno. (1973 Supp.) § 20-4-408; West's Wis.Stats.Anno. (1973 Supp.) § 904.08.

The Conference adopts the Senate amendment.

ADVISORY COMMITTEE'S NOTE (2006 AMENDMENT)

Rule 408 has been amended to settle some questions in the courts about the scope of the Rule, and to make it easier to read. First, the amendment provides that Rule 408 does not prohibit the introduction in a criminal case of statements or conduct during compromise negotiations regarding a civil dispute by a government regulatory, investigative, or enforcement agency. *See, e.g.*, *United States v. Prewitt*, 34 F.3d 436, 439 (7th Cir. 1994) (admissions of fault made in compromise of a civil securities enforcement action were admissible against the accused in a subsequent criminal action for mail fraud). Where an individual makes a statement in the presence of government agents, its subsequent admission in a criminal case should not be unexpected. The individual can seek to protect against subsequent disclosure through negotiation and agreement with the civil regulator or an attorney for the government.

Statements made in compromise negotiations of a claim by a government agency may be excluded in criminal cases where the circumstances so warrant under Rule 403. For example, if an individual was unrepresented at the time the statement was made in a civil enforcement proceeding, its probative value in a subsequent criminal case may be minimal. But there is no absolute exclusion imposed by Rule 408.

In contrast, statements made during compromise negotiations of other disputed claims are not admissible in subsequent criminal litigation, when offered to prove liability for, invalidity of, or amount of those claims. When private parties enter into compromise negotiations they cannot protect against the subsequent use of statements in criminal cases by way of private ordering. The inability to guarantee protection against subsequent use could lead to parties refusing to admit fault, even if by doing so they could favorably settle the private matter. Such a chill on settlement negotiations would be contrary to the policy of Rule 408.

The amendment distinguishes statements and conduct (such as a direct admission of fault) made in compromise negotiations of a civil claim by a government agency from an offer or acceptance of a compromise of such a claim. An offer or acceptance of a compromise of any civil claim is excluded under the Rule if offered against the defendant as an admission of fault. In that case, the predicate for the evidence would be that the defendant, by compromising with the government agency, has admitted the validity and amount of the civil claim, and that this admission has sufficient probative value to be considered as evidence of guilt. But unlike a direct statement of fault, an offer or acceptance of a compromise is not very probative of the defendant's guilt. Moreover, admitting such an offer or acceptance could deter defendants from settling a civil regulatory action, for fear of evidentiary use in a subsequent criminal action. *See, e.g.*, Fishman, *Jones on Evidence, Civil and Criminal*, § 22:16 at 199, n.83 (7th ed. 2000) ("A target of a potential criminal investigation may be unwilling to settle civil claims against him if by doing so he increases the risk of prosecution and conviction.").

The amendment retains the language of the original rule that bars compromise evidence only when offered as evidence of the "validity," "invalidity," or "amount" of the disputed claim. The intent is to retain the extensive case law finding Rule 408 inapplicable when compromise evidence is offered for a purpose other than to prove the validity, invalidity, or amount of a disputed claim. *See, e.g.*, *Athey v. Farmers Ins. Exchange*, 234 F.3d 357 (8th Cir. 2000) (evidence of settlement offer by insurer was properly admitted to prove insurer's bad faith); *Coakley & Williams v. Structural Concrete Equip.*, 973 F.2d 349 (4th Cir. 1992) (evidence of settlement is not precluded by Rule 408 where offered to prove a party's intent with respect to the scope of a release); *Cates v. Morgan Portable Bldg. Corp.*, 708 F.2d 683 (7th Cir. 1985) (Rule 408 does not bar evidence of a settlement when offered to prove a breach of the settlement agreement, as the purpose of the evidence is to prove the fact of settlement as opposed to the validity or amount of the underlying claim); *Uforma/Shelby Bus. Forms, Inc. v. NLRB*, 111 F.3d 1284 (6th Cir. 1997) (threats made in settlement negotiations were admissible; Rule 408 is inapplicable when the claim is based upon a wrong that is committed during the course of settlement negotiations). So for example, Rule 408 is inapplicable if offered to show that a party made fraudulent statements in order to settle a litigation.

The amendment does not affect the case law providing that Rule 408 is inapplicable when evidence of the compromise is offered to prove notice. *See, e.g., United States v. Austin*, 54 F.3d 394 (7th Cir. 1995) (no error to admit evidence of the defendant's settlement with the FTC, because it was offered to prove that the defendant was on notice that subsequent similar conduct was wrongful); *Spell v. McDaniel*, 824 F.2d 1380 (4th Cir. 1987) (in a civil rights action alleging that an officer used excessive force, a prior settlement by the City of another brutality claim was properly admitted to prove that the City was on notice of aggressive behavior by police officers).

The amendment prohibits the use of statements made in settlement negotiations when offered to impeach by prior inconsistent statement or through contradiction. Such broad impeachment would tend to swallow the exclusionary rule and would impair the public policy of promoting settlements. *See McCormick on Evidence* at 186 (5th ed. 1999) ("Use of statements made in compromise negotiations to impeach the testimony of a party, which is not specifically treated in Rule 408, is fraught with danger of misuse of the statements to prove liability, threatens frank interchange of information during negotiations, and generally should not be permitted."). *See also EEOC v. Gear Petroleum, Inc.*, 948 F.2d 1542 (10th Cir. 1991) (letter sent as part of settlement negotiation cannot be used to impeach defense witnesses by way of contradiction or prior inconsistent statement; such broad impeachment would undermine the policy of encouraging uninhibited settlement negotiations).

The amendment makes clear that Rule 408 excludes compromise evidence even when a party seeks to admit its own settlement offer or statements made in settlement negotiations. If a party were to reveal its own statement or offer, this could itself reveal the fact that the adversary entered into settlement negotiations. The protections of Rule 408 cannot be waived unilaterally because the Rule, by definition, protects both parties from having the fact of negotiation disclosed to the jury. Moreover, proof of statements and offers made in settlement would often have to be made through the testimony of attorneys, leading to the risks and costs of disqualification. *See generally Pierce v. F.R. Tripler & Co.*, 955 F.2d 820, 828 (2d Cir. 1992) (settlement offers are excluded under Rule 408 even if it is the offeror who seeks to admit them; noting that the "widespread admissibility of the substance of settlement offers could bring with it a rash of motions for disqualification of a party's chosen counsel who would likely become a witness at trial").

The sentence of the Rule referring to evidence "otherwise discoverable" has been deleted as superfluous. *See, e.g.*, Advisory Committee Note to Maine Rule of Evidence 408 (refusing to include the sentence in the Maine version of Rule 408 and noting that the sentence "seems to state what the law would be if it were omitted"); Advisory Committee Note to Wyoming Rule of Evidence 408 (refusing to include the sentence in Wyoming Rule 408 on the ground that it was "superfluous"). The intent of the sentence was to prevent a party from trying to immunize admissible information, such as a pre-existing document, through the pretense of disclosing it during compromise negotiations. *See Ramada Development Co. v. Rauch*, 644 F.2d 1097 (5th Cir. 1981). But even without the sentence, the Rule cannot be read to protect pre-existing information simply because it was presented to the adversary in compromise negotiations.

ADVISORY COMMITTEE'S NOTE (2011 AMENDMENT)

The language of Rule 408 has been amended as part of the general restyling of the Evidence Rules to make them more easily understood and to make style and terminology consistent throughout the rules. These changes are intended to be stylistic only. There is no intent to change any result in any ruling on evidence admissibility.

Rule 408 previously provided that evidence was not excluded if offered for a purpose not explicitly prohibited by the Rule. To improve the language of the Rule, it now provides that the court may admit evidence if offered for a permissible purpose. There is no intent to change the process for admitting evidence covered by the Rule. It remains the case that if offered for an impermissible purpose, it must be excluded, and if offered for a purpose not barred by the Rule, its admissibility remains governed by the general principles of Rules 402, 403, 801, etc.

The Committee deleted the reference to "liability" on the ground that the deletion makes the Rule flow better and easier to read, and because "liability" is covered by the broader term "validity." Courts have not made substantive decisions on the basis of any distinction between validity and liability. No change in current practice or in the coverage of the Rule is intended.

Florida Stat. § 90.408. Compromise and Offers to Compromise

Evidence of an offer to compromise a claim which was disputed as to validity or amount, as well as any relevant conduct or statements made in negotiations concerning a compromise, is inadmissible to prove liability or absence of liability for the claim or its value.

SPONSORS' NOTE (1976 ENACTMENT)

Except for the phrase, "as well as any relevant conduct or statements made in negotiations concerning a compromise," this section codifies existing Florida law. Jordan v. City of Coral Gables, 191 So. 2d 38 (Fla. 1966); Mutual Benefit Health & Acc. Ass'n v. Bunting, 133 Fla. 646, 183 So. 321 (1938); Dade County v. Clarson, 240 So. 2d 828 (Fla. 3rd Dist. 1970) (District Court seemingly adopted view of Section 90.408 in excluding statement made by agent during settlement negotiations that the defendant was liable). The exclusion may be based on two grounds. (1) The evidence is irrelevant, since "such an offer does not ordinarily proceed from and imply a belief that the adversary's claim is well founded, but rather that the further prosecution of the claim, whether well founded or not, would in any event cause such annoyance as is preferably avoided by the payment of the sum offered." Mutual Benefit Health & Acc. Ass'n v. Bunting, supra at 326. (2) "The public policy of this state favors amicable settlement of disputes and the avoidance of litigation." City of Coral Gables v. Jordan, 186 So. 2d 60, 63, aff'd, 191 So. 2d 38 (Fla. 1966).

Florida purports to follow the common-law rule that the exclusion does not apply to admission of fact. Mutual Benefit Health & Acc. Ass'n v. Bunting, supra; McCormick, Evidence § 274 (2nd ed. 1972). No Florida cases were found, however, where the use of such evidence had been appealed and ruled on.

An inevitable effect of this exception permitting admissions of fact to be used as evidence is to inhibit freedom of communication with respect to compromise, and to serve as a trap for the unwary. These considerations account for the expansion of the rule to include evidence of conduct or statements made in compromise negotiations.

While the rule has ordinarily been phrased in terms of offers to compromise a similar attitude is taken with respect to completed compromises when offered against a party thereto. This latter situation would occur, for instance, when a party to the present litigation has compromised with a third person.

The policy considerations which underlie this section do not come into play when the effect is to induce a creditor to settle an admittedly due amount for a lesser sum. The section requires that the claim be disputed as to either validity or amount.

COMMENTARY ON FEDERAL AND FLORIDA RULE DIFFERENCES

Florida Stat. § 90.408 and its federal counterpart, Federal Rule 408, regulate the admissibility of evidence of compromises and offers to comprise.

Both the Florida and federal rules bar evidence of an offer to compromise a disputed claim, as well as evidence of conduct or statements made during compromise negotiations, when offered to prove the validity of a claim or its value. *See* FED. R. EVID. 408; FLA. STAT. § 90.408. Offers to settle with third parties, as well as completed settlements with third parties, are likewise subject to exclusion under both rules when offered to prove the validity or value of the claim being litigated. *See Rease v. Anheuser-Busch, Inc.*, 644 So. 2d 1383, 1388-89 (Fla. 1st DCA 1994); *Dallis v. Aetna Life Ins. Co.*, 768 F.2d 1303, 1306-07 (11th Cir. 1985); Advisory Committee's Note to FED. R. EVID. 408; Sponsors' Note to FLA. STAT. § 90.408.

Neither the federal nor the Florida rule is applicable unless either the validity *or* the amount of a claim is disputed; thus, for example, evidence of an effort by a debtor to induce a creditor to settle an admittedly due amount for a lesser sum is not subject to exclusion under either rule. *See* Advisory Committee's Note to FED. R. EVID. 408; Sponsors' Note to FLA. STAT. § 90.408. Under the federal rule, it is not necessary that a lawsuit actually be filed or threatened before a dispute is deemed to exist; it suffices that an actual dispute or difference of opinion exists between the parties. *See Dallis*, 768 F.2d at 1307; *Affiliated Mfr's., Inc. v. ALCOA*, 56 F.3d 521, 527-28 (3d Cir. 1995). Under Florida law, it is unclear whether the rule applies to statements and conduct that precede the initiation of litigation. *See Rease*, 644 So. 2d at 1389 n.6 (citing one case holding that it does not apply to anything that occurs before initiating litigation, but suggesting in dicta that it should apply before litigation is filed or threatened).

Federal Rule 408 was amended effective December 1, 2006, to provide that evidence of compromises and offers to compromise are inadmissible in civil and criminal cases, and that evidence of conduct or statements made in compromise negotiations is inadmissible in all cases *except* when offered in a criminal case and the negotations related to a claim by a public office or agency in the exercise of regulatory, investigative, or enforcement authority. *See* FED. R. EVID. 408(a); Advisory Committee's Note to 2006 Amendment to FED. R. EVID. 408. By contrast, the Florida rule can be invoked to bar the admission of compromises only in civil cases, not in criminal prosecutions. *See State v. Walters*, 719 So. 2d 1027, 1028 (Fla. 3d DCA 1998).

Federal Rule 408 was amended effective December 1, 2006, to bar the use of statements made in compromise negotiations to impeach a witness by prior inconsistent statement or contradiction. *See* FED. R. EVID. 408(a); Advisory Committee's Note to 2006 Amendment to FED. R. EVID. 408. The Florida rule, by contrast, does not prohibit such use of statements made in compromise negotiations.

Federal Rule 408 has an explicit sentence at the end of it indicating that it does not bar evidence of compromises, offers to compromise, or conduct or statements made during compromise negotiations when offered for reasons other than those expressly prohibited by it, and lists examples of such other uses (one of which is to prove the bias or prejudice of a witness). *See* FED. R. EVID. 408(b). However, even when offered for such other purposes, the trial court may still exclude it under Federal Rule 403 when there is a risk that the evidence might be misused by the jury for the purposes forbidden by Federal Rule 408. *See, e.g., Weir v. Federal Ins. Co.*, 811 F.2d 1387, 1395-96 (10th Cir. 1987). In contrast, Section 90.408 contains no such explicit language, and the Florida Supreme Court recently rejected an argument that evidence of a completed settlement between a witness and a party was admissible under an implied exception to Section 90.408 to demonstrate the bias or prejudice of the witness. *Saleeby v. Rocky Elson Const., Inc.*, 3 So. 3d 1078 (Fla. 2009).

Federal Rule 409. Offers to Pay Medical and Similar Expenses

Evidence of furnishing, promising to pay, or offering to pay medical, hospital, or similar expenses resulting from an injury is not admissible to prove liability for the injury.

ADVISORY COMMITTEE'S NOTE

The considerations underlying this rule parallel those underlying Rules 407 and 408, which deal respectively with subsequent remedial measures and offers of compromise. As stated in Annot., 20 A.L.R.2d 291, 293:

"[G]enerally, evidence of payment of medical, hospital, or similar expenses of an injured party by the opposing party, is not admissible, the reason often given being that such payment or offer is usually made from humane impulses and not from an admission of liability, and that to hold otherwise would tend to discourage assistance to the injured person."

Contrary to Rule 408, dealing with offers of compromise, the present rule does not extend to conduct or statements not a part of the act of furnishing or offering or promising to pay. This difference in treatment arises from fundamental differences in nature. Communication is essential if compromises are to be effected, and consequently broad protection of statements is needed. This is not so in cases of payments or offers or promises to pay medical expenses, where factual statements may be expected to be incidental in nature.

For rules on the same subject, but phrased in terms of "humanitarian motives," see Uniform Rule 52; California Evidence Code § 1152; Kansas Code of Civil Procedure § 60-452; New Jersey Evidence Rule 52.

ADVISORY COMMITTEE'S NOTE (2011 AMENDMENT)

The language of Rule 409 has been amended as part of the restyling of the Evidence Rules to make them more easily understood and to make style and terminology consistent throughout the rules. These changes are intended to be stylistic only. There is no intent to change any result in any ruling on evidence admissibility.

Florida Stat. § 90.409. Payment of Medical and Similar Expenses

Evidence of furnishing, or offering or promising to pay, medical or hospital expenses or other damages occasioned by an injury or accident is inadmissible to prove liability for the injury or accident.

SPONSORS' NOTE (1976 ENACTMENT)

The considerations underlying this rule are similar to those underlying Section 90.408. However, since factual statements are not inherent in the communications relating to the payment of medical or other expenses, this section does not extend to them. Similar provisions are found in Calif. Evid. Code § 1152; Kansas Code of Civ. Pro. § 60-452; New Jersey Evid. Rule 52 and Fed. Rule Evid. 409. Florida law is in accord. Babcock v. Flowers, 144 Fla. 479, 198 So. 326 (1940).

COMMENTARY ON FEDERAL AND FLORIDA RULE DIFFERENCES

Florida Stat. § 90.409 and its federal counterpart, Federal Rule 409, regulate the admissibility of evidence of furnishing, offering or promising to pay certain expenses of an injured person's medical, hospital and other expenses.

Both the Florida and federal rules only exclude such evidence when offered to prove liability, not when offered for other purposes. *See, e.g., Williams v. Missouri Pacific R.R. Co.*, 11 F.3d 132, 135 (10th Cir. 1993); *Savoie v. Otto Candies, Inc.*, 692 F.2d 363, 370 n.7 (5th Cir. 1982). Moreover, both rules exclude only evidence of furnishing, offering, or promising to pay such expenses, not factual statements made in the course of such a tender. *See Advisory Committee's Note to* FED. R. EVID. 409; *Sponsors' Note to* FLA. STAT. § 90.409.

While the federal rule refers to "medical, hospital, or *similar expenses resulting from an injury*", the Florida rule appears to be broader, referring to "medical or hospital expenses or *other damages occasioned by an injury or accident*." While there is no Florida authority on point, rules worded similarly to the Florida rule are interpreted to be broader than the federal rule, including such things as lost wages and damage to property. *See* Commentary to N.C. RULE EVID. 409; Official Comment to IOWA RULE EVID. 5.409. *See also Savoie*, 692 F.2d at 370 n.7 (questioning whether maintenance payments would qualify as "similar expenses" under Federal Rule 409).

The Florida rule can be invoked only in a civil case, not in a criminal prosecution. *See Johnson v. State*, 625 So. 2d 1297, 1299 (Fla. 1st DCA 1993). No decisions have addressed any such limitation for Federal Rule 409. *But see* Commentary to FED. R. EVID. 408 and FLA. STAT. § 90.408 (discussing a split in the federal courts before Federal Rule 408 was amended in 2006 on the question whether it could be invoked in criminal prosecutions).

Federal Rule 410. Pleas, Plea Discussions, and Related Statements

(a) Prohibited Uses. In a civil or criminal case, evidence of the following is not admissible against the defendant who made the plea or participated in the plea discussions:

    (1) a guilty plea that was later withdrawn;

    (2) a nolo contendere plea;

    (3) a statement made during a proceeding on either of those pleas under Federal Rule of Criminal Procedure 11 or a comparable state procedure; or

    (4) a statement made during plea discussions with an attorney for the prosecuting authority if the discussions did not result in a guilty plea or they resulted in a later-withdrawn guilty plea.

(b) Exceptions. The court may admit a statement described in Rule 410(a)(3) or (4):

    (1) in any proceeding in which another statement made during the same plea or plea discussions has been introduced, if in fairness the statements ought to be considered together; or

    (2) in a criminal proceeding for perjury or false statement, if the defendant made the statement under oath, on the record, and with counsel present.

ADVISORY COMMITTEE'S NOTE

Withdrawn pleas of guilty were held inadmissible in federal prosecutions in Kercheval v. United States, 274 U.S. 220 (1927). The Court pointed out that to admit the withdrawn plea would effectively set at naught the allowance of withdrawal and place the accused in a dilemma utterly inconsistent with the decision to award him a trial. The New York Court of Appeals, in People v. Spitaleri, 9 N.Y.2d 168 (1961), reexamined and overturned its earlier decisions which had allowed admission. In addition to the reasons set forth in Kercheval, which was quoted at length, the court pointed out that the effect of admitting the plea was to compel defendant to take the stand by way of explanation and to open the way for the prosecution to call the lawyer who had represented him at the time of entering the plea. State court decisions for and against admissibility are collected in Annot., 86 A.L.R.2d 326.

Pleas of *nolo contendere* are recognized by Rule 11 of the Rules of Criminal Procedure, although the law of numerous States is to the contrary. The present rule gives effect to the principal traditional characteristic of the *nolo* plea, i.e. avoiding the admission of guilt which is inherent in pleas of guilty. This position is consistent with the construction of Section 5 of the Clayton Act, 15 U.S.C. § 16(a), recognizing the inconclusive and compromise nature of judgments based on *nolo* pleas. General Electric Co. v. City of San Antonio, 334 F.2d 480 (5th Cir. 1964); Commonwealth Edison Co. v. Allis-Chalmers Mfg. Co., 323 F.2d 412 (7th Cir. 1963), cert. denied 376 U.S. 939; Armco Steel Corp. v. North Dakota, 376 F.2d 206 (8th Cir. 1967); City of Burbank v. General Electric Co., 329 F.2d 825 (9th Cir. 1964). See also state court decisions in Annot., 18 A.L.R.2d 1287, 1314.

Exclusion of offers to plead guilty or *nolo* has as its purpose the promotion of disposition of criminal cases by compromise. As pointed out in McCormick § 251, p. 543

"Effective criminal law administration in many localities would hardly be possible if a large proportion of the charges were not disposed of by such compromises."

See also People v. Hamilton, 60 Cal.2d 105 (1963), discussing legislation designed to achieve this result. As with compromise offers generally, Rule 408, free communication is needed, and security against having an offer of compromise or related statement admitted in evidence effectively encourages it.

Limiting the exclusionary rule to use against the accused is consistent with the purpose of the rule, since the possibility of use for or against other persons will not impair the effectiveness of withdrawing pleas or the freedom of discussion which the rule is designed to foster. See A.B.A. Standards Relating to Pleas of Guilty § 2.2 (1968). See also the narrower provisions of New Jersey Evidence Rule 52(2) and the unlimited exclusion provided in California Evidence Code § 1153.

REPORT OF HOUSE COMMITTEE ON THE JUDICIARY

The Committee added the phrase "Except as otherwise provided by Act of Congress" to Rule 410 as submitted by the Court in order to preserve particular congressional policy judgments as to the effect of a plea of guilty or of nolo contendere. See 15 U.S.C. 16(a). The Committee intends that its amendment refers to both present statutes and statutes subsequently enacted.

REPORT OF SENATE COMMITTEE ON THE JUDICIARY

As adopted by the House, rule 410 would make inadmissible pleas of guilty or nolo contendere subsequently withdrawn as well as offers to make such pleas. Such a rule is clearly justified as a means of encouraging pleading. However, the House rule would then go on to render inadmissible for any purpose statements made in connection with these pleas or offers as well.

The committee finds this aspect of the House rule unjustified. Of course, in certain circumstances such statements should be excluded. If, for example, a plea is vitiated because of coercion, statements made in connection with the plea may also have been coerced and should be inadmissible on that basis. In other cases, however, voluntary statements of an accused made in court on the record, in connection with a plea, and determined by a court to be reliable should be admissible even though the plea is subsequently withdrawn. This is particularly true in those cases where, if the House rule were in effect, a defendant would be able to contradict his previous statements and thereby lie with impunity.[14] To prevent such an

---

[14] See *Harris v. New York*, 401 U.S. 222 (1971).

injustice, the rule has been modified to permit the use of such statements for the limited purposes of impeachment and in subsequent perjury or false statement prosecutions.

CONFERENCE REPORT

The House bill provides that evidence of a guilty or nolo contendere plea, of an offer of either plea, or of statements made in connection with such pleas or offers of such pleas, is inadmissible in any civil or criminal action, case or proceeding against the person making such plea or offer. The Senate amendment makes the rule inapplicable to a voluntary and reliable statement made in court on the record where the statement is offered in a subsequent prosecution of the declarant for perjury or false statement.

The issues raised by Rule 410 are also raised by proposed Rule 11(e)(6) of the Federal Rules of Criminal Procedure presently pending before Congress. This proposed rule, which deals with the admissibility of pleas of guilty or nolo contendere, offers to make such pleas, and statements made in connection with such pleas, was promulgated by the Supreme Court on April 22, 1974, and in the absence of congressional action will become effective on August 1, 1975. The conferees intend to make no change in the presently-existing case law until that date, leaving the courts free to develop rules in this area on a case-by-case basis.

The Conferees further determined that the issues presented by the use of guilty and nolo contendere pleas, offers of such pleas, and statements made in connection with such pleas or offers, can be explored in greater detail during Congressional consideration of Rule 11(e)(6) of the Federal Rules of Criminal Procedure. The Conferees believe, therefore, that it is best to defer its effective date until August 1, 1975. The Conferees in tend that Rule 410 would be superseded by any subsequent Federal Rule of Criminal Procedure or act of Congress with which it is inconsistent, if the Federal Rule of Criminal Procedure or Act of Congress takes effect or becomes law after the date of the enactment of the act establishing the rules of evidence.

The conference adopts the Senate amendment with an amendment that expresses the above intentions.

ADVISORY COMMITTEE'S NOTE (2011 AMENDMENT)

The language of Rule 410 has been amended as part of the restyling of the Evidence Rules to make them more easily understood and to make style and terminology consistent throughout the rules. These changes are intended to be stylistic only. There is no intent to change any result in any ruling on evidence admissibility.

Florida Stat. § 90.410. Offer to Plead Guilty; Nolo Contendere; Withdrawn Pleas of Guilty

Evidence of a plea of guilty, later withdrawn; a plea of nolo contendere; or an offer to plead guilty or nolo contendere to the crime charged or any other crime is inadmissible in any civil or criminal proceeding. Evidence of statements made in connection with any of the pleas or offers is inadmissible, except when such statements are offered in a prosecution under chapter 837.

SPONSORS' NOTE (1976 ENACTMENT)

Withdrawn pleas of guilty were held inadmissible in federal prosecution, in Kercheval v. United States, 274 U.S. 220, 47 S.Ct. 582, 71 L.Ed. 1009 (1927). The Court pointed out that to admit the withdrawn plea would effectively negate the allowance of withdrawal and place the accused in a dilemma utterly inconsistent with the decision to award him a trial. In <u>Green v. State</u>, 40 Fla. 474, 24 So. 537 (1898), the Florida Supreme Court stated that "when an accused first pleads guilty to a charge, and afterwards, by permission of the court, is allowed to withdraw such plea, and put in general issue, the plea of confession allowed to be withdrawn cannot be put in evidence on the trial."

Exclusion of offer to plead guilty or <u>nolo</u> has as its purpose the promotion of disposition of criminal cases by compromise.

Prior to the acceptance of a plea of guilty or <u>nolo contendere</u> by the court, Fla. R. Crim. Pro. 3.170(j) requires the court to determine in open court "that the circumstances surrounding the plea reflect a full understanding of the plea and its voluntariness, and that there is a factual basis for the plea of guilty." If statements are made during this inquiry, they are not subsequently admissible against him if he withdraws a guilty plea, pleads <u>nolo contendere</u> or offers to plead <u>nolo contendere</u> or guilty.

COMMENTARY ON FEDERAL AND FLORIDA RULE DIFFERENCES

Florida Stat. § 90.410 and its federal counterpart, Federal Rule 410, govern the admissibility of evidence of withdrawn guilty pleas, pleas of *nolo contendere*, offers to plead guilty or *nolo contendere*, and statements made in connection with such pleas or offers. To different degrees, this type of evidence is barred under the Florida and federal rules as a means of encouraging plea negotiations. *See* Sponsors' Note to FLA. STAT. § 90.410; Advisory Committee's Note to FED. R. EVID. 410.

The Florida rule is drafted in sweeping terms, and has been interpreted not only to bar such evidence when offered against the defendant who made the plea or offer, but also to bar such evidence when offered by that defendant, such as where the accused seeks to offer evidence that he rejected an offer by the prosecution to plead guilty to a lesser charge. *See Donaldson v. State*, 722 So. 2d 177, 188 (Fla. 1998). By contrast, the federal rule, in terms, applies only when the evidence is offered "against the defendant who made the plea or participated in the plea discussions." *See* FED. R. EVID. 410; Advisory Committee's Note to FED. R. EVID. 410; *U.S. v. Mezzanatto*, 513 U.S. 196, 205-06 (1995); *U.S. v. Biaggi*, 909 F.2d 662, 690-91 (2d Cir. 1990).

Both the Florida and federal rules bar, in any civil or criminal proceeding, evidence of a withdrawn guilty plea or a plea of *nolo contendere*. *See* FED. R. EVID. 410(a)(1)-(2); FLA. STAT. § 90.410, Moreover, under both rules, statements made in the course of proceedings in which such pleas are entered are likewise inadmissible. *See* FED. R. EVID. 410(a)(3); FLA. STAT. § 90.410; Sponsors' Note to FLA. STAT. § 90.410. However, although evidence of a *plea* of *nolo contendere* is not admissible under either rule, evidence of a *conviction* based on such a plea *is* admissible, such as when the prior conviction is used to impeach the credibility of a witness. See *U.S. v. Williams*, 642 F.2d 136, 138-40 (5th Cir. Unit B 1981); *Cira v. Dillinger*, 903 So. 2d 367, 373 (Fla. 2d DCA 2005).

Under the Florida rule, evidence of "an offer to plead guilty or nolo contendere," as well as evidence of any statements made "in connection with" an offer to plead guilty or nolo contendere is likewise inadmissible. *See* FLA. STAT. § 90.410. Unsolicited, unilateral statements do not qualify as statements made "in connection with" an offer to plead. *See Calabro v. State*, 995 So. 2d 307, (Fla. 2008); *Owen v. Crosby*, 854 So. 2d 182, 189 (Fla. 2003). Rather, to qualify as being made "in connection with" an offer to plead, the court must determine both that the accused exhibited an actual, subjective expectation to negotiate a plea at the time of the discussion and that his expectation was objectively reasonable given the totality of the circumstances. *Owen*, 854 So. 2d at 189. This test is modeled after one created under the federal rule, which, until 1980, contained nearly identical language. *See Bottoson v. State*, 443 So. 2d 962, 965 (Fla. 1983); *U.S. v. Robertson*, 582 F.2d 1356, 1366-67 (5th Cir. 1978) (en banc). However, that language was eliminated from the federal rule and replaced with a provision excluding evidence of "a statement made during plea discussions with an attorney for the prosecuting authority if the discussions did not result in a guilty plea or they resulted in a later-withdrawn guilty plea." *See* FED. R. EVID. 410(a)(4). Thus, the current version of the federal rule *appears* to differ from the Florida rule in two ways: it does not appear to exclude unilateral *offers* to plead guilty or *nolo contendere*, and it appears only to exclude statements made in the course of a plea discussion with an attorney for the prosecuting authority. With respect to the first apparent difference, it seems that an offer to plead guilty or *nolo contendere* will by definition be made in a context that qualifies as a "plea discussion." With respect to the second apparent difference some federal authority holds that a statement to a law enforcement officer can be protected by the rule when the officer is found to have express or implied authority to act for the prosecuting government attorney. *See U.S. v. Greene*, 995 F.2d 793, 799-800 (8th Cir. 1993).

An exception exists to both the Florida and federal rules when the evidence is offered in a prosecution for perjury or false statement. *See* FED. R. EVID. 410(b)(2); FLA. STAT. § 90.410 (creating an exception for "a prosecution under chapter 837," which covers perjury and false statements). The federal rule also contains an exception in any proceeding in which another statement made in the course of the same plea or plea discussions has been introduced and the statement ought, in fairness, to be considered contemporaneously with it. *See* FED. R. EVID. 410(b)(1). The Florida rule contains no comparable exception, but that may be because the Florida rule, unlike the federal rule, is drafted in blanket terms that do not permit the defendant to introduce statements made in such pleas and plea discussions, making it unlikely that a situation will arise in which another statement made in the course of the plea or plea discussions would be introduced. There are no other exceptions to the federal or Florida rules. While the Florida rule originally contained an exception that would permit statements made in connection with pleas and plea discussions to be used to impeach a person who later testified in an inconsistent manner, the rule was amended to eliminate that exception. *See Landrum v. State*, 430 So. 2d 549, 550 (Fla. 2d DCA 1983). The drafters of the federal rule rejected an impeachment exception to the rule as well. *See U.S. v. Lawson*, 683 F.2d 688, 690-93 (2d Cir. 1982).

Federal Rule 411. Liability Insurance

Evidence that a person was or was not insured against liability is not admissible to prove whether the person acted negligently or otherwise wrongfully. But the court may admit this evidence for another purpose, such as proving a witness's bias or prejudice or proving agency, ownership, or control.

ADVISORY COMMITTEE'S NOTE

The courts have with substantial unanimity rejected evidence of liability insurance for the purpose of proving fault, and absence of liability insurance as proof of lack of fault. At best the inference of fault from the fact of insurance coverage is a tenuous one, as is its converse. More important, no doubt, has been the feeling that knowledge of the presence or absence of liability insurance would induce juries to decide cases on improper grounds. McCormick § 168; Annot., 4 A.L.R.2d 761. The rule is drafted in broad terms so as to include contributory negligence or other fault of a plaintiff as well as fault of a defendant.

The second sentence points out the limits of the rule, using well established illustrations. *Id.*

For similar rules see Uniform Rule 54; California Evidence Code § 1155; Kansas Code of Civil Procedure § 60-454; New Jersey Evidence Rule 54.

ADVISORY COMMITTEE'S NOTE (2011 AMENDMENT)

The language of Rule 411 has been amended as part of the general restyling of the Evidence Rules to make them more easily understood and to make style and terminology consistent throughout the rules. These changes are intended to be stylistic only. There is no intent to change any result in any ruling on evidence admissibility.

Rule 411 previously provided that evidence was not excluded if offered for a purpose not explicitly prohibited by the Rule. To improve the language of the Rule, it now provides that the court may admit evidence if offered for a permissible purpose. There is no intent to change the process for admitting evidence covered by the Rule. It remains the case that if offered for an impermissible purpose, it must be excluded, and if offered for a purpose not barred by the Rule, its admissibility remains governed by the general principles of Rules 402, 403, 801, etc.

COMMENTARY ON FEDERAL AND FLORIDA RULE DIFFERENCES

Federal Rule 411 bars evidence that a person was or was not insured against liability when offered on the issue whether the person acted negligently or otherwise wrongfully. Such evidence is not subject to exclusion under Rule 411 when it is offered for other purposes, see FED. R. EVID. 411, although it may be subject to exclusion under Federal Rule 403 to the extent that there is a risk that the evidence might be misused by the jury for the purposes forbidden by Rule 411. *See, e.g., Pinkham v. Burgess*, 933 F.2d 1066, 1071-72 (1st Cir. 1991). The federal courts are divided on the question whether indemnification agreements are covered by the rule. *Compare D.S.C. Communications Corp. v. Next Level Communications*, 929 F.Supp. 239, 242-45 (E.D. Tex. 1996) (not covered), *with Kirchoff v. Flynn*, 786 F.2d 320, 324 (7th Cir. 1986) (covered).

There is no equivalent provision in the Florida Evidence Code. The only rule that makes mention of insurance is Florida Stat. § 90.403, which provides that "[t]his section shall not be construed to mean that evidence of the existence of available third-party benefits is inadmissible." However, Florida decisional law provides for the exclusion of evidence of insurance coverage when offered on the issue of liability. *See Carls Markets, Inc. v. Meyer*, 69 So. 2d 789, 793 (Fla. 1953); *South Motor Co. of Dade Cty. v. Accountable Constr. Co.*, 707 So. 2d 909, 911-12 (Fla. 3d 1998). As with the federal rule, however, such evidence may be admissible if offered for other purposes. *See Nevarez v. Friskney*, 817 So. 2d 856, 857 (Fla. 5th DCA 2002).

Federal Rule 412. Sex-Offense Cases: The Victim's Sexual Behavior or Predisposition

(a) **Prohibited Uses.** The following evidence is not admissible in a civil or criminal proceeding involving alleged sexual misconduct:

(1) evidence offered to prove that a victim engaged in other sexual behavior; or

(2) evidence offered to prove a victim's sexual predisposition.

(b) **Exceptions.**

(1) *Criminal Cases.* The court may admit the following evidence in a criminal case:

(A) evidence of specific instances of a victim's sexual behavior, if offered to prove that someone other than the defendant was the source of semen, injury, or other physical evidence;

(B) evidence of specific instances of a victim's sexual behavior with respect to the person accused of the sexual misconduct, if offered by the defendant to prove consent or if offered by the prosecutor; and

(C) evidence whose exclusion would violate the defendant's constitutional rights.

(2) *Civil Cases.* In a civil case, the court may admit evidence offered to prove a victim's sexual behavior or sexual predisposition if its probative value substantially outweighs the danger of harm to any victim and of unfair prejudice to any party. The court may admit evidence of a victim's reputation only if the victim has placed it in controversy.

(c) Procedure to Determine Admissibility.

(1) *Motion.* If a party intends to offer evidence under Rule 412(b), the party must:

(A) file a motion that specifically describes the evidence and states the purpose for which it is to be offered;

(B) do so at least 14 days before trial unless the court, for good cause, sets a different time;

(C) serve the motion on all parties; and

(D) notify the victim or, when appropriate, the victim's guardian or representative.

(2) *Hearing.* Before admitting evidence under this rule, the court must conduct an in camera hearing and give the victim and parties a right to attend and be heard. Unless the court orders otherwise, the motion, related materials, and the record of the hearing must be and remain sealed.

(d) Definition of "Victim." In this rule, "victim" includes an alleged victim.

ADVISORY COMMITTEE'S NOTE (1994 AMENDMENT)

Rule 412 has been revised to diminish some of the confusion engendered by the original rule and to expand the protection afforded alleged victims of sexual misconduct. Rule 412 applies to both civil and criminal proceedings. The rule aims to safeguard the alleged victim against the invasion of privacy, potential embarrassment and sexual stereotyping that is associated with public disclosure of intimate sexual details and the infusion of sexual innuendo into the factfinding process. By affording victims protection in most instances, the rule also encourages victims of sexual misconduct to institute and to participate in legal proceedings against alleged offenders.

Rule 412 seeks to achieve these objectives by barring evidence relating to the alleged victim's sexual behavior or alleged sexual predisposition, whether offered as substantive evidence or for impeachment, except in designated circumstances in which the probative value of the evidence significantly outweighs possible harm to the victim.

The revised rule applies in all cases involving sexual misconduct without regard to whether the alleged victim or person accused is a party to the litigation. Rule 412 extends to "pattern" witnesses in both criminal and civil cases whose testimony about other instances of sexual misconduct by the person accused is otherwise admissible. When the case does not involve alleged sexual misconduct, evidence relating to a third-party witness' alleged sexual activities is not within the ambit of Rule 412. The witness will, however, be protected by other rules such as Rules 404 and 608, as well as Rule 403.

The terminology "alleged victim" is used because there will frequently be a factual dispute as to whether sexual misconduct occurred. It does not connote any requirement that the misconduct be alleged in the pleadings. Rule 412 does not, however, apply unless the person against whom the evidence is offered can reasonably be characterized as a "victim of alleged sexual misconduct." When this is not the case, as for instance in a defamation action involving statements concerning sexual misconduct in which the evidence is offered to show that the alleged defamatory statements were true or did not damage the plaintiff's reputation, neither Rule 404 nor this rule will operate to bar the evidence; Rule 401 and 403 will continue to control. Rule 412 will, however, apply in a Title VII action in which the plaintiff has alleged sexual harassment.

The reference to a person "accused" is also used in a non-technical sense. There is no requirement that there be a criminal charge pending against the person or even that the misconduct would constitute a criminal offense. Evidence offered to prove allegedly false prior claims by the victim is not barred by Rule 412. However, the evidence is subject to the requirements of Rule 404.

Subdivision (a). As amended, Rule 412 bars evidence offered to prove the victim's sexual behavior and alleged sexual predisposition. Evidence, which might otherwise be admissible under Rules 402, 404(b), 405, 607, 608, 609 or some other evidence rule, must be excluded if Rule 412 so requires. The word "other" is used to suggest some flexibility in admitting evidence "intrinsic" to the alleged sexual misconduct. *Cf.* Committee Note to 1991 amendment to Rule 404(b).

Past sexual behavior connotes all activities that involve actual physical conduct, i.e. sexual intercourse and sexual contact, or that imply sexual intercourse or sexual contact. *See, e.g., United States v. Galloway*, 937 F.2d 542 (10th Cir. 1991), *cert. denied*, 113 S.Ct. 418 (1992) (use of contraceptives inadmissible since use implies sexual activity); *United States v. One Feather*, 702 F.2d 736 (8th Cir. 1983) (birth of an illegitimate child inadmissible); *State v. Carmichael*, 727 P.2d 918, 925 (Kan. 1986) (evidence of venereal disease inadmissible). In addition, the word "behavior" should be construed to include activities of the mind, such as fantasies or dreams. *See* 23 C. Wright and K. Graham, Jr., *Federal Practice and Procedure*, § 5384 at p. 548 (1980) ("While there may be some doubt under statutes that require 'conduct,' it would seem that the language of Rule 412 is broad enough to encompass the behavior of the mind.").

The rule has been amended to also exclude all other evidence relating to an alleged victim of sexual misconduct that is offered to prove a sexual predisposition. This amendment is designed to exclude evidence that does not directly refer to sexual activities or thoughts but that the proponent believes may have a sexual connotation for the factfinder. Admission of such evidence would contravene Rule 412's objectives of shielding the alleged victim from potential embarrassment and safeguarding the victim against stereotypical thinking. Consequently, unless the (b)(2) exception is satisfied, evidence such as that relating to the alleged victim's mode of dress, speech, or life-style will not be admissible.

The introductory phrase in subdivision (a) was deleted because it lacked clarity and contained no explicit reference to the other provisions of the law that were intended to be overridden. The conditional clause, "except as provided in subdivisions (b) and (c)" is intended to make clear that evidence of the types described in subdivision (a) is admissible only under the strictures of those sections.

The reason for extending the rule to all criminal cases is obvious. The strong social policy of protecting a victim's privacy and encouraging victims to come forward to report criminal acts is not confined to cases that involve a charge of sexual assault. The need to protect the victim is equally great when a defendant is charged with kidnapping, and evidence is offered, either to prove motive or as background, that the defendant sexually assaulted the victim.

The reason for extending Rule 412 to civil cases is equally obvious. The need to protect alleged victims against invasions of privacy, potential embarrassment, and unwarranted sexual stereotyping, and the wish to encourage victims to come forward when they have been sexually molested do not disappear because the context has shifted from a criminal prosecution to a claim for damages or injunctive relief. There is a strong social policy in not only punishing those who engage in sexual misconduct, but in also providing relief to the victim. Thus, Rule 412 applies in any civil case in which a person claims to be the victim of sexual misconduct, such as actions for sexual battery or sexual harassment.

Subdivision (b). Subdivision (b) spells out the specific circumstances in which some evidence may be admissible that would otherwise be barred by the general rule expressed in subdivision (a). As amended, Rule 412 will be virtually unchanged in criminal cases, but will provide protection to any person alleged to be a victim of sexual misconduct regardless of the charge actually brought against an accused. A new exception has been added for civil cases.

In a criminal case, evidence may be admitted under subdivision (b)(1) pursuant to three possible exceptions, provided the evidence also satisfies other requirements for admissibility specified in the Federal Rules of Evidence, including Rule 403. Subdivisions (b)(1)(A) and (b)(1)(B) require proof in the form of specific instances of sexual behavior in recognition of the limited probative value and dubious reliability of evidence of reputation or evidence in the form of an opinion.

Under subdivision (b)(1)(A), evidence of specific instances of sexual behavior with persons other than the person whose sexual misconduct is alleged may be admissible if it is offered to prove that another person was the source of semen, injury or other physical evidence. Where the prosecution has directly or indirectly asserted that the physical evidence originated with the accused, the defendant must be afforded an opportunity to prove that another person was responsible. *See United States v. Begay*, 937 F.2d 515, 523 n. 10 (10th Cir. 1991). Evidence offered for the specific purpose identified in this subdivision may still be excluded if it does not satisfy Rules 401 or 403. *See, e.g., United States v. Azure*, 845 F.2d 1503, 1505–06 (8th Cir. 1988) (10 year old victim's injuries indicated recent use of force; court excluded evidence of consensual sexual activities with witness who testified at in camera hearing that he had never hurt victim and failed to establish recent activities).

Under the exception in subdivision (b)(1)(B), evidence of specific instances of sexual behavior with respect to the person whose sexual misconduct is alleged is admissible if offered to prove consent, or offered by the prosecution. Admissible pursuant to this exception might be evidence of prior instances of sexual activities between the alleged victim and the accused, as well as statements in which the alleged victim expresses an intent to engage in sexual intercourse with the accused, or voiced sexual fantasies involving that specific accused. In a prosecution for child sexual abuse, for example, evidence of uncharged sexual activity between the accused and the alleged victim offered by the prosecution may be admissible pursuant to Rule 404(b) to show a pattern of behavior. Evidence relating to the victim's alleged sexual predisposition is not admissible pursuant to this exception.

Under subdivision (b)(1)(C), evidence of specific instances of conduct may not be excluded if the result would be to deny a criminal defendant the protections afforded by the Constitution. For example, statements in which the victim has expressed an intent to have sex with the first person encountered on a particular occasion might not be excluded without violating the due process right of a rape defendant seeking to prove consent. Recognition of this basic principle was expressed in subdivision (b)(1) of the original rule. The United States Supreme Court has recognized that in various circumstances a defendant may have a right to introduce evidence otherwise precluded by an evidence rule under the Confrontation Clause. *See, e.g., Olden v. Kentucky*, 488 U.S. 227 (1988) (defendant in rape cases had right to inquire into alleged victim's cohabitation with another man to show bias).

Subdivision (b)(2) governs the admissibility of otherwise proscribed evidence in civil cases. It employs a balancing test rather than the specific exceptions stated in subdivision (b)(1) in recognition of the difficulty of foreseeing future developments in the law. Greater flexibility is needed to accommodate evolving causes of action such as claims for sexual harassment.

The balancing test requires the proponent of the evidence, whether plaintiff or defendant, to convince the court that the probative value of the proffered evidence "substantially outweighs the danger of harm to any victim and of unfair prejudice of any party." This test for admitting evidence offered to prove sexual behavior or sexual propensity in civil cases differs in three respects from the general rule governing admissibility set forth in Rule 403. First, it reverses the usual procedure spelled out in Rule 403 by shifting the burden to the proponent to demonstrate admissibility rather than making the opponent justify exclusion of the evidence. Second, the standard expressed in subdivision (b)(2) is more stringent than in the original rule; it raises the threshold for admission by requiring that the probative value of the evidence substantially outweigh the specified dangers. Finally, the Rule 412 test puts "harm to the victim" on the scale in addition to prejudice to the parties.

Evidence of reputation may be received in a civil case only if the alleged victim has put his or her reputation into controversy. The victim may do so without making a specific allegation in a pleading. *Cf.* Fed.R.Civ.P. 35(a).

Subdivision (c). Amended subdivision (c) is more concise and understandable than the subdivision it replaces. The requirement of a motion before trial is continued in the amended rule, as is the provision that a late motion may be permitted for good cause shown. In deciding whether to permit late filing, the court may take into account the conditions previously included in the rule: namely whether the evidence is newly discovered and could not have been obtained earlier through the existence of due diligence, and whether the issue to which such evidence relates has newly arisen in the case. The rule recognizes that in some instances the circumstances that justify an application to introduce evidence otherwise barred by Rule 412 will not become apparent until trial.

The amended rule provides that before admitting evidence that falls within the prohibition of Rule 412(a), the court must hold a hearing in camera at which the alleged victim and any party must be afforded the right to be present and an opportunity to be heard. All papers connected with the motion and any record of a hearing on the motion must be kept and remain under seal during the course of trial and appellate proceedings unless otherwise ordered. This is to assure that the privacy of the alleged victim is preserved in all cases in which the court rules that proffered evidence is not admissible, and in which the hearing refers to matters that are not received, or are received in another form.

The procedures set forth in subdivision (c) do not apply to discovery of a victim's past sexual conduct or predisposition in civil cases, which will be continued to be governed by Fed.R.Civ.P. 26. In order not to undermine the rationale of Rule 412, however, courts should enter appropriate orders pursuant to Fed.R.Civ.P. 26 (c) to protect the victim against unwarranted inquiries and to ensure confidentiality. Courts should presumptively issue protective orders barring discovery unless the party seeking discovery makes a showing that the evidence sought to be discovered would be relevant under the facts and theories of the particular case, and cannot be obtained except through discovery. In an action for sexual harassment, for instance, while some evidence of the alleged victim's sexual behavior and/or predisposition in the workplace may perhaps be relevant, non-work place conduct will usually be irrelevant. *Cf. Burns v. McGregor Electronic Industries, Inc.,* 989 F.2d 959, 962–63 (8th Cir. 1993) (posing for a nude magazine outside work hours is irrelevant to issue of unwelcomeness of sexual advances at work). Confidentiality orders should be presumptively granted as well.

One substantive change made in subdivision (c) is the elimination of the following sentence: "Notwithstanding subdivision (b) of Rule 104, if the relevancy of the evidence which the accused seeks to offer in the trial depends upon the fulfillment of a condition of fact, the court, at the hearing in chambers or at a subsequent hearing in chambers scheduled for such purpose, shall accept evidence on the issue of whether such condition of fact is fulfilled and shall determine such issue." On its face, this language would appear to authorize a trial judge to exclude evidence of past sexual conduct between an alleged victim and an accused or a defendant in a civil case based upon the judge's belief that such past acts did not occur. Such an authorization raises questions of invasion of the right to a jury trial under the Sixth and Seventh Amendments. *See* 1 S. Saltzburg & M. Martin, *Federal Rules of Evidence Manual*, 396–97 (5th ed. 1990).

The Advisory Committee concluded that the amended rule provided adequate protection for all persons claiming to be the victims of sexual misconduct, and that it was inadvisable to continue to include a provision in the rule that has been confusing and that raises substantial constitutional issues.

ADVISORY COMMITTEE'S NOTE (2011 AMENDMENT)

The language of Rule 412 has been amended as part of the restyling of the Evidence Rules to make them more easily understood and to make style and terminology consistent throughout the rules. These changes are intended to be stylistic only. There is no intent to change any result in any ruling on evidence admissibility.

Florida Stat. § 794.022. Rules of Evidence [in Sexual Assault Cases]

(1) The testimony of the victim need not be corroborated in a prosecution under s. 794.011.

(2) Specific instances of prior consensual sexual activity between the victim and any person other than the offender shall not be admitted into evidence in a prosecution under s. 794.011. However, such evidence may be admitted if it is first established to the court in a proceeding in camera that such evidence may prove that the defendant was not the source of the semen, pregnancy, injury, or disease; or, when consent by the victim is at issue, such evidence may be admitted if it is first established to the court in a proceeding in camera that such evidence tends to establish a pattern of conduct or behavior on the part of the victim which is so similar to the conduct or behavior in the case that it is relevant to the issue of consent.

(3) Notwithstanding any other provision of law, reputation evidence relating to a victim's prior sexual conduct or evidence presented for the purpose of showing that manner of dress of the victim at the time of the offense incited the sexual battery shall not be admitted into evidence in a prosecution under s. 794.011.

(4) When consent of the victim is a defense to prosecution under s. 794.011, evidence of the victim's mental incapacity or defect is admissible to prove that the consent was not intelligent, knowing, or voluntary; and the court shall instruct the jury accordingly.

(5) An offender's use of a prophylactic device, or a victim's request that an offender use a prophylactic device, is not, by itself, relevant to either the issue of whether or not the offense was committed or the issue of whether or not the victim consented.

COMMENTARY ON FEDERAL AND FLORIDA RULE DIFFERENCES

While Federal Rule 404 and Florida Stat. § 90.404 in general freely allow evidence of a victim's character to show action in conformity therewith, Florida Stat. § 794.022 and its federal counterpart, Federal Rule 412, significantly restrict the admissibility of such evidence in certain proceedings involving claims of sexual misconduct.

Under the federal rule, unless an exception applies, evidence in any form (specific instances, reputation, or opinion) offered to prove that a victim engaged in other sexual behavior or to prove a victim's sexual predisposition is inadmissible. *See* FED. R. EVID. 412(a). The Florida rule, while worded somewhat differently, covers most of the same types of evidence, providing that unless an exception applies, evidence of specific instances of prior consensual sexual activity between the victim and a person other than the accused, reputation evidence regarding the victim's prior sexual conduct, and any evidence presented for the purpose of showing that the victim's manner of dress at the time of the offense incited the sexual battery are inadmissible. *See* FLA. STAT. § 794.022(2)-(3).

The federal rule applies in a broader scope of proceedings than does the Florida rule. While the federal rule applies in "a civil or criminal proceeding involving alleged sexual misconduct," *see* FED. R. EVID. 412(a), the Florida rule applies only in criminal prosecutions for sexual battery. *See* FLA. STAT. §§ 794.011, 794.022. However, in civil cases, evidence normally barred by Federal Rule 412 is admissible if its probative value substantially outweighs the danger of harm to any victim and unfair prejudice to any party (although even then, reputation evidence is admissible only if it has been placed in controversy by the victim). *See* FED. R. EVID. 412(b)(2); *Judd v. Rodman*, 105 F.3d 1339, 1341-43 (11th Cir. 1997).

In criminal cases, both the federal and Florida rules permit evidence of specific instances of sexual behavior between the victim and the accused offered by the accused to prove consent or offered by the prosecution. *See* FED. R. EVID. 412(b)(1)(B); FLA. STAT. § 794.022(2); *Minus v. State*, 901 So. 2d 344, 349 (Fla. 4th DCA 2005). Both rules in criminal cases also permit evidence of specific instances of sexual behavior by the victim offered to prove that a person other than the accused was the source of semen, injury, or other physical evidence. *See* FED. R. EVID. 412(b)(1)(A); FLA. STAT. § 794.022(2). This latter exception can be invoked, however, only if the prosecution first brings up the existence of the semen, injury, or other physical evidence. *See U.S. v. Richards*, 118 F.3d 622, 623-24 (8th Cir. 1997); *Deel v. State*, 481 So. 2d 15, 16 (Fla. 5th DCA 1985).

In criminal cases, the federal rule contains an exception for "evidence whose exclusion would violate the defendant's constitutional rights." *See* FED. R. EVID. 412(b)(1)(C). While the Florida rule contains no analogous provision, the Florida courts recognize that evidence otherwise excluded by the rule must be admitted if excluding it would violate the defendant's Confrontation Clause right or other constitutional rights. *See Lewis v. State*, 591 So. 2d 922, 925 (Fla. 1991).

The Florida rule contains an exception that allows for evidence of specific instances of prior sexual activity between the victim and persons other than the accused when it "tends to establish a pattern of conduct or behavior on the part of the victim which is so similar to the conduct or behavior in the case that it is relevant to the issue of consent." *See* FLA. STAT. § 794.022(2). For this exception to apply, the pattern "must be so distinctive and so closely resemble the defendant's version of the encounter that it tends to prove that the complainant consented to the acts charged or behaved in such a manner as to lead the defendant reasonably to believe that the complainant consented." *Carlyle v. State*, 945 So. 2d 540, 546 (Fla. 2d DCA 2006); *Kaplan v. State*, 451 So. 2d 1386, 1387 (Fla. 4th DCA 1984). There is no comparable exception to the federal rule.

Florida precedent holds that evidence that the victim has *not* engaged in sexual behavior (i.e., evidence of her chastity or virginity) is *not* barred by the rule. *See Rancourt v. State*, 766 So. 2d 1071, 1073-74 (Fla. 2d DCA 2000); *McLean v. State*, 754 So. 2d 176, 181-82 (Fla. 2d DCA 2000). By contrast, federal authority holds that such evidence is barred by the rule, deeming it to be evidence of "sexual behavior." *See U.S. v. Blue Bird*, 372 F.3d 989, 995 (8th Cir. 2004).

The Florida rule contains several provisions not present in the federal rule. First, it provides that the testimony of the victim need not be corroborated in a prosecution for sexual battery, meaning that her testimony alone is legally sufficient to sustain a conviction. *See* FLA. STAT. § 794.022(1); *Saleem v. State*, 773 So. 2d 89, 89-90 (Fla. 5th DCA 2000). As this addresses the substantive question of sufficiency and not a question of admissibility, the issue is not addressed in the federal rules of evidence.

Second, the Florida rule provides that when consent of the victim is a defense, evidence of the victim's mental incapacity or defect is admissible to prove that the consent was not intelligent, knowing, or voluntarily, and requires that the jury be so instructed. *See* FLA. STAT. § 794.022(4).

Third, the Florida rule provides that evidence that the offender used a prophylactic device either of his own accord or at the victim's request is not, standing alone, "relevant" to the issue whether the offense was committed or whether the victim consented. *See* FLA. STAT. § 794.022(5). This has been interpreted to mean that evidence of condom use is admissible and is a factor that can be argued by counsel and considered by the trier of fact, but is not dispositive, and must be considered in light of other evidence. *See Strong v. State*, 853 So. 2d 1095, 1097-98 (Fla. 3d DCA 2003). Furthermore, although, unlike the previous section, this section does not mandate that a jury instruction be given, the trial court may instruct the jury accordingly. *See id.*

Under the federal rule, a party seeking to invoke any of the exceptions must file written notice at least 14 days before trial, serve the motion on all parties and notify the victim. *See* FED. R. EVID. 412(c)(1). Moreover, the court must hold a hearing *in camera*, give the victim and the parties a right to attend and be heard, and keep the records related to the hearing sealed unless it orders otherwise. *See* FED. R. EVID. 412(c)(2). The Florida rule contains no pre-trial notice requirement, but requires hearings to be held *in camera* when seeking to offer evidence under the exception for evidence that a person other than the accused was the source of semen, injury, or other physical evidence or for evidence of the victim's distinctive pattern of conduct or behavior. *See* FLA. STAT. § 794.022(2).

Federal Rule 413. Similar Crimes in Sexual-Assault Cases

(a) Permitted Uses. In a criminal case in which a defendant is accused of a sexual assault, the court may admit evidence that the defendant committed any other sexual assault. The evidence may be considered on any matter to which it is relevant.

(b) Disclosure to the Defendant. If the prosecutor intends to offer this evidence, the prosecutor must disclose it to the defendant, including witnesses' statements or a summary of the expected testimony. The prosecutor must do so at least 15 days before trial or at a later time that the court allows for good cause.

(c) Effect on Other Rules. This rule does not limit the admission or consideration of evidence under any other rule.

(d) Definition of "Sexual Assault." In this rule and Rule 415, "sexual assault" means a crime under federal law or under state law (as "state" is defined in 18 U.S.C. § 513) involving:

(1) any conduct prohibited by 18 U.S.C. chapter 109A;

(2) contact, without consent, between any part of the defendant's body — or an object — and another person's genitals or anus;

(3) contact, without consent, between the defendant's genitals or anus and any part of another person's body;

(4) deriving sexual pleasure or gratification from inflicting death, bodily injury, or physical pain on another person; or

(5) an attempt or conspiracy to engage in conduct described in subparagraphs (1)–(4).

CONGRESSIONAL DISCUSSION

Floor Statement of the Principal House Sponsor, Representative Susan Molinari, Concerning the Prior Crimes Evidence Rules for Sexual Assault and Child Molestation Cases (Cong.Rec. H8991-92, Aug. 21, 1994):

Mr. Speaker, the revised conference bill contains a critical reform that I have long sought to protect the public from crimes of sexual violence—general rules of admissibility in sexual assault and child molestation cases for evidence that the defendant has committed offenses of the same type on other occasions. The enactment of this reform is first and foremost a triumph for the public—for the women who will not be raped and the children who will not be molested because we have strengthened the legal system's tools for bringing the perpetrators of these atrocious crimes to justice.

Senator Dole and I initially proposed this reform in February of 1991 in the Women's Equal Opportunity Act bill, and we later re-introduced it in the Sexual Assault Prevention Act bills of the 102d and 103d Congresses. The proposal also enjoyed the strong support of the Administration in the 102d Congress, and was included in President Bush's violent crime bill of that Congress, S. 635. The Senate passed the proposed rules on Nov. 5, 1993, by a vote of 75 to 19, in a crime bill amendment offered by Senator Dole. This Chamber endorsed the same rules on June 29, 1994, by a vote of 348 to 62, through a motion to instruct conferees that I offered.

The rules in the revised conference bill are substantially identical to our earlier proposals. We have agreed to a temporary deferral of the effective date of the new rules, pending a report by the Judicial Conference, in order to accommodate procedural objections raised by opponents of the reform. However, regardless of what the Judicial Conference may recommend, the new rules will take effect within at most 300 days of the enactment of this legislation, unless repealed or modified by subsequent legislation.

The need for these rules, their precedential support, their interpretation, and the issues and policy questions they raise have been analyzed at length in the legislative history of this proposal. I would direct the Members' attention particularly to two earlier statements:

The first is the portion of the section-by-section analysis accompanying these rules in section 801 of S. 635, which President Bush transmitted to Congress in 1991. That statement appears on pages S 3238 [to] S 3242 of the daily edition of the Congressional Record for March 13, 1991.

The second is the prepared text of an address—entitled "Evidence of Propensity and Probability in Sex Offense Cases and Other Cases"—by Senior Counsel David J. Karp of the Office of Policy Development of the U.S. Department of Justice. Mr. Karp, who is the author of the new evidence rules, presented this statement on behalf of the Justice Department to the Evidence Section of the Association of American Law Schools on January 9, 1993. The statement provided a detailed account of the views of the legislative sponsors and the Administration concerning the proposed reform, and should also be considered an authoritative part of its legislative history.

These earlier statements address the issues raised by this reform in considerable detail. In my present remarks, I will simply emphasize the following essential points:

The new rules will supersede in sex offense cases the restrictive aspects of Federal Rule of Evidence 404(b). In contrast to Rule 404(b)'s general prohibition of evidence of character or propensity, the new rules for sex offense cases authorize admission and consideration of evidence of an uncharged offense for its bearing "on any matter to which it is relevant." This includes the defendant's propensity to commit sexual assault or child molestation offenses, and assessment of the probability or improbability that the defendant has been falsely or mistakenly accused of such an offense.

In other respects, the general standards of the rules of evidence will continue to apply, including the restrictions on hearsay evidence and the court's authority under Evidence Rule 403 to exclude evidence whose probative value is substantially outweighed by its prejudicial effect. Also, the government (or the plaintiff in a civil case) will generally have to disclose to the defendant any evidence that is to be offered under the new rules at least 15 days before trial.

The proposed reform is critical to the protection of the public from rapists and child molesters, and is justified by the distinctive characteristics of the cases it will affect. In child molestation cases, for example, a history of similar acts tends to be exceptionally probative because it shows an unusual disposition of the defendant—a sexual or sadosexual interest in children— that simply does not exist in ordinary people. Moreover, such cases require reliance on child victims whose credibility can readily be attacked in the absence of substantial corroboration. In such cases, there is a compelling public interest in admitting all significant evidence that will illumine the credibility of the charge and any denial by the defense.

Similarly, adult-victim sexual assault cases are distinctive, and often turn on difficult credibility determinations. Alleged consent by the victim is rarely an issue in prosecutions for other violent crimes—the accused mugger does not claim that the victim freely handed over [his] wallet as a gift—but the defendant in a rape case often contends that the victim engaged in consensual sex and then falsely accused him. Knowledge that the defendant has committed rapes on other occasions is frequently critical in assessing the relative plausibility of these claims and accurately deciding cases that would otherwise become unresolvable swearing matches.

The practical effect of the new rules is to put evidence of uncharged offenses in sexual assault and child molestation cases on the same footing as other types of relevant evidence that are not subject to a special exclusionary rule. The presumption is in favor of admission. The underlying legislative judgment is that the evidence admissible pursuant to the proposed rules is typically relevant and probative, and that its probative value is normally not outweighed by any risk of prejudice or other adverse effects.

In line with this judgment, the rules do not impose arbitrary or artificial restrictions on the admissibility of evidence. Evidence of offenses for which the defendant has not previously been prosecuted or convicted will be admissible, as well as evidence of prior convictions. No time limit is imposed on the uncharged offenses for which evidence may be admitted; as a practical matter, evidence of other sex offenses by the defendant is often probative and properly admitted, notwithstanding very substantial lapses of time in relation to the charged offense or offenses. See, e.g., United States v. Hadley, 918 F.2d 848, 850–51 (9th Cir. 1990), cert. dismissed, 113 S.Ct. 486 (1992) (evidence of offenses occurring up to 15 years earlier admitted); State v. Plymate, 345 N.W.2d 327 (Neb.1984) (evidence of defendant's commission of other child molestations more than 20 years earlier admitted).

Finally, the practical efficacy of these rules will depend on faithful execution by judges of the will of Congress in adopting this critical reform. To implement the legislative intent, the courts must liberally construe these rules to provide the basis for a fully informed decision of sexual assault and child molestation cases, including assessment of the defendant's propensities and questions of probability in light of the defendant's past conduct.

ADVISORY COMMITTEE'S NOTE (2011 AMENDMENT)

The language of Rule 413 has been amended as part of the restyling of the Evidence Rules to make them more easily understood and to make style and terminology consistent throughout the rules. These changes are intended to be stylistic only. There is no intent to change any result in any ruling on evidence admissibility.

Florida Stat. § 90.404. Character Evidence; When Admissible

....

(2) Other crimes, wrongs, or acts.

....

(c) 1. In a criminal case in which the defendant is charged with a sexual offense, evidence of the defendant's commission of other crimes, wrongs, or acts involving a sexual offense is admissible and may be considered for its bearing on any matter to which it is relevant.

2. For the purposes of this paragraph, the term "sexual offense" means conduct proscribed by s. 787.025(2)(c), s. 794.011, excluding s. 794.011(10), s. 794.05, s. 796.03, s. 796.035, s. 796.045, s. 825.1025(2)(b), s. 827.071, s. 847.0135(5), s. 847.0145, or s. 985.701(1).

(d) 1. When the state in a criminal action intends to offer evidence of other criminal offenses under paragraph (a), paragraph (b), or paragraph (c), no fewer than 10 days before trial, the state shall furnish to the defendant or to the defendant's counsel a written statement of the acts or offenses it intends to offer, describing them with the particularity required of an indictment or information. No notice is required for evidence of offenses used for impeachment or on rebuttal.

2. When the evidence is admitted, the court shall, if requested, charge the jury on the limited purpose for which the evidence is received and is to be considered. After the close of the evidence, the jury shall be instructed on the limited purpose for which the evidence was received and that the defendant cannot be convicted for a charge not included in the indictment or information.

....

COMMENTARY ON FEDERAL AND FLORIDA RULE DIFFERENCES

Florida Stat. § 90.404(2)(c) and its federal counterpart, Federal Rule 413 deem admissible in criminal cases in which the defendant is charged with sexual assault evidence of the defendant's commission of other acts of sexual assault. Unlike "other acts" evidence used under Federal Rule 404(b)(2) or Florida Stat. § 90.404(2)(a), such evidence may be considered for its bearing on any matter to which it is relevant, including as showing that the defendant has a propensity to engage in such acts. *See, e.g.*, *U.S. v. Sioux*, 362 F.3d 1241, 1244 (9th Cir. 2004).

Both rules allow for the admission of not only evidence of misconduct for which the accused was convicted, but also evidence of uncharged misconduct. For such evidence to be admitted under the federal rule, the trial court need only determine that there is sufficient evidence that the jury could find by a preponderance of the evidence that the incident occurred, thus treating it as a question of conditional relevancy. *See* *U.S. v. Enjady*, 134 F.3d 1427, 1433 (10th Cir. 1998). The Florida rule was enacted by the legislature in 2011 and so there is no precedent directly on point. However, the Florida Supreme Court has interpreted the analogous provision dealing with evidence of child molestation to permit admission only if the trial court finds by clear and convincing evidence that the person committed the prior act, thus *not* treating it as a question of conditional relevancy and setting a higher standard of proof. *See* *McLean v. State*, 934 So. 2d 1248, 1256 (Fla. 2006).

The types of other acts encompassed by the two rules differ slightly, with the federal rule referencing acts defined under federal statutes as well as other types of specified acts, and the Florida rule referencing acts defined under Florida statutes. *Compare* FED. R. EVID. 413(d), *with* FLA. STAT. § 90.404(2)(c)(2).

If a party intends to offer evidence under the federal provision, they are required to disclose the evidence to the defendant at least 15 days before trial unless the court for good cause permits disclosure to occur at a later date. *See* FED. R. EVID. 413(b). Under the Florida rule, such disclosure must occur 10 days before trial. *See* FLA. STAT. § 90.404(2)(d)(1).

As with all evidence offered under Florida Stat. § 90.404(2), upon request, the trial court must instruct the jury of the limited purpose for which the evidence has been admitted. *See* FLA. STAT. § 90.404(2)(d)(2). While a similar provision is not contained in the federal rule, the same result can be achieved by invoking the general rule governing limited admissibility. *See* FED. R. EVID. 105.

Even if evidence satisfies the requirements of these rules, both federal and Florida cases hold that such evidence is still subject to exclusion under Florida Stat. § 90.403 or Federal Rule 403, respectively. *See, e.g.*, *U.S. v. Julian*, 427 F.3d 471, 487 (7th Cir. 2005); *McLean*, 934 So. 2d at 1259-62.

Federal Rule 414. Similar Crimes in Child-Molestation Cases

(a) **Permitted Uses.** In a criminal case in which a defendant is accused of child molestation, the court may admit evidence that the defendant committed any other child molestation. The evidence may be considered on any matter to which it is relevant.

(b) **Disclosure to the Defendant.** If the prosecutor intends to offer this evidence, the prosecutor must disclose it to the defendant, including witnesses' statements or a summary of the expected testimony. The prosecutor must do so at least 15 days before trial or at a later time that the court allows for good cause.

(c) **Effect on Other Rules.** This rule does not limit the admission or consideration of evidence under any other rule.

(d) **Definition of "Child" and "Child Molestation."** In this rule and Rule 415:

(1) "child" means a person below the age of 14; and

(2) "child molestation" means a crime under federal law or under state law (as "state" is defined in 18 U.S.C. § 513) involving:

(A) any conduct prohibited by 18 U.S.C. chapter 109A and committed with a child;

(B) any conduct prohibited by 18 U.S.C. chapter 110;

(C) contact between any part of the defendant's body — or an object — and a child's genitals or anus;

(D) contact between the defendant's genitals or anus and any part of a child's body;

(E) deriving sexual pleasure or gratification from inflicting death, bodily injury, or physical pain on a child; or

(F) an attempt or conspiracy to engage in conduct described in subparagraphs (A)–(E).

CONGRESSIONAL DISCUSSION

See Floor Statement following Rule 413.

ADVISORY COMMITTEE'S NOTE (2011 AMENDMENT)

The language of Rule 414 has been amended as part of the restyling of the Evidence Rules to make them more easily understood and to make style and terminology consistent throughout the rules. These changes are intended to be stylistic only. There is no intent to change any result in any ruling on evidence admissibility.

Florida Stat. § 90.404. Character Evidence; When Admissible

....

(2) Other crimes, wrongs, or acts.

....

(b) 1. In a criminal case in which the defendant is charged with a crime involving child molestation, evidence of the defendant's commission of other crimes, wrongs, or acts of child molestation is admissible, and may be considered for its bearing on any matter to which it is relevant.

2. For the purposes of this paragraph, the term "child molestation" means conduct proscribed by s. 787.025(2)(c), s. 794.011, excluding s. 794.011(10), s. 794.05, s. 796.03, s. 796.035, s. 796.045, s. 800.04, s. 827.071, s. 847.0135(5), s. 847.0145, or s. 985.701(1) when committed against a person 16 years of age or younger.

....

(d) 1. When the state in a criminal action intends to offer evidence of other criminal offenses under paragraph (a), paragraph (b), or paragraph (c), no fewer than 10 days before trial, the state shall furnish to the defendant or to the defendant's counsel a written statement of the acts or offenses it intends to offer, describing them with the particularity required of an indictment or information. No notice is required for evidence of offenses used for impeachment or on rebuttal.

2. When the evidence is admitted, the court shall, if requested, charge the jury on the limited purpose for which the evidence is received and is to be considered. After the close of the evidence, the jury shall be instructed on the limited purpose for which the evidence was received and that the defendant cannot be convicted for a charge not included in the indictment or information.

....

COMMENTARY ON FEDERAL AND FLORIDA RULE DIFFERENCES

Florida Stat. § 90.404(2)(b) and its federal counterpart, Federal Rule 414, deem admissible in criminal cases in which the defendant is charged with child molestation evidence of the defendant's commission of other acts of child molestation. Unlike "other acts" evidence used under Federal Rule 404(b)(2) or Florida Stat. § 90.404(2)(a), such evidence may be considered for its bearing on any matter to which it is relevant, including as showing that the defendant has a propensity to engage in such acts. See, e.g., U.S. v. LeMay, 260 F.3d 1018, 1024-26 (9th Cir. 2001). The Florida rule is modeled after and described as "virtually identical" to the federal rule, see McLean v. State, 854 So. 2d 796, 802 (Fla. 2d DCA 2003); Fla. S. Comm. on Com., CS for SB 2012 (2001) Staff Analysis (Apr. 18, 2001). Nonetheless, there are a number of differences between the two provisions.

First, while the word "child" as used in the federal rule refers to a person below the age of fourteen, that word as used in the Florida rule refers to a person sixteen years of age or younger. Compare FED. R. EVID. 414(d)(1), with FLA. STAT. § 90.404(2)(b)(2). Second, the definitions of "child molestation" are slightly different under the two rules, with the federal rule referencing acts defined under federal statutes as well as other types of specified acts, and the Florida rule referencing acts defined under Florida statutes. Compare FED. R. EVID. 414(d)(2), with FLA. STAT. § 90.404(2)(b)(2).

Both rules allow for the admission of not just evidence of misconduct for which the accused was convicted, but also evidence of uncharged misconduct. For such evidence to be admitted under the federal rule, the trial court need only determine that there is sufficient evidence that the jury could find by a preponderance of the evidence that the incident occurred, thus treating it as a question of conditional relevancy. *U.S. v. Norris*, 428 F.3d 907, 913-14 (9th Cir. 2005). By contrast, such evidence is admissible under the Florida rule only if the trial court finds by clear and convincing evidence that the person committed the prior act, thus *not* treating it as a question of conditional relevancy and setting a higher standard of proof. *See McLean v. State*, 934 So. 2d 1248, 1256 (Fla. 2006).

If a party intends to offer evidence under the federal provision, they are required to disclose the evidence to the defendant at least 15 days before trial unless the court for good cause permits disclosure to occur at a later date. *See* FED. R. EVID. 414(b). Under the Florida rule, such disclosure must occur 10 days before trial. *See* FLA. STAT. § 90.404(2)(d)(1).

As with all evidence offered under Florida Stat. § 90.404(2), upon request, the trial court must instruct the jury of the limited purpose for which the evidence has been admitted. *See* FLA. STAT. § 90.404(2)(d)(2). While a similar provision is not contained in the federal rule, the same result can be achieved by invoking the general rule governing limited admissibility. *See* FED. R. EVID. 105.

Even if evidence satisfies the requirements of these rules, both federal and Florida cases hold that such evidence is still subject to exclusion under Florida Stat. § 90.403 or Federal Rule 403, respectively. *See U.S. v. Carino*, 368 Fed. Appx. 929, 930 (11th Cir. 2010); *U.S. v. LeMay*, 260 F.3d 1018, 1026-27 (9th Cir. 2001); *U.S. v. Castillo*, 140 F.3d 874, 882 (10th Cir. 1998); *McLean*, 934 So. 2d at 1259-62.

Federal Rule 415. Similar Acts in Civil Cases Involving Sexual Assault or Child Molestation

(a) **Permitted Uses.** In a civil case involving a claim for relief based on a party's alleged sexual assault or child molestation, the court may admit evidence that the party committed any other sexual assault or child molestation. The evidence may be considered as provided in Rules 413 and 414.

(b) **Disclosure to the Opponent.** If a party intends to offer this evidence, the party must disclose it to the party against whom it will be offered, including witnesses' statements or a summary of the expected testimony. The party must do so at least 15 days before trial or at a later time that the court allows for good cause.

(c) **Effect on Other Rules.** This rule does not limit the admission or consideration of evidence under any other rule.

CONGRESSIONAL DISCUSSION

See Floor Statement following Rule 413.

ADVISORY COMMITTEE'S NOTE (2011 AMENDMENT)

The language of Rule 415 has been amended as part of the restyling of the Evidence Rules to make them more easily understood and to make style and terminology consistent throughout the rules. These changes are intended to be stylistic only. There is no intent to change any result in any ruling on evidence admissibility.

COMMENTARY ON FEDERAL AND FLORIDA RULE DIFFERENCES

Federal Rule 415 deems admissible in civil cases in which a claim is predicated on a party's alleged commission of conduct constituting an offense of sexual assault or child molestation, evidence of the party's commission of other acts of sexual assault or child molestation. Unlike "other acts" evidence used under Federal Rule 404(b), such evidence may be considered for its bearing on any matter to which it is relevant, including as showing that the defendant has a propensity to engage in such acts. *See Doe ex. rel. Rudy-Glanzer v. Glanzer*, 232 F.3d 1258, 1267-68 (9th Cir. 2000).

The rule allows for the admission of not only evidence of misconduct for which the accused was convicted, but also evidence of uncharged misconduct. For such evidence to be admitted, the trial court need only determine that there is sufficient evidence that the jury could find by a preponderance of the evidence that the incident occurred, thus treating it as a question of conditional relevancy. *See, e.g., Johnson v. Elk Lake Sch. Dist.*, 283 F.3d 138, 151-55 (3d Cir. 2002).

If a party intends to offer evidence under this provision, they are required to disclose the evidence to the defendant at least 15 days before trial unless the court for good cause permits disclosure to occur at a later date. *See* FED. R. EVID. 415(b).

Even if evidence satisfies the requirements of Federal Rule 415, such evidence is still subject to exclusion under Federal Rule 403. *See Blind-Doan v. Sanders*, 291 F.3d 1079, 1082-83 (9th Cir. 2002); *Johnson*, 283 F.3d at 155.

There is no comparable provision in the Florida Evidence Code. While the Florida legislature recently enacted provisions equivalent to Federal Rules 413 (evidence of similar crimes in sexual-assault cases) and 414 (evidence of similar crimes in child molestation cases), *see* Commentary to FED. R. EVID. 413, 414 and FLA. STAT. § 90.404, it did not create one equivalent to Federal Rule 415. Evidence of "other acts" of sexual assault can be offered in sexual assault prosecutions in Florida courts under Florida Stat. § 90.404(2)(a) to prove such things as motive, opportunity, intent, preparation, plan, knowledge, identity, or absence of mistake or accident, but unlike with Federal Rule 415, cannot be offered to prove a propensity to engage in such acts. *See Zack v. State*, 753 So. 2d 9, 16-17 (Fla. 2000); *Houston v. State*, 852 So. 2d 425, 426-27 (Fla. 5th DCA 2003); *Geldreich v. State*, 763 So. 2d 1114, 1117-18 (Fla. 4th DCA 1999); *Johnson v. State*, 717 So. 2d 1057, 1065 (Fla. 1st DCA 1998); *Vural v. State*, 717 So. 2d 65, 66-67 (3d DCA 1998). While no cases specifically hold that evidence of other acts of sexual assault or child molestation are admissible in a civil case in which a claim is predicated on a party's alleged commission of conduct constituting an offense of sexual assault or child molestation, the Florida courts have, in dicta, indicated that Florida Stat. § 90.404(2)(a) can be invoked in a civil case. *See State v. Storer*, 920 So. 2d 754, 756-57 (Fla. 2d DCA 2006); *Washington v. State*, 737 So. 2d 1208, 1223 (Fla. 1st DCA 1999).

ARTICLE V. PRIVILEGES

Federal Rule	Florida Stat. §	Description
501	90.501	Privilege in General
—	90.5015	Journalist's Privilege
—	90.502	Lawyer-Client Privilege
—	90.5021	Fiduciary Lawyer-Client Privilege
—	90.503	Psychotherapist-Patient Privilege
—	90.5035	Sexual Assault Counselor-Victim Privilege
—	90.5036	Domestic Violence Advocate-Victim Privilege
—	90.504	Husband-Wife Privilege
—	90.505	Privilege With Respect to Communications to Clergy
—	90.5055	Accountant-Client Privilege
—	90.506	Privilege With Respect to Trade Secrets
502	90.507	Waiver of Privilege by Voluntary Disclosure
—	90.508	Privileged Matter Disclosed Under Compulsion or Without Opportunity to Claim Privilege
—	90.509	Application of Privileged Communication
—	90.510	Privileged Communication Necessary to Adverse Party

Federal Rule 501. Privilege in General

The common law — as interpreted by United States courts in the light of reason and experience — governs a claim of privilege unless any of the following provides otherwise:

- the United States Constitution;

- a federal statute; or

- rules prescribed by the Supreme Court.

But in a civil case, state law governs privilege regarding a claim or defense for which state law supplies the rule of decision.

REPORT OF HOUSE COMMITTEE ON THE JUDICIARY

Article V as submitted to Congress contained thirteen Rules. Nine of those Rules defined specific non-constitutional privileges which the federal courts must recognize (i.e. required reports, lawyer-client, psychotherapist-patient, husband-wife, communications to clergymen, political vote, trade secrets, secrets of state and other official information, and identity of informer.) Another Rule provided that only those privileges set forth in Article V or in some other Act of Congress could be recognized by the federal courts. The three remaining Rules addressed collateral problems as to waiver of privilege by voluntary disclosure, privileged matter disclosed under compulsion or without opportunity to claim privilege, comment upon or inference from a claim of privilege, and jury instruction with regard thereto.

The Committee amended Article V to eliminate all of the Court's specific Rules on privileges. Instead, the Committee, through a single Rule, 501, left the law of privileges in its present state and further provided that privileges shall continue to be developed by the courts of the United States under a uniform standard applicable both in civil and criminal cases. That standard, derived from Rule 26 of the Federal Rules of Criminal Procedure, mandates the application of the principles of the common law as interpreted by the courts of the United States in the light of reason and experience. The words "person, government, State, or political subdivision thereof " were added by the Committee to the lone term "witnesses" used in Rule 26 to make clear that, as under present law, not only witnesses may have privileges. The Committee also included in its amendment a proviso modeled after Rule 302 and similar to language added by the Committee to Rule 601 relating to the competency of witnesses. The proviso is designed to require the application of State privilege law in civil actions and proceedings governed by *Erie R. Co.* v. *Tompkins*, 304 U.S. 64 (1938), a result in accord with current federal court decisions. See *Republic Gear Co.* v. *Borg-Warner Corp.*, 381 F.2d 551, 555–556 n. 2 (2nd Cir. 1967). The Committee deemed the proviso to be necessary in the light of the Advisory Committee's view (see its note to Court Rule 501) that this result is not mandated under *Erie*.

The rationale underlying the proviso is that federal law should not supersede that of the States in substantive areas such as privilege absent a compelling reason. The Committee believes that in civil cases in the federal courts where an element of a claim or defense is not grounded upon a federal question, there is no federal interest strong enough to justify departure from State policy. In addition, the Committee considered that the Court's proposed Article V would have promoted forum shopping in some civil actions, depending upon differences in the privilege law applied as among the State and federal courts. The Committee's proviso, on the other hand, under which the federal courts are bound to apply the State's privilege law in actions founded upon a State-created right or defense, removes the incentive to "shop."

REPORT OF SENATE COMMITTEE ON THE JUDICIARY

Article V as submitted to Congress contained 13 rules. Nine of those rules defined specific nonconstitutional privileges which the Federal courts must recognize (i.e. required reports, lawyer-client, psychotherapist-patient, husband-wife, communications to clergymen, political vote, trade secrets, secrets of state and other official information, and identity of informer). Many of these rules contained controversial modifications or restrictions upon common law privileges. As noted supra, the House amended article V to eliminate all of the Court's specific rules on privileges. Through a single rule, 501, the House provided that privileges shall be governed by the principles of the common law as interpreted by the courts of the United States in the light of reason and experience (a standard derived from rule 26 of the Federal Rules of Criminal Procedure) except in the case of an element of a civil claim or defense as to which State law supplies the rule of decision in which event state privilege law was to govern.

The committee agrees with the main thrust of the House amendment: that a federally developed common law based on modern reason and experience shall apply except where the State nature of the issues renders deference to State privilege law the wiser course, as in the usual diversity case. The committee understands that thrust of the House amendment to require that State privilege law be applied in "diversity" cases (actions on questions of State law between citizens of different States arising under 28 U.S.C. § 1332). The language of the House amendment, however, goes beyond this in some respects, and falls short of it in others: State privilege law applies even in nondiversity, Federal question civil cases, where an issue governed by State substantive law is the object of the evidence (such issues do sometimes arise in such cases); and, in all instances where State privilege law is to be applied, e.g., on proof of a State issue in a diversity case, a close reading reveals that State privilege law is not to be applied unless the matter to be proved is an element of that state claim or defense, as distinguished from a step along the way in the proof of it.

The committee is concerned that the language used in the House amendment could be difficult to apply. It provides that "in civil actions...with respect to an element of a claim or defense as to which State law supplies the rule of decision," State law on privilege applies. The question of what is an element of a claim or defense is likely to engender considerable litigation. If the matter in question constitutes an element of a claim, State law supplies the privilege rule; whereas if it is a mere item of proof with respect to a claim, then, even though State law might supply the rule of decision, Federal law on the privilege would apply. Further, disputes will arise as to how the rule should be applied in an antitrust action or in a tax case where the Federal statute is silent as to a particular aspect of the substantive law in question, but Federal cases had incorporated State law by reference to State law.[15] Is a claim (or defense) based on such a reference a claim or defense as to which federal or State law supplies the rule of decision?

Another problem not entirely avoidable is the complexity or difficulty the rule introduces into the trial of a Federal case containing a combination of Federal and State claims and defenses, e.g. an action involving Federal antitrust and State unfair competition claims. Two different bodies of privilege law would need to be consulted. It may even develop that the same witness-testimony might be relevant on both counts and privileged as to one but not the other.[16]

The formulation adopted by the House is pregnant with litigious mischief. The committee has, therefore, adopted what we believe will be a clearer and more practical guideline for determining when courts should respect State rules of privilege. Basically, it provides that in criminal and Federal question civil cases, federally evolved rules on privilege should apply since it is Federal policy which is being enforced.[17] Conversely, in diversity cases where the litigation in question turns on a substantive question

---

[15] For a discussion of reference to State substantive law, see note on Federal Incorporation by Reference of State Law, Hart & Wechsler, The Federal Courts and the Federal System, pp. 491–94 (2d ed. 1973).

[16] The problems with the House formulation are discussed in Rothstein, The Proposed Amendments to the Federal Rules of Evidence, 62 Georgetown University Law Journal 125 (1973) at notes 25, 26 and 70–74 and accompanying text.

[17] It is also intended that the Federal law of privileges should be applied with respect to pendant State law claims when they arise in a Federal question case.

of State law, and is brought in the Federal courts because the parties reside in different States, the committee believes it is clear that State rules of privilege should apply unless the proof is directed at a claim or defense for which Federal law supplies the rule of decision (a situation which would not commonly arise.)[18] It is intended that the State rules of privilege should apply equally in original diversity actions and diversity actions removed under 28 U.S.C. § 1441(b).

Two other comments on the privilege rule should be made. The committee has received a considerable volume of correspondence from psychiatric organizations and psychiatrists concerning the deletion of rule 504 of the rule submitted by the Supreme Court. It should be clearly understood that, in approving this general rule as to privileges, the action of Congress should not be understood as disapproving any recognition of a psychiatrist-patient, or husband-wife, or any other of the enumerated privileges contained in the Supreme Court rules. Rather, our action should be understood as reflecting the view that the recognition of a privilege based on a confidential relationship and other privileges should be determined on a case-by-case basis.

Further, we would understand that the prohibition against spouses testifying against each other is considered a rule of privilege and covered by this rule and not by rule 601 of the competency of witnesses.

CONFERENCE REPORT

Rule 501 deals with the privilege of a witness not to testify. Both the House and Senate bills provide that federal privilege law applies in criminal cases. In civil actions and proceedings, the House bill provides that state privilege law applies "to an element of a claim or defense as to which State law supplies the rule of decision." The Senate bill provides that "in civil actions and proceedings arising under 28 U.S.C. § 1332 or 28 U.S.C. § 1335, or between citizens of different States and removed under 28 U.S.C. § 1441(b) the privilege of a witness, person, government, State or political subdivision thereof is determined in accordance with State law, unless with respect to the particular claim or defense, Federal law supplies the rule of decision."

The wording of the House and Senate bills differs in the treatment of civil actions and proceedings. The rule in the House bill applies to evidence that relates to "an element of a claim or defense." If an item of proof tends to support or defeat a claim or defense, or an element of a claim or defense, and if state law supplies the rule of decision for that claim or defense, then state privilege law applies to that item of proof.

Under the provision in the House bill, therefore, state privilege law will usually apply in diversity cases. There may be diversity cases, however, where a claim or defense is based upon federal law. In such instances, federal privilege law will apply to evidence relevant to the federal claim or defense. See *Sola Electric Co.* v. *Jefferson Electric Co.*, 317 U.S. 173 (1942).

In nondiversity jurisdiction civil cases, federal privilege law will generally apply. In those situations where a federal court adopts or incorporates state law to fill interstices or gaps in federal statutory phrases, the court generally will apply federal privilege law. As Justice Jackson has said:

---

[18] While such a situation might require use of two bodies of privilege law, federal and state, in the same case, nevertheless the occasions on which this would be required are considerably reduced as compared with the House version, and confined to situations where the Federal and State interests are such as to justify application of neither privilege law to the case as a whole. If the rule proposed here results in two conflicting bodies of privilege law applying to the same piece of evidence in the same case, it is contemplated that the rule favoring reception of the evidence should be applied. This policy is based on the present rule 43(a) of the Federal Rules of Civil Procedure which provides: In any case, the statute or rule which favors the reception of the evidence governs and the evidence shall be presented according to the most convenient method prescribed in any of the statutes or rules to which reference is herein made.

A federal court sitting in a non-diversity case such as this does not sit as a local tribunal. In some cases it may see fit for special reasons to give the law of a particular state highly persuasive or even controlling effect, but in the last analysis its decision turns upon the law of the United States, not that of any state.

D'Oench, Duhme & Co. v. Federal Deposit Insurance Corp., 315 U.S. 447, 471 (1942) (Jackson, J., concurring). When a federal court chooses to absorb state law, it is applying the state law as a matter of federal common law. Thus, state law does not supply the rule of decision (even though the federal court may apply a rule derived from state decisions), and state privilege law would not apply. See C.A. Wright, *Federal Courts* 251–252 (2d ed. 1970); *Holmberg v. Armbrecht*, 327 U.S. 392 (1946); *DeSylva v. Ballentine*, 351 U.S. 570, 581 (1956); 9 Wright & Miller, *Federal Rules and Procedure* § 2408.

In civil actions and proceedings, where the rule of decision as to a claim or defense or as to an element of a claim or defense is supplied by state law, the House provision requires that state privilege law apply.

The Conference adopts the House provision.

ADVISORY COMMITTEE'S NOTE (2011 AMENDMENT)

The language of Rule 501 has been amended as part of the restyling of the Evidence Rules to make them more easily understood and to make style and terminology consistent throughout the rules. These changes are intended to be stylistic only. There is no intent to change any result in any ruling on evidence admissibility.

Florida Stat. § 90.501. Privileges Recognized Only as Provided

Except as otherwise provided by this chapter, any other statute, or the Constitution of the United States or of the State of Florida, no person in a legal proceeding has a privilege to:

(1) Refuse to be a witness.

(2) Refuse to disclose any matter.

(3) Refuse to produce any object or writing.

(4) Prevent another from being a witness, from disclosing any matter, or from producing any object or writing.

SPONSORS' NOTE (1976 ENACTMENT)

This section abolishes all common-law privileges existing in Florida and makes the creation of privileges dependent upon legislative action or pursuant to the Supreme Court's rule-making power.

This chapter does not address itself to constitutional protections surrounding an accused. For example, the privilege against self-incrimination is not affected. See Boynton v. State, 75 So. 2d 211, 213 (Fla. 1954). The privilege to exclude unlawfully seized evidence and illegally obtained confessions is provided for under Rule 3.190 of the Florida Rules of Criminal Procedure. Similarly, this chapter does not affect the prosecution's privilege not to reveal the identity of an informer under certain circumstances. These areas of the law receive the continual attention of both state and federal court systems, making a current codification of enduring validity a difficult, if not impossible, task.

Similar provisions are contained in Fed. Rule Evid. 501 and Calif. Evid. Code § 911.

COMMENTARY ON FEDERAL AND FLORIDA RULE DIFFERENCES

Florida Stat. § 90.501 and its federal counterpart, Federal Rule 501, set forth the general rule with respect to privileges.

As originally drafted, the federal rules of evidence would have set forth nine specific testimonial privileges that would have applied to all proceedings in federal court, with the courts having no authority to create new privileges or alter existing privileges through common law decisionmaking. *See* Proposed FED. R. EVID. 501-513. However, Congress rejected that proposal and replaced it with a single rule, Federal Rule 501. Under that rule, the existence and scope of federal privileges are to be governed by the principles of the common law as they may be interpreted by the courts of the United States "in the light of reason and experience."

The Supreme Court has, in a series of cases, identified several factors that the courts are to take into account in determining whether "reason and experience" support the creation of a new privilege or the modification or elimination of an existing one. *See, e.g., Jaffee v. Redmond*, 518 U.S. 1 (1996); *University of Pennsylvania v. EEOC*, 493 U.S. 182 (1990); *U.S. v. Gillock*, 445 U.S. 360 (1980); *Trammel v. United States*, 445 U.S. 40 (1980). First, a court is to determine whether the privilege furthers an important public interest by asking whether and how recognizing or modifying a privilege would alter behavior, and whether such changes advance a public good. Second, a court is to balance this benefit against the cost of recognizing the privilege, namely, the extent to which it would impair the truth-seeking process by excluding relevant, reliable evidence. Third, a court should consider how many states have recognized or modified the privilege. The existence of a broad consensus in state law supporting the privilege indicates that "reason and experience" support recognition of the privilege under federal law. Fourth, a court should look to whether or not the privilege was among the nine evidentiary privileges recommended by the Advisory Committee and rejected by Congress, with inclusion on that original list weighing in favor of recognizing the privilege and exclusion weighing against recognition. Finally, a court should be extremely reluctant to recognize a privilege under Rule 501 if Congress has considered the question whether to create such a privilege by way of statute but has declined to do so. *See In re Subpoena Issued to Commodity Futures Trading Commission*, 370 F. Supp. 2d 201, 208-09 (D.D.C. 2005) (summarizing Supreme Court precedent), *aff'd in part on other grounds*, 439 F.3d 740 (D.C. Cir. 2006).

The treatment of privileges under the Florida Evidence Code, by contrast, closely resembles the proposed but rejected scheme under the federal rules of evidence. FLA. STAT. § 90.501 provides that, unless otherwise provided in the Florida Evidence Code or other source of law, a person has no privilege to refuse to be a witness, refuse to disclose any matter, refuse to produce an object or writing, or prevent another person from doing the same. Thus, unlike Federal Rule 501, which gives the courts flexibility to develop the rules of privilege on a case-by-case basis, the Florida courts are barred from developing new privileges through common law decisionmaking. *See Guerrier v. State*, 811 So. 2d 852, 854 (Fla. 5th DCA 2002); *State v. Castellano*, 460 So. 2d 480, 481 (Fla. 2d DCA 1984); *Marshall v. Anderson*, 459 So. 2d 384, 386 (Fla. 3d DCA 1984).

The Florida Evidence Code sets forth nine different privileges. *See* FLA. STAT. §§ 90.5015-90.506. The commentary following each of those provisions examines the existence and scope of those privileges under the case law applying Federal Rule 501. In addition, certain Florida laws outside of the evidence code are relevant in determining whether or not evidence is privileged. *See, e.g.,* FLA. STAT. § 39.204 (abrogating all privileges except the attorney-client and clergy privileges for communications involving the alleged perpetrator in any situation involving known or suspected child abuse, abandonment, or neglect).

Under Federal Rule 501, in civil actions in which state law supplies the rule of decision—typically diversity actions—the court applies state rather than federal privilege law. A federal court exercising jurisdiction over such a claim looks at the law of the state in which it sits, including that state's choice of law rules, to determine which state's privilege law to apply in disputes with multi-state contacts. *See Pritchard-Keang Nam Corp. v. Jaworski*, 751 F.2d 277, 281 n.4 (8th Cir. 1984). If a federal court is adjudicating a mix of federal and state law claims, federal privilege law applies, even if the witness' testimony is relevant to a state law claim that would otherwise be controlled by a contrary state privilege. *See Hancock v. Hobbs*, 967 F.2d 462, 466-67 (11th Cir. 1992). By contrast, the Florida courts, even when adjudicating only a federal claim, apply Florida privilege law. *See Royal Caribbean Corp. v. Modesto*, 614 So. 2d 517, 519 (Fla. 3d DCA 1992).

Florida Stat. § 90.5015. Journalist's Privilege

(1) Definitions. For purposes of this section, the term:

(a) "Professional journalist" means a person regularly engaged in collecting, photographing, recording, writing, editing, reporting, or publishing news, for gain or livelihood, who obtained the information sought while working as a salaried employee of, or independent contractor for, a newspaper, news journal, news agency, press association, wire service, radio or television station, network, or news magazine. Book authors and others who are not professional journalists, as defined in this paragraph, are not included in the provisions of this section.

(b) "News" means information of public concern relating to local, statewide, national, or worldwide issues or events.

(2) Privilege. A professional journalist has a qualified privilege not to be a witness concerning, and not to disclose the information, including the identity of any source, that the professional journalist has obtained while actively gathering news. This privilege applies only to information or eyewitness observations obtained within the normal scope of employment and does not apply to physical evidence, eyewitness observations, or visual or audio recording of crimes. A party seeking to overcome this privilege must make a clear and specific showing that:

(a) The information is relevant and material to unresolved issues that have been raised in the proceeding for which the information is sought;

(b) The information cannot be obtained from alternative sources; and

(c) A compelling interest exists for requiring disclosure of the information.

(3) Disclosure. A court shall order disclosure pursuant to subsection (2) only of that portion of the information for which the showing under subsection (2) has been made and shall support such order with clear and specific findings made after a hearing.

(4) Waiver. A professional journalist does not waive the privilege by publishing or broadcasting information.

(5) Construction. This section must not be construed to limit any privilege or right provided to a professional journalist under law.

(6) Authentication. Photographs, diagrams, video recordings, audio recordings, computer records, or other business records maintained, disclosed, provided, or produced by a professional journalist, or by the employer or principal of a professional journalist, may be authenticated for admission in evidence upon a showing, by affidavit of the professional journalist, or other individual with personal knowledge, that the photograph, diagram, video recording, audio recording, computer record, or other business record is a true and accurate copy of the original, and that the copy truly and accurately reflects the observations and facts contained therein.

(7) Accuracy of evidence. If the affidavit of authenticity and accuracy, or other relevant factual circumstance, causes the court to have clear and convincing doubts as to the authenticity or accuracy of the proferred evidence, the court may decline to admit such evidence.

(8) Severability. If any provision of this section or its application to any particular person or circumstance is held invalid, that provision or its application is severable and does not affect the validity of other provisions or applications of this section.

COMMENTARY ON FEDERAL AND FLORIDA RULE DIFFERENCES

Florida Stat. § 90.5015 gives a professional journalist a privilege not to be a witness concerning, and not to disclose, information (including the identity of a source) obtained while actively gathering news. See FLA. STAT. § 90.5015(2). The phrase "professional journalist" is narrowly defined to include only those regularly engaged in collecting, photographing, recording, writing, editing, reporting, or publishing news for gain or livelihood who obtained the information while working as a salaried employee of, or independent contractor for, a newspaper, news journal, news agency, press association, wire service, radio or television station, network, or news magazine. See FLA. STAT. § 90.5015(1)(a). All others, including book authors, are excluded from the definition. See id. Moreover, the privilege applies only to information or eyewitness observations obtained within the normal scope of employment and does not apply to physical evidence of crimes, eyewitness observations of crimes, or visual or audio recordings of crimes. See FLA. STAT. § 90.5015(2); News-Journal Corp. v. Carson, 741 So. 2d 572, 574-75 (Fla. 5th DCA 1999). Unlike most other privileges, it applies to confidential as well as non-confidential information. See Ulrich v. Coast Dental Servs., Inc., 739 So. 2d 142, 143 (Fla. 5th DCA 1999).

However, even if the requirements for invoking the privilege are satisfied, the privilege is only a qualified one, and can be overcome by a clear and specific showing that (1) the information is relevant and material to unresolved issues that have been raised in the proceeding for which the information is sought; (2) the information cannot be obtained from alternative sources; and (3) a compelling interest exists for requiring disclosure. See FLA. STAT. § 90.5015(2). An order requiring disclosure must be supported with clear and specific findings made after a hearing. See FLA. STAT. § 90.5015(3).

Some lower federal courts, including the Eleventh Circuit, have held that a reporter has a qualified privilege, grounded in the First Amendment, not to disclose information, including the identity of her source. See Price v. Time, Inc., 416 F.3d 1327, 1343 (11th Cir. 2005); U.S. v. Smith, 135 F.3d 963, 971-72 (5th Cir. 1998); U.S. v. Caporale, 806 F.2d 1487, 1504 (11th Cir. 1986). But see McKevitt v. Pallasch, 339 F.3d 530, 532-33 (7th Cir. 2003); In re Grand Jury Proceedings, 810 F.2d 580, 583-86 (6th Cir. 1987). However, this privilege is not absolute, and can be overcome by a showing that the information is highly relevant, necessary to the proper presentation of the case, and unobtainable from other sources. See Caporale, 806 F.2d at 1504. The federal courts are split on whether this privilege can be invoked in criminal cases, compare U.S. v. Burke, 700 F.2d 70, 77 (2d Cir. 1983) (applicable in criminal cases), with Smith, 135 F.3d at 972 (not applicable in criminal cases), as well as whether it protects non-confidential information, compare Gonzalez v. National Broadcasting Co., 194 F.3d 29, 33 (2d Cir. 1999) (protects non-confidential information), with Smith, 135 F.3d at 972 (does not protect non-confidential information). The federal courts have also struggled with who qualifies as a journalist. See generally In re Madden, 151 F.3d 125, 128-30 (3d Cir. 1998).

One early federal decision grounded its holding at least in part on Federal Rule 501, see Riley v. City of Chester, 612 F.2d 708, 713-18 (3d Cir. 1979), but the circuit later re-characterized the decision as a First Amendment one, see In re Madden, 151 F.3d at 128. A recent panel of the D.C. Circuit splintered three ways on the question whether a journalist's privilege exists under Federal Rule 501. See In re: Grand Jury Subpoena, Judith Miller, 438 F.3d 1141, 1149-50 (D.C. Cir. 2006).

Florida Stat. § 90.502. Lawyer-Client Privilege

(1) For purposes of this section:

(a) A "lawyer" is a person authorized, or reasonably believed by the client to be authorized, to practice law in any state or nation.

(b) A "client" is any person, public officer, corporation, association, or other organization or entity, either public or private, who consults a lawyer with the purpose of obtaining legal services or who is rendered legal services by a lawyer.

(c) A communication between lawyer and client is "confidential" if it is not intended to be disclosed to third persons other than:

1. Those to whom disclosure is in furtherance of the rendition of legal services to the client.

2. Those reasonably necessary for the transmission of the communication.

(2) A client has a privilege to refuse to disclose, and to prevent any other person from disclosing, the contents of confidential communications when such other person learned of the communications because they were made in the rendition of legal services to the client.

(3) The privilege may be claimed by:

(a) The client.

(b) A guardian or conservator of the client.

(c) The personal representative of a deceased client.

(d) A successor, assignee, trustee in dissolution, or any similar representative of an organization, corporation, or association or other entity, either public or private, whether or not in existence.

(e) The lawyer, but only on behalf of the client. The lawyer's authority to claim the privilege is presumed in the absence of contrary evidence.

(4) There is no lawyer-client privilege under this section when:

(a) The services of the lawyer were sought or obtained to enable or aid anyone to commit or plan to commit what the client knew was a crime or fraud.

(b) A communication is relevant to an issue between parties who claim through the same deceased client.

(c) A communication is relevant to an issue of breach of duty by the lawyer to the client or by the client to the lawyer, arising from the lawyer-client relationship.

(d) A communication is relevant to an issue concerning the intention or competence of a client executing an attested document to which the lawyer is an attesting witness, or concerning the execution or attestation of the document.

(e) A communication is relevant to a matter of common interest between two or more clients, or their successors in interest, if the communication was made by any of them to a lawyer retained or consulted in common when offered in a civil action between the clients or their successors in interest.

(5) Communications made by a person who seeks or receives services from the Department of Revenue under the child support enforcement program to the attorney representing the department shall be confidential and privileged as provided for in this section. Such communications shall not be disclosed to anyone other than the agency except as provided for in this section. Such disclosures shall be protected as if there were an attorney-client relationship between the attorney for the agency and the person who seeks services from the department.

(6) A discussion or activity that is not a meeting for purposes of s. 286.011 shall not be construed to waive the attorney-client privilege established in this section. This shall not be construed to constitute an exemption to either s. 119.07 or s. 286.011.

SPONSORS' NOTE (1976 ENACTMENT)

Subsection (1) This subsection defines a "lawyer" as a person licensed to practice law or one who holds himself out to the public as qualified to practice law in any state or nation. "Lawyer" also includes a person whom the client reasonably believes to be a lawyer. This subsection does not affect the qualification and admission of lawyers to practice in Florida, which is regulated and administered by the Florida Bar.

The definition of "client" includes both public and private corporations and governmental bodies. See Radiant Burners, Inc. v. American Gas Ass'n., 320 F.2d 314 (7th Cir. 1963) (private corporations) and Connecticut Mutual Life In[s]. Co. v. Shields, 18 F.R.D. 448 (S.D.N.Y. 1955) (public bodies). Consistent with existing Florida law, the privilege applies to communications relevant to retaining an attorney, although actual employment does not result. In Keir v. State, 152 Fla. 389, 394, 11 So. 2d 886, 888 (1943), the Supreme Court stated: "[C]ommunications made by a person to an attorney with the view to employing him professionally fall within the...[privilege], although the attorney is not subsequently employed."

The determinative factor in establishing the confidentiality of a communication is intent. When a communication from a client is expressly confidential or made under circumstances that should be understood by the attorney to be so, the requisite confidentiality is achieved. When the communication is made in public or divulged by the client to disinterested third persons, the intent to keep the communication confidential is lacking and the privilege cannot be claimed. See McCormick, Evidence § 91 (2nd ed. 1972).

Practicality requires that some disclosure outside the immediate lawyer-client circle be allowed without impairing confidentiality. This section allows disclosure to those persons "to whom disclosure is in furtherance of the rendition of professional legal services," which may include a spouse, parent, business associate or joint client.

Disclosure is also permitted to those persons "reasonably necessary for the transmission of the communication." This definition includes employees or agents of a lawyer who routinely receive communications from the client for transmission to the attorney.

Similar provisions are contained in Prop. Fed. Rule Evid. 503 and Calif. Evid. Code § 952.

Subsection (2) This subsection provides that confidential communications which are made for the purpose of rendering legal services to a client are privileged. The lawyer-client privilege encourages full disclosure by the client to the attorney in the furtherance of the administration of justice. McCormick, Evidence § 89 (2nd ed. 1972). The section provides that the privilege belongs to the client and is applicable only when a communication is for the purpose of facilitating the rendition of professional legal services to the client. No communication, no matter how confidential or relevant to the client's business or personal affairs, is privileged unless it materially facilitates the rendition of legal services by a lawyer.

In <u>Modern Woodmen of America v. Watkins</u>, 132 F.2d 352, 354 (5th Cir. 1942), a case appealed from the United States District Court for the Southern District of Florida, the court stated:

> The privilege...does not extend to every statement made to a lawyer. If the statement is about matters unconnected with the business at hand, or in a general conversation, or to the lawyer merely as a personal friend, the matter is not privileged.

Dean Wigmore has consistently maintained that the means of preserving the confidentiality of communication are in the hands of the client. He argues, therefore, that it is improper to extend the privilege to those who overhear, surreptitiously or otherwise, communications between attorney and client. 8 Wigmore, <u>Evidence</u> § 2326 (McNaughton rev. 1961); See <u>Horn v. State</u>, 298 So. 2d 194 (Fla. 1st Dist. 1974) (overheard marital conversation). However, the current sophisticated techniques for eavesdropping and interception make this position untenable. This section protects against these kinds of invasions of the privilege, and is in accord with Fla. Stat. § 934.08 which provides that communications, otherwise privileged, do not lose their privileged status if they are intercepted regardless of whether the interception is authorized by statute or is in violation thereof.

The privilege is applicable to persons who learn of confidential communications made for the purpose of facilitating the rendition of legal services. Therefore, the privilege is applicable to individuals who are utilized in addition to the lawyer's employees who already are involved in the communication process. For example, persons retained to assist the lawyer in a specialized area of a case or to prepare for litigation may claim the lawyer-client privilege to the same extent as the principal attorney. The lawyer-client privilege is extended to those communications between lawyer and client which are channeled through intermediaries routinely used in the communication process, e.g., clerks, agents, secretaries. See <u>Vann v. State</u>, 85 So. 2d 133 (Fla. 1956); see Prop. Fed. Rule Evid. 503.

When clients with similar interest retain separate attorneys, this subsection permits each client to prevent disclosure of his own statements, but not those of the other party. A primary reason for retaining separate counsel may be the potentially conflicting interests in addition to the common interests that brought them together. If one party desires to disclose his own statements made during a joint conference, he may do so. It is assumed that no party would disclose material prejudicial to his own or a joint interest. If all of the parties decline to disclose their own statements, no disclosure will occur. The situation should be distinguished from a conference when the parties meet on a purely adversary basis. There, any statements made, if otherwise admissible, could be used by the other party. When one attorney represents two or more parties with opposing interests, communications between the parties in the attorney's presence are not privileged since the parties have adverse interests and there is no expectation of privacy. The attorney, however, may not disclose information given to him by one client in the absence of the other party. See <u>Dominguez v. Citizens' Bank & Trust Co.</u>, 62 Fla. 148, 56 So. 682 (1911).

A similar provision is contained in Prop. Fed. Rule Evid. 503.

<u>Subsection (3)</u> This subsection provides that the privilege and the exercise thereof is firmly assigned to the client. His guardian or personal representative may claim it on his behalf. In the case of a corporation or association, any representative may claim the privilege.

A lawyer may not claim the privilege on his own behalf but may claim it on behalf of the client at the appropriate time. Under both existing law and this section, the privilege continues when an attorney is called to testify even though the employment relationship has terminated. See <u>Seaboard Air Line R.R. v. Parker</u>, 65 Fla. 543, 62 So. 589 (1913). Additionally, Ethical Consideration 4-4 of the Code of Professional Responsibility requires an attorney to act in a manner which preserves the confidentiality of the privilege. In the absence of contradictory evidence, an attorney is presumed to have the requisite authority to claim the privilege.

Similar provisions are contained in Prop. Fed. Rule Evid. 503 and Calif. Evid. Code § 953. See McCormick, Evidence § 92 (2nd ed. 1972).

Subsection (4) This subsection codifies several well-established exceptions to the privilege:

(a) When the services of the attorney are sought to be utilized in the commission of a crime or fraud, the privilege does not attach. McCormick, Evidence § 95 (2nd ed. 1972); 8 Wigmore, Evidence § 2298 (McNaughton rev. 1961). Since the modern justification for the privilege is to promote the administration of justice, the privilege should not be used to obstruct justice. In Kneale v. Williams, 158 Fla. 811, 818, 30 So. 2d 284, 287 (1947) the Supreme Court stated:

> It appears to be well settled that the perpetration of a fraud is outside the scope of the professional duty of an attorney and no privileges attach to a communication and transaction between an attorney and client with respect to transactions constituting the making of a false claim or the perpetration of a fraud.

See Prop. Fed. Rule Evid. 503.

(b) When multiple parties claim through the same decedent, as in a will contest or a challenge to testate or intestate succession, each party claims to best represent the interests of the deceased. To allow any or all parties to invoke the lawyer-client privilege prevents the swift resolution of the conflict and frustrates the public policy of expeditiously distributing estates in accordance with the testator's wishes. McCormick, Evidence § 94 (2nd ed. 1972). This subsection simply disallows the privilege in favor of the policies stated above. This exception should not be confused with the right of a personal representative to claim the privilege in an action where a party is not claiming through the deceased, but adverse to the estate. See Section 90.504(3)(c).

In denying the privilege to questions of testate or intestate succession involving parties claiming through an estate, the desired goal is full disclosure of the facts to facilitate distribution in accordance with the testator's wishes. On these same grounds, this section denies the privilege to communications relevant to an inter vivos transaction which is challenged through the estate after the decedent's death.

Similar provisions are contained in Prop. Fed. Rule Evid. 503 and Calif. Evid. Code § 957; New Jersey Evid. Rule 26(2)(b) and Kansas Code of Civ. Pro. § 60-426(b)(2).

(c) This exception states existing Florida law that there is no privilege when the communication is relevant to an issue relating to the breach of a duty which arose in the context of a lawyer-client relationship. In Herrin v. Abbe, 55 Fla. 769, 773, 46 So. 183, 185 (1908) the Supreme Court stated:

> [T]he testimony is of statements made by the defendant to the witness in discussing matters of indebtedness between them – not professional matters as to which the defendant could claim the privilege of silence on the part of counsel.

The same rationale would apply where the issue is the adequacy of representation or allegations of professional misconduct. See McCormick, Evidence § 91 (2nd ed. 1972).

(d) When a lawyer acts as an attesting witness for his client, a communication relevant to the intention or competence of a client in executing the document is not privileged since it is in the client's interest that the attorney testify that the witnessed document was properly executed. If the privilege included these communications, it would prevent a lawyer from performing the task he undertook when he witnessed the document.

This subsection limits the exception to communications relevant to the attestation. All other communications concerning the document remain privileged. While a lawyer should be allowed to act as an attesting witness, that action should not remove the privilege from communications between client and lawyer where the lawyer is acting as counselor and advisor. See Calif. Evid. Code § 959.

(e) This exception excludes from the privilege communications made when two persons consult a single lawyer and their joint communications are later offered into evidence when the parties subsequently become adversaries. This exception is an extension of existing Florida law as expressed in <u>Dominguez v. Citizen's Bank & Trust Co.</u>, 62 Fla. 148, 56 So. 682 (1911), where the Florida Supreme Court held that an attorney who represents adverse parties to an action may not refuse to testify as to matters discussed in a joint conference. In such circumstances, the critical factor of confidentiality is missing and the defendant should be able to utilize in his defense the relevant statements made by the plaintiff.

This exception preserves an additional holding of the <u>Dominguez</u> case, i.e., that an attorney may refuse to testify to matters relevant to issues which one of the parties told him in confidence, in the absence of the other party.

Similar provisions are contained in Prop. Fed. Rule Evid. 503; Calif. Evid. Code § 962; Kansas Code of Civ. Pro. § 60-426(b)(4); New Jersey Evid. Rule 26(2).

COMMENTARY ON FEDERAL AND FLORIDA RULE DIFFERENCES

Florida Stat. § 90.502 gives a client a privilege to refuse to disclose—and to prevent any other person from disclosing—the contents of confidential communications when such other person learned of the communications because they were made in the rendition of legal services by a lawyer to a client. See FLA. STAT. § 90.502(2). The Florida privilege is modeled after Proposed Federal Rule 503. Under Federal Rule 501, the U.S. Supreme Court has recognized a privilege for confidential communications by a client to an attorney made for the purpose of obtaining legal assistance. See *Fisher v. U.S.*, 425 U.S. 391, 403 (1976). Neither rule privileges communications just because they happen to be made to a lawyer; they are privileged only if made to a lawyer in his capacity as such for the purpose of obtaining legal services. See *U.S. v. Evans*, 113 F.3d 1457, 1463 (7th Cir. 1997); *State v. Branham*, 952 So. 2d 618, 620-21 (Fla. 2d DCA 2007); *Hoch v. Rissman, Weisberg, Barrett*, 742 So. 2d 451, 458 (Fla. 5th DCA 1999). Under both Florida and federal law, the privilege may be claimed by the client or on her behalf by her attorney, guardian, conservator, personal representative, and if the client is an entity, by a successor, assignee, trustee in dissolution, or similar representative. See FLA. STAT. § 90.502(3); *Citibank, N.A. v. Andros*, 666 F.2d 1192, 1195 (8th Cir. 1981) (citing, with approval, Proposed FED. R. EVID. 503(c)).

Both the Florida and federal versions of the attorney-client privilege protect a communication not only if it is made to a person actually authorized to practice law in any state or nation, but also if made to a person reasonably believed by the client so to be. See Fla. Stat. § 90.502(1)(a); *U.S. v. Boffa*, 513 F. Supp. 517, 523 (D. Del. 1981). Moreover, while both Florida and federal law protect only *confidential* communications between attorney and client, a communication is still considered confidential if it is made in the presence of or disclosed to persons other than the attorney, so long as such disclosure is in furtherance of the rendition of legal services to the client or the person to whom it is disclosed serves as a conduit for the transmission of the communication between client and attorney. See FLA. STAT. § 90.502(1)(c); *In re Lindsey*, 158 F.3d 1263, 1279-82 (D.C. Cir. 1998); *U.S. v. Kovel*, 296 F.2d 918, 921 (2d Cir. 1961).

The attorney-client privilege under both Florida and federal law protects certain communications between employees of a corporation and the corporation's attorney. Under Florida law, a communication between an employee and corporate counsel is protected by the privilege if: (1) it would not have been made but for the contemplation of legal services; (2) the employee made the communication at the direction of her corporate superior; (3) the superior made the request as part of the corporation's effort to secure legal advice or services; (4) the content of the communication relates to the legal services being rendered, and the subject matter of the communication is within the scope of the employee's duties; and (5) the communication is not disseminated beyond persons who, because of the corporate structure, need to know its contents. *See Southern Bell Tel. & Tel. Co. v. Deason*, 632 So. 2d 1377, 1383 (Fla. 1994). Under federal law, communications between a corporate employee and a corporate attorney are privileged if: (1) made for the purpose of securing legal advice; (2) made by the employee at the direction of her corporate superior; (3) the superior made the request so that the corporation could secure legal advice; (3) the subject matter of the communication is within the scope of the employee's corporate duties; and (5) the communication is not disseminated beyond persons who, because of the corporate structure, need to know its contents. *See In re Bieter Co.*, 16 F.3d 929, 935-36 (8th Cir. 1994); *see also Upjohn Co. v. U.S.*, 449 U.S. 383, 394-97 (1981) (declining to adopt a particular test but holding that communication is privileged when these elements are present).

There are a number of exceptions to both the Florida and federal privileges. First, both Florida and federal law have a crime-fraud exception to the attorney-client privilege under which communications between client and attorney are not privileged if they were sought or obtained for the purpose of enabling someone to commit or plan to commit a crime or fraud. *See* FLA. STAT. § 90.502(4)(a); *U.S. v. Zolin*, 491 U.S. 554, 562-63 (1989); *In re Grand Jury Investigation (Schroeder)*, 842 F.2d 1223, 1226 (11th Cir. 1987). Under federal law, once a party seeking to invoke the crime-fraud exception makes a prima facie showing—defined to mean something more than a suspicion but less than a preponderance of the evidence, *see U.S. v. Chen*, 99 F.3d 1495, 1503 (9th Cir. 1996)—that the exception applies, the burden shifts to the party invoking the privilege to prove that the crime-fraud exception is inapplicable. *See Gutter v. E.I. Dupont De Nemours*, 124 F. Supp. 2d 1291, 1307 (S.D. Fla. 2000). Moreover, in making that determination, the court may engage in *in camera* review of the disputed communication itself, provided that the party seeking to invoke the exception makes a showing of a factual basis sufficient to support a good faith belief by a reasonable person that the exception applies. *See Zolin*, 491 U.S. at 572. Similarly, under Florida law, once the party seeking to invoke the exception makes a prima facie showing that it applies, the burden shifts to the party invoking the privilege to prove that the crime-fraud exception is inapplicable. *See American Tobacco Co. v. State*, 697 So. 2d 1249, 1256 (Fla. 4th DCA 1997). However, unlike under federal practice, the court cannot rely on the disputed communication itself in making that determination. *See First Union Nat. Bank v. Turney*, 824 So. 2d 172, 183 (Fla. 1st DCA 2001).

Second, under both Florida and federal law, the privilege does not apply to a communication relevant to an issue between parties who claim through the same deceased client, such as in a will contest or a challenge to testate or intestate succession. *See* FLA. STAT. § 90.502(4)(b); Sponsors' Note to FLA. STAT. § 90.502(4)(b); *Swidler & Berlin v. U.S.*, 524 U.S. 399, 404-06 (1998); *Caputo v. Nouskhajian*, 871 So. 2d 266, 270 (Fla. 5th DCA 2004).

Third, under both Florida and federal law, the privilege does not apply to a communication relevant to an issue of breach of duty by the lawyer to the client or by the client to the lawyer, arising from the lawyer-client relationship, such as an action by the client against the attorney for malpractice. *See* FLA. STAT. § 90.502(4)(c); *Shafnaker v. Clayton*, 680 So. 2d 1109, 1111 (Fla. 1st DCA 1996); *Willy v. Administrative Review Bd.*, 423 F.3d 483, 495-99 (5th Cir. 2005). However, the exception is construed narrowly to permit only disclosure of what is necessary to make or defend against the claim of breach of duty. *See Willy*, 423 F.3d at 498; *Shafnaker*, 680 So. 2d at 1111.

Fourth, under Florida law, when a lawyer acts as an attesting witness for a client, the attorney-client privilege does not apply to a communication relevant to the intention or competence of the client in executing the document. *See* FLA. STAT. § 90.502(4)(d). No cases address the issue under federal law, but the same result seems likely. *See* Proposed FED. R. EVID. 503(d)(4).

Fifth, under both Florida and federal law, a communication relevant to a matter of common interest between two or more clients (or their successors in interest) is not privileged if made by any of them to a lawyer retained or consulted in common when offered in litigation between the clients (or their successors in interest). *See* FLA. STAT. § 90.502(4)(e); *U.S. v. Almeida*, 341 F.3d 1318, 1324-26 (11th Cir. 2003). While the Florida exception applies only in subsequent *civil* litigation between the clients, the federal decisions apply it in subsequent criminal prosecutions in which the clients are co-defendants. *Compare* FLA. STAT. § 90.502(4)(e), *with Almeida*, 341 F.3d at 1324-26.

Finally, as a general rule under federal law, certain basic facts about the attorney-client relationship are not deemed privileged, including the identity of the client and the source of payment of the attorney's legal fees. *See In re Grand Jury Matter No. 91-01386*, 969 F.2d 995, 997 (11th Cir. 1992). Under Eleventh Circuit precedent, however, the attorney-client privilege protects such non-privileged basic facts if disclosing them would also disclose other, privileged communications and when the incriminating nature of the privileged communications has created in the client a reasonable expectation that the information would be kept confidential. *See In re Grand Jury Matter No. 91-01386*, 969 F.2d at 997-98. Under Florida law, the precedents conflict on the question whether such basic facts are deemed privileged. *Compare In re State Attorney's Office Investigative Subpoena Dated Nov. 2, 1983*, 444 So. 2d 592, 594 (Fla. 2d DCA 1984), *with Corry v. Meggs*, 498 So. 2d 508, 511 (Fla. 1st DCA 1986). In any event, assuming that such basic facts do not normally fall within the scope of the Florida privilege, Florida precedent recognizes an exception when disclosing the information will yield "substantively probative links in an existing chain of incriminating evidence" against the person. *See Corry*, 498 So. 2d at 512-13.

Florida Stat. § 90.5021. Fiduciary Lawyer-Client Privilege

(1) For the purpose of this section, a client acts as a fiduciary when serving as a personal representative or a trustee as defined in ss. 731.201 and 736.0103, an administrator ad litem as described in s. 733.308, a curator as described in s. 733.501, a guardian or guardian ad litem as defined in s. 744.102, a conservator as defined in s. 710.102, or an attorney in fact as described in chapter 709.

(2) A communication between a lawyer and a client acting as a fiduciary is privileged and protected from disclosure under s. 90.502 to the same extent as if the client were not acting as a fiduciary. In applying s. 90.502 to a communication under this section, only the person or entity acting as a fiduciary is considered a client of the lawyer.

(3) This section does not affect the crime or fraud exception to the lawyer-client privilege provided in s. 90.502(4)(a).

COMMENTARY ON FEDERAL AND FLORIDA RULE DIFFERENCES

Florida Stat. § 90.5021 makes clear that communications between an attorney and a client who is acting as a fiduciary are protected from disclosure to the same extent as they would be if the client were not acting as a fiduciary. *See* FLA. STAT. § 90.5021(2). It thus clarifies that, for purposes of the attorney-client privilege, only the person or entity acting as a fiduciary—and not others, such as the beneficiaries of the fiduciary relationship—is considered to be the client. *See* FLA. STAT. § 90.5021(2).

Section 90.5021—which was enacted in 2011—differs significantly from the common law, which has long recognized a "fiduciary exception" to the attorney-client privilege whereby the beneficiary of the fiduciary relationship is considered to be the "real" client and thus has a right to obtain and make evidentiary use of communications between the attorney and the fiduciary. *See generally U.S. v. Jicarilla Apache Nation*, 131 S. Ct. 2313 (2011). The U.S. Supreme Court recently assumed without deciding that the fiduciary exception exists as a matter of federal common law. *See id.*

Florida Stat. § 90.503. Psychotherapist-Patient Privilege

(1) For purposes of this section:

(a) A "psychotherapist" is:

1. A person authorized to practice medicine in any state or nation, or reasonably believed by the patient so to be, who is engaged in the diagnosis or treatment of a mental or emotional condition, including alcoholism and other drug addiction;

2. A person licensed or certified as a psychologist under the laws of any state or nation, who is engaged primarily in the diagnosis or treatment of a mental or emotional condition, including alcoholism and other drug addiction;

3. A person licensed or certified as a clinical social worker, marriage and family therapist, or mental health counselor under the laws of this state, who is engaged primarily in the diagnosis or treatment of a mental or emotional condition, including alcoholism and other drug addiction; or

4. Treatment personnel of facilities licensed by the state pursuant to chapter 394, chapter 395, or chapter 397, of facilities designated by the Department of Children and Family Services pursuant to chapter 394 as treatment facilities, or of facilities defined as community mental health centers pursuant to s. 394.907(1), who are engaged primarily in the diagnosis or treatment of a mental or emotional condition, including alcoholism and other drug addiction; or

5. An advanced registered nurse practitioner certified under s. 464.012, whose primary scope of practice is the diagnosis or treatment of mental or emotional conditions, including chemical abuse, and limited only to actions performed in accordance with part I of chapter 464.

(b) A "patient" is a person who consults, or is interviewed by, a psychotherapist for purposes of diagnosis or treatment of a mental or emotional condition, including alcoholism and other drug addiction.

(c) A communication between psychotherapist and patient is "confidential" if it is not intended to be disclosed to third persons other than:

1. Those persons present to further the interest of the patient in the consultation, examination, or interview.

2. Those persons necessary for the transmission of the communication.

3. Those persons who are participating in the diagnosis and treatment under the direction of the psychotherapist.

(2) A patient has a privilege to refuse to disclose, and to prevent any other person from disclosing, confidential communications or records made for the purpose of diagnosis or treatment of the patient's mental or emotional condition, including alcoholism and other drug addiction, between the patient and the psychotherapist, or persons who are participating in the diagnosis or treatment under the direction of the psychotherapist. This privilege includes any diagnosis made, and advice given, by the psychotherapist in the course of that relationship.

(3) The privilege may be claimed by:

(a) The patient or the patient's attorney on the patient's behalf.

(b) A guardian or conservator of the patient.

(c) The personal representative of a deceased patient.

(d) The psychotherapist, but only on behalf of the patient. The authority of a psychotherapist to claim the privilege is presumed in the absence of evidence to the contrary.

(4) There is no privilege under this section:

(a) For communications relevant to an issue in proceedings to compel hospitalization of a patient for mental illness, if the psychotherapist in the course of diagnosis or treatment has reasonable cause to believe the patient is in need of hospitalization.

(b) For communications made in the course of a court-ordered examination of the mental or emotional condition of the patient.

(c) For communications relevant to an issue of the mental or emotional condition of the patient in any proceeding in which the patient relies upon the condition as an element of his or her claim or defense or, after the patient's death, in any proceeding in which any party relies upon the condition as an element of the party's claim or defense.

SPONSORS' NOTE (1976 ENACTMENT)

At the common law, no privilege existed between physician and patient concerning confidential information given to a doctor. McCormick, Evidence § 98 (2nd ed. 1972). When a patient consults a doctor he seeks a cure for his illness or injury, and

> the thought of some later disclosure of his confidences in the courtroom would not usually be a substantial factor in curbing his freedom of communication with his doctor. Accordingly, the justification in the need for encouraging the frank disclosure of information to the doctor seems to have slight relevancy to the actual play of forces upon the average patient.

McCormick, Evidence § 105 (2nd ed. 1972). Florida has followed the common-law rule and has not adopted a statute to extend the privilege. See Morrison v. Malmquist, 62 So. 2d 415 (Fla. 1953).

When a patient seeks treatment for emotional or mental disorders, the need for a testimonial privilege increases. In order to be effective, the psychotherapist must be able to persuade the patient to talk freely and fully. This may only be possible when the patient is assured that the communications will remain confidential. It is fairly well settled that confidentiality is essential to the conduct of successful psychiatric care. See Report No. 45, Group for the Advancement of Psychiatry 92 (1960); Slovenko, Psychiatry and a Second Look at the Medical Privilege, 6 Wayne L. Rev. 175 (1960). Florida has agreed with this general requirement for confidentiality by adopting two statutes, § 90.242 and § 490.32, providing for psychiatrist-patient and psychologist-patient privileges. This section combines the two existing privileges under the single heading of "psychotherapist-patient privilege."

Subsection (1) This subsection makes the privilege applicable to certain communications to persons authorized to practice medicine in any state or nation or reasonably believed by the patient to be so, while engaged in the diagnosis or treatment of a mental or emotional condition, including alcoholism or other drug addiction. Existing Fla.Stat. § 90.242 is expanded from recognizing the privilege for only psychiatrists to all persons licensed to practice medicine who are involved in the enumerated treatment. This privilege is also applied to licensed or certified psychotherapists.

A "patient" is defined as one seeking treatment for a mental or emotional disorder as opposed to one consulting a psychotherapist for business or other professional purposes. The rationale for extending confidentiality to the psychotherapist-patient relationship is to assist successful treatment, and there is no plausible reason to extend it to communications where a businessman seeks psychological advice on consumer purchasing motivations or a lawyer prepares materials for a law review article concerning psychiatry or psychology and its relation to law.

A communication is "confidential" if made in the interest of treatment by the psychotherapist and not intended for general dissemination. The same considerations affecting confidentiality in the lawyer-client privilege apply. This subsection allows the psychotherapist to enlist the assistance of persons necessary for adequate treatment without destroying the concept of confidentiality.

Alcoholism and other drug addiction are included as an emotional or mental disorder in order to be consistent with current approaches to drug abuse problems. This approach is evidenced by the legislative intent of chapter 397 of the Florida Statutes to provide for the rehabilitation of drug users and drug dependent persons.

Similar provisions are contained in Prop. Fed. Rule Evid. 504 and Calif. Evid. Code §§ 1010-12.

Subsection (2) The psychotherapist-patient privilege belongs to the patient and protects those communications made for the diagnosis or treatment of his mental or emotional condition, including drug addiction. It includes all these communications made in the presence of those participating in the treatment at the psychotherapist's direction. It does not apply where the communication is made to unparticipating individuals or in circumstances where confidentiality is reasonably anticipated. Because of the contemporary concern with the wide incidence of drug abuse, the inclusion of treatment for drug addiction within the privilege is justified since inclusion encourages individuals requiring assistance to seek rehabilitation. See Fla. Stat. § 397.011.

A similar provision is contained in Prop. Fed. Rule Evid. 504.

Subsection (3) As indicated in subsection (2), the privilege and the exercise thereof belong to the patient. Since it may not be possible for the patient to claim the privilege in his own behalf, the subsection provides that the patient's attorney, guardian or conservator may claim the privilege. As with other privileges, the personal representative of a deceased patient may also claim the privilege.

The psychotherapist may invoke the privilege on behalf of the patient. Since the primary purpose of the privilege is to assist in successful treatment, denial of the ability to invoke the privilege by the psychotherapist would effectively destroy the privilege. Consistent with other privileges, the psychotherapist is assumed to have the authority to invoke the privilege in the absence of contrary evidence.

Similar provisions are contained in Prop. Fed. Rule Evid. 504 and Calif. Evid. Code § 1013.

Subsection (4) This subsection provides three exceptions to the privilege which reflect the experiences of the Connecticut and federal evidence codes of when disclosure of the communications better serves the interests of the patient and society, see Goldstein & Katz, Psychiatrist-Patient Privilege: The GAP Proposal and the Connecticut Statute, 36 Conn. B.J. 175 (1962); Advisory Committee's Note to Prop. Fed. Rule Evid. 504 (1972). Persuasive arguments have been made that the nature of the psychotherapist-patient relationship requires that communications between psychotherapist and patient be totally immune from legally coerced disclosure. See Louisell, The Psychologist in Today's Legal World: Part II, 41 Minn. L. Rev. 731, 746 (1957).

(a) Because of the serious nature of commitment proceedings, the harm to the psychotherapist-patient relationship is outweighed by the harm to society in general if relevant information is excluded from them. In Florida, the statutory scheme regulating hospitalization for mental illness (The Baker Act, Fla. Stat. ch. 394) provides for both voluntary and involuntary hospitalization. When the hospitalization is voluntary, the patient is cooperating with the psychotherapist to promote recovery, and it is reasonable to assume that the question of privilege will not arise. When the hospitalization is involuntary, the philosophy of the Baker Act (requiring the patient to be mentally ill and likely to injure himself or others) indicates that the privilege should be disallowed to protect the patient and society. The language of this subsection provides that the psychotherapist need only have "reasonable cause to believe" that the patient requires hospitalization. Such a standard is considered adequate because of the built-in safeguards of the Baker Act, e.g., the administrator of the receiving facility must recommend hospitalization, based upon the opinions of at least two physicians who have personally examined the patient within the preceding five days.

(b) An exception is present when a judge orders an examination of the mental or emotional condition of the patient. Communications made in the course thereof are not privileged with respect to the particular purpose for which the examination is ordered unless the judge orders otherwise.

Florida Rule of Crim. Pro. 3.210 permits a trial court, inter alia, upon its motion or that of defense counsel, to conduct a hearing to determine a criminal defendant's mental condition. Florida Rule of Civ. Pro. 1.360 allows a court to order, upon motion for good cause, an examination of the mental condition of a party or a person under the legal control of a party. These rules, respectively, prevent the trial of a defendant unable to assist in his own defense and assist a party in a civil suit in obtaining relevant information about the mental condition of other parties. To allow a claim of privilege to attach to these examinations would frustrate the purpose of the examinations.

This exception does not result in the admission of all communications made by the patient during the examination. The privilege attaches to those communications which are made during a court-ordered examination but are not relevant to the purpose for which the examination was ordered. In Parkin v. State, 238 So. 2d 817 (Fla. 1970), the Florida Supreme Court held that the purpose of a mental examination for criminal defendants was to determine sanity, not guilt or innocence. Consequently, any matters outside the scope of the examination, i.e., the question of the defendant's sanity, are not within the exception and are privileged.

Further, the exception recognizes the trial judge's discretion to allow a claim of privilege when the benefits of disclosure are outweighed by the harm to the patient's interests.

In addition, an accused's privilege against self-incrimination prohibits a:

> psychiatrist from testifying directly as to the facts surrounding the crime, where such facts have been elicited from the defendant during the course of a compulsory mental examination....[H]owever, if the defendant's counsel opens the inquiry to collateral issues, admissions or guilt, the State's redirect examination properly could inquire within the scope opened by the defense.

State v. Parkin, 238 So. 2d 817, 820 (Fla. 1970).

(c) The last exception to the privilege arises when a patient, as a litigant, puts his mental condition in issue. Existing Florida Statute § 90.242(3)(b) and § 490.32(2)(b) contain similar provisions. When one party makes a claim or defense regarding his mental or emotional condition, it would be inimical to the interest of justice to deny the other party an opportunity to show otherwise. This possible inequity is remedied in the Florida Rules of Crim. Pro. 3.210 and Fla. Rule Civ. Pro. 1.360 by allowing the state and adverse parties, respectively, to obtain a court order for mental examination of the patient-litigant. The language of this exception insures that the nonprivileged communications are those that are relevant to the issue of mental condition rather than ultimate guilt or innocence. The exception is equally applicable in civil and criminal proceedings.

Similar exceptions are contained in Prop. Fed. Rule Evid. 504; Calif. Evid. Code §§ 1016, 1017, 1024; New Jersey Evid. Rule 28 and Kansas Code of Civ. Pro. § 60-427.

COMMENTARY ON FEDERAL AND FLORIDA RULE DIFFERENCES

Florida Stat. § 90.503 gives a patient a privilege to refuse to disclose—and to prevent any other person from disclosing—confidential communications between the patient and a psychotherapist or records made for the purpose of diagnosis or treatment of the patient's mental or emotional condition, including any diagnosis made or advice given by the psychotherapist. See FLA. STAT. § 90.503(2). The privilege may be claimed by the patient or on his behalf by his attorney, guardian, conservator, personal representative, or the psychotherapist. See FLA. STAT. § 90.503(3).

The Florida privilege extends not only to communications with physicians engaged in diagnosis or treatment of mental or emotional conditions (i.e., psychiatrists), but also to licensed or certified psychologists, clinical social workers, marriage and family therapists, mental health counselors, and treatment personnel at certain types of facilities licensed by the state. See FLA. STAT. § 90.503(1)(a)(1)-(4). Moreover, effective July 1, 2006, the rule extends the privilege to communications with advanced registered nurse practitioners whose primary scope of practice is the diagnosis or treatment of mental or emotional conditions, including chemical abuse. See id. § 90.503(1)(a)(5). See also In re Amendments to the Florida Evidence Code, 960 So.2d 762, 762-64 (Fla. 2007) (order by Florida Supreme Court adopting amendment to § 90.503 to the extent that it is procedural). The privilege applies if the patient reasonably but mistakenly believes the person to be a physician, but not if he reasonably so believes the person to be a psychologist or to fall within one of the other categories. See id. § 90.503(1)(a); Thompson v. State, 615 So. 2d 737, 742 (Fla. 1st DCA 1993).

The Florida privilege covers only communications; it does not cover such things as the fact that treatment was occurring, the dates of treatment, and the like. See Wilder v. Wilder, 993 So. 2d 182, 185 (2d DCA 2008).

Under the Florida statute, the psychotherapist privilege does not apply to communications relevant to an issue in involuntary commitment proceedings, for communications made in the course of a court-ordered examination of the patient's mental or emotional condition, for communications relevant to the patient's mental or emotional condition in any proceeding in which he puts it at issue by relying on it as an element of a claim or defense—or after the patient's death—if any party puts it at issue by relying on it as an element of a claim or defense. See FLA. STAT. § 90.503(4); State v. Famiglietti, 817 So. 2d 901, 903 (Fla. 3d DCA 2002). Other statutes have been interpreted to create additional exceptions to the privilege, including a "dangerous patient" exception that permits a psychotherapist to testify that the patient expressed an intent to harm someone, see Guerrier v. State, 811 So. 2d 852, 855-56 (Fla. 5th DCA 2002) (relying on FLA. STAT. § 456.059), and an exception for communications involving the alleged perpetrator in any situation involving known or suspected child abuse, abandonment, or neglect, see Hill v. State, 846 So. 2d 1208, 1213-14 (Fla. 5th DCA 2003) (relying on FLA. STAT. § 39.204). However, the courts will not create additional exceptions through common law decisionmaking. See Famiglietti, 817 So. 2d at 903-06.

The Florida statute is very similar to Proposed Federal Rule 504. The U.S. Supreme Court has held that, under Federal Rule 501, a privilege exists for communications made by a patient to a psychotherapist. See Jaffee v. Redmond, 518 U.S. 1 (1996). The federal privilege extends not only to communications to psychiatrists and psychologists, but also to licensed social workers when providing psychotherapy. See id. at 15. Moreover, lower courts have held that the privilege applies to a person reasonably believed by a patient to be a psychotherapist, see Speaker v. County of San Bernardino, 82 F. Supp. 2d 1105, 1112-14 (C.D. Cal. 2000), as well as to unlicensed employee assistance program counselors. See Oleszko v. State Compensation Ins. Fund, 243 F.3d 1154, 1156-59 (9th Cir. 2001). The privilege can be invoked by the patient or by the psychotherapist on her behalf. See U.S. v. Hansen, 955 F. Supp. 1225, 1226 (D. Mont. 1997). The lower courts have recognized a crime-fraud exception to the psychotherapist privilege comparable to the exception to the attorney-client privilege. See In re Grand Jury Proceedings (Gregory P. Violette), 183 F.3d 71, 78 (1st Cir. 1999). They have split, however, on the question whether a "dangerous patient" exception exists that permits a psychotherapist to testify that a patient expressed an intent to harm someone. *Compare U.S. v. Glass*, 133 F.3d 1356, 1357 (10th Cir. 1998) (recognizing such an exception), *with U.S. v. Chase*, 340 F.3d 978, 985-92 (9th Cir. 2003) (en banc) (joining the Sixth Circuit in refusing to recognize such an exception).

As under Florida law, a patient can waive the privilege by putting his mental or emotional state at issue, but the federal courts have split on what constitutes doing so. Under one approach, a party waives the privilege by making any claim for emotional distress. Under a second approach, a party waives the privilege when he introduces some of the privileged communications or calls the particular psychotherapist as a witness. Under a third approach, a party waives the privilege by offering evidence of psychiatric treatment or offering medical expert testimony to establish a claim of emotional harm. Under the fourth approach, garden variety claims of emotional distress do not waive the privilege, but complex claims such as those that the person suffered a specific psychological disorder or was prevented from working do waive it. *See Merrill v. Waffle House, Inc.*, 227 F.R.D. 467, 474-75 (N.D. Tex. 2005) (collecting cases).

Florida Stat. § 90.5035. Sexual Assault Counselor-Victim Privilege

(1) For purposes of this section:

(a) A "rape crisis center" is any public or private agency that offers assistance to victims of sexual assault or sexual battery and their families.

(b) A "sexual assault counselor" is any employee of a rape crisis center whose primary purpose is the rendering of advice, counseling, or assistance to victims of sexual assault or sexual battery.

(c) A "trained volunteer" is a person who volunteers at a rape crisis center, has completed 30 hours of training in assisting victims of sexual violence and related topics provided by the rape crisis center, is supervised by members of the staff of the rape crisis center, and is included on a list of volunteers that is maintained by the rape crisis center.

(d) A "victim" is a person who consults a sexual assault counselor or a trained volunteer for the purpose of securing advice, counseling, or assistance concerning a mental, physical, or emotional condition caused by a sexual assault or sexual battery, an alleged sexual assault or sexual battery, or an attempted sexual assault or sexual battery.

(e) A communication between a sexual assault counselor or trained volunteer and a victim is "confidential" if it is not intended to be disclosed to third persons other than:

1. Those persons present to further the interest of the victim in the consultation, examination, or interview.

2. Those persons necessary for the transmission of the communication.

3. Those persons to whom disclosure is reasonably necessary to accomplish the purposes for which the sexual assault counselor or the trained volunteer is consulted.

(2) A victim has a privilege to refuse to disclose, and to prevent any other person from disclosing, a confidential communication made by the victim to a sexual assault counselor or trained volunteer or any record made in the course of advising, counseling, or assisting the victim. Such confidential communication or record may be disclosed only with the prior written consent of the victim. This privilege includes any advice given by the sexual assault counselor or trained volunteer in the course of that relationship.

(3) The privilege may be claimed by:

(a) The victim or the victim's attorney on his or her behalf.

(b) A guardian or conservator of the victim.

(c) The personal representative of a deceased victim.

(d) The sexual assault counselor or trained volunteer, but only on behalf of the victim. The authority of a sexual assault counselor or trained volunteer to claim the privilege is presumed in the absence of evidence to the contrary.

COMMENTARY ON FEDERAL AND FLORIDA RULE DIFFERENCES

Florida Stat. § 90.5035 gives victims of sexual battery a privilege to refuse to disclose—and to prevent any other person from disclosing—a confidential communication made by the victim to a sexual assault counselor or trained volunteer, any record made in the course of advising, counseling, or assisting the victim, and any advice given by the counselor or volunteer in the course of the relationship. See FLA. STAT. § 90.5035(2). The privilege may be claimed by the victim or on her behalf by her attorney, guardian, conservator, personal representative, the sexual assault counselor or the trained volunteer. See FLA. STAT. § 90.5035(3). The communication or record so privileged may be disclosed only with the victim's prior written consent. See FLA. STAT. § 90.5035(2).

Unlike most of the privileges recognized under Florida law, this privilege is absolute, and contains no exceptions. See State v. Pinder, 678 So. 2d 410, 414 (Fla. 4th DCA 1996). Thus, only if a defendant in a criminal case successfully shows that he is entitled to such evidence under the Due Process or Confrontation Clauses will the privilege be overcome. See id. at 416.

There are very few federal decisions addressing this issue. One federal district court has held that, under Federal Rule 501, a client of a rape counseling center holds some form of privilege for communications with a rape crisis counselor, but found it unnecessary to determine whether the privilege was absolute or qualified as it found it had been waived. See U.S. v. Lowe, 948 F. Supp. 97, 99-100 (D. Mass. 1996). Another federal district court has held that a privilege exists under Federal Rule 501 for "professional counselors," but only if they are licensed, see Jane Student 1 v. Williams, 206 F.R.D. 306, 307-10 (S.D. Ala. 2002), which is not a requirement of Florida Stat. § 90.5035.

Florida Stat. § 90.5036. Domestic Violence Advocate-Victim Privilege

(1) For purposes of this section:

(a) A "domestic violence center" is any public or private agency that offers assistance to victims of domestic violence, as defined in s. 741.28, and their families.

(b) A "domestic violence advocate" means any employee or volunteer who has 30 hours of training in assisting victims of domestic violence and is an employee of or volunteer for a program for victims of domestic violence whose primary purpose is the rendering of advice, counseling, or assistance to victims of domestic violence.

(c) A "victim" is a person who consults a domestic violence advocate for the purpose of securing advice, counseling, or assistance concerning a mental, physical, or emotional condition caused by an act of domestic violence, an alleged act of domestic violence, or an attempted act of domestic violence.

(d) A communication between a domestic violence advocate and a victim is "confidential" if it relates to the incident of domestic violence for which the victim is seeking assistance and if it is not intended to be disclosed to third persons other than:

1. Those persons present to further the interest of the victim in the consultation, assessment, or interview.

2. Those persons to whom disclosure is reasonably necessary to accomplish the purpose for which the domestic violence advocate is consulted.

(2) A victim has a privilege to refuse to disclose, and to prevent any other person from disclosing, a confidential communication made by the victim to a domestic violence advocate or any record made in the course of advising, counseling, or assisting the victim. The privilege applies to confidential communications made between the victim and the domestic violence advocate and to records of those communications only if the advocate is registered under s. 39.905 at the time the communication is made. This privilege includes any advice given by the domestic violence advocate in the course of that relationship.

(3) The privilege may be claimed by:

(a) The victim or the victim's attorney on behalf of the victim.

(b) A guardian or conservator of the victim.

(c) The personal representative of a deceased victim.

(d) The domestic violence advocate, but only on behalf of the victim. The authority of a domestic violence advocate to claim the privilege is presumed in the absence of evidence to the contrary.

COMMENTARY ON FEDERAL AND FLORIDA RULE DIFFERENCES

Florida Stat. § 90.5036 gives victims of domestic violence a privilege to refuse to disclose—and to prevent any other person from disclosing—a confidential communication made by the victim to a domestic violence advocate, any record made in the course of advising, counseling, or assisting the victim, and any advice given by the advocate in the course of the relationship. *See* FLA. STAT. § 90.5036(2). The privilege may be claimed by the victim or on her behalf by her attorney, guardian, conservator, personal representative, or the domestic violence advocate. *See* FLA. STAT. § 90.5036(3). For the privilege to apply, the advocate must have been registered in accordance with the requirements of Florida Stat. § 39.905 at the time the communication was made. *See* FLA. STAT. § 90.5036(2).

There are no federal decisions directly addressing this issue. One federal district court has held that, under Federal Rule 501, a client of a rape counseling center holds some form of privilege for communications with a rape crisis counselor, but found it unnecessary to determine whether the privilege was absolute or qualified as it found it had been waived. *See U.S. v. Lowe*, 948 F. Supp. 97, 99-100 (D. Mass. 1996). Another federal district court has held that a privilege exists under Federal Rule 501 for "professional counselors," but only if they are licensed, *see Jane Student 1 v. Williams*, 206 F.R.D. 306, 307-10 (S.D. Ala. 2002).

Florida Stat. § 90.504. Husband-Wife Privilege

(1) A spouse has a privilege during and after the marital relationship to refuse to disclose, and to prevent another from disclosing, communications which were intended to be made in confidence between the spouses while they were husband and wife.

(2) The privilege may be claimed by either spouse or by the guardian or conservator of a spouse. The authority of a spouse, or guardian or conservator of a spouse, to claim the privilege is presumed in the absence of contrary evidence.

(3) There is no privilege under this section:

(a) In a proceeding brought by or on behalf of one spouse against the other spouse.

(b) In a criminal proceeding in which one spouse is charged with a crime committed at any time against the person or property of the other spouse, or the person or property of a child of either.

(c) In a criminal proceeding in which the communication is offered in evidence by a defendant-spouse who is one of the spouses between whom the communication was made.

SPONSORS' NOTE (1976 ENACTMENT)

The common law recognized three impediments to testimony by spouses: 1) a rule of incompetency, where one spouse was disqualified to testify for the other; 2) a privilege of refusing to testify against a spouse, including the ability of one spouse to prevent the other from testifying against him and; 3) a privilege to exclude confidential communications between the spouses. See McCormick, Evidence § 78 (2nd ed. 1972). Florida has abrogated the first two of these rules by statute. Existing Fla. Stat. § 90.04 established that neither the husband nor the wife shall be excluded as witness in civil cases, and § 914.07 adopted a similar rule in criminal cases. This section codifies the marital communications privilege, which has been recognized in Florida since Henderson v. Chaires, 25 Fla. 26, 6 So. 164 (1889).

Subsection (1) This subsection permits one spouse to refuse to disclose, and to prevent the other spouse from disclosing, confidential communications made during coverture. To be privileged, the communications must be made when confidentiality could be anticipated. The privilege is limited to expressions intended by one spouse to convey a meaning or message to the other and not to other "actions" or "facts." See Ross v. State, 202 So. 2d 582 (Fla. 1st Dist. 1967); Gates v. State, 201 So. 2d 786 (Fla. 3rd Dist. 1967); McCormick, Evidence § 79 (2nd ed. 1972). The privilege survives death or divorce, to insure total freedom of communication by removing the apprehension of disclosure. 8 Wigmore, Evidence § 2340 (McNaughton rev. 1961).

Similar provisions are contained in Calif. Evid. Code § 980; N.J. Evid. Rule 28; Kansas Code of Civ. Pro. § 60-428.

Subsection (2) The assertion of the privilege rests with that principal directly involved, i.e., the spouse. A guardian or conservator of an incompetent spouse may claim the privilege in the spouse's behalf, but no provision is made to allow a personal representative of a deceased spouse to claim the privilege. After a spouse's death, the privilege may only be claimed by or on behalf of the surviving spouse. To avoid unnecessary complications, the claimant of the privilege is presumed to have the requisite authority unless contrary evidence is presented.

Similar provisions are contained in Calif. Evid. Code § 980 and Kansas Code of Civ. Pro. § 60-428.

Subsection (3) This subsection sets forth the instances when confidential intraspousal communications are not privileged. When one spouse seeks to utilize the judicial process against the other spouse, e.g., a divorce or child custody case, a prompt and satisfactory settlement would be frustrated if the other spouse could prevent the giving of relevant testimony by invoking the privilege. The subsection is in accord with existing law, Section 88.261 of the Florida Statutes, which disallows the husband-wife privilege in any proceedings pursuant to the Uniform Reciprocal Enforcement of Support Law. See McCormick, Evidence § 85 (2nd ed. 1972).

In criminal proceedings in which one spouse is a defendant, the privilege does not exist when the spouse has committed a crime against the other or their children. There is no justifiable reason to allow the privilege to obstruct justice. This policy is reflected in existing § 828.04(10), Florida Statutes, which denies the husband-wife privilege in litigation growing out of child-abuse cases. Similarly, when a spouse perpetrates a crime against a third party in the course of a crime against the other spouse, the privilege does not apply since relevant testimony would be suppressed by the offending spouse without benefiting the marital relation. See McCormick, Evidence § 85 (2nd ed. 1972).

Finally, when a spouse is a defendant in a criminal case and offers marital communications as evidence, the privilege is not applicable since it should not be possible for the other spouse to frustrate the offer and deny the defendant-spouse a complete defense.

Similar provisions are contained in Calif. Evid. Code §§ 984, 985, 987; Kansas Code of Civ. Pro. § 60-428. Prop. Fed. Rule Evid. 505 provides only that a person has a privilege to prevent any testimony of his spouse from being admitted in evidence in a criminal proceeding against him.

COMMENTARY ON FEDERAL AND FLORIDA RULE DIFFERENCES

Florida Stat. § 90.504 gives a spouse a privilege during and after the marital relationship to refuse to disclose—and to prevent another person from disclosing—confidential communications made between the spouses while they were husband and wife. *See* FLA. STAT. § 90.504(1). Marital communications are presumed confidential absent evidence to the contrary. *See Yokie v. State*, 773 So. 2d 115, 117 (Fla. 4th DCA 2000). The privilege may be claimed by either spouse or the guardian or conservator of a spouse. *See* FLA. STAT. § 90.504(2). Save for one exception, discussed below, one spouse cannot unilaterally waive the privilege over the other spouse's objection. *See, e.g., Yokie*, 773 So. 2d at 117.

The Florida privilege does not prevent all testimony by one spouse against the other, but only testimony regarding confidential communications made while the two were married to one another. *See Taylor v. State*, 855 So. 2d 1, 26 (Fla. 2003). Thus, for example, it cannot be invoked to prevent one spouse from testifying about what she witnessed the other spouse do on a particular occasion. *See Bolin v. State*, 793 So. 2d 894, 897 n.3 (Fla. 2001); Sponsors' Note to Florida Stat. § 90.504(1). Nor does it apply to confidential communications that occurred before the couple was married. *See State v. Stewartson*, 443 So. 2d 1074, 1076 (Fla. 5th DCA 1984). Pre-rules case law indicates that the word "communications" includes assertive conduct, such as signs and gestures. *See Kerlin v. State*, 352 So. 2d 45, 51 (Fla. 1977). The privilege protects only the *content* of marital communications, not the *fact* that a husband and wife communicated with one another. *See Humphrey v. State*, 979 So. 2d 283, 285 (Fla. 2d DCA 2008).

The Florida privilege survives divorce in that even after the couple has divorced, the privilege can be invoked to bar testimony about confidential communications made *while* they were married. *See Bolin v. State*, 650 So. 2d 21, 23 (Fla. 1995). However, communications made after the spouses have divorced are not protected, and indeed, communications may not be protected if made while the couple was still legally married but permanently separated. *See Valentine v. State*, 688 So. 2d 313, 318 (Fla. 1996) (Grimes, J., concurring). The privilege also survives the death of one spouse in that it can be invoked by the surviving spouse, but the deceased spouse's personal representative lacks the authority to claim it on the deceased spouse's behalf. *See* Sponsors' Note to FLA. STAT. §§ 90.504(1)-(2).

There are several exceptions to the Florida marital privilege. First, it does not apply in proceedings brought by or on behalf one spouse against the other. *See* FLA. STAT. § 90.504(3)(a).

Second, it is inapplicable in criminal proceedings in which one spouse is charged with a crime committed against the person or property of the other spouse or the person or property of either spouse's child. *See* FLA. STAT. § 90.504(3)(b); *Floyd v. State*, 18 So. 3d 432, 448 (Fla. 2009). Third, the privilege does not apply in a criminal case in which the communication is offered in evidence by the defendant-spouse; thus, in such cases, the defendant-spouse alone has the power to waive the privilege. *See* FLA. STAT. § 90.504(3)(c). Unlike with the federal privilege, discussed below, there is no "joint participants" exception to the Florida privilege. *See Johnson v. State*, 451 So. 2d 1024, 1024 (Fla. 1st DCA 1984).

Federal decisions interpreting Federal Rule 501 recognize two different types of marital privilege: a marital confidential communications privilege and an adverse spousal testimonial privilege. *See U.S. v. Abram*, 171 Fed. Appx. 304, 309 (11th Cir. 2006); *U.S. v. Singleton*, 260 F.3d 1295, 1297-98 & n.2 (11th Cir. 2001).

The federal marital confidential communications privilege, like the Florida privilege, does not bar all testimony by one spouse against the other, but rather applies only to confidential communications made during the marriage, *see Abram*, 171 Fed. Appx. at 309-10, although the word "communications" includes assertive conduct. *See U.S. v. Bahe*, 128 F.3d 1440, 1443 (10th Cir. 1997). As under Florida law, marital communications are presumed confidential absent evidence to the contrary. *See Singleton*, 260 F.3d at 1300. And like the Florida privilege, the federal marital confidential communications privilege is held by both spouses, and thus cannot be unilaterally waived by one of the spouses. *See U.S. v. Montgomery*, 384 F.3d 1050, 1057-59 (9th Cir. 2004). Moreover, like the Florida privilege, the federal marital confidential communications survives divorce in that even after the couple has divorced, the privilege can be invoked to bar testimony about confidential communications made *while* they were married. *See Singleton*, 260 F.3d at 1297 n.2. However, the federal privilege does not apply to communications between spouses who are permanently separated (defined as "living separately with no reasonable expectation of reconciliation") even if at the time they were legally married to one another. *See id.* at 1298-1300. As with the Florida privilege, an exception exists to the federal privilege in criminal proceedings in which one spouse is charged with a crime committed against the person or property of the other spouse or the person or property of either spouse's child. *See Trammel v. United States*, 445 U.S. 40, 46 n.7 (1980); *see also Bahe*, 128 F.3d at 1446 (extending exception to child molestation case in which neither spouse is parent of child). However, unlike with the Florida privilege, there is a "joint participants" exception to the federal marital communications privilege, making it inapplicable to conversations between spouses about crimes in which they are jointly participating. *See Abram*, 171 Fed. Appx. at 310.

The second marital privilege, the adverse spousal testimonial privilege, is recognized under federal law but not under Florida law. This privilege is broader in scope than the marital confidential communications privilege in that it categorically blocks any testimony by one spouse against the other, including testimony on non-confidential matters and matters that occurred before the couple was married. *See U.S. v. Byrd*, 750 F.2d 585, 590-91 (7th Cir. 1984). However, unlike the marital communications privilege, the adverse spousal testimony privilege does not survive a terminated marriage, and thus cannot be invoked if the couple is no longer married at the time the testimony is sought. *See Singleton*, 260 F.3d at 1297 n.2. Nor can it be invoked if, at the time the testimony is sought, the couple is permanently separated. *See id.* at 1300. In addition, unlike with the marital communications privilege, the adverse spousal testimonial privilege is held by the witness-spouse, who is free to unilaterally waive it over the other spouse's objection. *See Trammel*, 445 U.S. at 53. As with the marital communications privilege, an exception exists to the federal adverse spousal testimonial privilege in criminal proceedings in which one spouse is charged with a crime committed against the person or property of the other spouse or the person or property of either spouse's child. *See id.* at 46 n.7. The federal courts are split on the question whether a "joint participants" exception exists to the adverse spousal testimonial privilege, with some courts holding that no such exception exists even while recognizing such an exception to the martial communications privilege. *See, e.g., U.S. v. Sims*, 755 F.2d 1239, 1240-43 (6th Cir. 1985) (collecting cases). Moreover, federal decisions suggest that, in general, the adverse spousal testimonial privilege can be invoked only in criminal, not civil, cases save for those civil cases that are "tethered" to a criminal proceeding, such as when the government brings a civil forfeiture action parallel with a criminal prosecution against a person. *See U.S. v. Sririam*, 2001 WL 59055, at *3-4 (N.D. Ill. 2001) (collecting cases).

Florida Stat. § 90.505. Privilege With Respect to Communications to Clergy

(1) For the purposes of this section:

(a) A "member of the clergy" is a priest, rabbi, practitioner of Christian Science, or minister of any religious organization or denomination usually referred to as a church, or an individual reasonably believed so to be by the person consulting him or her.

(b) A communication between a member of the clergy and a person is "confidential" if made privately for the purpose of seeking spiritual counsel and advice from the member of the clergy in the usual course of his or her practice or discipline and not intended for further disclosure except to other persons present in furtherance of the communication.

(2) A person has a privilege to refuse to disclose, and to prevent another from disclosing, a confidential communication by the person to a member of the clergy in his or her capacity as spiritual adviser.

(3) The privilege may be claimed by:

(a) The person.

(b) The guardian or conservator of a person.

(c) The personal representative of a deceased person.

(d) The member of the clergy, on behalf of the person. The member of the clergy's authority to do so is presumed in the absence of evidence to the contrary.

SPONSORS' NOTE (1976 ENACTMENT)

This section recognizes as privileged, a communication made by a person to a clergyman, or to an individual reasonably believed to be a clergyman, when it is made privately for the purpose of seeking spiritual guidance. See McCormick, Evidence § 77 (2nd ed. 1972). Although the privilege was not recognized at the common law, a majority of the states, including Florida, has enacted a statutory privilege covering religious denominations and organizations in general. See 8 Wigmore, Evidence § 2394-95 (McNaughton rev. 1961).

Subsection (1) Consistent with the existing statutory definition in Section 90.241, a clergyman is defined as a spiritual representative of a religious denomination or organization. The definition excludes self-denominated "ministers." There is no requirement that the functionary be engaged on a full-time basis as a clergyman. A clergyman is one who engages in those activities that generally conform to those of a priest, rabbi or minister.

Although not provided in the existing statute, when a person reasonably believes an individual to be a clergyman, he is permitted to invoke the privilege to prevent disclosure of communications made in good faith. The attorney-client and psychotherapist-patient privileges contain similar provisions.

Consistent with other privileges, communications to clergymen will not be privileged unless made in the course of seeking spiritual counsel and advice and under circumstances to insure confidentiality. Consequently, communications made in the presence of third parties not necessary to the furtherance of the communication or under circumstances where confidentiality cannot be expected, e.g., in public facilities or large groups, are not privileged.

Similar provisions are contained in Prop. Fed. Rule Evid. 506; Calif. Evid. Code §§ 1030, 1032; N.J. Evid. Rule 29; Kansas Code of Civ. Pro. § 60-429.

Subsection (2) This subsection states the clergyman-penitent privilege; that a person seeking spiritual counsel may prevent the clergyman or eavesdropper from disclosing the communication. The existing statute, section 90.241, recognizes that the privilege protects all confidential communication with a clergyman as spiritual advisor rather than only a "confession." There are apparently no reported Florida cases dealing with the clergyman's privilege.

Similar provisions are contained in Prop. Fed. Rule Evid. 506; Calif. Evid. Code § 1032; N.J. Evid. Rule 29; Kansas Code of Civ. Pro. § 60-429.

Subsection (3) The ability to assert the privilege is assigned to the person seeking the communication with a clergyman. If he is unable to do so, those who purport to best represent his interests, i.e., guardian, conservator or personal representative, may claim the privilege in his behalf. As with the attorney-client and psychotherapist-patient privileges, the clergyman may claim the privilege on behalf of the person. In the interest of simplified procedure, a clergyman is presumed to have the requisite authority to claim the privilege.

Similar provisions are contained in Prop. Fed. Rule Evid. 506; Wisc. Rule Evid. 905.06.

COMMENTARY ON FEDERAL AND FLORIDA RULE DIFFERENCES

Florida Stat. § 90.505 gives a person a privilege to refuse to disclose—and to prevent any other person from disclosing—a confidential communication made for the purpose of seeking spiritual counsel and advice by that person to a member of the clergy in her capacity as a spiritual adviser. *See* FLA. STAT. § 90.505(1)(b), (2). The privilege may be claimed by the person or on his behalf by his guardian, conservator, personal representative, or the clergymember. *See* FLA. STAT. § 90.505(3).

For the Florida privilege to apply, the communication must be made (1) to a member of the clergy (2) for the purpose of seeking spiritual counseling and advice (3) in the usual course of the clergymember's practice or discipline (4) privately and not for further disclosure except to other persons present in furtherance of the communication. *See Nussbaumer v. State*, 882 So. 2d 1067, 1074 (Fla. 2d DCA 2004). Florida law defines the phrase "member of the clergy" broadly to include a priest, rabbi, practitioner of Christian Science, a minister of any religious organization usually referred to as a church, or an individual reasonably believed so to be by the person consulting him. *See* FLA. STAT. § 90.505(1)(a); *Woodard v. Jupiter Christian School, Inc.*, 913 So. 2d 1188, 1191 (Fla. 4th DCA 2005). The requirement that the communication be made for the purpose of seeking spiritual counseling and advice means that the privilege does not protect communications made for "wholly secular purposes." *See Nussbaumer*, 882 So. 2d at 1075. It is not a requirement of the statute that the person who communicates with the member of the clergy be a member of that church or religious organization. *See id.* at 1079.

Unlike most of the privileges recognized under Florida law, this privilege is absolute, and contains no exceptions. *See State v. Pinder*, 678 So. 2d 410, 414 (Fla. 4th DCA 1996). Only if a defendant in a criminal case successfully shows that he is entitled to such evidence under the Due Process or Confrontation Clauses can an absolute privilege be overcome. *See id.* at 416.

The Florida privilege is very similar to Proposed Federal Rule 506. Federal decisions have held that, under Federal Rule 501, a privilege exists for communications made (1) to a clergyperson (2) in her spiritual and professional capacity (3) with a reasonable expectation of privacy. *See In re Grand Jury Investigation*, 918 F.2d 374, 384 (3d Cir. 1990). Like the Florida statute, federal decisions define clergyperson broadly to include a minister, priest, rabbi, or other similar functionary of a religious organization, or an individual reasonably believed so to be. *See id.* at 384-85 & n.13. Under the federal privilege, the presence of third persons when the communication is made does not destroy the privilege if their presence is essential to and in furtherance of the communication. *See id.* at 384. The privilege can be invoked by the person or on his behalf by the clergymember. *See id.* at 385 n.15. The federal courts have left open the question whether any exceptions exist to the privilege. *See id.* at 385.

Florida Stat. § 90.5055. Accountant-Client Privilege

(1) For purposes of this section:

(a) An "accountant" is a certified public accountant or a public accountant.

(b) A "client" is any person, public officer, corporation, association, or other organization or entity, either public or private, who consults an accountant with the purpose of obtaining accounting services.

(c) A communication between an accountant and the accountant's client is "confidential" if it is not intended to be disclosed to third persons other than:

1. Those to whom disclosure is in furtherance of the rendition of accounting services to the client.

2. Those reasonably necessary for the transmission of the communication.

(2) A client has a privilege to refuse to disclose, and to prevent any other person from disclosing, the contents of confidential communications with an accountant when such other person learned of the communications because they were made in the rendition of accounting services to the client. This privilege includes other confidential information obtained by the accountant from the client for the purpose of rendering accounting advice.

(3) The privilege may be claimed by:

(a) The client.

(b) A guardian or conservator of the client.

(c) The personal representative of a deceased client.

(d) A successor, assignee, trustee in dissolution, or any similar representative of an organization, corporation, or association or other entity, either public or private, whether or not in existence.

(e) The accountant, but only on behalf of the client. The accountant's authority to claim the privilege is presumed in the absence of contrary evidence.

(4) There is no accountant-client privilege under this section when:

(a) The services of the accountant were sought or obtained to enable or aid anyone to commit or plan to commit what the client knew or should have known was a crime or fraud.

(b) A communication is relevant to an issue of breach of duty by the accountant to the accountant's client or by the client to his or her accountant.

(c) A communication is relevant to a matter of common interest between two or more clients, if the communication was made by any of them to an accountant retained or consulted in common when offered in a civil action between the clients.

COMMENTARY ON FEDERAL AND FLORIDA RULE DIFFERENCES

Florida Stat. § 90.5055 provides a client with a privilege to refuse to disclose—and to prevent other persons from disclosing—the contents of confidential communications with an accountant when made for the purpose of rendering accounting services to the client. *See* FLA. STAT. § 90.5055(2). The privilege may be claimed by the client or on her behalf by her guardian, conservator, personal representative, or the accountant, and if the client is an entity, by a successor, assignee, trustee in dissolution, or similar representative. *See* FLA. STAT. § 90.5055(3).

There are three exceptions to the Florida accountant-client privilege: first, a crime-fraud exception that makes the privilege inapplicable if the accountant's services were sought or obtained to enable anyone to commit or plan to commit what the client knew or should have known was a crime or fraud, *see* FLA. STAT. § 90.5055(4)(a); second, an exception for communications relevant to an issue of breach of duty by the accountant to the client or vice-versa, *see* FLA. STAT. § 90.5055(4)(b); third, an exception for communications relevant to a matter of common interest between multiple clients, if made by any of them to an accountant retained or consulted in common, when offered in a civil action between those clients, *see* FLA. STAT. § 90.5055(4)(c). The third exception applies even if all clients were not present when the communication was made. *See Transmark, U.S.A., Inc. v. State, Dep't of Ins.*, 631 So. 2d 1112, 1116-17 (Fla. 1st DCA 1994).

By contrast, the federal courts have refused to recognize an accountant-client privilege under Federal Rule 501. *See, e.g., Matter of International Horizons, Inc.*, 689 F.2d 996, 1003-04 (11th Cir. 1982). In 1998, Congress enacted a statute that creates an extremely narrow privilege for communications between a "federally authorized tax practitioner" and a client involving "tax advice" that applies in non-criminal tax matters before the IRS or in non-criminal tax proceedings in federal court brought by or against the United States. *See* 26 U.S.C. § 7525. However, this statute only covers a communication that would be considered privileged if made to an attorney. *See id.* § 7525(a)(1). The case law makes clear that the statute creates only a limited privilege for non-lawyers (including tax preparers, many of whom are accountants) who are permitted under federal law to practice before the IRS; it does not create a privilege for such non-lawyer practitioners when they are engaged in non-legal work, such as providing accounting or tax preparation services. *See U.S. v. BDO Seidman*, 337 F.3d 802, 810 (7th Cir. 2003); *U.S. v. Frederick*, 182 F.3d 496, 502 (7th Cir. 1999).

Florida Stat. § 90.506. Privilege With Respect to Trade Secrets

A person has a privilege to refuse to disclose, and to prevent other persons from disclosing, a trade secret owned by that person if the allowance of the privilege will not conceal fraud or otherwise work injustice. When the court directs disclosure, it shall take the protective measures that the interests of the holder of the privilege, the interests of the parties, and the furtherance of justice require. The privilege may be claimed by the person or the person's agent or employee.

SPONSORS' NOTE (1976 ENACTMENT)

This section recognizes a privilege to refuse to disclose trade secrets if the lack of disclosure does not tend to conceal fraud or otherwise work injustice. When a court orders disclosure, the section provides for the issuance of a protective order.

The issue of trade-secret privilege usually arises when a litigant seeks to compel disclosure of secret information which is commercially valuable to his opponent. Florida Rule of Civ. Pro. 1.280(c)(7) which permits the trial judge, upon motion of a party from whom discovery is sought, to issue a protective order "that a trade secret or other confidential research, development, or commercial information not be disclosed or be disclosed only in a designated way" is extended by this section to evidentiary matters at trial. The difference in circumstances at the discovery stage and at the trial may be such as to require a different ruling at the trial.

The purpose of the privilege is to prohibit a party from using the duty of a witness to testify as a method of obtaining a valuable trade secret when the lack of disclosure will not jeopardize more important interests. It is widely recognized that the trade-secret privilege is not absolute. 8 Wigmore, Evidence § 2212(3) (McNaughton rev. 1961). In each case the judge must weigh the importance of protecting the claimant's secret against the interests in facilitating the trial and promoting a just end to the litigation. See 15 Wayne L. Rev. 1286, 1347 (1969). Such factors as the potential impact of disclosure upon the holder's business, see Note, Protection of Trade Secrets in Florida: Are Present Remedies Adequate?, 24 U. Fla. L. Rev. 721 (1972), protection afforded by copyright and patent laws, see Calif. Evid. Code § 1060 (Law Revision Commission Comment), and necessity of disclosure to the presentation of the opponent's case, see 15 Wayne L. Rev. 1286, 1349 (1969), may guide the judge in deciding whether to order disclosure. However, the judge is afforded wide discretion to permit the privilege to be invoked so long as the wrongdoer is not allowed to conceal his acts.

This section permits the judge to order disclosure in any manner designed to protect the secret. While the most common means would probably be the in camera proceeding, other possible means of protecting the secret may include sealing the part of the record describing the secret, prohibiting disclosure of the secret to a witness, omitting details of the secret from the record, and wording the opinion in terms avoiding disclosure of the secret. See Annot., Safeguarding Trade Secrets, 62 A.L.R.2d 509 (1958).

While problems of trade-secret privilege arise most frequently when the secret itself is the subject of the litigation, see, e.g., Segal Lock & Hardware Co., v. FTC, 143 F.2d 935 (2nd Cir. 1944), the privilege may be applicable in a wide range of situations, see Putney v. Du Bois Co., 240 Mo. App. 1075, 226 S.W. 2d 737 (1950) (action for injuries resulting from use of defendant's product); Fla. Stat. § 817.81(6) (civil investigation of unfair trade practices). The type of trade secrets contemplated under this section includes not only chemical formulas and mechanical designs but also such commercial secrets as know-how, see Hawkland, Some Recent American Developments in the Protection of Know-How, 20 Buffalo L. Rev. 119 (1970), and certain customer lists, see Inland Rubber Corp. v. Helman, 237 So. 2d 291 (Fla. 1st Dist. 1970).

This section does not affect existing statutory provisions which specifically provide for the use or admission of such evidence. See Fla. Stat. § 403.111.

For similar provisions, see Calif. Evid. Code § 1060; Uniform Rule 32; Model Code Rule 226; Prop. Fed. Rule Evid. 508.

COMMENTARY ON FEDERAL AND FLORIDA RULE DIFFERENCES

Florida Stat. § 90.506 gives the owner of a trade secret a privilege to refuse to disclose—and to prevent other persons from disclosing—the trade secret, so long as doing so will not conceal fraud or otherwise work injustice. The privilege may be claimed by the owner or his agent or employee.

The Florida trade secret privilege is not absolute, and can be overcome by a sufficient showing of a need for the information. *See Freedom Newspapers, Inc. v. Egly*, 507 So. 2d 1180, 1184 (Fla. 2d DCA 1987); Sponsors' Note to FLA. STAT. § 90.506. When the privilege is claimed, the court must conduct an *in camera* inspection of the materials to determine whether they contain trade secrets; if it determines that they do, it must then make a determination whether the party seeking production has shown reasonable necessity for the requested materials. *See Ameritrust Ins. Corp. v. O'Donnell Landscapes, Inc.*, 899 So. 2d 1205, 1207 (Fla. 2d DCA 2005); *Sheridan Healthcorp, Inc. v. Total Health Choice, Inc.*, 770 So. 2d 221, 222 (Fla. 3d DCA 2000).

The Florida trade secrets privilege is nearly identical to Proposed Federal Rule 508, a factor that weighs in favor of recognizing such a privilege under Federal Rule 501. *See* Commentary to FED. R. EVID. 501 and FLA. STAT. § 90.501. While no cases appear to address the existence of such a privilege under Federal Rule 501, similar protection is provided under the Federal Rules of Civil Procedure. *See* FED. R. CIV. P. 26(c)(1)(G).

Florida Stat. § 90.507. Waiver of Privilege by Voluntary Disclosure

A person who has a privilege against the disclosure of a confidential matter or communication waives the privilege if the person, or the person's predecessor while holder of the privilege, voluntarily discloses or makes the communication when he or she does not have a reasonable expectation of privacy, or consents to disclosure of, any significant part of the matter or communication. This section is not applicable when the disclosure is itself a privileged communication.

SPONSORS' NOTE (1976 ENACTMENT)

This section provides for a waiver of a privilege by voluntary disclosure. As the Florida Supreme Court stated in the leading case of Savino v. Luciano, 92 So. 2d 817, 819 (Fla. 1957):

[A]s in all confidential and privileged communications, "[t]he justification for the privilege lies not in the fact of communication, but in the interest of the persons concerned that the subject matter should not become public."...When a party himself ceases to treat a matter as confidential, it loses its confidential character.

Recently, in Tibado v. Brees, 212 So. 2d 61, 63 (Fla. 2nd Dist. 1968); the defendant voluntarily testified in a deposition to confidential communications between him and his wife. In denying the husband's objection to the introduction of the deposition during the trial, the Court stated:
It is clear that under the law of Florida that a personal privilege may be waived and when Mr. Tibado voluntarily and without objection testified on deposition to the privileged communications they lost their confidential character.

Waiver by voluntary disclosure occurs only when the substance of the privileged information is revealed. Thus, when a witness upon cross-examination testifies without objection that he has not made a certain statement to his attorney, he has not waived his attorney-client privilege since the contents of the statement have not been revealed. Seaboard Air Line R.R. v. Parker, 65 Fla. 543, 62 So. 589 (1913); see McCormick, Evidence § 93 (2nd ed. 1972).

For similar provisions, see Prop. Fed. Rule Evid. 511; Wisc. Evid. Rule 905.11. See also Calif. Evid. Code § 912.

Federal Rule 502. Attorney-Client Privilege and Work Product; Limitations on Waiver

The following provisions apply, in the circumstances set out, to disclosure of a communication or information covered by the attorney-client privilege or work-product protection.

(a) Disclosure Made in a Federal Proceeding or to a Federal Office or Agency; Scope of a Waiver. When the disclosure is made in a federal proceeding or to a federal office or agency and waives the attorney-client privilege or work-product protection, the waiver extends to an undisclosed communication or information in a federal or state proceeding only if:

(1) the waiver is intentional;

(2) the disclosed and undisclosed communications or information concern the same subject matter; and

(3) they ought in fairness to be considered together.

(b) Inadvertent Disclosure. When made in a federal proceeding or to a federal office or agency, the disclosure does not operate as a waiver in a federal or state proceeding if:

(1) the disclosure is inadvertent;

(2) the holder of the privilege or protection took reasonable steps to prevent disclosure; and

(3) the holder promptly took reasonable steps to rectify the error, including (if applicable) following Federal Rule of Civil Procedure 26(b)(5)(B).

(c) Disclosure Made in a State Proceeding. When the disclosure is made in a state proceeding and is not the subject of a state-court order concerning waiver, the disclosure does not operate as a waiver in a federal proceeding if the disclosure:

(1) would not be a waiver under this rule if it had been made in a federal proceeding; or

(2) is not a waiver under the law of the state where the disclosure occurred.

(d) Controlling Effect of a Court Order. A federal court may order that the privilege or protection is not waived by disclosure connected with the litigation pending before the court — in which event the disclosure is also not a waiver in any other federal or state proceeding.

(e) Controlling Effect of a Party Agreement. An agreement on the effect of disclosure in a federal proceeding is binding only on the parties to the agreement, unless it is incorporated into a court order.

(f) Controlling Effect of this Rule. Notwithstanding Rules 101 and 1101, this rule applies to state proceedings and to federal court-annexed and federal court-mandated arbitration proceedings, in the circumstances set out in the rule. And notwithstanding Rule 501, this rule applies even if state law provides the rule of decision.

(g) Definitions. In this rule:

(1) "attorney-client privilege" means the protection that applicable law provides for confidential attorney-client communications; and

(2) "work-product protection" means the protection that applicable law provides for tangible material (or its intangible equivalent) prepared in anticipation of litigation or for trial.

ADVISORY COMMITTEE'S NOTE

This new rule has two major purposes:

1) It resolves some longstanding disputes in the courts about the effect of certain disclosures of communications or information protected by the attorney-client privilege or as work product—specifically those disputes involving inadvertent disclosure and subject matter waiver.

2) It responds to the widespread complaint that litigation costs necessary to protect against waiver of attorney-client privilege or work product have become prohibitive due to the concern that any disclosure (however innocent or minimal) will operate as a subject matter waiver of all protected communications or information. This concern is especially troubling in cases involving electronic discovery. *See, e.g., Hopson v. City of Baltimore,* 232 F.R.D. 228, 244 (D.Md. 2005) (electronic discovery may encompass "millions of documents" and to insist upon "record-by-record pre-production privilege review, on pain of subject matter waiver, would impose upon parties costs of production that bear no proportionality to what is at stake in the litigation").

The rule seeks to provide a predictable, uniform set of standards under which parties can determine the consequences of a disclosure of a communication or information covered by the attorney-client privilege or work-product protection. Parties to litigation need to know, for example, that if they exchange privileged information pursuant to a confidentiality order, the court's order will be enforceable. Moreover, if a federal court's confidentiality order is not enforceable in a state court then the burdensome costs of privilege review and retention are unlikely to be reduced.

The rule makes no attempt to alter federal or state law on whether a communication or information is protected under the attorney-client privilege or work product immunity as an initial matter. Moreover, while establishing some exceptions to waiver, the rule does not purport to supplant applicable waiver doctrine generally.

The rule governs only certain waivers by disclosure. Other common-law waiver doctrines may result in a finding of waiver even where there is no disclosure of privileged information or work product. *See, e.g., Nguyen v. Excel Corp.,* 197 F.3d 200 (5th Cir. 1999) (reliance on an advice of counsel defense waives the privilege with respect to attorney-client communications pertinent to that defense); *[B]yers v. Burleson,* 100 F.R.D. 436 (D.D.C. 1983) (allegation of lawyer malpractice constituted a waiver of confidential communications under the circumstances). The rule is not intended to displace or modify federal common law concerning waiver of privilege or work product where no disclosure has been made.

Subdivision (a). The rule provides that a voluntary disclosure in a federal proceeding or to a federal office or agency, if a waiver, generally results in a waiver only of the communication or information disclosed; a subject matter waiver (of either privilege or work product) is reserved for those unusual situations in which fairness requires a further disclosure of related, protected information, in order to prevent a selective and misleading presentation of evidence to the disadvantage of the adversary. *See, e.g., In re United Mine Workers of America Employee Benefit Plans Litig.,* 159 F.R.D. 307, 312 (D.D.C. 1994)(waiver of work product limited to materials actually disclosed, because the party did not deliberately disclose documents in an attempt to gain a tactical advantage). Thus, subject matter waiver is limited to situations in which a party intentionally puts protected information into the litigation in a selective, misleading and unfair manner. It follows that an inadvertent disclosure of protected information can never result in a subject matter waiver. *See* Rule 502(b). The rule rejects the result in *In re Sealed Case,* 877 F.2d 976 (D.C.Cir. 1989), which held that inadvertent disclosure of documents during discovery automatically constituted a subject matter waiver.

The language concerning subject matter waiver—"ought in fairness"—is taken from Rule 106, because the animating principle is the same. Under both Rules, a party that makes a selective, misleading presentation that is unfair to the adversary opens itself to a more complete and accurate presentation.

To assure protection and predictability, the rule provides that if a disclosure is made at the federal level, the federal rule on subject matter waiver governs subsequent state court determinations on the scope of the waiver by that disclosure.

Subdivision (b). Courts are in conflict over whether an inadvertent disclosure of a communication or information protected as privileged or work product constitutes a waiver. A few courts find that a disclosure must be intentional to be a waiver. Most courts find a waiver only if the disclosing party acted carelessly in disclosing the communication or information and failed to request its return in a timely manner. And a few courts hold that any inadvertent disclosure of a communication or information protected under the attorney-client privilege or as work product constitutes a waiver without regard to the protections taken to avoid such a disclosure. *See generally Hopson v. City of Baltimore*, 232 F.R.D. 228 (D.Md. 2005), for a discussion of this case law.

The rule opts for the middle ground: inadvertent disclosure of protected communications or information in connection with a federal proceeding or to a federal office or agency does not constitute a waiver if the holder took reasonable steps to prevent disclosure and also promptly took reasonable steps to rectify the error. This position is in accord with the majority view on whether inadvertent disclosure is a waiver.

Cases such as *Lois Sportswear, U.S.A., Inc. v. Levi Strauss & Co.*, 104 F.R.D. 103, 105 (S.D.N.Y. 1985) and *Hartford Fire Ins. Co. v. Garvey*, 109 F.R.D. 323, 332 (N.D.Cal. 1985), set out a multi-factor test for determining whether inadvertent disclosure is a waiver. The stated factors (none of which are dispositive) are the reasonableness of precautions taken, the time taken to rectify the error, the scope of discovery, the extent of disclosure and the overriding issue of fairness. The rule does not explicitly codify that test, because it is really a set of non-determinative guidelines that vary from case to case. The rule is flexible enough to accommodate any of those listed factors. Other considerations bearing on the reasonableness of a producing party's efforts include the number of documents to be reviewed and the time constraints for production. Depending on the circumstances, a party that uses advanced analytical software applications and linguistic tools in screening for privilege and work product may be found to have taken "reasonable steps" to prevent inadvertent disclosure. The implementation of an efficient system of records management before litigation may also be relevant.

The rule does not require the producing party to engage in a post-production review to determine whether any protected communication or information has been produced by mistake. But the rule does require the producing party to follow up on any obvious indications that a protected communication or information has been produced inadvertently.

The rule applies to inadvertent disclosures made to a federal office or agency, including but not limited to an office or agency that is acting in the course of it regulatory, investigative or enforcement authority. The consequences of waiver, and the concomitant costs of pre-production privilege review, can be as great with respect to disclosures to offices and agencies as they are in litigation.

Subdivision (c). Difficult questions can arise when 1) a disclosure of a communication or information protected by the attorney-client privilege or as work product is made in a state proceeding, 2) the communication or information is offered in a subsequent federal proceeding on the ground that the disclosure waived the privilege or protection, and 3) the state and federal laws are in conflict on the question of waiver. The Committee determined that the proper solution for the federal court is to apply the law that is most protective of privilege and work product. If the state law is more protective (such as where the state law is that an inadvertent disclosure can never be a waiver), the holder of the privilege or protection may well have relied on that law when making the disclosure in the state proceeding. Moreover, applying a more restrictive federal law of waiver could impair the state objective of preserving the privilege or work-product protection for disclosures made in state proceedings. On the other hand, if the federal law is more protective, applying the state law of waiver to determine admissibility in federal court is likely to undermine the federal objective of limiting the costs of production.

The rule does not address the enforceability of a state court confidentiality order in a federal proceeding, as that question is covered both by statutory law and principles of federalism and comity. *See* 28 U.S.C. § 1738 (providing that state judicial proceedings "shall have the same full faith and credit in every court within the United States . . . as they have by law or usage in the courts of such State . . . from which they are taken"). *See also Tucker v. Ohtsu Tire & Rubber Co.*, 191 F.R.D. 495, 499 (D.Md. 2000) (noting that a federal court considering the enforceability of a state confidentiality order is "constrained by principles of comity, courtesy, and . . . federalism"). Thus, a state court order finding no waiver in connection with a disclosure made in a state court proceeding is enforceable under existing law in subsequent federal proceedings.

Subdivision (d). Confidentiality orders are becoming increasingly important in limiting the costs of privilege review and retention, especially in cases involving electronic discovery. But the utility of a confidentiality order in reducing discovery costs is substantially diminished if it provides no protection outside the particular litigation in which the order is entered. Parties are unlikely to be able to reduce the costs of pre-production review for privilege and work product if the consequence of disclosure is that the communications or information could be used by non-parties to the litigation.

There is some dispute on whether a confidentiality order entered in one case is enforceable in other proceedings. *See generally Hopson v. City of Baltimore*, 232 F.R.D. 228 (D.Md. 2005), for a discussion of this case law. The rule provides that when a confidentiality order governing the consequences of disclosure in that case is entered in a federal proceeding, its terms are enforceable against non-parties in any federal or state proceeding. For example, the court order may provide for return of documents without waiver irrespective of the care taken by the disclosing party; the rule contemplates enforcement of "claw-back" and "quick peek" arrangements as a way to avoid the excessive costs of pre-production review for privilege and work product. *See Zubulake v. UBS Warburg LLC*, 216 F.R.D. 280, 290 (S.D.N.Y. 2003) (noting that parties may enter into "so-called 'claw-back' agreements that allow the parties to forego privilege review altogether in favor of an agreement to return inadvertently produced privilege documents"). The rule provides a party with a predictable protection from a court order—predictability that is needed to allow the party to plan in advance to limit the prohibitive costs of privilege and work product review and retention.

Under the rule, a confidentiality order is enforceable whether or not it memorializes an agreement among the parties to the litigation. Party agreement should not be a condition of enforceability of a federal court's order.

Under subdivision (d), a federal court may order that disclosure of privileged or protected information "in connection with" a federal proceeding does not result in waiver. But subdivision (d) does not allow the federal court to enter an order determining the waiver effects of a separate disclosure of the same information in other proceedings, state or federal. If a disclosure has been made in a state proceeding (and is not the subject of a state-court order on waiver), then subdivision (d) is inapplicable. Subdivision (c) would govern the federal court's determination whether the state-court disclosure waived the privilege or protection in the federal proceeding.

Subdivision (e). Subdivision (e) codifies the well-established proposition that parties can enter an agreement to limit the effect of waiver by disclosure between or among them. Of course such an agreement can bind only the parties to the agreement. The rule makes clear that if parties want protection against non-parties from a finding of waiver by disclosure, the agreement must be made part of a court order.

Subdivision (f). The protections against waiver provided by Rule 502 must be applicable when protected communications or information disclosed in federal proceedings are subsequently offered in state proceedings. Otherwise the holders of protected communications and information, and their lawyers, could not rely on the protections provided by the Rule, and the goal of limiting costs in discovery would be substantially undermined. Rule 502(f) is intended to resolve any potential tension between the provisions of Rule 502 that apply to state proceedings and the possible limitations on the applicability of the Federal Rules of Evidence otherwise provided by Rules 101 and 1101.

The rule is intended to apply in all federal court proceedings, including court-annexed and court-ordered arbitrations, without regard to any possible limitations of Rules 101 and 1101. This provision is not intended to raise an inference about the applicability of any other rule of evidence in arbitration proceedings more generally.

The costs of discovery can be equally high for state and federal causes of action, and the rule seeks to limit those costs in all federal proceedings, regardless of whether the claim arises under state or federal law. Accordingly, the rule applies to state law causes of action brought in federal court.

Subdivision (g). The rule's coverage is limited to attorney-client privilege and work product. The operation of waiver by disclosure, as applied to other evidentiary privileges, remains a question of federal common law. Nor does the rule purport to apply to the Fifth Amendment privilege against compelled self-incrimination.

The definition of work product "materials" is intended to include both tangible and intangible inforation. *See In re Cendant Corp. Sec. Litig.*, 343 F.3d 658, 662 (3d Cir. 2003) ("work product protection extends to both tangible and intangible work product").

ADVISORY COMMITTEE'S NOTE (2011 AMENDMENT)

Rule 502 has been amended by changing the initial letter of a few words from uppercase to lowercase as part of the restyling of the Evidence Rules to make style and terminology consistent throughout the rules. There is no intent to change any result in any ruling on evidence admissibility.

COMMENTARY ON FEDERAL AND FLORIDA RULE DIFFERENCES

Florida Stat. § 90.507 provides that a person who otherwise has a privilege against disclosure of a confidential communication or document waives the privilege if the person (or his predecessor while holder of the privilege) voluntarily discloses the matter, makes the communication when she does not have a reasonable expectation of privacy, or consents to disclosure of any significant part of the matter.

Under the Florida rule, a failure to object to the introduction of otherwise privileged matter constitutes a waiver. See *Woodel v. State*, 804 So. 2d 316, 323 (Fla. 2001). When disclosure is inadvertent, Florida law neither views the privilege as automatically waived nor necessarily preserved, but instead follows a multi-factored "relevant circumstances" test to determine whether the privilege has been waived. See *Nova Southeastern Univ. v. Jacobson*, 25 So. 3d 82, 86 (Fla. 4th DCA 2009); *Abamar Housing & Dev., Inc. v. Lisa Daly Lady Décor, Inc.*, 698 So. 2d 276, 278-79 (Fla. 3d DCA 1997). When a partial disclosure of otherwise privileged matter is voluntarily made, it constitutes a waiver of all other privileged matter relevant to the matter already disclosed. See *Coates v. Akerman, Senterfitt & Eidson, P.A.*, 940 So. 2d 504, 511 (Fla. 2d DCA 2006); *Eastern Air Lines v. Gellert*, 431 So. 2d 329, 332-33 (Fla. 3d DCA 1983).

There is no *general* federal rule of evidence governing waiver. However, in 2008, Congress enacted into law Federal Rule 502, which governs waiver of the attorney-client privilege. Under that provision, when inadvertent disclosure of privileged matter occurs in a federal proceeding or to a federal office or agency, it does *not* constitute waiver of the attorney-client privilege if (a) the holder of the privilege took reasonable steps to prevent disclosure; and (b) the holder promptly took steps to rectify the error. See FED. R. EVID. 502(b). When a partial disclosure of otherwise privileged matter is *intentionally* made, it constitutes a waiver of all other privileged matter concerning the same subject matter when the court finds that they ought in fairness to be considered together. See FED. R. EVID. 502(a). However, such "subject matter" waiver does not occur when the partial disclosure was *inadvertent*. See *id.*; Advisory Committee's Note to FED. R. EVID. 502(a). As under Florida practice, a failure to object to the introduction of otherwise privileged matter constitutes a waiver. *See, e.g., U.S. v. Vo*, 413 F.3d 1010, 1017 (9th Cir. 2005); *Nguyen v. Excel Corp.*, 197 F.3d 200, 206 & n.12 (5th Cir. 1999).

Florida Stat. § 90.508. Privileged Matter Disclosed Under Compulsion or Without Opportunity to Claim Privilege

Evidence of a statement or other disclosure of privileged matter is inadmissible against the holder of the privilege if the statement or disclosure was compelled erroneously by the court or made without opportunity to claim the privilege.

SPONSORS' NOTE (1976 ENACTMENT)

This section prevents the use of privileged information against the holder of the privilege when disclosure of the information was compelled erroneously. While confidentiality, once destroyed, is not susceptible of restoration, prohibiting the use of privileged information against the holder is believed to afford some remedy for the holder's expectation of confidentiality.

This section is consistent with the principle of Davis v. State, 233 So. 2d 641, 642 (Fla. 2nd Dist. 1970) that "a coerced waiver [of a privilege] is invalid," and obviates the concern of the court in Tibado v. Brees, 212 So. 2d 61 (Fla. 2nd Dist. 1968) that a witness, to preserve the privilege, must endure the "hazard of being cited and punished for contempt" for refusing to testify and seeking remedy in a petition for habeas corpus. If the privileged information is erroneously compelled, the effect of disclosure will be mitigated by preventing the use of the testimony at retrial, which will most often be the principle concern of the holder.

This section also excludes as evidence against the holder privileged information disclosed where the holder had no opportunity to claim the privilege. Existing Florida law is in accord. In Schetter v. Schetter, 239 So. 2d 51, 52 (Fla. 4th Dist. 1970), an attorney had turned over to a psychiatrist tape-recordings of his conversations with his client. The testimony of the psychiatrist based upon the tapes was held to be inadmissible since the unauthorized disclosure of the communications was a violation of the attorney-client privilege. Although disclosure to the psychiatrist destroyed the confidentiality which the privilege was designed to protect, the client did not have an opportunity to object to its disclosure and was permitted to suppress its use against him.

For similar provisions, see Prop. Fed. Rule Evid. 512; Wisc. Evid. Rule 905.12; Calif. Evid. Code § 912(a).

COMMENTARY ON FEDERAL AND FLORIDA RULE DIFFERENCES

Florida Stat. § 90.508 provides that privileged communications or documents are inadmissible against the holder of the privilege if the evidence was compelled erroneously by the court or was disclosed without an opportunity to claim the privilege.

This provision is nearly identical to Proposed Federal Rule 512, and under federal case law evidence does not lose its privileged status if a court erroneously compels its disclosure or if it is disclosed without opportunity to claim the privilege. *See In re Vargas*, 723 F.2d 1461, 1466 & n.4 (10th Cir. 1983); *Transamerica Computer Co. v. IBM Corp.*, 573 F.2d 646, 651 (9th Cir. 1978).

Florida Stat. § 90.509. Application of Privileged Communication

Nothing in this act shall abrogate a privilege for any communication which was made prior to July 1, 1979, if such communication was privileged at the time it was made.

SPONSORS' NOTE (1976 ENACTMENT)

This section was added by the House Judiciary Committee to insure that statements which were made prior to the effective date of the Code and were privileged when they were made would not have their privileged nature destroyed because of the enactment of the Code.

COMMENTARY ON FEDERAL AND FLORIDA RULE DIFFERENCES

Florida Stat. § 90.509 provides that no communication that was, under pre-existing law, privileged when made shall have its privileged nature destroyed by the enactment of the Florida Evidence Code, to the extent that the scope of any pre-existing privilege was narrowed under the Code.

There is no comparable provision in the federal rules of evidence. When a federal court determines under Federal Rule 501 that "reason and experience" call for the narrowing of a pre-existing privilege, that holding is made applicable to communications made prior to that date, even if those communications were privileged under pre-existing law. *See In re Grand Jury Subpoena Duces Tecum*, 112 F.3d 910, 925 (8th Cir. 1997).

Florida Stat. § 90.510. Privileged Communication Necessary to Adverse Party

In any civil case or proceeding in which a party claims a privilege as to a communication necessary to an adverse party, the court, upon motion, may dismiss the claim for relief or the affirmative defense to which the privileged testimony would relate. In making its determination, the court may engage in an in camera inquiry into the privilege.

COMMENTARY ON FEDERAL AND FLORIDA RULE DIFFERENCES

Florida Stat. § 90.510 provides that in a civil case in which a party claims a privilege as to a communication deemed necessary to an adverse party, the court, if requested, may dismiss the claim or affirmative defense to which the privileged testimony relates. In making this determination, the court is given the authority under the rule to engage in an *in camera* inquiry into the privilege. The provision is inapplicable in criminal cases. *See State v. Famiglietti*, 817 So. 2d 901, 905 (Fla. 3d DCA 2002).

There is no comparable provision in the federal rules of evidence. *See In re Forfeiture of $13,000.00 U.S. Currency*, 522 So. 2d 408, 409 (Fla. 5th DCA 1988).

ARTICLE VI. WITNESSES

Federal Rule	Florida Stat. §	Description
601	90.601	Competency to Testify in General
—	90.603	Disqualification of Witness
602	90.604	Need for Personal Knowledge
603	90.605	Oath or Affirmation to Testify Truthfully
604	90.606, 90.6063	Interpreter
605	90.607	Judge's Competency as a Witness
606	90.607	Juror's Competency as a Witness
607	90.608	Who May Impeach a Witness
608	90.609	A Witness's Character for Truthfulness or Untruthfulness
609	90.610	Impeachment by Evidence of a Criminal Conviction
610	90.611	Religious Beliefs or Opinions
611	90.612	Mode and Order of Examining Witnesses and Presenting Evidence
612	90.613	Writing Used to Refresh a Witness's Memory
613	90.614	Witness's Prior Statement
614	90.615	Court's Calling or Examining a Witness
615	90.616	Excluding Witnesses

Federal Rule 601. Competency to Testify in General

Every person is competent to be a witness unless these rules provide otherwise. But in a civil case, state law governs the witness's competency regarding a claim or defense for which state law supplies the rule of decision.

ADVISORY COMMITTEE'S NOTE

This general ground-clearing eliminates all grounds of incompetency not specifically recognized in the succeeding rules of this Article. Included among the grounds thus abolished are religious belief, conviction of crime, and connection with the litigation as a party or interested person or spouse of a party or interested person. With the exception of the so-called Dead Man's Acts, American jurisdictions generally have ceased to recognize these grounds.

The Dead Man's Acts are surviving traces of the common law disqualification of parties and interested persons. They exist in variety too great to convey conviction of their wisdom and effectiveness. These rules contain no provision of this kind. For the reasoning underlying the decision not to give effect to state statutes in diversity cases, see the Advisory Committee's Note to Rule 501.

No mental or moral qualifications for testifying as a witness are specified. Standards of mental capacity have proved elusive in actual application. A leading commentator observes that few witnesses are disqualified on that ground. Weihofen, Testimonial Competence and Credibility, 34 Geo.Wash.L.Rev. 53 (1965). Discretion is regularly exercised in favor of allowing the testimony. A witness wholly without capacity is difficult to imagine. The question is one particularly suited to the jury as one of weight and credibility, subject to judicial authority to review the sufficiency of the evidence. 2 Wigmore §§ 501, 509. Standards of moral qualification in practice consist essentially of evaluating a person's truthfulness in terms of his own answers about it. Their principal utility is in affording an opportunity on voir dire examination to impress upon the witness his moral duty. This result may, however, be accomplished more directly, and without haggling in terms of legal standards, by the manner of administering the oath or affirmation under Rule 603.

Admissibility of religious belief as a ground of impeachment is treated in Rule 610. Conviction of crime as a ground of impeachment is the subject of Rule 609. Marital relationship is the basis for privilege under Rule 505. Interest in the outcome of litigation and mental capacity are, of course, highly relevant to credibility and require no special treatment to render them admissible along with other matters bearing upon the perception, memory, and narration of witnesses.

REPORT OF HOUSE COMMITTEE ON THE JUDICIARY

Rule 601 as submitted to the Congress provided that "Every person is competent to be a witness except as otherwise provided in these rules." One effect of the Rule as proposed would have been to abolish age, mental capacity, and other grounds recognized in some State jurisdictions as making a person incompetent as a witness. The greatest controversy centered around the Rule's rendering inapplicable in the federal courts the so-called Dead Man's Statutes which exist in some States. Acknowledging that there is substantial disagreement as to the merit of Dead Man's Statutes, the Committee nevertheless believed that where such statutes have been enacted they represent State policy which should not be overturned in the absence of a compelling federal interest. The Committee therefore amended the Rule to make competency in civil actions determinable in accordance with State law with respect to elements of claims or defenses as to which State law supplies the rule of decision. Cf. Courtland v. Walston & Co., Inc., 340 F.Supp. 1076, 1087–1092 (S.D.N.Y.1972).

REPORT OF SENATE COMMITTEE ON THE JUDICIARY

The amendment to rule 601 parallels the treatment accorded rule 501 discussed immediately above.

CONFERENCE REPORT

Rule 601 deals with competency of witnesses. Both the House and Senate bills provide that federal competency law applies in criminal cases. In civil actions and proceedings, the House bill provides that state competency law applies "to an element of a claim or defense as to which State law supplies the rule of decision." The Senate bill provides that "in civil actions and proceedings arising under 28 U.S.C. § 1332 or 28 U.S.C. § 1335, or between citizens of different States and removed under 28 U.S.C. § 1441(b) the competency of a witness, person, government, State or political subdivision thereof is determined in accordance with State law, unless with respect to the particular claim or defense, Federal law supplies the rule of decision."

The wording of the House and Senate bills differs in the treatment of civil actions and proceedings. The rule in the House bill applies to evidence that relates to "an element of a claim or defense." If an item of proof tends to support or defeat a claim or defense, or an element of a claim or defense, and if state law supplies the rule of decision for that claim or defense, then state competency law applies to that item of proof.

For reasons similar to those underlying its action on Rule 501, the Conference adopts the House provision.

ADVISORY COMMITTEE'S NOTE (2011 AMENDMENT)

The language of Rule 601 has been amended as part of the restyling of the Evidence Rules to make them more easily understood and to make style and terminology consistent throughout the rules. These changes are intended to be stylistic only. There is no intent to change any result in any ruling on evidence admissibility.

Florida Stat. § 90.601. General Rule of Competency

Every person is competent to be a witness, except as otherwise provided by statute.

SPONSORS' NOTE (1976 ENACTMENT)

This section, which is substantially qualified by other provisions in this Act, makes it clear that grounds for disqualification of a witness must be based upon statute. Included among the grounds abolished by this Act are religious belief, conviction of a crime, and connection with litigation as a party or interested person or being the spouse of a party or interested person.

The existing Florida law on competency of witnesses is similar to this section. While there is no existing statute which generally grants competency, Section 90.04 of the Florida Statutes provides that both a husband and wife are competent witnesses in civil actions, Section 90.06 provides that atheists and agnostics are competent witnesses, Section 90.08 provides that the prior conviction of a crime does not disqualify a witness in any court, and Section 914.07 provides that the law regarding the competency of witnesses in civil cases is applicable in criminal cases. Furthermore, Section 90.07, which made a convicted perjurer incompetent to testify, has been repealed. Rather than setting forth all of the grounds that will not make a witness incompetent, this section affirmatively provides for the elimination of all disqualifications unless specifically provided. The matters treated in the aforementioned existing statutory provisions, which are not included in this section, are included elsewhere in this Act.

The common law rule of incompetency of all persons having a direct pecuniary or proprietary interest in the litigation has been abolished by Section 90.05 of the Florida Statutes.

COMMENTARY ON FEDERAL AND FLORIDA RULE DIFFERENCES

Florida Stat. § 90.601 and its federal counterpart, Federal Rule 601, set forth the default rule on witness competency. Under both the federal and Florida rules, unless otherwise provided in some other rule, every person is competent to be a witness, creating a presumption in favor of competency. *Rutherford v. Moore*, 774 So. 2d 637, 646 (Fla. 2000); *U.S. v. Allen J.*, 127 F.3d 1292, 1294 (10th Cir. 1997). Thus, the rules abolish such common law grounds for declaring a witness incompetent as religious belief, conviction of crime, and connection with the litigation as a party, interested person, or spouse of a party or interested person. *See* Advisory Committee's Note to FED. R. EVID. 601; Sponsors' Note to FLA. STAT. § 90.601.

Under the federal rule, in civil actions and proceedings, the competency of a witness with respect to an element of a claim or defense as to which state law governs is to be determined in accordance with state law. A federal court exercising jurisdiction over such a claim looks at the law of the state in which it sits, including that state's choice of law rules, to determine which state's competency law to apply in disputes with multi-state contacts. *See Equitable Life Assur. Soc'y of U.S. v. McKay*, 837 F.2d 904, 905 (9th Cir. 1988). Although applicable to any state law ground of incompetency, Congress's primary concern in enacting this provision was to give effect to state Dead Man's Acts in diversity cases, *see* Advisory Committee's Note to FED. R. EVID. 601, which Florida once had but has since repealed. *See* 2005 Florida Laws ch. 2005-46, § 1 (repealing FLA. STAT. § 90.602). *See also In re Amendments to the Florida Evidence Code*, 960 So. 2d 762, 762-64 (Fla. 2007) (order by Florida Supreme Court concurring in repeal of § 90.602 to the extent that it is procedural). By contrast, the Florida rule does not direct the Florida courts to apply federal law when adjudicating a federal claim.

Florida Stat. § 90.603. Disqualification of Witness

A person is disqualified to testify as a witness when the court determines that the person is:

(1) Incapable of expressing himself or herself concerning the matter in such a manner as to be understood, either directly or through interpretation by one who can understand him or her.

(2) Incapable of understanding the duty of a witness to tell the truth.

SPONSORS' NOTE (1976 ENACTMENT)

This section is a codification of existing Florida law. In <u>Clinton v. State</u>, 53 Fla. 98, 43 So. 312, 315 (1907), the Supreme Court said:

> Where it appears that...[a witness] has sufficient intelligence to receive just impressions of the facts respecting which he is to testify, and sufficient capacity to relate them correctly, and has received sufficient instruction to appreciate the nature and obligation of an oath, he should be admitted to testify....

Children and persons suffering from mental impairment are permitted to testify when they meet the criteria of this Act. Florida has adopted this view towards the competency of children, <u>Bell v. State</u>, 93 So.2d 575 (Fla. 1957), <u>Cross v. State</u>, 89 Fla. 212, 103 So. 636 (1925), and mentally defective persons, <u>Florida Power and Light Co. v. Robinson</u>, 68 So.2d 406, 413 (Fla. 1953).

The question of competency is to be determined by the trial court under existing law and Section 90.104 of this Act. See <u>Clinton v. State</u>, <u>supra</u>; <u>Ramey v. State</u>, 202 So.2d 221 (Fla. 3rd Dist. 1967). See Calif. Evid. Code § 701; Fed. Rule Evid. 601.

COMMENTARY ON FEDERAL AND FLORIDA RULE DIFFERENCES

Florida Stat. § 90.603 provides that a person cannot testify as a witness if the court determines that he is either incapable of directly or indirectly communicating in a manner that can be understood or he is incapable of understanding the duty of a witness to tell the truth. The rule is typically invoked with respect to children and those who are mentally incapacitated. *See Tampa Brass & Aluminum Corp. v. American Employers' Ins. Co.*, 709 So. 2d 548, 548-49 (Fla. 2d DCA 1998). However, Florida law does not set a minimum age limit for testifying, *see Griffin v. State*, 526 So. 2d 752, 753 (Fla. 1st DCA 1988), nor is someone disqualified from testifying just because she is insane, *see Belcher v. Johnson*, 834 So. 2d 422, 422 (Fla. 2d DCA 2003); *Zabrani v. Riveron*, 495 So. 2d 1195, 1197-98 (Fla. 3d DCA 1986).

Together with Florida Stat. § 90.604 (requirement of personal knowledge), this rule has been interpreted as requiring that a witness be disqualified if the court determines that she is (1) unable to communicate to the jury; (2) unable to understand the duty to tell the truth; or (3) unable to perceive and remember events. *See Rutherford v. Moore*, 774 So. 2d 637, 646 (Fla. 2000). When a challenge is made to a witness's qualification to testify, the trial court must permit voir dire on the issue and make a case-specific determination of the witness's qualification to testify. *See Palazzolo v. State*, 754 So. 2d 731, 738 (Fla. 2d DCA 2000). The fact that someone is a known liar—even a convicted perjurer—does not disqualify him under this section; he can be disqualified only if there is evidence of a "mental inability to understand the concept of an oath to tell the truth." *Tampa Brass*, 709 So. 2d at 549.

There is no analogous provision in the federal rules of evidence, as the thrust of those rules is that the witness's limitations can be brought to the jury's attention and be weighed accordingly. *See* Advisory Committee's Note to FED. R. EVID. 601; *U.S. v. Bedonie*, 913 F.2d 782, 798-801 (10th Cir. 1990). However, the federal courts have found the authority to exclude the testimony of a witness so impaired that she cannot give meaningful testimony under other provisions, including Federal Rule 403 (probative worth substantially outweighs prejudicial effect), Federal Rule 603 (inability of witness to take or comprehend oath), and Federal Rule 602 (impaired to the point that he is not testifying from personal knowledge). *See U.S. v. Ramirez*, 871 F.2d 582, 584 (6th Cir. 1989).

Federal Rule 602. Need for Personal Knowledge

A witness may testify to a matter only if evidence is introduced sufficient to support a finding that the witness has personal knowledge of the matter. Evidence to prove personal knowledge may consist of the witness's own testimony. This rule does not apply to a witness's expert testimony under Rule 703.

ADVISORY COMMITTEE'S NOTE

" . . . [T]he rule requiring that a witness who testifies to a fact which can be perceived by the senses must have had an opportunity to observe, and must have actually observed the fact" is a "most pervasive manifestation" of the common law insistence upon "the most reliable sources of information."

McCormick § 10, p. 19. These foundation requirements may, of course, be furnished by the testimony of the witness himself; hence personal knowledge is not an absolute but may consist of what the witness thinks he knows from personal perception. 2 Wigmore § 650. It will be observed that the rule is in fact a specialized application of the provisions of Rule 104(b) on conditional relevancy.

This rule does not govern the situation of a witness who testifies to a hearsay statement as such, if he has personal knowledge of the making of the statement. Rules 801 and 805 would be applicable. This rule would, however, prevent him from testifying to the subject matter of the hearsay statement, as he has no personal knowledge of it.

The reference to Rule 703 is designed to avoid any question of conflict between the present rule and the provisions of that rule allowing an expert to express opinions based on facts of which he does not have personal knowledge.

ADVISORY COMMITTEE'S NOTE (2011 AMENDMENT)

The language of Rule 602 has been amended as part of the restyling of the Evidence Rules to make them more easily understood and to make style and terminology consistent throughout the rules. These changes are intended to be stylistic only. There is no intent to change any result in any ruling on evidence admissibility.

Florida Stat. § 90.604. Lack of Personal Knowledge

Except as otherwise provided in s. 90.702, a witness may not testify to a matter unless evidence is introduced which is sufficient to support a finding that the witness has personal knowledge of the matter. Evidence to prove personal knowledge may be given by the witness's own testimony.

SPONSORS' NOTE (1976 ENACTMENT)

This section recognizes that a witness who has actually perceived and observed the fact is the most reliable source of information. The foundation requirement may be supplied by the witness. However, Section 90.703 provides that expert witnesses may be allowed to base their testimony on hypothetical questions presented by counsel rather than requiring that they have personal knowledge of the matters to which they testify.

The existing law is in accord with this Section. See Herndon v. State, 73 Fla. 451, 74 So. 511 (1917); Kennard v. State, 42 Fla. 581, 28 So. 858 (1900). Occasionally the witness has made a personal observation but does not have a definite "impression," "e.g., he saw a man, and 'thought' it was the accused. To this defect in the quality of the impression the law makes no objection, but receives it for what it is worth." Kennard v. State, supra at 859.

See Calif. Evid. Code § 702; New Jersey Evid. Rule 19; Fed. Rule Evid. 602.

COMMENTARY ON FEDERAL AND FLORIDA RULE DIFFERENCES

Florida Stat. § 90.604 and its federal counterpart, Federal Rule 602, set forth the requirement that a witness may not testify to a matter unless sufficient evidence is introduced to support a finding that the witness has personal knowledge of the matter.

Under both rules, whether the witness has personal knowledge is a question of conditional relevancy, as the judge only makes a finding that there is evidence sufficient to support a finding that the witness has personal knowledge. *See* Advisory Committee's Note to FED. R. EVID. 602; FLA. STAT. § 90.105(2); FED. R. EVID. 104(b). Moreover, under both rules, the witness's own testimony can serve as the basis for such a finding. Finally, an exception to both rules exists for expert witnesses, who are permitted to express opinions based on facts of which they lack personal knowledge. *See* Advisory Committee's Note to FED. R. EVID. 602; Sponsors' Note to FLA. STAT. § 90.604.

Federal Rule 603. Oath or Affirmation to Testify Truthfully

Before testifying, a witness must give an oath or affirmation to testify truthfully. It must be in a form designed to impress that duty on the witness's conscience.

ADVISORY COMMITTEE'S NOTE

The rule is designed to afford the flexibility required in dealing with religious adults, atheists, conscientious objectors, mental defectives, and children. Affirmation is simply a solemn undertaking to tell the truth; no special verbal formula is required. As is true generally, affirmation is recognized by federal law. "Oath" includes affirmation, 1 U.S.C. § 1; judges and clerks may administer oaths and affirmations, 28 U.S.C. §§ 459, 953; and affirmations are acceptable in lieu of oaths under Rule 43(d) of the Federal Rules of Civil Procedure. Perjury by a witness is a crime, 18 U.S.C. § 1621.

ADVISORY COMMITTEE'S NOTE (2011 AMENDMENT)

The language of Rule 603 has been amended as part of the restyling of the Evidence Rules to make them more easily understood and to make style and terminology consistent throughout the rules. These changes are intended to be stylistic only. There is no intent to change any result in any ruling on evidence admissibility.

Florida Stat. § 90.605. Oath or Affirmation of Witness

(1) Before testifying, each witness shall declare that he or she will testify truthfully, by taking an oath or affirmation in substantially the following form: "Do you swear or affirm that the evidence you are about to give will be the truth, the whole truth, and nothing but the truth?" The witness's answer shall be noted in the record.

(2) In the court's discretion, a child may testify without taking the oath if the court determines the child understands the duty to tell the truth or the duty not to lie.

SPONSORS' NOTE (1976 ENACTMENT)

[This section is designed to afford the flexibility required in dealing with religious adults, atheists, conscientious objectors, mental defectives, and children. No special verbal formula is required. See Calif. Evid. Code § 710; New Jersey Evid. Rule 18; Fed. Rule Evid. 603.][19]

The existing law also permits a witness to declare that he will testify truthfully, either by oath or affirmation. Fla.Stat. § 90.02. Perjury, as defined in non-judicial proceedings by Fla. Stat. § 837.01, includes willful false swearing and affirming.

---

[19] Editor's Note: The bracketed language refers to the original version of the rule, which was subsequently amended by the legislature to provide for a uniform oath.

COMMENTARY ON FEDERAL AND FLORIDA RULE DIFFERENCES

Florida Stat. § 90.605 and its federal counterpart, Federal Rule 603, set forth a general requirement that every witness must, before testifying, declare by oath or affirmation that he will testify truthfully. The rules differ in two respects.

First, the Florida rule specifies that the oath should be in a specific form: "Do you swear or affirm that the evidence you are about to give will be the truth, the whole truth, and nothing but the truth?" The drafters of the Florida rule added this language "to insure a uniform oath or affirmation." Sponsors' Note to FLA. STAT. § 90.605. By contrast, the federal rule requires only that the oath be in a form designed to impress the duty to testify truthfully on the witness's conscience, and does not dictate a specific verbal formula. See *U.S. v. Ward*, 989 F.2d 1015, 1019 (9th Cir. 1992); Advisory Committee's Note to FED. R. EVID. 603.

Second, the Florida rule gives the trial court discretion to permit a child to testify without taking the oath if the court determines that the child understands the duty to tell the truth. To invoke this exception, the trial court must determine whether the child has a "moral sense" of the duty to tell the truth. See *Griffin v. State*, 526 So. 2d 752, 755 (Fla. 1st DCA 1988). While the federal rule does not permit a judge to dispense with the oath or affirmation requirement, it does give the trial court flexibility to fashion an oath or affirmation that is meaningful to a child witness. See *U.S. v. Thai*, 29 F.3d 785, 811-12 (2d Cir. 1994).

Federal Rule 604. Interpreter

An interpreter must be qualified and must give an oath or affirmation to make a true translation.

ADVISORY COMMITTEE'S NOTE

The rule implements Rule 43(f) of the Federal Rules of Civil Procedure and Rule 28(b) of the Federal Rules of Criminal Procedure, both of which contain provisions for the appointment and compensation of interpreters.

ADVISORY COMMITTEE'S NOTE (2011 AMENDMENT)

The language of Rule 604 has been amended as part of the restyling of the Evidence Rules to make them more easily understood and to make style and terminology consistent throughout the rules. These changes are intended to be stylistic only. There is no intent to change any result in any ruling on evidence admissibility.

Florida Stat. § 90.606. Interpreters and Translators

(1)   (a) When a judge determines that a witness cannot hear or understand the English language, or cannot express himself or herself in English sufficiently to be understood, an interpreter who is duly qualified to interpret for the witness shall be sworn to do so.

(b) This section is not limited to persons who speak a language other than English, but applies also to the language and descriptions of any person, such as a child or a person who is mentally or developmentally disabled, who cannot be reasonably understood, or who cannot understand questioning, without the aid of an interpreter.

(2) A person who serves in the role of interpreter or translator in any action or proceeding is subject to all the provisions of this chapter relating to witnesses.

(3) An interpreter shall take an oath that he or she will make a true interpretation of the questions asked and the answers given and that the interpreter will make a true translation into English of any writing which he or she is required by his or her duties to decipher or translate.

SPONSORS' NOTE (1976 ENACTMENT)

When a witness is not able to communicate in the English language, an interpreter or translator must be sought. This section applies not only to those persons who speak a foreign language, but also to persons organically unable to use words, e.g., deaf-mutes. The provisions in subsection requiring the interpreter to be an expert must be read with § 90.702 which defines an expert as one so qualified by knowledge, skill, experience, training, or education. Therefore, a person who is demonstrated to have sufficient knowledge of a foreign language would be qualified, despite his lack of specialized formal education of it.

This section is in accord with the existing Florida law in having the trial judge make the determination of when an interpreter is needed. See Watson v. State, 190 So.2d 161 (Fla.), cert. denied 389 U.S. 960, 88 S.Ct. 339, 19 L.Ed.2d 369 (1966). The other requirements of this section are included in Kelly v. State, 118 So. 1 (Fla.1928). See Calif. Evid. Code §§ 750-54; Fed. Rule Evid. 604.

Florida Stat. § 90.6063. Interpreter Services for Deaf Persons

(1) The Legislature finds that it is an important concern that the rights of deaf citizens be protected. It is the intent of the Legislature to ensure that appropriate and effective interpreter services be made available to Florida's deaf citizens.

(2) In all judicial proceedings and in sessions of a grand jury wherein a deaf person is a complainant, defendant, witness, or otherwise a party, or wherein a deaf person is a juror or grand juror, the court or presiding officer shall appoint a qualified interpreter to interpret the proceedings or deliberations to the deaf person and to interpret the deaf person's testimony, statements, or deliberations to the court, jury, or grand jury. A qualified interpreter shall be appointed, or other auxiliary aid provided as appropriate, for the duration of the trial or other proceeding in which a deaf juror or grand juror is seated.

(3) (a) "Deaf person" means any person whose hearing is so seriously impaired as to prohibit the person from understanding oral communications when spoken in a normal, conversational tone.

(b) For the purposes of this section, the term "qualified interpreter" means an interpreter certified by the National Registry of Interpreters for the Deaf or the Florida Registry of Interpreters for the Deaf or an interpreter whose qualifications are otherwise determined by the appointing authority.

(4) Every deaf person whose appearance before a proceeding entitles him or her to an interpreter shall notify the appointing authority of his or her disability not less than 5 days prior to any appearance and shall request at such time the services of an interpreter. Whenever a deaf person receives notification of the time of an appearance before a proceeding less than 5 days prior to the proceeding, the deaf person shall provide his or her notification and request as soon thereafter as practicable. In any case, nothing in this subsection shall operate to relieve an appointing authority's duty to provide an interpreter for a deaf person so entitled, and failure to strictly comply with the notice requirement will not be deemed a waiver of the right to an interpreter. An appointing authority may require a person requesting the appointment of an interpreter to furnish reasonable proof of the person's disability when the appointing authority has reason to believe that the person is not so disabled.

(5) The appointing authority may channel requests for qualified interpreters through:

(a) The Florida Registry of Interpreters for the Deaf;

(b) The Division of Vocational Rehabilitation of the Department of Education; or

(c) Any other resource wherein the appointing authority knows that qualified interpreters can be found.

(6) No qualified interpreter shall be appointed unless the appointing authority and the deaf person make a preliminary determination that the interpreter is able to communicate readily with the deaf person and is able to repeat and translate statements to and from the deaf person accurately.

(7) Before a qualified interpreter may participate in any proceedings subsequent to an appointment under the provisions of this act, such interpreter shall make an oath or affirmation that he or she will make a true interpretation in an understandable manner to the deaf person for whom the interpreter is appointed and that he or she will repeat the statements of the deaf person in the English language to the best of his or her skill and judgment. Whenever a deaf person communicates through an interpreter to any person under such circumstances that the communication would be privileged, and the recipient of the communication could not be compelled to testify as to the communication, this privilege shall apply to the interpreter.

(8) An interpreter appointed by the court in a criminal matter or in a civil matter shall be entitled to a reasonable fee for such service, in addition to actual expenses for travel, to be paid out of general county funds.

COMMENTARY ON FEDERAL AND FLORIDA RULE DIFFERENCES

Florida Stat. §§ 90.606 and 90.6063 and their federal counterpart, Federal Rule 604, govern the use of interpreters at trial. In addition, detailed provisions governing the appointment of interpreters in federal court are set forth in 28 U.S.C. § 1827.

Under both Florida and federal law, the interpreter is required to take a more specific oath or affirmation than is required of witnesses under Florida Stat. § 90.605 and its federal counterpart, Federal Rule 603, to wit, an oath to make a "true" translation. *See* FLA. STAT. § 90.606(3); *id.* § 90.6063(7); FED. R. EVID. 604. Moreover, under both Florida and federal law, the interpreter must be qualified as an expert witness. *See* FLA. STAT. § 90.606(1)(a); Sponsors' Note to FLA. STAT. § 90.606(1)(a); FED. R. EVID. 604. In addition, both the federal and Florida laws encompass not just foreign-language interpreters but also interpreters for the hearing impaired, and both have been interpreted to permit an interpreter to accompany a hearing-impaired juror into the jury room to assist her in deliberations. *See U.S. v. Dempsey*, 830 F.2d 1084, 1088-91 (10th Cir. 1987); *Dilorenzo v. State*, 711 So. 2d 1362, 1362-63 (Fla. 4th DCA 1998).

There are a few significant differences, however, between the two rules. First, the Florida rule appears to be broader in that it covers not just interpreters for the hearing impaired and for those who speak languages other than English, but also to those who help interpret communications by children and the mentally or developmentally disabled who cannot be understood without the aid of an interpreter. *See* FLA. STAT. § 90.606(1)(b). Furthermore, while under Florida law the requirement of a special oath appears to apply even to those who only translate foreign *documents, see* FLA. STAT. § 90.606(3); *B.C.S., S.r.l. v. Wise*, 910 So. 2d 871, 874 & n.5 (Fla. 5th DCA 2005), the federal rule requires the special oath only for those who translate the testimony of a witness, not for those who merely translate documents. *See U.S. v. Armijo*, 5 F.3d 1229, 1235 (9th Cir. 1993).

Federal Rule 605. Judge's Competency as a Witness

The presiding judge may not testify as a witness at the trial. A party need not object to preserve the issue.

ADVISORY COMMITTEE'S NOTE

In view of the mandate of 28 U.S.C. § 455 that a judge disqualify himself in "any case in which he...is or has been a material witness," the likelihood that the presiding judge in a federal court might be called to testify in the trial over which he is presiding is slight. Nevertheless the possibility is not totally eliminated.

The solution here presented is a broad rule of incompetency, rather than such alternatives as incompetency only as to material matters, leaving the matter to the discretion of the judge, or recognizing no incompetency. The choice is the result of inability to evolve satisfactory answers to questions which arise when the judge abandons the bench for the witness stand. Who rules on objections? Who compels him to answer? Can he rule impartially on the weight and admissibility of his own testimony? Can he be impeached or cross-examined effectively? Can he, in a jury trial, avoid conferring his seal of approval on one side in the eyes of the jury? Can he, in a bench trial, avoid an involvement destructive of impartiality? The rule of general incompetency has substantial support. See Report of the Special Committee on the Propriety of Judges Appearing as Witnesses, 36 A.B.A.J. 630 (1950); cases collected in Annot. 157 A.L.R. 311; McCormick § 68, p. 147; Uniform Rule 42; California Evidence Code § 703; Kansas Code of Civil Procedure § 60-442; New Jersey Evidence Rule 42. Cf. 6 Wigmore § 1909, which advocates leaving the matter to the discretion of the judge, and statutes to that effect collected in Annot., 157 A.L.R. 311.

The rule provides an "automatic" objection. To require an actual objection would confront the opponent with a choice between not objecting, with the result of allowing the testimony, and objecting, with the probable result of excluding the testimony but at the price of continuing the trial before a judge likely to feel that his integrity had been attacked by the objector.

ADVISORY COMMITTEE'S NOTE (2011 AMENDMENT)

The language of Rule 605 has been amended as part of the restyling of the Evidence Rules to make them more easily understood and to make style and terminology consistent throughout the rules. These changes are intended to be stylistic only. There is no intent to change any result in any ruling on evidence admissibility.

Federal Rule 606. Juror's Competency as a Witness

(a) **At the Trial.** A juror may not testify as a witness before the other jurors at the trial. If a juror is called to testify, the court must give a party an opportunity to object outside the jury's presence.

(b) **During an Inquiry into the Validity of a Verdict or Indictment.**

(1) *Prohibited Testimony or Other Evidence.* During an inquiry into the validity of a verdict or indictment, a juror may not testify about any statement made or incident that occurred during the jury's deliberations; the effect of anything on that juror's or another juror's vote; or any juror's mental processes concerning the verdict or indictment. The court may not receive a juror's affidavit or evidence of a juror's statement on these matters.

(2) *Exceptions.* A juror may testify about whether:

(A) extraneous prejudicial information was improperly brought to the jury's attention;

(B) an outside influence was improperly brought to bear on any juror; or

(C) a mistake was made in entering the verdict on the verdict form.

ADVISORY COMMITTEE'S NOTE

Subdivision (a). The considerations which bear upon the permissibility of testimony by a juror in the trial in which he is sitting as juror bear an obvious similarity to those evoked when the judge is called as a witness. See Advisory Committee's Note to Rule 605. The judge is not, however in this instance so involved as to call for departure from usual principles requiring objection to be made; hence the only provision on objection is that opportunity be afforded for its making out of the presence of the jury. Compare Rule 605.

Subdivision (b). Whether testimony, affidavits, or statements of jurors should be received for the purpose of invalidating or supporting a verdict or indictment, and if so, under what circumstances, has given rise to substantial differences of opinion. The familiar rubric that a juror may not impeach his own verdict, dating from Lord Mansfield's time, is a gross oversimplification. The values sought to be promoted by excluding the evidence include freedom of deliberation, stability and finality of verdicts, and protection of jurors against annoyance and embarrassment. McDonald v. Pless, 238U.S. 264 (1915). On the other hand, simply putting verdicts beyond effective reach can only promote irregularity and injustice. The rule offers an accommodation between these competing considerations.

The mental operations and emotional reactions of jurors in arriving at a given result would, if allowed as a subject of inquiry, place every verdict at the mercy of jurors and invite tampering and harassment. See Grenz v. Werre, 129 N.W.2d 681 (N.D.1964). The authorities are in virtually complete accord in excluding the evidence. Fryer, Note on Disqualification of Witnesses, Selected Writings on Evidence and Trial 345, 347 (Fryer ed. 1957); Maguire, Weinstein, et al., Cases on Evidence 887 (5th ed. 1965); 8 Wigmore § 2349 (McNaughton Rev.1961). As to matters other than mental operations and emotional reactions of jurors, substantial authority refuses to allow a juror to disclose irregularities which occur in the jury room, but allows his testimony as to irregularities occurring outside and allows outsiders to testify as to occurrences both inside and out. 8 Wigmore § 2354 (McNaughton Rev.1961). However, the door of the jury room is not necessarily a satisfactory dividing point, and the Supreme Court has refused to accept it for every situation. Mattox v. United States, 146 U.S. 140 (1892).

Under the federal decisions the central focus has been upon insulation of the manner in which the jury reached its verdict, and this protection extends to each of the components of deliberation, including arguments, statements, discussions, mental and emotional reactions, votes, and any other feature of the process. Thus testimony or affidavits of jurors have been held incompetent to show a compromise verdict, Hyde v. United States, 225 U.S. 347, 382 (1912); a quotient verdict, McDonald v. Pless, 238 U.S. 264 (1915); speculation as to insurance coverage, Holden v. Porter, 405 F.2d 878 (10th Cir. 1969); Farmers Coop. Elev. Ass'n v. Strand, 382 F.2d 224, 230 (8th Cir. 1967), cert. denied 389 U.S. 1014; misinterpretation of instructions, Farmers Coop. Elev. Ass'n v. Strand, *supra*; mistake in returning verdict, United States v. Chereton, 309 F.2d 197 (6th Cir. 1962); interpretation of guilty plea by one defendant as implicating others, United States v. Crosby, 294 F.2d 928, 949 (2d Cir. 1961). The policy does not, however, foreclose testimony by jurors as to prejudicial extraneous information or influences injected into or brought to bear upon the deliberative process. Thus a juror is recognized as competent to testify to statements by the bailiff or the introduction of a prejudicial newspaper account into the jury room, Mattox v. United States, 146 U.S. 140 (1892). See also Parker v. Gladden, 385 U.S. 363 (1966).

This rule does not purport to specify the substantive grounds for setting aside verdicts for irregularity; it deals only with the competency of jurors to testify concerning those grounds. Allowing them to testify as to matters other than their own inner reactions involves no particular hazard to the values sought to be protected. The rule is based upon this conclusion. It makes no attempt to specify the substantive grounds for setting aside verdicts for irregularity.

See also Rule 6(e) of the Federal Rules of Criminal Procedure and 18 U.S.C. § 3500, governing the secrecy of grand jury proceedings. The present rule does not relate to secrecy and disclosure but to the competency of certain witnesses and evidence.

REPORT OF HOUSE COMMITTEE ON THE JUDICIARY

As proposed by the Court, Rule 606(b) limited testimony by a juror in the course of an inquiry into the validity of a verdict or indictment. He could testify as to the influence of extraneous prejudicial information brought to the jury's attention (e.g. a radio newscast or a newspaper account) or an outside influence which improperly had been brought to bear upon a juror (e.g. a threat to the safety of a member of his family), but he could not testify as to other irregularities which occurred in the jury room. Under this formulation a quotient verdict could not be attacked through the testimony of a juror, nor could a juror testify to the drunken condition of a fellow juror which so disabled him that he could not participate in the jury's deliberations.

The 1969 and 1971 Advisory Committee drafts would have permitted a member of the jury to testify concerning these kinds of irregularities in the jury room. The Advisory Committee Note in the 1971 draft stated that "... the door of the jury room is not a satisfactory dividing point, and the Supreme Court has refused to accept it." The Advisory Committee further commented that—

The trend has been to draw the dividing line between testimony as to mental processes, on the one hand, and as to the existence of conditions or occurrences of events calculated improperly to influence the verdict, on the other hand, without regard to whether the happening is within or without the jury room.... The jurors are the persons who know what really happened. Allowing them to testify as to matters other than their own reactions involves no particular hazard to the values sought to be protected. The rule is based upon this conclusion. It makes no attempt to specify the substantive grounds for setting aside verdicts for irregularity.

Objective jury misconduct may be testified to in California, Florida, Iowa, Kansas, Nebraska, New Jersey, North Dakota, Ohio, Oregon, Tennessee, Texas, and Washington.

Persuaded that the better practice is that provided for in the earlier drafts, the Committee amended subdivision (b) to read in the text of those drafts.

REPORT OF SENATE COMMITTEE ON THE JUDICIARY

As adopted by the House, this rule would permit the impeachment of verdicts by inquiry into, not the mental processes of the jurors, but what happened in terms of conduct in the jury room. This extension of the ability to impeach a verdict is felt to be unwarranted and ill-advised.

The rule passed by the House embodies a suggestion by the Advisory Committee of the Judicial Conference that is considerably broader than the final version adopted by the Supreme Court, which embodied long-accepted Federal law. Although forbidding the impeachment of verdicts by inquiry into the jurors' mental processes, it deletes from the Supreme Court version the proscription against testimony "as to any matter or statement occurring during the course of the jury's deliberations." This deletion would have the effect of opening verdicts up to challenge on the basis of what happened during the jury's internal deliberations, for example, where a juror alleged that the jury refused to follow the trial judge's instructions or that some of the jurors did not take part in deliberations.

Permitting an individual to attack a jury verdict based upon the jury's internal deliberations has long been recognized as unwise by the Supreme Court. In *McDonald* v. *Pless*, the Court stated:

> [L]et it once be established that verdicts solemnly made and publicly returned into court can be attacked and set aside on the testimony of those who took part in their publication and all verdicts could be, and many would be, followed by an inquiry in the hope of discovering something which might invalidate the finding. Jurors would be harassed and beset by the defeated party in an effort to secure from them evidence of facts which might establish misconduct sufficient to set aside a verdict. If evidence thus secured could be thus used, the result would be to make what was intended to be a private deliberation, the constant subject of public investigation—to the destruction of all frankness and freedom of discussion and conference.[20]

As it stands then, the rule would permit the harassment of former jurors by losing parties as well as the possible exploitation of disgruntled or otherwise badly-motivated ex-jurors.

Public policy requires a finality to litigation. And common fairness requires that absolute privacy be preserved for jurors to engage in the full and free debate necessary to the attainment of just verdicts. Jurors will not be able to function effectively if their deliberations are to be scrutinized in post-trial litigation. In the interest of protecting the jury system and the citizens who make it work, rule 606 should not permit any inquiry into the internal deliberations of the jurors.

CONFERENCE REPORT

Rule 606(b) deals with juror testimony in an inquiry into the validity of a verdict or indictment. The House bill provides that a juror cannot testify about his mental processes or about the effect of anything upon his or another juror's mind as influencing him to assent to or dissent from a verdict or indictment. Thus, the House bill allows a juror to testify about objective matters occurring during the jury's deliberation, such as the misconduct of another juror or the reaching of a quotient verdict. The Senate bill does not permit juror testimony about any matter or statement occurring during the course of the jury's deliberations. The Senate bill does provide, however, that a juror may testify on the question whether extraneous prejudicial information was improperly brought to the jury's attention and on the question whether any outside influence was improperly brought to bear on any juror.

The Conference adopts the Senate amendment. The Conferees believe that jurors should be encouraged to be conscientious in promptly reporting to the court misconduct that occurs during jury deliberations.

ADVISORY COMMITTEE'S NOTE (2006 AMENDMENT)

Rule 606(b) has been amended to provide that juror testimony may be used to prove that the verdict reported was the result of a mistake in entering the verdict on the verdict form. The amendment responds to a divergence between the text of the Rule and the case law that has established an exception for proof of clerical errors. *See, e.g., Plummer v. Springfield Term. Ry.*, 5 F.3d 1, 3 (1st Cir. 1993) ("A number of circuits hold, and we agree, that juror testimony regarding an alleged clerical error, such as announcing a verdict different than that agreed upon, does not challenge the validity of the verdict or the deliberation of mental processes, and therefore is not subject to Rule 606(b)."); *Teevee Toons, Inc., v.*

---

[20] 238 U.S. 264, at 267 (1914).

MP3.Com, Inc., 148 F.Supp.2d 276, 278 (S.D.N.Y. 2001) (noting that Rule 606(b) has been silent regarding inquiries designed to confirm the accuracy of a verdict).

In adopting the exception for proof of mistakes in entering the verdict on the verdict form, the amendment specifically rejects the broader exception, adopted by some courts, permitting the use of juror testimony to prove that the jurors were operating under a misunderstanding about the consequences of the result that they agreed upon. *See, e.g., Attridge v. Cencorp Div. of Dover Techs. Int'l, Inc.*, 836 F.2d 113, 116 (2d Cir. 1987); *Eastridge Development Co., v. Halpert Associates, Inc.*, 853 F.2d 772 (10th Cir. 1988). The broader exception is rejected because an inquiry into whether the jury misunderstood or misapplied an instruction goes to the jurors' mental processes underlying the verdict, rather than the verdict's accuracy in capturing what the jurors had agreed upon. *See, e.g., Karl v. Burlington Northern R.R.*, 880 F.2d 68, 74 (8th Cir. 1989) (error to receive juror testimony on whether verdict was the result of jurors' misunderstanding of instructions: "The jurors did not state that the figure written by the foreman was different from that which they agreed upon, but indicated that the figure the foreman wrote down was intended to be a net figure, not a gross figure. Receiving such statements violates Rule 606(b) because the testimony relates to how the jury interpreted the court's instructions, and concerns the jurors' 'mental processes,' which is forbidden by the rule."); *Robles v. Exxon Corp.*, 862 F.2d 1201, 1208 (5th Cir. 1989) ("the alleged error here goes to the substance of what the jury was asked to decide, necessarily implicating the jury's mental processes insofar as it questions the jury's understanding of the court's instructions and application of those instructions to the facts of the case"). Thus, the exception established by the amendment is limited to cases such as "where the jury foreperson wrote down, in response to an interrogatory, a number different from that agreed upon by the jury, or mistakenly stated that the defendant was 'guilty' when the jury had actually agreed that the defendant was not guilty." *Id.*

It should be noted that the possibility of error in the verdict form will be reduced substantially by polling the jury. Rule 606(b) does not, of course, prevent this precaution. *See* 8C. Wigmore, *Evidence,* § 2350 at 691 (McNaughten ed. 1961) (noting that the reasons for the rule barring juror testimony, "namely, the dangers of uncertainty and of tampering with the jurors to procure testimony, disappear in large part if such investigation as may be desired is *made by the judge* and takes place *before the jurors' discharge* and separation") (emphasis in original). Errors that come to light after polling the jury "may be corrected on the spot, or the jury may be sent out to continue deliberations, or, if necessary, a new trial may be ordered." C. Mueller & L. Kirkpatrick, *Evidence Under the Rules* at 671 (2d ed. 1999) (citing *Sincox v. United States,* 571 F.2d 876, 878–79 (5th Cir. 1978)).

ADVISORY COMMITTEE'S NOTE (2011 AMENDMENT)

The language of Rule 606 has been amended as part of the restyling of the Evidence Rules to make them more easily understood and to make style and terminology consistent throughout the rules. These changes are intended to be stylistic only. There is no intent to change any result in any ruling on evidence admissibility.

Florida Stat. § 90.607. Competency of Certain Persons as Witnesses

(1) (a) Except as provided in paragraph (b), the judge presiding at the trial of an action is not competent to testify as a witness in that trial. An objection is not necessary to preserve the point.

(b) By agreement of the parties, the trial judge may give evidence on a purely formal matter to facilitate the trial of the action.

(2) (a) A member of the jury is not competent to testify as a witness in a trial when he or she is sitting as a juror. If the juror is called to testify, the opposing party shall be given an opportunity to object out of the presence of the jury.

(b) Upon an inquiry into the validity of a verdict or indictment, a juror is not competent to testify as to any matter which essentially inheres in the verdict or indictment.

SPONSORS' NOTE (1976 ENACTMENT)

Subsection (1) In view of the mandate of Fla.Stat. § 38.02 that a judge disqualify himself upon the filing of a proper suggestion of disqualification if "said judge is a material witness for or against one of the parties to said cause,...." the likelihood that a trial judge will be called to testify is small. See generally, Hooks v. State, 207 So.2d 459 (Fla. 2nd Dist. 1968). This section totally eliminates the possibility by adopting a broad rule of incompetency. The automatic objection eliminates trying a case before a judge who possibly feels that his integrity has been attacked by the objector.

This section is supported by the United States Supreme Court which has said in Glasser v. United States, 315 U.S. 60, 82, 62 S.Ct. 457, 86 L.Ed. 680, 706 (1942) that in a criminal case it "is, of course, improper for a judge to assume the role of a witness;..."

See Special Committee on the Propriety of Judges Appearing as Witnesses, 36 A.B.A.J. 630 (1950); Uniform Rule 42; Calif. Evid. Code § 703; Kansas Code of Evid. § 60-442; New Jersey Evid. Rule 42; Fed.Rule Evid. 605.

Subsection (2) Paragraph (a) modifies the common law view that a juror may testify and return to the box, 6 Wigmore, Evidence § 1910 (1940), and adopt the disqualification of Uniform Rule 43. There is no contrary Florida case. Section 913.03(11) of the Florida Statutes provides that a juror may be challenged for cause if he is to be a witness for either party at the trial.

Paragraph (b) does not allow inquiry into any matter concerning the juror's mind, emotions, mental processes or mistaken beliefs which he received about the law in his determination of the verdict, but does allow a juror's testimony or affidavit which shows misconduct during the trial or in the jury room to be used to avoid a verdict as long as the conduct does not inhere in the verdict. The court in McAllister Hotel, Inc. v. Porte, 123 So.2d 339, 344 (Fla. 1960), explained "[T]he law does not permit a juror to avoid his verdict for any reason which essentially inheres in the verdict itself, as that he 'did not assent to the verdict; that he misunderstood the instructions of the Court; the statements of witnesses or the pleadings in the case; that he was unduly influenced by the statements or otherwise of his fellow jurors, or mistaken in his calculations or judgment, or other matters resting alone in the juror's breast."

Under this subsection jurors may testify to evidence of overt acts which might have prejudicially affected the jury in reaching their own verdict. This section distinguishes between a juror's own thought processes and conduct which might affect all the jurors and thus does not inhere in the verdict. For example, the Florida court has avoided quotient verdicts. In Marks v. State Road Department, 69 So.2d 771 (Fla. 1954), the court said:

> Quotient verdicts are universally condemned. To constitute a quotient verdict, however, it is essential that there be a preliminary agreement or understanding among the jurors that each will select a figure as representing his opinion of value or damage and that the sum of said amounts divided by the number of jurors will be accepted by each as his or her verdict, and is in fact so accepted.

See 53 Iowa L. Rev. 1366 (1968) for a listing of the twelve states adopting this view and other examples of the various types of misconduct which do not inhere in the verdict.

See Calif. Evid. Code §§ 704, 1150; Fed. Rule Evid. 606.

This subsection does not purport to specify the substantiating grounds for setting aside verdicts for irregularity but deals only with the competency of jurors to testify concerning those grounds.

COMMENTARY ON FEDERAL AND FLORIDA RULE DIFFERENCES

Florida Stat. § 90.607 and its federal counterparts, Federal Rules 605 and 606, regulate the competency of the presiding judge and members of the jury to testify as witnesses.

Under both the federal and Florida rules, a judge is deemed incompetent to testify as a witness at a trial over which he presides. See FLA. STAT. § 90.607(1)(a); FED. R. EVID. 605. Moreover, under both rules, an objection need not be made in order to preserve this point for review on appeal. See FLA. STAT. § 90.607(1)(a); FED. R. EVID. 605. However, the Florida rule permits the parties to agree to permit the judge to give evidence on a "purely formal matter," while the federal rule contains no such exception. See FLA. STAT. § 90.607(1)(b).

Under both rules, a person is deemed incompetent to testify as a witness at any trial in which she is sitting as a member of the jury. See FLA. STAT. § 90.607(2)(a); FED. R. EVID. 606(a). While neither rule dispenses with the requirement that a party object to preserve this point for appellate review, both rules provide that the opposing party be given the opportunity to do so outside of the jury's presence. See FLA. STAT. § 90.607(2)(a); FED. R. EVID. 606(a).

Even after the jury has rendered its verdict (or, in the case of a grand jury, its indictment), a juror is—subject to certain exceptions—barred from testifying at a proceeding in which an inquiry is being made into the validity of the verdict or indictment. See FLA. STAT. § 90.607(2)(b); FED. R. EVID. 606(b). The Florida rule provides that a juror cannot testify as to any matter which "essentially inheres in" the verdict or indictment. FLA. STAT. § 90.607(2)(b). The federal rule, by contrast, is more specific, providing that a juror may not testify to *any* matter or statement occurring during jury deliberations *or* to the effect of anything upon that or any other juror's mind or emotions or concerning the juror's mental processes, but creating exceptions for evidence of "extraneous prejudicial information" improperly brought to the jury's attention, an "outside influence" improperly brought to bear upon any juror, or making a mistake in entering the verdict on the verdict form. See FED. R. EVID. 606(b).

In most circumstances, the different verbal formulations used in the federal and Florida rules arrive at the same conclusion. Thus, under both the federal and Florida rules, a juror may testify that a member of the jury was approached or threatened by someone or that information about the case was brought to the attention of jurors, such as through a newspaper or communication from a court employee or other individual, or through outside research by a juror. See *Tanner v. U.S.*, 483 U.S. 107, 117-18, 122-25 (1987); *Sea Hawk Seafoods, Inc. v. Alyeska Pipeline Service Co.*, 206 F.3d 900, 906 (9th Cir. 2000); *Marshall v. State*, 854 So. 2d 1235, 1240 (Fla. 2003); *Powell v. Allstate Ins. Co.*, 652 So. 2d 354, 357 n.5 (Fla. 1995). Moreover, under both the federal and Florida rules, a juror may *not* testify about such things as a misunderstanding or failure to follow jury instructions, such as testimony that a juror considered evidence that the judge instructed the jury not to consider or testimony that jurors made an error in calculating damages, or that he was pressured or unduly influenced by fellow jurors. See *U.S. v. Rodriguez*, 116 F.3d 1225, 1227 (8th Cir. 1997); *Plummer v. Springfield Terminal Ry. Co.*, 5 F.3d 1, 2-5 (1st Cir. 1993); *U.S. v. Roach*, 164 F.3d 403, 412-13 (8th Cir. 1998); *Simpson v. State*, 3 So. 3d 1135, 1143-44 (Fla. 2009); *Jones v. State*, 928 So. 2d 1178, 1191-92 (Fla. 2006); *Devoney v. State*, 717 So. 2d 501, 502-04 (Fla. 1998); *Baptist Hosp. of Miami, Inc. v. Maler*, 579 So. 2d 97, 99 (Fla. 1991); *Short v. Abukhdeir*, 738 So. 2d 408, 409-10 (Fla. 2d DCA 1999).

However, there are a number of instances in which juror testimony is permitted under the Florida rule but not permitted under the federal rule. First, while the Florida rule permits juror testimony that the jurors agreed to decide through lot, game, or chance or rendered a quotient verdict, *see Baptist Hosp.*, 579 So. 2d at 100, the federal rule does not permit such testimony. *See Tanner*, 483 U.S. at 122-25; *Scogin v. Century Fitness, Inc.*, 780 F.2d 1316, 1318-20 (8th Cir, 1985).

Second, while the Florida rule permits juror testimony that other jurors made open appeals to racial bias during the deliberations, *see Powell*, 652 So. 2d at 357-58, the federal rule does not. *See Marcavage v. Board of Trustees of Temple Univ.*, 400 F. Supp. 2d 801, 806-07 (E.D. Pa. 2005); *Neilson v. Basit*, 1994 WL 30980, at *9 (N.D. Ill. 1994). *But see U.S. v. Villar*, 586 F.3d 76 (1st Cir. 2009) (holding that the Sixth Amendment requires admission of such evidence). Third, while the Florida rule has been interpreted to permit a juror to testify to any *express* agreement among jurors to disregard their oaths and instructions (as contrasted with their doing so without such an agreement), there are no decisions interpreting the federal rule to permit such testimony. *See Reaves v. State*, 826 So. 2d 932, 943 (Fla. 2002); *Devoney v. State*, 717 So. 2d 501, 504 (Fla. 1998). Finally, while the U.S. Supreme Court has held that testimony by jurors that other jurors used drugs or alcohol during the deliberations is barred by the federal rule, *see Tanner*, 483 U.S. at 121-26, the Florida courts have not been confronted with the issue, although the Florida Supreme Court has cited the U.S. Supreme Court's decision with approval in interpreting the scope of the Florida rule in a different context. *See Devoney*, 717 So. 2d at 504.

The federal rule was amended, effective December 1, 2006, to permit inquiry into whether there was a mistake in entering the verdict onto the verdict form. *See* FED. R. EVID. 606(b)(2)(C); Advisory Committee's Note to 2006 Amendment to FED. R. EVID. 606. The exception is extremely narrow, and is limited to cases in which the jury foreperson wrote down, in response to an interrogatory, a number different from that agreed upon by the jury, or mistakenly stated that the defendant was guilty when the jury had actually agreed that he was not guilty. *See* Advisory Committee's Note to 2006 Amendment to FED. R. EVID. 606. In so amending the rule, the Advisory Committee explicitly rejected a broader exception to the rule implied by Second Circuit precedent, under which inquiry was permitted into such things as whether the damages amount determined by the jury was intended to be a net rather than a gross figure. *See id.* (rejecting *Attridge v. Cencorp. Div. of Dover Techs. Int'l, Inc.*, 836 F.2d 113, 116 (2d Cir. 1987)). There is no analogous provision in the Florida rule.

Under both the Florida and federal rules, even if a juror is deemed competent to testify, he may only testify about the *fact* that the misconduct occurred, *not* its effect on his or any other juror's vote. *See U.S. v. Rutherford*, 371 F.3d 634, 644 (9th Cir. 2004); *Powell*, 652 So. 2d at 357; *State v. Hamilton*, 574 So. 2d 124, 128-31 (Fla. 1991). In determining whether the misconduct had an impact on the verdict or indictment, a judge must thus make an objective inquiry into its probable effect. *Manley v. Ambase Corp.*, 337 F.3d 237, 252 (2d Cir. 2003); *Hamilton*, 574 So. 2d at 128-31.

It is important to keep in mind that the Florida and federal rules ban only testimony by the jurors themselves, and not testimony by non-jurors who may have witnessed the alleged misconduct. *See Tanner*, 483 U.S. at 127; FLA. STAT. § 90.607(2)(b). However, neither rule permits a party to circumvent the rule by having a third party testify to what a juror said to him regarding what took place during deliberations. *See* FED. R. EVID. 606(b) ("The court may not receive a juror's affidavit or evidence of a juror's statement on these matters."); *Baptist Hosp.*, 579 So. 2d at 98-100 (affidavits by attorneys who spoke with jurors).

Federal Rule 607. Who May Impeach a Witness

Any party, including the party that called the witness, may attack the witness's credibility.

ADVISORY COMMITTEE'S NOTE

The traditional rule against impeaching one's own witness is abandoned as based on false premises. A party does not hold out his witnesses as worthy of belief, since he rarely has a free choice in selecting them. Denial of the right leaves the party at the mercy of the witness and the adversary. If the impeachment is by a prior statement, it is free from hearsay dangers and is excluded from the category of hearsay under Rule 801(d)(1). Ladd, Impeachment of One's Own Witness—New Developments, 4 U.Chi.L.Rev. 69 (1936); McCormick § 38; 3 Wigmore §§ 896–918. The substantial inroads into the old rule made over the years by decisions, rules, and statutes are evidence of doubts as to its basic soundness and workability. Cases are collected in 3 Wigmore § 905. Revised Rule 32(a)(1) of the Federal Rules of Civil Procedure allows any party to impeach a witness by means of his deposition, and Rule 43(b) has allowed the calling and impeachment of an adverse party or person identified with him. Illustrative statutes allowing a party to impeach his own witness under varying circumstances are Ill.Rev.Stats.1967, c. 110, § 60; Mass.Laws Annot. 1959, c. 233, § 23; 20 N.M.Stats. Annot. 1953, § 20-2-4; N.Y. CPLR § 4514 (McKinney 1963); 12 Vt.Stats. Annot. 1959, §§ 1641a, 1642. Complete judicial rejection of the old rule is found in United States v. Freeman, 302 F.2d 347 (2d Cir. 1962). The same result is reached in Uniform Rule 20; California Evidence Code § 785; Kansas Code of Civil Procedure § 60-420. See also New Jersey Evidence Rule 20.

ADVISORY COMMITTEE'S NOTE (2011 AMENDMENT)

The language of Rule 607 has been amended as part of the restyling of the Evidence Rules to make them more easily understood and to make style and terminology consistent throughout the rules. These changes are intended to be stylistic only. There is no intent to change any result in any ruling on evidence admissibility.

Florida Stat. § 90.608. Who May Impeach

Any party, including the party calling the witness, may attack the credibility of a witness by:

(1) Introducing statements of the witness which are inconsistent with the witness's present testimony.

(2) Showing that the witness is biased.

(3) Attacking the character of the witness in accordance with the provisions of s. 90.609 or s. 90.610.

(4) Showing a defect of capacity, ability, or opportunity in the witness to observe, remember, or recount the matters about which the witness testified.

(5) Proof by other witnesses that material facts are not as testified to by the witness being impeached.

SPONSORS' NOTE (1976 ENACTMENT)

[Subsection (1) This section retains the traditional rule against impeaching a party's own witness and enumerates the methods of attacking witness credibility. See McCormick, Evidence §§ 33, 38 (2nd ed. 1972)][21]

Subsection (2) [Renumbered as Subsections (1) through (5)] Under existing law, Fla. Stat. § 90.09, when a witness produced by a party proves adverse, the witness may be impeached by prior inconsistent statements and other contradictory evidence, but not by general evidence of bad character. The application of the statute has been limited by judicial interpretation. It has been applied only to adverse witnesses who give "evidence that is prejudicial to the party producing the witness." Johnson v. State, 178 So.2d 724, 728 (Fla. 2nd Dist. 1965). Thus if the witness fails to give the testimony expected of him, the statute is not applicable unless the testimony given is also prejudicial. Hernandez v. State, 22 So.2d 781 (Fla. 1945). Moreover, the party seeking to impeach his own witness must be surprised or entrapped by the testimony. Foremost Dairies, Inc. v. Cutler, 212 So.2d 37 (Fla. 4th Dist. 1968). This subsection

---

[21] Editor's Note: The bracketed language refers to the original version of the rule, which was subsequently amended to eliminate the rule against impeaching one's own witness.

eliminates the necessity of surprise in order to use prior inconsistent statements to impeach an adverse witness.

Florida Rule of Civil Procedure 1.450(a) provides that a party may call as a witness an adverse party (or an officer, director, or managing agent of a public or private corporation or of a partnership or association which is an adverse party) and interrogate, contradict and impeach him in all respects as if he had been called by the adverse party. The adverse party is treated as if he had been previously called by his own counsel and the testimony is treated as if it were cross-examination. See Wigginton, New Florida Common Law Rules, 3 U. Fla. L. Rev. 1, 26 (1950). Apparently, the scope of impeachment of an adverse party is that of any other witness upon cross-examination and is not limited to inconsistent statements or by the doctrines of surprise and prejudice. Cf. Foremost Dairies, Inc. v. Cutler, 212 So.2d 37 (Fla. 4th Dist. 1968).

This section does not eliminate the limitation on impeachment stated in Johnson v. State, 178 So.2d 724, 729 (Fla. 2nd Dist. 1965):

> Where it is sought to impeach a witness on the basis of testimony given on cross-examination, the testimony must, of course, be relevant and material....[T]he test of relevancy and materiality is whether the cross-examining party could have, for any purpose other than impeachment, introduced evidence on the subject in chief.

See Tully v. State, 69 Fla. 662, 68 So. 934 (1915); Lockwood v. State, 107 So.2d 770 (Fla. 2nd Dist. 1959). On cross-examination of a witness on collateral or irrelevant matters the answer given by the witness is conclusive and it is error to permit opposing counsel to introduce evidence contradicting the witness's answer. See Statewright v. State, 278 So.2d 652 (Fla. 4th Dist. 1973).

Section 90.10 of the existing law permits impeachment of witnesses by prior inconsistent statements if certain prerequisites are met. Section 90.614 of this Act covers these matters.

COMMENTARY ON FEDERAL AND FLORIDA RULE DIFFERENCES

Florida Stat. § 90.608 and its federal counterpart, Federal Rules 607, set forth the basic rule for impeaching the credibility of a witness. Both rules reject the voucher rule of the common law, thus permitting a witness's credibility to be attacked by any party, including the party who called the person as a witness. Yet while Florida Stat. § 90.608 sets forth the various methods of impeaching a witness's credibility, Federal Rule 607 does not specify the methods of impeachment; some methods are discussed in other federal rules, see, e.g., FED. R. EVID. 608, 609, while other methods are defined in the case law. See, e.g., U.S. v. Abel, 469 U.S. 45, 45-46 (1984).

Both federal and Florida law provide for impeachment by prior inconsistent statement, even when it is not admissible for substantive purposes. See FLA. STAT. § 90.608(1); Williamson v. State, 961 So. 2d 229, 235 (Fla. 2007); Wilson v. City of Aliceville, 779 F.2d 631, 636 (11th Cir. 1986). When impeaching a witness with a prior inconsistent statement, a party must lay the foundation required by Florida Stat. § 90.614 or its federal counterpart, Federal Rule of Evidence 613. See Pearce v. State, 880 So. 2d 561, 569-70 (Fla. 2004); U.S. v. Saget, 991 F.2d 702, 710 (11th Cir. 1993). Under both rules, extrinsic evidence of the prior inconsistent statement cannot be offered when impeaching the witness on a collateral matter, in other words, when the evidence is not relevant for any purpose other than to contradict the witness. See Pearce, 880 So. 2d at 569; Daeda v. State, 841 So. 2d 632, 635-36 (Fla. 2d DCA 2003); U.S. v. Roulette, 75 F.3d 418, 423 (8th Cir. 1996). Finally, notwithstanding the rejection of the voucher rule under both Florida and federal law, both federal and Florida case law provide that the trial court may prevent a party from impeaching his own witness pursuant to Federal Rule 403 or Florida Stat. § 90.403 when it appears that the party called the witness for the primary purpose of impeaching him with—and thus getting before the jury—what would otherwise be inadmissible evidence. Morton v. State, 689 So. 2d 259, 262-64 (Fla. 1997), receded from on other *grounds, Rodriguez v. State*, 753 So. 2d 29 (Fla. 2000); *Laur v. State*, 781 So. 2d 452, 454-55 (Fla. 4th DCA 2001); *Balogh's of Coral Gables, Inc. v. Getz*, 798 F.2d 1356, 1358 n.2 (11th Cir. 1986).

Both Florida and federal law provide for impeachment of a witness by showing that she is biased. *See* FLA. STAT. § 90.608(2); *Abel*, 469 U.S. at 51-52. The term "bias" is defined broadly under both federal and Florida law to include any motivation that a witness might have to testify untruthfully, including interest in the outcome of the case, dislike of a party, and the like. *See Abel*, 469 U.S. at 52; *Bell v. State*, 965 So. 2d 48, 56 (Fla. 2007); *Williams v. State*, 912 So. 2d 66, 68 (Fla. 4th DCA 2005). Bias may be demonstrated through the introduction of extrinsic evidence. *See Abel*, 469 U.S. at 52; *Sorge v. State*, 915 So. 2d 707, 708 (Fla. 1st DCA 2005); *Hair v. State*, 428 So. 2d 760, 761-62 (Fla. 3d DCA 1983).

Both Florida and federal law provide for impeachment of a witness through an attack on his character, either through the testimony of character witnesses or by introducing evidence of the witness's prior convictions for certain crimes. *See* FLA. STAT. § 90.608(3); FED. R. EVID. 608, 609. The details of these methods of impeachment are set forth in the commentary to Federal Rules of Evidence 608 and 609 and Florida Stat. §§ 90.609, 90.610.

Florida and federal law permit a witness to be impeached by showing a defect in the witness's capacity, ability or opportunity to observe, remember, or recount the events to which he testified, including such things as problems with memory, eyesight, or hearing, or mental illness impacting the witness's ability to perceive. *See* FLA. STAT. § 90.608(4); *Gamble v. State*, 492 So. 2d 1132, 1133-34 (Fla. 5th DCA 1986); *U.S. v. Pryce*, 938 F.2d 1343, 1346 (D.C. Cir. 1991). Moreover, under both federal and Florida practice, inquiry can be had into the witness's use of drugs or alcohol at the time of the witness's observation of the events in dispute or while testifying, but not generally into chronic use of alcohol or drugs absent proof that such chronic use impacts the witness's ability to perceive and remember. *See Edwards v. State*, 548 So. 2d 656, 657-58 (Fla. 1989); *U.S. v. DiPaolo*, 804 F.2d 225, 229-30 (2d Cir. 1986). Evidence of a defect in sensory perception may be proved through extrinsic evidence. *See Gelabert v. State*, 407 So. 2d 1007, 1009-10 (Fla. 5th DCA 1981); *Behler v. Hanlon*, 199 F.R.D. 553, 558 (D. Md. 2001).

Finally, both Florida and federal law permit a witness to be impeached through contradiction, to wit, that the facts are not as testified to by the witness. *See* FLA. STAT. § 90.608(5); *U.S. v. Russell*, 717 F.2d 518, 520 (11th Cir. 1983). However, extrinsic evidence cannot be offered to contradict a witness on a collateral matter. *See Eaton Corp. v. Votour*, 895 So. 2d 466, 468 (Fla. 1st DCA 2005); *Griffin v. State*, 827 So. 2d 1098, 1099 (Fla. 1st DCA 2000); *Russell*, 717 F.2d at 520.

Federal Rule 608. A Witness's Character for Truthfulness or Untruthfulness

(a) **Reputation or Opinion Evidence.** A witness's credibility may be attacked or supported by testimony about the witness's reputation for having a character for truthfulness or untruthfulness, or by testimony in the form of an opinion about that character. But evidence of truthful character is admissible only after the witness's character for truthfulness has been attacked.

(b) **Specific Instances of Conduct.** Except for a criminal conviction under Rule 609, extrinsic evidence is not admissible to prove specific instances of a witness's conduct in order to attack or support the witness's character for truthfulness. But the court may, on cross-examination, allow them to be inquired into if they are probative of the character for truthfulness or untruthfulness of:

(1) the witness; or

(2) another witness whose character the witness being cross-examined has testified about.

By testifying on another matter, a witness does not waive any privilege against self-incrimination for testimony that relates only to the witness's character for truthfulness.

ADVISORY COMMITTEE'S NOTE

Subdivision (a). In Rule 404(a) the general position is taken that character evidence is not admissible for the purpose of proving that the person acted in conformity therewith, subject, however, to several exceptions, one of which is character evidence of a witness as bearing upon his credibility. The present rule develops that exception.

In accordance with the bulk of judicial authority, the inquiry is strictly limited to character for veracity, rather than allowing evidence as to character generally. The result is to sharpen relevancy, to reduce surprise, waste of time, and confusion, and to make the lot of the witness somewhat less unattractive. McCormick § 44.

The use of opinion and reputation evidence as means of proving the character of witnesses is consistent with Rule 405(a). While the modern practice has purported to exclude opinion, witnesses who testify to reputation seem in fact often to be giving their opinions, disguised somewhat misleadingly as reputation. See McCormick § 44. And even under the modern practice, a common relaxation has allowed inquiry as to whether the witnesses would believe the principal witness under oath. United States v. Walker, 313 F.2d 236 (6th Cir. 1963), and cases cited therein; McCormick § 44, pp. 94–95, n. 3.

Character evidence in support of credibility is admissible under the rule only after the witness' character has first been attacked, as has been the case at common law. Maguire, Weinstein, et al., Cases on Evidence 295 (5th ed. 1965); McCormick § 49, p. 105; 4 Wigmore § 1104. The enormous needless consumption of time which a contrary practice would entail justifies the limitation. Opinion or reputation that the witness is untruthful specifically qualifies as an attack under the rule, and evidence of misconduct, including conviction of crime, and of corruption also fall within this category. Evidence of bias or interest does not. McCormick § 49; 4 Wigmore §§ 1106, 1107. Whether evidence in the form of contradiction is an attack upon the character of the witness must depend upon the circumstances. McCormick § 49. Cf. 4 Wigmore §§ 1108, 1109.

As to the use of specific instances on direct by an opinion witness, see the Advisory Committee's Note to Rule 405, *supra*.

Subdivision (b). In conformity with Rule 405, which forecloses use of evidence of specific incidents as proof in chief of character unless character is an issue in the case, the present rule generally bars evidence of specific instances of conduct of a witness for the purpose of attacking or supporting his credibility. There are, however, two exceptions:

(1) specific instances are provable when they have been the subject of criminal conviction, and (2) specific instances may be inquired into on cross-examination of the principal witness or of a witness giving an opinion of his character for truthfulness.

(1) Conviction of crime as a technique of impeachment is treated in detail in Rule 609, and here is merely recognized as an exception to the general rule excluding evidence of specific incidents for impeachment purposes.

(2) Particular instances of conduct, though not the subject of criminal conviction, may be inquired into on cross-examination of the principal witness himself or of a witness who testifies concerning his character for truthfulness. Effective cross-examination demands that some allowance be made for going into matters of this kind, but the possibilities of abuse are substantial. Consequently safeguards are erected in the form of specific requirements that the instances inquired into be probative of truthfulness

or its opposite and not remote in time. Also, the overriding protection of Rule 403 requires that probative value not be outweighed by danger of unfair prejudice, confusion of issues, or misleading the jury, and that of Rule 611 bars harassment and undue embarrassment.

The final sentence constitutes a rejection of the doctrine of such cases as People v. Sorge, 301 N.Y. 198 (1950), that any past criminal act relevant to credibility may be inquired into on cross-examination, in apparent disregard of the privilege against self-incrimination. While it is clear that an ordinary witness cannot make a partial disclosure of incriminating matter and then invoke the privilege on cross-examination, no tenable contention can be made that merely by testifying he waives his right to foreclose inquiry on cross-examination into criminal activities for the purpose of attacking his credibility. So to hold would reduce the privilege to a nullity. While it is true that an accused, unlike an ordinary witness, has an option whether to testify, if the option can be exercised only at the price of opening up inquiry as to any and all criminal acts committed during his lifetime, the right to testify could scarcely be said to possess much vitality. In Griffin v. California, 380 U.S. 609 (1965), the Court held that allowing comment on the election of an accused not to testify exacted a constitutionally impermissible price, and so here. While no specific provision in terms confers constitutional status on the right of an accused to take the stand in his own defense, the existence of the right is so completely recognized that a denial of it or substantial infringement upon it would surely be of due process dimensions. See Ferguson v. Georgia, 365 U.S. 570 (1961); McCormick § 131; 8 Wigmore § 2276 (McNaughton Rev.1961). In any event, wholly aside from constitutional considerations, the provision represents a sound policy.

REPORT OF HOUSE COMMITTEE ON THE JUDICIARY

Rule 608(a) as submitted by the Court permitted attack to be made upon the character for truthfulness or untruthfulness of a witness either by reputation or opinion testimony. For the same reason underlying its decision to eliminate the admissibility of opinion testimony in Rule 405(a), the Committee amended Rule 608(a) to delete the reference to opinion testimony.

The second sentence of Rule 608(b) as submitted by the Court permitted specific instances of misconduct of a witness to be inquired into on cross-examination for the purpose of attacking his credibility, if probative of truthfulness or untruthfulness, "and not remote in time". Such cross-examination could be of the witness himself or of another witness who testifies as to "his" character for truthfulness or untruthfulness.

The Committee amended the Rule to emphasize the discretionary power of the court in permitting such testimony and deleted the reference to remoteness in time as being unnecessary and confusing (remoteness from time of trial or remoteness from the incident involved?). As recast, the Committee amendment also makes clear the antecedent of "his" in the original Court proposal.

REPORT OF SENATE COMMITTEE ON THE JUDICIARY

The Senate amendment adds the words "opinion or" to conform the first sentence of the rule with the remainder of the rule.

CONFERENCE REPORT

The Conference adopts the Senate amendment.

ADVISORY COMMITTEE'S NOTE (2003 AMENDMENT)

The Rule has been amended to clarify that the absolute prohibition on extrinsic evidence applies only when the sole reason for proffering that evidence is to attack or support the witness' character for truthfulness. *See United States v. Abel*, 469 U.S. 45 (1984); *United States v. Fusco*, 748 F.2d 996 (5th Cir. 1984) (Rule 608(b) limits the use of evidence "designed to show that the witness has done things, unrelated to the suit being tried, that make him more or less believable per se"); Ohio R.Evid. 608(b). On occasion the Rule's use of the overbroad term "credibility" has been read "to bar extrinsic evidence for bias, competency and contradiction impeachment since they too deal with credibility." American Bar Association Section of Litigation, *Emerging Problems Under the Federal Rules of Evidence* at 161 (3d ed. 1998). The amendment conforms the language of the Rule to its original intent, which was to impose an absolute bar on extrinsic evidence only if the sole purpose for offering the evidence was to prove the witness' character for veracity. *See* Advisory Committee Note to Rule 608(b) (stating that the Rule is "[i]n conformity with Rule 405, which forecloses use of evidence of specific incidents as proof in chief of character unless character is in issue in the case...").

By limiting the application of the Rule to proof of a witness' character for truthfulness, the amendment leaves the admissibility of extrinsic evidence offered for other grounds of impeachment (such as contradiction, prior inconsistent statement, bias and mental capacity) to Rules 402 and 403. *See, e.g., United States v. Winchenbach*, 197 F.3d 548 (1st Cir. 1999) (admissibility of a prior inconsistent statement offered for impeachment is governed by Rules 402 and 403, not Rule 608(b)); *United States v. Tarantino*, 846 F.2d 1384 (D.C. Cir. 1988) (admissibility of extrinsic evidence offered to contradict a witness is governed by Rules 402 and 403); *United States v. Lindemann*, 85 F.3d 1232 (7th Cir. 1996) (admissibility of extrinsic evidence of bias is governed by Rules 402 and 403).

It should be noted that the extrinsic evidence prohibition of Rule 608(b) bars any reference to the consequences that a witness might have suffered as a result of an alleged bad act. For example, Rule 608(b) prohibits counsel from mentioning that a witness was suspended or disciplined for the conduct that is the subject of impeachment, when that conduct is offered only to prove the character of the witness. *See United States v. Davis*, 183 F.3d 231, 257 n.12 (3d Cir. 1999) (emphasizing that in attacking the defendant's character for truthfulness "the government cannot make reference to Davis's forty-four day suspension or that Internal Affairs found that he lied about" an incident because "[s]uch evidence would not only be hearsay to the extent it contains assertion of fact, it would be inadmissible extrinsic evidence under Rule 608(b)"). *See also* Stephen A. Saltzburg, *Impeaching the Witness: Prior Bad Acts and Extrinsic Evidence*, 7 Crim. Just. 28, 31 (Winter 1993) ("counsel should not be permitted to circumvent the no-extrinsic-evidence provision by tucking a third person's opinion about prior acts into a question asked of the witness who has denied the act").

For purposes of consistency the term "credibility" has been replaced by the term "character for truthfulness" in the last sentence of subdivision (b). The term "credibility" is also used in subdivision (a). But the Committee found it unnecessary to substitute "character for truthfulness" for "credibility" in Rule 608(a), because subdivision (a)(1) already serves to limit impeachment to proof of such character.

Rules 609(a) and 610 also use the term "credibility" when the intent of those Rules is to regulate impeachment of a witness' character for truthfulness. No inference should be derived from the fact that the Committee proposed an amendment to Rule 608(b) but not to Rules 609 and 610.

ADVISORY COMMITTEE'S NOTE (2011 AMENDMENT)

The language of Rule 608 has been amended as part of the general restyling of the Evidence Rules to make them more easily understood and to make style and terminology consistent throughout the rules. These changes are intended to be stylistic only. There is no intent to change any result in any ruling on evidence admissibility.

The Committee is aware that the Rule's limitation of bad-act impeachment to "cross-examination" is trumped by Rule 607, which allows a party to impeach witnesses on direct examination. Courts have not relied on the term "on cross-examination" to limit impeachment that would otherwise be permissible under Rules 607 and 608. The Committee therefore concluded that no change to the language of the Rule was necessary in the context of a restyling project.

Florida Stat. § 90.609. Character of Witness as Impeachment

A party may attack or support the credibility of a witness, including an accused, by evidence in the form of reputation, except that:

(1) The evidence may refer only to character relating to truthfulness.

(2) Evidence of a truthful character is admissible only after the character of the witness for truthfulness has been attacked by reputation evidence.

SPONSORS' NOTE (1976 ENACTMENT)

Section 90.404 provides that evidence of a person's character is only admissible in the instances enumerated therein. This section develops the exception involving permitting the credibility of a witness to be attacked by evidence of his truth and veracity, rather than evidence of general moral character. See Pandula v. Fonseca, 145 Fla. 395, 199 So. 358 (1941); Taylor v. State, 139 Fla. 542, 190 So. 691, 694 (1939); Andrews v. State, 172 So.2d 505 (Fla. 1st Dist. 1965); Fla. Stat. § 90.08.

The credibility of a witness may not be supported by evidence until such time as the witness's credibility is attacked, Williams v. State, 110 So.2d 654 (Fla. 1959); Andrews v. State, 172 So.2d 505 (Fla. 1st Dist. 1965). See 4 Wigmore, Evidence §§ 1104-09 (Chadbourn rev.1972). If an accused testifies in his own behalf, under Section 90.608 his credibility may be attacked by showing that he had been previously convicted of certain crimes.

The use of opinion as well as reputation testimony is consistent with § 90.405.

COMMENTARY ON FEDERAL AND FLORIDA RULE DIFFERENCES

Florida Stat. § 90.609 and its federal counterpart, Federal Rule 608, regulate the use of evidence of a witness's character to impeach or rehabilitate his credibility. In addition, the federal rule regulates the use of evidence of specific instances of the witness's conduct that are probative of truthfulness or untruthfulness to impeach or rehabilitate his credibility.

Under both the federal and Florida rules, the only type of character evidence that can be used to impeach or rehabilitate a witness's credibility is his character for truthfulness (or lack thereof). See FLA. STAT. § 90.609(1); FED. R. EVID. 608(a)(1). However, consistent with their general treatment of character evidence, see FLA. STAT. § 90.405; FED. R. EVID. 405, the federal rule permits such testimony to be in the form of opinion or reputation, while the Florida rule permits only reputation testimony, not testimony in the form of an opinion. See FLA. STAT. § 90.609(1); FED. R. EVID. 608(a)(1); General Tel. Co. v. Wallace, 417 So. 2d 1022, 1024 (Fla. 2d DCA 1982). Before reputation testimony can be offered under either rule, a proper foundation must be laid establishing that the character witness is familiar with the person and the community in which the person's reputation has been formed, and that the testimony is based on discussions among a broad group of people rather than rumor or conversations with a narrow group of people. *Blackburn v. United Parcel Serv., Inc.*, 179 F.3d 81, 100-01 (3d Cir. 1999); *U.S. v. Watson*, 669 F.2d 1374, 1381 (11th Cir. 1982); *Ibar v. State*, 938 So. 2d 451, 468-69 (Fla. 2006); *Morrison v. State*, 818 So. 2d 432, 449 (Fla. 2002). The character witness giving reputation testimony thus must have been familiar with the person and his community for more than a brief period of time, and since the focus is on the person's character at the time of trial, the period of familiarity must not be remote in time. *See Watson*, 669 F.2d at 1381-82 & n.5; *Carter v. State*, 485 So. 2d 1292, 1294-95 (Fla. 4th DCA 1986). The foundation requirement for opinion testimony under the federal rule is less stringent, and is not conditioned on long acquaintance or recent information about the witness but only personal knowledge sufficient to form an impression of the person's character for truthfulness. *See Watson*, 669 F.2d at 1382.

Under the federal rule, evidence that a witness has a truthful character is admissible only after the witness's character for truthfulness has first been attacked. *See* Fed. R. Evid. 608(a). The sorts of impeachment that open the door to admitting evidence of a witness's character for truthfulness under this provision include introducing evidence of bad character under Federal Rule 608(a), inquiring about bad acts under Federal Rule 608(b), introducing evidence of prior convictions under Federal Rule 609, or a sustained cross-examination that amounts to an indirect attack on truthfulness; introducing evidence of bias or introducing evidence that contradicts that of the witness, or pointing out inconsistencies in the witness's testimony, however, does not. *See U.S. v. Dring*, 930 F.2d 687, 690-92 (9th Cir. 1991); *U.S. v. Danehy*, 680 F.2d 1311, 1314 (11th Cir. 1982). The Florida rule in terms provides only that an attack "by reputation evidence" opens the door to introducing evidence of a witness's truthful character, *see* Fla. Stat. § 90.609(2), but the case law holds that the rule does not change the pre-code law, which permitted such evidence to be introduced in response to a sustained cross-examination that amounts to an indirect attack on truthfulness. *See Arias v. State*, 593 So. 2d 260, 264-65 (Fla. 3d DCA 1992).

The most significant difference between the Florida and federal rules is with respect to the use of evidence of specific instances of the witness's conduct that are probative of truthfulness or untruthfulness to impeach or rehabilitate his credibility. While the federal rule does not permit extrinsic evidence of such conduct to be introduced, it does permit inquiry on cross-examination of a witness (concerning either her own conduct or that of another witness as to whose character the witness has testified). *See* Fed. R. Evid. 608(b). Under the federal rule, the questioner must have a good-faith belief that the conduct occurred, *see U.S. v. Silverman*, 745 F.2d 1386, 1397 (11th Cir. 1984), and because of the bar on extrinsic evidence, the questioner must take the witness's answer. *U.S. v. Matthews*, 168 F.3d 1234, 1244 (11th Cir. 1999). By contrast, there is no provision in the Florida rule for inquiring about conduct that is probative of truthfulness, and the case law makes clear that this is not a permissible method of impeachment under Florida law. *See Pantoja v. State*, 59 So. 3d 1092, 1096-97 (Fla. 2011); *Fernandez v. State*, 730 So. 2d 277, 282-83 (Fla. 1999); *Hitchcock v. State*, 413 So. 2d 741, 744 (Fla. 1982).

Federal Rule 609. Impeachment by Evidence of a Criminal Conviction

(a) **In General.** The following rules apply to attacking a witness's character for truthfulness by evidence of a criminal conviction:

    (1) for a crime that, in the convicting jurisdiction, was punishable by death or by imprisonment for more than one year, the evidence:

        (A) must be admitted, subject to Rule 403, in a civil case or in a criminal case in which the witness is not a defendant; and

    (B) must be admitted in a criminal case in which the witness is a defendant, if the probative value of the evidence outweighs its prejudicial effect to that defendant; and

    (2) for any crime regardless of the punishment, the evidence must be admitted if the court can readily determine that establishing the elements of the crime required proving — or the witness's admitting — a dishonest act or false statement.

(b) Limit on Using the Evidence After 10 Years. This subdivision (b) applies if more than 10 years have passed since the witness's conviction or release from confinement for it, whichever is later. Evidence of the conviction is admissible only if:

    (1) its probative value, supported by specific facts and circumstances, substantially outweighs its prejudicial effect; and

    (2) the proponent gives an adverse party reasonable written notice of the intent to use it so that the party has a fair opportunity to contest its use.

(c) Effect of a Pardon, Annulment, or Certificate of Rehabilitation. Evidence of a conviction is not admissible if:

    (1) the conviction has been the subject of a pardon, annulment, certificate of rehabilitation, or other equivalent procedure based on a finding that the person has been rehabilitated, and the person has not been convicted of a later crime punishable by death or by imprisonment for more than one year; or

    (2) the conviction has been the subject of a pardon, annulment, or other equivalent procedure based on a finding of innocence.

(d) Juvenile Adjudications. Evidence of a juvenile adjudication is admissible under this rule only if:

    (1) it is offered in a criminal case;

    (2) the adjudication was of a witness other than the defendant;

    (3) an adult's conviction for that offense would be admissible to attack the adult's credibility; and

    (4) admitting the evidence is necessary to fairly determine guilt or innocence.

(e) Pendency of an Appeal. A conviction that satisfies this rule is admissible even if an appeal is pending. Evidence of the pendency is also admissible.

ADVISORY COMMITTEE'S NOTE

As a means of impeachment, evidence of conviction of crime is significant only because it stands as proof of the commission of the underlying criminal act. There is little dissent from the general proposition that at least some crimes are relevant to credibility but much disagreement among the cases and commentators about which crimes are usable for this purpose. See McCormick § 43; 2 Wright, Federal Practice and Procedure: Criminal § 416 (1969). The weight of traditional authority has been to allow use of felonies generally, without regard to the nature of the particular offense, and of *crimen falsi* without regard to the grade of the offense. This is the view accepted by Congress in the 1970 amendment of § 14-305 of the District of Columbia Code, P.L. 91-358, 84 Stat. 473. Uniform Rule 21 and Model Code Rule 106 permit only crimes involving "dishonesty or false statement." Others have thought that the trial judge should have discretion to exclude convictions if the probative value of the evidence of the crime is substantially outweighed by the danger of unfair prejudice. Luck v. United States, 348 F.2d 763 (1965); McGowan, Impeachment of Criminal Defendants by Prior Convictions, 1970 Law & Soc.Order 1. Whatever may be the merits of those views, this rule is drafted to accord with the Congressional policy manifested in the 1970 legislation.

The proposed rule incorporates certain basic safeguards, in terms applicable to all witnesses but of particular significance to an accused who elects to testify. These protections include the imposition of definite time limitations, giving effect to demonstrated rehabilitation, and generally excluding juvenile adjudications.

Subdivision (a). For purposes of impeachment, crimes are divided into two categories by the rule: (1) those of what is generally regarded as felony grade, without particular regard to the nature of the offense, and (2) those involving dishonesty or false statement, without regard to the grade of the offense. Probable convictions are not limited to violations of federal law. By reason of our constitutional structure, the federal catalog of crimes is far from being a complete one, and resort must be had to the laws of the states for the specification of many crimes. For example, simple theft as compared with theft from interstate commerce. Other instances of borrowing are the Assimilative Crimes Act, making the state law of crimes applicable to the special territorial and maritime jurisdiction of the United States, 18 U.S.C. § 13, and the provision of the Judicial Code disqualifying persons as jurors on the grounds of state as well as federal convictions, 28 U.S.C. § 1865. For evaluation of the crime in terms of seriousness, reference is made to the congressional measurement of felony (subject to imprisonment in excess of one year) rather than adopting state definitions which vary considerably. See 28 U.S.C. § 1865, *supra*, disqualifying jurors for conviction in state or federal court of crime punishable by imprisonment for more than one year.

Subdivision (b). Few statutes recognize a time limit on impeachment by evidence of conviction. However, practical considerations of fairness and relevancy demand that some boundary be recognized. See Ladd, Credibility Tests — Current Trends, 89 U.Pa.L.Rev. 166, 176–177 (1940). This portion of the rule is derived from the proposal advanced in Recommendation Proposing in Evidence Code, § 788(5), p. 142, Cal.Law Rev.Comm'n (1965), though not adopted. See California Evidence Code § 788.

Subdivision (c). A pardon or its equivalent granted solely for the purpose of restoring civil rights lost by virtue of a conviction has no relevance to an inquiry into character. If, however, the pardon or other proceeding is hinged upon a showing of rehabilitation the situation is otherwise. The result under the rule is to render the conviction inadmissible. The alternative of allowing in evidence both the conviction and the rehabilitation has not been adopted for reasons of policy, economy of time, and difficulties of evaluation.

A similar provision is contained in California Evidence Code § 788. Cf. A.L.I. Model Penal Code, Proposed Official Draft § 306.6(3)(e) (1962), and discussion in A.L.I. Proceedings 310 (1961).

Pardons based on innocence have the effect, of course, of nullifying the conviction *ab initio*.

Subdivision (d). The prevailing view has been that a juvenile adjudication is not usable for impeachment. Thomas v. United States, 121 F.2d 905 (1941); Cotton v. United States, 355 F.2d 480 (10th Cir. 1966). This conclusion was based upon a variety of circumstances. By virtue of its informality, frequently diminished quantum of required proof, and other departures from accepted standards for criminal trials under the theory of *parens patriae*, the juvenile adjudication was considered to lack the precision and general probative value of the criminal conviction. While In re Gault, 387 U.S. 1 (1967), no doubt eliminates these characteristics insofar as objectionable, other obstacles remain. Practical problems of administration are raised by the common provisions in juvenile legislation that records be kept confidential and that they be destroyed after a short time. While *Gault* was skeptical as to the realities of confidentiality of juvenile records, it also saw no constitutional obstacles to improvement. 387 U.S. at 25. See also Note, Rights and Rehabilitation in the Juvenile Courts, 67 Colum.L.Rev. 281, 289 (1967). In addition, policy considerations much akin to those which dictate exclusion of adult convictions after rehabilitation has been established strongly suggest a rule of excluding juvenile adjudications. Admittedly, however, the rehabilitative process may in a given case be a demonstrated failure, or the strategic importance of a given witness may be so great as to require the overriding of general policy in the interests of particular justice. See Giles v. Maryland, 386 U.S. 66 (1967). Wigmore was outspoken in his condemnation of the disallowance of juvenile adjudications to impeach, especially when the witness is the complainant in a case of molesting a minor. 1 Wigmore § 196; 3 *id.* §§ 924a, 980. The rule recognizes discretion in the judge to effect an accommodation among these various factors by departing from the general principle of exclusion. In deference to the general pattern and policy of juvenile statutes, however, no discretion is accorded when the witness is the accused in a criminal case.

Subdivision (e). The presumption of correctness which ought to attend judicial proceedings supports the position that pendency of an appeal does not preclude use of a conviction for impeachment. United States v. Empire Packing Co., 174 F.2d 16 (7th Cir. 1949), cert. denied 337 U.S. 959; Bloch v. United States, 226 F.2d 185 (9th Cir. 1955), cert. denied 350 U.S. 948 and 353 U.S. 959; and see Newman v. United States, 331 F.2d 968 (8th Cir. 1964). Contra, Campbell v. United States, 176 F.2d 45 (1949). The pendency of an appeal is, however, a qualifying circumstance properly considerable.

REPORT OF HOUSE COMMITTEE ON THE JUDICIARY

Rule 609(a) as submitted by the Court was modeled after Section 133(a) of Public Law 91-358, 14 D.C.Code 305(b)(1), enacted in 1970. The Rule provided that:

> For the purpose of attacking the credibility of a witness, evidence that he has been convicted of a crime is admissible but only if the crime (1) was punishable by death or imprisonment in excess of one year under the law under which he was convicted or (2) involved dishonesty or false statement regardless of the punishment.

As reported to the Committee by the Subcommittee, Rule 609(a) was amended to read as follows:

> For the purpose of attacking the credibility of a witness, evidence that he has been convicted of a crime is admissible only if the crime (1) was punishable by death or imprisonment in excess of one year, unless the court determines that the danger of unfair prejudice outweighs the probative value of the evidence of the conviction, or (2) involved dishonesty or false statement.

In full committee, the provision was amended to permit attack upon the credibility of a witness by prior conviction only if the prior crime involved dishonesty or false statement. While recognizing that the prevailing doctrine in the federal courts and in most States allows a witness to be impeached by evidence of prior felony convictions without restriction as to type, the Committee was of the view that, because of the danger of unfair prejudice in such practice and the deterrent effect upon an accused who might wish to testify, and even upon a witness who was not the accused, cross-examination by evidence of prior conviction should be limited to those kinds of convictions bearing directly on credibility, *i.e.*, crimes involving dishonesty or false statement.

Rule 609(b) as submitted by the Court was modeled after Section 133(a) of Public Law 91-358, 14 D.C.Code 305(b)(2)(B), enacted in 1970. The Rule provided:

> Evidence of a conviction under this rule is not admissible if a period of more than ten years has elapsed since the date of the release of the witness from confinement imposed for his most recent conviction, or the expiration of the period of his parole, probation, or sentence granted or imposed with respect to his most recent conviction, whichever is the later date.

Under this formulation, a witness' entire past record of criminal convictions could be used for impeachment (provided the conviction met the standard of subdivision (a)), if the witness had been most recently released from confinement, or the period of his parole or probation had expired, within ten years of the conviction.

The Committee amended the Rule to read in the text of the 1971 Advisory Committee version to provide that upon the expiration of ten years from the date of a conviction of a witness, or of his release from confinement for that offense, that conviction may no longer be used for impeachment. The Committee was of the view that after ten years following a person's release from confinement (or from the date of his conviction) the probative value of the conviction with respect to that person's credibility diminished to a point where it should no longer be admissible.

Rule 609(c) as submitted by the Court provided in part that evidence of a witness' prior conviction is not admissible to attack his credibility if the conviction was the subject of a pardon, annulment, or other equivalent procedure, based on a showing of rehabilitation, and the witness has not been convicted of a subsequent crime. The Committee amended the Rule to provide that the "subsequent crime" must have been "punishable by death or imprisonment in excess of one year", on the ground that a subsequent conviction of an offense not a felony is insufficient to rebut the finding that the witness has been rehabilitated. The Committee also intends that the words "based on a finding of the rehabilitation of the person convicted" apply not only to "certificate of rehabilitation, or other equivalent procedure", but also to "pardon" and "annulment."

REPORT OF SENATE COMMITTEE ON THE JUDICIARY

As proposed by the Supreme Court, the rule would allow the use of prior convictions to impeach if the crime was a felony or a misdemeanor if the misdemeanor involved dishonesty or false statement. As modified by the House, the rule would admit prior convictions for impeachment purposes only if the offense, whether felony or misdemeanor, involved dishonesty or false statement.

The committee has adopted a modified version of the House-passed rule. In your committee's view, the danger of unfair prejudice is far greater when the accused, as opposed to other witnesses, testifies, because the jury may be prejudiced not merely on the question of credibility but also on the ultimate question of guilt or innocence. Therefore, with respect to defendants, the committee agreed with the House limitation that only offenses involving false statement or dishonesty may be used. By that phrase, the committee means crimes such as perjury or subornation of perjury, false statement, criminal fraud, embezzlement or false pretense, or any other offense, in the nature of crimen falsi the commission of which involves some element of untruthfulness, deceit or falsification bearing on the accused's propensity to testify truthfully.

With respect to other witnesses, in addition to any prior conviction involving false statement or dishonesty, any other felony may be used to impeach if, and only if, the court finds that the probative value of such evidence outweighs its prejudicial effect against the party offering that witness.

Notwithstanding this provision, proof of any prior offense otherwise admissible under rule 404 could still be offered for the purposes sanctioned by that rule. Furthermore, the committee intends that notwithstanding this rule, a defendant's misrepresentation regarding the existence or nature of prior convictions may be met by rebuttal evidence, including the record of such prior convictions. Similarly, such records may be offered to rebut representations made by the defendant regarding his attitude toward or willingness to commit a general category of offense, although denials or other representations by the defendant regarding the specific conduct which forms the basis of the charge against him shall not make prior convictions admissible to rebut such statement.

In regard to either type of representation, of course, prior convictions may be offered in rebuttal only if the defendant's statement is made in response to defense counsel's questions or is made gratuitously in the course of cross-examination. Prior convictions may not be offered as rebuttal evidence if the prosecution has sought to circumvent the purpose of this rule by asking questions which elicit such representations from the defendant.

One other clarifying amendment has been added to this subsection, that is, to provide that the admissibility of evidence of a prior conviction is permitted only upon cross-examination of a witness. It is not admissible if a person does not testify. It is to be understood, however, that a court record of a prior conviction is admissible to prove that conviction if the witness has forgotten or denies its existence.

Although convictions over ten years old generally do not have much probative value, there may be exceptional circumstances under which the conviction substantially bears on the credibility of the witness. Rather than exclude all convictions over 10 years old, the committee adopted an amendment in the form of a final clause to the section granting the court discretion to admit convictions over 10 years old, but only upon a determination by the court that the probative value of the conviction supported by specific facts and circumstances, substantially outweighs its prejudicial effect.

It is intended that convictions over 10 years old will be admitted very rarely and only in exceptional circumstances. The rules provide that the decision be supported by specific facts and circumstances thus requiring the court to make specific findings on the record as to the particular facts and circumstances it has considered in determining that the probative value of the conviction substantially outweighs its prejudicial impact. It is expected that, in fairness, the court will give the party against whom the conviction is introduced a full and adequate opportunity to contest its admission.

CONFERENCE REPORT

Rule 609 defines when a party may use evidence of a prior conviction in order to impeach a witness. The Senate amendments make changes in two subsections of Rule 609.

The House bill provides that the credibility of a witness can be attacked by proof of prior conviction of a crime only if the crime involves dishonesty or false statement. The Senate amendment provides that a witness' credibility may be attacked if the crime (1) was punishable by death or imprisonment in excess of one year under the law under which he was convicted or (2) involves dishonesty or false statement, regardless of the punishment.

The Conference adopts the Senate amendment with an amendment. The Conference amendment provides that the credibility of a witness, whether a defendant or someone else, may be attacked by proof of a prior conviction but only if the crime: (1) was punishable by death or imprisonment in excess of one year under the law under which he was convicted and the court determines that the probative value of the conviction outweighs its prejudicial effect to the defendant; or (2) involved dishonesty or false statement regardless of the punishment.

By the phrase "dishonesty and false statement" the Conference means crimes such as perjury or subornation of perjury, false statement, criminal fraud, embezzlement, or false pretense, or any other offense in the nature of crimen falsi, the commission of which involves some element of deceit, untruthfulness, or falsification bearing on the accused's propensity to testify truthfully.

The admission of prior convictions involving dishonesty and false statement is not within the discretion of the Court. Such convictions are peculiarly probative of credibility and, under this rule, are always to be admitted. Thus, judicial discretion granted with respect to the admissibility of other prior convictions is not applicable to those involving dishonesty or false statement.

With regard to the discretionary standard established by paragraph (1) of rule 609(a), the Conference determined that the prejudicial effect to be weighed against the probative value of the conviction is specifically the prejudicial effect *to the defendant*. The danger of prejudice to a witness other than the defendant (such as injury to the witness' reputation in his community) was considered and rejected by the Conference as an element to be weighed in determining admissibility. It was the judgment of the Conference that the danger of prejudice to a nondefendant witness is outweighed by the need for the trier of fact to have as much relevant evidence on the issue of credibility as possible. Such evidence should only be excluded where it presents a danger of improperly influencing the outcome of the trial by persuading the trier of fact to convict the defendant on the basis of his prior criminal record.

The House bill provides in subsection (b) that evidence of conviction of a crime may not be used for impeachment purposes under subsection (a) if more than ten years have elapsed since the date of the conviction or the date the witness was released from confinement imposed for the conviction, whichever is later. The Senate amendment permits the use of convictions older than ten years, if the court determines, in the interests of justice, that the probative value of the conviction, supported by specific facts and circumstances, substantially outweighs its prejudicial effect.

The Conference adopts the Senate amendment with an amendment requiring notice by a party that he intends to request that the court allow him to use a conviction older than ten years. The Conferees anticipate that a written notice, in order to give the adversary a fair opportunity to contest the use of the evidence, will ordinarily include such information as the date of the conviction, the jurisdiction, and the offense or statute involved. In order to eliminate the possibility that the flexibility of this provision may impair the ability of a party-opponent to prepare for trial, the Conferees intend that the notice provision operate to avoid surprise.

ADVISORY COMMITTEE'S NOTE (1990 AMENDMENT)

The amendment to Rule 609(a) makes two changes in the rule. The first change removes from the rule the limitation that the conviction may only be elicited during cross-examination, a limitation that virtually every circuit has found to be inapplicable. It is common for witnesses to reveal on direct examination their convictions to "remove the sting" of the impeachment. See e.g., United States v. Bad Cob, 560 F.2d 877 (8th Cir. 1977). The amendment does not contemplate that a court will necessarily permit proof of prior convictions through testimony, which might be time-consuming and more prejudicial than proof through a written record. Rules 403 and 611(a) provide sufficient authority for the court to protect against unfair or disruptive methods of proof.

The second change effected by the amendment resolves an ambiguity as to the relationship of Rules 609 and 403 with respect to impeachment of witnesses other than the criminal defendant. See, Green v. Bock Laundry Machine Co., 490 U.S. 504 (1989). The amendment does not disturb the special balancing test for the criminal defendant who chooses to testify. Thus, the rule recognizes that, in virtually every case in which prior convictions are used to impeach the testifying defendant, the defendant faces a unique risk of prejudice—i.e., the danger that convictions that would be excluded under Fed.R.Evid. 404 will be misused by a jury as propensity evidence despite their introduction solely for impeachment purposes. Although the rule does not forbid all use of convictions to impeach a defendant, it requires that the government show that the probative value of convictions as impeachment evidence outweighs their prejudicial effect.

Prior to the amendment, the rule appeared to give the defendant the benefit of the special balancing test when defense witnesses other than the defendant were called to testify. In practice, however, the concern about unfairness to the defendant is most acute when the defendant's own convictions are offered as evidence. Almost all of the decided cases concern this type of impeachment, and the amendment does not deprive the defendant of any meaningful protection, since Rule 403 now clearly protects against unfair impeachment of any defense witness other than the defendant. There are cases in which a defendant might be prejudiced when a defense witness is impeached. Such cases may arise, for example, when the witness bears a special relationship to the defendant such that the defendant is likely to suffer some spill-over effect from impeachment of the witness.

The amendment also protects other litigants from unfair impeachment of their witnesses. The danger of prejudice from the use of prior convictions is not confined to criminal defendants. Although the danger that prior convictions will be misused as character evidence is particularly acute when the defendant is impeached, the danger exists in other situations as well. The amendment reflects the view that it is desirable to protect all litigants from the unfair use of prior convictions, and that the ordinary balancing test of Rule 403, which provides that evidence shall not be excluded unless its prejudicial effect substantially outweighs its probative value, is appropriate for assessing the admissibility of prior convictions for impeachment of any witness other than a criminal defendant.

The amendment reflects a judgment that decisions interpreting Rule 609(a) as requiring a trial court to admit convictions in civil cases that have little, if anything, to do with credibility reach undesirable results. See, e.g., Diggs v. Lyons, 741 F.2d 577 (3d Cir. 1984), cert. denied, 105 S.Ct. 2157 (1985). The amendment provides the same protection against unfair prejudice arising from prior convictions used for impeachment purposes as the rules provide for other evidence. The amendment finds support in decided cases. See, e.g., Petty v. Ideco, 761 F.2d 1146 (5th Cir. 1985); Czaka v. Hickman, 703 F.2d 317 (8th Cir. 1983).

Fewer decided cases address the question whether Rule 609(a) provides any protection against unduly prejudicial prior convictions used to impeach government witnesses. Some courts have read Rule 609(a) as giving the government no protection for its witnesses. See, e.g., United States v. Thorne, 547 F.2d 56 (8th Cir. 1976); United States v. Nevitt, 563 F.2d 406 (9th Cir. 1977), cert. denied, 444 U.S. 847 (1979). This approach also is rejected by the amendment. There are cases in which impeachment of government witnesses with prior convictions that have little, if anything, to do with credibility may result in unfair prejudice to the government's interest in a fair trial and unnecessary embarrassment to a witness. Fed.R.Evid. 412 already recognizes this and excluded certain evidence of past sexual behavior in the context of prosecutions for sexual assaults.

The amendment applies the general balancing test of Rule 403 to protect all litigants against unfair impeachment of witnesses. The balancing test protects civil litigants, the government in criminal cases, and the defendant in a criminal case who calls other witnesses. The amendment addresses prior convictions offered under Rule 609, not for other purposes, and does not run afoul, therefore, of Davis v. Alaska, 415 U.S. 308 (1974). Davis involved the use of a prior juvenile adjudication not to prove a past law violation, but to prove bias. The defendant in a criminal case has the right to demonstrate the bias of a witness and to be assured a fair trial, but not to unduly prejudice a trier of fact. See generally Rule 412. In any case in which the trial court believes that confrontation rights require admission of impeachment evidence, obviously the Constitution would take precedence over the rule.

The probability that prior convictions of an ordinary government witness will be unduly prejudicial is low in most criminal cases. Since the behavior of the witness is not the issue in dispute in most cases, there is little chance that the trier of fact will misuse the convictions offered as impeachment evidence as propensity evidence. Thus, trial courts will be skeptical when the government objects to impeachment of its witnesses with prior convictions. Only when the government is able to point to a real danger of prejudice that is sufficient to outweigh substantially the probative value of the conviction for impeachment purposes will the conviction be excluded.

The amendment continues to divide subdivision (a) into subsections (1) and (2) thus facilitating retrieval under current computerized research programs which distinguish the two provisions. The Committee recommended no substantive change in subdivision (a)(2), even though some cases raise a concern about the proper interpretation of the words "dishonesty or false statement." These words were used but not explained in the original Advisory Committee Note accompanying Rule 609. Congress extensively debated the rule, and the Report of the House and Senate Conference Committee states that "[b]y the phrase 'dishonesty and false statement,' the Conference means crimes such as perjury, subornation of perjury, false statement, criminal fraud, embezzlement, or false pretense, or any other offense in the nature of *crimen falsi*, commission of which involves some element of deceit, untruthfulness, or falsification bearing on the accused's propensity to testify truthfully." The Advisory Committee concluded that the Conference Report provides sufficient guidance to trial courts and that no amendment is necessary, notwithstanding some decisions that take an unduly broad view of "dishonesty," admitting convictions such as for bank robbery or bank larceny. Subsection (a)(2) continues to apply to any witness, including a criminal defendant.

Finally, the Committee determined that it was unnecessary to add to the rule language stating that, when a prior conviction is offered under Rule 609, the trial court is to consider the probative value of the prior conviction *for impeachment*, not for other purposes. The Committee concluded that the title of the rule, its first sentence, and its placement among the impeachment rules clearly establish that evidence offered under Rule 609 is offered only for purposes of impeachment.

ADVISORY COMMITTEE'S NOTE (2006 AMENDMENT)

The amendment provides that Rule 609(a)(2) mandates the admission of evidence of a conviction only when the conviction required the proof of (or in the case of a guilty plea, the admission of) an act of dishonesty or false statement. Evidence of all other convictions is inadmissible under this subsection, irrespective of whether the witness exhibited dishonesty or made a false statement in the process of the commission of the crime of conviction. Thus, evidence that a witness was convicted for a crime of violence, such as murder, is not admissible under Rule 609(a)(2), even if the witness acted deceitfully in the course of committing the crime.

The amendment is meant to give effect to the legislative intent to limit the convictions that are to be automatically admitted under subsection (a)(2). The Conference Committee provided that by "dishonesty and false statement" it meant "crimes such as perjury, subornation of perjury, false statement, criminal fraud, embezzlement, or false pretense, or any other offense in the nature of *crimen falsi*, the commission of which involves some element of deceit, untruthfulness, or falsification bearing on the [witness's] propensity to testify truthfully." Historically, offenses classified as *crimina falsi* have included only those crimes in which the ultimate criminal act was itself an act of deceit. *See* Green, *Deceit and the Classification of Crimes: Federal Rule of Evidence 609(a)(2) and the Origins of* Crimen Falsi, 90 J. Crim. L. & Criminology 1087 (2000).

Evidence of crimes in the nature of *crimina falsi* must be admitted under Rule 609(a)(2), regardless of how such crimes are specifically charged. For example, evidence that a witness was convicted of making a false claim to a federal agent is admissible under this subsection regardless of whether the crime was charged under a section that expressly references deceit (e.g., 18 U.S.C. § 1001, Material Misrepresentation to the Federal Government) or a section that does not (e.g., 18 U.S.C. § 1503, Obstruction of Justice).

The amendment requires that the proponent have ready proof that the conviction required the factfinder to find, or the defendant to admit, an act of dishonesty or false statement. Ordinarily, the statutory elements of the crime will indicate whether it is one of dishonesty or false statement. Where the deceitful nature of the crime is not apparent from the statute and the face of the judgment—as, for example, where the conviction simply records a finding of guilt for a statutory offense that does not reference deceit expressly—a proponent may offer information such as an indictment, a statement of admitted facts, or jury instructions to show that the factfinder had to find, or the defendant had to admit, an act of dishonesty or false statement in order for the witness to have been convicted. *Cf. Taylor v. United States*, 495 U.S. 575, 602 (1990) (providing that a trial court may look to a charging instrument or jury instructions to ascertain the nature of a prior offense where the statute is insufficiently clear on its face); *Shepard v. United States*, 125 S.Ct. 1254 (2005) (the inquiry to determine whether a guilty plea to a crime defined by a nongeneric statute necessarily admitted elements of the generic offense was limited to the charging document's terms, the terms of a plea agreement or transcript of colloquy between judge and defendant in which the factual basis for the plea was confirmed by the defendant, or a comparable judicial record). But the amendment does not contemplate a "mini-trial" in which the court plumbs the record of the previous proceeding to determine whether the crime was in the nature of *crimen falsi*.

The amendment also substitutes the term "character for truthfulness" for the term "credibility" in the first sentence of the Rule. The limitations of Rule 609 are not applicable if a conviction is admitted for a purpose other than to prove the witness's character for untruthfulness. *See, e.g., United States v. Lopez*, 979 F.2d 1024 (5th Cir. 1992) (Rule 609 was not applicable where the conviction was offered for purposes of contradiction). The use of the term "credibility" in subsection (d) is retained, however, as that subdivision is intended to govern the use of a juvenile adjudication for any type of impeachment.

ADVISORY COMMITTEE'S NOTE (2011 AMENDMENT)

The language of Rule 609 has been amended as part of the restyling of the Evidence Rules to make them more easily understood and to make style and terminology consistent throughout the rules. These changes are intended to be stylistic only. There is no intent to change any result in any ruling on evidence admissibility.

Florida Stat. § 90.610. Conviction of Certain Crimes as Impeachment

(1) A party may attack the credibility of any witness, including an accused, by evidence that the witness has been convicted of a crime if the crime was punishable by death or imprisonment in excess of 1 year under the law under which the witness was convicted, or if the crime involved dishonesty or a false statement regardless of the punishment, with the following exceptions:

(a) Evidence of any such conviction is inadmissible in a civil trial if it is so remote in time as to have no bearing on the present character of the witness.

(b) Evidence of juvenile adjudications are inadmissible under this subsection.

(2) The pendency of an appeal or the granting of a pardon relating to such crime does not render evidence of the conviction from which the appeal was taken or for which the pardon was granted inadmissible. Evidence of the pendency of the appeal is admissible.

(3) Nothing in this section affects the admissibility of evidence under s. 90.404 or s. 90.608.

SPONSORS' NOTE (1976 ENACTMENT)

<u>Subsection (1)</u> This subsection recognizes that conviction of certain crimes may be used to test credibility. There has been disagreement over which crimes may be so used. Only crimes involving dishonesty or false statement are permitted under Uniform Rule 21 and Model Code of Evidence Rule 106. Other jurisdictions have required the trial judge to determine that the probative value of the evidence of the crime is not substantially outweighed by the danger of unfair prejudice. See <u>Luck v. United States</u>, 348 F.2d 763 (D.C. Cir.1965).

The existing Florida law allows a witness to be impeached upon cross-examination "by reason of conviction of any crime." Fla. Stat. § 90.08. Therefore, a witness may be impeached by felonies or misdemeanors, whether or not they involve moral turpitude, <u>Hendrick v. Strazzula</u>, 135 So.2d 1 (Fla. 1961), but not for violations of municipal ordinances. <u>Roe v. State</u>, 96 Fla. 723, 119 So. 118 (1928). Interrogation as to former arrests or accusations of crimes is also improper. <u>Jordan v. State</u>, 107 Fla. 333,

144 So. 669 (1932); but see Wallace v. State, 41 Fla. 547, 26 So. 713, 719 (Fla. 1899). McArthur v. Cook, 99 So.2d 565 (Fla. 1957) sets forth the accepted procedure for using prior convictions to impeach. Note that it is improper to name the specific crime involved.

[This subsection allows only the use of crimes involving dishonesty and false statements. When the credibility of a witness is under attack the character traits of truth and veracity are under dispute. Only crimes involving dishonesty and false statement are relevant.][22]

Fed. Rule Evid. 609 also allows the use of crimes which were punishable by death or imprisonment in excess of one year if the court determines that the probative value of admitting this evidence outweighs its prejudicial effect to the defendant.

[Subsection (1)(a) This subsection recognizes that a conviction can become too remote to effect credibility and therefore lacks probative value. McCormick, Evidence § 43 (2nd ed. 1972); Ladd, Credibility Tests—Current Trends, 89 U. Pa. L. Rev. 166, 177 (1941). If a witness has been released from custody for ten years, the crimes may not be used.

See Toms v. State, 200 S.W.2d 174 (Tex. Crim. App. 1947); Mass. Gen. Laws 233 § 21 (1973); and Fed. Rule Evid. 609(b) which have adopted various times after which the conviction becomes inadmissible.

The existing law does not bar the introduction of remote convictions, but permits the opposing counsel to show remoteness on redirect. McArthur v. Cook, 99 So.2d 565 (Fla. 1957).][23]

[Subsection (1)(b) This section recognizes that when a conviction has been pardoned it should not be used to impeach the witness. Under existing law, opposing counsel can show the pardon on redirect to minimize the effect of the conviction. See McArthur v. Cook, 99 So.2d 565, 567 (Fla. 1955); 3A Wigmore, Evidence § 980 (Chadbourn rev. 1970).

Fed. Rule Evid. 609 and Calif. Evid. Code § 788 prohibit the use of a conviction only when a pardon was granted because the witness was innocent or rehabilitated but allow the conviction's use where the pardon was granted to restore the witness's civil rights.][24]

Subsection (1)(c) [Renumbered as Section 1(b)] This section is consistent with Fla. Stat. § 39.10(3) (adjudication of child as dependent or delinquent is not a conviction) and § 39.12(6) (generally prohibiting the use of juvenile court records in other civil or criminal actions).

The majority view is reflected by this subsection. However, Fed. Rule Evid. 609, adopts the view of 1 Wigmore, Evidence § 196 and 3A Wigmore, Evidence §§ 924a, 980 (Chadbourn rev. 1970) and allows the court discretion in a criminal case to admit the juvenile adjudication if the evidence is necessary for a fair trial.

This section does not adopt the discretionary view, but extends the policy of the Florida Juvenile Court Act in protecting the juvenile and recognizes the lack of some procedural rights in juvenile proceedings. See McCormick, Evidence § 43 (2nd ed. 1972).

---

[22] Editor's Note: The bracketed language refers to the original version of the rule, which was subsequently amended to permit the use of crimes other than those involving dishonesty and false statement to impeach a witness.

[23] Editor's Note: The bracketed language refers to the original version of the rule, which was subsequently amended to eliminate a specific cutoff date for determining remoteness and to limit the applicability of the provision to civil cases.

[24] Editor's Note: The bracketed language refers to the original version of the rule, which was subsequently amended to eliminate the bar on using a conviction for which a pardon was granted.

Subsection (2) This section makes admissible a conviction after a guilty verdict has been returned. A final appellate determination is not required in order to use the conviction in light of the increasing number of subsequent attacks upon convictions, which can indefinitely prolong the litigation. See Fed. Rule Evid. 609(e).

COMMENTARY ON FEDERAL AND FLORIDA RULE DIFFERENCES

Florida Stat. § 90.610 and its federal counterpart, Federal Rule 609, regulate the use of a witness's prior criminal convictions to impeach her credibility. Both rules permit only two types of convictions to be used to impeach a witness: those for crimes punishable by death or imprisonment in excess of one year (hereinafter "felony-grade crime") and those for crimes that involve a dishonest act or false statement, regardless of punishment. See FLA. STAT. § 90.610(1); FED. R. EVID. 609(a)(1)-(2). Beyond that, however, there are significant differences between the two rules.

The federal rule has a complicated set of balancing tests that treat differently the admissibility of convictions depending on their age and type, as well as on whether they are being offered against the accused in a criminal case or some other witness. Under the federal rule, evidence that a witness *other than* the accused in a criminal case has been convicted of a felony-grade crime shall be admitted, subject to exclusion only under Federal Rule 403. See FED. R. EVID. 609(a)(1)(A). By contrast, evidence that the defendant in a criminal case has been convicted of a felony-grade crime is to be admitted if he testifies as a witness only if the court determines that the probative value outweighs its prejudicial effect. See FED. R. EVID. 609(a)(1)(B). If a witness has been convicted of a crime involving a dishonest act or false statement, federal courts *must* admit that evidence, and have *no* discretion to exclude the evidence under Federal Rule 403, regardless of the potential sentence and regardless of whether the witness is the accused in a criminal case or not. See FED. R. EVID. 609(a)(2); *U.S. v. Toney*, 615 F.2d 277, 279-80 (11th Cir. 1980). Finally, under the federal rule, convictions that are more than 10 years old (measured from the date of release or conviction, whichever is later) are not admissible unless the adverse party is given advance written notice of intent to use it and the probative value *substantially* outweighs its prejudicial effect. See FED. R. EVID. 609(b). This latter provision creates a presumption against admissibility for older convictions. See *U.S. v. Pritchard*, 973 F.2d 905, 908 (11th Cir. 1992). Factors considered in weighing probative worth against prejudicial effect include the nature of the prior conviction, its age, the frequency of prior convictions, similarity between the past and charged crimes, importance of the defendant's testimony, and the centrality of credibility in the case. See *U.S. v. Burston*, 159 F.3d 1328, 1335-36 (11th Cir. 1998); *Pritchard*, 973 F.2d at 908-09.

The Florida rule, by contrast, has a much simpler regulatory scheme that does not differentiate based on type of conviction or whether it is being used to impeach the accused in a criminal case or not. Rather, all such convictions may be used to impeach a witness, subject to an exception in civil cases if the conviction is "so remote in time as to have no bearing on the present character of the witness." FLA. STAT. § 90.610(1)(a). Thus, unlike with the federal rule, the drafters of the Florida rule "expressly declined to adopt an 'arbitrary number of years' to be used in assessing remoteness and admissibility." *Trowell v. J.C. Penney Co., Inc.*, 813 So. 2d 1042, 1043 (Fla. 4th DCA 2002). Under this provision, even if a conviction is very old, that the person continued to acquire felony convictions after that one suggests that the older conviction does have a bearing on present character. See *Pryor v. State*, 855 So. 2d 134, 136-37 (Fla. 1st DCA 2003); *Trowell*, 813 So. 2d at 1043-44. While this provision only in terms applies in civil cases, see *Peoples v. State*, 576 So. 2d 783, 789 (Fla. 5th DCA 1991), Florida Stat. § 90.403 has been held to provide a basis for excluding convictions for remoteness in criminal cases, see *Pryor*, 855 So. 2d at 137, and indeed has been held generally to apply to all convictions offered under Florida Stat. § 90.610 based on such factors as the nature of the prior crime and its remoteness in time. See *Riechmann v. State*, 581 So. 2d 133, 140 (Fla. 1991); *State v. Page*, 449 So. 2d 813, 816 (Fla. 1984).

Under both the federal and Florida rules, a "conviction" includes a judgment of conviction that follows either a jury verdict or a plea of guilty. See *State v. McFadden*, 772 So. 2d 1209, 1211-13 (Fla.

2000); *U.S. v. Kane*, 944 F.2d 1406, 1412-13 (7th Cir. 1991). Moreover, under both rules, if the trial court withholds adjudication after such a plea or verdict, it is not a "conviction." *See McFadden*, 772 So. 2d at 1211-13; *U.S. v. Georgalis*, 631 F.2d 1199, 1203 n.3 (5th Cir. 1980). It is clear that a conviction based on a plea of nolo contendere is admissible under the federal rule, *see U.S. v. Williams*, 642 F.2d 136, 138-40 (5th Cir. Unit B 1981), and it also appears that such evidence is admissible under the Florida rule as well. *See Cira v. Dillinger*, 903 So. 2d 367, 373 (Fla. 2d DCA 2005). Under both the Florida and federal rules, a foreign conviction counts as a "conviction" so long as the foreign system of justice is not deemed to be unfair. *Riechmann*, 581 So. 2d at 139; *U.S. v. Wilson*, 556 F.2d 1177, 1178 (4th Cir. 1977).

Another significant difference between the two rules is that the Florida courts take a broad view of the phrase "dishonesty or a false statement," holding that it includes not only crimes such as jury tampering, *see Tampling v. State*, 610 So. 2d 100, 101 (Fla. 1st DCA 1992), bribery, *see Peterson v. State*, 645 So.2d 10, 13 (Fla. 4th DCA 1994), or passing bad checks, *see Children's Palace, Inc. v. Johnson*, 609 So.2d 755, 756 (Fla. 1st DCA 1993), but any crime that has as its basis lying, cheating, deceiving, stealing, or defrauding, such as robbery or theft, *see Page*, 449 So. 2d at 815-16, or even joy-riding, *see Belton v. State*, 475 So. 2d 275 (Fla. 3d DCA 1985). By contrast, the federal courts in Florida take a much narrower view of the scope of the analogous phrase "a dishonest act or false statement," holding that it does not apply to "crimes such as theft, robbery, or shoplifting," *see U.S. v. Sellers*, 906 F.2d 597, 603 (11th Cir. 1990), evidently limiting it to crimes such as "perjury or subornation of perjury, false statement, criminal fraud, embezzlement, or false pretense, or any other offense in the nature of crimen falsi, the commission of which involves some element of deceit, untruthfulness, or falsification bearing on the accused's propensity to testify truthfully." Conference Report to FED. R. EVID. 609. In this regard, the Florida Supreme Court recognizes that its "interpretation of the statute differs from the federal construction of identical language contained in federal rule 609," and that it has adopted the "minority view." *Page*, 449 So. 2d at 815. Yet even under the Florida rule, violent crimes are not deemed to involve "dishonesty or false statement. *See Cullen v. State*, 920 So. 2d 1155 (Fla. 4th DCA 2006) (statutory rape); *Riechmann*, 581 So. 2d at 140 (involuntary manslaughter).

Moreover, an amendment to the federal rule that took effect on December 1, 2006, makes clear that the mere fact that a person makes a false statement or exhibits dishonesty in the course of committing a crime does not make it a crime of "dishonesty or false statement" within the meaning of the rule; only if an act of dishonesty or false statement is an *element* of the offense does it qualify. *See* Advisory Committee's Note to 2006 Amendment to FED. R. EVID. 609.

Yet another significant difference between the federal and Florida rules is the amount of information regarding the prior convictions that is admitted. Under the federal rule, the nature and date of each conviction is admitted, *see Burston*, 159 F.3d at 1335, either through a certified copy of the conviction or by eliciting it from the witness on cross-examination, *see Wilson v. Attaway*, 757 F.2d 1227, 1244 (11th Cir. 1985). By contrast, under Florida case law, the proper method to impeach a witness with his prior convictions is to ask him if he has ever been convicted of a felony (and if so, how many times) or of a crime involving dishonesty or false statement (and if so, how many times). If the witness answers the questions correctly, counsel may not ask further questions. If he denies ever being convicted or misstates the number of previous convictions, counsel may impeach him by introducing into evidence records of past convictions, but in any event, can ask no further questions and in no event can counsel delve into the nature of the crimes. *See Dessaure v. State*, 891 So. 2d 455, 469 (Fla. 2004); *Brown v. State*, 787 So. 2d 136, 138-39 (Fla. 4th DCA 2001); *Porter v. State*, 593 So. 2d 1158, 1159 (Fla. 2d DCA 1992); *Cummings v. State*, 412 So. 2d 436, 438 (Fla. 4th DCA 1982). Only certified copies of the judgment of conviction can be used to rebut the witness's denial, and if counsel lacks such copies, she is stuck with the witness's denial (except with respect to foreign judgments from countries for which such records are extremely hard to access). *See Peterson*, 645 So. 2d at 12; *Peoples*, 576 So. 2d at 789. The Florida decisions reason that the fact of conviction alone is sufficient to cast doubt on the witness's credibility, and that any additional light that the specific nature of the crime sheds on credibility is outweighed by the risk of prejudice. *See Bobb v. State*, 647 So. 2d 881, 883 (Fla. 4th DCA 1995); *Reeser v. Boats Unlimited, Inc.*, 432 So. 2d 1346, 1349 (Fla. 4th DCA 1983). The witness who has been impeached, however, can volunteer to reveal the nature of the crime. *Cummings*, 412 So. 2d at 438. Moreover, if in the course of disclosing his prior convictions a defendant-witness engages in "spin control" by characterizing them in a way favorable to his case at trial, the state is entitled to inquire further regarding the convictions so as to dispel any misleading impression. *See Rogers v. State*, 964 So. 2d 221, 222-23 (Fla. 4th DCA 2007)

The Florida and federal rules differ in their treatment of a conviction that has been the subject of a pardon. Under the Florida rule, that a pardon was granted does not render inadmissible evidence of the conviction to impeach the witness's credibility. *See* FLA. STAT. § 90.610(2). By contrast, under the federal rule, a conviction that has been the subject of a pardon, annulment, or similar procedure based on a finding of innocence cannot be used to impeach a witness's credibility; one that is based on a finding of rehabilitation likewise cannot be used to impeach a witness's credibility unless the person has been convicted of a subsequent crime punishable by death or imprisonment in excess of one year. *See* FED. R. EVID. 609(c).

The Florida and federal rules also differ slightly with respect to evidence of juvenile adjudications. The Florida rule in all circumstances bars the admission of juvenile adjudications to impeach a witness's credibility. *See* FLA. STAT. § 90.610(1)(b). The federal rule provides that such adjudications are "generally not admissible," but gives the trial court discretion to admit them for a witness other than the accused if it would otherwise be admissible and is necessary to a fair determination of guilt or innocence. *See* FED. R. EVID. 609(d). However, implicit in the Florida decisions is that the absolute bar would be relaxed in a case in which the defendant's Confrontation Clause rights required it. *See Martin v. State*, 710 So. 2d 58, 59 (Fla. 4th DCA 1998).

Finally, under both the Florida and federal rules, the pendency of an appeal from a conviction does not render inadmissible evidence of that conviction to impeach the witness's credibility, although evidence of the pendency of the appeal is made admissible under both rules. *See* FLA. STAT. § 90.610(2); FED. R. EVID. 609(e).

Federal Rule 610. Religious Beliefs or Opinions

Evidence of a witness's religious beliefs or opinions is not admissible to attack or support the witness's credibility.

ADVISORY COMMITTEE'S NOTE

While the rule forecloses inquiry into the religious beliefs or opinions of a witness for the purpose of showing that his character for truthfulness is affected by their nature, an inquiry for the purpose of showing interest or bias because of them is not within the prohibition. Thus disclosure of affiliation with a church which is a party to the litigation would be allowable under the rule. Cf. Tucker v. Reil, 51 Ariz. 357 (1938). To the same effect, though less specifically worded, is California Evidence Code § 789. See 3 Wigmore § 936.

ADVISORY COMMITTEE'S NOTE (2011 AMENDMENT)

The language of Rule 610 has been amended as part of the restyling of the Evidence Rules to make them more easily understood and to make style and terminology consistent throughout the rules. These changes are intended to be stylistic only. There is no intent to change any result in any ruling on evidence admissibility.

Florida Stat. § 90.611. Religious Beliefs or Opinions

Evidence of the beliefs or opinions of a witness on matters of religion is inadmissible to show that the witness's credibility is impaired or enhanced thereby.

SPONSORS' NOTE (1976 ENACTMENT)

This section adopts the prevailing view that there is no basis for believing that lack of faith in God's avenging wrath is relevant to the issue of truthfulness. McCormick, Evidence, § 48 (2nd ed. 1972). It is in accord with existing Fla. Stat. § 90.06: "Atheists, agnostics, and all persons who do not believe in the doctrine of future rewards and punishments shall be permitted to testify in any of the courts of this state." In Taylor v. State, 139 Fla. 542, 190 So. 691, 694 (1939), the court omitted "religious beliefs" from its listing of the evidence which could be used to attack the credibility of a witness.

This section does not bar inquiry into religious matters to show interest or bias, i.e., to show church affiliation when a church is a litigant.

COMMENTARY ON FEDERAL AND FLORIDA RULE DIFFERENCES

Both Florida Stat. § 90.611 and its federal counterpart, Federal Rule 610, regulate the admissibility of evidence of a witness's religious beliefs or opinions. Under both rules, such evidence is not admissible when offered for the purpose of showing that the witness' credibility is impaired *or* enhanced due to his religious affiliation (or lack thereof). *Tisdale v. Federal Express Corp.*, 415 F.3d 516, 536 (6th Cir. 2005); *Norquoy v. Metcalf*, 575 So. 2d 322, 323 (Fla. 4th DCA 1991). Moreover, a party is unlikely to be able to circumvent the rule by re-characterizing evidence of a person's religious beliefs as evidence of a lack of sensory or mental capacity. *See Reeves v. State*, 862 So. 2d 60, 61-62 (Fla. 1st DCA 2003) (rejecting argument that Florida Stat. § 90.611 does not bar evidence that the victim said "she saw Jesus standing in the room" because it is evidence offered to demonstrate that witness lacks the ability to differentiate between fantasy and reality in perceiving things).

However, evidence of a witness' religious beliefs or opinions is *not* excluded by either Florida Stat. § 90.611 or Federal Rule 610 when it is offered for some purpose other than to suggest that the witness' credibility is impaired or enhanced *as a result of* such beliefs. Thus, for example, evidence that a witness may be *biased* in favor of a party because of their common membership in the same church would not be barred by either rule, *see Firemen's Fund Ins. Co. v. Thien*, 63 F.3d 754, 761 (8th Cir. 1995); Advisory Committee's Note to FED. R. EVID. 610; Sponsors' Note to FLA. STAT. § 90.611, although under Federal Rule 403 or Florida Stat. § 90.403 a court might hold that to avoid the potential risk of prejudice against a party because of his specific religion, only evidence of common membership and not the name of the religious denomination should be introduced. *See Finch v. Hercules, Inc.*, 1995 WL 785100, at *5 (D. Del. 1995).

Moreover, neither rule bars inquiry into religious matters when such matters are relevant to the issues in the case. *See U.S. v. Beasley*, 72 F.3d 1518, 1527-28 (11th Cir. 1996) (does not bar evidence offered in racketeering prosecution that defendant used his position as head of a religious cult to get followers to commit racketeering acts); *Colbert v. Rolls*, 746 So. 2d 1134, 1135-36 (Fla. 5th DCA 1999) (does not bar evidence offered in medical malpractice suit that defendant allowed his religious beliefs to influence his medical decisions).

The Florida courts describe the Florida and federal rules as "virtually the same," and thus find federal decisions interpreting Federal Rule 610 persuasive in interpreting Florida Stat. § 90.611. *Reeves*, 862 So. 2d at 62 n.2.

Federal Rule 611. Mode and Order of Examining Witnesses and Presenting Evidence

(a) Control by the Court; Purposes. The court should exercise reasonable control over the mode and order of examining witnesses and presenting evidence so as to:

(1) make those procedures effective for determining the truth;

(2) avoid wasting time; and

(3) protect witnesses from harassment or undue embarrassment.

(b) Scope of Cross-Examination. Cross-examination should not go beyond the subject matter of the direct examination and matters affecting the witness's credibility. The court may allow inquiry into additional matters as if on direct examination.

(c) Leading Questions. Leading questions should not be used on direct examination except as necessary to develop the witness's testimony. Ordinarily, the court should allow leading questions:

(1) on cross-examination; and

(2) when a party calls a hostile witness, an adverse party, or a witness identified with an adverse party.

ADVISORY COMMITTEE'S NOTE

Subdivision (a). Spelling out detailed rules to govern the mode and order of interrogating witnesses and presenting evidence is neither desirable nor feasible. The ultimate responsibility for the effective working of the adversary system rests with the judge. The rule sets forth the objectives which he should seek to attain.

Item (1) restates in broad terms the power and obligation of the judge as developed under common law principles. It covers such concerns as whether testimony shall be in the form of a free narrative or responses to specific questions, McCormick § 5, the order of calling witnesses and presenting evidence, 6 Wigmore § 1867, the use of demonstrative evidence, McCormick § 179, and the many other questions arising during the course of a trial which can be solved only by the judge's common sense and fairness in view of the particular circumstances.

Item (2) is addressed to avoidance of needless consumption of time, a matter of daily concern in the disposition of cases. A companion piece is found in the discretion vested in the judge to exclude evidence as a waste of time in Rule 403(b).

Item (3) calls for a judgment under the particular circumstances whether interrogation tactics entail harassment or undue embarrassment. Pertinent circumstances include the importance of the testimony, the nature of the inquiry, its relevance to credibility, waste of time, and confusion. McCormick § 42. In Alford v. United States, 282 U.S. 687 (1931), the Court pointed out that, while the trial judge should protect the witness from questions which "go beyond the bounds of proper cross-examination merely to harass, annoy or humiliate," this protection by no means forecloses efforts to discredit the witness. Reference to the transcript of the prosecutor's cross-examination in Berger v. United States, 295 U.S. 78 (1935), serves to lay at rest any doubts as to the need for judicial control in this area.

The inquiry into specific instances of conduct of a witness allowed under Rule 608(b) is, of course, subject to this rule.

Subdivision (b). The tradition in the federal courts and in numerous state courts has been to limit the scope of cross-examination to matters testified to on direct, plus matters bearing upon the credibility of the witness. Various reasons have been advanced to justify the rule of limited cross-examination. (1) A party vouches for his own witness but only to the extent of matters elicited on direct. Resurrection Gold Mining Co. v. Fortune Gold Mining Co., 129 F. 668, 675 (8th Cir. 1904), quoted in Maguire, Weinstein, et al., Cases on Evidence 277, n. 38 (5th ed. 1965). But the concept of vouching is discredited, and Rule 607 rejects it. (2) A party cannot ask his own witness leading questions. This is a problem properly solved in terms of what is necessary for a proper development of the testimony rather than by a mechanistic formula similar to the vouching concept. See discussion under subdivision (c). (3) A practice of limited cross-examination promotes orderly presentation of the case. Finch v. Weiner, 109 Conn. 616 (1929). While this latter reason has merit, the matter is essentially one of the order of presentation and not one in which involvement at the appellate level is likely to prove fruitful. See, for example, Moyer v. Aetna Life Ins. Co., 126 F.2d 141 (3rd Cir. 1942); Butler v. New York Central R. Co., 253 F.2d 281 (7th Cir. 1958); United States v. Johnson, 285 F.2d 35 (9th Cir. 1960); Union Automobile Indemnity Ass'n v. Capitol Indemnity Ins. Co., 310 F.2d 318 (7th Cir. 1962). In evaluating these considerations, McCormick says:

"The foregoing considerations favoring the wide-open or restrictive rules may well be thought to be fairly evenly balanced. There is another factor, however, which seems to swing the balance overwhelmingly in favor of the wide-open rule. This is the consideration of economy of time and energy. Obviously, the wide-open rule presents little or no opportunity for dispute in its application. The restrictive practice in all its forms, on the other hand, is productive in many court rooms, of continual bickering over the choice of the numerous variations of the 'scope of the direct' criterion, and of their application to particular cross-questions. These controversies are often reventilated on appeal, and reversals for error in their determination are frequent. Observance of these vague and ambiguous restrictions is a matter of constant and hampering concern to the cross-examiner. If these efforts, delays and misprisions were the necessary incidents to the guarding of substantive rights or the fundamentals of fair trial, they might be worth the cost. As the price of the choice of an obviously debatable regulation of the order of evidence, the sacrifice seems misguided. The American Bar Association's Committee for the Improvement of the Law of Evidence for the year 1937–38 said this:

'The rule limiting cross-examination to the precise subject of the direct examination is probably the most frequent rule (except the Opinion rule) leading in the trial practice today to refined and technical quibbles which obstruct the progress of the trial, confuse the jury, and give rise to appeal on technical grounds only. Some of the instances in which Supreme Courts have ordered new trials for the mere transgression of this rule about the order of evidence have been astounding.

'We recommend that the rule allowing questions upon any part of the issue known to the witness...be adopted....'" McCormick, §27, p. 51. See also 5 Moore's Federal Practice ¶ 43.10 (2nd ed. 1964).

The provision of the second sentence, that the judge may in the interests of justice limit inquiry into new matters on cross-examination, is designed for those situations in which the result otherwise would be confusion, complication, or protraction of the case, not as a matter of rule but as demonstrable in the actual development of the particular case.

The rule does not purport to determine the extent to which an accused who elects to testify thereby waives his privilege against self-incrimination. The question is a constitutional one, rather than a mere matter of administering the trial. Under Simmons v. United States, 390 U.S. 377 (1968), no general waiver occurs when the accused testifies on such preliminary matters as the validity of a search and seizure or the admissibility of a confession. Rule 104(d), *supra*. When he testifies on the merits, however, can he foreclose inquiry into an aspect or element of the crime by avoiding it on direct? The affirmative answer given in Tucker v. United States, 5 F.2d 818 (8th Cir. 1925), is inconsistent with the description of the waiver as extending to "all other relevant facts" in Johnson v. United States, 318 U.S. 189, 195 (1943). See also Brown v. United States, 356 U.S. 148 (1958). The situation of an accused who desires to testify on some but not all counts of a multiple-count indictment is one to be approached, in the first instance at least, as a problem of severance under Rule 14 of the Federal Rules of Criminal Procedure. Cross v. United States, 335 F.2d 987 (1964). Cf. United States v. Baker, 262 F.Supp. 657, 686 (D.D.C. 1966). In all events, the extent of the waiver of the privilege against self-incrimination ought not to be determined as a by-product of a rule on scope of cross-examination.

Subdivision (c). The rule continues the traditional view that the suggestive powers of the leading question are as a general proposition undesirable. Within this tradition, however, numerous exceptions have achieved recognition: The witness who is hostile, unwilling, or biased; the child witness or the adult with communication problems; the witness whose recollection is exhausted; and undisputed preliminary matters. 3 Wigmore §§ 774–778. An almost total unwillingness to reverse for infractions has been manifested by appellate courts. See cases cited in 3 Wigmore § 770. The matter clearly falls within the area of control by the judge over the mode and order of interrogation and presentation and accordingly is phrased in words of suggestion rather than command.

The rule also conforms to tradition in making the use of leading questions on cross-examination a matter of right. The purpose of the qualification "ordinarily" is to furnish a basis for denying the use of leading questions when the cross-examination is cross-examination in form only and not in fact, as for example the "cross-examination" of a party by his own counsel after being called by the opponent (savoring more of re-direct) or of an insured defendant who proves to be friendly to the plaintiff.

The final sentence deals with categories of witnesses automatically regarded and treated as hostile. Rule 43(b) of the Federal Rules of Civil Procedure has included only "an adverse party or an officer, director, or managing agent of a public or private corporation or of a partnership or association which is an adverse party." This limitation virtually to persons whose statements would stand as admissions is believed to be an unduly narrow concept of those who may safely be regarded as hostile without further demonstration. See, for example, Maryland Casualty Co. v. Kador, 225 F.2d 120 (5th Cir. 1955), and Degelos v. Fidelity and Casualty Co., 313 F.2d 809 (5th Cir. 1963), holding despite the language of Rule 43(b) that an insured fell within it, though not a party in an action under the Louisiana direct action statute. The phrase of the rule, "witness identified with" an adverse party, is designed to enlarge the category of persons thus callable.

REPORT OF HOUSE COMMITTEE ON THE JUDICIARY

As submitted by the Court, Rule 611(b) provided:

A witness may be cross-examined on any matter relevant to any issue in the case, including credibility. In the interests of justice, the judge may limit cross-examination with respect to matters not testified to on direct examination.

The Committee amended this provision to return to the rule which prevails in the federal courts and thirty-nine State jurisdictions. As amended, the Rule is in the text of the 1969 Advisory Committee draft. It limits cross-examination to credibility and to matters testified to on direct examination, unless the judge permits more, in which event the cross-examiner must proceed as if on direct examination. This traditional rule facilitates orderly presentation by each party at trial. Further, in light of existing discovery procedures, there appears to be no need to abandon the traditional rule.

The third sentence of Rule 611(c)[25] as submitted by the Court provided that:

> In civil cases, a party is entitled to call an adverse party or witness identified with him and interrogate by leading questions.

---

[25] Editor's Note: This refers to subsection (c)(2) of the restyled version of the rule.

The Committee amended this Rule to permit leading questions to be used with respect to any hostile witness, not only an adverse party or person identified with such adverse party. The Committee also substituted the word "When" for the phrase "In civil cases" to reflect the possibility that in criminal cases a defendant may be entitled to call witnesses identified with the government, in which event the Committee believed the defendant should be permitted to inquire with leading questions.

REPORT OF SENATE COMMITTEE ON THE JUDICIARY

Rule 611(b) as submitted by the Supreme Court permitted a broad scope of cross-examination: "cross-examination on any matter relevant to any issue in the case" unless the judge, in the interests of justice, limited the scope of cross-examination.

The House narrowed the Rule to the more traditional practice of limiting cross-examination to the subject matter of direct examination (and credibility), but with discretion in the judge to permit inquiry into additional matters in situations where that would aid in the development of the evidence or otherwise facilitate the conduct of the trial.

The committee agrees with the House amendment. Although there are good arguments in support of broad cross-examination from perspectives of developing all relevant evidence, we believe the factors of insuring an orderly and predictable development of the evidence weigh in favor of the narrower rule, especially when discretion is given to the trial judge to permit inquiry into additional matters. The committee expressly approves this discretion and believes it will permit sufficient flexibility allowing a broader scope of cross-examination whenever appropriate.

The House amendment providing broader discretionary cross-examination permitted inquiry into additional matters only as if on direct examination. As a general rule, we concur with this limitation, however, we would understand that this limitation would not preclude the utilization of leading questions if the conditions of subsection (c) of this rule were met, bearing in mind the judge's discretion in any case to limit the scope of cross-examination.[26]

Further, the committee has received correspondence from Federal judges commenting on the applicability of this rule to section 1407 of title 28. It is the committee's judgment that this rule as reported by the House is flexible enough to provide sufficiently broad cross-examination in appropriate situations in multidistrict litigation.

As submitted by the Supreme Court, the rule provided: "In civil cases, a party is entitled to call an adverse party or witness identified with him and interrogate by leading questions."

The final sentence of subsection (c)[27] was amended by the House for the purpose of clarifying the fact that a "hostile witness" — that is a witness who is hostile in fact — could be subject to interrogation by leading questions. The rule as submitted by the Supreme Court declared certain witnesses hostile as a matter of law and thus subject to interrogation by leading questions without any showing of hostility in fact. These were adverse parties or witnesses identified with adverse parties. However, the wording of the first sentence of subsection (c) while generally prohibiting the use of leading questions on direct examination, also provides "except as may be necessary to develop his testimony." Further, the first paragraph of the Advisory Committee Note explaining the subsection makes clear that they intended that leading questions could be asked of a hostile witness or a witness who was unwilling or biased and even though that witness was not associated with an adverse party. Thus, we question whether the House amendment was necessary.

---

[26] See McCormick on Evidence, §§ 24–26 (especially 24) (2d ed. 1972).
[27] Editor's Note: This refers to subsection (c)(2) of the restyled version of the rule.

However, concluding that it was not intended to affect the meaning of the first sentence of the subsection and was intended solely to clarify the fact that leading questions are permissible in the interrogation of a witness, who is hostile in fact, the committee accepts that House amendment.

The final sentence of this subsection was also amended by the House to cover criminal as well as civil cases. The committee accepts this amendment, but notes that it may be difficult in criminal cases to determine when a witness is "identified with an adverse party," and thus the rule should be applied with caution.

ADVISORY COMMITTEE'S NOTE (2011 AMENDMENT)

The language of Rule 611 has been amended as part of the restyling of the Evidence Rules to make them more easily understood and to make style and terminology consistent throughout the rules. These changes are intended to be stylistic only. There is no intent to change any result in any ruling on evidence admissibility.

Florida Stat. § 90.612. Mode and Order of Interrogation and Presentation

(1) The judge shall exercise reasonable control over the mode and order of the interrogation of witnesses and the presentation of evidence, so as to:

(a) Facilitate, through effective interrogation and presentation, the discovery of the truth.

(b) Avoid needless consumption of time.

(c) Protect witnesses from harassment or undue embarrassment.

(2) Cross-examination of a witness is limited to the subject matter of the direct examination and matters affecting the credibility of the witness. The court may, in its discretion, permit inquiry into additional matters.

(3) Leading questions should not be used on the direct examination of a witness except as may be necessary to develop the witness's testimony. Ordinarily, leading questions should be permitted on cross-examination. When a party calls a hostile witness, an adverse party, or a witness identified with an adverse party, interrogation may be by leading questions.

The judge shall take special care to protect a witness under age 14 from questions that are in a form that cannot reasonably be understood by a person of the age and understanding of the witness, and shall take special care to restrict the unnecessary repetition of questions.

SPONSORS' NOTE (1976 ENACTMENT)

Subsection (1) This subsection restates the common law power and obligation of the judge to exercise reasonable control over the mode and order of interrogating witnesses and the presentation of witnesses. Existing law, in recognizing that the primary object of the examination of witnesses is to make known the truth, Coogler v. Rhodes, 38 Fla. 240, 21 So. 109, 111 (1897), allows the trial court to exercise its discretion to "regulate the order of the introduction of evidence," Wilson v. Jernigan, 49 So. 44, 47 (Fla. 1909); to exclude repetitious or wasteful questions, Eatman v. State, 37 So. 576 (Fla. 1904); and to maintain the dignity of the courtroom, which includes the protection of witnesses under examination,

Baisden v. State, 203 So.2d 194 (Fla. 4th Dist. 1967), from harassment or embarrassment, Loftin v. Morgenstern, 60 So.2d 732 (Fla. 1952).

Subsection (2) This subsection limits cross-examination to the scope of direct and is justified by the promotion of the orderly presentation of the examiner's case. The existing Florida law is in accord with this subsection.

In Padgett v. State, 64 Fla. 389, 397, 59 So. 946, 949 (1912), the court recognizes:

> the well established rule that a party has no right to cross-examine a witness except as to facts and circumstances connected with matters testified about on his direct examination. If he desires to inquire into other matters, he must make the witness his own....While this is true, we bear in mind that a wide range should be allowed on the cross-examination of a witness when the questions propounded seek to elicit the motives, interest, or animus of the witness as connected with the cause or the parties thereto, upon which matters he may be contradicted by other evidence. Likewise, considerable latitude should be permitted in the propounding of questions on cross-examination which seek to test the memory or credibility of the witness....The conduct of the cross-examination generally and...the range which it shall be permitted to take rests in the sound discretion of the trial court.

The court further said in Embrey v. Southern Gas & Elec. Corp., 63 So.2d 258, 262 (Fla. 1953) that:

> cross-examination of a witness should always be relative to the subject of the main inquiry...it should not be limited or confined to the identical details testified in chief, but should extend to its entire subject matter, and all matter that may modify, supplement, contradict, rebut or make clearer the facts testified to in chief by the witness on cross-examination.

Questions on cross-examination are not objectional because they tend to establish a defense. See Embrey v. Southern Gas & Elec. Corp., 63 So.2d 258 (Fla. 1953); Coco v. State, 62 So.2d 892 (Fla. 1953). If an event has been testified to in general terms, the witness may be interrogated about the details, Johnson v. State, 178 So.2d 724 (Fla. 2nd Dist. 1965).

In criminal cases the state "is not to be confined strictly to the subjects" of the direct examination when cross-examining the accused, Thomas v. State, 249 So.2d 510 (Fla. 3rd Dist. 1971). The breadth of the scope is apparent in Haager v. State, 83 Fla. 41, 49, 90 So. 812, 815 (1922) where the court said:

> it was proper for counsel on cross-examination to interrogate the witness about everything that was said or done either by...[the defendant or the victim] from the time the difficulty began until...[the defendant] left the scene of the difficulty. The state's attorney could not limit investigation into the entire transaction by asking the witness about only a part of the difficulty, and the defendant['s counsel] had a right to inquire if the defendant said anything else.

While enunciating certain guidelines, the appellate courts seem to follow the statement made in Atlantic Coast Line R.R. v. Watkins, 97 Fla. 350, 360, 121 So. 95, 99 (1929) that: "counsel are often allowed to go far afield in the cross-examination of a witness and the limit often rests within the courts' discretion...."

It should be noted that under existing law it is possible for counsel to inquire into matters outside the scope of proper cross-examination if he makes the witness his own. Shargaa v. State, 84 So.2d 42 (Fla. 1955). Then counsel would not be able to impeach the witness.

The final section of subsection (2) allows the court, in its discretion, to permit inquiry into new matters which would otherwise result in confusion, complication or protraction.

Subsection (3) This subsection restates the existing law on the use of leading questions. During the examination of a party's own witness "a leading question should be permitted only when it appears essential to promote justice." <u>Coker v. Hayes</u>, 16 Fla. 368, 373 (1878). Permission to use leading questions is within the discretion of the trial judge. <u>Anderson v. State</u>, 88 Fla. 93, 101 So. 202 (1924); <u>Penton v. State</u>, 64 Fla. 411, 60 So. 343 (1912). The courts have upheld the use of leading questions for one's own witness when the witness was young and "very ignorant," <u>Ellis v. State</u>, 25 Fla. 702, 6 So. 768 (1889), was persistently unwilling or biased, <u>Coker v. Hayes</u>, 16 Fla. 368, 373 (1978); and was hostile, <u>Caldwell v. State</u>, 243 So.2d 422 (Fla. 1st Dist. 1971).

In addition to providing for the limited use of leading questions with unwilling, hostile or adverse witnesses, Fla. R. Civ. Pro. 1.450(a) provides for the calling and interrogation of an adverse party.

Calif. Evid. Code § 767 and Fed. Rule Evid. 611(c) are similar. See 3 Wigmore §§ 769-780 (Chadbourn rev. 1970).

COMMENTARY ON FEDERAL AND FLORIDA RULE DIFFERENCES

Florida Stat. § 90.612 and its federal counterpart, Federal Rule 611, set forth the rules governing the mode and order of interrogating witnesses and presenting evidence. Each rule has a general provision empowering the trial court to exercise control over the mode and order of interrogating witnesses and presenting evidence, followed by provisions defining the scope of cross-examination and regulating the use of leading questions.

In exercising control over the mode and order of interrogating witnesses, judges in both the federal and Florida courts are supposed to be guided by the goals of facilitating the discovery of the truth, avoiding needless consumption of time, and protecting witnesses from harassment or undue embarrassment. FLA. STAT. § 90.612(1); FED. R. EVID. 611(a). Both rules empower the judge to do such things as place reasonable time limits on witness testimony, see *Sullivan v. Sullivan*, 736 So. 2d 103, 105-06 (Fla. 4th DCA 1999); *Akouri v. State of Florida Dept. of Transp.*, 408 F.3d 1338, 1346 (11th Cir. 2005), or permit a party to re-open her case, see *Register v. State*, 718 So. 2d 350, 353 (Fla. 5th DCA 1998); *Blinzler v. Marriott Int'l, Inc.*, 81 F.3d 1148, 1160 (1st Cir. 1996).

Both the federal and Florida rules provide that leading questions should not be used on direct examination except where necessary to develop a witness's testimony (such as a witness who is young, timid, or mentally incapacitated) or when a party calls a hostile witness, an adverse party, or a witness identified with an adverse party. FLA. STAT. § 90.612(3); FED. R. EVID. 611(c)(2); Advisory Committee's Note to FED. R. EVID. 611(c); Sponsors' Note to FLA. STAT. § 90.612(3). Similarly, both rules permit the use of leading questions on cross-examination, see FLA. STAT. § 90.612(3); FED. R. EVID. 611(c)(1).

Both the federal and Florida rules as a general rule limit the scope of cross-examination of a witness to the subject matter of direct examination and matters affecting the credibility of the witness, yet both rules give the trial court discretion to deviate from this rule and permit inquiry into matters beyond the scope of the subject matter of the direct examination. FLA. STAT. § 90.612(2); FED. R. EVID. 611(b). The only significant difference between the two rules in this regard is that while the Federal rule provides that inquiry into such additional matters shall proceed "as if on direct examination," the Florida rule is not so limited. The purpose of this proviso in the federal rule is to require that when a cross-examining party goes beyond the scope of direct, he should only be able to make use of leading questions in those instances in which leading questions would normally be allowed on direct examination. See *MDU Resources Group v. W.R. Grace and Co.*, 14 F.3d 1274, 1282 (8th Cir. 1994). Whether this omission is likely to make a difference in practice is unlikely since the Florida courts give the provision governing the use of leading questions a practical rather than a rigid interpretation. See *Erp v. Carroll*, 438 So. 2d 31, 37 (Fla. 5th DCA 1983) ("an obviously willing, forthright and candid witness need not, and should not, be led without regard to the witness' formal status or interest or whether the witness is being directly examined by the person calling the witness or cross-examined by anyone else.... the test for permitting or prohibiting leading

questions is ultimately and essentially independent of the superficial circumstance as to which party originally put the witness on the stand.").

The Florida rule contains a provision at the end of it instructing the judge to take special care to protect witnesses under the age of 14 from questions that cannot reasonably be understood by a person of the witness's age and understanding, and to take special care to restrict the unnecessary repetition of questions. *See* FLA. STAT. § 90.612. No comparable instruction exists in the federal rule, although federal judges no doubt have the authority to accommodate the needs of child witnesses through the exercise of their powers under Federal Rule 611(a).

Federal Rule 612. Writing Used to Refresh a Witness's Memory

(a) **Scope.** This rule gives an adverse party certain options when a witness uses a writing to refresh memory:

    (1) while testifying; or

    (2) before testifying, if the court decides that justice requires the party to have those options.

(b) **Adverse Party's Options; Deleting Unrelated Matter.** Unless 18 U.S.C. § 3500 provides otherwise in a criminal case, an adverse party is entitled to have the writing produced at the hearing, to inspect it, to cross-examine the witness about it, and to introduce in evidence any portion that relates to the witness's testimony. If the producing party claims that the writing includes unrelated matter, the court must examine the writing in camera, delete any unrelated portion, and order that the rest be delivered to the adverse party. Any portion deleted over objection must be preserved for the record.

(c) **Failure to Produce or Deliver the Writing.** If a writing is not produced or is not delivered as ordered, the court may issue any appropriate order. But if the prosecution does not comply in a criminal case, the court must strike the witness's testimony or — if justice so requires — declare a mistrial.

ADVISORY COMMITTEE'S NOTE

The treatment of writings used to refresh recollection while on the stand is in accord with settled doctrine. McCormick § 9, p. 15. The bulk of the case law has, however, denied the existence of any right to access by the opponent when the writing is used prior to taking the stand, though the judge may have discretion in the matter. Goldman v. United States, 316 U.S. 129 (1942); Needelman v. United States, 261 F.2d 802 (5th Cir. 1958), cert. dismissed 362 U.S. 600, rehearing denied 363 U.S. 858, Annot., 82 A.L.R.2d 473, 562 and 7 A.L.R.3d 181, 247. An increasing group of cases has repudiated the distinction. People v. Scott, 29 Ill.2d 97, 193 (1963); State v. Mucci, 25 N.J. 423 (1957); State v. Hunt, 25 N.J. 514 (1958); State v. Deslovers, 40 R.I. 89 (1917), and this position is believed to be correct. As Wigmore put it, "the risk of imposition and the need of safeguard is just as great" in both situations. 3 Wigmore § 762, p. 111. To the same effect is McCormick, § 9, p. 17.

The purpose of the phrase "for the purpose of testifying" is to safeguard against using the rule as a pretext for wholesale exploration of an opposing party's files and to insure that access is limited only to those writings which may fairly be said in fact to have an impact upon the testimony of the witness.

The purpose of the rule is the same as that of the *Jencks* statute, 18 U.S.C. § 3500: to promote the search of credibility and memory. The same sensitivity to disclosure of government files may be involved; hence the rule is expressly made subject to the statute, subdivision (a) of which provides: "In any criminal prosecution brought by the United States, no statement or report in the possession of the United States which was made by a Government witness or prospective Government witness (other than the defendant) shall be the subject of subpoena, discovery, or inspection until said witness has testified on direct examination in the trial of the case." Items falling within the purview of the statute are producible only as provided by its terms, Palermo v. United States, 360 U.S. 343, 351 (1959), and disclosure under the rule is limited similarly by the statutory conditions. With this limitation in mind, some differences of application may be noted. The *Jencks* statute applies only to statements of witnesses; the rule is not so limited. The statute applies only to criminal cases; the rule applies to all cases. The statute applies only to government witnesses; the rule applies to all witnesses. The statute contains no requirement that the statement be consulted for purposes of refreshment before or while testifying; the rule so requires. Since many writings would qualify under either statute or rule, a substantial overlap exists, but the identity of procedures makes this of no importance.

The consequences of nonproduction by the government in a criminal case are those of the *Jencks* statute, striking the testimony or in exceptional cases a mistrial. 18 U.S.C. § 3500(d). In other cases these alternatives are unduly limited, and such possibilities as contempt, dismissal, finding issues against the offender, and the like are available. See Rule 16(g) of the Federal Rules of Criminal Procedure and Rule 37(b) of the Federal Rules of Civil Procedure for appropriate sanctions.

REPORT OF HOUSE COMMITTEE ON THE JUDICIARY

As submitted to Congress, Rule 612 provided that except as set forth in 18 U.S.C. § 3500, if a witness uses a writing to refresh his memory for the purpose of testifying, "either before or while testifying," an adverse party is entitled to have the writing produced at the hearing, to inspect it, to cross-examine the witness on it, and to introduce in evidence those portions relating to the witness' testimony. The Committee amended the Rule so as still to require the production of writings used by a witness while testifying, but to render the production of writings used by a witness to refresh his memory before testifying discretionary with the court in the interests of justice, as is the case under existing federal law. See *Goldman* v. *United States*, 316 U.S. 129 (1942). The Committee considered that permitting an adverse party to require the production of writings used before testifying could result in fishing expeditions among a multitude of papers which a witness may have used in preparing for trial.

The Committee intends that nothing in the Rule be construed as barring the assertion of a privilege with respect to writings used by a witness to refresh his memory.

ADVISORY COMMITTEE'S NOTE (2011 AMENDMENT)

The language of Rule 612 has been amended as part of the restyling of the Evidence Rules to make them more easily understood and to make style and terminology consistent throughout the rules. These changes are intended to be stylistic only. There is no intent to change any result in any ruling on evidence admissibility.

Florida Stat. § 90.613. Refreshing the Memory of a Witness

When a witness uses a writing or other item to refresh memory while testifying, an adverse party is entitled to have such writing or other item produced at the hearing, to inspect it, to cross-examine the witness thereon, and to introduce it, or, in the case of a writing, to introduce those portions which relate to the testimony of the witness, in evidence. If it is claimed that the writing contains matters not related to the subject matter of the testimony, the judge shall examine the writing in camera, excise any portions not so related, and order delivery of the remainder to the party entitled thereto. Any portion withheld over objection shall be preserved and made available to the appellate court in the event of an appeal. If a writing or other item is not produced or delivered pursuant to order under this section, the testimony of the witness concerning those matters shall be stricken.

SPONSORS' NOTE (1976 ENACTMENT)

Florida cases recognize that a writing may be used to refresh the recollection of a witness. In addition:

> The opposite party in both criminal and civil cases has a right to see and examine the memorandums used by the witness, so as to be in a position to cross-examine the witness in regard to the testimony given on direct examination...[B]asic principle[s] of fair play...require that the opposite party be permitted to examine the notes...so that the accuracy of his statements may be verified. Allen v. State, 243 So.2d 448 (Fla. 1st Dist. 1971).

In order to refresh his memory a witness must testify on the basis of his independent recollection of the subject in question. The range of permissible means by which recollection may be jogged is considerably wider than when the witness relies on a past recollection recorded. See § 90.803(5), infra. The two situations were distinguished in Volusia County Bank v. Bigelow, 45 Fla. 638, 646, 33 So. 704, 706 (1933) where the court said:

> There is a clear and obvious distinction between the use of a memorandum for the purpose of stimulating the memory and its use as a basis for testimony regarding transactions to which there is no independent recollection. In the former case it's immaterial what constitutes the spur to the memory, as the testimony, when given, rests solely upon the independent recollection of the witness. (emphasis added.)

Not only may the witness refresh his memory with an item not admissible as independent evidence, see e.g., Atlanta & St. A.B.R.R. v. Ewing, 112 Fla. 483, 150 So. 586 (1933) (copy of original entries on tally sheet), but also, under this section, the item to refresh recollection may be admissible for examination by the jury. See McCormick, Evidence § 9 (2nd ed. 1972); cf. § 90.803(5), infra.

Where the writing or other item used to refresh the witness' memory is not delivered to the opposing party on demand, the testimony of witness related to the item demanded must be stricken. As noted by the District Court of Appeals:

> If appellant's counsel had been permitted...to examine the [witness'] notes...we can only speculate as to whether by the use of such notes appellant's counsel would have been able by cross-examination to impeach or discredit in some manner the witness' testimony. Allen v. State, supra, at 450.

For similar provisions, see Calif. Evid. Code § 771, Fed. Rule Evid. 612.

COMMENTARY ON FEDERAL AND FLORIDA RULE DIFFERENCES

Florida Stat. § 90.613 and its federal counterpart, Federal Rule 612, set forth the rights of an adverse party with respect to writings and other items used to refresh a witness's memory. The two rules are similar in that under both, when a witness uses certain items to refresh their memory, the adverse party has the right to inspect it, to cross-examine the witness thereon, and to introduce into evidence those portions that relate to the witness's testimony. However, the two rules differ in several key respects.

First, while the federal rule only applies to writings used to refresh a witness's memory, the Florida rule applies to writings *or other items*. Thus, while the Florida rule would provide opposing counsel the above-delineated rights with respect to objects, audio-recordings, and other items used to refresh a witness's memory, the federal rule in terms provides no comparable right. However, it is unclear whether the federal rule is interpreted in practice as narrowly as its text suggests. *See 20th Century Wear, Inc. v. Sanmark-Stardust Inc.*, 747 F.2d 81, 93 n.17 (2d Cir. 1984) (stating that Fed. R. Evid. 612 gives adverse counsel a "right to inspect at trial whatever is used to refresh recollection," and suggesting this includes an audiotape).

Second, while the Florida rule applies only to writings or other items relied on by a witness to refresh his memory *while* testifying, the federal rule applies to writings relied on by a witness to refresh his memory while *or before* testifying. *See* FED. R. EVID. 612(a); *Proskauer Rose LLP v. Boca Airport, Inc.*, 987 So. 2d 116, 117-18 (4th DCA 2008). However, the federal rule treats these two types of documents differently, providing an automatic right with respect to writings relied on by a witness while testifying, but only a qualified right with respect to writings relied on by a witness before testifying when the trial court in its discretion determines that "justice requires" it. *See* FED. R. EVID. 612(a)(2); *Suss v. MSX Int'l Eng'g Servs., Inc.*, 212 F.R.D. 159, 163 (S.D.N.Y. 2002). In exercising that discretion, the trial court balances the policies underlying the work product doctrine with the need for disclosure to promote effective cross-examination and impeachment. *See Nutramax Labs., Inc. v. Twin Labs., Inc.*, 183 F.R.D. 458, 468 (D. Md. 1998).

Third, while the federal rule is subject to the provisions of the *Jencks* statute, 18 U.S.C. § 3500, the Florida rule is not made subject to any comparable statutory provision. The key limitation that this provision places on the federal rule is that it exempts disclosure of statements or reports made by a government witness or prospective government witness until the witness has testified on direct examination. *See* Advisory Committee's Note to FED. R. EVID. 612.

Both the federal and Florida rules provide that if a writing relied upon by a witness is claimed to contain matters not related to the subject matter of the witness's testimony, the court must examine the writing *in camera*, excise the unrelated portions of the writing, and deliver the remainder to the adverse party. *See* FED. R. EVID. 612(b); FLA. STAT. § 90.613.

The Florida and federal rules provide somewhat different sanctions for failing to comply with an order to produce a writing or other item used to refresh a witness's memory. Under the Florida rule, the testimony of the witness must be stricken. By contrast, under the federal rule, the trial court is given discretion to make "any appropriate order," except that in a criminal case in which the prosecution fails to comply, the court must strike the witness's testimony or, in its discretion, may declare a mistrial. *See* FED. R. EVID. 612(c); FLA. STAT. § 90.613.

Federal Rule 613. Witness's Prior Statement

(a) **Showing or Disclosing the Statement During Examination.** When examining a witness about the witness's prior statement, a party need not show it or disclose its contents to the witness. But the party must, on request, show it or disclose its contents to an adverse party's attorney.

(b) **Extrinsic Evidence of a Prior Inconsistent Statement.** Extrinsic evidence of a witness's prior inconsistent statement is admissible only if the witness is given an opportunity to explain or deny the statement and an adverse party is given an opportunity to examine the witness about it, or if justice so requires. This subdivision (b) does not apply to an opposing party's statement under Rule 801(d)(2).

ADVISORY COMMITTEE'S NOTE

Subdivision (a). The Queen's Case, 2 Br. & B. 284, 129 Eng.Rep. 976 (1820), laid down the requirement that a cross-examiner, prior to questioning the witness about his own prior statement in writing, must first show it to the witness. Abolished by statute in the country of its origin, the requirement nevertheless gained currency in the United States. The rule abolishes this useless impediment, to cross-examination. Ladd, Some Observations on Credibility: Impeachment of Witnesses, 52 Cornell L.Q. 239, 246–247 (1967); McCormick § 28; Wigmore §§ 1259–1260. Both oral and written statements are included.

The provision for disclosure to counsel is designed to protect against unwarranted insinuations that a statement has been made when the fact is to the contrary.

The rule does not defeat the application of Rule 1002 relating to production of the original when the contents of a writing are sought to be proved. Nor does it defeat the application of Rule 26(b)(3) of the Rules of Civil Procedure, as revised, entitling a person on request to a copy of his own statement, though the operation of the latter may be suspended temporarily.

Subdivision (b). The familiar foundation requirement that an impeaching statement first be shown to the witness before it can be proved by extrinsic evidence is preserved but with some modifications. See Ladd, Some Observations on Credibility: Impeachment of Witnesses, 52 Cornell L.Q. 239, 247 (1967). The traditional insistence that the attention of the witness be directed to the statement on cross-examination is relaxed in favor of simply providing the witness an opportunity to explain and the opposite party an opportunity to examine on the statement, with no specification of any particular time or sequence. Under this procedure, several collusive witnesses can be examined before disclosure of a joint prior inconsistent statement. See Comment to California Evidence Code § 770. Also, dangers of oversight are reduced. See McCormick § 37, p. 68.

In order to allow for such eventualities as the witness becoming unavailable by the time the statement is discovered, a measure of discretion is conferred upon the judge. Similar provisions are found in California Evidence Code § 770 and New Jersey Evidence Rule 22(b).

Under principles of *expression unius* the rule does not apply to impeachment by evidence of prior inconsistent conduct. The use of inconsistent statements to impeach a hearsay declaration is treated in Rule 806.

ADVISORY COMMITTEE'S NOTE (2011 AMENDMENT)

The language of Rule 613 has been amended as part of the restyling of the Evidence Rules to make them more easily understood and to make style and terminology consistent throughout the rules. These changes are intended to be stylistic only. There is no intent to change any result in any ruling on evidence admissibility.

Florida Stat. § 90.614. Prior Statements of Witnesses

(1) When a witness is examined concerning the witness's prior written statement or concerning an oral statement that has been reduced to writing, the court, on motion of the adverse party, shall order the statement to be shown to the witness or its contents disclosed to him or her.

(2) Extrinsic evidence of a prior inconsistent statement by a witness is inadmissible unless the witness is first afforded an opportunity to explain or deny the prior statement and the opposing party is afforded an opportunity to interrogate the witness on it, or the interests of justice otherwise require. If a witness denies making or does not distinctly admit making the prior inconsistent statement, extrinsic evidence of such statement is admissible. This subsection is not applicable to admissions of a party-opponent as defined in s. 90.803(18).

SPONSORS' NOTE (1976 ENACTMENT)

Subsection (1) Existing Florida law requires that prior to cross-examination of a witness concerning a prior inconsistent statement, the substance of the statement or the statement must be revealed to him.

Thus in <u>Smith v. State</u>, 95 So.2d 525, 526 (Fla. 1957), in dealing with the use on cross-examination of a witness' prior testimony to the State Attorney, the Supreme Court noted:

> Such testimony cannot, for the purpose of impeachment, be read to the jury, unless it be produced and shown to the witness, and his attention called to the contradictory statements, in order that he may explain them if he can....[The witness] cannot, of course, be cross-examined as to the contents of this testimony without showing him the evidence or allowing him to hear it read. The rule on this subject has been regarded as settled since the Queen's case, 2 Brod. & B. 284 (1820).

This section represents a change in existing law, in situations where the witness' statement is part of the private files of counsel. In <u>Whitaker v. Blackburn</u>, 74 So.2d 794, 795-97 (Fla. 1954), the Supreme Court noted:

> [I]t is error to compel delivery of a transcript of a <u>private and unofficial nature</u> to opposing counsel merely because it is used as an aid in examination....[T]he transcript [of the witness' prior statements] used by defense counsel on cross-examination was the private property of defense counsel, which the trial judge had no authority to compel him to deliver to [opposing counsel] for use by the latter in redirect examination.

The rationale behind this rule was based on a concern that "an attorney's private papers and written data—his private notes made to aid memory on the trial" would no longer be "safe or sacred" were the rule otherwise. <u>Id.</u>, at 796. However, since under this subsection only the statement of the witness himself must be disclosed, the sanctity of counsel's private thoughts, and the privacy of his original memoranda, are preserved.

The impeachment of the declarant of a hearsay declaration by use of his inconsistent statements is treated in Section 90.806.

Calif. Evid. Code § 769 and Fed. Evid. Rule 613(a) do not require that the statement be shown to a former witness prior to questioning him about it.

<u>Subsection (2)</u> This subsection retains, with some modification, the traditional foundation requirements for proof of a prior inconsistent statement.

Existing Fla. Stat. § 90.10 provides:

> If a witness, upon cross-examination as to a former statement made by him relative to the subject matter of the cause and inconsistent with his present testimony, does not distinctly admit that he has made such statement, proof may be given that he did in fact make it; but before such proof can be given, the circumstances of the supposed statement, sufficient to designate the particular occasion, must be mentioned to witness, and he must be asked whether or not he made such statements.

Under this subsection, the witness must be given an opportunity to "explain, confess or deny" a prior statement before the statement can be used for the purpose of impeachment. <u>Hancock v. McDonald</u>, 148 So.2d 56, 58 (Fla. 1st Dist. 1963). Additionally, the opposite party must be given an opportunity on redirect examination to question the witness concerning the prior statement. <u>Stewart v. State</u>, 58 Fla. 97, 50 So. 642 (1910).

COMMENTARY ON FEDERAL AND FLORIDA RULE DIFFERENCES

Florida Stat. § 90.614 and its federal counterpart, Federal Rule 613, regulate the process for examining a witness concerning her prior inconsistent statements and admitting extrinsic evidence of the same.

Under the Florida rule, when a witness is being examined concerning her prior inconsistent statement, the statement—if she wrote it or if it concerns an oral statement of hers that has been reduced to writing (such as a deposition transcript)—must, upon motion by the adverse party, be shown to the witness or its contents disclosed to her. See FLA. STAT. § 90.614(1). The federal rule, by contrast, requires only that the same be shown or disclosed to opposing *counsel*, although it is to some extent broader than the Florida rule in that it applies to all oral and written statements. See FED. R. EVID. 613(a); Advisory Committee's Note to FED. R. EVID. 613(a).

Moreover, under the Florida rule, extrinsic evidence of a witness's prior inconsistent statement is not admissible unless the witness is *first* afforded an opportunity to explain or deny the statement and opposing counsel is afforded an opportunity to interrogate the witness on it. See FLA. STAT. § 90.614(2). Unlike Florida Stat. § 90.614(1), this requirement applies to *all* prior inconsistent statements, whether in written or oral form. See, e.g., Gudinas v. State, 693 So. 2d 953, 964 (Fla. 1997) (applying it to tape-recorded statement); *Williams v. State*, 472 So. 2d 1350, 1352 (Fla. 2d DCA 1985) (applying it to oral statement). So as to afford them such an opportunity, the attorney seeking to make use of the prior inconsistent statement must draw the witness's attention to the specific time, place and person to whom the statement was made. See *Pearce v. State*, 880 So. 2d 561, 569-70 (Fla. 2004); *see also Penske Truck Leasing Co., LP v. Moore*, 702 So. 2d 1295, 1300 (Fla. 4th DCA 1997) (insufficient to ask witness if he has ever told "anyone" something that is inconsistent with what he has testified to). Under the Florida rule, if the witness admits making the statement, examining counsel may *not* offer extrinsic evidence to prove the statement was made. *Pearce*, 880 So. 2d at 570. Only if the witness "denies making or does not distinctly admit making" the prior statement is extrinsic evidence of the same admissible. See FLA. STAT. § 90.614(2); *Pearce*, 880 So. 2d at 570. A statement by the witness that she does not recall making the statement is sufficient to permit the admission of extrinsic evidence. See *Rodriguez v. State*, 65 So. 3d 1133, 1135-36 (Fla. 4th DCA 2011); *MBL Life Assur. Corp. v. Suarez*, 768 So. 2d 1129, 1135 (Fla. 3d DCA 2000). The federal rule, while also requiring that the witness be given an opportunity to explain or deny, does not require that such opportunity be given *before* the extrinsic evidence of the prior inconsistent statement is introduced, but only that the witness be given the opportunity at some point. See Advisory Committee's Note to FED. R. EVID. 613(b); *Rush v. Illinois Cent. R.R. Co.*, 399 F.3d 705, 722 (6th Cir. 2005). Nonetheless, federal trial courts retain discretion to *require* that such opportunity be given *before* the extrinsic evidence is introduced. See, e.g., *U.S. v. Schnapp*, 322 F.3d 564, 571 (8th Cir. 2003).

Under both federal and state practice, the restrictions on the use of extrinsic evidence are inapplicable when one offers an inconsistent statement of a hearsay declarant to impeach him. See FED. R. EVID. 806; FLA. STAT. § 90.806; *Blanton v. State*, 880 So. 2d 798, 801 n.4 (Fla. 5th DCA 2004), *approved in part, disapproved in part on other grounds*, 978 So. 2d 149 (2008). The restrictions likewise are inapplicable to prior inconsistent statements that qualify as an opposing party's statement as defined in Federal Rule 801(d)(2) or Florida Stat. § 90.803(18). See FED. R. EVID. 613(b); FLA. STAT. § 90.614(2).

Finally, both the federal and Florida rules permit the trial court to dispense with the requirement that the witness be given an opportunity to deny or explain where justice so requires, an exception that might apply in the rare instance in which the party does not learn of the prior inconsistent statement until after the witness has testified and is no longer available. See Advisory Committee's Note to FED. R. EVID. 613(b).

Federal Rule 614. Court's Calling or Examining a Witness

(a) **Calling.** The court may call a witness on its own or at a party's request. Each party is entitled to cross-examine the witness.

(b) Examining. The court may examine a witness regardless of who calls the witness.

(c) Objections. A party may object to the court's calling or examining a witness either at that time or at the next opportunity when the jury is not present.

ADVISORY COMMITTEE'S NOTE

Subdivision (a). While exercised more frequently in criminal than in civil cases, the authority of the judge to call witnesses is well established. McCormick § 8, p. 14; Maguire, Weinstein, et al., Cases on Evidence 303–304 (5th ed. 1965); 9 Wigmore § 2484. One reason for the practice, the old rule against impeaching one's own witness, no longer exists by virtue of Rule 607, *supra*. Other reasons remain, however, to justify the continuation of the practice of calling court's witnesses. The right to cross-examine, with all it implies, is assured. The tendency of juries to associate a witness with the party calling him, regardless of technical aspects of vouching, is avoided. And the judge is not imprisoned within the case as made by the parties.

Subdivision (b). The authority of the judge to question witnesses is also well established. McCormick § 8, pp. 12–13; Maguire, Weinstein, et al., Cases on Evidence 737–739 (5th ed. 1965); 3 Wigmore § 784. The authority is, of course, abused when the judge abandons his proper role and assumes that of advocate, but the manner in which interrogation should be conducted and the proper extent of its exercise are not susceptible of formulation in a rule. The omission in no sense precludes courts of review from continuing to reverse for abuse.

Subdivision (c). The provision relating to objections is designed to relieve counsel of the embarrassment attendant upon objecting to questions by the judge in the presence of the jury, while at the same time assuring that objections are made in apt time to afford the opportunity to take possible corrective measures. Compare the "automatic" objection feature of Rule 605 when the judge is called as a witness.

ADVISORY COMMITTEE'S NOTE (2011 AMENDMENT)

The language of Rule 614 has been amended as part of the restyling of the Evidence Rules to make them more easily understood and to make style and terminology consistent throughout the rules. These changes are intended to be stylistic only. There is no intent to change any result in any ruling on evidence admissibility.

Florida Stat. § 90.615. Calling Witnesses by the Court

(1) The court may call witnesses whom all parties may cross-examine.

(2) When required by the interests of justice, the court may interrogate witnesses, whether called by the court or by a party.

SPONSORS' NOTE (1976 ENACTMENT)

Subsection (1) This subsection restates existing Florida law which allows the court in its discretion to call witnesses who can be cross-examined by both parties. See Hall v. State, 136 Fla. 644, 187 So. 392, 407 (1939). In the leading case, Brown v. State, 91 Fla. 682, 108 So. 842, 845 (1926), the Supreme Court said:

It is in the discretion of the court to call any witness who was present at the transaction, or whose name is on the indictment, not called by the prosecution, and when so called, the witness may be examined and cross-examined by both sides. He is not a witness for either party.

See Lowe v. State, 130 Fla. 835, 178 So. 872 (1937).

See Fed. Rule Evid. 614; Model Code of Evid. 105(d); McCormick, Evidence § 8, pp. 12-13 (2nd ed. 1972).

Subsection (2) The court's interrogation of witnesses has been long recognized in Florida. In Watson v. State, 190 So.2d 161, 164, cert. denied 389 U.S. 960, 88 S.Ct. 339, 19 L.Ed.2d 369 (1967) the court said:

[A] trial judge, in order to ascertain the truth, may, if he deems it necessary, ask questions of witnesses and clear up uncertainties as to issues in cases that appear to require it....Error is committed only when it appears that the judge departs from neutrality or expresses bias or prejudice in his comments in the presence of the jury.

In Bumby and Stimpson, Inc. v. Peninsula Utilities Corp., 169 So.2d 499 (Fla. 3rd Dist. 1964) the judge was allowed to ask questions and extensively participate in the questioning as long as the questions did not usurp the functions of counsel by being too extensive and causing prejudice. See Sims v. State, 184 So.2d 217 (Fla. 2nd Dist. 1966).

COMMENTARY ON FEDERAL AND FLORIDA RULE DIFFERENCES

Under both the Florida and federal rules, a trial court judge has the authority to call witnesses, either on his own motion or at a party's suggestion. See FED. R. EVID. 614(a); FLA. STAT. § 90.615(1); *Shere v. State*, 579 So. 2d 86, 92-93 (Fla. 1991). While there is no limitation on this authority under federal law, the scope of this authority is somewhat uncertain under Florida law. Until 1990, Florida law generally barred a party from impeaching its own witness; thus, Florida Stat. § 90.615(1) played a particularly important role, since a witness called by the court was not one called by either party and thus could be impeached by either party. To avoid the risk that the rule would be used to circumvent the rule barring a party from impeaching his own witnesses, the Florida Supreme Court held that the rule could only be invoked in situations in which no party was able to vouch for the witness's credibility and the person was an eyewitness to the events at issue. *Shere*, 579 So. 2d at 90-93. It seems unlikely that this limitation survives the elimination of Florida's voucher rule, although no cases have addressed the issue since the voucher rule was eliminated.

Under both the Florida and federal rules, the court has the power to interrogate witnesses that it calls as well as those called by the parties. See Federal Rule of Evidence 614(b); Florida Stat. § 90.615(2). Under both rules, the trial court commits error if, in its questioning, it appears that it is not neutral or has expressed bias or prejudice. See *R.O. v. State*, 46 So. 3d 124, 126 (Fla. 3d DCA 2010); *Perry v. State*, 776 So. 2d 1102, 1103 (Fla. 5th DCA 2001); *U.S. v. Wright*, 392 F.3d 1269, 1274-75 (11th Cir. 2004). The Florida rule limits the ability of a trial judge to question witnesses to situations in which "the interests of justice" require; although no similar language appears in the federal rule, it is interpreted as not permitting a judge to interject himself into the case by questioning the witnesses when the attorneys are competently conducting their cases. See *U.S. v. Blackburn*, 165 Fed. Appx. 721, 724-25 (11th Cir. 2006).

A key difference between the Florida and federal rules is that under the federal rule, an objection to the calling or interrogation of a witness by the court is deemed timely even if not made at the time of the calling or interrogation of the witness but instead at the first available opportunity when the jury is not present, a provision designed to "relieve counsel of the embarrassment attendant upon objecting to questions by the judge in the presence of the jury." Advisory Committee's Note to FED. R. EVID. 614(c). No comparable provision exists in the Florida rule, thus evidently requiring counsel to conform to the normal rule requiring a contemporaneous objection.

Federal Rule 615. Excluding Witnesses

At a party's request, the court must order witnesses excluded so that they cannot hear other witnesses' testimony. Or the court may do so on its own. But this rule does not authorize excluding:

(a) a party who is a natural person;

(b) an officer or employee of a party that is not a natural person, after being designated as the party's representative by its attorney;

(c) a person whose presence a party shows to be essential to presenting the party's claim or defense; or

(d) a person authorized by statute to be present.

ADVISORY COMMITTEE'S NOTE

The efficacy of excluding or sequestering witnesses has long been recognized as a means of discouraging and exposing fabrication, inaccuracy, and collusion. 6 Wigmore §§ 1837–1838. The authority of the judge is admitted, the only question being whether the matter is committed to his discretion or one of right. The rule takes the latter position. No time is specified for making the request.

Several categories of persons are excepted. ([a]) Exclusion of persons who are parties would raise serious problems of confrontation and due process. Under accepted practice they are not subject to exclusion. 6 Wigmore § 1841. ([b]) As the equivalent of the right of a natural-person party to be present, a party which is not a natural person is entitled to have a representative present. Most of the cases have involved allowing a police officer who has been in charge of an investigation to remain in court despite the fact that he will be a witness. United States v. Infanzon, 235 F.2d 318 (2d Cir. 1956); Portomene v. United States, 221 F.2d 582 (5th Cir. 1955); Powell v. United States, 208 F.2d 618 (6th Cir. 1953); Jones v. United States, 252 F.Supp. 781 (W.D.Okl. 1966). Designation of the representative by the attorney rather than by the client may at first glance appear to be an inversion of the attorney-client relationship, but it may be assumed that the attorney will follow the wishes of the client, and the solution is simple and workable. See California Evidence Code § 777. ([c]) The category contemplates such persons as an agent who handled the transaction being litigated or an expert needed to advise counsel in the management of the litigation. See 6 Wigmore § 1841, n. 4.

REPORT OF SENATE COMMITTEE ON THE JUDICIARY

Many district courts permit government counsel to have an investigative agent at counsel table throughout the trial although the agent is or may be a witness. The practice is permitted as an exception to the rule of exclusion and compares with the situation defense counsel finds himself in—he always has the client with him to consult during the trial. The investigative agent's presence may be extremely important to government counsel, especially when the case is complex or involves some specialized subject matter. The agent, too, having lived with the case for a long time, may be able to assist in meeting trial surprises where the best-prepared counsel would otherwise have difficulty. Yet, it would not seem the Government could often meet the burden under rule 615 of showing that the agent's presence is essential. Furthermore, it could be dangerous to use the agent as a witness as early in the case as possible, so that he might then help counsel as a nonwitness, since the agent's testimony could be needed in rebuttal. Using another, nonwitness agent from the same investigative agency would not generally meet government counsel's needs.

This problem is solved if it is clear that investigative agents are within the group specified under the second exception made in the rule, for "an officer or employee of a party which is not a natural person designated as its representative by its attorney." It is our understanding that this was the intention of the House committee. It is certainly this committee's construction of the rule.

ADVISORY COMMITTEE'S NOTE (1998 AMENDMENT)

The amendment is in response to: (1) the Victim's Rights and Restitution Act of 1990, 42 U.S.C. § 10606, which guarantees, within certain limits, the right of a crime victim to attend the trial; and (2) the Victim Rights Clarification Act of 1997 (18 U.S.C. § 3510).

ADVISORY COMMITTEE'S NOTE (2011 AMENDMENT)

The language of Rule 615 has been amended as part of the restyling of the Evidence Rules to make them more easily understood and to make style and terminology consistent throughout the rules. These changes are intended to be stylistic only. There is no intent to change any result in any ruling on evidence admissibility.

Florida Stat. § 90.616. Exclusion of Witnesses

(1) At the request of a party the court shall order, or upon its own motion the court may order, witnesses excluded from a proceeding so that they cannot hear the testimony of other witnesses except as provided in subsection (2).

(2) A witness may not be excluded if the witness is:

(a) A party who is a natural person.

(b) In a civil case, an officer or employee of a party that is not a natural person. The party's attorney shall designate the officer or employee who shall be the party's representative.

(c) A person whose presence is shown by the party's attorney to be essential to the presentation of the party's cause.

(d) In a criminal case, the victim of the crime, the victim's next of kin, the parent or guardian of a minor child victim, or a lawful representative of such person, unless, upon motion, the court determines such person's presence to be prejudicial.

COMMENTARY ON FEDERAL AND FLORIDA RULE DIFFERENCES

Florida Stat. § 90.616 and its federal counterpart, Federal Rule 615, provide for the exclusion of witnesses from judicial proceedings so as to prevent them from hearing the testimony of other witnesses. The purpose underlying the rules is to prevent witnesses from tailoring their testimony to match that given by other witnesses. See *Capeway Roofing Sys., Inc. v. Chao*, 391 F.3d 56, 58 (1st Cir. 2004); *Knight v. State*, 746 So. 2d 423, 430 (Fla. 1999). Florida authority holds that in enacting Florida Stat. § 90.616, the Florida legislature "essentially adopted the federal rule," and accordingly finds federal decisions interpreting Federal Rule 615 persuasive in interpreting Florida Stat. § 90.616. See *Goodman v. West Coast Brace & Limb, Inc.*, 580 So. 2d 193, 195 (Fla. 2d DCA 1991).

Under both rules, the trial court must issue such an order if a party requests it. In addition, both rules give the trial court discretion to make such an order in the absence of such a request. Each rule contains four exceptions that are similar but not identical.

First, neither rule can be invoked to exclude a natural person who is a party to a case. *See* FED. R. EVID. 615(a); FLA. STAT. § 90.616(2)(a). In the case of a party that is not a natural person (such as a corporation), both the federal and Florida rules provide that an officer or employee designated by its attorney as the party's representative is likewise not subject to exclusion. *See* FED. R. EVID. 615(b); FLA. STAT. § 90.616(2)(b). Whether this latter provision creates a right to designate multiple representatives or only a single representative is an open question in the federal courts, *compare U.S. v. Pulley*, 922 F.2d 1283, 1285-86 (6th Cir. 1991) (limited to one representative), *with U.S. v. Jackson*, 60 F.3d 128, 134 (2d Cir. 1995) (not limited), and has not been addressed by the Florida courts. In one respect, however, the two rules are clearly different: while the Florida rule makes this exception applicable only "[i]n a civil case," the federal rule is not so limited. Thus, while under the federal rule, the government in a criminal case can designate the investigating agent as its representative and thus prevent his exclusion as of right, *see, e.g., U.S. v. Butera*, 677 F.2d 1376, 1381 (11th Cir. 1982); *In re U.S.*, 584 F.2d 666, 667 (5th Cir. 1978), no such automatic right exists under Florida practice.

Under both the Florida and federal rules, a witness will also not be excluded if he is shown to be essential to presenting the party's claim or defense. *See* FED. R. EVID. 615(c); FLA. STAT. § 90.616(2)(c). This provision is most often applied to permit an expert witness to remain in the courtroom. *See, e.g., U.S. v. Seschillie*, 310 F.3d 1208, 1213 (9th Cir. 2002); *Knight v. State*, 746 So. 2d 423, 430 (Fla. 1999). However, it can be invoked in the federal courts to permit a second officer or employee of a non-natural party to remain in the courtroom in the event that Rule 615(b) only provides for the designation of one such representative, *see, e.g., U.S. v. Green*, 324 F.3d 375, 380 (5th Cir. 2003), and it can be invoked in a criminal case in the Florida courts to permit an investigating agent to remain in the courtroom, *see, e.g., Knight*, 746 So. 2d at 430. However, unlike the first two exceptions to the Florida and federal rules, which except certain individuals automatically, this exception can be invoked only if the trial court is persuaded that the witness is essential to the presentation of the party's cause. *See Hernandez v. State*, 4 So. 3d 642, 662-63 (Fla. 2009).

Finally, under both the Florida and federal rules, an exception exists in criminal cases for crime victims and their families, allowing them to remain in the courtroom even if they will be testifying as witnesses at trial. The Florida rule specifically creates an exception in a criminal case for "the victim of the crime, the victim's next of kin, the parent or guardian of a minor child victim, or a lawful representative of such person," FLA. STAT. § 90.616(3)(d), while the federal rule refers only to "a person authorized by statute to be present," FED. R. EVID. 615(d). The statute referenced by the federal provision gives the victim a right not to be excluded from public court proceedings related to the offense, *see* 18 U.S.C. § 3771(a)(3); *U.S. v. Edwards*, 526 F.3d 747, 757-58 (11th Cir. 2008); if the direct victim of the crime is a minor, deceased, incompetent, or incapacitated, this right is given to the victim's legal guardian, the representative of the victim's estate, family members, or any other persons appointed as suitable by the court, *see id.* § 3771(e). Under both the federal and Florida provisions, however, the trial court retains the authority to exclude the victim and or a family member: under the federal rule, it may do so if it determines by clear and convincing evidence that her testimony would be "materially altered" if she heard other testimony at trial, *see id.* § 3771(a)(3); *Edwards*, 526 F.3d at 757-58, while under the Florida rule it may do so if it determines that her presence at trial to be "prejudicial," which, like the federal rule, focuses on the likelihood that her testimony will be affected by hearing that of other witnesses. *See Cain v. State*, 758 So. 2d 1257, 1258 (Fla. 4th DCA 2000).

ARTICLE VII. OPINIONS AND EXPERT TESTIMONY

Federal Rule	Florida Stat. §	Description
701	90.701	Opinion Testimony by Lay Witnesses
702	90.702	Testimony by Expert Witnesses
703	90.704	Bases of an Expert's Opinion Testimony
704	90.703	Opinion on an Ultimate Issue
705	90.705	Disclosing the Facts or Data Underlying an Expert's Opinion
706	—	Court-Appointed Expert Witnesses

Federal Rule 701. Opinion Testimony by Lay Witnesses

If a witness is not testifying as an expert, testimony in the form of an opinion is limited to one that is:

(a) rationally based on the witness's perception;

(b) helpful to clearly understanding the witness's testimony or to determining a fact in issue; and

(c) not based on scientific, technical, or other specialized knowledge within the scope of Rule 702.

ADVISORY COMMITTEE'S NOTE

The rule retains the traditional objective of putting the trier of fact in possession of an accurate reproduction of the event.

Limitation (a) is the familiar requirement of first-hand knowledge or observation.

Limitation (b) is phrased in terms of requiring testimony to be helpful in resolving issues. Witnesses often find difficulty in expressing themselves in language which is not that of an opinion or conclusion. While the courts have made concessions in certain recurring situations, necessity as a standard for permitting opinions and conclusions has proved too elusive and too unadaptable to particular situations for purposes of satisfactory judicial administration. McCormick § 11. Moreover, the practical impossibility of determining by rule what is a "fact," demonstrated by a century of litigation of the question of what is a fact for purposes of pleading under the Field Code, extends into evidence also. 7 Wigmore § 1919. The rule assumes that the natural characteristics of the adversary system will generally lead to an acceptable result, since the detailed account carries more conviction than the broad assertion, and a lawyer can be expected to display his witness to the best advantage. If he fails to do so, cross-examination and argument will point up the weakness. See Ladd, Expert Testimony, 5 Vand.L.Rev. 414, 415–417 (1952). If, despite these considerations, attempts are made to introduce meaningless assertions which amount to little more than choosing up sides, exclusion for lack of helpfulness is called for by the rule.

The language of the rule is substantially that of Uniform Rule 56(1). Similar provisions are California Evidence Code § 800; Kansas Code of Civil Procedure § 60-456(a); New Jersey Evidence Rule 56(1).

ADVISORY COMMITTEE'S NOTE (2000 AMENDMENT)

Rule 701 has been amended to eliminate the risk that the reliability requirements set forth in Rule 702 will be evaded through the simple expedient of proffering an expert in lay witness clothing. Under the amendment, a witness' testimony must be scrutinized under the rules regulating expert opinion to the extent that the witness is providing testimony based on scientific, technical, or other specialized knowledge within the scope of Rule 702. *See generally Asplundh Mfg. Div. v. Benton Harbor Eng'g*, 57 F.3d 1190 (3d Cir. 1995). By channeling testimony that is actually expert testimony to Rule 702, the amendment also ensures that a party will not evade the expert witness disclosure requirements set forth in Fed.R.Civ.P. 26 and Fed.R.Crim.P. 16 by simply calling an expert witness in the guise of a layperson. *See* Joseph, *Emerging Expert Issues Under the 1993 Disclosure Amendments to the Federal Rules of Civil Procedure*, 164 F.R.D. 97, 108 (1996) (noting that "there is no good reason to allow what is essentially surprise expert testimony[,]" and that "the Court should be vigilant to preclude manipulative conduct designed to thwart the expert disclosure and discovery process")[.] *See also United States v. Figueroa-Lopez*, 125 F.3d 1241, 1246 (9th Cir. 1997) (law enforcement agents testifying that the defendant's conduct was consistent with that of a drug trafficker could not testify as lay witnesses; to permit such testimony under Rule 701 "subverts the requirements of Federal Rule of Criminal Procedure 16(a)(1)(E)").

The amendment does not distinguish between expert and lay *witnesses*, but rather between expert and lay *testimony*. Certainly it is possible for the same witness to provide both lay and expert testimony in a single case. *See, e.g., United States v. Figueroa-Lopez*, 125 F.3d 1241, 1246 (9th Cir. 1997) (law enforcement agents could testify that the defendant was acting suspiciously, without being qualified as experts; however, the rules on experts were applicable where the agents testified on the basis of extensive experience that the defendant was using code words to refer to drug quantities and prices). The amendment makes clear that any part of a witness' testimony that is based upon scientific, technical, or other specialized knowledge within the scope of Rule 702 is governed by the standards of Rule 702 and the corresponding disclosure requirements of the Civil and Criminal Rules.

The amendment is not intended to affect the "prototypical example[s] of the type of evidence contemplated by the adoption of Rule 701 relat[ing] to the appearance of persons or things, identity, the manner of conduct, competency of a person, degrees of light or darkness, sound, size, weight, distance, and an endless number of items that cannot be described factually in words apart from inferences." *Asplundh Mfg. Div. v. Benton Harbor Eng'g*, 57 F.3d 1190, 1196 (3d Cir. 1995).

For example, most courts have permitted the owner or officer of a business to testify to the value or projected profits of the business, without the necessity of qualifying the witness as an accountant, appraiser, or similar expert. *See, e.g., Lightning Lube, Inc. v. Witco Corp.*, 4 F.3d 1153 (3d Cir. 1993) (no abuse of discretion in permitting the plaintiff's owner to give lay opinion testimony as to damages, as it was based on his knowledge and participation in the day-to-day affairs of the business). Such opinion testimony is admitted not because of experience, training or specialized knowledge within the realm of an expert, but because of the particularized knowledge that the witness has by virtue of his or her position in the business. The amendment does not purport to change this analysis. Similarly, courts have permitted lay witnesses to testify that a substance appeared to be a narcotic, so long as a foundation of familiarity with the substance is established. *See, e.g., United States v. Westbrook*, 896 F.2d 330 (8th Cir. 1990) (two lay witnesses who were heavy amphetamine users were properly permitted to testify that a substance was amphetamine; but it was error to permit another witness to make such an identification where she had no experience with amphetamines). Such testimony is not based on specialized knowledge within the scope of Rule 702, but rather is based upon a layperson's personal knowledge. If, however, that witness were to describe how a narcotic was manufactured, or to describe the intricate workings of a narcotic distribution network, then the witness would have to qualify as an expert under Rule 702. *United States v. Figueroa-Lopez*, supra.

The amendment incorporates the distinctions set forth in *State v. Brown*, 836 S.W.2d 530, 549 (1992), a case involving former Tennessee Rule of Evidence 701, a rule that precluded lay witness testimony based on "special knowledge." In *Brown*, the court declared that the distinction between lay and expert witness testimony is that lay testimony "results from a process of reasoning familiar in everyday life," while expert testimony "results from a process of reasoning which can be mastered only by specialists in the field." The court in *Brown* noted that a lay witness with experience could testify that a substance appeared to be blood, but that a witness would have to qualify as an expert before he could testify that bruising around the eyes is indicative of skull trauma. That is the kind of distinction made by the amendment to this Rule.

ADVISORY COMMITTEE'S NOTE (2011 AMENDMENT)

The language of Rule 701 has been amended as part of the general restyling of the Evidence Rules to make them more easily understood and to make style and terminology consistent throughout the rules. These changes are intended to be stylistic only. There is no intent to change any result in any ruling on evidence admissibility.

The Committee deleted all reference to an "inference" on the grounds that the deletion made the Rule flow better and easier to read, and because any "inference" is covered by the broader term "opinion." Courts have not made substantive decisions on the basis of any distinction between an opinion and an inference. No change in current practice is intended.

Florida Stat. § 90.701. Opinion Testimony of Lay Witnesses

If a witness is not testifying as an expert, the witness's testimony about what he or she perceived may be in the form of inference and opinion when:

(1) The witness cannot readily, and with equal accuracy and adequacy, communicate what he or she has perceived to the trier of fact without testifying in terms of inferences or opinions and the witness's use of inferences or opinions will not mislead the trier of fact to the prejudice of the objecting party; and

(2) The opinions and inferences do not require a special knowledge, skill, experience, or training.

SPONSORS' NOTE (1976 ENACTMENT)

The common-law general rule is that lay witnesses must testify to facts which they observed and are not permitted to testify in terms of inferences or opinions based upon those facts. Jones v. State, 44 Fla. 74, 32 So. 793 (1902). Courts have permitted exceptions to this general rule when (1) the facts upon which the opinion or inference is based cannot otherwise be made intelligible, or (2) the opinion is of a condition that cannot be reproduced and made comprehensible to the trier of the facts by description. Opinion evidence as to such things as distance, time, size, weight, form, and identity has usually been admitted by the courts. See Evidence in Florida, The Florida Bar Continuing Legal Edu. § 4.30 The Opinion Rule.

This section retains the traditional objective of putting the trier of fact in possession of an accurate reproduction of the event, while permitting the witness to testify in language more characteristic of ordinary conversation. The Comment to Model Code of Evidence Rule 401 explains:

> Where a witness is attempting to communicate the impressions made upon his senses by what he has perceived, any attempt to distinguish between so-called fact and opinion is likely to result in profitless quibbling. Analytically no such distinction is possible. The English common law does not attempt to prevent a witness from describing his experiences in terms including inferences. If he hasn't the skill or experience required for drawing inferences, he will not be allowed to state them. His inferences, when received may not be worth much, but they can do no harm. The court will not permit them to be given more weight than the basis upon which they are built will sustain, and that basis can be uncovered on cross-examination if the judge has not required that it be given in advance.

Provisions similar to this section are found in Calif. Evid. Code § 800; Kansas Code of Civ. Pro. § 60-456(a); New Jersey Evid. Rule 56(1); Fed. Rule Evid. 701.

The extent to which lay witnesses have been permitted to testify in terms of opinions and inferences in Florida courts is not clear. In South Venice Corp. v. Caspersen, 229 So.2d 652 (Fla. 2nd Dist. 1969) the appellant contended that the trial court had erred in admitting into evidence the opinion testimony of a layman that an island was located in a bay. The court stated that it was unable to find any Florida case directly on point but said that generally the admission of opinion by non-expert witnesses is largely within the discretion of the trial judge. However the court avoided a direct ruling by holding that there was sufficient testimony and evidence to support the verdict without reference to this opinion testimony. In another case, Scott v. Barfield, 202 So.2d 591, 594 (Fla. 4th Dist. 1967), the court stated that when the testimony of the lay witness "enters into that of opinion or supposition, it invades the province of the jury." Florida cases were found which sanction the admissibility, or define, in general terms, circumstances under which a non-expert witness may testify in terms of inferences and opinion. Many cases have held that ordinary witnesses may testify concerning specific situations, e.g., speed and distance, identity, mental condition.

Although the effect of this section may be a liberalization of the circumstances under which non-experts may testify in terms of inferences and opinion, the purpose of the section is to de-emphasize the fact-opinion distinction in order to give the trier of fact a more complete and accurate reproduction of the event.

COMMENTARY ON FEDERAL AND FLORIDA RULE DIFFERENCES

Florida Stat. § 90.701 and its federal counterpart, Federal Rule 701, delineate the circumstances under which a lay witness may testify in the form of an opinion or inference.

Both the federal and Florida rules require that lay witness opinion testimony be based solely on the witness's own first-hand perceptions. See FED. R. EVID. 701(a); FLA. STAT. § 90.701. Although this requirement simply re-states the personal knowledge requirement, see FED. R. EVID. 602; FLA. STAT. § 90.604, it differs from the rules governing expert witnesses, who are permitted to render an opinion based on facts of which they lack personal knowledge. See FED. R. EVID. 703; FLA. STAT. § 90.704. The federal rule expressly provides that the testimony must be "rationally" based on the witness's perceptions, which has been interpreted to mean that the opinion must be one that a normal person would form from those perceptions. See Agro Air Assocs., Inc. v. Houston Cas. Co., 128 F.3d 1452, 1456 (11th Cir. 1997); Lubbock Feed Lots, Inc. v. Iowa Beef Processors, 630 F.2d 250, 263 (5th Cir. 1980). While the Florida rule does not contain similar language, it has been similarly interpreted. See, e.g., Somerville v. State, 626 So. 2d 1070, 1071-72 (Fla. 1st DCA 1993) (rejecting testimony by purchaser of stolen property that when buying it, he "felt" that it was stolen).

The second requirement under the federal rule is that the testimony be "helpful" to understanding the witness's testimony or determining a fact in issue. See FED. R. EVID. 701(b). Testimony in the form of an opinion or inference will not be "helpful" when the jury is in as good a position as the witness to draw the inference or form the opinion. See, e.g., Hester v. BIC Corp., 225 F.3d 178, 185 (2d Cir. 2000) (in employment discrimination action, error to permit lay witness to testify that he believed defendant was motivated by discriminatory animus); Lynch v. City of Boston, 180 F.3d 1, 17 (1st Cir. 1999). By contrast, testimony in the form of an opinion or inference is "helpful" when the witness is in a better position than the trier of fact to draw the inference or form the opinion, or when the witness is testifying about a matter that "cannot be described factually in words apart from inferences," such as testimony regarding a person's appearance (including how old they appeared to be or that they seemed excited or angry or looked healthy), a person's mental state, the identity of a person, the speed of a vehicle, distance, size, weight, and the like. Asplundh Mfg. Div. v. Benton Harbor Eng'g, 57 F.3d 1190, 1195-98 (3d Cir. 1995); Advisory Committee's Note to 2000 Amendment to FED. R. EVID. 701.

The second requirement under the Florida rule is worded differently, but in practice appears to be no different than the second requirement under the Federal rule. Under the Florida rule, a witness can testify in the form of an opinion or inference if he "cannot readily and with equal accuracy and adequacy" convey his perceptions without testifying in such form and testifying in such form will not mislead the trier of fact. See FLA. STAT. § 90.701(1). As is the case with the federal rule, testimony in the form of an opinion is inadmissible when the jury is in as good a position as the witness to draw the inference or form the opinion. See Essex v. State, 917 So. 2d 953, 957 (Fla. 4th DCA 2005). Moreover, the situations in which a witness is deemed not to be able to "readily and with equal accuracy and adequacy" convey his perceptions under the Florida rule appear to mirror those in which it would be "helpful" to the trier of fact for the witness to testify in the form of an opinion or inference under the federal rule. See, e.g., Bolin v. State, 41 So. 3d 151, 155-58 (Fla. 2010) (testimony that something appeared to be stained with blood); *Bush v. State*, 809 So. 2d 107, 119-20 (Fla. 4th DCA 2002) (testimony that person looks healthy); *Lee v. State*, 729 So. 2d 975, 979 (Fla. 1st DCA 1999) (testimony that person looks angry); *Lewek v. State*, 702 So. 2d 527, 532 (Fla. 4th DCA 1997) (testimony regarding vehicle speed); *The Fla. Bar v. Clement*, 662 So. 2d 690, 697 (Fla. 1995) (testimony regarding person's mental state); *Fino v. Nodine*, 646 So. 2d 746, 748-49 (Fla. 4th DCA 1994) (testimony regarding distance, size, time, weight, form, and identity); *State v. Cordia*, 564 So. 2d 601, 601-02 (Fla. 2d DCA 1990) (identification of speaker based upon knowledge of person's voice); *Zwinge v. Hettinger*, 530 So. 2d 318, 323 (Fla. 2d DCA 1988) (testimony regarding intoxication).

Finally, under both the Florida and federal rules, lay opinion testimony is admissible only if it is *not* based on scientific, technical, or other specialized knowledge. *See* FED. R. EVID. 701(c); FLA. STAT. § 90.701(2). Testimony based on such specialized knowledge requires that the foundation requirements for expert witness testimony be satisfied. *See* FED. R. EVID. 702; FLA. STAT. § 90.702.

Federal Rule 702. Testimony by Expert Witnesses

A witness who is qualified as an expert by knowledge, skill, experience, training, or education may testify in the form of an opinion or otherwise if:

(a) the expert's scientific, technical, or other specialized knowledge will help the trier of fact to understand the evidence or to determine a fact in issue;

(b) the testimony is based on sufficient facts or data;

(c) the testimony is the product of reliable principles and methods; and

(d) the expert has reliably applied the principles and methods to the facts of the case.

ADVISORY COMMITTEE'S NOTE

An intelligent evaluation of facts is often difficult or impossible without the application of some scientific, technical, or other specialized knowledge. The most common source of this knowledge is the expert witness, although there are other techniques for supplying it.

Most of the literature assumes that experts testify only in the form of opinions. The assumption is logically unfounded. The rule accordingly recognizes that an expert on the stand may give a dissertation or exposition of scientific or other principles relevant to the case, leaving the trier of fact to apply them to the facts. Since much of the criticism of expert testimony has centered upon the hypothetical question, it seems wise to recognize that opinions are not indispensable and to encourage the use of expert testimony in nonopinion form when counsel believes the trier can itself draw the requisite inference. The use of opinions is not abolished by the rule, however. It will continue to be permissible for the experts to take the further step of suggesting the inference which should be drawn from applying the specialized knowledge to the facts. See Rules 703 to 705.

Whether the situation is a proper one for the use of expert testimony is to be determined on the basis of assisting the trier. "There is no more certain test for determining when experts may be used than the common sense inquiry whether the untrained layman would be qualified to determine intelligently and to the best possible degree the particular issue without enlightenment from those having a specialized understanding of the subject involved in the dispute." Ladd, Expert Testimony, 5 Vand.L.Rev. 414, 418 (1952). When opinions are excluded, it is because they are unhelpful and therefore superfluous and a waste of time. 7 Wigmore § 1918.

The rule is broadly phrased. The fields of knowledge which may be drawn upon are not limited merely to the "scientific" and "technical" but extend to all "specialized" knowledge. Similarly, the expert is viewed, not in a narrow sense, but as a person qualified by "knowledge, skill, experience, training or education." Thus within the scope of the rule are not only experts in the strictest sense of the word, e.g. physicians, physicists, and architects, but also the large group sometimes called "skilled" witnesses, such as bankers or landowners testifying to land values.

ADVISORY COMMITTEE'S NOTE (2000 AMENDMENT)

Rule 702 has been amended in response to *Daubert v. Merrell Dow Pharmaceuticals, Inc.*, 509 U.S. 579 (1993), and to the many cases applying *Daubert*, including *Kumho Tire Co. v. Carmichael*, 119 S.Ct. 1167 (1999). In *Daubert* the Court charged trial judges with the responsibility of acting as gatekeepers to exclude unreliable expert testimony, and the Court in *Kumho* clarified that this gatekeeper function applies to all expert testimony, not just testimony based in science. *See also Kumho*, 119 S.Ct. at 1178 (citing the Committee Note to the proposed amendment to Rule 702, which had been released for public comment before the date of the *Kumho* decision). The amendment affirms the trial court's role as gatekeeper and provides some general standards that the trial court must use to assess the reliability and helpfulness of proffered expert testimony. Consistently with *Kumho*, the Rule as amended provides that all types of expert testimony present questions of admissibility for the trial court in deciding whether the evidence is reliable and helpful. Consequently, the admissibility of all expert testimony is governed by the principles of Rule 104(a). Under that Rule, the proponent has the burden of establishing that the pertinent admissibility requirements are met by a preponderance of the evidence. *See Bourjaily v. United States*, 483 U.S. 171 (1987).

Daubert set forth a non-exclusive checklist for trial courts to use in assessing the reliability of scientific expert testimony. The specific factors explicated by the *Daubert* Court are (1) whether the expert's technique or theory can be or has been tested—that is, whether the expert's theory can be challenged in some objective sense, or whether it is instead simply a subjective, conclusory approach that cannot reasonably be assessed for reliability; (2) whether the technique or theory has been subject to peer review and publication; (3) the known or potential rate of error of the technique or theory when applied; (4) the existence and maintenance of standards and controls; and (5) whether the technique or theory has been generally accepted in the scientific community. The Court in *Kumho* held that these factors might also be applicable in assessing the reliability of non-scientific expert testimony, depending upon "the particular circumstances of the particular case at issue." 119 S.Ct. at 1175.

No attempt has been made to "codify" these specific factors. *Daubert* itself emphasized that the factors were neither exclusive nor dispositive. Other cases have recognized that not all of the specific Daubert factors can apply to every type of expert testimony. In addition to *Kumho*, 119 S.Ct. at 1175, *see Tyus v. Urban Search Management*, 102 F.3d 256 (7th Cir. 1996) (noting that the factors mentioned by the Court in *Daubert* do not neatly apply to expert testimony from a sociologist). *See also Kannankeril v. Terminix Int'l, Inc.*, 128 F.3d 802, 809 (3d Cir. 1997) (holding that lack of peer review or publication was not dispositive where the expert's opinion was supported by "widely accepted scientific knowledge"). The standards set forth in the amendment are broad enough to require consideration of any or all of the specific *Daubert* factors where appropriate.

Courts both before and after *Daubert* have found other factors relevant in determining whether expert testimony is sufficiently reliable to be considered by the trier of fact. These factors include:

> (1) Whether experts are "proposing to testify about matters growing naturally and directly out of research they have conducted independent of the litigation, or whether they have developed their opinions expressly for purposes of testifying." *Daubert v. Merrell Dow Pharmaceuticals*, Inc., 43 F.3d 1311, 1317 (9th Cir. 1995).

(2) Whether the expert has unjustifiably extrapolated from an accepted premise to an unfounded conclusion. *See General Elec. Co. v. Joiner*, 522 U.S. 136, 146 (1997) (noting that in some cases a trial court "may conclude that there is simply too great an analytical gap between the data and the opinion proffered").

(3) Whether the expert has adequately accounted for obvious alternative explanations. *See Claar v. Burlington N.R.R.*, 29 F.3d 499 (9th Cir. 1994) (testimony excluded where the expert failed to consider other obvious causes for the plaintiff's condition). *Compare Ambrosini v. Labarraque*, 101 F.3d 129 (D.C. Cir. 1996) (the possibility of some uneliminated causes presents a question of weight, so long as the most obvious causes have been considered and reasonably ruled out by the expert).

(4) Whether the expert "is being as careful as he would be in his regular professional work outside his paid litigation consulting." *Sheehan v. Daily Racing Form, Inc.*, 104 F.3d 940, 942 (7th Cir. 1997). *See Kumho Tire Co. v. Carmichael*, 119 S.Ct. 1167, 1176 (1999) (*Daubert* requires the trial court to assure itself that the expert "employs in the courtroom the same level of intellectual rigor that characterizes the practice of an expert in the relevant field").

(5) Whether the field of expertise claimed by the expert is known to reach reliable results for the type of opinion the expert would give. *See Kumho Tire Co. v. Carmichael*, 119 S.Ct. 1167, 1175 (1999) (*Daubert*'s general acceptance factor does not "help show that an expert's testimony is reliable where the discipline itself lacks reliability, as for example, do theories grounded in any so-called generally accepted principles of astrology or necromancy."), *Moore v. Ashland Chemical, Inc.*, 151 F.3d 269 (5th Cir. 1998) (en banc) (clinical doctor was properly precluded from testifying to the toxicological cause of the plaintiff's respiratory problem, where the opinion was not sufficiently grounded in scientific methodology); *Sterling v. Velsicol Chem. Corp.*, 855 F.2d 1188 (6th Cir. 1988) (rejecting testimony based on "clinical ecology" as unfounded and unreliable).

All of these factors remain relevant to the determination of the reliability of expert testimony under the Rule as amended. Other factors may also be relevant. *See Kumho*, 119 S.Ct. 1167, 1176 ("[W]e conclude that the trial judge must have considerable leeway in deciding in a particular case how to go about determining whether particular expert testimony is reliable."). Yet no single factor is necessarily dispositive of the reliability of a particular expert's testimony. *See, e.g., Heller v. Shaw Industries, Inc.*, 167 F.3d 146, 155 (3d Cir. 1999) ("not only must each stage of the expert's testimony be reliable, but each stage must be evaluated practically and flexibly without bright-line exclusionary (or inclusionary) rules."); *Daubert v. Merrell Dow Pharmaceuticals, Inc.*, 43 F.3d 1311, 1317, n.5 (9th Cir. 1995) (noting that some expert disciplines "have the courtroom as a principal theatre of operations" and as to these disciplines "the fact that the expert has developed an expertise principally for purposes of litigation will obviously not be a substantial consideration.").

A review of the caselaw after *Daubert* shows that the rejection of expert testimony is the exception rather than the rule. *Daubert* did not work a "seachange over federal evidence law," and "the trial court's role as gatekeeper is not intended to serve as a replacement for the adversary system." *United States v. 14.38 Acres of Land Situated in Leflore County, Mississippi*, 80 F.3d 1074, 1078 (5th Cir. 1996). As the Court in *Daubert* stated: "Vigorous cross-examination, presentation of contrary evidence, and careful instruction on the burden of proof are the traditional and appropriate means of attacking shaky but admissible evidence." 509 U.S. at 595. Likewise, this amendment is not intended to provide an excuse for an automatic challenge to the testimony of every expert. *See Kumho Tire Co. v. Carmichael*, 119 S.Ct. 1167, 1176 (1999) (noting that the trial judge has the discretion "both to avoid unnecessary 'reliability' proceedings in ordinary cases where the reliability of an expert's methods is properly taken for granted, and to require appropriate proceedings in the less usual or more complex cases where cause for questioning the expert's reliability arises.").

When a trial court, applying this amendment, rules that an expert's testimony is reliable, this does not necessarily mean that contradictory expert testimony is unreliable. The amendment is broad enough to permit testimony that is the product of competing principles or methods in the same field of expertise.

See, e.g., Heller v. Shaw Industries, Inc., 167 F.3d 146, 160 (3d Cir. 1999) (expert testimony cannot be excluded simply because the expert uses one test rather than another, when both tests are accepted in the field and both reach reliable results). As the court stated in *In re Paoli R.R. Yard PCB Litigation*, 35 F.3d 717, 744 (3d Cir. 1994), proponents "do not have to demonstrate to the judge by a preponderance of the evidence that the assessments of their experts are correct, they only have to demonstrate by a preponderance of evidence that their opinions are reliable.... The evidentiary requirement of reliability is lower than the merits standard of correctness." *See also Daubert v. Merrell Dow Pharmaceuticals, Inc.*, 43 F.3d 1311, 1318 (9th Cir. 1995) (scientific experts might be permitted to testify if they could show that the methods they used were also employed by "a recognized minority of scientists in their field."); *Ruiz-Troche v. Pepsi Cola*, 161 F.3d 77, 85 (1st Cir. 1998) ("*Daubert* neither requires nor empowers trial courts to determine which of several competing scientific theories has the best provenance.").

The Court in *Daubert* declared that the "focus, of course, must be solely on principles and methodology, not on the conclusions they generate." 509 U.S. at 595. Yet as the Court later recognized, "conclusions and methodology are not entirely distinct from one another." *General Elec. Co. v. Joiner*, 522 U.S. 136, 146 (1997). Under the amendment, as under *Daubert*, when an expert purports to apply principles and methods in accordance with professional standards, and yet reaches a conclusion that other experts in the field would not reach, the trial court may fairly suspect that the principles and methods have not been faithfully applied. *See Lust v. Merrell Dow Pharmaceuticals, Inc.*, 89 F.3d 594, 598 (9th Cir. 1996). The amendment specifically provides that the trial court must scrutinize not only the principles and methods used by the expert, but also whether those principles and methods have been properly applied to the facts of the case. As the court noted in *In re Paoli R.R. Yard PCB Litig.*, 35 F.3d 717, 745 (3d Cir. 1994), "*any* step that renders the analysis unreliable...renders the expert's testimony inadmissible. *This is true whether the step completely changes a reliable methodology or merely misapplies that methodology.*"

If the expert purports to apply principles and methods to the facts of the case, it is important that this application be conducted reliably. Yet it might also be important in some cases for an expert to educate the factfinder about general principles, without ever attempting to apply these principles to the specific facts of the case. For example, experts might instruct the factfinder on the principles of thermodynamics, or bloodclotting, or on how financial markets respond to corporate reports, without ever knowing about or trying to tie their testimony into the facts of the case. The amendment does not alter the venerable practice of using expert testimony to educate the factfinder on general principles. For this kind of generalized testimony, Rule 702 simply requires that: (1) the expert be qualified; (2) the testimony address a subject matter on which the factfinder can be assisted by an expert; (3) the testimony be reliable; and (4) the testimony "fit" the facts of the case.

As stated earlier, the amendment does not distinguish between scientific and other forms of expert testimony. The trial court's gatekeeping function applies to testimony by any expert. *See Kumho Tire Co. v. Carmichael*, 119 S.Ct. 1167, 1171 (1999) ("We conclude that *Daubert*'s general holding—setting forth the trial judge's general 'gatekeeping' obligation—applies not only to testimony based on 'scientific' knowledge, but also to testimony based on 'technical' and 'other specialized' knowledge."). While the relevant factors for determining reliability will vary from expertise to expertise, the amendment rejects the premise that an expert's testimony should be treated more permissively simply because it is outside the realm of science. An opinion from an expert who is not a scientist should receive the same degree of scrutiny for reliability as an opinion from an expert who purports to be a scientist. *See Watkins v. Telsmith, Inc.*, 121 F.3d 984, 991 (5th Cir. 1997) ("[I]t seems exactly backwards that experts who purport to rely on general engineering principles and practical experience might escape screening by the district court simply by stating that their conclusions were not reached by any particular method or technique."). Some types of expert testimony will be more objectively verifiable, and subject to the expectations of falsifiability, peer review, and publication, than others. Some types of expert testimony will not rely on anything like a scientific method, and so will have to be evaluated by reference to other standard principles attendant to the particular area of expertise. The trial judge in all cases of proffered expert testimony must find that it is properly grounded, well-reasoned, and not speculative before it can be admitted. The expert's testimony must be grounded in an accepted body of learning or experience in the expert's field, and the expert must explain how the conclusion is so grounded. *See, e.g.*, American College of Trial Lawyers, *Standards and Procedures for Determining the Admissibility of Expert Testimony after Daubert*, 157 F.R.D. 571, 579 (1994) ("[W] hether the testimony concerns economic principles, accounting standards, property valuation or other non-scientific subjects, it should be evaluated by reference to the 'knowledge and experience' of that particular field.").

The amendment requires that the testimony must be the product of reliable principles and methods that are reliably applied to the facts of the case. While the terms "principles" and "methods" may convey a certain impression when applied to scientific knowledge, they remain relevant when applied to testimony based on technical or other specialized knowledge. For example, when a law enforcement agent testifies regarding the use of code words in a drug transaction, the principle used by the agent is that participants in such transactions regularly use code words to conceal the nature of their activities. The method used by the agent is the application of extensive experience to analyze the meaning of the conversations. So long as the principles and methods are reliable and applied reliably to the facts of the case, this type of testimony should be admitted.

Nothing in this amendment is intended to suggest that experience alone—or experience in conjunction with other knowledge, skill, training or education—may not provide a sufficient foundation for expert testimony. To the contrary, the text of Rule 702 expressly contemplates that an expert may be qualified on the basis of experience. In certain fields, experience is the predominant, if not sole, basis for a great deal of reliable expert testimony. *See, e.g., United States v. Jones*, 107 F.3d 1147 (6th Cir. 1997) (no abuse of discretion in admitting the testimony of a handwriting examiner who had years of practical experience and extensive training, and who explained his methodology in detail); *Tassin v. Sears Roebuck*, 946 F.Supp. 1241, 1248 (M.D.La. 1996) (design engineer's testimony can be admissible when the expert's opinions "are based on facts, a reasonable investigation, and traditional technical/mechanical expertise, and he provides a reasonable link between the information and procedures he uses and the conclusions he reaches"). *See also Kumho Tire Co. v. Carmichael*, 119 S.Ct. 1167, 1178 (1999) (stating that "no one denies that an expert might draw a conclusion from a set of observations based on extensive and specialized experience.").

If the witness is relying solely or primarily on experience, then the witness must explain how that experience leads to the conclusion reached, why that experience is a sufficient basis for the opinion, and how that experience is reliably applied to the facts. The trial court's gatekeeping function requires more than simply "taking the expert's word for it." *See Daubert v. Merrell Dow Pharmaceuticals, Inc.*, 43 F.3d 1311, 1319 (9th Cir. 1995) ("We've been presented with only the experts' qualifications, their conclusions and their assurances of reliability. Under *Daubert*, that's not enough."). The more subjective and controversial the expert's inquiry, the more likely the testimony should be excluded as unreliable. *See O'Conner v. Commonwealth Edison Co.*, 13 F.3d 1090 (7th Cir. 1994) (expert testimony based on a completely subjective methodology held properly excluded). *See also Kumho Tire Co. v. Carmichael*, 119 S.Ct. 1167, 1176 (1999) ("[I]t will at times be useful to ask even of a witness whose expertise is based purely on experience, say, a perfume tester able to distinguish among 140 odors at a sniff, whether his preparation is of a kind that others in the field would recognize as acceptable.").

Subpart ([b]) of Rule 702 calls for a quantitative rather than qualitative analysis. The amendment requires that expert testimony be based on sufficient underlying "facts or data." The term "data" is intended to encompass the reliable opinions of other experts. See the original Advisory Committee Note to Rule 703. The language "facts or data" is broad enough to allow an expert to rely on hypothetical facts that are supported by the evidence. *Id.*

When facts are in dispute, experts sometimes reach different conclusions based on competing versions of the facts. The emphasis in the amendment on "sufficient facts or data" is not intended to authorize a trial court to exclude an expert's testimony on the ground that the court believes one version of the facts and not the other.

There has been some confusion over the relationship between Rules 702 and 703. The amendment makes clear that the sufficiency of the basis of an expert's testimony is to be decided under Rule 702.

Rule 702 sets forth the overarching requirement of reliability, and an analysis of the sufficiency of the expert's basis cannot be divorced from the ultimate reliability of the expert's opinion. In contrast, the "reasonable reliance" requirement of Rule 703 is a relatively narrow inquiry. When an expert relies on inadmissible information, Rule 703 requires the trial court to determine whether that information is of a type reasonably relied on by other experts in the field. If so, the expert can rely on the information in reaching an opinion. However, the question whether the expert is relying on a *sufficient* basis of information—whether admissible information or not—is governed by the requirements of Rule 702.

The amendment makes no attempt to set forth procedural requirements for exercising the trial court's gatekeeping function over expert testimony. *See* Daniel J. Capra, *The Daubert Puzzle*, 38 Ga.L.Rev. 699, 766 (1998) ("Trial courts should be allowed substantial discretion in dealing with *Daubert* questions; any attempt to codify procedures will likely give rise to unnecessary changes in practice and create difficult questions for appellate review."). Courts have shown considerable ingenuity and flexibility in considering challenges to expert testimony under *Daubert*, and it is contemplated that this will continue under the amended Rule. *See, e.g., Cortes-Irizarry v. Corporacion Insular*, 111 F.3d 184 (1st Cir. 1997) (discussing the application of *Daubert* in ruling on a motion for summary judgment); *In re Paoli R.R. Yard PCB Litig.*, 35 F.3d 717, 736, 739 (3d Cir. 1994) (discussing the use of *in limine* hearings); *Claar v. Burlington N.R.R.*, 29 F.3d 499, 502–05 (9th Cir. 1994) (discussing the trial court's technique of ordering experts to submit serial affidavits explaining the reasoning and methods underlying their conclusions).

The amendment continues the practice of the original Rule in referring to a qualified witness as an "expert." This was done to provide continuity and to minimize change. The use of the term "expert" in the Rule does not, however, mean that a jury should actually be informed that a qualified witness is testifying as an "expert." Indeed, there is much to be said for a practice that prohibits the use of the term "expert" by both the parties and the court at trial. Such a practice "ensures that trial courts do not inadvertently put their stamp of authority" on a witness's opinion, and protects against the jury's being "overwhelmed by the so-called 'experts'." Hon. Charles Richey, *Proposals to Eliminate the Prejudicial Effect of the Use of the Word "Expert" Under the Federal Rules of Evidence in Criminal and Civil Jury Trials*, 154 F.R.D. 537, 559 (1994) (setting forth limiting instructions and a standing order employed to prohibit the use of the term "expert" injury trials).

ADVISORY COMMITTEE'S NOTE (2011 AMENDMENT)

The language of Rule 702 has been amended as part of the restyling of the Evidence Rules to make them more easily understood and to make style and terminology consistent throughout the rules. These changes are intended to be stylistic only. There is no intent to change any result in any ruling on evidence admissibility.

Florida Stat. § 90.702. Testimony by Experts

If scientific, technical, or other specialized knowledge will assist the trier of fact in understanding the evidence or in determining a fact in issue, a witness qualified as an expert by knowledge, skill, experience, training, or education may testify about it in the form of an opinion; however, the opinion is admissible only if it can be applied to evidence at trial.

SPONSORS' NOTE (1976 ENACTMENT)

Whether the situation is a proper one for the use of expert testimony is to be determined on the basis of whether it will assist the trier of fact. "There is no more certain test for determining when experts may be used than the common sense inquiry whether the untrained layman would be qualified to determine intelligently and to the best possible degree the particular issue without enlightenment from those having a specialized understanding of the subject involved in the dispute." Ladd, <u>Expert Evidence</u>, 5 Vand. L.

Rev. 414, 418 (1952). If the issue involves a matter of common knowledge about which the ordinary layman would be capable of forming a correct judgment, expert testimony is not admissible. If the triers of fact have a general knowledge of a matter, but an expert's testimony would aid their understanding of the issue, it would be admissible. The Florida courts are in substantial accord with this position. "The opinion of an expert should be excluded where the facts testified to are of a kind that do not require any special knowledge or experience in order to form a conclusion, or are of such character that they may be presumed to be within the common experience of all men moving in ordinary walks of life." Mills v. Redwing Carriers, Inc., 127 So.2d 453, 456 (Fla. 2nd Dist. 1961).

The fields of knowledge that may be drawn upon are not limited merely to the scientific or technical but extend to all specialized knowledge. Included within the scope of the rule are such "skilled" witnesses as bankers or landowners testifying to land values, as well as more formally trained persons such as physicians and architects.

Since much of the criticism of expert testimony has centered on the hypothetical question, it seems wise to encourage the use of expert testimony in non-opinion forms when counsel believes the trier can itself draw the requisite inference. The expert may give a dissertation or an explanation of scientific or other principles relevant to a case, leaving the trier of fact to apply these principles to the facts. The use of opinion is not abolished, however, and it will continue to be permissible for the expert to take the further step of suggesting the inference which should be drawn from applying the specialized knowledge to the facts.

The Advisory Committee's Note to Proposed Federal Rule of Evidence 702 states that "When opinions are excluded, it is because they are unhelpful and therefore superfluous and a waste of time." Although Florida courts generally speak in terms of "an invasion of [the] jury's province," when excluding expert testimony, such decisions are based on whether the jury is competent to make its own deductions without hearing the expert. See Smaglick v. Jersey Ins. Co., 209 So.2d 475 (Fla. 4th Dist. 1968). Consequently, the rule in this section should not alter the circumstances under which an expert's testimony will be excluded.

The definition of an expert is similar to that of Section 90.231 of the Florida Statutes and of Florida Rule of Civil Procedure 1.390 which define an expert as "one possessed of special knowledge or skill about the subject upon which he is called to testify." See Fed. Rule Evid. 702.

COMMENTARY ON FEDERAL AND FLORIDA RULE DIFFERENCES

Florida Stat. § 90.702 and its federal counterpart, Federal Rule 702, govern the admissibility of expert witness testimony. Under each rule, expert testimony is admissible only if the trial court finds that three requirements are satisfied: reliability, witness qualification, and helpfulness. *Ramirez v. State*, 651 So. 2d 1164, 1166-67 (Fla. 1995); *Cook ex rel. Estate of Tessier v. Sheriff of Monroe County, Fla.*, 402 F.3d 1092, 1107 (11th Cir. 2005).

Under both the Florida and federal rules, expert testimony is admissible only if the scientific theory or technique on which it is based is reliable. However, the tests for reliability under the two rules differ substantially. Florida follows the so-called *Frye* test, under which a scientific theory or principle will be deemed reliable if it has gained "general acceptance" in the field to which it belongs. *Castillo v. E.I. Du Pont De Nemours & Co.*, 854 So. 2d 1264, 1268 (Fla. 2003). To be generally accepted, it need not be universally accepted, but it must be supported by a "clear majority" of members of the relevant scientific community, with weight given not solely to the quantity of opinions but also their authoritativeness. *See Hadden v. State*, 690 So. 2d 573, 576 n.2 (Fla. 1997); *Brim v. State*, 695 So. 2d 268, 272 (Fla. 1997). In making this determination, courts look to expert testimony, scientific and legal writings, and judicial opinions. *See Castillo*, 854 So. 2d at 1268. The burden is on the proponent of the expert testimony to establish general acceptance by a preponderance of the evidence. *See Ramirez v. State*, 651 So. 2d 1164, 1168 (Fla. 1995). Appellate review of the trial court's application of the general acceptance test is *de novo*, with the appellate court asking whether the theory or principle is generally accepted *at the time of review. Castillo,* 854 So. 2d at 1268; *Hadden,* 690 So. 2d at 579. "Pure opinion" testimony that is based on the expert's personal experience and training, such as an expert's opinion that someone is incompetent or a medical diagnosis—if it does not rely on any study, test, procedure, or methodology that constitutes new or novel scientific evidence—is not subject to the *Frye* test. *See Marsh v. Valyou,* 977 So. 2d 543, 547-49 (Fla. 2007).

By contrast, the reliability of expert testimony under Federal Rule 702 involves a multi-factored inquiry by the trial court judge in which general acceptance is but one of many factors that the trial court may consider. *See Daubert v. Merrell Dow Pharm., Inc.,* 509 U.S. 579 (1993). Other factors that the trial court may (but need not) consider in determining reliability include: (1) whether the technique or theory can be or has been tested; (2) whether it has been subject to peer review and publication; (3) the known or potential rate of error; (4) existence and maintenance of standards and controls. *See id.* at 593-95; Advisory Committee's Note to 2000 Amendment to FED. R. EVID. 702. As with the Florida rule, the burden is on the proponent of the expert testimony to establish reliability by a preponderance of the evidence. *See Cook,* 402 F.3d at 1107. However, appellate review of that determination is under the extremely deferential abuse of discretion standard, not only for the ultimate determination of reliability, but also in deciding what factors to consider in determining reliability. *See Kumho Tire Co. v. Carmichael,* 526 U.S. 137, 150-53 (1999); *General Elec. Co. v. Joiner,* 522 U.S. 136, 141-43 (1997).

The Florida Supreme Court views the *Frye* test that it follows as setting a "higher standard of reliability" than does the *Daubert* test. *See Brim,* 695 So. 2d at 271-72. In at least one respect, however, the reliability inquiry under the federal rule is stricter than the reliability inquiry under the Florida rule. Under the federal rule, not only must the underlying theory or principle be shown to be reliable; it must also be shown that it was applied reliably to the facts of the case. *See* FED. R. EVID. 702(3); Advisory Committee's Note to 2000 Amendment to FED. R. EVID. 702. By contrast, the reliability inquiry under the Florida rule looks only to the reliability of the underlying theory or principle, with the question whether the theory was applied reliably in the case viewed as a question of weight for the jury to assess. *Castillo,* 854 So. 2d at 1276; *State v. Sercey,* 825 So. 2d 959, 980-81 (Fla. 1st DCA 2002).

The second requirement under both the Florida and federal rules is that the witness be qualified. Formal education is not the only way to be qualified under either rule; both permit a witness to be qualified solely on the basis of experience. *See Chavez v. State,* 12 So. 3d 199, 205 (Fla. 2009); *Waldorf v. Shuta,* 142 F.3d 601, 625-26 (3d Cir. 1998). Indeed, under both the federal and Florida rules, a witness has been deemed qualified to testify as an expert on identifying drugs based on his prior experience as a user or dealer of drugs. *See Brooks v. State,* 762 So. 2d 879, 892-93 (Fla. 2000); *United States v. Johnson,* 575 F.2d 1347, 1360-61 (5th Cir. 1978). Moreover, under both the federal and Florida rules, the determination that a witness is qualified is reviewed deferentially on appeal. *See Ramirez v. State,* 542 So. 2d 352, 355 (Fla. 1989); *Waldorf,* 142 F.3d at 626-27.

The third requirement of both the Florida and federal rules is that the testimony be helpful in that it assists the trier of fact to understand the evidence or determine a fact at issue. Expert testimony is not helpful if it refers to matters within the common knowledge and experience of jurors. *See Chesnoff v. State,* 840 So. 2d 423, 425 (Fla. 5th DCA 2003); Advisory Committee's Note to FED. R. EVID. 702. Testimony is also not helpful if it invades the province of the jury, such as testimony that a witness is or is not credible, *see McLean v. State,* 754 So. 2d 176, 181 (Fla. 2d DCA 2000); *Nichols v. American Nat'l Ins. Co.,* 154 F.3d 875, 883 (8th Cir. 1998), that is phrased in terms of a legal conclusion, such as testimony that someone was negligent, *see Town of Palm Beach v. Palm Beach County,* 460 So. 2d 879, 882 (Fla. 1984); *U.S. v. Barile,* 286 F.3d 749, 759-62 (4th Cir. 2002), or that simply tells the jury what result to reach, *see Town of Palm Beach,* 460 So. 2d at 882; *Woods v. Lecureaux,* 110 F.3d 1215, 1220 (6th Cir. 1997). However, expert testimony is helpful when it would explain behavior that would otherwise be puzzling to a jury in light of their common knowledge and experience, such as testimony regarding battered woman syndrome. *See Terry v. State,* 467 So. 2d 761, 764 (Fla. 4th DCA 1985); *Arcoren v. U.S.,* 929 F.2d 1235, 1240-41 (8th Cir.

1991). Under both the federal and Florida rules, the determination that expert testimony is helpful is reviewed on appeal only for abuse of discretion. *See Angrand v. Key*, 657 So. 2d 1146, 1149 (Fla. 1995); *Arcoren*, 929 F.2d at 1241.

Finally, even if testimony satisfies all of the requirements under Florida Stat. § 90.702 or Federal Rule 702, the trial court retains the authority to exclude the evidence under Florida Stat. § 90.403 or Federal Rule 403. *See Ramirez v. State*, 810 So. 2d 836, 842 (Fla. 2001); *Allison v. McGhan Medical Corp.*, 184 F.3d 1300, 1310 (11th Cir. 1999).

Federal Rule 703. Bases of an Expert's Opinion Testimony

An expert may base an opinion on facts or data in the case that the expert has been made aware of or personally observed. If experts in the particular field would reasonably rely on those kinds of facts or data in forming an opinion on the subject, they need not be admissible for the opinion to be admitted. But if the facts or data would otherwise be inadmissible, the proponent of the opinion may disclose them to the jury only if their probative value in helping the jury evaluate the opinion substantially outweighs their prejudicial effect.

ADVISORY COMMITTEE'S NOTE

Facts or data upon which expert opinions are based may, under the rule, be derived from three possible sources. The first is the firsthand observation of the witness with opinions based thereon traditionally allowed. A treating physician affords an example. Rheingold, The Basis of Medical Testimony, 15 Vand.L.Rev. 473, 489 (1962). Whether he must first relate his observations is treated in Rule 705. The second source, presentation at the trial, also reflects existing practice. The technique may be the familiar hypothetical question or having the expert attend the trial and hear the testimony establishing the facts. Problems of determining what testimony the expert relied upon, when the latter technique is employed and the testimony is in conflict, may be resolved by resort to Rule 705. The third source contemplated by the rule consists of presentation of data to the expert outside of court and other than by his own perception. In this respect the rule is designed to broaden the basis for expert opinions beyond that current in many jurisdictions and to bring the judicial practice into line with the practice of the experts themselves when not in court. Thus a physician in his own practice bases his diagnosis on information from numerous sources and of considerable variety, including statements by patients and relatives, reports and opinions from nurses, technicians and other doctors, hospital records, and X rays. Most of them are admissible in evidence, but only with the expenditure of substantial time in producing and examining various authenticating witnesses. The physician makes life-and-death decisions in reliance upon them. His validation, expertly performed and subject to cross-examination, ought to suffice for judicial purposes. Rheingold, *supra*, at 531; McCormick § 15. A similar provision is California Evidence Code § 801(b).

The rule also offers a more satisfactory basis for ruling upon the admissibility of public opinion poll evidence. Attention is directed to the validity of the techniques employed rather than to relatively fruitless inquiries whether hearsay is involved. See Judge Feinberg's careful analysis in Zippo Mfg. Co. v. Rogers Imports, Inc., 216 F.Supp. 670 (S.D.N.Y. 1963). See also Blum et al., The Art of Opinion Research: A Lawyer's Appraisal of an Emerging Service, 24 U.Chi.L.Rev. 1 (1956); Bonynge, Trademark Surveys and Techniques and Their Use in Litigation, 48 A.B.A.J. 329 (1962); Zeisel, The Uniqueness of Survey Evidence, 45 Cornell L.Q. 322 (1960); Annot., 76 A.L.R.2d 919.

If it be feared that enlargement of permissible data may tend to break down the rules of exclusion unduly, notice should be taken that the rule requires that the facts or data "be of a type reasonably relied upon by experts in the particular field." The language would not warrant admitting in evidence the opinion of an "accidentologist" as to the point of impact in an automobile collision based on statements of bystanders, since this requirement is not satisfied. See Comment, Cal.Law Rev.Comm'n, Recommendation Proposing an Evidence Code 148–150 (1965).

ADVISORY COMMITTEE'S NOTE (2000 AMENDMENT)

Rule 703 has been amended to emphasize that when an expert reasonably relies on inadmissible information to form an opinion or inference, the underlying information is not admissible simply because the opinion or inference is admitted. Courts have reached different results on how to treat inadmissible information when it is reasonably relied upon by an expert in forming an opinion or drawing an inference. *Compare United States v. Rollins*, 862 F.2d 1282 (7th Cir. 1988) (admitting, as part of the basis of an FBI agent's expert opinion on the meaning of code language, the hearsay statements of an informant), *with United States v. 0.59 Acres of Land*, 109 F.3d 1493 (9th Cir. 1997) (error to admit hearsay offered as the basis of an expert opinion, without a limiting instruction). Commentators have also taken differing views. *See e.g.*, Ronald Carlson, *Policing the Bases of Modern Expert Testimony*, 39 Vand.L.Rev. 577 (1986) (advocating limits on the jury's consideration of otherwise inadmissible evidence used as the basis for an expert opinion); Paul Rice, *Inadmissible Evidence as a Basis for Expert Testimony: A Response to Professor Carlson*, 40 Vand.L.Rev. 583 (1987) (advocating unrestricted use of information reasonably relied upon by an expert).

When information is reasonably relied upon by an expert and yet is admissible only for the purpose of assisting the jury in evaluating an expert's opinion, a trial court applying this Rule must consider the information's probative value in assisting the jury to weigh the expert's opinion on the one hand, and the risk of prejudice resulting from the jury's potential misuse of the information for substantive purposes on the other. The information may be disclosed to the jury, upon objection, only if the trial court finds that the probative value of the information in assisting the jury to evaluate the expert's opinion substantially outweighs its prejudicial effect. If the otherwise inadmissible information is admitted under this balancing test, the trial judge must give a limiting instruction upon request, informing the jury that the underlying information must not be used for substantive purposes. *See* Rule 105. In determining the appropriate course, the trial court should consider the probable effectiveness or lack of effectiveness of a limiting instruction under the particular circumstances.

The amendment governs only the disclosure to the jury of information that is reasonably relied on by an expert, when that information is not admissible for substantive purposes. It is not intended to affect the admissibility of an expert's testimony. Nor does the amendment prevent an expert from relying on information that is inadmissible for substantive purposes.

Nothing in this Rule restricts the presentation of underlying expert facts or data when offered by an adverse party. *See* Rule 705. Of course, an adversary's attack on an expert's basis will often open the door to a proponent's rebuttal with information that was reasonably relied upon by the expert, even if that information would not have been discloseable initially under the balancing test provided by this amendment. Moreover, in some circumstances the proponent might wish to disclose information that is relied upon by the expert in order to "remove the sting" from the opponent's anticipated attack, and thereby prevent the jury from drawing an unfair negative inference. The trial court should take this consideration into account in applying the balancing test provided by this amendment.

This amendment covers facts or data that cannot be admitted for any purpose other than to assist the jury to evaluate the expert's opinion. The balancing test provided in this amendment is not applicable to facts or data that are admissible for any other purpose but have not yet been offered for such a purpose at the time the expert testifies.

The amendment provides a presumption against disclosure to the jury of information used as the basis of an expert's opinion and not admissible for any substantive purpose, when that information is offered by the proponent of the expert. In a multi-party case, where one party proffers an expert whose testimony is also beneficial to other parties, each such party should be deemed a "proponent" within the meaning of the amendment.

ADVISORY COMMITTEE'S NOTE (2011 AMENDMENT)

The language of Rule 703 has been amended as part of the general restyling of the Evidence Rules to make them more easily understood and to make style and terminology consistent throughout the rules. These changes are intended to be stylistic only. There is no intent to change any result in any ruling on evidence admissibility.

The Committee deleted all reference to an "inference" on the grounds that the deletion made the Rule flow better and easier to read, and because any "inference" is covered by the broader term "opinion." Courts have not made substantive decisions on the basis of any distinction between an opinion and an inference. No change in current practice is intended.

Florida Stat. § 90.704. Basis of Opinion Testimony by Experts

The facts or data upon which an expert bases an opinion or inference may be those perceived by, or made known to, the expert at or before the trial. If the facts or data are of a type reasonably relied upon by experts in the subject to support the opinion expressed, the facts or data need not be admissible in evidence.

SPONSORS' NOTE (1976 ENACTMENT)

Facts or data upon which expert opinion are based may be derived from three possible sources: (1) Firsthand observation of the witness, (2) presentation of evidence at the trial, and (3) presentation of data to the expert outside of court and other than by his own perception. The first two sources reflect existing practice. Inclusion of the third source is designed to broaden the basis of expert opinion beyond that currently allowed and to bring the judicial practice into line with the practice of the experts themselves when not in court. Thus, a physician in his own practice bases his diagnosis on information from numerous sources and of considerable variety, including statements by patients and relatives, reports and opinions of nurses, technicians, and other doctors, hospital records, and X-rays. The reasonableness of experts' reliance on this data may be questioned on cross-examination.

This section also offers a satisfactory basis for a ruling upon the admissibility of public opinion poll evidence. Attention is directed to the validity of the techniques employed rather than to relatively fruitless inquiries whether hearsay is involved. See Zippo Mfg. Co. v. Rogers Imports, Inc., 216 F.Supp. 670 (S.D.N.Y. 1963).

Although Florida case law does not speak in terms similar to the language in this section, in at least one situation the effect is that of substantial accord. Numerous Florida cases uphold the admissibility of opinion evidence by a treating physician based, at least partially, on information supplied to him by the patient. Steiger v. Massachusetts Cas. Ins. Co., 253 So.2d 882 (Fla. 3rd Dist. 1971); Raydel Ltd. v. Medcalfe, 162 So.2d 910 (Fla. 3rd Dist. 1964), quashed on other grounds 178 So.2d 569 (1965).

If it is feared that enlargement of permissible data may tend to break down the rules of exclusion unduly, notice should be taken that the section requires that the facts or data "are of a type reasonably relied upon by experts in the particular subject."

This section is the same as Fed. Rule Evid. 703. A similar provision is contained in Calif. Evid. Code § 801(b).

COMMENTARY ON FEDERAL AND FLORIDA RULE DIFFERENCES

Florida Stat. § 90.704 and its federal counterpart, Federal Rule 703 (upon which it is modeled, see *Schwarz v. State*, 695 So. 2d 452, 454 (Fla. 4th DCA 1997)), set forth the permissible bases for opinion testimony by expert witnesses. Unlike lay witnesses, whose opinion testimony must be based on facts within their personal knowledge, see FLA. STAT. § 90.701; FED. R. EVID. 701, expert witnesses under both Florida and federal law are permitted to base their opinions on facts of which they lack personal knowledge.

The Florida and federal rules recognize three possible bases for expert witness testimony. First, like a lay witness, an expert may base his opinion on his firsthand observations, as would be the case with a treating physician. See Advisory Committee's Note to FED. R. EVID. 703; Sponsors' Note to FLA. STAT. § 90.704. Second, an expert may base his opinion on facts made known to him at trial, either through having the expert attend the trial and listening to witness testimony (in which case, the expert might be exempt from a sequestration order under Florida Stat. § 90.616 or its federal counterpart, Federal Rule 615, see *U.S. v. Seschillie*, 310 F.3d 1208, 1212-13 (9th Cir. 2002); *Knight v. State*, 746 So. 2d 423, 430 (Fla. 1998)) or by means of a hypothetical question posed by counsel that is based on the evidence presented at trial. See Advisory Committee's Note to FED. R. EVID. 703; Sponsors' Note to FLA. STAT. § 90.704. Third, an expert may base his opinion on facts made known to him in advance of trial, such as in the case of a medical expert who renders a diagnosis based on a review of a patient's records and conversations with his treating physician. See Advisory Committee's Note to FED. R. EVID. 703; Sponsors' Note to FLA. STAT. § 90.704.

Under both the Federal and Florida rules, if facts or data are of the type that experts in the field would "reasonably rel[y] upon" in forming opinions, those facts or data need *not* be admissible in evidence in order for the opinion to be admitted. See *Bigham v. State*, 995 So. 2d 207, 215 (Fla. 2008). The determination whether experts in the field reasonably rely on such facts or data in forming their opinions is made by the trial court, see *C.W. v. Dept. of Children & Family Servs.*, 904 So. 2d 588, 590 (Fla. 3d DCA 2005); *Black v. M & W Gear Co.*, 269 F.3d 1220, 1244 (10th Cir. 2001), and in making that determination, it can consider the expert's own testimony, the testimony of other experts, and treatises, and may also take judicial notice regarding the types of data reasonably relied upon by experts in the field. *U.S. v. Stone*, 222 F.R.D. 334, 340 (E.D. Tenn. 2004).

One potential difference between the Florida and federal rules is the extent to which otherwise inadmissible facts or data underlying an opinion may be disclosed to the jury by the proponent of the opinion as a means of helping the jury to evaluate the expert's opinion (disclosure at the opponent's request is addressed in Florida Stat. § 90.705 and its federal counterpart, Federal Rule 705). Under the federal rule, as amended in 2000, such facts or data may be disclosed to the jury at the proponent's request only if the court determines that the probative value in assisting the jury in evaluating the expert's opinion *substantially* outweighs their prejudicial effect, a much more stringent balancing test than that of Federal Rule 403. See Advisory Committee's Note to 2000 Amendment to FED. R. EVID. 703. While the Florida rule lacks similar language, thus subjecting disclosure to the normal balancing test of Florida Stat. § 90.403, the Florida courts have been reluctant to permit such disclosure coupled with a limiting instruction not to use the otherwise inadmissible evidence for substantive purposes, reasoning that "[t]he distinction will likely escape the jury." See *Department of Corr. v. Williams*, 549 So. 2d 1071, 1071-72 & n.1 (Fla. 5th DCA 1989). Moreover, the Florida Supreme Court has held that trial courts must take care to ensure that the expert not merely serve as a conduit for otherwise inadmissible hearsay. See *Dufour v. State*, 2011 WL 320985, at *16 (Fla. 2011); *Linn v. Fossum*, 946 So. 2d 1032, 1037-38 (Fla. 2006).

Federal Rule 704. Opinion on an Ultimate Issue

(a) **In General — Not Automatically Objectionable.** An opinion is not objectionable just because it embraces an ultimate issue.

(b) Exception. In a criminal case, an expert witness must not state an opinion about whether the defendant did or did not have a mental state or condition that constitutes an element of the crime charged or of a defense. Those matters are for the trier of fact alone.

ADVISORY COMMITTEE'S NOTE

The basic approach to opinions, lay and expert, in these rules is to admit them when helpful to the trier of fact. In order to render this approach fully effective and to allay any doubt on the subject, the so-called "ultimate issue" rule is specifically abolished by the instant rule.

The older cases often contained strictures against allowing witnesses to express opinions upon ultimate issues, as a particular aspect of the rule against opinions. The rule was unduly restrictive, difficult of application, and generally served only to deprive the trier of fact of useful information. 7 Wigmore §§ 1920, 1921; McCormick § 12. The basis usually assigned for the rule, to prevent the witness from "usurping the province of the jury," is aptly characterized as "empty rhetoric." 7 Wigmore § 1920, p. 17. Efforts to meet the felt needs of particular situations led to odd verbal circumlocutions which were said not to violate the rule. Thus a witness could express his estimate of the criminal responsibility of an accused in terms of sanity or insanity, but not in terms of ability to tell right from wrong or other more modern standard. And in cases of medical causation, witnesses were sometimes required to couch their opinions in cautious phrases of "might or could," rather than "did," though the result was to deprive many opinions of the positiveness to which they were entitled, accompanied by the hazard of a ruling of insufficiency to support a verdict. In other instances the rule was simply disregarded, and, as concessions to need, opinions were allowed upon such matters as intoxication, speed, handwriting, and value, although more precise coincidence with an ultimate issue would scarcely be possible.

Many modern decisions illustrate the trend to abandon the rule completely. People v. Wilson, 25 Cal.2d 341 (1944), whether abortion necessary to save life of patient; Clifford-Jacobs Forging Co. v. Industrial Comm., 19 Ill.2d 236 (1960), medical causation; Dowling v. L. H. Shattuck, Inc., 91 N.H. 234 (1941), proper method of shoring ditch; Schweiger v. Solbeck, 191 Or. 454 (1951), cause of landslide. In each instance the opinion was allowed.

The abolition of the ultimate issue rule does not lower the bars so as to admit all opinions. Under Rules 701 and 702, opinions must be helpful to the trier of fact, and Rule 403 provides for exclusion of evidence which wastes time. These provisions afford ample assurances against the admission of opinions which would merely tell the jury what result to reach, somewhat in the manner of the oath-helpers of an earlier day. They also stand ready to exclude opinions phrased in terms of inadequately explored legal criteria. Thus the question, "Did T have capacity to make a will?" would be excluded, while the question, "Did T have sufficient mental capacity to know the nature and extent of his property and the natural objects of his bounty and to formulate a rational scheme of distribution?" would be allowed. McCormick § 12.

For similar provisions see Uniform Rule 56(4); California Evidence Code § 805; Kansas Code of Civil Procedure § 60-456(d); New Jersey Evidence Rule 56(3).

ADVISORY COMMITTEE'S NOTE (2011 AMENDMENT)

The language of Rule 704 has been amended as part of the general restyling of the Evidence Rules to make them more easily understood and to make style and terminology consistent throughout the rules. These changes are intended to be stylistic only. There is no intent to change any result in any ruling on evidence admissibility.

The Committee deleted all reference to an "inference" on the grounds that the deletion made the Rule flow better and easier to read, and because any "inference" is covered by the broader term "opinion." Courts have not made substantive decisions on the basis of any distinction between an opinion and an inference. No change in current practice is intended.

Florida Stat. § 90.703. Opinion on Ultimate Issue

Testimony in the form of an opinion or inference otherwise admissible is not objectionable because it includes an ultimate issue to be decided by the trier of fact.

SPONSORS' NOTE (1976 ENACTMENT)

Many cases contain prohibitions against allowing witnesses to express opinion on ultimate issues on the grounds that to do so would invade the province of the jury. This rule has been criticized as being unduly restrictive, difficult of application, and generally serving only to deprive the trier of fact of useful information. 7 Wigmore, Evidence §§ 1920, 1921 (3rd ed. 1940); McCormick, Evidence § 12 (2nd ed. 1972). Although some early Florida cases seemingly follow this older "ultimate issue" exclusionary rule; the Florida Supreme Court in North v. State, 65 So.2d 77, 88 (Fla. 1952), in allowing a physician to express his opinion as to the cause of the bruises and contusions on the victim's throat, adopted the position stated in 20 Am. Jur. 654, Evidence § 782:

> It is certainly contrary to the unmistakable trend of authority to exclude expert opinion testimony merely upon the ground that it amounts to an opinion upon ultimate facts. The modern tendency is to make no distinction between evidential and ultimate facts subject to expert opinion. The courts consider that it is more important to get to the truth of the matter than to quibble over distinctions in this regard which are in many cases impracticable.

This view has prevailed in Florida. See Gifford v. Galaxie Homes, Inc., 223 So.2d 108, 111 (Fla. 2nd Dist. 1969), where, in permitting expert testimony that a ramp was not constructed and maintained according to reasonably safe construction and engineering standards of the community, it was further reasoned:

> It is still the sole province of the jury to accept or reject the testimony of the expert witness, regardless of how respectable and qualified that witness may be, and the jury is in no wise bound by the expert's conclusions, any more than it is bound by the testimony of any other witness.

The abolition of the "ultimate issue" exclusionary rule does not admit all opinion testimony. Section 90.701 prohibits opinions and inferences of a lay witness when the witness lacks the knowledge, skill, experience, or training to rationally form such opinions, and permits the exclusion of opinions of a lay witness when the lay witness can just as adequately and accurately relate what he has perceived without testifying in terms of inferences and opinions. Section 90.702 limits expert opinion testimony to circumstances where the trier of fact will be assisted by such testimony in understanding the evidence or determining a fact in issue. Section 90.403 provides for exclusion of evidence for waste of time.

These sections, together with Section 90.705, which permits the judge to require disclosure of facts or data underlying an expert's opinion, afford ample assurance that the admission of opinions which would merely tell the jury what result to reach will be excluded. In addition, an opinion phrased in terms of inadequately explored legal criteria where there was not a sufficient foundation to show expertise in determining the legal effect of the facts could be excluded. The question, "Did T have capacity to make a will?" could be excluded, while the question, "Did T have sufficient mental capacity to know the nature and extent of his property and the natural objects of his bounty and to formulate a rational scheme of distribution?" would be allowed. See generally, Morris, The Role of Expert Testimony in the Trial of Negligence Issues, 26 Texas L. Rev. 1, 10-23 (1947).

For similar provisions see Uniform Rule 56(4); Calif. Evid. Code § 805; Kansas Code of Civ. Pro. § 60-456(d); New Jersey Evidence Rule 56(3); Fed. Rule Evid. 704.

COMMENTARY ON FEDERAL AND FLORIDA RULE DIFFERENCES

Florida Stat. § 90.703 and its federal counterpart, Federal Rule 704, abolish the common law rule under which both lay and expert witnesses were barred from testifying in the form of an opinion that embraced an "ultimate issue" in the case (such as testimony regarding causation in a negligence action).

However, as indicated in the legislative history to both rules, elimination of the ultimate issue rule does not mean that all opinions on ultimate issues are automatically admissible; they must still satisfy other evidentiary rules, including, in particular, the helpfulness requirement of Florida Stat. § 90.702 or Federal Rule 702. See Advisory Committee's Note to FED. R. EVID. 704; Sponsors' Note to FLA. STAT. § 90.703. Thus, testimony that invades the province of the jury—such as testimony that a witness is or is not credible, see McLean v. State, 754 So. 2d 176, 181 (Fla. 2d DCA 2000); Nichols v. American Nat'l Ins. Co., 154 F.3d 875, 883 (8th Cir. 1998), that is phrased in terms of a legal conclusion, such as testimony that someone was negligent, see Town of Palm Beach v. Palm Beach County, 460 So. 2d 879, 882 (Fla. 1984); U.S. v. Barile, 286 F.3d 749, 759-62 (4th Cir. 2002), or that simply tells the jury what result to reach, see Schneer v. Allstate Indem. Co., 767 So. 2d 485, 488-489 (Fla. 3d DCA 2000); Woods v. Lecureaux, 110 F.3d 1215, 1220 (6th Cir. 1997)—will be excluded not because it reaches an ultimate issue in the case, but rather because it does not satisfy the helpfulness requirement.

A significant difference between the two rules arises in criminal cases in which expert testimony is offered on the question whether the defendant did or did not have a mental state or condition constituting an element of a crime or defense. The federal rule was amended in 1984 to reinstate the ultimate issue rule in this circumstance, barring expert opinion testimony on the question whether the defendant did or did not have such mental state or condition. See FED. R. EVID. 704(b). The federal rule bars not only direct testimony on this issue, but also indirect testimony by means of a thinly veiled hypothetical that mirrors the pertinent characteristics of the defendant, although it does not bar an explanation of a disease and its typical effect on a person's mental state. See U.S. v. Thigpen, 4 F.3d 1573, 1580 (11th Cir. 1993). By contrast, the Florida rule contains no such limitation, and Florida law permits an expert to testify on the question whether the defendant had a mental state or condition constituting an element of a crime or defense. See Reynolds v. State, 837 So. 2d 1044, 1046-48 (Fla. 4th DCA 2002).

Federal Rule 705. Disclosing the Facts or Data Underlying an Expert's Opinion

Unless the court orders otherwise, an expert may state an opinion — and give the reasons for it — without first testifying to the underlying facts or data. But the expert may be required to disclose those facts or data on cross-examination.

ADVISORY COMMITTEE'S NOTE

The hypothetical question has been the target of a great deal of criticism as encouraging partisan bias, affording an opportunity for summing up in the middle of the case, and as complex and time consuming. Ladd, Expert Testimony, 5 Vand.L.Rev. 414, 426–427 (1952). While the rule allows counsel to make disclosure of the underlying facts or data as a preliminary to the giving of an expert opinion, if he chooses, the instances in which he is required to do so are reduced. This is true whether the expert bases his opinion on data furnished him at secondhand or observed by him at firsthand.

The elimination of the requirement of preliminary disclosure at the trial of underlying facts or data has a long background of support. In 1937 the Commissioners on Uniform State Laws incorporated a provision to this effect in their Model Expert Testimony Act, which furnished the basis for Uniform Rules 57 and 58. Rule 4515, N.Y. CPLR (McKinney 1963), provides:

"Unless the court orders otherwise, questions calling for the opinion of an expert witness need not be hypothetical in form, and the witness may state his opinion and reasons without first specifying the data upon which it is based. Upon cross-examination, he may be required to specify the data...."

See also California Evidence Code § 802; Kansas Code of Civil Procedure §§ 60-456, 60457; New Jersey Evidence Rules 57, 58.

If the objection is made that leaving it to the cross-examiner to bring out the supporting data is essentially unfair, the answer is that he is under no compulsion to bring out any facts or data except those unfavorable to the opinion. The answer assumes that the cross-examiner has the advance knowledge which is essential for effective cross-examination. This advance knowledge has been afforded, though imperfectly, by the traditional foundation requirement. Rule 26(b)(4) of the Rules of Civil Procedure, as revised, provides for substantial discovery in this area, obviating in large measure the obstacles which have been raised in some instances to discovery of findings, underlying data, and even the identity of the experts. Friedenthal, Discovery and Use of an Adverse Party's Expert Information, 14 Stan.L.Rev. 455 (1962).

These safeguards are reinforced by the discretionary power of the judge to require preliminary disclosure in any event.

ADVISORY COMMITTEE'S NOTE (1993 AMENDMENT)

This rule, which relates to the manner of presenting testimony at trial, is revised to avoid an arguable conflict with revised Rule 26(a)(2)(B) and 26(e)(1) of the Federal Rules of Civil Procedure or with revised Rule 16 of the Federal Rules of Criminal Procedure, which require disclosure in advance of trial of the basis and reasons for an expert's opinions.

If a serious question is raised under Rule 702 or 703 as to the admissibility of expert testimony, disclosure of the underlying facts or data on which opinions are based may, of course, be needed by the court before deciding whether, and to what extent, the person should be allowed to testify. This rule does not preclude such an inquiry.

ADVISORY COMMITTEE'S NOTE (2011 AMENDMENT)

The language of Rule 705 has been amended as part of the general restyling of the Evidence Rules to make them more easily understood and to make style and terminology consistent throughout the rules. These changes are intended to be stylistic only. There is no intent to change any result in any ruling on evidence admissibility.

The Committee deleted all reference to an "inference" on the grounds that the deletion made the Rule flow better and easier to read, and because any "inference" is covered by the broader term "opinion." Courts have not made substantive decisions on the basis of any distinction between an opinion and an inference. No change in current practice is intended.

Florida Stat. § 90.705. Disclosure of Facts or Data Underlying Expert Opinion

(1) Unless otherwise required by the court, an expert may testify in terms of opinion or inferences and give reasons without prior disclosure of the underlying facts or data. On cross-examination the expert shall be required to specify the facts or data.

(2) Prior to the witness giving the opinion, a party against whom the opinion or inference is offered may conduct a voir dire examination of the witness directed to the underlying facts or data for the witness's opinion. If the party establishes prima facie evidence that the expert does not have a sufficient basis for the opinion, the opinions and inferences of the expert are inadmissible unless the party offering the testimony establishes the underlying facts or data.

SPONSORS' NOTE (1976 ENACTMENT)

Subsection (1) This subsection eliminates the requirement of preliminary disclosure at the trial of underlying facts or data. Counsel is allowed to make disclosure of the underlying facts or data as a preliminary to the giving of an expert opinion, if he chooses, but the instances in which he is required to do so are reduced. This is true whether the expert bases his opinion on data furnished him secondhand, or observed by him firsthand.

The change which this section represents was prompted by the criticism which has been leveled at the use of the hypothetical question. As was stated in 2 Wigmore, Evidence § 686 (3rd ed. 1940):

> The hypothetical question, misused by the clumsy and abused by the clever, has in practice led to intolerable obstruction of truth. In the first place, it has artificially clamped the mouth of the expert witness, so that his answer to a complex question may not express his actual opinion on the actual case. This is because the question may be so built up and contrived by counsel as to represent only a partisan conclusion. In the second place, it has tended to mislead the jury so as to purport of actual expert opinion. This is due to the same reason. In the third place, it has tended to confuse the jury, so that its employment becomes a mere waste of time and a futile obstruction.

The cross-examiner has the opportunity to bring out the supporting data, if he should so desire. It is assumed that the cross-examiner has the advance knowledge that is essential for effective cross-examination. The judge also has the discretionary power to require preliminary disclosure.

This section is in apparent conflict with existing Florida law. However, in at least one situation the Florida courts recognize the philosophy of this section in allowing a psychiatrist in a criminal case to state his opinion to the jury without first relating the facts upon which the opinion is based. Cirack v. State, 201 So.2d 706 (Fla. 1967) (court-appointed psychiatrist called after both sides rested); Blocker v. State, 92 Fla. 878, 110 So. 547 (1926) (psychiatrist called by the prosecution). In considering the factual record necessary to support a hypothetical question the court stated in Nat Harrison Associates, Inc. v. Byrd, 256 So.2d 50, 53 (Fla. 4th Dist. 1971) that:

> The facts submitted to the expert in the hypothetical question propounded on direct examination must be supported by competent substantial evidence in the record at the time the question is asked or by reasonable inferences from such evidence....Adherence to this form for the direct examination of an expert prevents the expert from expressing an opinion based on unstated and perhaps unwarranted factual assumptions concerning the event; facilitates cross examination and rebuttal; and fosters an understanding of the opinion by the trier of fact.

The elimination of the requirement of preliminary disclosure has a long background of support. See Honigman, The Hypothetical Question Meets Its Answer, 36 Mich. S.B.J. No. 11 at 12 (1957). In 1937 the Commissioners on Uniform State Laws incorporated a provision to this effect in their Model Expert

Testimony Act, which furnished the basis for Uniform Rules 57 and 58. For similar provisions see Calif. Evid. Code § 802; Kansas Code of Civ. Pro. §§ 60-456, 60-457; New Jersey Evid. Rules 57, 58; Rule 4515, New York C.P.L.R. (McKinney 1963); Fed. Rule Evid. 705.

Subsection (2) This subsection provides protection for opposing counsel that expert opinion which is completely unqualified will not be admitted and risk prejudicing the jury. In this instance, the protection of using cross-examination to expose the flaws in the opinion is not sufficient in all cases.

COMMENTARY ON FEDERAL AND FLORIDA RULE DIFFERENCES

Florida Stat. § 90.705 and its federal counterpart, Federal Rule 705, sets forth the rules governing when an expert must disclose the facts or data underlying his opinion.

As a general rule, both Florida and federal law permit an expert to give his opinion without first testifying to the underlying facts or data, unless the court orders otherwise. See FLA. STAT. § 90.705(1); FED. R. EVID. 705. Thus, as a general rule, the expert can give his opinion first and subsequently disclose the underlying facts or data (to the extent that such disclosure is not barred by Federal Rule 703 or its Florida equivalent), or not disclose the underlying facts or data at all on direct examination.

However, under both the Florida and federal rules, the opposing party has the right to require him to specify the facts or data on cross-examination. See FLA. STAT. § 90.705(1); FED. R. EVID. 705. One potential difference between the Florida and federal rules in this regard is that the federal rule provides that the expert *may* be required to disclose the underlying facts or data on cross-examination, and has been interpreted to permit the trial court to bar such disclosure under Federal Rule 403, see *U.S. v. Gillis*, 773 F.2d 549, 553-54 (4th Cir. 1985), while the Florida rule states that such facts or data *shall* be disclosed on cross-examination.

The Florida rule provides that before the witness gives her opinion, the opposing party may conduct a voir dire examination directed at the facts and data underlying the opinion to test the sufficiency of the witness's basis for her opinion; if in doing so he establishes that the witness lacks a sufficient basis for the opinion, her testimony is inadmissible (unless the party offering her testimony establishes the underlying basis). See FLA. STAT. § 90.705(2); *Esty v. State*, 642 So. 2d 1074, 1078 (Fla. 1994). While the federal rule contains no comparable language, it is understood not to bar inquiry by the court to determine the admissibility of the expert's testimony. See *U.S. v. Brien*, 59 F.3d 274, 278 (1st Cir. 1995); Advisory Committee's Note to 1993 Amendment to FED. R. EVID. 705.

Federal Rule 706. Court-Appointed Expert Witnesses

(a) Appointment Process. On a party's motion or on its own, the court may order the parties to show cause why expert witnesses should not be appointed and may ask the parties to submit nominations. The court may appoint any expert that the parties agree on and any of its own choosing. But the court may only appoint someone who consents to act.

(b) Expert's Role. The court must inform the expert of the expert's duties. The court may do so in writing and have a copy filed with the clerk or may do so orally at a conference in which the parties have an opportunity to participate. The expert:

(1) must advise the parties of any findings the expert makes;

(2) may be deposed by any party;

(3) may be called to testify by the court or any party; and

(4) may be cross-examined by any party, including the party that called the expert.

(c) Compensation. The expert is entitled to a reasonable compensation, as set by the court. The compensation is payable as follows:

(1) in a criminal case or in a civil case involving just compensation under the Fifth Amendment, from any funds that are provided by law; and

(2) in any other civil case, by the parties in the proportion and at the time that the court directs — and the compensation is then charged like other costs.

(d) Disclosing the Appointment to the Jury. The court may authorize disclosure to the jury that the court appointed the expert.

(e) Parties' Choice of Their Own Experts. This rule does not limit a party in calling its own experts.

ADVISORY COMMITTEE'S NOTE

The practice of shopping for experts, the venality of some experts, and the reluctance of many reputable experts to involve themselves in litigation, have been matters of deep concern. Though the contention is made that court appointed experts acquire an aura of infallibility to which they are not entitled, Levy, Impartial Medical Testimony—Revisited, 34 Temple L.Q. 416 (1961), the trend is increasingly to provide for their use. While experience indicates that actual appointment is a relatively infrequent occurrence, the assumption may be made that the availability of the procedure in itself decreases the need for resorting to it. The ever-present possibility that the judge *may* appoint an expert in a given case must inevitably exert a sobering effect on the expert witness of a party and upon the person utilizing his services.

The inherent power of a trial judge to appoint an expert of his own choosing is virtually unquestioned. Scott v. Spanjer Bros., Inc., 298 F.2d 928 (2d Cir. 1962); Danville Tobacco Assn. v. Bryant-Buckner Associates, Inc., 333 F.2d 202 (4th Cir. 1964); Sink, The Unused Power of a Federal Judge to Call His Own Expert Witnesses, 29 S.Cal.L.Rev. 195 (1956); 2 Wigmore § 563, 9 *id.* § 2484; Annot., 95 A.L.R.2d 383. Hence the problem becomes largely one of detail.

The New York plan is well known and is described in Report by Special Committee of the Association of the Bar of the City of New York: Impartial Medical Testimony (1956). On recommendation of the Section of Judicial Administration, local adoption of an impartial medical plan was endorsed by the American Bar Association. 82 A.B.A.Rep. 184–185 (1957). Descriptions and analyses of plans in effect in various parts of the country are found in Van Dusen, A United States District Judge's View of the Impartial Medical Expert System, 32 F.R.D. 498 (1963); Wick and Kightlinger, Impartial Medical Testimony Under the Federal Civil Rules: A Tale of Three Doctors, 34 Ins. Counsel J. 115 (1967); and numerous articles collected in Klein, Judicial Administration and the Legal Profession 393 (1963). Statutes and rules include California Evidence Code §§ 730–733; Illinois Supreme Court Rule 215(d), Ill.Rev.Stat.1969, c. 110A, § 215(d); Burns Indiana Stats.1956, § 9-1702; Wisconsin Stats.Annot.1958, § 957.27.

In the federal practice, a comprehensive scheme for court appointed experts was initiated with the adoption of Rule 28 of the Federal Rules of Criminal Procedure in 1946. The Judicial Conference of the United States in 1953 considered court appointed experts in civil cases, but only with respect to whether they should be compensated from public funds, a proposal which was rejected. Report of the Judicial Conference of the United States 23 (1953). The present rule expands the practice to include civil cases.

Subdivision[s (a) and (b) are] based on Rule 28 of the Federal Rules of Criminal Procedure, with a few changes, mainly in the interest of clarity. Language has been added to provide specifically for the appointment either on motion of a party or on the judge's own motion. A provision subjecting the court appointed expert to deposition procedures has been incorporated. The rule has been revised to make definite the right of any party, including the party calling him, to cross-examine.

Subdivision ([c]) combines the present provision for compensation in criminal cases with what seems to be a fair and feasible handling of civil cases, originally found in the Model Act and carried from there into Uniform Rule 60. See also California Evidence Code §§ 730–731. The special provision for Fifth Amendment compensation cases is designed to guard against reducing constitutionally guaranteed just compensation by requiring the recipient to pay costs. See Rule 71A(*l*) of the Rules of Civil Procedure.

Subdivision ([d]) seems to be essential if the use of court appointed experts is to be fully effective. Uniform Rule 61 so provides.

Subdivision ([e]) is in essence the last sentence of Rule 28(a) of the Federal Rules of Criminal Procedure.

ADVISORY COMMITTEE'S NOTE (2011 AMENDMENT)

The language of Rule 706 has been amended as part of the restyling of the Evidence Rules to make them more easily understood and to make style and terminology consistent throughout the rules. These changes are intended to be stylistic only. There is no intent to change any result in any ruling on evidence admissibility.

COMMENTARY ON FEDERAL AND FLORIDA RULE DIFFERENCES

Federal Rule 706 provides federal trial courts with authority to appoint expert witnesses. The rule gives trial courts discretion to make such an appointment on their own motion or at the request of a party, with the expert so appointed one agreed upon by the parties or of the judge's own choosing. See FED. R. EVID. 706(a). Such an appointment does not prevent the parties from retaining and calling experts of their own choosing. See FED. R. EVID. 706(e). The trial court may, but need not, disclose to the jury that the expert was appointed by the court. See FED. R. EVID. 706(d). The rule provides the parties with certain rights with respect to court-appointed experts, including the right to be advised of the expert's findings, the right to take the expert's deposition, the right to call the expert to testify, and the right to cross-examine the expert. See FED. R. EVID. 706(b). The rule provides for compensation of the expert with public funds in criminal cases and just compensation actions, but by the parties (as directed by the court) in other cases. See FED. R. EVID. 706(c).

There is no comparable rule in the Florida Evidence Code. However, a number of specific Florida statutes and rules give trial courts the power (and sometimes the duty) to appoint experts in specific situations, such as before ordering chemical castration, see FLA. STAT. § 794.0235(2)(a), to determine the mental condition of a criminal defendant, see FLA. STAT. § 916.115, to determine whether a person facing a death sentence is mentally retarded, see FLA. STAT. § 921.137, to determine whether an indigent criminal defendant is incompetent to stand trial, see FLA. R. CRIM. P. 3.216, or to determine whether a criminal defendant facing a death sentence is insane at the time of execution, see FLA. R. CRIM. P. 3.812. In addition, Florida authority recognizes that Fla. Stat. § 90.615(1)—which gives trial courts discretion to call witnesses in general—can be invoked not only to call lay witnesses, but also expert ones. See Committee Note to FLA. FAM. L. R. P. 12.365; *Ritter v. Jimenez*, 343 So. 2d 659, 660-61 (Fla. 3d DCA 1977).

ARTICLE VIII. HEARSAY

Federal Rule	Florida Stat. §	Description
801	90.801; 90.803(18)	Definitions That Apply to This Article; Exclusions from Hearsay
802	90.802	The Rule Against Hearsay
803	90.803; 90.706	Exceptions to the Rule Against Hearsay — Regardless of Whether the Declarant Is Available as a Witness
804	90.804	Exceptions to the Rule Against Hearsay — When the Declarant Is Unavailable as a Witness
805	90.805	Hearsay Within Hearsay
806	90.806	Attacking and Supporting the Declarant's Credibility
807	—	Residual Exception

Federal Rule 801. Definitions That Apply to This Article; Exclusions from Hearsay

(a) Statement. "Statement" means a person's oral assertion, written assertion, or nonverbal conduct, if the person intended it as an assertion.

(b) Declarant. "Declarant" means the person who made the statement.

(c) Hearsay. "Hearsay" means a statement that:

(1) the declarant does not make while testifying at the current trial or hearing; and

(2) a party offers in evidence to prove the truth of the matter asserted in the statement.

(d) Statements That Are Not Hearsay. A statement that meets the following conditions is not hearsay:

(1) *A Declarant-Witness's Prior Statement.* The declarant testifies and is subject to cross-examination about a prior statement, and the statement:

    (A) is inconsistent with the declarant's testimony and was given under penalty of perjury at a trial, hearing, or other proceeding or in a deposition;

    (B) is consistent with the declarant's testimony and is offered to rebut an express or implied charge that the declarant recently fabricated it or acted from a recent improper influence or motive in so testifying; or

    (C) identifies a person as someone the declarant perceived earlier.

(2) *An Opposing Party's Statement.* The statement is offered against an opposing party and:

    (A) was made by the party in an individual or representative capacity;

    (B) is one the party manifested that it adopted or believed to be true;

    (C) was made by a person whom the party authorized to make a statement on the subject;

    (D) was made by the party's agent or employee on a matter within the scope of that relationship and while it existed; or

    (E) was made by the party's coconspirator during and in furtherance of the conspiracy.

The statement must be considered but does not by itself establish the declarant's authority under (C); the existence or scope of the relationship under (D); or the existence of the conspiracy or participation in it under (E).

ADVISORY COMMITTEE'S NOTE

INTRODUCTORY NOTE: THE HEARSAY PROBLEM

The factors to be considered in evaluating the testimony of a witness are perception, memory, and narration. Morgan, Hearsay Dangers and the Application of the Hearsay Concept, 62 Harv.L. Rev. 177 (1948), Selected Writings on Evidence and Trial 764, 765 (Fryer ed. 1957); Shientag, Cross-

Examination—A Judge's Viewpoint, 3 Record 12 (1948); Strahorn, A Reconsideration of the Hearsay Rule and Admissions, 85 U.Pa. L. Rev. 484, 485 (1937), Selected Writings, *supra*, 756, 757; Weinstein, Probative Force of Hearsay, 46 Iowa L. Rev. 331 (1961). Sometimes a fourth is added, sincerity, but in fact it seems merely to be an aspect of the three already mentioned.

In order to encourage the witness to do his best with respect to each of these factors, and to expose any inaccuracies which may enter in, the Anglo-American tradition has evolved three conditions under which witnesses will ideally be required to testify: (1) under oath, (2) in the personal presence of the trier of fact, (3) subject to cross-examination.

(1) Standard procedure calls for the swearing of witnesses. While the practice is perhaps less effective than in an earlier time, no disposition to relax the requirement is apparent, other than to allow affirmation by persons with scruples against taking oaths.

(2) The demeanor of the witness traditionally has been believed to furnish trier and opponent with valuable clues. *Universal Camera Corp. v. N.L.R.B.*, 340 U.S. 474, 495 496 (1951); Sahm, Demeanor Evidence: Elusive and Intangible Imponderables, 47 A.B.A.J. 580 (1961), quoting numerous authorities. The witness himself will probably be impressed with the solemnity of the occasion and the possibility of public disgrace. Willingness to falsify may reasonably become more difficult in the presence of the person against whom directed. Rules 26 and 43(a) of the Federal Rules of Criminal and Civil Procedure, respectively, include the general requirement that testimony be taken orally in open court. The Sixth Amendment right of confrontation is a manifestation of these beliefs and attitudes.

(3) Emphasis on the basis of the hearsay rule today tends to center upon the condition of cross-examination. All may not agree with Wigmore that cross-examination is "beyond doubt the greatest legal engine ever invented for the discovery of truth," but all will agree with his statement that it has become a "vital feature" of the Anglo-American system. 5 Wigmore § 1367, p. 29. The belief, or perhaps hope, that cross-examination is effective in exposing imperfections of perception, memory, and narration is fundamental. Morgan, Foreword to Model Code of Evidence 37 (1942).

The logic of the preceding discussion might suggest that no testimony be received unless in full compliance with the three ideal conditions. No one advocates this position. Common sense tells that much evidence which is not given under the three conditions may be inherently superior to much that is. Moreover, when the choice is between evidence which is less than best and no evidence at all, only clear folly would dictate an across-the-board policy of doing without. The problem thus resolves itself into effecting a sensible accommodation between these considerations and the desirability of giving testimony under the ideal conditions.

The solution evolved by the common law has been a general rule excluding hearsay but subject to numerous exceptions under circumstances supposed to furnish guarantees of trustworthiness. Criticisms of this scheme are that it is bulky and complex, fails to screen good from bad hearsay realistically, and inhibits the growth of the law of evidence.

Since no one advocates excluding all hearsay, three possible solutions may be considered: (1) abolish the rule against hearsay and admit all hearsay; (2) admit hearsay possessing sufficient probative force, but with procedural safeguards; (3) revise the present system of class exceptions.

(1) Abolition of the hearsay rule would be the simplest solution. The effect would not be automatically to abolish the giving of testimony under ideal conditions. If the declarant were available, compliance with the ideal conditions would be optional with either party. Thus the proponent could call the declarant as a witness as a form of presentation more impressive than his hearsay statement. Or the opponent could call the declarant to be cross-examined upon his statement. This is the tenor of Uniform Rule 63(1), admitting the hearsay declaration of a person "who is present at the hearing and available for cross-examination." Compare the treatment of declarations of available declarants in Rule 801(d)(1) of the instant rules. If the declarant were unavailable, a rule of free admissibility would make no distinctions in

terms of degrees of noncompliance with the ideal conditions and would exact no quid pro quo in the form of assurances of trustworthiness. Rule 503 of the Model Code did exactly that, providing for the admissibility of any hearsay declaration by an unavailable declarant, finding support in the Massachusetts act of 1898, enacted at the instance of Thayer, Mass.Gen.L. 1932, c. 233 § 65, and in the English act of 1938, St.1938, c. 28, Evidence. Both are limited to civil cases. The draftsmen of the Uniform Rules chose a less advanced and more conventional position. Comment, Uniform Rule 63. The present Advisory Committee has been unconvinced of the wisdom of abandoning the traditional requirement of some particular assurance of credibility as a condition precedent to admitting the hearsay declaration of an unavailable declarant.

In criminal cases, the Sixth Amendment requirement of confrontation would no doubt move into a large part of the area presently occupied by the hearsay rule in the event of the abolition of the latter. The resultant split between civil and criminal evidence is regarded as an undesirable development.

(2) Abandonment of the system of class exceptions in favor of individual treatment in the setting of the particular case, accompanied by procedural safeguards, has been impressively advocated. Weinstein, The Probative Force of Hearsay, 46 Iowa L. Rev. 331 (1961). Admissibility would be determined by weighing the probative force of the evidence against the possibility of prejudice, waste of time, and the availability of more satisfactory evidence. The bases of the traditional hearsay exceptions would be helpful in assessing probative force. Ladd, The Relationship of the Principles of Exclusionary Rules of Evidence to the Problem of Proof, 18 Minn.L. Rev. 506 (1934). Procedural safeguards would consist of notice of intention to use hearsay, free comment by the judge on the weight of the evidence, and a greater measure of authority in both trial and appellate judges to deal with evidence on the basis of weight. The Advisory Committee has rejected this approach to hearsay as involving too great a measure of judicial discretion, minimizing the predictability of rulings, enhancing the difficulties of preparation for trial, adding a further element to the already over-complicated congeries of pretrial procedures, and requiring substantially different rules for civil and criminal cases. The only way in which the probative force of hearsay differs from the probative force of other testimony is in the absence of oath, demeanor, and cross-examination as aids in determining credibility. For a judge to exclude evidence because he does not believe it has been described as "altogether atypical, extraordinary...." Chadbourn, Bentham and the Hearsay Rule—A Benthamic View of Rule 63(4)(c) of the Uniform Rules of Evidence, 75 Harv.L. Rev. 932, 947 (1962).

(3) The approach to hearsay in these rules is that of the common law, i.e., a general rule excluding hearsay, with exceptions under which evidence is not required to be excluded even though hearsay. The traditional hearsay exceptions are drawn upon for the exceptions, collected under two rules, one dealing with situations where availability of the declarant is regarded as immaterial and the other with those where unavailability is made a condition to the admission of the hearsay statement. Each of the two rules concludes with a provision for hearsay statements not within one of the specified exceptions "but having comparable circumstantial guarantees of trustworthiness." Rules 803(24) and [804(b)(5)]. This plan is submitted as calculated to encourage growth and development in this area of the law, while conserving the values and experience of the past as a guide to the future.

CONFRONTATION AND DUE PROCESS

Until very recently, decisions invoking the confrontation clause of the Sixth Amendment were surprisingly few, a fact probably explainable by the former inapplicability of the clause to the states and by the hearsay rule's occupancy of much the same ground. The pattern which emerges from the earlier cases invoking the clause is substantially that of the hearsay rule, applied to criminal cases: an accused is entitled to have the witnesses against him testify under oath, in the presence of himself and trier, subject to cross-examination; yet considerations of public policy and necessity require the recognition of such exceptions as dying declarations and former testimony of unavailable witnesses. *Mattox v. United States*, 156 U.S. 237 (1895); *Motes v. United States*, 178 U.S. 458 (1900); *Delaney v. United States*, 263 U.S. 586

(1924). Beginning with *Snyder v. Massachusetts*, 291 U.S. 97 (1934), the Court began to speak of confrontation as an aspect of procedural due process, thus extending its applicability to state cases and to federal cases other than criminal. The language of Snyder was that of an elastic concept of hearsay. The deportation case of *Bridges v. Wixon*, 326 U.S. 135 (1945), may be read broadly as imposing a strictly construed right of confrontation in all kinds of cases or narrowly as the product of a failure of the Immigration and Naturalization Service to follow its own rules. *In re Oliver*, 333 U.S. 257 (1948), ruled that cross-examination was essential to due process in a state contempt proceeding, but in *United States v. Nugent*, 346 U.S. 1 (1953), the court held that it was not an essential aspect of a "hearing" for a conscientious objector under the Selective Service Act. *Stein v. New York*, 346 U.S. 156, 196 (1953), disclaimed any purpose to read the hearsay rule into the Fourteenth Amendment, but in *Greene v. McElroy*, 360 U.S. 474 (1959), revocation of security clearance without confrontation and cross-examination was held unauthorized, and a similar result was reached in *Willner v. Committee on Character*, 373 U.S. 96 (1963). Ascertaining the constitutional dimensions of the confrontation-hearsay aggregate against the background of these cases is a matter of some difficulty, yet the general pattern is at least not inconsistent with that of the hearsay rule.

In 1965 the confrontation clause was held applicable to the states. *Pointer v. Texas*, 380 U.S. 400 (1965). Prosecution use of former testimony given at a preliminary hearing where petitioner was not represented by counsel was a violation of the clause. The same result would have followed under conventional hearsay doctrine read in the light of a constitutional right to counsel, and nothing in the opinion suggests any difference in essential outline between the hearsay rule and the right of confrontation. In the companion case of *Douglas v. Alabama*, 380 U.S. 415 (1965), however, the result reached by applying the confrontation clause is one reached less readily via the hearsay rule. A confession implicating petitioner was put before the jury by reading it to the witness in portions and asking if he made that statement. The witness refused to answer on grounds of self-incrimination. The result, said the Court, was to deny cross-examination, and hence confrontation. True, it could broadly be said that the confession was a hearsay statement which for all practical purposes was put in evidence. Yet a more easily accepted explanation of the opinion is that its real thrust was in the direction of curbing undesirable prosecutorial behavior, rather than merely applying rules of exclusion, and that the confrontation clause was the means selected to achieve this end. Comparable facts and a like result appeared in *Brookhart v. Janis*, 384 U.S. 1 (1966).

The pattern suggested in *Douglas* was developed further and more distinctly in a pair of cases at the end of the 1966 term. *United States v. Wade*, 388 U.S. 218 (1967), and *Gilbert v. California*, 388 U.S. 263 (1967), hinged upon practices followed in identifying accused persons before trial. This pretrial identification was said to be so decisive an aspect of the case that accused was entitled to have counsel present; a pretrial identification made in the absence of counsel was not itself receivable in evidence and, in addition, might fatally infect a courtroom identification. The presence of counsel at the earlier identification was described as a necessary prerequisite for "a meaningful confrontation at trial." *United States v. Wade, supra*, 388 U.S. at p. 236. *Wade* involved no evidence of the fact of a prior identification and hence was not susceptible of being decided on hearsay grounds. In *Gilbert*, witnesses did testify to an earlier identification, readily classifiable as hearsay under a fairly strict view of what constitutes hearsay. The Court, however, carefully avoided basing the decision on the hearsay ground, choosing confrontation instead. 388 U.S. 263, 272, n.3. See also *Parker v. Gladden*, 385 U.S. 363 (1966), holding that the right of confrontation was violated when the bailiff made prejudicial statements to jurors, and Note, 75 Yale L.J. 1434 (1966).

Under the earlier cases, the confrontation clause may have been little more than a constitutional embodiment of the hearsay rule, even including traditional exceptions but with some room for expanding them along similar lines. But under the recent cases the impact of the clause clearly extends beyond the confines of the hearsay rule. These considerations have led the Advisory Committee to conclude that a hearsay rule can function usefully as an adjunct to the confrontation right in constitutional areas and independently in nonconstitutional areas. In recognition of the separateness of the confrontation clause and the hearsay rule, and to avoid inviting collisions between them or between the hearsay rule and other exclusionary principles, the exceptions set forth in Rules 803 and 804 are stated in terms of exemption from the general exclusionary mandate of the hearsay rule, rather than in positive terms of admissibility. See Uniform Rule 63(1) to (31) and California Evidence Code §§ 1200–1340.

Subdivision (a). The definition of "statement" assumes importance because the term is used in the definition of hearsay in subdivision (c). The effect of the definition of "statement" is to exclude from the operation of the hearsay rule all evidence of conduct, verbal or nonverbal, not intended as an assertion. The key to the definition is that nothing is an assertion unless intended to be one.

It can scarcely be doubted that an assertion made in words is intended by the declarant to be an assertion. Hence verbal assertions readily fall into the category of "statement." Whether nonverbal conduct should be regarded as a statement for purposes of defining hearsay requires further consideration. Some nonverbal conduct, such as the act of pointing to identify a suspect in a lineup, is clearly the equivalent of words, assertive in nature, and to be regarded as a statement. Other nonverbal conduct, however, may be offered as evidence that the person acted as he did because of his belief in the existence of the condition sought to be proved, from which belief the existence of the condition may be inferred. This sequence is, arguably, in effect an assertion of the existence of the condition and hence properly includable within the hearsay concept. See Morgan, Hearsay Dangers and the Application of the Hearsay Concept, 62 Harv.L.Rev. 177, 214, 217 (1948), and the elaboration in Finman, Implied Assertions as Hearsay: Some Criticisms of the Uniform Rules of Evidence, 14 Stan.L.Rev. 682 (1962). Admittedly evidence of this character is untested with respect to the perception, memory, and narration (or their equivalents) of the actor, but the Advisory Committee is of the view that these dangers are minimal in the absence of an intent to assert and do not justify the loss of the evidence on hearsay grounds. No class of evidence is free of the possibility of fabrication, but the likelihood is less with nonverbal than with assertive verbal conduct. The situations giving rise to the nonverbal conduct are such as virtually to eliminate questions of sincerity. Motivation, the nature of the conduct, and the presence or absence of reliance will bear heavily upon the weight to be given the evidence. Falknor, The "Hear-Say" Rule as a "See-Do" Rule: Evidence of Conduct, 33 Rocky Mt.L.Rev. 133 (1961). Similar considerations govern nonassertive verbal conduct and verbal conduct which is assertive but offered as a basis for inferring something other than the matter asserted, also excluded from the definition of hearsay by the language of subdivision (c).

When evidence of conduct is offered on the theory that it is not a statement, and hence not hearsay, a preliminary determination will be required to determine whether an assertion is intended. The rule is so worded as to place the burden upon the party claiming that the intention existed; ambiguous and doubtful cases will be resolved against him and in favor of admissibility. The determination involves no greater difficulty than many other preliminary questions of fact. Maguire, The Hearsay System: Around and Through the Thicket, 14 Vand.L.Rev. 741, 765–767 (1961).

For similar approaches, see Uniform Rule 62(1); California Evidence Code §§ 225, 1200; Kansas Code of Civil Procedure § 60-459(a); New Jersey Evidence Rule 62(1).

Subdivision (c). The definition follows along familiar lines in including only statements offered to prove the truth of the matter asserted. McCormick § 225; 5 Wigmore § 1361, 6 *id.* § 1766. If the significance of an offered statement lies solely in the fact that it was made, no issue is raised as to the truth of anything asserted, and the statement is not hearsay. Emich Motors Corp. v. General Motors Corp., 181 F.2d 70 (7th Cir. 1950), rev'd on other grounds 340 U.S. 558, letters of complaint from customers offered as a reason for cancellation of dealer's franchise, to rebut contention that franchise was revoked for refusal to finance sales through affiliated finance company. The effect is to exclude from hearsay the entire category of "verbal acts" and "verbal parts of an act," in which the statement itself affects the legal rights of the parties or is a circumstance bearing on conduct affecting their rights.

The definition of hearsay must, of course, be read with reference to the definition of statement set forth in subdivision (a).

Testimony given by a witness in the course of court proceedings is excluded since there is compliance with all the ideal conditions for testifying.

Subdivision (d). Several types of statements which would otherwise literally fall within the definition are expressly excluded from it:

(1) *Prior statement by witness.* Considerable controversy has attended the question whether a prior out-of-court statement by a person now available for cross-examination concerning it, under oath and in the presence of the trier of fact, should be classed as hearsay. If the witness admits on the stand that he made the statement and that it was true, he adopts the statement and there is no hearsay problem. The hearsay problem arises when the witness on the stand denies having made the statement or admits having made it but denies its truth. The argument in favor of treating these latter statements as hearsay is based upon the ground that the conditions of oath, cross-examination, and demeanor observation did not prevail at the time the statement was made and cannot adequately be supplied by the later examination. The logic of the situation is troublesome. So far as concerns the oath, its mere presence has never been regarded as sufficient to remove a statement from the hearsay category, and it receives much less emphasis than cross-examination as a truth-compelling device. While strong expressions are found to the effect that no conviction can be had or important right taken away on the basis of statements not made under fear of prosecution for perjury, Bridges v. Wixon, 326 U.S. 135 (1945), the fact is that, of the many common law exceptions to the hearsay rule, only that for reported testimony has required the statement to have been made under oath. Nor is it satisfactorily explained why cross-examination cannot be conducted subsequently with success. The decisions contending most vigorously for its inadequacy in fact demonstrate quite thorough exploration of the weaknesses and doubts attending the earlier statement. State v. Saporen, 205 Minn. 358 (1939); Ruhala v. Roby, 379 Mich. 102 (1967); People v. Johnson, 68 Cal.2d 646 (1968). In respect to demeanor, as Judge Learned Hand observed in Di Carlo v. United States, 6 F.2d 364 (2d Cir. 1925), when the jury decides that the truth is not what the witness says now, but what he said before, they are still deciding from what they see and hear in court. The bulk of the case law nevertheless has been against allowing prior statements of witnesses to be used generally as substantive evidence. Most of the writers and Uniform Rule 63(1) have taken the opposite position.

The position taken by the Advisory Committee in formulating this part of the rule is founded upon an unwillingness to countenance the general use of prior prepared statements as substantive evidence, but with a recognition that particular circumstances call for a contrary result. The judgment is one more of experience than of logic. The rule requires in each instance, as a general safeguard, that the declarant actually testify as a witness, and it then enumerates three situations in which the statement is excepted from the category of hearsay. Compare Uniform Rule 63(1) which allows any out-of-court statement of a declarant who is present at the trial and available for cross-examination.

(A) Prior inconsistent statements traditionally have been admissible to impeach but not as substantive evidence. Under the rule they are substantive evidence. As has been said by the California Law Revision Commission with respect to a similar provision:

"Section 1235 admits inconsistent statements of witnesses because the dangers against which the hearsay rule is designed to protect are largely nonexistent. The declarant is in court and may be examined and cross-examined in regard to his statements and their subject matter. In many cases, the inconsistent statement is more likely to be true than the testimony of the witness at the trial because it was made nearer in time to the matter to which it relates and is less likely to be influenced by the controversy that gave rise to the litigation. The trier of fact has the declarant before it and can observe his demeanor and the nature of his testimony as he denies or tries to explain away the inconsistency. Hence, it is in as good a position to determine the truth or falsity of the prior statement as it is to determine the truth or falsity of the inconsistent testimony given in court. Moreover, Section 1235 will provide a party with desirable protection against the 'turncoat' witness who changes his story on the stand and deprives the party calling him of evidence essential to his case." Comment, California Evidence Code § 1235. See also McCormick § 39. The Advisory Committee finds these views more convincing than those expressed in People v. Johnson, 68 Cal.2d 646 (1968). The constitutionality of the Advisory Committee's view was upheld in California v. Green, 399 U.S. 149 (1970). Moreover, the requirement that the statement be inconsistent with the testimony given assures a thorough exploration of both versions while the witness is on the stand and bars any general and indiscriminate use of previously prepared statements.

(B) Prior consistent statements traditionally have been admissible to rebut charges of recent fabrication or improper influence or motive but not as substantive evidence. Under the rule they are substantive evidence. The prior statement is consistent with the testimony given on the stand, and, if the opposite party wishes to open the door for its admission in evidence, no sound reason is apparent why it should not be received generally.

(C) The admission of evidence of identification finds substantial support, although it falls beyond a doubt in the category of prior out-of-court statements. Illustrative are People v. Gould, 54 Cal.2d 621 (1960); Judy v. State, 218 Md. 168 (1958); State v. Simmons, 63 Wash.2d 17 (1963); California Evidence Code § 1238; New Jersey Evidence Rule 63(1)(c); N.Y.Code of Criminal Procedure § 393-b. Further cases are found in 4 Wigmore § 1130. The basis is the generally unsatisfactory and inconclusive nature of courtroom identifications as compared with those made at an earlier time under less suggestive conditions. The Supreme Court considered the admissibility of evidence of prior identification in Gilbert v. California, 388 U.S. 263 (1967). Exclusion of lineup identification was held to be required because the accused did not then have the assistance of counsel. Significantly, the Court carefully refrained from placing its decision on the ground that testimony as to the making of a prior out-of-court identification ("That's the man") violated either the hearsay rule or the right of confrontation because not made under oath, subject to immediate cross-examination, in the presence of the trier. Instead the Court observed:

"There is a split among the States concerning the admissibility of prior extra-judicial identifications, as independent evidence of identity, both by the witness and third parties present at the prior identification. See 71 A.L.R.2d 449. It has been held that the prior identification is hearsay, and, when admitted through the testimony of the identifier, is merely a prior consistent statement. The recent trend, however, is to admit the prior identification under the exception that admits as substantive evidence a prior communication by a witness who is available for cross-examination at the trial. See 5 A.L.R.2d Later Case Service 1225–1228...." 388 U.S. at 272, n. 3.

(2) *Admissions.* Admissions by a party-opponent are excluded from the category of hearsay on the theory that their admissibility in evidence is the result of the adversary system rather than satisfaction of the conditions of the hearsay rule. Strahorn, A Reconsideration of the Hearsay Rule and Admissions, 85 U.Pa.L.Rev. 484, 564 (1937); Morgan, Basic Problems of Evidence 265 (1962); 4 Wigmore § 1048. No guarantee of trustworthiness is required in the case of an admission. The freedom which admissions have enjoyed from technical demands of searching for an assurance of trustworthiness in some against-interest circumstance, and from the restrictive influences of the opinion rule and the rule requiring firsthand knowledge, when taken with the apparently prevalent satisfaction with the results, calls for generous treatment of this avenue to admissibility.

The rule specifies five categories of statements for which the responsibility of a party is considered sufficient to justify reception in evidence against him:

(A) A party's own statement is the classic example of an admission. If he has a representative capacity and the statement is offered against him in that capacity, no inquiry whether he was acting in the representative capacity in making the statement is required; the statement need only be relevant to represent affairs. To the same effect is California Evidence Code § 1220. Compare Uniform Rule 63(7), requiring a statement to be made in a representative capacity to be admissible against a party in a representative capacity.

(B) Under established principles an admission may be made by adopting or acquiescing in the statement of another. While knowledge of contents would ordinarily be essential, this is not inevitably so: "X is a reliable person and knows what he is talking about." See McCormick § 246, p. 527, n. 15. Adoption or acquiescence may be manifested in any appropriate manner. When silence is relied upon, the theory is that the person would, under the circumstances, protest the statement made in his presence, if untrue. The decision in each case calls for an evaluation in terms of probable human behavior. In civil cases, the results have generally been satisfactory. In criminal cases, however, troublesome questions have been raised by decisions holding that failure to deny is an admission: the inference is a fairly weak one, to begin with; silence may be motivated by advice of counsel or realization that "anything you say may be used against you"; unusual opportunity is afforded to manufacture evidence; and encroachment upon the privilege against self-incrimination seems inescapably to be involved. However, recent decisions of the Supreme Court relating to custodial interrogation and the right to counsel appear to resolve these difficulties. Hence the rule contains no special provisions concerning failure to deny in criminal cases.

(C) No authority is required for the general proposition that a statement authorized by a party to be made should have the status of an admission by the party. However, the question arises whether only statements to third persons should be so regarded, to the exclusion of statements by the agent to the principal. The rule is phrased broadly so as to encompass both. While it may be argued that the agent authorized to make statements to his principal does not speak for him, Morgan, Basic Problems of Evidence 273 (1962), communication to an outsider has not generally been thought to be an essential characteristic of an admission. Thus a party's books or records are usable against him, without regard to any intent to disclose to third persons. 5 Wigmore § 1557. See also McCormick § 78, pp. 159–161. In accord is New Jersey Evidence Rule 63(8)(a). Cf. Uniform Rule 63(8)(a) and California Evidence Code § 1222 which limit status as an admission in this regard to statements authorized by the party to be made "for" him, which is perhaps an ambiguous limitation to statements to third persons. Falknor, Vicarious Admissions and the Uniform Rules, 14 Vand.L.Rev. 855, 860–861 (1961).

(D) The tradition has been to test the admissibility of statements by agents, as admissions, by applying the usual test of agency. Was the admission made by the agent acting in the scope of his employment? Since few principals employ agents for the purpose of making damaging statements, the usual result was exclusion of the statement. Dissatisfaction with this loss of valuable and helpful evidence has been increasing. A substantial trend favors admitting statements related to a matter within the scope of the agency or employment. Grayson v. Williams, 256 F.2d 61 (10th Cir. 1958); Koninklijke Luchtvaart Maatschappij N.V. KLM Royal Dutch Airlines v. Tuller, 292 F.2d 775, 784 (1961); Martin v. Savage Truck Lines, Inc., 121 F.Supp. 417 (D.D.C. 1954), and numerous state court decisions collected in 4 Wigmore, 1964 Supp. pp. 66–73, with comments by the editor that the statements should have been excluded as not within scope of agency. For the traditional view see Northern Oil Co. v. Socony Mobil Oil Co., 347 F.2d 81, 85 (2d Cir. 1965) and cases cited therein. Similar provisions are found in Uniform Rule 63(9)(a), Kansas Code of Civil Procedure § 60-460(i)(1), and New Jersey Evidence Rule 63(9)(a).

(E) The limitation upon the admissibility of statements of co-conspirators to those made "during the course and in furtherance of the conspiracy" is in the accepted pattern. While the broadened view of agency taken in item (iv) might suggest wider admissibility of statements of co-conspirators, the agency theory of conspiracy is at best a fiction and ought not to serve as a basis for admissibility beyond that already established. See Levie, Hearsay and Conspiracy, 52 Mich.L.Rev. 1159 (1954); Comment, 25 U.Chi.L.Rev. 530 (1958). The rule is consistent with the position of the Supreme Court in denying admissibility to statements made after the objectives of the conspiracy have either failed or been achieved. Krulewitch v. United States, 336 U.S. 440 (1949); Wong Sun v. United States, 371 U.S. 471, 490 (1963). For similarly limited provisions see California Evidence Code § 1223 and New Jersey Rule 63(9)(b). Cf. Uniform Rule 63(9)(b).

REPORT OF HOUSE COMMITTEE ON THE JUDICIARY

Present federal law, except in the Second Circuit, permits the use of prior inconsistent statements of a witness for impeachment only. Rule 801(d)(1) as proposed by the Court would have permitted all such statements to be admissible as substantive evidence, an approach followed by a small but growing number of State jurisdictions and recently held constitutional in *California* v. *Green*, 399 U.S. 149

(1970). Although there was some support expressed for the Court Rule, based largely on the need to counteract the effect of witness intimidation in criminal cases, the Committee decided to adopt a compromise version of the Rule similar to the position of the Second Circuit. The Rule as amended draws a distinction between types of prior inconsistent statements (other than statements of identification of a person made after perceiving him which are currently admissible, see *United States* v. *Anderson*, 406 F.2d 719, 720 (4th Cir.), cert. denied, 395 U.S. 967 (1969)) and allows only those made while the declarant was subject to cross-examination at a trial or hearing or in a deposition, to be admissible for their truth. Compare *United States* v. *DeSisto*, 329 F.2d 929 (2nd Cir.), cert. denied, 377 U.S. 979 (1964); *United States* v. *Cunningham*, 446 F.2d 194 (2nd Cir. 1971) (restricting the admissibility of prior inconsistent statements as substantive evidence to those made under oath in a formal proceeding, but not requiring that there have been an opportunity for cross-examination). The rationale for the Committee's decision is that (1) unlike in most other situations involving unsworn or oral statements, there can be no dispute as to whether the prior statement was made; and (2) the context of a formal proceeding, an oath, and the opportunity for cross-examination provide firm additional assurances of the reliability of the prior statement.

REPORT OF SENATE COMMITTEE ON THE JUDICIARY

Rule 801 defines what is and what is not hearsay for the purpose of admitting a prior statement as substantive evidence. A prior statement of a witness at a trial or hearing which is inconsistent with his testimony is, of course, always admissible for the purpose of impeaching the witness' credibility.

As submitted by the Supreme Court, subdivision (d)(1)(A) made admissible as substantive evidence the prior statement of a witness inconsistent with his present testimony.

The House severely limited the admissibility of prior inconsistent statements by adding a requirement that the prior statement must have been subject to cross-examination, thus precluding even the use of grand jury statements. The requirement that the prior statement must have been subject to cross-examination appears unnecessary since this rule comes into play only when the witness testifies in the present trial. At that time, he is on the stand and can explain an earlier position and be cross-examined as to both.

The requirement that the statement be under oath also appears unnecessary. Notwithstanding the absence of an oath contemporaneous with the statement, the witness, when on the stand, qualifying or denying the prior statement, is under oath. In any event, of all the many recognized exceptions to the hearsay rule, only one (former testimony) requires that the out-of-court statement have been made under oath. With respect to the lack of evidence of the demeanor of the witness at the time of the prior statement, it would be difficult to improve upon Judge Learned Hand's observation that when the jury decides that the truth is not what the witness says now but what he said before, they are still deciding from what they see and hear in court.[28]

The rule as submitted by the Court has positive advantages. The prior statement was made nearer in time to the events, when memory was fresher and intervening influences had not been brought into play. A realistic method is provided for dealing with the turncoat witness who changes his story on the stand.[29]

New Jersey, California, and Utah have adopted a rule similar to this one; and Nevada, New Mexico, and Wisconsin have adopted the identical Federal rule.

For all of these reasons, we think the House amendment should be rejected and the rule as submitted by the Supreme Court reinstated.[30]

---

[28] Di Carlo v. United States, 6 F.2d 364 (2d Cir. 1925).
[29] See Comment, California Evidence Code § 1235; McCormick, Evidence, § 38 (2nd ed. 1972).

As submitted by the Supreme Court and as passed by the House, subdivision (d)(1)(C) of rule 801 made admissible the prior statement identifying a person made after perceiving him. The committee decided to delete this provision because of the concern that a person could be convicted solely upon evidence admissible under this subdivision.

The House approved the long-accepted rule that "a statement by a coconspirator of a party during the course and in furtherance of the conspiracy" is not hearsay as it was submitted by the Supreme Court. While the rule refers to a coconspirator, it is this committee's understanding that the rule is meant to carry forward the universally accepted doctrine that a joint venturer is considered as a coconspirator for the purposes of this rule even though no conspiracy has been charged. *United States* v. *Rinaldi*, 393 F.2d 97, 99 (2d Cir.), cert. denied 393 U.S. 913 (1968); *United States* v. *Spencer*, 415 F.2d 1301, 1304 (7th Cir. 1969).

CONFERENCE REPORT

Rule 801 supplies some basic definitions for the rules of evidence that deal with hearsay. Rule 801(d)(1) defines certain statements as not hearsay. The Senate amendments make two changes in it.

The House bill provides that a statement is not hearsay if the declarant testifies and is subject to cross-examination concerning the statement and if the statement is inconsistent with his testimony and was given under oath subject to cross-examination and subject to the penalty of perjury at a trial or hearing or in a deposition. The Senate amendment drops the requirement that the prior statement be given under oath subject to cross-examination and subject to the penalty of perjury at a trial or hearing or in a deposition.

The Conference adopts the Senate amendment with an amendment, so that the rule now requires that the prior inconsistent statement be given under oath subject to the penalty of perjury at a trial, hearing, or other proceeding, or in a deposition. The rule as adopted covers statements before a grand jury. Prior inconsistent statements may, of course, be used for impeaching the credibility of a witness. When the prior inconsistent statement is one made by a defendant in a criminal case, it is covered by Rule 801(d)(2).

The House bill provides that a statement is not hearsay if the declarant testifies and is subject to cross-examination concerning the statement and the statement is one of identification of a person made after perceiving him. The Senate amendment eliminated this provision.

The Conference adopts the Senate amendment.

ADVISORY COMMITTEE'S NOTE (1997 AMENDMENT)

Rule 801(d)(2) has been amended in order to respond to three issues raised by *Bourjaily* v. *United States*, 483 U.S. 171 (1987). First, the amendment codifies the holding in *Bourjaily* by stating expressly that a court shall consider the contents of a coconspirator's statement in determining "the existence of

---

30 It would appear that some of the opposition to this Rule is based on a concern that a person could be convicted solely upon evidence admissible under this Rule. The Rule, however, is not addressed to the question of the sufficiency of evidence to send a case to the jury, but merely as to its admissibility. Factual circumstances could well arise where, if this were the sole evidence, dismissal would be appropriate.

the conspiracy and the participation therein of the declarant and the party against whom the statement is offered." According to *Bourjaily*, Rule 104(a) requires these preliminary questions to be established by a preponderance of the evidence.

Second, the amendment resolves an issue on which the Court had reserved decision. It provides that the contents of the declarant's statement do not alone suffice to establish a conspiracy in which the declarant and the defendant participated. The court must consider in addition the circumstances surrounding the statement, such as the identity of the speaker, the context in which the statement was made, or evidence corroborating the contents of the statement in making its determination as to each preliminary question. This amendment is in accordance with existing practice. Every court of appeals that has resolved this issue requires some evidence in addition to the contents of the statement. *See, e.g., United States v. Beckham*, 968 F.2d 47, 51 (D.C.Cir. 1992); *United States v. Sepulveda*, 15 F.3d 1161, 1181–82 (1st Cir. 1993), *cert. denied*, 114 S.Ct. 2714 (1994); *United States v. Daly*, 842 F.2d 1380, 1386 (2d Cir.), *cert. denied*, 488 U.S. 821 (1988); *United States v. Clark*, 18 F.3d 1337, 1341–42 (6th Cir.), *cert. denied*, 115 S.Ct. 152 (1994); *United States v. Zambrana*, 841 F.2d 1320, 1344–45 (7th Cir. 1988); *United States v. Silverman*, 861 F.2d 571, 577 (9th Cir. 1988); *United States v. Gordon*, 844 F.2d 1397, 1402 (9th Cir. 1988); *United States v. Hernandez*, 829 F.2d 988, 993 (10th Cir. 1987), *cert. denied*, 485 U.S. 1013 (1988); *United States v. Byrom*, 910 F.2d 725, 736 (11th Cir. 1990).

Third, the amendment extends the reasoning of *Bourjaily* to statements offered under subdivisions (C) and (D) of Rule 801(d)(2). In *Bourjaily*, the Court rejected treating foundational facts pursuant to the law of agency in favor of an evidentiary approach governed by Rule 104(a). The Advisory Committee believes it appropriate to treat analogously preliminary questions relating to the declarant's authority under subdivision (C), and the agency or employment relationship and scope thereof under subdivision (D).

ADVISORY COMMITTEE'S NOTE (2011 AMENDMENT)

The language of Rule 801 has been amended as part of the general restyling of the Evidence Rules to make them more easily understood and to make style and terminology consistent throughout the rules. These changes are intended to be stylistic only. There is no intent to change any result in any ruling on evidence admissibility.

Statements falling under the hearsay exclusion provided by Rule 801(d)(2) are no longer referred to as "admissions" in the title to the subdivision. The term "admissions" is confusing because not all statements covered by the exclusion are admissions in the colloquial sense — a statement can be within the exclusion even if it "admitted" nothing and was not against the party's interest when made. The term "admissions" also raises confusion in comparison with the Rule 804(b)(3) exception for declarations against interest. No change in application of the exclusion is intended.

Florida Stat. § 90.801. Hearsay; Definitions; Exceptions

(1) The following definitions apply under this chapter:

(a) A "statement" is:

1. An oral or written assertion; or

2. Nonverbal conduct of a person if it is intended by the person as an assertion.

(b) A "declarant" is a person who makes a statement.

(c) "Hearsay" is a statement, other than one made by the declarant while testifying at the trial or hearing, offered in evidence to prove the truth of the matter asserted.

(2) A statement is not hearsay if the declarant testifies at the trial or hearing and is subject to cross-examination concerning the statement and the statement is:

(a) Inconsistent with the declarant's testimony and was given under oath subject to the penalty of perjury at a trial, hearing, or other proceeding or in a deposition;

(b) Consistent with the declarant's testimony and is offered to rebut an express or implied charge against the declarant of improper influence, motive, or recent fabrication; or

(c) One of identification of a person made after perceiving the person.

SPONSORS' NOTE (1976 ENACTMENT)

<u>Subsection (1)</u> This subsection which defines "statement" for the purpose of the application of the hearsay rule, adopts the generally accepted view that assertive conduct is subject to the hearsay rule and non-assertive conduct is not. See McCormick, <u>Evidence</u> § 250 (2nd ed. 1972); The Florida Bar, <u>Evidence in Florida</u> § 511 (1971). The effect of this definition is to exclude from the definitions of hearsay all conduct, both verbal and non-verbal, which is not intended by a person to be an assertion.

When evidence of conduct is offered by a party who claims that the evidence is not hearsay because it is not a statement, the court will make a preliminary determination as to whether the offering party has met its burden of showing that the assertion was not intended. If a witness points to a person in a lineup to identify him, the action is the equivalent of words being spoken by the witness and is a "statement."

The Advisory Committee Note to Proposed Federal Rule of Evidence 801 comments on the exclusion of implied assertions from the definition of hearsay:

> Other nonverbal conduct, however, may be offered as evidence that the person acted as he did because of his belief in the existence of the condition sought to be proved, from which belief the existence of the condition may be inferred. This sequence is, arguably, in effect an assertion of the existence of the condition and hence properly includable within the hearsay concept. See Morgan, Hearsay Dangers and the Application of the Hearsay Concept, 62 Harv. L. Rev. 177, 214, 217 (1948), and the elaboration in Finman, Implied Assertions as Hearsay: Some Criticisms of the Uniform Rules of Evidence, 14 Stan. L. Rev. 682 (1962). Admittedly evidence of this character is untested with respect to the perception, memory, and narration (or their equivalents) of the actor, but the Advisory Committee is of the view that these dangers are minimal in the absence of an intent to assert and do not justify the loss of the evidence on hearsay grounds. No class of evidence is free of the possibility of fabrication, but the likelihood is less with nonverbal than with assertive verbal conduct. The situations giving rise to the nonverbal conduct are such as virtually to eliminate questions of sincerity. Motivation, the nature of the conduct, and the presence or absence of reliance will bear heavily upon the weight to be given the evidence. Falknor, The "Hear-Say" Rule as a "See-Do" Rule: Evidence of Conduct, 33 Rocky Mt. L. Rev. 133 (1961). Similar considerations govern nonassertive verbal conduct and verbal conduct which is assertive but offered as a basis for inferring something other than the matter asserted, also excluded from the definition of hearsay....

See Calif. Evid. Code §§ 225, 1200; Kansas Code of Civ. Pro. § 60-459(a); New Jersey Evid. Rule 62(1); Fed. Rule Evid. 801(a).

This subsection adopts the generally accepted definition of hearsay. Professor McCormick states that hearsay evidence is:

testimony in court, or written evidence, of a statement made out of court, <u>the statement being offered as an assertion to show the truth of matters asserted</u> therein, and thus resting for its value upon the credibility of the out-of-court asserter. McCormick, <u>Evidence</u> § 246 (2nd ed. 1972) (emphasis added).

See <u>State Farm Mut. Auto. Ins. Co. v. Ganz</u>, 119 So. 2d 319 (Fla. 3rd Dist. 1960); Calif. Evid. Code § 1200; New Jersey Evid. Rule 63; Fed. Rule Evid. 801(c).

This subsection does not include verbal acts, i.e., when the significance of an offered statement lies solely in that it was made and not in its truthfulness. "[T]he state's witnesses testified to statements amounting to verbal acts. It is well settled that such statements are admissible in evidence and in nowise run afoul of the hearsay rule." <u>Pauline v. Lee</u>, 147 So.2d 359, 363 (Fla. 2nd Dist. 1962), <u>cert. denied</u>, 156 So.2d 389 (Fla. 1963). See <u>Chacon v. State</u>, 102 So.2d 578, 591 (Fla. 1958) (on rehearing).

<u>Subsection (2)</u> This subsection specifically excludes certain statements which otherwise would be hearsay, as defined in Subsection [(1)(c)]. See generally Ladd, <u>Some Highlights of the New Federal Rules of Evidence</u>, 1 Fla. St. U.L. Rev. 191, 197-214 (1973).

<u>Paragraph (a)</u> This paragraph excludes from the definition of hearsay certain out-of-court statements by a witness who testifies at the trial or hearing and is subject to cross-examination. Since the declarant is in court and may be cross-examined in regard to the statement, the dangers inherent in hearsay testimony are minimized. See 5 Wigmore, <u>Evidence</u> §§ 1361-1362 (3rd ed. 1940). The prior statement may be used as substantive evidence. It is unrealistic to believe that a jury properly discriminates when told to accept certain evidence as bearing only on the credibility of the witness. The prior statement may be more reliable than the present testimony.

As Dean Ladd stated in Ladd, <u>Some Highlights of the New Federal Rules of Evidence</u>, 1 Fla. St. U.L. Rev. 191, 200 (1973):

> The...rule is sound in reason and is practical and realistic. The witness who perceived the events in issue is present in court and has given testimony of those events under oath. If he admits making the inconsistent statement, he has the opportunity to explain it. If his explanation is not acceptable to the triers of fact, they may use what he admitted to be a prior inconsistent statement to discredit his testimony. If the triers of fact believed the witness spoke the truth in the prior statement that he admitted making, it is not reasonable to expect the triers to limit its use to credibility in their decision-making process regardless of a court's instruction that it may be used to discredit but not to prove. The mental gymnastics required to articulate and segregate the use of prior statements for impeachment purposes only makes the limitation rule a formalistic fiction in disregard of realism.

The constitutionality of a similar provision was upheld in <u>California v. Green</u>, 399 U.S. 149, 90 S.Ct. 1930, 26 L.Ed.2d 489 (1970).

Existing Florida law does not permit this broad use of inconsistent statements as substantive evidence. It was noted in <u>Tomlinson v. Peninsular Naval Stores Co.</u>, 61 Fla. 453, 55 So. 548 (1911) that, "[P]rior inconsistent statements may affect credibility, but they are not evidence to prove a fact, not otherwise shown." Apparently, the appellate courts were not again confronted with this issue until <u>Wallace v. Rashkow</u>, 270 So.2d 743, 744-45 (Fla. 3rd Dist. 1972), where, after commenting on the considerable criticism that the rule had drawn, the court distinguished the <u>Tomlinson</u> case and held it applicable only to situations in which there was not before the court other evidence of the facts in the statement:

> While the [Tomlinson] case is by no means illuminating on the legal issue involved, it appears to assert certain qualifying language to the general rule. That language is the last three words of the quoted phrase, to-wit: "not otherwise shown." In the decisions cited by the appellant, each involve a prior extrajudicial statement which is the <u>only</u> (court's emphasis) evidence contrary to

that offered by the appealing party. In this case, there is considerable testimony of the witnesses and parties, exclusive of the extrajudicial statement, upon which the jury could find that Wallace was contributorily negligent. In other words, the extrajudicial statement in this case would appear to be admissible under the qualifying language of the Tomlinson decision....

After explaining the limited application of the Tomlinson decision, the court went on to comment that the introduction of the statement was at the most harmless error.

Thus under the Wallace rationale, if there is other evidence introduced on the matter contained in the inconsistent statement, the prior statement can be used as affirmative proof. This section goes beyond that interpretation and allows the use of prior inconsistent statements as substantive evidence regardless of whether other evidence of the same facts is introduced.

In order for prior inconsistent statements to be introduced, Section 90.614 requires that generally the witness must be afforded an opportunity to explain or deny the statement before it is admissible.

See Calif. Evid. Code § 1235. Fed.Rule Evid. 801(d)(1) permits the use of this testimony only when it was given under oath, subject to the penalty of perjury, at a trial, hearing or deposition.

Paragraph (b) This section permits the use of prior consistent statements as substantive evidence when offered to rebut a charge of recent fabrication or improper influence or motive. Existing Florida law is in accord, with the exception that the statements are not always treated as substantive, see comment to paragraph (a). In Van Gallon v. State, 50 So.2d 882 (Fla.1951), the court stated:

We recognize the rule that a witness's testimony may not be corroborated by his own prior consistent statement and the exception that such a statement may become relevant if an attempt is made to show a recent fabrication. The exception is based on the theory that once the witness's story is undertaken, by imputation, insinuation, or direct evidence, to be assailed as a recent fabrication, the admission of an earlier consistent statement rebuts the suggestion of improper motive and the challenge of his integrity.

This rule has been followed in Sosa v. State, 215 So.2d 736, 743 (Fla. 1968) (concurring opinion) and Jackman v. State, 140 So.2d 627 (Fla. 3rd Dist. 1962) (statements established motive to falsify). See Fed. Rule Evid. 801(d)(1).

Paragraph (c) This paragraph makes admissible as substantive evidence a statement of identification made by a person soon after his perception, if the person who made the identification testifies and is available for cross-examination concerning the identification. The identification was made at a time closer to the event in controversy when the mind of the witness was clearer. Both the testimony of the person making the identification and of witnesses who were present when the identification occurred would be admissible. This paragraph does not make admissible unconstitutional line-up identifications, Gilbert v. California, 388 U.S. 263, 87 S.Ct. 1951, 18 L.Ed. 2d 1178 (1967); United States v. Wade, 388 U.S. 218, 87 S.Ct. 1926, 18 L.Ed. 2d 1149 (1967). For similar provisions, see Calif. Evid. Code § 1238; New Jersey Evid. Rule 63(1); New York Code of Crim. Pro. § 393(b); Fed. R. Evid. 801(d)(1).

The existing Florida rule on admissibility of statements concerning identification of a person made after perceiving him is something of a compromise between admissibility and inadmissibility. Such testimony is "admissible in rebuttal of testimony tending to impeach or discredit the testimony of the identifying witness, or to rebut a charge, imputation, or suggestion of falsity....[S]uch...may be considered in corroboration of the testimony of the identifying witness at the trial." Willis v. State, 208 So. 2d 458, 459 (Fla. 1st Dist.), aff'd, 217 So. 2d 106 (Fla. 1968). A later case, Stevens v. State, 251 So.2d 565 (Fla. 3rd Dist. 1971), makes it clear that such evidence is inadmissible as "original or substantive" evidence.

Florida Stat. § 90.803(18). Hearsay Exceptions; Availability of Declarant Immaterial [Admissions]

The provision of s. 90.802 to the contrary notwithstanding, the following are not inadmissible as evidence, even though the declarant is available as a witness:

....

(18) Admissions. A statement that is offered against a party and is:

(a) The party's own statement in either an individual or a representative capacity;

(b) A statement of which the party has manifested an adoption or belief in its truth;

(c) A statement by a person specifically authorized by the party to make a statement concerning the subject;

(d) A statement by the party's agent or servant concerning a matter within the scope of the agency or employment thereof, made during the existence of the relationship; or

(e) A statement by a person who was a coconspirator of the party during the course, and in furtherance, of the conspiracy. Upon request of counsel, the court shall instruct the jury that the conspiracy itself and each member's participation in it must be established by independent evidence, either before the introduction of any evidence or before evidence is admitted under this paragraph.

....

SPONSORS' NOTE (1976 ENACTMENT)

This subsection provides that admissions by a party are admissible as exceptions to hearsay. Existing law treats admissions as an exception to the hearsay rule although it tends to confuse "admissions" with "declarations against interest" and terms them "admissions against interest."

> It is well settled that an admission against interest may be introduced into evidence as substantive evidence of the truth of the matter stated. This is so even though the person making the admission against interest subsequently denies making such admission.

Seaboard Coast Line R.R. Co. v. Nieuwendaal, 253 So.2d 451, 452 (Fla.2nd Dist. 1971).

There are five types of statements included as admissions.

(1) This category includes admissions by a party in either his individual or representative capacity. If the party has a representative capacity, e.g., executor, and the admission is offered against him in that capacity, it does not matter whether the party was acting as an individual or a representative when he made the statement. See Calif. Evid. Code § 1220; Fed. Rule Evid. 801(d)(2)(A).

(2) Also admissible as an exception to the hearsay rule are adoptive admissions, e.g., those made by adopting or acquiescing in the statement of another, Sullivan v. McMillan, 26 Fla. 543, 8 So. 450 (1890). For example, if A makes a discrediting statement about B, in the presence of B and under circumstances that would call for a protest, silence by B would manifest a belief in the truth of the statement and constitute an admission by conduct. See McCormick, Evidence §§ 269-70 (2nd ed. 1972).

The constitutional right to remain silent in criminal cases, Miranda v. Arizona, 384 U.S. 436, 86 S.Ct. 1602, 16 L.Ed.2d 694 (1966), is not affected by this provision, and an alleged tacit admission in a criminal case is not admissible when the defendant is privileged to remain silent, see State v. Galasso, 217

So.2d 326 (Fla. 1968); <u>Horton v. State</u>, 285 So.2d 418 (Fla. 2nd Dist. 1973); <u>Jones v. State</u>, 200 So.2d 574 (Fla. 3rd Dist. 1967).

For similar provisions, see Calif. Evid. Code § 1221; Fed. Rule Evid. 801(d)(2)(B).

(3) A statement which a party authorizes another to make is generally treated as an admission of the party. Disagreement occurs when the statement is not to a third person but rather is a statement by the agent <u>to</u> the person authorizing the statement. Such statements generally take the form of reports and tend to be highly reliable. Under this provision, a party's books and records can be used against him without regard to any intent to disclose to third persons. "The high degree of trustworthiness of intra-company reports is equal to that of business records, which are admissible as an exception to the hearsay rule although they may be self-serving. Furthermore, there is no privilege that would preclude their use." Ladd, <u>supra</u> at 211. See 5 Wigmore, <u>Evidence</u> § 1557 (3rd ed. 1940) (citing cases).

See New Jersey Evid. Rule 63(8)(a); Fed. Rule Evid. 801(d)(2)(C). Calif. Evid. Code § 1222 limits the use of these admissions to statements which are authorized to be made to third parties.

(4) Statements by an agent or servant which are related to matters within the scope of his agency or employment are admissible against the principal or employer. Florida has adopted this rule, rejecting the common-law view that the statements would not be admissible when there had been no authority to speak. <u>Myrick v. Lloyd</u>, 158 Fla. 47, 27 So.2d 615 (1946). In <u>Gordon v. Hotel Seville, Inc.</u>, 105 So.2d 175, 177 (Fla. 3rd Dist. 1958) <u>cert. denied</u>, 109 So.2d 767 (Fla. 1959) the court stated:

> An admission against interest made by an employee in the course of and within the scope of his employment and relating to a matter which is not beyond the penumbra of his duties or employment, is a recognized exception to the hearsay rule, and such a statement by the employee will be admissible against the employer as an admission against interest.

For similar provisions, see New Jersey Evid. Rule 63(9)(a); Kansas Code Civ. Pro. § 60-460(i)(1); Fed. Rule Evid. 801(d)(2)(D).

(5) Statements by a co-conspirator are admissible against the other conspirators when they are made in the course and furtherance of the conspiracy. Before this rule may be invoked, there must be evidence of a conspiracy and of the objecting party's participation in it. This provision is consistent with existing Florida law. See <u>Honchell v. State</u>, 257 So.2d 889 (Fla. 1971); <u>Farnell v. State</u>, 214 So.2d 753 (Fla. 2nd Dist. 1968).

For similar provisions, see Calif. Evid. Code § 1223; New Jersey Evid. Rule 63(9)(b); Fed. Rule Evid. 801(d)(2)(E).

COMMENTARY ON FEDERAL AND FLORIDA RULE DIFFERENCES

Federal Rule 801 and its Florida counterparts, Florida Stat. §§ 90.801 and 90.803(18), set forth the basic definition of hearsay, which, subject to certain exceptions, is inadmissible pursuant to Federal Rule 802 and Florida Stat. § 90.802.

Both the Florida and federal rules define the term "hearsay" as a statement (save for one made by the declarant while testifying at the trial or hearing), offered in evidence to prove the truth of the matter asserted. *See* FED. R. EVID. 801(c); FLA. STAT. § 90.801(1)(c). In turn, both rules define the term "statement" as including an oral or written assertion or nonverbal conduct of a person that is intended by the person as an assertion. *See* FED. R. EVID. 801(a); FLA. STAT. § 90.801(1)(a). Accordingly, something is hearsay, and thus presumptively inadmissible unless an exception applies, if it is an oral, written, or nonverbal assertion offered into evidence to prove the truth of the matter asserted. Thus, to be deemed hearsay, something must *both* be an assertion *and* be offered to prove the truth of the matter asserted. See U.S. v. Cruz, 805 F.2d 1464, 1477-78 (11th Cir. 1986); Banks v. State, 790 So. 2d 1094, 1097 (Fla. 2001). Stated somewhat differently, evidence is not hearsay, and thus not excluded by the hearsay rule, if it is not an assertion or if it is not offered into evidence to prove the truth of the matter asserted.

Under both the Florida and federal rules, if a statement is significant simply because the statement was made, and it is offered into evidence for that reason, it is not being offered to prove the truth of the matter asserted and thus is not hearsay. See Advisory Committee's Note to FED. R. EVID. 801(c); Sponsors' Note to FLA. STAT. § 90.801(1)(c). One example is a witness's prior inconsistent statement offered to impeach his credibility as a witness; what matters is not the *truth* of the earlier statement but the *fact* that it was made and that it contradicts the witness's current testimony, raising doubts about his credibility. See Fitzpatrick v. State, 900 So. 2d 495, 515 (Fla. 2005); U.S. v. Grant, 256 F.3d 1146, 1156 (11th Cir. 2001). A second example is when a statement is offered to show the effect that a statement had on a person who heard the statement; what matters is not the *truth* of the statement but rather showing the effect it had on the person who heard it. See Hotelera Naco, Inc. v. Chinea, 708 So. 2d 961, 962 (Fla. 3d DCA 1998); Cruz, 805 F.2d at 1478. A third example is a statement that has legal significance simply because it was made, such as defamatory statements, threatening statements, statements offering a bribe, statements of offer and acceptance, demands, and the like; the mere *fact* that such statements are made is legally significant, without regard to the truth or falsity of the statement made. See Banks, 790 So. 2d at 1097-98; Georgetown Manor, Inc. v. Ethan Allen, Inc., 991 F.2d 1533, 1540 (11th Cir. 1993). To be sure, a statement may be significant both for the truth of the matter asserted *and* simply because it was made, in which case a limiting instruction is appropriate, or if the risk is too great that the jury may use it for the hearsay purpose, it may be excluded under Federal Rule 403 or Florida Stat. § 90.403. See State v. Baird, 572 So. 2d 904, 906 (Fla. 1990); Georgetown Manor, 991 F.2d at 1540.

Under both the Florida and federal rules, oral, written, or non-verbal conduct qualifies as an assertion, and is thus hearsay, only if the declarant *intended* to assert something. See Advisory Committee's Note to FED. R. EVID. 801(a); Sponsors' Note to FLA. STAT. § 90.801(1)(a). Under both the federal and Florida rules, an *implied assertion* is not hearsay because the declarant did not intend to assert the thing that is implied from his statement or conduct. See U.S. v. Zenni, 492 F. Supp. 464, 469 (E.D. Ky. 1980); Hernandez v. State, 863 So. 2d 484, 486 (Fla. 4th DCA 2004); Advisory Committee's Note to FED. R. EVID. 801(c); Sponsors' Note to FLA. STAT. § 90.801(1)(c). One potential difference between the federal and Florida rules is who bears the burden of proving an intent to assert or the lack thereof. Under the federal rule, it appears that the party seeking to have a statement excluded as hearsay bears the burden of proving that it is assertive, while under the Florida rule, it appears that the party who seeks to have the statement admitted bears the burden of proving that it is non-assertive. Compare Advisory Committee's Note to FED. R. EVID. 801(a), *with* Sponsors' Note to FLA. STAT. § 90.801(1).

Under both the Florida and federal rules, three types of prior statements by a witness who testifies at trial and is subject to cross-examination concerning the prior statement are deemed not to fall within the definition of hearsay, even though they are assertions and are offered to prove the truth of the matter asserted. See FED. R. EVID. 801(d)(1); FLA. STAT. § 90.801(2). For any of these types of prior statements, the requirement that the witness be "subject to cross-examination" sets a rather low threshold, and is indeed satisfied so long as the witness is on the stand under oath and responds willingly to questions; even if the person appears on the stand and claims not to remember making the prior statement, that is sufficient to satisfy the requirement that the person be subject to cross-examination. See A.E.B. v. State, 818 So. 2d 534, 535-36 (Fla. 2d DCA 2002); U.S. v. Owens, 484 U.S. 554, 561-64 (1988).

First, under both rules, a prior inconsistent statement of a witness is admissible as proof of the truth of the matter asserted therein if it was given under penalty of perjury at a trial, hearing, or other proceeding, or in a deposition. See FED. R. EVID. 801(d)(1)(A); FLA. STAT. § 90.801(2)(a). Under both rules, the phrase "other proceeding" includes testimony before a grand jury, see Ibar v. State, 938 So. 2d 451, 462-63 (Fla. 2006); Moore v. State, 452 So. 2d 559, 562 (Fla. 1984); U.S. v. Jacoby, 955 F.2d 1527, 1539 (11th Cir. 1992), but it does not include such things as a statement made under oath during an interview conducted by the police or prosecutor, even if it is made under oath subject to penalty of perjury. *See Pearce v. State*, 880 So. 2d 561, 569 (Fla. 2004); *U.S. v. Dietrich*, 854 F.2d 1056, 1060-62 (7th Cir. 1988). To qualify as an "other proceeding" under either rule, the proceeding must have formalities comparable to those in grand jury proceedings or depositions, and should also be the sort of proceedings in which verbatim transcripts are produced. *See Ellis v. State*, 622 So. 2d 991, 997-98 (Fla. 1993); *Dietrich*, 854 F.2d at 1060-62. In addition, under Florida law, a distinction is drawn in criminal cases between discovery depositions and regular depositions, and only the latter, not the former, fall within the scope of the phrase "deposition" as used in the Florida rule. *See State v. Green*, 667 So. 2d 756, 760 (Fla. 1995).

Second, under both the federal and Florida rules, a prior *consistent* statement of a witness is admissible as proof of the truth of the matter asserted therein; unlike with prior inconsistent statements, the setting in which the prior statement was made is irrelevant, but such statements are admissible only after a charge is made against the witness of improper influence or motive or recent fabrication. *See* FED. R. EVID. 801(d)(1)(B); FLA. STAT. § 90.801(2)(b). Moreover, although not explicit in the text of either rule, both the federal and Florida rules have been interpreted to admit only those statements that were made *before* the alleged improper influence or motive to fabricate arose. *See Tome v. U.S.*, 513 U.S. 150 (1995); *Taylor v. State*, 855 So. 2d 1, 23 (Fla. 2003). If multiple improper influences or motives are alleged, and the prior consistent statement pre-dates some of those influences or motives and post-dates others, it is still admissible under both the Florida and federal rules to rebut the influence or motive that it pre-dates. *See Chandler v. State*, 702 So. 2d 186, 198 (Fla. 1997); *U.S. v. Wilson*, 355 F.3d 358, 361 (5th Cir. 2003). Moreover, under both the federal and Florida rules, a prior consistent statement, even if not admissible for substantive purposes because it does not fit the requirements of this provision, may still be admissible for rehabilitative purposes. *See U.S. v. Simonelli*, 237 F.3d 19, 25-28 (1st Cir. 2001); *Monday v. State*, 792 So. 2d 1278, 1281 (Fla. 1st DCA 2001).

Third, under both the federal and Florida rules, a prior statement of identification of a person made after perceiving the person is admissible as proof of the truth of the matter asserted therein; there is no requirement that it be consistent or inconsistent with the witness's testimony, nor is there a requirement that it be made in any particular type of setting or that it rebut a charge of improper influence or motive. *See* FED. R. EVID. 801(d)(1)(C); FLA. STAT. § 90.801(2)(c). Under both rules, perception includes not only perception by sight, but also through other senses, such as hearing. *See State v. Richards*, 843 So. 2d 962, 967 (Fla. 3d DCA 2003); *U.S. v. Ramirez*, 45 F.3d 1096, 1101 n.1 (7th Cir. 1995). The Florida rule has been interpreted narrowly to encompass only statements identifying a particular person, such as by saying "X is the one who did it" or picking a particular person out of a lineup or set of photos; a prior statement describing the person who committed a particular offense is not deemed to be a statement of "identification" under the Florida rule. *See Ibar*, 938 So. 2d at 461 n.3; *Puryear v. State*, 810 So. 2d 901, 906 (Fla. 2002). By contrast, the federal rule has been interpreted to include statements in the form of a description. *See U.S. v. Brink*, 39 F.3d 419, 425-26 (3d Cir. 1994).

Under the federal rule, five categories of statements made by a party or by certain people associated with a party, when offered against a party, are deemed to be outside the definition of hearsay. *See* FED. R. EVID. 801(d)(2). The Florida rule paves the way to admitting those same five categories of "admissions" (a term no longer used in the federal rule) by a slightly different route, viewing them as within the definition of hearsay but creating exceptions to the hearsay rule for such statements. *See* FLA. STAT. § 90.803(18).

Under both the Florida and federal rules, it is not necessary that the statement be based on the declarant's personal knowledge. *See Metropolitan Dade County v. Yearby*, 580 So. 2d 186, 189 (Fla. 3d DCA 1991); Advisory Committee's Note to FED. R. EVID. 801(d)(2). Moreover, under both rules, the statement must be offered *against* the party who made it (or the party associated with the person who made it); a party cannot invoke either rule to get his *own* statements admitted (or the statements of those with whom he is associated). *See Christopher v. State*, 583 So. 2d 642, 645 (Fla. 1991); *U.S. v. Marin*, 669 F.2d 73, 84 (2d Cir. 1982).

The first category under both rules is the individual statement; both rules pave the way for admitting a party's own statement against that party. See FED. R. EVID. 801(d)(2)(A); FLA. STAT. § 90.803(18)(a). There is no requirement under either rule that the statement be against the interests of the party who made the statement. See State v. Dreggors, 813 So. 2d 170, 172 n.1 (Fla. 5th DCA 2002); U.S. v. Reed, 227 F.3d 763, 770 (7th Cir. 2000).

The second category under both rules is an adopted statement; both rules provide for admitting a statement of which a party has manifested an adoption or belief in its truth. See FED. R. EVID. 801(d)(2)(B); FLA. STAT. § 90.803(18)(b). Under both Florida and federal practice, a statement by one person can be adopted by a party through that party's silence, provided that the statement was heard and understood by the party, that the party had the ability and opportunity to deny the statement, and it is the sort of statement that, if untrue, would have caused a reasonable person in the party's position to deny the statement. See Globe v. State, 877 So. 2d 663, 673 (Fla. 2004); Nelson v. State, 748 So. 2d 237, 242-43 (Fla. 1999); U.S. v. Carter, 760 F.2d 1568, 1579-80 (11th Cir. 1985).

The third category is an authorized statement; under both rules, statements by a party's speaking agent, that is, by a person specifically authorized by the party to speak on his behalf, are admissible against the party. See FED. R. EVID. 801(d)(2)(C); FLA. STAT. § 90.803(18)(c).

The fourth category under both federal and Florida practice is a vicarious statement; under both rules, a statement by a party's agent or servant concerning a matter within the scope of the agency or employment made during the existence of the relationship is admissible against the party. See FED. R. EVID. 801(d)(2)(D); FLA. STAT. § 90.803(18)(d). To be within the scope of employment or agency, it must concern a matter which is connected with a duty within the scope of the person's employment or agency. See Lee v. Department of Health and Rehab. Servs., 698 So. 2d 1194, 1200 (Fla. 1997); Wilkinson v. Carnival Cruise Lines, Inc., 920 F.2d 1560, 1564-66 (11th Cir. 1991). Under the Florida rule, a government agent is viewed as an agent for purposes of Florida Stat. § 90.803(18)(d), so as to permit his statements to be offered against the government in a criminal prosecution brought by the government. See Garland v. State, 834 So. 2d 265, 266-68 (Fla. 4th DCA 2002). By contrast, the federal courts are divided on the question whether, in a criminal case, a government agent is an "agent" for purposes of Federal Rule 801(d)(2)(D). Compare U.S. v. Yildiz, 355 F.3d 80, 82 (2d Cir. 2004) (holding that common law rule that statements of government agents are not admissions of the sovereign is incorporated into Rule 801(d)(2)(D)), with U.S. v. Branham, 97 F.3d 835, 850-51 (6th Cir. 1996) (statements by government agents can be admitted as admissions against the government in criminal cases).

The fifth category under both the federal and Florida rules is a coconspirator statement; under both rules, a statement by a coconspirator of a party made during the course and in furtherance of the conspiracy is admissible against the party. See FED. R. EVID. 801(d)(2)(E); FLA. STAT. § 90.803(18)(e). It is not necessary that a conspiracy be charged in order to invoke either provision. See Brown v. State, 648 So. 2d 268, 270-71 (Fla. 4th DCA 1995); U.S. v. Cagnina, 697 F.2d 915, 922 (11th Cir. 1983). Moreover, to invoke the exception, the trial court need only find by a preponderance of the evidence that a conspiracy existed between the declarant and the party, as is the case generally with preliminary questions. See Romani v. State, 542 So. 2d 984, 985 n.3 (Fla. 1989); Bourjaily v. U.S., 483 U.S. 171, 175-76 (1987). An important difference between the Florida and federal rules is that under the federal rule, the trial court can rely on the statement itself to determine whether or not a conspiracy existed between the declarant and the party, while under the Florida rule, the trial court must make that determination based solely on independent evidence. Compare Romani, 542 So. 2d at 985-86, with Bourjaily, 483 U.S. at 178-79. However, even under the federal rule, while the contents of the statement itself can be considered in determining the existence of a conspiracy between the declarant and the party for coconspirator statements (as well as the declarant's authority for authorized statements and the agency or employment relationship and the scope thereof for vicarious statements), the statement's contents are not alone sufficient to establish those points; there must be some additional, independent evidence. See FED. R. EVID. 801(d)(2). Unlike the federal rule, the Florida rule provides that, upon request, the jury is to be instructed—before the introduction of any evidence or before any evidence is admitted under this provision—that the conspiracy itself must be established by independent evidence. *See Tresvant v. State*, 396 So. 2d 733, 737 n.7 (Fla. 3d DCA 1981). Finally, under both the Florida and federal rules, the trial court has discretion to either require that a party first show by a preponderance of the evidence that the foundational prerequisites for invoking the exception exist before being allowed to introduce the coconspirator statements into evidence, or instead may conditionally admit the statements subject to eventual proof by the party of the foundational prerequisites to invoking the exception. *See U.S. v. Barshov*, 733 F.2d 842, 849-50 (11th Cir. 1984); *Tresvant*, 396 So. 2d at 737 n.7.

Federal Rule 802. The Rule Against Hearsay

Hearsay is not admissible unless any of the following provides otherwise:

- a federal statute;

- these rules; or

- other rules prescribed by the Supreme Court.

ADVISORY COMMITTEE'S NOTE

The provision excepting from the operation of the rule hearsay which is made admissible by other rules adopted by the Supreme Court or by Act of Congress continues the admissibility thereunder of hearsay which would not qualify under these Evidence Rules. The following examples illustrate the working of the exception:

Federal Rules of Civil Procedure

> Rule 4(g): proof of service by affidavit.
> Rule 32: admissibility of depositions.
> Rule 43(e): affidavits when motion based on facts not appearing of record.
> Rule 56: affidavits in summary judgment proceedings.
> Rule 65(b): showing by affidavit for temporary restraining order.

Federal Rules of Criminal Procedure

> Rule 4(a): affidavits to show grounds for issuing warrants.
> Rule 12(b)(4): affidavits to determine issues of fact in connection with motions.

Acts of Congress

> 10 U.S.C. § 7730: affidavits of unavailable witnesses in actions for damages caused by vessel in naval service, or towage or salvage of same, when taking of testimony or bringing of action delayed or stayed on security grounds.
> 29 U.S.C. § 161(4): affidavit as proof of service in NLRB proceedings.
> 38 U.S.C. § 5206: affidavit as proof of posting notice of sale of unclaimed property by Veterans Administration.

ADVISORY COMMITTEE'S NOTE (2011 AMENDMENT)

The language of Rule 802 has been amended as part of the restyling of the Evidence Rules to make them more easily understood and to make style and terminology consistent throughout the rules. These changes are intended to be stylistic only. There is no intent to change any result in any ruling on evidence admissibility.

Florida Stat. § 90.802. Hearsay Rule

Except as provided by statute, hearsay evidence is inadmissible.

SPONSORS' NOTE (1976 ENACTMENT)

This section restates the general rule that excludes hearsay testimony. In State Farm Mut. Auto. Ins. Co. v. Ganz, 119 So.2d 319, 321 (Fla. 3rd Dist. 1960) the court stated:

> The general rule which bars the admission of evidence falling within the definition of hearsay is so firmly established and so well known that the citation of authority affirming the general principle seems hardly warranted.

The main objection to the introduction of hearsay testimony is the lack of an opportunity for the adverse party to cross-examine the declarant. In addition, the hearsay statement is usually not under oath and the jury does not have the opportunity to observe the demeanor of the witness. See McCormick, Evidence § 245 (2nd ed. 1972).

Exceptions to the hearsay rules are contained in subsequent statutory provisions. In addition, certain types of statements, which are technically included in the definition of hearsay, are admissible under the Rules of Procedure. For example, Fla. R. Civ. Pro. 1.330(a)(3) provides inter alia for the use of a deposition at trial when the witness is at a greater distance than 100 miles from the place of trial or hearing.

COMMENTARY ON FEDERAL AND FLORIDA RULE DIFFERENCES

Florida Stat. § 90.802 and its federal counterpart, Federal Rule 802, set forth the rule against hearsay. Under both rules, hearsay—which is defined in Florida Stat. § 90.801 and its federal counterpart, Federal Rule 801—is not admissible except as otherwise provided by law. The exceptions to this rule are set forth in Florida Stat. §§ 90.803-90.804 and Federal Rules 803-804 and 807. In addition, a few specialized statutes and rules of procedure create exceptions to the rule. See Advisory Committee's Note to FED. R. EVID. 802; Sponsors' Note to FLA. STAT. § 90.802.

Federal Rule 803(1), (2). Exceptions to the Rule Against Hearsay — Regardless of Whether the Declarant Is Available as a Witness [Present Sense Impression; Excited Utterance]

The following are not excluded by the rule against hearsay, regardless of whether the declarant is available as a witness:

(1) *Present Sense Impression.* A statement describing or explaining an event or condition, made while or immediately after the declarant perceived it.

(2) *Excited Utterance.* A statement relating to a startling event or condition, made while the declarant was under the stress of excitement that it caused.

....

ADVISORY COMMITTEE'S NOTE

The exceptions are phrased in terms of nonapplication of the hearsay rule, rather than in positive terms of admissibility, in order to repel any implication that other possible grounds for exclusion are eliminated from consideration.

The present rule proceeds upon the theory that under appropriate circumstances a hearsay statement may possess circumstantial guarantees of trustworthiness sufficient to justify nonproduction of the declarant in person at the trial even though he may be available. The theory finds vast support in the many exceptions to the hearsay rule developed by the common law in which unavailability of the declarant is not a relevant factor. The present rule is a synthesis of them, with revision where modern developments and conditions are believed to make that course appropriate.

In a hearsay situation, the declarant is, of course, a witness, and neither this rule nor Rule 804 dispenses with the requirement of firsthand knowledge. It may appear from his statement or be inferable from circumstances. See Rule 602.

Exceptions (1) and (2). In considerable measure these two examples overlap, though based on somewhat different theories. The most significant practical difference will lie in the time lapse allowable between event and statement.

The underlying theory of Exception (1) is that substantial contemporaneity of event and statement negative the likelihood of deliberate or conscious misrepresentation. Moreover, if the witness is the declarant, he may be examined on the statement. If the witness is not the declarant, he may be examined as to the circumstances as an aid in evaluating the statement. Morgan, Basic Problems of Evidence 340–341 (1962).

The theory of Exception (2) is simply that circumstances may produce a condition of excitement which temporarily stills the capacity of reflection and produces utterances free of conscious fabrication. 6 Wigmore § 1747, p. 135. Spontaneity is the key factor in each instance, though arrived at by somewhat different routes. Both are needed in order to avoid needless niggling.

While the theory of Exception (2) has been criticized on the ground that excitement impairs accuracy of observation as well as eliminating conscious fabrication, Hutchins and Slesinger, Some Observations on the Law of Evidence: Spontaneous Exclamations, 28 Colum.L.Rev. 432 (1928), it finds support in cases without number. See cases in 6 Wigmore § 1750; Annot. 53 A.L.R.2d 1245 (statements as to cause of or responsibility for motor vehicle accident); Annot., 4 A.L.R.3d 149 (accusatory statements by homicide victims). Since unexciting events are less likely to evoke comment, decisions involving Exception (1) are far less numerous. Illustrative are Tampa Elec. Co. v. Getrost, 151 Fla. 558, 10 So.2d 83 (1942); Houston Oxygen Co. v. Davis, 139 Tex. 1 (1942); and cases cited in McCormick § 273, p. 585, n. 4.

With respect to the *time element*, Exception (1) recognizes that in many, if not most, instances precise contemporaneity is not possible and hence a slight lapse is allowable. Under Exception (2) the standard of measurement is the duration of the state of excitement. "How long can excitement prevail? Obviously there are no pat answers and the character of the transaction or event will largely determine the significance of the time factor." Slough, Spontaneous Statements and State of Mind, 46 Iowa L.Rev. 224, 243 (1961); McCormick § 272, p. 580.

Participation by the declarant is not required: a non-participant may be moved to describe what he perceives, and one may be startled by an event in which he is not an actor. Slough, supra; McCormick, supra; 6 Wigmore § 1755; Annot., 78 A.L.R.2d 300.

Whether *proof of the startling event* may be made by the statement itself is largely an academic question, since in most cases there is present at least circumstantial evidence that something of a startling nature must have occurred. For cases in which the evidence consists of the condition of the declarant (injuries, state of shock), see Insurance Co. v. Mosely, 75 U.S. (8 Wall.) 397 (1869); Wheeler v. United States, 211 F.2d 19 (1953), cert. denied 347 U.S. 1019; Wetherbee v. Safety Casualty Co., 219 F.2d 274 (5th Cir. 1955); Lampe v. United States, 229 F.2d 43 (1956). Nevertheless, on occasion the only evidence may be the content of the statement itself, and rulings that it may be sufficient are described as "increasing," Slough, *supra* at 246, and as the "prevailing practice," McCormick § 272, p. 579. Illustrative are Armour & Co. v. Industrial Commission, 78 Colo. 569 (1926); Young v. Stewart, 191 N.C. 297 (1926). Moreover, under Rule 104(a) the judge is not limited by the hearsay rule in passing upon preliminary questions of fact.

Proof of declarant's perception by his statement presents similar considerations when declarant is identified. People v. Poland, 22 Ill.2d 175 (1961). However, when declarant is an unidentified bystander, the cases indicate hesitancy in upholding the statement alone as sufficient, Garrett v. Howden, 73 N.M. 307 (1963); Beck v. Dye, 200 Wash. 1 (1939), a result which would under appropriate circumstances be consistent with the rule.

Permissible *subject matter* of the statement is limited under Exception (1) to description or explanation of the event or condition, the assumption being that spontaneity, in the absence of a startling event, may extend no farther. In Exception (2), however, the statement need only "relate" to the startling event or condition, thus affording a broader scope of subject matter coverage. 6 Wigmore §§ 1750, 1754. See Sanitary Grocery Co. v. Snead, 90 F.2d 374 (1937), slip-and-fall case sustaining admissibility of clerk's statement. "That has been on the floor for a couple of hours," and Murphy Auto Parts Co., Inc. v. Ball, 249 F.2d 508 (1957), upholding admission, on issue of driver's agency, of his statement that he had to call on a customer and was in a hurry to get home. Quick, Hearsay, Excitement, Necessity and the Uniform Rules: A Reappraisal of Rule 63(4), 6 Wayne L.Rev. 204, 206–209 (1960).

Similar provisions are found in Uniform Rule 63(4)(a) and (b); California Evidence Code § 1240 (as to Exception (2) only); Kansas Code of Civil Procedure § 60-460(d)(1) and (2); New Jersey Evidence Rule 63(4).

....

ADVISORY COMMITTEE'S NOTE (2011 AMENDMENT)

The language of Rule 803 has been amended as part of the restyling of the Evidence Rules to make them more easily understood and to make style and terminology consistent throughout the rules. These changes are intended to be stylistic only. There is no intent to change any result in any ruling on evidence admissibility.

Florida Stat. § 90.803(1), (2). Hearsay Exceptions; Availability of Declarant Immaterial [Spontaneous Statement; Excited Utterance]

The provision of s. 90.802 to the contrary notwithstanding, the following are not inadmissible as evidence, even though the declarant is available as a witness:

(1) Spontaneous statement. A spontaneous statement describing or explaining an event or condition made while the declarant was perceiving the event or condition, or immediately thereafter, except when such statement is made under circumstances that indicate its lack of trustworthiness.

(2) Excited utterance. A statement or excited utterance relating to a startling event or condition made while the declarant was under the stress of excitement caused by the event or condition.

....

SPONSORS' NOTE (1976 ENACTMENT)

These two exceptions provide admissibility for the bulk of the evidence that has heretofore been admissible under the so-called res gestae exception. The term res gestae, which has been criticized often, does not appear in this code, as it does not in the Federal Rules of Evidence. For example, the court in Green v. State, 93 Fla. 1076, 1080, 113 So. 121, 123 (1927), referred to the term as "a sort of 'catch-all' in which to save a point when it may not be clearly brought under some better and more clearly defined head." 6 Wigmore, Evidence § 1767 (3rd ed. 1940) was quoted with approval in Williams v. State, 188 So.2d 320, 323 (Fla. 2nd Dist. 1966), modified, 198 So.2d 21 (Fla. 1967):

> The phrase "res gestae" has long been not only entirely useless, but even positively harmful. It is useless, because every rule of Evidence to which it has ever been applied exists as a part of some well established principle and can be explained in the terms of that principle. It is harmful, because by its ambiguity it invites the confusion of one rule with another and thus creates uncertainty as to the limitations of both. It ought therefore wholly to be repudiated, as a vicious element in our legal phraseology. No rule of Evidence can be created or applied by the mere muttering of a shibboleth.

The expansiveness and lack of precision with which the term res gestae has been used is illustrated in Morgan, The Law of Evidence, 1941-45, 59 Harv. L. Rev. 481, 568 (1946), where it was stated that:

Courts and lawyers constantly use res gestae to describe:

> (a) part of a relevant transaction the offered evidence of which has no hearsay aspect,
>
> (b) declarations of presently existing subjective symptoms offered in evidence as tending to prove the existence of those symptoms,
>
> (c) declarations of a presently existing mental condition offered in evidence as tending to prove that condition, its probable continuance and its previous existence, and to prove conduct in accord with that mental condition,
>
> (d) declarations of a past mental condition or of past symptoms, and
>
> (e) spontaneous statements or statements made contemporaneously with a relevant event or condition, evidence of which is offered as tending to prove the truth of the matter stated.

Florida courts have similarly used the term res gestae to cover a wide variety of circumstances. See The Florida Bar, Evidence in Florida, Chap. 9, Hearsay Exceptions—Res Gestae (1971). Under this code the evidence that has been admitted in Florida under the res gestae label will continue to be admissible, but it will be admissible either as not involving hearsay, or under more precisely stated exceptions.

A few Florida cases apply res gestae to circumstances which do not involve oral statements and therefore apply the concept although no hearsay exception was required for admissibility. In Browne v. State, 92

Fla. 699, 109 So. 811 (1926), the clothes of a deceased worn at the time of an alleged murder were admissible as res gestae evidence. In Powell v. State, 131 Fla. 254, 175 So. 213 (1937), a prosecution of a husband for the murder of his wife, both the wife and his mother-in-law were murdered at the same time, but not by the same physical act, and both bodies were disposed of in the same manner and in the same place. The court found that evidence in regard to the circumstances surrounding the death of the mother-in-law constituted a part of the res gestae of the death and circumstances surrounding the murder of the wife and was therefore admissible. The use of the res gestae doctrine would appear to be improper in both these cases. The admissibility of such evidence should depend on relevancy alone, since hearsay is not involved.

Although there is considerable overlap in subsection (1), the spontaneous statement exception, and subsection (2), the excited-utterance exception, the drafters of the Federal Rules thought them both necessary in order to avoid "needless niggling." In general, the exceptions to the exclusionary rule proceed upon a theory that under appropriate circumstances a hearsay statement may possess circumstantial guarantees of trustworthiness sufficient to justify introduction of the evidence at the trial even though the declarant may be available. The circumstantial guarantee of subsection (1) is that when a spontaneous statement of narration is made simultaneously with perception, the substantial contemporaneity of event and statement negative the likelihood of deliberate or conscious misinterpretation. The theory of subsection (2) is simply that when an excited utterance is made, the circumstances produce a condition of excitement which temporarily stills the capacity of reflection and produces utterance free of conscious fabrication. The key element in both is spontaneity.

Permissible subject matter is somewhat different under the two subsections. Under subsection (1) it is limited to description or explanation of the event or condition. In subsection (2), the statement need only "relate" to the startling event or condition.

Decisions involving subsection (1) are far less numerous than those involving subsection (2), since unexciting events are less likely to evoke memorable comment. Apparently, illustrative of subsection (1) is Tampa Elec. Co. v. Getrost, 151 Fla. 588, 10 So.2d 83 (1942), where an assistant to an electric lineman was permitted to testify that the lineman told him that he had called the plant and ordered the power in the line cut off. The lineman had proceeded to work on the wire and was electrocuted. The court observed that at the time the utterance was made there was no occasion for it to have resulted from reflection or premeditation, nor was there any motive that would make it self-serving. The court asked whether the hearsay vices were present, and finding that they were not, held that the conversation was admissible.

Subsection (2) is illustrated in Gauck v. Meleski, 346 F.2d 433 (5th Cir. 1965), where after a rear-end collision of trucks in the Northern District of Florida, the first witness to arrive at the scene of the accident stated that he found the decedent alive and that he said, "He hit me from behind." The court indicated that on remand the evidence would be admissible. In Foster v. Thornton, 125 Fla. 699, 170 So. 459 (1936) an action against a chiropractor for malpractice, it was held that statements made by the patient immediately after regaining consciousness were admissible as res gestae since they were an outgrowth of the treatment, explanatory of it, excluded any idea of design or deliberation and were corroborated by the evidence of several other witnesses. Similar provisions are found in Uniform Rule 63(4)(a) and (b); Calif. Evid. Code § 1240 (as to subsection (2) only); Kansas Code of Civ. Pro. § 60-460(d)(1) and (2); New Jersey Evid. Rule 63(4); Fed. Rule Evid. 803(1) and (2).

COMMENTARY ON FEDERAL AND FLORIDA RULE DIFFERENCES

Florida Stat. § 90.803 and its federal counterpart, Federal Rule 803, set forth a series of unrestricted exceptions to the hearsay rule, so denominated because evidence falling within the scope of these exceptions is viewed as having sufficient indicia of reliability that it can be admitted without regard to the declarant's availability to appear at trial and testify as a witness. See Advisory Committee's Note to FED. R. EVID. 803; Sponsors' Note to FLA. STAT. § 90.803(1)-(2). Because of the sheer number of exceptions that exist under each rule, the rules, their legislative history, and the commentary to the rules is broken down by exception (or in some cases, in small, related groups of exceptions).

Florida Stat. §§ 90.803(1)-(2) and their federal counterparts, Federal Rules 803(1)-(2), create exceptions to the hearsay rule for present sense impressions ("spontaneous statement" in the Florida rule) and excited utterances. The two exceptions overlap to some degree, see Advisory Committee's Note to FED. R. EVID. 803(1)-(2); Sponsors' Note to FLA. STAT. § 90.803(1)-(2), and are often considered by courts in tandem with one another.

Federal Rule 803(1) creates an exception to the hearsay rule for "[a] statement describing or explaining an event or condition, made while or immediately after the declarant perceived it.." See FED. R. EVID. 803(1). The analogous provision in the Florida rule is similar, but inserts the word "spontaneous" before the word "statement" and also has a proviso at the end barring such evidence if "made under circumstances that indicate its lack of trustworthiness." See FLA. STAT. § 90.803(1). The Florida courts have interpreted the requirement that the statement be "spontaneous" to mean that it was made without first engaging in reflective thought. See Deparvine v. State, 995 So. 2d 351, 369 (Fla. 2008); J.M. v. State, 665 So. 2d 1135, 1137 (Fla. 5th DCA 1996). While not explicit in Federal Rule 803(1), some federal courts have read into it a similar requirement, namely, that the court find that the statement was made "without calculated narration." See, e.g., Cody v. Harris, 409 F.3d 853, 860 (7th Cir. 2005). The trustworthiness proviso at the end of the Florida rule has typically been invoked to exclude statements by an unidentified bystander, in the absence of evidence to establish that the declarant perceived the event. See, e.g., Deparvine, 995 So. 2d at 367-68; Wal-Mart Stores, Inc. v. Jenkins, 739 So. 2d 171, 171-72 (Fla. 5th DCA 1999). While the federal rule does not contain a similar proviso, federal courts have likewise refused to admit statements by unidentified bystanders in the absence of evidence that they perceived the event. See Miller v. Crown Amusements, Inc., 821 F. Supp. 703, 705-06 (S.D. Ga. 1993).

Federal Rule 803(2) creates an exception to the hearsay rule for "[a] statement relating to a startling event or condition, made while the declarant was under the stress of excitement that it caused." The Florida rule is very similar, adding the words "or excited utterance" after the word "statement," language that has been invoked by the Florida Supreme Court to hold that something can be admitted under the exception even if the declarant's voice was calm when they made the statement. See Hudson v. State, 992 So. 2d 96, 108 (Fla. 2008).

To qualify as an excited utterance under either exception, there must have been an event startling enough to create nervous excitement, the statement must have been made while the person was under the stress of excitement caused by the event, and it must have been made before the person had time to contrive or misrepresent. See Hudson, 992 So. 2d at 107; State v. Jano, 524 So. 2d 660, 661-62 (Fla. 1988); U.S. v. Hadley, 431 F.3d 484, 496 (6th Cir. 2005); U.S. v. Alarcon-Simi, 300 F.3d 1172, 1175 (9th Cir. 2002). The requirements that the person was under the stress of excitement and that the statement was made before the person had time to contrive or misrepresent are interwoven: so long as the person remains under the stress of excitement, it is unlikely that the declarant contrived or misrepresented. See Bell v. State, 847 So. 2d 558, 561 (Fla. 3d DCA 2003). Corroboration of the startling event is not required; the declarant's condition and the declaration itself are sufficient to establish that the startling event occurred. See State v. Wright, 678 So. 2d 493, 494 (Fla. 4th DCA 1996); U.S. v. Ruiz, 249 F.3d 643, 647 (7th Cir. 2001).

Although the excited utterance and spontaneous statement exceptions overlap, there are two key differences between them under both federal and Florida law. The first difference is the permissible time lapse between the event and the statement: the spontaneous statement must be made while perceiving the event or immediately thereafter, while there is no specific time limit for the excited utterance. See Jano, 524 So. 2d at 663; Miller v. Keating, 754 F.2d 507, 512 (3d Cir. 1985). Yet while there is no specific time limit for excited utterances, the duration of time between the event or condition and when the statement was made is nonetheless an important consideration, for the more time that has elapsed, the less likely it is that the person was still under the stress of excitement, and the more likely it is that she will have had time to engage in reflective thought that allows her to contrive or misrepresent. *See Hudson*, 992 So. 2d at 107-08; *Jano*, 524 So. 2d at 661-63; *Strong v. State*, 947 So. 2d 552, 554-55 (Fla. 3d DCA 2006); *Haggins v. Warden, Fort Pillow State Farm*, 715 F.2d 1050, 1057-58 (6th Cir. 1983). Rarely will it be the case that someone will be deemed to be excited if the statement was made more than several hours after the event. *See Jano*, 524 So. 2d at 663; *U.S. v. Taveras*, 380 F.3d 532, 537 (1st Cir. 2004) ("The time lapse in most excited utterance cases is usually a few seconds or a few minutes. In extreme circumstances, we have even accepted a delay of a few hours."). *But see U.S. v. Belfast*, 611 F.3d 783, 817 (11th Cir. 2010) (stressing that it is "the totality of the circumstances, not simply the length of time that has passed between the event and the statement, that determines whether a hearsay statement was an excited utterance," and citing cases admitting statements made up to 12 hours after the event as excited utterances). Other factors to consider in determining whether the declarant was excited when she made the statement include the age of the declarant, her physical and mental condition, the characteristics of the event and the subject matter of the statements. *See Jano*, 524 So. 2d at 661; *U.S. v. Alexander*, 331 F.3d 116, 122-23 (D.C. Cir. 2003).

The second key difference between the two provisions is the permissible subject matter of the statement: a spontaneous statement must *describe* the event, while an excited utterance need only *relate* to the event, thus providing for the admissibility of a statements covering a broader scope of subject matter. *See Johnson v. State*, 969 So. 2d 938, 950 (Fla. 2007); Advisory Committee's Note to FED. R. EVID. 803(1)-(2). Thus, for example, if upon observing a car accident, a witness says, "He left the party drunk!" that would not "describe" the event (such a statement would be limited to describing the accident itself), but it would "relate" to the event. *See Johnson*, 969 So. 2d at 950; *Edwards v. State*, 763 So. 2d 549, 550 (Fla. 3d DCA 2000).

Federal Rule 803(3). Exceptions to the Rule Against Hearsay — Regardless of Whether the Declarant Is Available as a Witness [Then-Existing Mental, Emotional, or Physical Condition]

The following are not excluded by the rule against hearsay, regardless of whether the declarant is available as a witness:

....

(3) *Then-Existing Mental, Emotional, or Physical Condition.* A statement of the declarant's then-existing state of mind (such as motive, intent, or plan) or emotional, sensory, or physical condition (such as mental feeling, pain, or bodily health), but not including a statement of memory or belief to prove the fact remembered or believed unless it relates to the validity or terms of the declarant's will.

....

ADVISORY COMMITTEE'S NOTE

....

Exception (3) is essentially a specialized application of Exception (1), presented separately to enhance its usefulness and accessibility. See McCormick §§ 265, 268.

The exclusion of "statements of memory or belief to prove the fact remembered or believed" is necessary to avoid the virtual destruction of the hearsay rule which would otherwise result from allowing state of mind, provable by a hearsay statement, to serve as the basis for an inference of the happening of the event which produced the state of mind. Shepard v. United States, 290 U.S. 96 (1933); Maguire, The

Hillmon Case — Thirty-three Years After, 38 Harv.L.Rev. 709, 719–731 (1925); Hinton, States of Mind and the Hearsay Rule, 1 U.Chi.L.Rev. 394, 421–423 (1934). The rule of Mutual Life Ins. Co. v. Hillmon, 145 U.S. 285 (1892), allowing evidence of intention as tending to prove the doing of the act intended, is, of course, left undisturbed.

The carving out, from the exclusion mentioned in the preceding paragraph, of declarations relating to the execution, revocation, identification, or terms of declarant's will represents an *ad hoc* judgment which finds ample reinforcement in the decisions, resting on practical grounds of necessity and expediency rather than logic. McCormick § 271, pp. 577–578; Annot., 34 A.L.R.2d 588, 62 A.L.R.2d 855. A similar recognition of the need for and practical value of this kind of evidence is found in California Evidence Code § 1260.

....

REPORT OF HOUSE COMMITTEE ON THE JUDICIARY

Rule 803(3) was approved in the form submitted by the Court to Congress. However, the Committee intends that the Rule be construed to limit the doctrine of *Mutual Life Insurance Co. v. Hillmon*, 145 U.S. 285, 295–300 (1892), so as to render statements of intent by a declarant admissible only to prove his future conduct, not the future conduct of another person.

....

Florida Stat. § 90.803(3). Hearsay Exceptions; Availability of Declarant Immaterial [Then-Existing Mental, Emotional, or Physical Condition]

The provision of s. 90.802 to the contrary notwithstanding, the following are not inadmissible as evidence, even though the declarant is available as a witness:

....

(3) Then-existing mental, emotional, or physical condition.

(a) A statement of the declarant's then-existing state of mind, emotion, or physical sensation, including a statement of intent, plan, motive, design, mental feeling, pain, or bodily health, when such evidence is offered to:

1. Prove the declarant's state of mind, emotion, or physical sensation at that time or at any other time when such state is an issue in the action.

2. Prove or explain acts of subsequent conduct of the declarant.

(b) However, this subsection does not make admissible:

1. An after-the-fact statement of memory or belief to prove the fact remembered or believed, unless such statement relates to the execution, revocation, identification, or terms of the declarant's will.

2. A statement made under circumstances that indicate its lack of trustworthiness.

....

SPONSORS' NOTE (1976 ENACTMENT)

This exception to the hearsay rule, which is generally accepted in most modern decisions, makes admissible evidence of extrajudicial statements made by a declarant of his bodily condition (symptoms, pain or other feelings) or mental state as they then exist. See 6 Wigmore, Evidence §§ 1725-30 (3rd ed. 1940); McCormick, Evidence §§ 291, 294 (2nd ed. 1972). Since these statements relate to an existing bodily or mental condition, they possess a spontaneous quality. Presumably they are the sincere and natural manifestation of a subjective condition. This exception does not admit a statement when it was made under circumstances indicating that the statement is not trustworthy.

A statement concerning bodily condition must describe existing symptoms and feeling and cannot relate to the cause or the nature of the injury. A statement of declarant's then existing state of mind is relevant to show the declarant's state of mind. Generally, the statement of then existing state of mind is admissible to show that the declarant did certain acts which he intended to do. However, under this exception a statement of memory or belief is not admissible to prove the fact remembered or believed, i.e., a past fact. If the evidence of state of mind were admissible to show that the fact remembered or believed actually occurred, any statement narrating a past event, would be admissible to prove that the event occurred. However, a statement of memory or belief is admissible to prove the fact remembered or believed if it relates to the execution, revocation, identification, or terms of declarant's will for reasons of expediency and necessity—it may very well be the best evidence available. For similar provisions, see Calif. Evid. Code §§ 1250-51; New Jersey Evid. Rule 63(12); Fed. Rule Evid. 803(3).

Although Florida case law has not developed this area extensively, there is substantial accord. Prior declarations were admitted to show intent in Wetjen v. Williamson, 196 So.2d 461 (Fla. 1st Dist. 1967), where, in determining whether chattels had been annexed to realty and become fixtures, the court allowed declarations of a party to be admitted in order to determine if he intended that the article be permanently annexed, and Bowen v. Keen, 154 Fla. 161, 171, 17 So.2d 706, 711 (1944), where the court stated that, "The rule is quite generally recognized that the statements of a deceased person as to the purpose and destination of a trip or journey he is about to take are admissible."

One rather old case, Jacksonville Elect. Co. v. Sloan, 52 Fla. 257, 42 So. 516 (1906), reached a conclusion contrary to this exception. Statements made by the deceased in the morning before the afternoon when he was killed concerning his physical condition were excluded from evidence as not being a part of the res gestae.

Existing Florida law is apparently in accord with the rule admitting statements of memory or belief relating to the execution, revocation, identification, or terms of a declarant's will to prove the fact remembered or believed. In Marshall v. Hewett, 156 Fla. 645, 24 So.2d 1 (1945), the testimony of the draftsman of a will concerning the verbal instructions given him by the testator was admissible for the purpose of making clear the desires and intent of the testator. See Calif. Evid. Code § 1260.

COMMENTARY ON FEDERAL AND FLORIDA RULE DIFFERENCES

Florida Stat. § 90.803(3) and its federal counterpart, Federal Rule of Evidence 803(3), create an exception to the hearsay rule under certain circumstances for statements by a person regarding her then-existing state of mind, emotion, or physical sensation, including statements of intent, plan, motive, design, mental feeling, pain, or bodily health. Both the Florida and federal rules exclude from the scope of this exception statements of memory or belief offered to prove the fact remembered or believed, unless it relates to the execution, revocation, identification, or terms of the declarant's will. See FED. R. EVID. 803(3); FLA. STAT. § 90.803(3)(b)(1).

Under both the federal and Florida rules, the exception can be invoked for the purpose of proving the declarant's state of mind, emotion, or physical sensation, as well as the future conduct of the declarant, *see* FED. R. EVID. 803(3); FLA. STAT. § 90.803(3)(a), assuming, of course, that it is somehow relevant in the case. *See U.S. v. Veltmann*, 6 F.3d 1483, 1493-94 (11th Cir. 1993); *Taylor v. State*, 855 So. 2d 1, 18 (Fla. 2003). Yet while under the Florida rule it is clear that a declarant's statement of intent to do something is admissible only to prove *his* own future conduct, *not* that of a third person, *see Ibar v. State*, 938 So. 2d 451, 465 (Fla. 2006); *Brooks v. State*, 787 So. 2d 765, 770-71 (Fla. 2001); FLORIDA STAT. § 90.803(3)(a)(2), the federal decisions hold that such evidence *can* be used to prove the conduct of a third person, with a split only on the question whether corroborating evidence is required. *See U.S. v. Houlihan*, 871 F. Supp. 1495, 1499-1500 (D. Mass. 1994) (collecting cases).

One other difference between the federal and Florida rules is that the latter contains a proviso that makes inadmissible a statement made under circumstances that indicate its lack of trustworthiness. *See* FLA. STAT. § 90.803(3)(b)(2). By contrast, federal courts do not have discretion to exclude evidence falling within the scope of this exception based on a finding of lack of trustworthiness. *See U.S. v. Torres*, 901 F.2d 205, 239 (2d Cir. 1990); *U.S. v. Peak*, 856 F.2d 825, 834 (7th Cir. 1988).

Federal Rule 803(4). Exceptions to the Rule Against Hearsay — Regardless of Whether the Declarant Is Available as a Witness [Statements Made for Medical Diagnosis or Treatment]

The following are not excluded by the rule against hearsay, regardless of whether the declarant is available as a witness:

....

(4) *Statement Made for Medical Diagnosis or Treatment.* A statement that:

(A) is made for — and is reasonably pertinent to — medical diagnosis or treatment; and

(B) describes medical history; past or present symptoms or sensations; their inception; or their general cause.

....

ADVISORY COMMITTEE'S NOTE

....

Exception (4). Even those few jurisdictions which have shied away from generally admitting statements of present condition have allowed them if made to a physician for purposes of diagnosis and treatment in view of the patient's strong motivation to be truthful. McCormick § 266, p. 563. The same guarantee of trustworthiness extends to statements of past conditions and medical history, made for purposes of diagnosis or treatment. It also extends to statements as to causation, reasonably pertinent to the same purposes, in accord with the current trend. Shell Oil Co. v. Industrial Commission, 2 Ill.2d 590 (1954); McCormick § 266, p. 564; New Jersey Evidence Rule 63(12)(c). Statements as to fault would not ordinarily qualify under this latter language. Thus a patient's statement that he was struck by an automobile would qualify but not his statement that the car was driven through a red light. Under the exception the statement need not have been made to a physician. Statements to hospital attendants, ambulance drivers, or even members of the family might be included.

Conventional doctrine has excluded from the hearsay exception, as not within its guarantee of truthfulness, statements to a physician consulted only for the purpose of enabling him to testify. While these statements were not admissible as substantive evidence, the expert was allowed to state the basis of his opinion, including statements of this kind. The distinction thus called for was one most unlikely to be made by juries. The rule accordingly rejects the limitation. This position is consistent with the provision of Rule 703 that the facts on which expert testimony is based need not be admissible in evidence if of a kind ordinarily relied upon by experts in the field.

....

REPORT OF HOUSE COMMITTEE ON THE JUDICIARY

....

After giving particular attention to the question of physical examination made solely to enable a physician to testify, the Committee approved Rule 803(4) as submitted to Congress, with the understanding that it is not intended in any way to adversely affect present privilege rules or those subsequently adopted.

....

REPORT OF SENATE COMMITTEE ON THE JUDICIARY

The House approved this rule as it was submitted by the Supreme Court "with the understanding that it is not intended in any way to adversely affect present privilege rules." We also approve this rule, and we would point out with respect to the question of its relation to privileges, it must be read in conjunction with rule 35 of the Federal Rules of Civil Procedure which provides that whenever the physical or mental condition of a party (plaintiff or defendant) is in controversy, the court may require him to submit to an examination by a physician. It is these examinations which will normally be admitted under this exception.

....

Florida Stat. § 90.803(4). Hearsay Exceptions; Availability of Declarant Immaterial [Statements for Purposes of Medical Diagnosis or Treatment]

The provision of s. 90.802 to the contrary notwithstanding, the following are not inadmissible as evidence, even though the declarant is available as a witness:

....

(4) Statements for purposes of medical diagnosis or treatment. Statements made for purposes of medical diagnosis or treatment by a person seeking the diagnosis or treatment, or made by an individual who has knowledge of the facts and is legally responsible for the person who is unable to communicate the facts, which statements describe medical history, past or present symptoms, pain, or sensations, or the inceptions or general character of the cause or external source thereof, insofar as reasonably pertinent to diagnosis or treatment.

....

SPONSORS' NOTE (1976 ENACTMENT)

Because of the strong motivation to be truthful when making statements to physicians for the purpose of diagnosis and treatments, the statements are treated as an exception to the hearsay rule. See McCormick, Evidence § 292 (2nd ed. 1972); 6 Wigmore, Evidence §§ 1719-20 (3rd ed. 1940); Annot., 37 A.L.R.3d 778 (1971). Existing Florida law apparently recognizes the admissibility as substantive evidence of statements made to the treating physician. This exception permits testimony relating to causation only when it is reasonably pertinent to diagnosis or treatment. See Brown v. Seaboard Airline R.R., 434 F.2d 1101 (5th Cir. 1970). The court in Wilkinson v. Grover, 181 So.2d 591 (Fla. 3rd Dist. 1966) seemed to exclude all statements to the physician relating to causation unless they were "admissions" or res gestae.

Under this subsection, statements need not have been made to a physician. Statements to hospital attendants, ambulance drivers, or even members of the family might be included.

While existing Florida law permits a treating physician to testify based on the history given by the patient, see Bill Kelley Chevrolet, Inc. v. Kerr, 258 So.2d 280 (Fla. 3rd Dist. 1972), the courts are currently divided over whether a physician who is consulted only for the purpose of qualifying him to testify may base his opinion even in part on information the patient tells him at the examination. Compare Bondy v. West, 219 So.2d 117 (Fla. 2nd Dist. 1969) (expert testimony based in part on patient's medical testimony is inadmissible) with Raydel, Ltd. v. Medcalfe, 162 So.2d 910 (Fla. 3rd Dist.1964), quashed on other grounds, 178 So.2d 569 (Fla. 1965) (expert allowed to testify from medical history given him by patient when he also bases his opinion on findings of his examination). To the extent that an examining physician is allowed to base his opinion on information supplied by the patient, such information must be in the record. While the information supplied by the patient to such an "examining" physician is admitted for the purpose of supplying a basis for the physician's opinion and not as substantive evidence, the distinction is one unlikely to be made by a juror. This section accordingly rejects this limitation.

This subsection is in accord with the Raydel position. The fact that an "examining" physician depends in part on information gained from the patient in addition to findings from his examination will not prevent the physician from testifying as an expert nor will it prevent the physician from relating statements made by the patient.

This subsection is consistent with the provisions of Section 90.704 which allow expert testimony to be based on facts which are not admissible in evidence if they are of a kind ordinarily relied upon by experts in the field.

See Wisc. Rule Evid. 908.03(4); Fed. Rule Evid. 803(4).

COMMENTARY ON FEDERAL AND FLORIDA RULE DIFFERENCES

Florida Stat. § 90.803(4) and its federal counterpart, Federal Rule of Evidence 803(4), create an exception to the hearsay rule for statements made for purposes of medical diagnosis or treatment that describe past or present symptoms, pain, or sensations, as well as the cause thereof insofar as reasonably pertinent to diagnosis or treatment. Under neither provision is it necessary that the statement be made to a physician, but may instead be a statement made to hospital attendants, ambulance drivers, family members and the like, so long as it is made for the purpose of obtaining medical diagnosis or treatment. *See* Advisory Committee's Note to FED. R. EVID. 803(4); Sponsors' Note to FLA. STAT. § 90.803(4); *Begley v. State*, 483 So. 2d 70, 73 (Fla. 4th DCA 1986).

The requirement under both provisions that statements regarding cause are admissible only insofar as reasonably pertinent to diagnosis or treatment means that statements as to fault—such as that a particular person caused the injury—are usually not admissible. *See U.S. v. Belfast*, 611 F.3d 783, 818-19 (11th Cir. 2010); Advisory Committee's Note to FED. R. EVID. 803(4); Sponsors' Note to FLA. STAT. § 90.803(4). However, the federal courts have held that statement by a child to a physician identifying a member of the household or family as the perpetrator *are* pertinent to diagnosis or treatment and thus admissible under Federal Rule 803(4), *see U.S. v. Joe*, 8 F.3d 1488, 1494 (10th Cir. 1993) (collecting cases), an interpretation of Florida Stat. § 90.803(4) that has been rejected by the Florida Supreme Court, *see State v. Jones*, 625 So. 2d 821, 826 (Fla. 1993).

The Florida provision is applicable only if the declarant is the "person seeking diagnosis or treatment, or...an individual who has knowledge of the facts and is legally responsible for the person who is unable to communicate the facts." *See* FLA. STAT. § 90.803(4). By contrast, so long as the statement is made for purposes of medical diagnosis or treatment, the federal rule imposes no limitation on who the declarant is, permitting statements by family members, bystanders, and others to fall within the scope of the exception. *See Bucci v. Essex Ins. Co.*, 393 F.3d 285, 298-99 (1st Cir. 2005).

Federal Rule 803(5). Exceptions to the Rule Against Hearsay — Regardless of Whether the Declarant Is Available as a Witness [Recorded Recollection]

The following are not excluded by the rule against hearsay, regardless of whether the declarant is available as a witness:

....

(5) *Recorded Recollection.* A record that:

(A) is on a matter the witness once knew about but now cannot recall well enough to testify fully and accurately;

(B) was made or adopted by the witness when the matter was fresh in the witness's memory; and

(C) accurately reflects the witness's knowledge.

If admitted, the record may be read into evidence but may be received as an exhibit only if offered by an adverse party.

....

ADVISORY COMMITTEE'S NOTE

....

Exception (5). A hearsay exception for recorded recollection is generally recognized and has been described as having "long been favored by the federal and practically all the state courts that have had occasion to decide the question." United States v. Kelly, 349 F.2d 720, 770 (2d Cir. 1965), citing numerous cases and sustaining the exception against a claimed denial of the right of confrontation. Many additional cases are cited in Annot., 82 A.L.R.2d 473, 520. The guarantee of trustworthiness is found in the reliability inherent in a record made while events were still fresh in mind and accurately reflecting them. Owens v. State, 67 Md. 307, 316 (1887).

The principal controversy attending the exception has centered, not upon the propriety of the exception itself, but upon the question whether a preliminary requirement of impaired memory on the part of the witness should be imposed. The authorities are divided. If regard be had only to the accuracy of the evidence, admittedly impairment of the memory of the witness adds nothing to it and should not be required. McCormick § 277, p. 593; 3 Wigmore § 738, p. 76; Jordan v. People, 151 Colo. 133 (1962), cert. denied 373 U.S. 944; Hall v. State, 223 Md. 158 (1960); State v. Bindhammer, 44 N.J. 372 (1965). Nevertheless, the absence of the requirement, it is believed, would encourage the use of statements carefully prepared for purposes of litigation under the supervision of attorneys, investigators, or claim adjusters. Hence the example includes a requirement that the witness not have "sufficient recollection to enable him to testify fully and accurately." To the same effect are California Evidence Code § 1237 and New Jersey Rule 63(1)(b), and this has been the position of the federal courts. Vicksburg & Meridian R.R. v. O'Brien, 119 U.S. 99 (1886); Ahern v. Webb, 268 F.2d 45 (10th Cir. 1959); and see N.L.R.B. v. Hudson Pulp and Paper Corp., 273 F.2d 660, 665 (5th Cir. 1960); N.L.R.B. v. Federal Dairy Co., 297 F.2d 487 (1st Cir. 1962). But cf. United States v. Adams, 385 F.2d 548 (2d Cir. 1967).

No attempt is made in the exception to spell out the method of establishing the initial knowledge or the contemporaneity and accuracy of the record, leaving them to be dealt with as the circumstances of the particular case might indicate. Multiple person involvement in the process of observing and recording, as in Rathbun v. Brancatella, 93 N.J.L. 222 (1919), is entirely consistent with the exception.

Locating the exception at this place in the scheme of the rules is a matter of choice. There were two other possibilities. The first was to regard the statement as one of the group of prior statements of a testifying witness which are excluded entirely from the category of hearsay by Rule 801(d)(1). That category, however, requires that declarant be "subject to cross-examination," as to which the impaired memory aspect of the exception raises doubts. The other possibility was to include the exception among those covered by Rule 804. Since unavailability is required by that rule and lack of memory is listed as a species of unavailability by the definition of the term in Rule 804(a)(3), that treatment at first impression would seem appropriate. The fact is, however, that the unavailability requirement of the exception is of a limited and peculiar nature. Accordingly, the exception is located at this point rather than in the context of a rule where unavailability is conceived of more broadly.

....

REPORT OF HOUSE COMMITTEE ON THE JUDICIARY

....

Rule 803(5) as submitted by the Court permitted the reading into evidence of a memorandum or record concerning a matter about which a witness once had knowledge but now has insufficient recollection to enable him to testify accurately and fully, "shown to have been made when the matter was fresh in his memory and to reflect that knowledge correctly." The Committee amended this Rule to add the words "or adopted by the witness" after the phrase "shown to have been made", a treatment consistent with the definition of "statement" in the Jencks Act, 18 U.S.C. 3500. Moreover, it is the Committee's understanding that a memorandum or report, although barred under this Rule, would nonetheless be admissible if it came within another hearsay exception. This last stated principle is deemed applicable to all the hearsay rules.

REPORT OF SENATE COMMITTEE ON THE JUDICIARY

....

Rule 803(5) as submitted by the Court permitted the reading into evidence of a memorandum or record concerning a matter about which a witness once had knowledge but now has insufficient recollection to enable him to testify accurately and fully, "shown to have been made when the matter was fresh in his memory and to reflect that knowledge correctly." The House amended the rule to add the words "or adopted by the witness" after the phrase "shown to have been made," language parallel to the Jencks Act.[31]

The committee accepts the House amendment with the understanding and belief that it was not intended to narrow the scope of applicability of the rule. In fact, we understand it to clarify the rule's applicability to a memorandum adopted by the witness as well as one made by him. While the rule as submitted by the Court was silent on the question of who made the memorandum, we view the House amendment as a helpful clarification, noting, however, that the Advisory Committee's note to this rule suggests that the important thing is the accuracy of the memorandum rather than who made it.

The committee does not view the House amendment as precluding admissibility in situations in which multiple participants were involved.

When the verifying witness has not prepared the report, but merely examined it and found it accurate, he has adopted the report, and it is therefore admissible. The rule should also be interpreted to cover other situations involving multiple participants, e.g., employer dictating to secretary, secretary making memorandum at direction of employer, or information being passed along a chain of persons, as in *Curtis* v. *Bradley*.[32]

The committee also accepts the understanding of the House that a memorandum or report, although barred under this rule, would nonetheless be admissible if it came within another hearsay exception. We consider this principle to be applicable to all the hearsay rules.

Florida Stat. § 90.803(5). Hearsay Exceptions; Availability of Declarant Immaterial [Recorded Recollection]

The provision of s. 90.802 to the contrary notwithstanding, the following are not inadmissible as evidence, even though the declarant is available as a witness:

....

(5) Recorded recollection. A memorandum or record concerning a matter about which a witness once had knowledge, but now has insufficient recollection to enable the witness to testify fully and accurately, shown to have been made by the witness when the matter was fresh in the witness's memory and to reflect that knowledge correctly. A party may read into evidence a memorandum or record when it is admitted, but no such memorandum or record is admissible as an exhibit unless offered by an adverse party.

....

SPONSORS' NOTE (1976 ENACTMENT)

---

[31] 18 U.S.C. § 3500.

[32] 65 Conn. 99 (1894). See, also, Rathbun v. Brancatella, 93 N.J.L. 222 (1919); see also, *McCormick on Evidence*, § 303 (2d ed. 1972).

The "past recollection recorded" exception is generally recognized in federal and state courts. See McCormick, Evidence §§ 299-303 (2nd ed. 1972). As stated in the Advisory Committee's Note to Proposed Federal Rule of Evidence 803:

> The principal controversy attending the exception has centered, not upon the propriety of the exception itself, but upon the question whether a preliminary requirement of impaired memory on the part of the witness should be imposed....[T]he absence of the requirement, it is believed, would encourage the use of statements carefully prepared for purposes of litigation under the supervision of investigators, or claim adjusters. Hence, the example includes a requirement that the witness not have "sufficient recollection to enable him to testify fully and accurately."

Existing Florida law is in agreement with this exception. Montgomery Ward & Co. v. Rosenquist, 112 So.2d 885 (Fla. 2nd Dist. 1959). See Smith v. Hinkley, 98 Fla. 132, 123 So. 564 (1929) (witness who had no present recollection allowed to testify from writing made when memory perfect). Cf. Great Atl. & Pac. Tea Co. v. Nobles, 202 So.2d 603 (Fla. 1st Dist. 1967).

For similar rules see Calif. Evid. Code § 1237; New Jersey Evid.Rule 63(1)(b); Wisc. Rule Evid. 908.03 (omits the last sentence of this exception); Fed. Rule Evid. 803(5).

COMMENTARY ON FEDERAL AND FLORIDA RULE DIFFERENCES

Florida Stat. § 90.803(5) and its federal counterpart, Federal Rule of Evidence 803(5), create an exception to the hearsay rule for so-called recorded recollections, defined under both rules to include a memorandum or record concerning a matter about which a witness once had knowledge but now lacks sufficient recollection to enable the witness to testify fully and accurately, provided that it was made by the witness when fresh in his memory and reflects that knowledge correctly. Under both rules, if the foundational requirements are established, the memorandum or record can be read into evidence but may not itself be received as an exhibit unless offered by an adverse party. Under both rules, a tape-recorded statement qualifies as a "record" and may be played to the jury if the foundational requirements are established. See U.S. v. Jones, 601 F.3d 1247, 1263-64 (11th Cir. 2010); U.S. v. Sollars, 979 F.2d 1294, 1298 (8th Cir. 1992); Smith v. State, 880 So. 2d 730, 736 (Fla. 2d DCA 2004).

While the Florida rule is limited to recorded recollections "made" by a witness, the Federal rule is broader, encompassing those "made or adopted" by the witness (the Florida rule originally contained the words "or adopted," but the legislature deleted them, see 1976 Fla. Laws ch. 78-361). Moreover, the federal courts have interpreted the exception as generally being applicable in other situations in which multiple people are involved in the process of making a record, such as when one person reports his observations to a second person who writes them down. See, e.g., U.S. v. Hernandez, 333 F.3d 1168, 1179 (10th Cir. 2003). Given the legislature's decision to narrow the scope of the Florida exception to statements made by a witness, it seems doubtful that the courts would interpret the provision to encompass recorded recollections created through the involvement of multiple people.

Federal Rule 803(6). Exceptions to the Rule Against Hearsay — Regardless of Whether the Declarant Is Available as a Witness [Records of a Regularly Conducted Activity]

The following are not excluded by the rule against hearsay, regardless of whether the declarant is available as a witness:

....

(6) *Records of a Regularly Conducted Activity.* A record of an act, event, condition, opinion, or diagnosis if:

(A) the record was made at or near the time by — or from information transmitted by — someone with knowledge;

(B) the record was kept in the course of a regularly conducted activity of a business, organization, occupation, or calling, whether or not for profit;

(C) making the record was a regular practice of that activity;

(D) all these conditions are shown by the testimony of the custodian or another qualified witness, or by a certification that complies with Rule 902(11) or (12) or with a statute permitting certification; and

(E) neither the source of information nor the method or circumstances of preparation indicate a lack of trustworthiness.

....

ADVISORY COMMITTEE'S NOTE

....

Exception (6) represents an area which has received much attention from those seeking to improve the law of evidence. The Commonwealth Fund Act was the result of a study completed in 1927 by a distinguished committee under the chairmanship of Professor Morgan. Morgan et al., The Law of Evidence: Some Proposals for its Reform 63 (1927). With changes too minor to mention, it was adopted by Congress in 1936 as the rule for federal courts. 28 U.S.C. § 1732. A number of states took similar action. The Commissioners on Uniform State Laws in 1936 promulgated the Uniform Business Records as Evidence Act, 9A U.L.A. 506, which has acquired a substantial following in the states. Model Code Rule 514 and Uniform Rule 63(13) also deal with the subject. Difference of varying degrees of importance exist among these various treatments.

These reform efforts were largely within the context of business and commercial records, as the kind usually encountered, and concentrated considerable attention upon relaxing the requirement of producing as witnesses, or accounting for the nonproduction of, all participants in the process of gathering, transmitting, and recording information which the common law had evolved as a burdensome and crippling aspect of using records of this type. In their areas of primary emphasis on witnesses to be called and the general admissibility of ordinary business and commercial records, the Commonwealth Fund Act and the Uniform Act appear to have worked well. The exception seeks to preserve their advantages.

On the subject of what witnesses must be called, the Commonwealth Fund Act eliminated the common law requirement of calling or accounting for all participants by failing to mention it. United States v. Mortimer, 118 F.2d 266 (2d Cir. 1941); La Porte v. United States, 300 F.2d 878 (9th Cir. 1962); McCormick § 290, p. 608. Model Code Rule 514 and Uniform Rule 63(13) did likewise. The Uniform Act, however, abolished the common law requirement in express terms, providing that the requisite foundation testimony might be furnished by "the custodian or other qualified witness." Uniform Business Records as Evidence Act, § 2; 9A U.L.A. 506. The exception follows the Uniform Act in this respect.

The element of unusual reliability of business records is said variously to be supplied by systematic checking, by regularity and continuity which produce habits of precision, by actual experience of business in relying upon them, or by a duty to make an accurate record as part of a continuing job or occupation. McCormick §§ 281, 286, 287; Laughlin, Business Entries and the Like, 46 Iowa L.Rev. 276 (1961). The model statutes and rules have sought to capture these factors and to extend their impact by employing the phrase "regular course of business," in conjunction with a definition of "business" far broader than its ordinarily accepted meaning. The result is a tendency unduly to emphasize a requirement of routineness and repetitiveness and an insistence that other types of records be squeezed into the fact patterns which give rise to traditional business records. The rule therefore adopts the phrase "the course of a regularly conducted activity" as capturing the essential basis of the hearsay exception as it has evolved and the essential element which can be abstracted from the various specifications of what is a "business."

Amplification of the kinds of activities producing admissible records has given rise to problems which conventional business records by their nature avoid. They are problems of the source of the recorded information, of entries in opinion form, of motivation, and of involvement as participant in the matters recorded.

Sources of information presented no substantial problem with ordinary business records. All participants, including the observer or participant furnishing the information to be recorded, were acting routinely, under a duty of accuracy, with employer reliance on the result, or in short "in the regular course of business." If, however, the supplier of the information does not act in the regular course, an essential link is broken; the assurance of accuracy does not extend to the information itself, and the fact that it may be recorded with scrupulous accuracy is of no avail. An illustration is the police report incorporating information obtained from a bystander: the officer qualifies as acting in the regular course but the informant does not. The leading case, Johnson v. Lutz, 253 N.Y. 124 (1930), held that a report thus prepared was inadmissible. Most of the authorities have agreed with the decision. Gencarella v. Fyfe, 171 F.2d 419 (1st Cir. 1948); Gordon v. Robinson, 210 F.2d 192 (3d Cir. 1954); Standard Oil Co. of California v. Moore, 251 F.2d 188, 214 (9th Cir. 1957), cert. denied 356 U.S. 975; Yates v. Bair Transport, Inc., 249 F.Supp. 681 (S.D.N.Y. 1965); Annot., 69 A.L.R.2d 1148. Cf. Hawkins v. Gorea Motor Express, Inc., 360 F.2d 933 (2d Cir. 1966); Contra, 5 Wigmore § 1530a, n. 1, pp. 391–392. The point is not dealt with specifically in the Commonwealth Fund Act, the Uniform Act, or Uniform Rule 63(13). However, Model Code Rule 514 contains the requirement "that it was the regular course of that business for one with personal knowledge...to make such a memorandum or record or to transmit information thereof to be included in such a memorandum or record...." The rule follows this lead in requiring an informant with knowledge acting in the course of the regularly conducted activity.

Entries in the form of opinions were not encountered in traditional business records in view of the purely factual nature of the items recorded, but they are now commonly encountered with respect to medical diagnoses, prognoses, and test results, as well as occasionally in other areas. The Commonwealth Fund Act provided only for records of an "act, transaction, occurrence, or event," while the Uniform Act, Model Code Rule 514, and Uniform Rule 63(13) merely added the ambiguous term "condition." The limited phrasing of the Commonwealth Fund Act, 28 U.S.C. § 1732, may account for the reluctance of some federal decisions to admit diagnostic entries. New York Life Ins. Co. v. Taylor, 147 F.2d 297 (1945); Lyles v. United States, 254 F.2d 725 (1957), cert. denied 356 U.S. 961; England v. United States, 174 F.2d 466 (5th Cir. 1949); Skogen v. Dow Chemical Co., 375 F.2d 692 (8th Cir. 1967). Other federal decisions, however, experienced no difficulty in freely admitting diagnostic entries. Reed v. Order of United Commercial Travelers, 123 F.2d 252 (2d Cir. 1941); Buckminster's Estate v. Commissioner of Internal Revenue, 147 F.2d 331 (2d Cir. 1944); Medina v. Erickson, 226 F.2d 475 (9th Cir. 1955); Thomas v. Hogan, 308 F.2d 355 (4th Cir. 1962); Glawe v. Rulon, 284 F.2d 495 (8th Cir. 1960). In the state courts, the trend favors admissibility. Borucki v. MacKenzie Bros. Co., 125 Conn. 92 (1938); Allen v. St. Louis Public Service Co., 365 Mo. 677, 285 S.W.2d 663, 55 A.L.R.2d 1022 (1956); People v. Kohlmeyer, 284 N.Y. 366 (1940); Weis v. Weis, 147 Ohio St. 416 (1947). In order to make clear its adherence to the latter position, the rule specifically includes both diagnoses and opinions, in addition to acts, events, and conditions, as proper subjects of admissible entries.

Problems of the motivation of the informant have been a source of difficulty and disagreement. In Palmer v. Hoffman, 318 U.S. 109 (1943), exclusion of an accident report made by the since deceased engineer, offered by defendant railroad trustees in a grade crossing collision case, was upheld. The report was not "in the regular course of business," not a record of the systematic conduct of the business as a business, said the Court. The report was prepared for use in litigating, not railroading. While the opinion mentions the motivation of the engineer only obliquely, the emphasis on records of routine operations is significant only by virtue of impact on motivation to be accurate. Absence of routineness raises lack of motivation to be accurate. The opinion of the Court of Appeals had gone beyond mere lack of motive to be accurate: the engineer's statement was "dripping with motivations to misrepresent." Hoffman v. Palmer, 129 F.2d 976, 991 (2d Cir. 1942). The direct introduction of motivation is a disturbing factor, since absence of motive to misrepresent has not traditionally been a requirement of the rule; that records might be self-serving has not been a ground for exclusion. Laughlin, Business Records and the Like, 46 Iowa L.Rev. 276, 285 (1961). As Judge Clark said in his dissent, "I submit that there is hardly a grocer's account book which could not be excluded on that basis." 129 F.2d at 1002. A physician's evaluation report of a personal injury litigant would appear to be in the routine of his business. If the report is offered by the party at whose instance it was made, however, it has been held inadmissible, Yates v. Bair Transport, Inc., 249 F.Supp. 681 (S.D.N.Y. 1965), otherwise if offered by the opposite party, Korte v. New York, N.H. & H.R. Co., 191 F.2d 86 (2d Cir. 1951), cert. denied 342 U.S. 868.

The decisions hinge on motivation and which party is entitled to be concerned about it. Professor McCormick believed that the doctor's report or the accident report were sufficiently routine to justify admissibility. McCormick § 287, p. 604. Yet hesitation must be experienced in admitting everything which is observed and recorded in the course of a regularly conducted activity. Efforts to set a limit are illustrated by Hartzog v. United States, 217 F.2d 706 (4th Cir. 1954), error to admit worksheets made by since deceased deputy collector in preparation for the instant income tax evasion prosecution, and United States v. Ware, 247 F.2d 698 (7th Cir. 1957), error to admit narcotics agents' records of purchases. See also Exception (8), *infra*, as to the public record aspects of records of this nature. Some decisions have been satisfied as to motivation of an accident report if made pursuant to statutory duty, United States v. New York Foreign Trade Zone Operators, 304 F.2d 792 (2d Cir. 1962); Taylor v. Baltimore & O.R. Co., 344 F.2d 281 (2d Cir. 1965), since the report was oriented in a direction other than the litigation which ensued. Cf. Matthews v. United States, 217 F.2d 409 (5th Cir. 1954). The formulation of specific terms which would assure satisfactory results in all cases is not possible. Consequently the rule proceeds from the base that records made in the course of a regularly conducted activity will be taken as admissible but subject to authority to exclude if "the sources of information or other circumstances indicate lack of trustworthiness."

Occasional decisions have reached for enhanced accuracy by requiring involvement as a participant in matters reported. Clainos v. United States, 163 F.2d 593 (1947), error to admit police records of convictions; Standard Oil Co. of California v. Moore, 251 F.2d 188 (9th Cir. 1957), cert. denied 356 U.S. 975, error to admit employees' records of observed business practices of others. The rule includes no requirement of this nature. Wholly acceptable records may involve matters merely observed, e.g. the weather.

The form which the "record" may assume under the rule is described broadly as a "memorandum, report, record, or data compilation, in any form." The expression "data compilation" is used as broadly descriptive of any means of storing information other than the conventional words and figures in written or documentary form. It includes, but is by no means limited to, electronic computer storage. The term is borrowed from revised Rule 34(a) of the Rules of Civil Procedure.

....

REPORT OF HOUSE COMMITTEE ON THE JUDICIARY

....

Rule 803(6) as submitted by the Court permitted a record made "in the course of a regularly conducted activity" to be admissible in certain circumstances. The Committee believed there were insufficient guarantees of reliability in records made in the course of activities falling outside the scope of "business" activities as that term is broadly defined in 28 U.S.C. 1732. Moreover, the Committee concluded that the additional requirement of Section 1732 that it must have been the regular practice of a business to make the record is a necessary further assurance of its trustworthiness. The Committee accordingly amended the Rule to incorporate these limitations.

....

REPORT OF SENATE COMMITTEE ON THE JUDICIARY

....

Rule 803(6) as submitted by the Supreme Court permitted a record made in the course of a regularly conducted activity to be admissible in certain circumstances. This rule constituted a broadening of the traditional business records hearsay exception which has been long advocated by scholars and judges active in the law of evidence.

The House felt there were insufficient guarantees of reliability of records not within a broadly defined business records exception. We disagree. Even under the House definition of "business" including profession, occupation, and "calling of every kind," the records of many regularly conducted activities will, or may be, excluded from evidence. Under the principle of *ejusdem generis*, the intent of "calling of every kind" would seem to be related to work-related endeavors—e.g., butcher, baker, artist, etc.

Thus, it appears that the records of many institutions or groups might not be admissible under the House amendments. For example, schools, churches, and hospitals will not normally be considered businesses within the definition. Yet, these are groups which keep financial and other records on a regular basis in a manner similar to business enterprises. We believe these records are of equivalent trustworthiness and should be admitted into evidence.

Three states, which have recently codified their evidence rules, have adopted the Supreme Court version of rule 803(6), providing for admission of memoranda of a "regularly conducted activity." None adopted the words "business activity" used in the House amendment.[33]

Therefore, the committee deleted the word "business" as it appears before the word "activity". The last sentence then is unnecessary and was also deleted.

It is the understanding of the committee that the use of the phrase "person with knowledge" is not intended to imply that the party seeking to introduce the memorandum, report, record, or data compilation must be able to produce, or even identify, the specific individual upon whose first-hand knowledge the memorandum, report, record or data compilation was based. A sufficient foundation for the introduction of such evidence will be laid if the party seeking to introduce the evidence is able to show that it was the regular practice of the activity to base such memorandums, reports, records, or data compilations upon a transmission from a person with knowledge, e.g., in the case of the content of a shipment of goods, upon a report from the company's receiving agent or in the case of a computer printout, upon a report from the company's computer programmer or one who has knowledge of the particular record system. In short, the scope of the phrase "person with knowledge" is meant to be

---

[33] See Nev.Rev.Stats. § 15.135; N.Mex.Stats. (1973 Supp.) § 20-4-803(6); West's Wis.Stats.Anno. (1973 Supp.) § 908.03(6).

coterminous with the custodian of the evidence or other qualified witness. The committee believes this represents the desired rule in light of the complex nature of modern business organizations.

....

CONFERENCE REPORT

Rule 803 defines when hearsay statements are admissible in evidence even though the declarant is available as a witness. The Senate amendments make three changes in this rule.

The House bill provides in subsection (6) that records of a regularly conducted "business" activity qualify for admission into evidence as an exception to the hearsay rule. "Business" is defined as including "business, profession, occupation and calling of every kind." The Senate amendment drops the requirement that the records be those of a "business" activity and eliminates the definition of "business." The Senate amendment provides that records are admissible if they are records of a regularly conducted "activity."

The Conference adopts the House provision that the records must be those of a regularly conducted "business" activity. The Conferees changed the definition of "business" contained in the House provision in order to make it clear that the records of institutions and associations like schools, churches and hospitals are admissible under this provision. The records of public schools and hospitals are also covered by Rule 803(8), which deals with public records and reports.

....

ADVISORY COMMITTEE'S NOTE (2000 AMENDMENT)

The amendment provides that the foundation requirements of Rule 803(6) can be satisfied under certain circumstances without the expense and inconvenience of producing time-consuming foundation witnesses. Under current law, courts have generally required foundation witnesses to testify. *See, e.g., Tongil Co., Ltd. v. Hyundai Merchant Marine Corp.*, 968 F.2d 999 (9th Cir. 1992) (reversing a judgment based on business records where a qualified person filed an affidavit but did not testify). Protections are provided by the authentication requirements of Rule 902(11) for domestic records, Rule 902(12) for foreign records in civil cases, and 18 U.S.C. § 3505 for foreign records in criminal cases.

Florida Stat. § 90.803(6). Hearsay Exceptions; Availability of Declarant Immaterial [Records of Regularly Conducted Business Activity]

The provision of s. 90.802 to the contrary notwithstanding, the following are not inadmissible as evidence, even though the declarant is available as a witness:

....

(6) Records of regularly conducted business activity.

(a) A memorandum, report, record, or data compilation, in any form, of acts, events, conditions, opinion, or diagnosis, made at or near the time by, or from information transmitted by, a person with knowledge, if kept in the course of a regularly conducted business activity and if it was the regular practice of that business activity to make such memorandum, report, record, or data compilation, all as shown by the testimony of the custodian or other qualified witness, or as shown by a certification or declaration that complies with paragraph (c) and s. 90.902(11), unless the sources of information or other circumstances show lack of trustworthiness. The term "business" as used in this paragraph includes a business, institution, association, profession, occupation, and calling of every kind, whether or not conducted for profit.

(b) Evidence in the form of an opinion or diagnosis is inadmissible under paragraph (a) unless such opinion or diagnosis would be admissible under ss. 90.701-90.705 if the person whose opinion is recorded were to testify to the opinion directly.

(c) A party intending to offer evidence under paragraph (a) by means of a certification or declaration shall serve reasonable written notice of that intention upon every other party and shall make the evidence available for inspection sufficiently in advance of its offer in evidence to provide to any other party a fair opportunity to challenge the admissibility of the evidence. If the evidence is maintained in a foreign country, the party intending to offer the evidence must provide written notice of that intention at the arraignment or as soon after the arraignment as is practicable or, in a civil case, 60 days before the trial. A motion opposing the admissibility of such evidence must be made by the opposing party and determined by the court before trial. A party's failure to file such a motion before trial constitutes a waiver of objection to the evidence, but the court for good cause shown may grant relief from the waiver.

....

SPONSORS' NOTE (1976 ENACTMENT)

This exception combines the "Shop-Book Rule" and "Business Record Act." The exception is generally recognized because of the reliability of business records supplied by systematic checking, by regularity and continuity which produce habits of precision, by actual experience of business in relying upon them, and by a duty to make an accurate record as part of a continuing job or occupation.

This exception restates existing § 92.36 of the Florida Statutes which provides, in part, that:

A record of an act, condition or event, including a record kept by means of electronic data processing, shall, in so far as relevant, be competent evidence if the custodian or other qualified witness testifies to its identity and the mode of its preparation, and if it was made in the regular course of business, at or near the time of the act, condition or event, and if, in the opinion of the court, the sources of information, method and time of preparation were such as to justify its admission.

This exception provides a change from existing law. Opinions and diagnoses which are in a qualified record are admissible as long as the opinion is one which the witness could give under Sections 90.701-90.705 if called to testify. The recorder of entries on a hospital chart makes the entry with the knowledge that life and death often hang in the balance. Whether these diagnostic entries are admissible has not been determined in Florida. However, in Brevard County v. Jacks, 238 So.2d 156, 158-59 (Fla. 4th Dist. 1970), the court found error in the trial judge's refusal to admit hospital records under the business records act. The court relied on 40 Am. Jur.2d Hospitals and Asylums § 43, p. 884, which it quoted as follows:

"Unless subject to such specific objections as irrelevancy, inadequate sources of information, self-serving character, or exceeding the bounds of legitimate expert opinion, the admissibility of hospital records in evidence under the Uniform Business Records Act may extend to such matters, among others, as the physical examination findings, the patient's symptoms and complaints, treatment and progress records, diagnoses by those qualified to make them, the results of analyses and laboratory tests, X-rays, and the behavior of the patient, and those parts of the patient's history inherently necessary or at least helpful to the observation, diagnosis, and the treatment of the patient."

See McCormick, Evidence §§ 307, 313 (2nd ed. 1972).

See Fed. Rule Evid. 803(6); New Jersey Evid. Rule 63(13), Calif. Evid. Code § 1271, Kansas Code of Civ. Pro. § 60-460(m).

Problems of the motivation of the informant have been a source of difficulty and disagreement. If the recorder's motive is not to be correct but rather is to prepare for litigation, the report is inadmissible. See Laughlin, Business Entries and the Like, 46 Iowa L. Rev. 276, 285 (1961). Because of the difficulty of stating in specific terms the circumstances of admissibility, the exception contains the phrase "unless the sources of information or other circumstances indicate lack of trustworthiness."

All participants must be acting routinely in the supplying and recording of the information. If the supplier of the information does not act in the regular course, an essential link is broken; the assurance of accuracy does not extend to the information itself, and the fact that it may be recorded with scrupulous accuracy is of no avail. For example, when a police report incorporates information obtained from a bystander, the officer qualifies as acting in the regular course but the informant does not. The report is thus inadmissible. See Johnson v. Lutz, 253 N.Y. 124, 170 N.E. 517 (1930).

Existing Section 92.37 is included in this exception. Under that section, shop books and books of account of a party in which charges and entries were made are admissible. The entry must have been made in the regular course of business, at or near the time of the act, condition, or event. E.Z.E. Inc. v. Jackson, 235 So.2d 337 (Fla. 4th Dist. 1970). This section is no longer necessary since the business records act is an extension of it, and was "intended to liberalize the rules as to the allowance of shop book memoranda." Exchange Nat. Bank v. Hospital & Welfare Bd., 181 So.2d 9, 11 (Fla. 2nd Dist. 1965).

COMMENTARY ON FEDERAL AND FLORIDA RULE DIFFERENCES

Florida Stat. § 90.803(6) and its federal counterpart, Federal Rule of Evidence 803(6), create an exception to the hearsay rule for business records, defined to include a memorandum, report, record, or data compilation of acts, events, conditions, opinions, or diagnoses, made at or near the time by, or from information transmitted by, a person with knowledge, if kept in the course of a regularly conducted business activity and if it was the regular practice of that business activity to make such a memorandum, report, record, or data compilation. Both rules encompass the records of a broad array of organizations whether or not conducted for profit, thus including such things as schools, churches, hospitals and the like along with traditional for-profit businesses. Both the Florida and federal rules permit these foundational requirements to be shown either through the testimony of the custodian of records or other qualified witness, or alternatively, with a certification as provided for in Federal Rules 902(11)-(12) or Florida Stat. § 90.902(11). The Florida rule contains certain notice requirements when a party intends to establish the foundational requirements through certification. See FLA. STAT. § 90.803(6)(c). While Federal Rule 803(6) itself does not set forth any notice requirements, such requirements are contained in Federal Rules 902(11)-(12), which are cross-referenced in Federal Rule 803(6).

Although neither the Florida nor the federal exception requires that the person who made the record have personal knowledge of the matters contained therein, only that it was transmitted to the person from someone with such personal knowledge, see U.S. v. Langford, 647 F.3d 1309, 1326-27 (11th Cir. 2011); King v. Auto Supply of Jupiter, Inc., 917 So. 2d 1015, 1019 (Fla. 1st DCA 2006), the source of the information must be a member of the organization; neither exception encompasses information contained in business records if the source who has personal knowledge is an outsider. See id.; T. Harris Young & Assoc., Inc. v. Marquette Elecs., Inc., 931 F.2d

816, 828 (11th Cir. 1991); Advisory Committee's Note to FED. R. EVID. 803(6); Sponsors' Note to FLA. STAT. § 90.803(6). If a business record contains information from an outsider, it is hearsay-within-hearsay, and it is admissible only if the inner layer also falls within an exception to the hearsay rule. *See Brooks v. State*, 918 So. 2d 181, 193 (Fla. 2005); *U.S. v. Bueno-Sierra*, 99 F.3d 375, 379 n.10 (11th Cir. 1996).

Even if the foundational requirements are satisfied, both rules provide an exception to admissibility if the source of information or method or circumstances of preparation indicate a lack of trustworthiness. The party opposing admissibility bears the burden of proving a lack of trustworthiness under both Florida and federal law. *See Love v. Garcia*, 634 So. 2d 158, 160 (Fla. 1994); *Shelton v. Consumer Prods. Safety Comm'n*, 277 F.3d 998, 1010 (8th Cir. 2002).

Under the Florida rule, a business record in the form of a diagnosis or opinion is admissible only if the person whose opinion is recorded would have been qualified to testify to the opinion directly under the provisions of Florida Stat. §§ 90.701-90.705. *See* FLA. STAT. § 90.803(6)(b). The text of the federal rule is silent on this issue, and one of the few cases addressing the issue declined to adopt a rule that business records containing expert opinion are admissible only if the proponent establishes the expert's qualifications under Rule 702. Rather, the court adopted a flexible approach that gives the trial court discretion to exclude such records under the trustworthiness proviso of Rule 803(6) in cases in which expert's qualifications are in serious doubt. *See U.S. v. Licavoli*, 604 F.2d 613, 622-23 (9th Cir. 1979).

The federal courts, including the Eleventh Circuit, hold that this exception cannot be invoked in a criminal case against a defendant to admit a public record if the same record would not be admissible under Federal Rule 803(8)(A)(ii) or (iii) because of the limitations set forth in those rules. *See U.S. v. Brown*, 9 F.3d 907, 911 (11th Cir. 1993). While no Florida decisions have directly addressed this issue, the Florida Supreme Court has stated generally that "[w]here government records are at issue, the records are often admissible both as business records and as public records." *Yisrael v. State*, 993 So. 2d 952, 959 (Fla. 2008).

Federal Rule 803(7). Exceptions to the Rule Against Hearsay — Regardless of Whether the Declarant Is Available as a Witness [Absence of a Record of a Regularly Conducted Activity]

The following are not excluded by the rule against hearsay, regardless of whether the declarant is available as a witness:

....

(7) *Absence of a Record of a Regularly Conducted Activity.* Evidence that a matter is not included in a record described in paragraph (6) if:

(A) the evidence is admitted to prove that the matter did not occur or exist;

(B) a record was regularly kept for a matter of that kind; and

(C) neither the possible source of the information nor other circumstances indicate a lack of trustworthiness.

....

ADVISORY COMMITTEE'S NOTE

....

Exception (7). Failure of a record to mention a matter which would ordinarily be mentioned is satisfactory evidence of its nonexistence. Uniform Rule 63(14), Comment. While probably not hearsay as defined in Rule 801, *supra*, decisions may be found which class the evidence not only as hearsay but also as not within any exception. In order to set the question at rest in favor of admissibility, it is specifically treated here. McCormick § 289, p. 609; Morgan, Basic Problems of Evidence 314 (1962); 5 Wigmore § 1531; Uniform Rule 63(14); California Evidence Code § 1272; Kansas Code of Civil Procedure § 60-460(n); New Jersey Evidence Rule 63(14).

....

REPORT OF HOUSE COMMITTEE ON THE JUDICIARY

....

Rule 803(7) as submitted by the Court concerned the *absence* of entry in the records of a "regularly conducted activity." The Committee amended this Rule to conform with its action with respect to Rule 803(6).

....

Florida Stat. § 90.803(7). Hearsay Exceptions; Availability of Declarant Immaterial [Absence of Entry in Records of Regularly Conducted Activity]

The provision of s. 90.802 to the contrary notwithstanding, the following are not inadmissible as evidence, even though the declarant is available as a witness:

....

(7) Absence of entry in records of regularly conducted activity. Evidence that a matter is not included in the memoranda, reports, records, or data compilations, in any form, of a regularly conducted activity to prove the nonoccurrence or nonexistence of the matter, if the matter was of a kind of which a memorandum, report, record, or data compilation was regularly made and preserved, unless the sources of information or other circumstances show lack of trustworthiness.

....

SPONSORS' NOTE (1976 ENACTMENT)

Technically, evidence of the absence of a record may not be hearsay, but in order to set the question to rest in favor of admissibility, it is specifically treated. The failure of a record to mention a matter that would be ordinarily mentioned can be viewed as circumstantial evidence of its nonexistence. Since the record is not offered to prove the truth of the facts it contains, the inference from the absence of an entry is arguably not hearsay. It may be argued that the lack of an entry is a negative assertion that the transaction did not occur and is therefore hearsay. Similar provisions are found in Calif. Evid. Code § 1272; Kansas Code of Civ. Pro. § 60-460(n); and New Jersey Evid. Rule 63(14); Wisc. Evid. Rule 908.03(7); Fed. Rule Evid. 803(7).

COMMENTARY ON FEDERAL AND FLORIDA RULE DIFFERENCES

Florida Stat. § 90.803(7) and its federal counterpart, Federal Rule 803(7), create an exception to the hearsay rule for evidence that a matter is not included in the memoranda, reports, records, or data compilations of a regularly conducted business activity, offered as proof of the nonoccurrence or nonexistence of the matter, if it was of a kind of which a memorandum, report, record, or data compilation was regularly made and preserved. Both rules contain a proviso excluding such evidence if the sources of information or other circumstances indicate a lack of trustworthiness.

There are no substantive differences between the federal and Florida rules.

Federal Rule 803(8). Exceptions to the Rule Against Hearsay — Regardless of Whether the Declarant Is Available as a Witness [Public Records]

The following are not excluded by the rule against hearsay, regardless of whether the declarant is available as a witness:

....

(8) *Public Records.* A record or statement of a public office if:

(A) it sets out:

(i) the office's activities;

(ii) a matter observed while under a legal duty to report, but not including, in a criminal case, a matter observed by law-enforcement personnel; or

(iii) in a civil case or against the government in a criminal case, factual findings from a legally authorized investigation; and

(B) neither the source of information nor other circumstances indicate a lack of trustworthiness.

....

ADVISORY COMMITTEE'S NOTE

....

Exception (8). Public records are a recognized hearsay exception at common law and have been the subject of statutes without number. McCormick § 291. See, for example, 28 U.S.C. § 1733, the relative narrowness of which is illustrated by its nonapplicability to nonfederal public agencies, thus necessitating resort to the less appropriate business record exception to the hearsay rule. Kay v. United States, 255 F.2d 476 (4th Cir. 1958). The rule makes no distinction between federal and nonfederal offices and agencies.

Justification for the exception is the assumption that a public official will perform his duty properly and the unlikelihood that he will remember details independently of the record. Wong Wing Foo v. McGrath, 196 F.2d 120 (9th Cir. 1952), and see Chesapeake & Delaware Canal Co. v. United States, 250 U.S. 123

(1919). As to items [(A)(i)] and [(A)(ii)], further support is found in the reliability factors underlying records of regularly conducted activities generally. See Exception (6), supra.

[(A)(i)] Cases illustrating the admissibility of records of the office's or agency's own activities are numerous. Chesapeake & Delaware Canal Co. v. United States, 250 U.S. 123 (1919), Treasury records of miscellaneous receipts and disbursements; Howard v. Perrin, 200 U.S. 71 (1906), General Land Office records; Ballew v. United States, 160 U.S. 187 (1895). Pension Office records.

[(A)(ii)] Cases sustaining admissibility of records of matters observed are also numerous. United States v. Van Hook, 284 F.2d 489 (7th Cir. 1960), remanded for resentencing 365 U.S. 609, letter from induction officer to District Attorney, pursuant to army regulations, stating fact and circumstances of refusal to be inducted; T'Kach v. United States, 242 F.2d 937 (5th Cir. 1957), affidavit of White House personnel officer that search of records showed no employment of accused, charged with fraudulently representing himself as an envoy of the President; Minnehaha County v. Kelley, 150 F.2d 356 (8th Cir. 1945); Weather Bureau records of rainfall; United States v. Meyer, 113 F.2d 387 (7th Cir. 1940), cert. denied 311 U.S. 706, map prepared by government engineer from information furnished by men working under his supervision.

[(A)(iii)] The more controversial area of public records is that of the so-called "evaluative" report. The disagreement among the decisions has been due in part, no doubt, to the variety of situations encountered, as well as to differences in principle. Sustaining admissibility are such cases as United States v. Dumas, 149 U.S. 278 (1893), statement of account certified by Postmaster General in action against postmaster; McCarty v. United States, 185 F.2d 520 (5th Cir. 1950), reh. denied 187 F.2d 234, Certificate of Settlement of General Accounting Office showing indebtedness and letter from Army official stating Government had performed, in action on contract to purchase and remove waste food from Army camp; Moran v. Pittsburgh-Des Moines Steel Co., 183 F.2d 467 (3d Cir. 1950), report of Bureau of Mines as to cause of gas tank explosion; Petition of W___, 164 F.Supp. 659 (E.D.Pa. 1958), report by Immigration and Naturalization Service investigator that petitioner was known in community as wife of man to whom she was not married. To the opposite effect and denying admissibility are Franklin v. Skelly Oil Co., 141 F.2d 568 (10th Cir. 1944), State Fire Marshal's report of cause of gas explosion; Lomax Transp. Co. v. United States, 183 F.2d 331 (9th Cir. 1950), Certificate of Settlement from General Accounting Office in action for naval supplies lost in warehouse fire; Yung Jin Teung v. Dulles, 229 F.2d 244 (2d Cir. 1956), "Status Reports" offered to justify delay in processing passport applications. Police reports have generally been excluded except to the extent to which they incorporate firsthand observations of the officer. Annot., 69 A.L.R.2d 1148. Various kinds of evaluative reports are admissible under federal statutes: 7 U.S.C. § 78, findings of Secretary of Agriculture prima facie evidence of true grade of grain; 7 U.S.C. § 210(f), findings of Secretary of Agriculture prima facie evidence in action for damages against stockyard owner; 7 U.S.C. § 292, order by Secretary of Agriculture prima facie evidence in judicial enforcement proceedings against producers association monopoly; 7 U.S.C. § 1622(h), Department of Agriculture inspection certificates of products shipped in interstate commerce prima facie evidence; 8 U.S.C. § 1440(c), separation of alien from military service on conditions other than honorable provable by certificate from department in proceedings to revoke citizenship; 18 U.S.C. § 4245, certificate of Director of Prisons that convicted person has been examined and found probably incompetent at time of trial prima facie evidence in court hearing on competency; 42 U.S.C. § 269(b), bill of health by appropriate official prima facie evidence of vessel's sanitary history and condition and compliance with regulations; 46 U.S.C. § 679, certificate of consul presumptive evidence of refusal of master to transport destitute seamen to United States. While these statutory exceptions to the hearsay rule are left undisturbed, Rule 802, the willingness of Congress to recognize a substantial measure of admissibility for evaluative reports is a helpful guide.

Factors which may be of assistance in passing upon the admissibility of evaluative reports include: (1) the timeliness of the investigation, McCormick, Can the Courts Make Wider Use of Reports of Official Investigations? 42 Iowa L.Rev. 363 (1957); (2) the special skill or experience of the official, id., (3) whether a hearing was held and the level at which conducted, Franklin v. Skelly Oil Co., 141 F.2d 568 (10th Cir. 1944); (4) possible motivation problems suggested by Palmer v. Hoffman, 318 U.S. 109 (1943).

Others no doubt could be added.

The formulation of an approach which would give appropriate weight to all possible factors in every situation is an obvious impossibility. Hence the rule, as in Exception (6), assumes admissibility in the first instance but with ample provision for escape if sufficient negative factors are present. In one respect, however, the rule with respect to evaluative reports under item [(A)(iii)] is very specific: they are admissible only in civil cases and against the government in criminal cases in view of the almost certain collision with confrontation rights which would result from their use against the accused in a criminal case.

....

REPORT OF HOUSE COMMITTEE ON THE JUDICIARY

....

The Committee approved Rule 803(8) without substantive change from the form in which it was submitted by the Court. The Committee intends that the phrase "factual findings" be strictly construed and that evaluations or opinions contained in public reports shall not be admissible under this Rule.

....

REPORT OF SENATE COMMITTEE ON THE JUDICIARY

....

The House approved rule 803(8), as submitted by the Supreme Court, with one substantive change. It excluded from the hearsay exception reports containing matters observed by police officers and other law enforcement personnel in criminal cases. Ostensibly, the reason for this exclusion is that observations by police officers at the scene of the crime or the apprehension of the defendant are not as reliable as observations by public officials in other cases because of the adversarial nature of the confrontation between the police and the defendant in criminal cases.

The committee accepts the House's decision to exclude such recorded observations where the police officer is available to testify in court about his observation. However, where he is unavailable as unavailability is defined in rule 804(a)(4) and (a)(5), the report should be admitted as the best available evidence. Accordingly, the committee has amended rule 803(8) to refer to the provision of rule 804(b)(5), which allows the admission of such reports, records or other statements where the police officer or other law enforcement officer is unavailable because of death, then existing physical or mental illness or infirmity, or not being successfully subject to legal process.[34]

The House Judiciary Committee report contained a statement of intent that "the phrase 'factual findings' in subdivision [(A)(iii)] be strictly construed and that evaluations or opinions contained in public reports shall not be admissible under this rule." The committee takes strong exception to this limiting understanding of the application of the rule. We do not think it reflects an understanding of the intended operation of the rule as explained in the Advisory Committee notes to this subsection. The Advisory Committee notes on subsection [(A)(iii)] of this subdivision point out that various kinds of evaluative reports are now admissible under Federal statutes. 7 U.S.C. § 78, findings of Secretary of Agriculture prima facie evidence of true grade of grain; 42 U.S.C. § 269(b), bill of health by appropriate official prima

---

[34] Editor's Note: The version of Rule 804(b)(5) discussed here was not included in the rules as enacted.

facie evidence of vessel's sanitary history and condition and compliance with regulations. These statutory exceptions to the hearsay rule are preserved. Rule 802. The willingness of Congress to recognize these and other such evaluative reports provides a helpful guide in determining the kind of reports which are intended to be admissible under this rule. We think the restrictive interpretation of the House overlooks the fact that while the Advisory Committee assumes admissibility in the first instance of evaluative reports, they are not admissible if, as the rule states, "the sources of information or other circumstances indicate lack of trustworthiness."

The Advisory Committee explains the factors to be considered:

> Factors which may be [of] assistance in passing upon the admissibility of evaluative reports include: (1) the timeliness of the investigation, McCormick, Can the Courts Make Wider Use of Reports of Official Investigations? 42 Iowa L.Rev. 363 (1957); (2) the special skill or experience of the official, *id.*; (3) whether a hearing was held and the level at which conducted, Franklin v. Skelly Oil Co., 141 F.2d 568 (9th Cir. 1944); (4) possible motivation problems suggested by Palmer v. Hoffman, 318 U.S. 109 (1943). Others no doubt could be added.[35]

The committee concludes that the language of the rule together with the explanation provided by the Advisory Committee furnish sufficient guidance on the admissibility of evaluative reports.

....

CONFERENCE REPORT

....

The Senate amendment adds language, not contained in the House bill, that refers to another rule that was added by the Senate in another amendment.

In view of its action on Rule 804(b)(5) (Criminal law enforcement records and reports), the Conference does not adopt the Senate amendment and restores the bill to the House version.

....

Florida Stat. § 90.803(8). Hearsay Exceptions; Availability of Declarant Immaterial [Public Records and Reports]

The provision of s. 90.802 to the contrary notwithstanding, the following are not inadmissible as evidence, even though the declarant is available as a witness:

....

(8) Public records and reports. Records, reports, statements reduced to writing, or data compilations, in any form, of public offices or agencies, setting forth the activities of the office or agency, or matters observed pursuant to duty imposed by law as to matters which there was a duty to report, excluding in criminal cases matters observed by a police officer or other law enforcement personnel, unless the sources of information or other circumstances show their lack of trustworthiness. The criminal case exclusion shall not apply to an affidavit otherwise admissible under s. 316.1934 or s. 327.354.

....

---

[35] Advisory Committee's notes, to Rule [803(8)(A)(iii)].

SPONSORS' NOTE (1976 ENACTMENT)

Public records are a recognized hearsay exception at common law. McCormick, Evidence § 315 (2nd ed. 1972). The exception recognizes the inconvenience that would result from requiring the officer who made the report to testify to the authenticity of the official document. The influence of an official duty to make accurate statements and the force of habit and routine provide the necessary assurance of reliability. It is also unlikely that a public official will remember details independently of the record.

While public records have been the subject of general statutes in a number of states, no statute is present in Florida. Existing Florida law is in accord with items (a) and (b). The leading case is Bell v. Kendrick, 25 Fla. 778, 785, 6 So. 868, 869 (1889), in which the court stated:

> Official registers or books kept by persons in public office in which they are required, whether by statute or by the nature of the office, to write down particular transactions occurring in the course of their public duties, and under their personal observation, are generally admissible in evidence, notwithstanding their authenticity is not confirmed by the ordinary test of truth, the obligation of an oath, and an opportunity to cross-examine the person on whose authority the truth of the document depends....It is not necessary to the admissibility in evidence of an official register of this kind that a statute should expressly require it to be kept, or that the nature of the office should render it indispensable.

See Branch v. State, 76 Fla. 558, 80 So. 482 (1919); Corbett v. Berg, 152 So.2d 196 (Fla. 3rd Dist. 1963).

Numerous cases in Florida have upheld the admissibility of hospital records under the public records exception because of the requirement of Fla. Stat. § 382.31 that hospitals maintain records concerning their patients. See, e.g., Wilkinson v. Grover, 181 So.2d 591 (Fla. 3rd Dist. 1965), cert. denied, 188 So.2d 824 (Fla. 1966); Comment, Evidence: The Admissibility of Hospital Records Under Florida Statutes, Section 382.31, 18 U. Fla. L. Rev. 512 (1965).

Nothing in this subsection affects existing statutes that make privileged specific public records, e.g., police accident reports, or that provide for the admissibility of specific government reports.

See New Jersey Evid. Rule 63(15) and Calif. Evid. Code § 1280.

Wisc. Rule Evid. 908.03(8) and Fed. Rule Evid. 803(8) are similar but specifically provide that factual findings resulting from investigations are admissible.

COMMENTARY ON FEDERAL AND FLORIDA RULE DIFFERENCES

Florida Stat. § 90.803(8) and its federal counterpart, Federal Rule of Evidence 803(8), create an exception to the hearsay rule for certain categories of records, reports, statements, or data compilations of public offices or agencies.

The federal rule divides public records into three different categories, and subjects each category to different treatment. The first category—records setting forth the activities of the office or agency—can be admitted under this exception without any special restrictions. See FED. R. EVID. 803(8)(A)(i). The second category—records setting forth matters observed pursuant to duty imposed by law as to which matters there was a duty to report—are admissible under this exception, subject to a proviso excluding from its scope in criminal cases matters observed by law-enforcement personnel. See FED. R. EVID. 803(8)(A)(ii). The federal courts are split on the question whether this proviso bars such evidence when offered in a criminal case by the accused. Compare U.S. v. Smith, 521 F.2d 957, 968-69 n.24 (D.C. Cir. 1975) (holding that it does not), with U.S. v.

FLORIDA AND FEDERAL EVIDENCE RULES

Insaulgarat, 378 F.3d 456, 465-66 (5th Cir. 2004) (holding that the plain language of the proviso does not distinguish between evidence offered by the prosecution and the defense). Moreover, the Eleventh Circuit has held that the proviso does not apply to police records prepared in a routine, non-adversarial setting. *See U.S. v. Caraballo,* 595 F.3d 1214, 1226 (11th Cir. 2010); *U.S. v. Agustino-Hernandez,* 14 F.3d 42, 43 (11th Cir. 1994). The third category—records setting forth factual findings resulting from an investigation made pursuant to authority granted by law—are admissible only in civil actions and against the government in criminal cases. *See* FED. R. EVID. 803(8)(A)(iii). The phrase "factual findings" is broadly construed to include conclusions and opinions contained in such reports. *See Beech Aircraft Corp. v. Rainey,* 488 U.S. 153, 162 (1988). Rule 803(8)(B) makes the exception inapplicable if the sources of information or other circumstances indicate lack of trustworthiness.

The Florida rule divides public records into two different categories, and subjects each category to different treatment. The first category—records setting forth the activities of the office or agency—can be admitted under this exception without any special restrictions, as is the case under the federal rule. The second category—records setting forth matters observed pursuant to duty imposed by law as to which matters there was a duty to report—are admissible under this exception, subject to a proviso excluding from its scope "in criminal cases matters observed by police officers and other law enforcement personnel," as is the case under the federal rule. However, the Florida rule differs from the federal rule with respect to this category in that the last sentence of the rule makes this proviso inapplicable to affidavits containing the results of tests measuring the presence of alcohol or controlled substances in a person's system, offered in a prosecution for driving a motor vehicle or vessel under the influence of alcohol or other controlled substance, thus making such affidavits admissible under the exception. *See, e.g., State v. Belvin,* 986 So. 2d 516, 519-20 (Fla. 2008). Unlike the federal rule, the Florida rule does not provide for the admission of records setting forth factual findings resulting from an investigation made pursuant to authority granted by law under any circumstances. *See Lee v. Department of Health and Rehab. Servs.,* 698 So. 2d 1194, 1200-01 (Fla. 1997). As under the federal rule, a proviso at the end of § 90.803(8) makes the hearsay exception inapplicable if "the sources of information or other circumstances show their lack of trustworthiness." *See* § 90.803(8).

As is the case with the exception for business records, the exception for public records does not encompass information contained in public records if the source who has personal knowledge is an outsider. *See United Tech. Corp. v. Mazer,* 556 F.3d 1260, 1278 (11th Cir. 2009); *Claussen v. State of Fla., Dep't of Transp.,* 750 So. 2d 79, 82 (Fla. 2d DCA 1999); *U.S. v. Mackey,* 117 F.3d 24, 28-29 (1st Cir. 1997).

The federal courts, including the Eleventh Circuit, hold that the business records exception cannot be invoked in a criminal case against a defendant to admit a public record if the same record would not be admissible under Federal Rule 803(8)(A)(ii) or (iii) because of the limitations set forth in those rules. *See U.S. v. Brown,* 9 F.3d 907, 911 (11th Cir. 1993). No Florida decisions have addressed this issue.

Federal Rule 803(9). Exceptions to the Rule Against Hearsay — Regardless of Whether the Declarant Is Available as a Witness [Public Records of Vital Statistics]

The following are not excluded by the rule against hearsay, regardless of whether the declarant is available as a witness:

....

(9) *Public Records of Vital Statistics.* A record of a birth, death, or marriage, if reported to a public office in accordance with a legal duty.

....

ADVISORY COMMITTEE'S NOTE

....

Exception (9). Records of vital statistics are commonly the subject of particular statutes making them admissible in evidence, Uniform Vital Statistics Act, 9C U.L.A. 350 (1957). The rule is in principle narrower than Uniform Rule 63(16) which includes reports required of persons performing functions authorized by statute, yet in practical effect the two are substantially the same. Comment Uniform Rule 63(16). The exception as drafted is in the pattern of California Evidence Code § 1281.

....

Florida Stat. § 90.803(9). Hearsay Exceptions; Availability of Declarant Immaterial [Records of Vital Statistics]

The provision of s. 90.802 to the contrary notwithstanding, the following are not inadmissible as evidence, even though the declarant is available as a witness:

....

(9) Records of vital statistics. Records or data compilations, in any form, of births, fetal deaths, deaths, or marriages, if a report was made to a public office pursuant to requirements of law. However, nothing in this section shall be construed to make admissible any other marriage of any party to any cause of action except for the purpose of impeachment as set forth in s. 90.610.

....

SPONSORS' NOTE (1976 ENACTMENT)

Records of vital statistics are commonly the subject of particular statutes making them admissible in evidence. 5 Wigmore, Evidence §§ 1643, 1644 (3rd ed. 1940). Existing Fla. Stat. § 382.20 makes certificates of birth, death or stillbirth admissible in evidence as prima facie evidence of the facts contained therein. Although Section 382.20 does not require the admissibility of marriage records, Section 382.23 requires the county judge to transmit marriage licenses to the bureau of vital statistics, and the common-law hearsay exception admitting public records would make them admissible. See comment to subsection (8). Consequently, this subsection is in substantial accord with existing Florida law.

See Calif. Evid. Code § 1281; Wisc. Evid. Rule 908.03(9); Fed. Rule Evid. 803(9).

COMMENTARY ON FEDERAL AND FLORIDA RULE DIFFERENCES

Florida Stat. § 90.803(9) and its federal counterpart, Federal Rule 803(9), create an exception to the hearsay rule for government records or data compilations of births, fetal deaths, deaths, and marriages. The exception applies only if the underlying information was reported to a public office pursuant to a requirement of law; it does not apply to information voluntarily reported to a public office or agency. See *Gibson v. County of Riverside*, 181 F. Supp. 2d 1057, 1066 (C.D. Cal. 2002). The exception is broader than that for public records generally in that it paves the way for admitting information contained in public records that is provided by outsiders. *Compare* Commentary on FED. R. EVID. 803(8) and FLA. STAT. § 90.803(8).

The Florida rule differs from the federal rule in that it has a second sentence that provides that the exception does not make admissible as substantive evidence a record containing information about any other marriage of a party, although it does not prevent such evidence from being used for purposes of impeachment pursuant to Florida Stat. § 90.610. The evident purpose of this sentence is to bar such a record from being used in a wrongful death action brought by the decedent's spouse as evidence that the plaintiff has since remarried. *See* 1 CHARLES W. EHRHARDT, FLORIDA PRACTICE: EVIDENCE § 803.9 (2005).

Federal Rule 803(10). Exceptions to the Rule Against Hearsay — Regardless of Whether the Declarant Is Available as a Witness [Absence of a Public Record]

The following are not excluded by the rule against hearsay, regardless of whether the declarant is available as a witness:

....

(10) *Absence of a Public Record.* Testimony — or a certification under Rule 902 — that a diligent search failed to disclose a public record or statement if the testimony or certification is admitted to prove that:

(A) the record or statement does not exist; or

(B) a matter did not occur or exist, if a public office regularly kept a record or statement for a matter of that kind.

....

ADVISORY COMMITTEE'S NOTE

....

Exception (10). The principle of proving nonoccurrence of an event by evidence of the absence of a record which would regularly be made of its occurrence, developed in Exception (7) with respect to regularly conducted activities, is here extended to public records of the kind mentioned in Exceptions (8) and (9). 5 Wigmore § 1633(6), p. 519. Some harmless duplication no doubt exists with Exception (7). For instances of federal statutes recognizing this method of proof, see 8 U.S.C. § 1284(b), proof of absence of alien crewman's name from outgoing manifest prima facie evidence of failure to detain or deport, and 42 U.S.C. § 405(c)(3), (4)(B), (4)(C), absence of HEW record prima facie evidence of no wages or self-employment income.

The rule includes situations in which absence of a record may itself be the ultimate focal point of inquiry, e.g. People v. Love, 310 Ill. 558 (1923), certificate of Secretary of State admitted to show failure to file documents required by Securities Law, as well as cases where the absence of a record is offered as proof of the non-occurrence of an event ordinarily recorded.

The refusal of the common law to allow proof by certificate of the lack of a record or entry has no apparent justification, 5 Wigmore § 1678(7), p. 752. The rule takes the opposite position, as do Uniform Rule 63(17); California Evidence Code § 1284; Kansas Code of Civil Procedure § 60-460(c); New Jersey Evidence Rule 63(17). Congress has recognized certification as evidence of the lack of a record. 8 U.S.C. §

1360(d), certificate of Attorney General or other designated officer that no record of Immigration and Naturalization Service of specified nature or entry therein is found, admissible in alien cases.

....

Florida Stat. § 90.803(10). Hearsay Exceptions; Availability of Declarant Immaterial [Absence of Public Record or Entry]

The provision of s. 90.802 to the contrary notwithstanding, the following are not inadmissible as evidence, even though the declarant is available as a witness:

....

(10) Absence of public record or entry. Evidence, in the form of a certification in accord with § 90.902, or in the form of testimony, that diligent search failed to disclose a record, report, statement, or data compilation or entry, when offered to prove the absence of the record, report, statement, or data compilation or the nonoccurrence or nonexistence of a matter of which a record, report, statement, or data compilation would regularly have been made and preserved by a public office and agency.

....

SPONSORS' NOTE (1976 ENACTMENT)

This subsection permits the proof of the non-occurrence of an event by evidence of the absence of a public record which would regularly be made of its occurrence. It applies to the public records of the kind mentioned in subsections (8) and (9) and is similar to subsection (7) which concerns records of a regularly conducted activity.

8 U.S.C. § 1284(b) recognizes this method of proof by providing that proof of absence of alien crewman's name from outgoing manifest is prima facie evidence of failure to detain or deport.

No Florida cases were found that are in accord with this exception. One old case, Parker, Holmes & Co. v. Cleveland, 37 Fla. 39, 19 So. 344 (1896), held that a clerk's certificate that certain land described had not been transferred or mortgaged was inadmissible on the grounds that: "The law as to certificates of clerks as custodians of records only extends to transcripts of such records. If their testimony is desired upon other points, they should be regularly sworn, and testify as other witnesses." Id. at 50-51, 19 So. at 346.

Dean Wigmore describes the principle that a custodian of documents lacked authority to certify that a specific document did not exist as one that:

> will some day be reckoned as one of the most stupid instances of legal pedantry in our annals. The certificate of a custodian that he has diligently searched for a document or an entry of a specified tenor and has been unable to find it ought to be usually as satisfactory for evidencing its non-existence in his office as his testimony on the stand to this effect would be....

5 Wigmore, Evidence § 1678(7), p. 754 (3rd ed. 1940).

For similar provisions see Fed. Rule Evid. 803(10); Uniform Rule 63(17); Calif. Evid. Code § 1284; Kansas Code of Civ. Pro. § 60-460(o); New Jersey Evid. Rule 63(17); and Wisc. Rule Evid. 908.03(10).

COMMENTARY ON FEDERAL AND FLORIDA RULE DIFFERENCES

Florida Stat. § 90.803(10) and its federal counterpart, Federal Rule 803(10), create an exception to the hearsay rule for evidence of the *absence* of a public record, report, statement, or data compilation offered as proof of the nonoccurrence or nonexistence of a matter of which such a record, report, statement, or data compilation would normally have been made and preserved by a public office or agency. Under both provisions, the evidence may be offered either in the form of testimony or a certification in accordance with Federal Rule 902 or Florida Stat. § 90.902. A prerequisite to invoking either provision is a showing that a "diligent search" was undertaken that failed to disclose any record of the matter.

The constitutionality of using the certification procedure against the accused in a criminal case is constitutionally suspect in light of the Supreme Court's recent decision in *Crawford v. Washington*, 541 U.S. 36 (2004). Indeed, a pending, proposed amendment to Federal Rule 803(10) would allow a certification to be admitted against the accused in a criminal case only if the prosecution provides advance notice of its intent to offer the certification and the defense fails to object.

Federal Rule 803(11). Exceptions to the Rule Against Hearsay — Regardless of Whether the Declarant Is Available as a Witness [Records of Religious Organizations Concerning Personal or Family History]

The following are not excluded by the rule against hearsay, regardless of whether the declarant is available as a witness:

....

(11) *Records of Religious Organizations Concerning Personal or Family History.* A statement of birth, legitimacy, ancestry, marriage, divorce, death, relationship by blood or marriage, or similar facts of personal or family history, contained in a regularly kept record of a religious organization.

....

ADVISORY COMMITTEE'S NOTE

....

Exception (11). Records of activities of religious organizations are currently recognized as admissible at least to the extent of the business records exception to the hearsay rule, 5 Wigmore § 1523, p. 371, and Exception (6) would be applicable. However, both the business record doctrine and Exception (6) require that the person furnishing the information be one in the business or activity. The result is such decisions as Daily v. Grand Lodge, 311 Ill. 184 (1924), holding a church record admissible to prove fact, date, and place of baptism, but not age of child except that he had at least been born at the time. In view of the unlikelihood that false information would be furnished on occasions of this kind, the rule contains no requirement that the informant be in the course of the activity. See California Evidence Code § 1315 and Comment.

....

Florida Stat. § 90.803(11). Hearsay Exceptions; Availability of Declarant Immaterial [Records of Religious Organizations]

The provision of s. 90.802 to the contrary notwithstanding, the following are not inadmissible as evidence, even though the declarant is available as a witness:

....

(11) Records of religious organizations. Statements of births, marriages, divorces, deaths, parentage, ancestry, relationship by blood or marriage, or other similar facts of personal or family history contained in a regularly kept record of a religious organization.

....

SPONSORS' NOTE (1976 ENACTMENT)

Church records are generally admissible as business records under Section 90.803(6) to prove the occurrence of a church activity such as baptism, confirmation, or marriage. 5 Wigmore, Evidence § 1523 (3rd ed. 1940). Because it is unlikely that Section 90.803(6) would permit such records to be used as evidence of the age or relationship of the participants, this subsection is included to permit church records to be used to prove certain additional information. Facts of family history, such as birth dates, relationships, marital histories, that are ordinarily reported to church authorities and recorded in connection with the church's baptismal, confirmation, marriage, and funeral records may be proven by such records. The justification for this exception is the unlikelihood that false information would be furnished on occasions of this kind.

Apparently, the only Florida case which comments on this exception is Cone v. Benjamin, 157 Fla. 800, 822, 27 So.2d 90, 102 (1946), in which the court stated that: "It is also well settled that entries as to births, deaths and marriages shown by family Bibles, Church registers and certificates and inscriptions on monuments . . . are admissible under certain circumstances." The court did not elaborate on what these circumstances were, and did not cite any earlier Florida cases as authority for this statement.

Calif. Evid. Code § 1315; Wisc. Rule Evid. 908.03(11) and Fed. Rule Evid. 803(11) are similar.

COMMENTARY ON FEDERAL AND FLORIDA RULE DIFFERENCES

Florida Stat. § 90.803(11) and its federal counterpart, Federal Rule 803(11), create an exception to the hearsay rule for statements of fact of personal or family history, such as births, marriages, divorces, deaths, ancestry, relationship by blood and marriage, and the like, contained in regularly kept records of religious organizations. While a religious organization qualifies as "business" so as to permit its records to be admitted as business records under Federal Rule 803(6) or Florida Stat. § 90.803(6), that rule does not pave the way for admitting information contained within such records obtained from sources outside of the business, such as parishioners; this provision paves the way for admitting such information. See Advisory Committee's Note to FED. R. EVID. 803(11); Sponsors' Note to FLA. STAT. § 90.803(11).

The only difference between the two rules is that in the list of examples of personal or family history, the federal rule uses the word "legitimacy" while the Florida rule uses the term "parentage."

Federal Rule 803(12). Exceptions to the Rule Against Hearsay — Regardless of Whether the Declarant Is Available as a Witness [Certificates of Marriage, Baptism, and Similar Ceremonies]

The following are not excluded by the rule against hearsay, regardless of whether the declarant is available as a witness:

....

(12) *Certificates of Marriage, Baptism, and Similar Ceremonies.* A statement of fact contained in a certificate:

(A) made by a person who is authorized by a religious organization or by law to perform the act certified;

(B) attesting that the person performed a marriage or similar ceremony or administered a sacrament; and

(C) purporting to have been issued at the time of the act or within a reasonable time after it.

....

ADVISORY COMMITTEE'S NOTE

....

Exception (12). The principle of proof by certification is recognized as to public officials in Exceptions (8) and (10), and with respect to authentication in Rule 902. The present exception is a duplication to the extent that it deals with a certificate by a public official, as in the case of a judge who performs a marriage ceremony. The area covered by the rule is, however, substantially larger and extends the certification procedure to clergymen and the like who perform marriages and other ceremonies or administer sacraments. Thus certificates of such matters as baptism or confirmation, as well as marriage, are included. In principle they are as acceptable evidence as certificates of public officers. See 5 Wigmore § 1645, as to marriage certificates. When the person executing the certificate is not a public official, the self-authenticating character of documents purporting to emanate from public officials, see Rule 902, is lacking and proof is required that the person was authorized and did make the certificate. The time element, however, may safely be taken as supplied by the certificate, once authority and authenticity are established, particularly in view of the presumption that a document was executed on the date it bears.

For similar rules, some limited to certificates of marriage, with variations in foundation requirements, see Uniform Rule 63(18); California Evidence Code § 1316; Kansas Code of Civil Procedure § 60-460(p); New Jersey Evidence Rule 63(18).

....

Florida Stat. § 90.803(12). Hearsay Exceptions; Availability of Declarant Immaterial [Marriage, Baptismal, and Similar Certificates]

The provision of s. 90.802 to the contrary notwithstanding, the following are not inadmissible as evidence, even though the declarant is available as a witness:

....

(12) Marriage, baptismal, and similar certificates. Statements of facts contained in a certificate that the maker performed a marriage or other ceremony or administered a sacrament, when such statement was certified by a member of the clergy, public official, or other person authorized by the rules or practices of a religious organization or by law to perform the act certified, and when such certificate purports to have been issued at the time of the act or within a reasonable time thereafter.

....

SPONSORS' NOTE (1976 ENACTMENT)

This subsection extends the certification procedure of a public official as provided in subsection (8) to clergymen and the like who perform marriages and other ceremonies or administer sacraments.

5 Wigmore, Evidence § 1645 (3rd ed. 1940) stated that:

> No doubt such certificates, or their equivalent, ought to be furnished, for convenient use in evidence by the parties to a marriage, especially in this our country of numerous jurisdictions and migratory population.

But Wigmore conceded that: "In the United States, there is little common-law authority, and that not harmonious."

Apparently the only Florida case that makes a statement concerning such certificates is Cone v. Benjamin, 157 Fla. 800, 822, 27 So.2d 90, 102 (1946) in which the court said that:

> It is...well settled that entries as to births, deaths, and marriages shown by family Bibles, Church registers and certificates and inscriptions on monuments; hospital records and hotel registers (under certain circumstances and for certain purposes); letters of deceased relatives containing statements as to family matters, although entitled to different degrees of credibility; recitals in wills, deeds of conveyance, and in marriage settlements and certificates; inscriptions on family portraits, rings, and other family memorials; school censuses and other books and public records which mention births, marriages, and deaths, are admissible under certain circumstances.

The court did not elaborate on what these "certain circumstances" were, but held that a privately published book containing a family history and genealogy was admissible to prove pedigree.

Admissibility under this subsection is limited to certified statements that the maker "performed" a marriage or other ceremony or administered a sacrament, and does not extend to other facts which might be stated in the certificate, such as the date of birth stated in a baptismal certificate.

The justification for this exception is the same as that for the exception for public documents: the assumption of regular performance of the act, and the unlikelihood of independent recollection.

When the person executing the certificate is not a public official, the self-authenticating character of documents purporting to emanate from public officials, see Section 90.902, is lacking and proof is required that the person was authorized and did make the certificate. However, the time element required in the subsection, may safely be taken as supplied by the certificate, once authority and authenticity are established, particularly in view of the presumption that a document was executed on the date it bears.

For similar provisions, some limited to certificates of marriage, with variations in foundation requirements, see Uniform Rule 63(18); Calif. Evid. Code § 1316; Kansas Code of Civ. Pro. § 60-460(p); New Jersey Evid. Rule 63(18); Fed. Rule Evid. 803(12).

COMMENTARY ON FEDERAL AND FLORIDA RULE DIFFERENCES

Florida Stat. § 90.803(12) and its federal counterpart, Federal Rule 803(12), create an exception to the hearsay rule for statements of fact contained in marriage, baptismal, confirmation, and similar certificates. The exception applies only if the person who made the certificate is authorized by law or by the rules or practices of a religious organization to perform the act certified. Moreover, it applies only if the certificate was issued at the time the act was performed or within a reasonable time thereafter.

Although worded slightly differently from one another, there are no substantive differences between the federal and Florida rules.

Federal Rule 803(13). Exceptions to the Rule Against Hearsay — Regardless of Whether the Declarant Is Available as a Witness [Family Records]

The following are not excluded by the rule against hearsay, regardless of whether the declarant is available as a witness:

....

    (13) *Family Records.* A statement of fact about personal or family history contained in a family record, such as a Bible, genealogy, chart, engraving on a ring, inscription on a portrait, or engraving on an urn or burial marker.

....

ADVISORY COMMITTEE'S NOTE

....

Exception (13). Records of family history kept in family Bibles have by long tradition been received in evidence. 5 Wigmore §§ 1495, 1496, citing numerous statutes and decisions. See also Regulations, Social Security Administration, 20 C.F.R. § 404.703(c), recognizing family Bible entries as proof of age in the absence of public or church records. Opinions in the area also include inscriptions on tombstones, publicly displayed pedigrees, and engravings on rings. Wigmore, *supra*. The rule is substantially identical in coverage with California Evidence Code § 1312.

....

REPORT OF HOUSE COMMITTEE ON THE JUDICIARY

....

The Committee approved this Rule in the form submitted by the Court, intending that the phrase "Statements of fact concerning personal or family history" be read to include the specific types of such statements enumerated in Rule 803(11).

....

Florida Stat. § 90.803(13). Hearsay Exceptions; Availability of Declarant Immaterial [Family Records]

The provision of s. 90.802 to the contrary notwithstanding, the following are not inadmissible as evidence, even though the declarant is available as a witness:

....

(13) Family records. Statements of fact concerning personal or family history in family Bibles, charts, engravings in rings, inscriptions on family portraits, engravings on urns, crypts, or tombstones, or the like.

....

SPONSORS' NOTE (1976 ENACTMENT)

Records of family history kept in family Bibles have long been received in evidence. 5 Wigmore, <u>Evidence</u> §§ 1495-96 (3rd ed. 1940) (citing numerous statutes and decisions from jurisdictions adopting this view). <u>Cone v. Benjamin</u>, 157 Fla. 800, 27 So.2d 90 (1946) expresses approval for the admission of such evidence. See also Regulations, Social Security Administration, 20 C.F.R. § 404.703(c), recognizing family Bible entries as proof of age in the absence of public or church records. See Fed. Rule Evid. 803(13); Wisc. Rule Evid. 908.03(13); Calif. Evid. Code § 1312.

COMMENTARY ON FEDERAL AND FLORIDA RULE DIFFERENCES

Florida Stat. § 90.803(13) and its federal counterpart, Federal Rule 803(13), create an exception to the hearsay rule for statements of fact concerning personal or family history contained in family Bibles, charts, inscriptions on family portraits, engravings on rings, urns, crypts, or tombstones, and the like. The only difference between the federal and Florida rules is that the former includes genealogies in its list while the latter does not, but that difference is probably not significant since the lists are only illustrative and the latter ends with the phrase "or the like."

Federal Rule 803(14). Hearsay Exceptions; Availability of Declarant Immaterial [Records of Documents That Affect an Interest in Property]

The following are not excluded by the rule against hearsay, regardless of whether the declarant is available as a witness:

....

(14) *Records of Documents That Affect an Interest in Property.* The record of a document that purports to establish or affect an interest in property if:

    (A) the record is admitted to prove the content of the original recorded document, along with its signing and its delivery by each person who purports to have signed it;

    (B) the record is kept in a public office; and

    (C) a statute authorizes recording documents of that kind in that office.

....

ADVISORY COMMITTEE'S NOTE

....

Exception (14). The recording of title documents is a purely statutory development. Under any theory of the admissibility of public records, the records would be receivable as evidence of the contents of the recorded document, else the recording process would be reduced to a nullity. When, however, the record is offered for the further purpose of proving execution and delivery, a problem of lack of first-hand knowledge by the recorder, not present as to contents, is presented. This problem is solved, seemingly in all jurisdictions, by qualifying for recording only those documents shown by a specified procedure, either acknowledgement or a form of probate, to have been executed and delivered. 5 Wigmore §§ 1647–1651. Thus what may appear in the rule, at first glance, as endowing the record with an effect independently of local law and inviting difficulties of an *Erie* nature under Cities Service Oil Co. v. Dunlap, 308 U.S. 208 (1939), is not present, since the local law in fact governs under the example.

....

Florida Stat. § 90.803(14). Hearsay Exceptions; Availability of Declarant Immaterial [Records of Documents Affecting an Interest in Property]

The provision of s. 90.802 to the contrary notwithstanding, the following are not inadmissible as evidence, even though the declarant is available as a witness:

....

(14) Records of documents affecting an interest in property. The record of a document purporting to establish or affect an interest in property, as proof of the contents of the original recorded or filed document and its execution and delivery by each person by whom it purports to have been executed, if the record is a record of a public office and an applicable statute authorized the recording or filing of the document in the office.

....

SPONSORS' NOTE (1976 ENACTMENT)

Public records of documents affecting an interest in property are admissible to prove the execution and delivery of the documents as well as their contents. A problem seemingly exists when the record is offered to prove execution and delivery, since the recorder lacks first-hand knowledge. This problem has been solved by qualifying for recording only those documents which have been executed and delivered. 5 Wigmore, Evidence §§ 1647-1651 (3rd ed. 1940). A public record must be receivable as evidence of the contents of the recorded document or the recording process is useless.

Existing Fla. Stat. § 92.121 is similar to this subsection in that it provides that deeds and records which have been proved for record and recorded according to law are admissible "as prima facie evidence in the courts of this state without requiring proof of the execution." That section limits the use of certified copies of the deeds and mortgages to those cases in which the original is not within the custody or control of the party offering such copy. This subsection would expand existing Section 92.121 by applying to all recorded documents affecting real property rather than just deeds and mortgages. See generally Fla. Stat. ch. 695 (Record of Conveyances of Real Estate).

See Wisc. Rule Evid. 908.03(14); Fed. Rule Evid. 803(14).

COMMENTARY ON FEDERAL AND FLORIDA RULE DIFFERENCES

Florida Stat. § 90.803(14) and its federal counterpart, Federal Rule 803(14), create an exception to the hearsay rule for the record of a document purporting to establish or affect an interest in property (such as a deed) when offered to prove the contents of the original recorded document and its execution and delivery by each person by whom it purports to have been executed. The exception applies only if an applicable statute authorizes the recording of such documents in the public office in which it was recorded. The exceptions are broader than those for public records generally in that they pave the way for admitting information contained in public records that is provided by outsiders, since the recorder at the public office typically does not have first-hand knowledge of execution and delivery. *See* Advisory Committee's Note to FED. R. EVID. 803(14); Sponsors' Note to FLA. STAT. § 90.803(14). *Compare* Commentary on FED. R. EVID. 803(8) and FLA. STAT. § 90.803(8).

The only difference between the federal and Florida rules is that the former refers only to "recorded" documents while the latter applies to "recorded or filed" documents, but there is no indication in the legislative history or the case law that this difference is significant.

Federal Rule 803(15). Exceptions to the Rule Against Hearsay — Regardless of Whether the Declarant Is Available as a Witness [Statements in Documents That Affect an Interest in Property]

The following are not excluded by the rule against hearsay, regardless of whether the declarant is available as a witness:

....

(15) *Statements in Documents That Affect an Interest in Property.* A statement contained in a document that purports to establish or affect an interest in property if the matter stated was relevant to the document's purpose — unless later dealings with the property are inconsistent with the truth of the statement or the purport of the document.

....

ADVISORY COMMITTEE'S NOTE

....

Exception (15). Dispositive documents often contain recitals of fact. Thus a deed purporting to have been executed by an attorney in fact may recite the existence of the power of attorney, or a deed may recite that the grantors are all the heirs of the last record owner. Under the rule, these recitals are exempted from the hearsay rule. The circumstances under which dispositive documents are executed and the requirement that the recital be germane to the purpose of the document are believed to be adequate guarantees of trustworthiness, particularly in view of the nonapplicability of the rule if dealings with the property have been inconsistent with the document. The age of the document is of no significance, though in practical application the document will most often be an ancient one. See Uniform Rule 63(29), Comment.

Similar provisions are contained in Uniform Rule 63(29); California Evidence Code § 1330; Kansas Code of Civil Procedure § 60-460(aa); New Jersey Evidence Rule 63(29).

....

Florida Stat. § 90.803(15). Hearsay Exceptions; Availability of Declarant Immaterial [Statements in Documents Affecting an Interest in Property]

The provision of s. 90.802 to the contrary notwithstanding, the following are not inadmissible as evidence, even though the declarant is available as a witness:

....

(15) Statements in documents affecting an interest in property. A statement contained in a document purporting to establish or affect an interest in property, if the matter stated was relevant to the purpose of the document, unless dealings with the property since the document was made have been inconsistent with the truth of the statement or the purport of the document.

....

SPONSORS' NOTE (1976 ENACTMENT)

This subsection, which makes admissible certain statements in documents affecting an interest in property, recognizes that litigation may arise years after a conveyance when the declarant of a statement in a deed would often be dead. Similarly, witnesses are often unavailable. The absence of other evidence creates the necessity of using the document to prove the recited fact. This exception is limited to those situations in which there have not been dealings which are inconsistent with the truth of the statement.

The Advisory Committee's Note to Proposed Federal Rule of Evidence 803(15), explains the reasons for including this rule as an exception to the hearsay exclusion

> Dispositive documents often contain recitals of fact. Thus a deed purporting to have been executed by an attorney in fact may recite the existence of the power of attorney, or a deed may recite that the grantors are all the heirs of the last record owner. Under the rule, these recitals are exempted from the hearsay rule. The circumstances under which dispositive documents are executed and the requirement that the recital be germane to the purpose of the document are believed to be adequate guarantees of trustworthiness, particularly in view of the nonapplicability of the rule if dealings with the property have been inconsistent with the document. The age of the document is of no significance, though in practical application the document will most often be an ancient one.

While existing Section 92.121 provides that recorded deeds and mortgages shall be taken as prima facie evidence, it is not clear whether this provision makes admissible a statement in the deed or mortgage.

Similar provisions are contained in Uniform Rule 63(29); Calif. Evid. Code § 1330; Kansas Code of Civ. Pro. § 60-460(aa); Wisc. Evid. Rule 908.03(15); Fed. Rule Evid. 803(15).

COMMENTARY ON FEDERAL AND FLORIDA RULE DIFFERENCES

Florida Stat. § 90.803(15) and its federal counterpart, Federal Rule 803(15), create an exception to the hearsay rule for statements contained in a document purporting to establish or affect an interest in property (such as a deed). Both exceptions are limited to statements that are relevant to the purpose of the document, and neither exception is applicable if dealings with the property since the document was made have been inconsistent with the truth of the statement or the purport of the document.

The federal and Florida rules are virtually identical in wording, and there appear to be no substantive differences between them. Some federal decisions have interpreted this exception broadly to include within its scope court judgments that affect an interest in property, *see U.S. v. Boulware*, 384 F.3d 794, 806-807 (9th Cir. 2004), although it seems doubtful that the Eleventh Circuit would so interpret the exception. *See U.S. v. Jones*, 29 F.3d 1549, 1554 (11th Cir. 1994) (refusing to interpret FED. R. EVID. 803(8) to admit judgments not within the scope of FED. R. EVID. 803(22)-(23)). There are no Florida decisions considering the application of this exception to such judgments.

Federal Rule 803(16). Exceptions to the Rule Against Hearsay — Regardless of Whether the Declarant Is Available as a Witness [Statements in Ancient Documents]

The following are not excluded by the rule against hearsay, regardless of whether the declarant is available as a witness:

....

(16) *Statements in Ancient Documents.* A statement in a document that is at least 20 years old and whose authenticity is established.

....

ADVISORY COMMITTEE'S NOTE

....

Exception (16). Authenticating a document as ancient, essentially in the pattern of the common law, as provided in Rule 901(b)(8), leaves open as a separate question the admissibility of assertive statements contained therein as against a hearsay objection. 7 Wigmore § 2145a. Wigmore further states that the ancient document technique of authentication is universally conceded to apply to all sorts of documents, including letters, records, contracts, maps, and certificates, in addition to title documents, citing numerous decisions. *Id.* § 2145. Since most of these items are significant evidentially only insofar as they are assertive, their admission in evidence must be as a hearsay exception. But see 5 *id.* § 1573, p. 429, referring to recitals in ancient deeds as a "limited" hearsay exception. The former position is believed to be the correct one in reason and authority. As pointed out in McCormick § 298, danger of mistake is minimized by authentication requirements, and age affords assurance that the writing antedates the present controversy. See Dallas County v. Commercial Union Assurance Co., 286 F.2d 388 (5th Cir. 1961), upholding admissibility of 58-year-old newspaper story. Cf. Morgan, Basic Problems of Evidence 364 (1962), but see *id.* 254.

For a similar provision, but with the added requirement that "the statement has since generally been acted upon as true by persons having an interest in the matter," see California Evidence Code § 1331.

....

Florida Stat. § 90.803(16). Hearsay Exceptions; Availability of Declarant Immaterial [Statements in Ancient Documents]

The provision of s. 90.802 to the contrary notwithstanding, the following are not inadmissible as evidence, even though the declarant is available as a witness:

....

(16) Statements in ancient documents. Statements in a document in existence 20 years or more, the authenticity of which is established.

....

SPONSORS' NOTE (1976 ENACTMENT)

This subsection provides that statements contained in ancient documents are admissible to prove the facts contained therein. See McCormick, Evidence § 323 (2nd ed. 1972). The justification lies in the propositions that ordinary testimonial evidence may be practically unavailable and the improbability that people would undertake the risk of forgery solely for posterity. 7 Wigmore, Evidence § 2137 (3rd ed. 1940). Authentication of ancient documents occurs under Section 90.901, but the admissibility of assertive statements contained therein as against a hearsay objection is a separate question. The ancient document technique of authentication is universally conceded to apply to all types of documents, including letters, records, contracts, maps, and certificates, in addition to title documents. 7 Wigmore, Evidence § 2145 (3rd ed. 1940).

This subsection provides admissibility for statements in all ancient documents authenticated per Section 90.901, and expands two existing statutory provisions. Fla. Stat. § 92.07 provides that judgments and decrees of record more than twenty years old are admissible to prove the facts recited, and Fla. Stat. § 92.08 provides that deeds and powers of attorney of record more than twenty years old are admissible to prove truth of facts recited.

See Wisc. Rule Evid. 908.03(16); Fed. Rule Evid. 803(16). Calif. Evid. Code § 1331 contains a similar provision, but with a 30-year time period and the added requirement that "the statement has since generally been acted upon as true by persons having an interest in the matter."

COMMENTARY ON FEDERAL AND FLORIDA RULE DIFFERENCES

Florida Stat. § 90.803(16) and its federal counterpart, Federal Rule 803(16), create an exception to the hearsay rule for so-called ancient documents—those that have been in existence twenty years or more—provided that their authenticity has been established. Federal Rule 901(b)(8) and Florida Stat. § 90.901 provide a method for authenticating ancient documents, and documents so authenticated automatically overcome a hearsay objection under these provisions. See Advisory Committee's Note to FED. R. EVID. 803(16); Sponsors' Note to FLA. STAT. § 90.803(16). The method of authenticating ancient documents is detailed in the Commentary to Federal Rule 901 and Florida Stat. § 90.901.

Federal Rule 803(17). Exceptions to the Rule Against Hearsay — Regardless of Whether the Declarant Is Available as a Witness [Market Reports and Similar Commercial Publications]

The following are not excluded by the rule against hearsay, regardless of whether the declarant is available as a witness:

....

(17) *Market Reports and Similar Commercial Publications.* Market quotations, lists, directories, or other compilations that are generally relied on by the public or by persons in particular occupations.

....

ADVISORY COMMITTEE'S NOTE

....

Exception (17). Ample authority at common law supported the admission in evidence of items falling in this category. While Wigmore's text is narrowly oriented to lists, etc., prepared for the use of a trade or profession, 6 Wigmore § 1702, authorities are cited which include other kinds of publications, for example, newspaper market reports, telephone directories, and city directories. *Id.* §§ 1702–1706. The basis of trustworthiness is general reliance by the public or by a particular segment of it, and the motivation of the compiler to foster reliance by being accurate.

For similar provisions, see Uniform Rule 63(30); California Evidence Code § 1340; Kansas Code of Civil Procedure § 60-460(bb); New Jersey Evidence Rule 63(30). Uniform Commercial Code § 2-724 provides for admissibility in evidence of "reports in official publications or trade journals or in newspapers or periodicals of general circulation published as the reports of such [established commodity] market."

....

Florida Stat. § 90.803(17). Hearsay Exceptions; Availability of Declarant Immaterial [Market Reports, Commercial Publications]

The provision of s. 90.802 to the contrary notwithstanding, the following are not inadmissible as evidence, even though the declarant is available as a witness:

....

(17) Market reports, commercial publications. Market quotations, tabulations, lists, directories, or other published compilations, generally used and relied upon by the public or by persons in particular occupations if, in the opinion of the court, the sources of information and method of preparation were such as to justify their admission.

....

SPONSORS' NOTE (1976 ENACTMENT)

Ample authority at common law supports the admission into evidence of items falling in this category. The basis of trustworthiness is the general reliance by the public, or by a particular segment of it, and the motivation of the compiler to foster reliance by being accurate. 6 Wigmore, <u>Evidence</u> §§ 1702-1706 (3rd ed. 1940). While Wigmore's text is narrowly oriented to lists and similar matters prepared for the use of a trade or profession, he cites authorities which include other kinds of publications, e.g., newspaper market reports, telephone directories, and city directories.

Florida has enacted the Uniform Commercial Code, including § 2-724 (Fla. Stat. § 672.724) which provides that:

> Whenever the prevailing price or value of any goods regularly bought and sold in any established commodity market is in issue, reports in official publications or trade journals or in newspapers or periodicals of general circulation published as the reports of such markets shall be admissible in evidence. The circumstances of the preparation of such a report may be shown to affect its weight but not its admissibility.

There appears to be no reported Florida case law on this subject.

For similar provisions, see Uniform Rule 63(30); Calif. Evid. Code § 1340; Kansas Code of Civ. Pro. § 60-460(bb); New Jersey Evid. Rule 63(30); Fed. Rule Evid. 803(17).

COMMENTARY ON FEDERAL AND FLORIDA RULE DIFFERENCES

Florida Stat. § 90.803(17) and its federal counterpart, Federal Rule 803(17), create an exception to the hearsay rule for market quotations, tabulations, lists, directories, or other published compilations generally used and relied upon by the public or by people in particular occupations. Examples include general publications such as newspaper market reports, telephone directories, and the like, *see* Advisory Committee's Note to FED. R. EVID. 803(17); Sponsors' Note to FLA. STAT. § 90.803(17), as well as specialized publications, such as *Gun Trader's Guide* or *County Comps. See U.S. v. Woods*, 321 F.3d 361, 364 (3d Cir. 2003) (collecting cases).

The Florida rule contains additional language providing that such evidence is admissible only "if, in the opinion of the court, the sources of information and method of preparation were such as to justify their admission." While such language is not present in the federal rule, federal courts require a showing that a published compilation is reliable before admitting it under the exception. *See Woods*, 321 F.3d at 364-65.

Federal Rule 803(18). Exceptions to the Rule Against Hearsay — Regardless of Whether the Declarant Is Available as a Witness [Statements in Learned Treatises, Periodicals, or Pamphlets]

The following are not excluded by the rule against hearsay, regardless of whether the declarant is available as a witness:

....

(18) *Statements in Learned Treatises, Periodicals, or Pamphlets.* A statement contained in a treatise, periodical, or pamphlet if:

(A) the statement is called to the attention of an expert witness on cross-examination or relied on by the expert on direct examination; and

(B) the publication is established as a reliable authority by the expert's admission or testimony, by another expert's testimony, or by judicial notice.

If admitted, the statement may be read into evidence but not received as an exhibit.

....

ADVISORY COMMITTEE'S NOTE

....

Exception (18). The writers have generally favored the admissibility of learned treatises, McCormick § 296, p. 621; Morgan, Basic Problems of Evidence 366 (1962); 6 Wigmore § 1692, with the support of occasional decisions and rules, City of Dothan v. Hardy, 237 Ala. 603 (1939); Lewandowski v. Preferred Risk Mut. Ins. Co., 33 Wis.2d 69 (1966), 66 Mich.L.Rev. 183 (1967); Uniform Rule 63(31); Kansas Code of Civil Procedure § 60-460(cc), but the great weight of authority has been that learned treatises are not admissible as substantive evidence though usable in the cross-examination of experts. The foundation of the minority view is that the hearsay objection must be regarded as unimpressive when directed against treatises since a high standard of accuracy is engendered by various factors: the treatise is written primarily and impartially for professionals, subject to scrutiny and exposure for inaccuracy, with the reputation of the writer at stake. 6 Wigmore § 1692. Sound as this position may be with respect to trustworthiness, there is, nevertheless, an additional difficulty in the likelihood that the treatise will be misunderstood and misapplied without expert assistance and supervision. This difficulty is recognized in the cases demonstrating unwillingness to sustain findings relative to disability on the basis of judicially noticed medical texts. Ross v. Gardner, 365 F.2d 554 (6th Cir. 1966); Sayers v. Gardner, 380 F.2d 940 (6th Cir. 1967); Colwell v. Gardner, 386 F.2d 56 (6th Cir. 1967); Glendenning v. Ribicoff, 213 F.Supp. 301 (W.D.Mo. 1962); Cook v. Celebrezze, 217 F.Supp. 366 (W.D.Mo. 1963); Sosna v. Celebrezze, 234 F.Supp. 289 (E.D.Pa. 1964); and see McDaniel v. Celebrezze, 331 F.2d 426 (4th Cir. 1964). The rule avoids the danger of misunderstanding and misapplication by limiting the use of treatises as substantive evidence to situations in which an expert is on the stand and available to explain and assist in the application of the treatise if desired. The limitation upon receiving the publication itself physically in evidence, contained in the last sentence, is designed to further this policy.

The relevance of the use of treatises on cross-examination is evident. This use of treatises has been the subject of varied views. The most restrictive position is that the witness must have stated expressly on direct his reliance upon the treatise. A slightly more liberal approach still insists upon reliance but allows it to be developed on cross-examination. Further relaxation dispenses with reliance but requires recognition as an authority by the witness, developable on cross-examination. The greatest liberality is found in decisions allowing use of the treatise on cross-examination when its status as an authority is established by any means. Annot., 60 A.L.R.2d 77. The exception is hinged upon this last position, which is that of the Supreme Court, Reilly v. Pinkus, 338 U.S. 269 (1949), and of recent well considered state court decisions, City of St. Petersburg v. Ferguson, 193 So.2d 648 (Fla.App. 1967), cert. denied Fla., 201 So.2d 556; Darling v. Charleston Memorial Community Hospital, 33 Ill.2d 326 (1965); Dabroe v. Rhodes Co., 64 Wash.2d 431 (1964).

In Reilly v. Pinkus, *supra*, the Court pointed out that testing of professional knowledge was incomplete without exploration of the witness' knowledge of and attitude toward established treatises in the field. The process works equally well in reverse and furnishes the basis of the rule.

The rule does not require that the witness rely upon or recognize the treatise as authoritative, thus avoiding the possibility that the expert may at the outset block cross-examination by refusing to concede reliance or authoritativeness. Dabroe v. Rhodes Co., supra. Moreover, the rule avoids the unreality of admitting evidence for the purpose of impeachment only, with an instruction to the jury not to consider it otherwise. The parallel to the treatment of prior inconsistent statements will be apparent. See Rules 613(b) and 801(d)(1).

....

Florida Stat. § 90.706. Authoritativeness of Literature for Use in Cross-Examination

Statements of facts or opinions on a subject of science, art, or specialized knowledge contained in a published treatise, periodical, book, dissertation, pamphlet, or other writing may be used in cross-examination of an expert witness if the expert witness recognizes the author or the treatise, periodical, book, dissertation, pamphlet, or other writing to be authoritative, or, notwithstanding nonrecognition by the expert witness, if the trial court finds the author or the treatise, periodical, book, dissertation, pamphlet, or other writing to be authoritative and relevant to the subject matter.

COMMENTARY ON FEDERAL AND FLORIDA RULE DIFFERENCES

Florida Stat. § 90.706 and its federal counterpart, Federal Rule 803(18), govern the use of learned treatises and other authoritative publications in examining expert witnesses.

Under the Florida rule, authoritative publications can be used only on cross-examination of an expert as a means of impeaching his opinion; they cannot be used to bolster the credibility of an expert or to supplement his opinion. *See Linn v. Fossum*, 946 So. 2d 1032, 1036 (Fla. 2006); *In re S.E.*, 946 So. 2d 620, 622 (Fla. 2d DCA 2007); *Donshik v. Sherman*, 861 So. 2d 53, 55-56 (Fla. 3d DCA 2003). Moreover, this is understood to mean true adversarial cross-examination; if what is involved is friendly cross-examination (such as by one defendant of a co-defendant's expert), the Florida rule does not permit their use. *See Tallahassee Mem'l Reg'l Med. Ctr. v. Mitchell*, 407 So. 2d 601, 602 (Fla. 1st DCA 1981). Neither this rule nor any other rule in the Florida Evidence Code creates a hearsay exception for learned treatises that permits them to be used as substantive evidence, and so their use is limited to being used for impeachment purposes. *See Donshik*, 861 So. 2d at 55-56.

By contrast, the Federal rule creates an exception to the hearsay rule that permits the learned treatise to be used by the trier of fact for substantive purposes. *See* FED. R. EVID. 803(18). Moreover, the federal rule permits the use of such material not only on cross-examination of an expert witness, but also on direct examination of a witness who has relied on such authoritative publications in forming his opinion. *See id.* However, if the publication is admitted it may only be read into evidence; it may not be received as an exhibit. *See id.*

A prerequisite to invoking both the Federal and Florida rules is a showing that the publication is authoritative. The mere fact that it is published in a reputable journal is insufficient; the article must still be shown to be authoritative. *See Whitfield v. State*, 859 So. 2d 529, 531 (Fla. 1st DCA 2003); *Costantino v. David M. Herzog, M.D., P.C.*, 203 F.3d 164, 172 (2d Cir. 2000). Often, authoritativeness is shown by getting the expert being cross-examined to concede its authoritativeness, but if he refuses to do so, authoritativeness must be established by some other means, such as by calling other expert witnesses or submitting their affidavits, or through judicial notice. *See Whitfield*, 859 So. 2d at 531; *Fravel v. Haughey*, 727 So. 2d 1033, 1034 (Fla. 5th DCA 1999) (en banc); *Kirkpatrick v. Wolford*, 704 So. 2d 708, 710 (Fla. 5th DCA 1998); *Chesterton v. Fisher*, 655 So. 2d 170, 171 (Fla. 3d DCA 1995); FED. R. EVID. 803(18). Under the federal rule, the trial court must find by a preponderance of the evidence that the publication is authoritative. *See* Daniel D. Blinka, *"Practical Inconvenience" or Conceptual Confusion: The Common-Law Genesis of Federal Rule of Evidence 703*, 20 AM. J. TRIAL ADVOC. 467 n.226 (1997). By contrast, under the Florida rule, the trial court need not make such a finding; since it is not being used as substantive evidence, there need only be "some credible evidence" that it is authoritative. *See Kirkpatrick*, 704 So. 2d at 710.

Federal Rule 803(19), (20), (21). Exceptions to the Rule Against Hearsay — Regardless of Whether the Declarant Is Available as a Witness [Reputation Concerning Personal or Family History, Boundaries or General History, or Character]

The following are not excluded by the rule against hearsay, regardless of whether the declarant is available as a witness:

....

(19) *Reputation Concerning Personal or Family History.* A reputation among a person's family by blood, adoption, or marriage — or among a person's associates or in the community — concerning the person's birth, adoption, legitimacy, ancestry, marriage, divorce, death, relationship by blood, adoption, or marriage, or similar facts of personal or family history.

(20) *Reputation Concerning Boundaries or General History.* A reputation in a community — arising before the controversy — concerning boundaries of land in the community or customs that affect the land, or concerning general historical events important to that community, state, or nation.

(21) *Reputation Concerning Character.* A reputation among a person's associates or in the community concerning the person's character.

....

ADVISORY COMMITTEE'S NOTE

....

Exceptions (19), (20), and (21). Trustworthiness in reputation evidence is found "when the topic is such that the facts are likely to have been inquired about and that persons having personal knowledge have disclosed facts which have thus been discussed in the community; and thus the community's conclusion, if any has been formed, is likely to be a trustworthy one." 5 Wigmore § 1580, p. 444, and see also § 1583. On this common foundation, reputation as to land boundaries, customs, general history, character, and marriage have come to be regarded as admissible. The breadth of the underlying principle suggests the formulation of an equally broad exception, but tradition has in fact been much narrower and more particularized, and this is the pattern of these exceptions in the rule.

Exception (19) is concerned with matters of personal and family history. Marriage is universally conceded to be a proper subject of proof by evidence of reputation in the community. 5 Wigmore § 1602. As to such items as legitimacy, relationship, adoption, birth, and death, the decisions are divided. *Id.* § 1605. All seem to be susceptible to being the subject of well founded repute. The "world" in which the reputation may exist may be family, associates, or community. This world has proved capable of expanding with changing times from the single uncomplicated neighborhood, in which all activities take place, to the multiple and unrelated worlds of work, religious affiliation, and social activity, in each of which a reputation may be generated. People v. Reeves, 360 Ill. 55 (1935); State v. Axilrod, 248 Minn. 204 (1956); Mass.Stat.1947, c. 410, M.G.L.A. c. 233 § 21A; 5 Wigmore § 1616. The family has often served as the point of beginning for allowing community reputation. 5 Wigmore § 1488. For comparable provisions see Uniform Rule 63(26), (27)(c); California Evidence Code §§ 1313, 1314; Kansas Code of Civil Procedure § 60-460(x), (y)(3); New Jersey Evidence Rule 63(26), (27)(c).

The first portion of Exception (20) is based upon the general admissibility of evidence of reputation as to land boundaries and land customs, expanded in this country to include private as well as public boundaries. McCormick § 299, p. 625. The reputation is required to antedate the controversy, though not to be ancient. The second portion is likewise supported by authority, *id.*, and is designed to facilitate proof of events when judicial notice is not available. The historical character of the subject matter dispenses with any need that the reputation antedate the controversy with respect to which it is offered. For similar provisions see Uniform Rule 63(27)(a), (b); California Evidence Code §§ 1320–1322; Kansas Code of Civil Procedure § 60-460(y), (1), (2); New Jersey Evidence Rule 63(27)(a), (b).

Exception (21) recognizes the traditional acceptance of reputation evidence as a means of proving human character. McCormick §§ 44, 158. The exception deals only with the hearsay aspect of this kind of evidence. Limitations upon admissibility based on other grounds will be found in Rules 404, relevancy of character evidence generally, and 608, character of witness. The exception is in effect a reiteration, in the context of hearsay, of Rule 405(a). Similar provisions are contained in Uniform Rule 63(28); California Evidence Code § 1324; Kansas Code of Civil Procedure § 60-460(z); New Jersey Evidence Rule 63(28).

....

Florida Stat. § 90.803(19), (20), (21). Hearsay Exceptions; Availability of Declarant Immaterial [Reputation Concerning Personal or Family History, Boundaries or General History, or Character]

The provision of s. 90.802 to the contrary notwithstanding, the following are not inadmissible as evidence, even though the declarant is available as a witness:

....

(19) Reputation concerning personal or family history. Evidence of reputation:

(a) Among members of a person's family by blood, adoption, or marriage;

(b) Among a person's associates; or

(c) In the community,

concerning a person's birth, adoption, marriage, divorce, death, relationship by blood, adoption, or marriage, ancestry, or other similar fact of personal or family history.

(20) Reputation concerning boundaries or general history. Evidence of reputation:

(a) In a community, arising before the controversy about the boundaries of, or customs affecting lands in, the community.

(b) About events of general history which are important to the community, state, or nation where located.

(21) Reputation as to character. Evidence of reputation of a person's character among associates or in the community.

....

SPONSORS' NOTE (1976 ENACTMENT)

"The courts are generally agreed that there exists, as an exception to the hearsay rule, a principle justifying the admission of evidence of reputation as to matters of general public interest and concern." Annot., Hearsay—Matter of Public Interest, 58 A.L.R.2d 615. The reputation is a testimonial inference introduced to prove the truth of the fact asserted.

Reputation as to land boundaries, customs, general history, character, and marriage have come to be regarded as admissible. Trustworthiness of reputation evidence is found "when the topic is such that the facts are likely to have been inquired about and that persons having personal knowledge have disclosed facts which have thus been discussed in the community; and thus the community's conclusion, if any has been formed, is likely to be a trustworthy one." 5 Wigmore, Evidence § 1580, p. 444 (3rd ed. 1940).

Subsection (19) concerns matters of personal and family history, which are commonly called "pedigree." The trustworthiness of reputation of marriage is based both on the fact that the husband and wife know of the consequences that would result from misrepresenting their relationship and in the constant exposure to observation and discussion by the community. Although marriage is generally conceded to be a proper subject of proof by evidence of reputation in the community, the decisions are divided as to such items as legitimacy, relationship, adoption, birth, and death. 5 Wigmore, Evidence §§ 1602, 1605 (3rd ed. 1940). The Advisory Committee's Note to Fed. Rule Evid. 803(19) comments on the expanded scope of the exception provided in the Federal Rules and adopted in this subsection:

> All seem to be susceptible to being the subject of well founded repute. The "world" in which the reputation may exist may be family, associates, or community. This world has proved capable of expanding with changing times from the single uncomplicated neighborhood, in which all activities take place, to the multiple and unrelated words and work, religious affiliation, and social activity, in each of which a reputation may be generated.

In Cone v. Benjamin, 157 Fla. 800, 821-22, 27 So.2d 90, 101-02 (1946) the Florida Supreme Court approved the use of "pedigree" testimony:

> Generally speaking, the theory underlying the acceptance of the declarations as to pedigree made by deceased persons who were members of or intimately connected with the family is based upon the theory that such persons were familiar with those matters of family history, tradition and repute with which the members of most families are familiar, although based upon hearsay within the family, and that, having been made before any controversy had arisen, there was no motive to speak other than the truth. As was said by Justice Paxson in the old case of Sitler v. Gehr, supra:
>
>> "Indeed we scarcely realize how little we actually know from our own observation and investigation. We learn the truths of history, the secrets of science and our knowledge of the world generally, from what we have read, or from what others have told us. What does a man know of his deceased ancestors but what he has learned from his immediate relatives? How was the plaintiff, who had never seen Balser Behr, to know that the latter was his uncle except from his mother? It is in such cases that the strict rules of evidence are relaxed as regards hearsay. If it were otherwise pedigree could not be proved at all in many cases, and in one sense it is primary not secondary evidence."

In General Properties Corp. v. Gore, 153 Fla. 236, 243, 14 So.2d 411, 415 (1943), the court quoted with approval 20 Am. Jur. Evidence § 473 (1939), "Declarations and general repute are admissible as proof of a marriage." In Stone v. State, 71 Fla. 514, 71 So. 634 (1916), the admission of hearsay testimony by an aunt concerning a child's age was approved because "ages are matters of common knowledge in families."

For comparable provisions see Uniform Rule 63(26), (27)(c); Calif. Evid. Code §§ 1313-14; Kansas Code of Civ. Pro. § 60-460(x), (y)(3); New Jersey Evid. Rule 63(26), (27)(c); Fed. Rule Evid. 803(19).

The first portion of Subsection (20) is based upon the general admissibility of evidence of reputation as to land boundaries and land customs, expanded in this country to include private as well as public boundaries. 6 Wigmore, Evidence §§ 1580, 1587 (3rd ed. 1940). The necessity for this evidence stems from the probable unavailability of witnesses and the absence of boundary markers. An ancient Florida case is in accord with this rule. In Daggett v. Willey, 6 Fla. 482, 511 (1863), the court stated that:

[R]eputation or hearsay,...taken in connection with other evidence, is entitled to respect in cases of boundary when the lapse of time is so great as to render it difficult, if not impossible, to prove the boundary by the existence of the primitive landmarks or other evidence than that of hearsay.

No Florida cases were found which deal with the requirement that the reputation arise prior to the controversy.

The second portion of this exception, which provides for admissibility of reputation evidence of general history, is likewise supported by authority. 5 Wigmore, Evidence §§ 1597, 1598 (3rd ed. 1940). The historical character of the subject matter negates the need that the reputation antedate the controversy with respect to which it is offered.

For similar provisions see Uniform Rule 63(27)(a), (b); Calif. Evid. Code §§ 1321-22; Kansas Code of Civ. Pro. § 60-460(1); New Jersey Evid. Rule 63(27)(a); Prop. Fed. Rule Evid. 803(20).

Subsection (21) recognizes the traditional acceptance of reputation evidence as a means of proving human character. 5 Wigmore, Evidence §§ 1608-1621 (3rd ed. 1940); Cornelius v. State, 49 So.2d 332 (Fla. 1950); Reddick v. State, 25 Fla. 112, 5 So. 704 (1889). This rule deals only with the hearsay aspect of this type of evidence. Limitations upon admissibility based on other grounds will be found in Section 90.404 (relevancy of character evidence generally) and in Section 90.609 (character of witness). Similar provisions are contained in Uniform Rule 63(28); Calif. Evid. Code § 1324; Kansas Code of Civ. Pro. § 60-460(z); New Jersey Evid. Rule 63(28); Prop. Fed. Rule Evid. 803(21).

COMMENTARY ON FEDERAL AND FLORIDA RULE DIFFERENCES

Florida Stat. §§ 90.803(19)-(21) and their federal counterparts, Federal Rules 803(19)-(21), create exceptions to the hearsay rule for various types of reputation testimony. Florida Stat. § 90.803(19) and Federal Rule 803(19) create an exception to the hearsay rule for reputation among members of a person's family (by blood, adoption or marriage), his associates, or the community, concerning his personal or family history, such as birth, death, marriage, divorce, ancestry, and the like. Florida Stat. § 90.803(20)(a) and Federal Rule 803(20) create an exception to the hearsay rule for reputation in the community—arising before the controversy—as to boundaries of or customs affecting lands in the community. Florida Stat. § 90.803(20)(b) and Federal Rule 803(20) create an exception to the hearsay rule for reputation as to events of general history important to the community or State or nation in which located. Finally, Florida Stat. § 90.803(21) and Federal Rule 803(21) create an exception to the hearsay rule for reputation of a person's character among associates or in the community.

To constitute "reputation" testimony within a community under any of the Florida or federal provisions, it must be shown that the witness is familiar with the person and the community in which the person's reputation has been formed, and that the testimony is based on discussions among a broad group of people rather than rumor or conversations with a narrow group of people. See Larzelere v. State, 676 So. 2d 394, 399-400 (Fla. 1996); Blackburn v. United Parcel Serv., Inc., 179 F.3d 81, 100-01 (3d Cir. 1999). The term "community" as used in both the Florida and federal rules is not limited to a person's residential community, but could instead be a work or school community. See U.S. v. Oliver, 492 F.2d 943, 945-46 (8th Cir. 1974); Webster v. State, 500 So. 2d 285, 287 (Fla. 1st DCA 1986). However, under Florida practice, some authority holds that one can offer evidence of a person's reputation in a non-residential community only if no character witnesses from the person's residential community are available. See Webster, 500 So. 2d at 287. With that caveat, there do not appear to be any substantive differences between the Florida and federal rules.

Federal Rule 803(22). Exceptions to the Rule Against Hearsay — Regardless of Whether the Declarant Is Available as a Witness [Judgment of a Previous Conviction]

The following are not excluded by the rule against hearsay, regardless of whether the declarant is available as a witness:

....

(22) *Judgment of a Previous Conviction.* Evidence of a final judgment of conviction if:

(A) the judgment was entered after a trial or guilty plea, but not a nolo contendere plea;

(B) the conviction was for a crime punishable by death or by imprisonment for more than a year;

(C) the evidence is admitted to prove any fact essential to the judgment; and

(D) when offered by the prosecutor in a criminal case for a purpose other than impeachment, the judgment was against the defendant.

The pendency of an appeal may be shown but does not affect admissibility.

....

ADVISORY COMMITTEE'S NOTE

....

Exception (22). When the status of a former judgment is under consideration in subsequent litigation, three possibilities must be noted: (1) the former judgment is conclusive under the doctrine of res judicata, either as a bar or a collateral estoppel; or (2) it is admissible in evidence for what it is worth; or (3) it may be of no effect at all. The first situation does not involve any problem of evidence except in the way that principles of substantive law generally bear upon the relevancy and materiality of evidence. The rule does not deal with the substantive effect of the judgment as a bar or collateral estoppel. When, however, the doctrine of res judicata does not apply to make the judgment either a bar or a collateral estoppel, a choice is presented between the second and third alternatives. The rule adopts the second for judgments of criminal conviction of felony grade. This is the direction of the decisions, Annot., 18 A.L.R.2d 1287, 1299, which manifest an increasing reluctance to reject *in toto* the validity of the law's factfinding processes outside the confines of res judicata and collateral estoppel. While this may leave a jury with the evidence of conviction but without means to evaluate it, as suggested by Judge Hinton, Note 27 Ill.L.Rev. 195 (1932), it seems safe to assume that the jury will give it substantial effect unless defendant offers a satisfactory explanation, a possibility not foreclosed by the provision. But see North River Ins. Co. v. Militello, 104 Colo. 28 (1939), in which the jury found for plaintiff on a fire policy despite the introduction of his conviction for arson. For supporting federal decisions see Clark, J., in New York & Cuba Mail S.S. Co. v. Continental Cas. Co., 117 F.2d 404, 411 (2d Cir. 1941); Connecticut Fire Ins. Co. v. Farrara, 277 F.2d 388 (8th Cir. 1960).

Practical considerations require exclusion of convictions of minor offenses, not because the administration of justice in its lower echelons must be inferior, but because motivation to defend at this level is often minimal or nonexistent. Cope v. Goble, 39 Cal.App.2d 448 (1940); Jones v. Talbot, 87 Idaho 498 (1964); Warren v. Marsh, 215 Minn. 615 (1943); Annot., 18 A.L.R.2d 1287, 1295–1297; 16 Brooklyn L.Rev. 286 (1950); 50 Colum.L.Rev. 529 (1950); 35 Cornell L.Q. 872 (1950). Hence the rule includes only convictions of felony grade, measured by federal standards.

Judgments of conviction based upon pleas of *nolo contendere* are not included. This position is consistent with the treatment of *nolo* pleas in Rule 410 and the authorities cited in the Advisory Committee's Note in support thereof.

While these rules do not in general purport to resolve constitutional issues, they have in general been drafted with a view to avoiding collision with constitutional principles. Consequently the exception does not include evidence of the conviction of a third person, offered against the accused in a criminal prosecution to prove any fact essential to sustain the judgment of conviction. A contrary position would seem clearly to violate the right of confrontation. Kirby v. United States, 174 U.S. 47 (1899), error to convict of possessing stolen postage stamps with the only evidence of theft being the record of conviction of the thieves. The situation is to be distinguished from cases in which conviction of another person is an element of the crime, e.g. 15 U.S.C. § 902(d), interstate shipment of firearms to a known convicted felon, and, as specifically provided, from impeachment.

For comparable provisions see Uniform Rule 63(20); California Evidence Code § 1300; Kansas Code of Civil Procedure § 60-460(r); New Jersey Evidence Rule 63(20).

....

COMMENTARY ON FEDERAL AND FLORIDA RULE DIFFERENCES

Federal Rule 803(22) creates an exception to the hearsay rule for evidence of certain types of final judgments in criminal cases offered to prove a fact essential to sustain the judgment. The exception is limited to judgments of conviction following a trial or a guilty plea for crimes punishable by death or imprisonment in excess of one year. It does not apply to judgments of conviction following a plea of *nolo contendere* or judgments of conviction for crimes punishable by one year or less in prison, *see U.S. v. Denetclaw*, 96 F.3d 454, 460 (10th Cir. 1996), nor does it apply to judgments of acquittal, which are hearsay not within any exception to the hearsay rule. *See U.S. v. Irvin*, 787 F.2d 1506, 1516-17 (11th Cir. 1986). That an appeal of the judgment is pending can be shown but does not affect its admissibility under this exception. The exception cannot be invoked by the government in a criminal prosecution to admit judgments against persons other than the accused (save for purposes of impeaching such other persons), a restriction designed to prevent a violation of a defendant's Confrontation Clause rights. *See* Advisory Committee's Note to FED. R. EVID. 803(22).

The Eleventh Circuit has held that the provision for admitting certain types of judgments under this exception and Federal Rule 803(23) implicitly restricts expansively interpreting any other hearsay exception (such as that for public records) to admit other types of judgments. *See U.S. v. Jones*, 29 F.3d 1549, 1554 (11th Cir. 1994).

The Florida Evidence Code has no comparable hearsay exception allowing the admission of prior convictions in subsequent litigation to prove an essential element of the convictions, and thus such judgments cannot overcome a hearsay objection. *See Napoli v. State*, 596 So. 2d 782, 786 (Fla. 1st DCA 1992); *State v. Dubose*, 11 So. 2d 477, 481 (Fla. 1943) (en banc).

Federal Rule 803(23). Exceptions to the Rule Against Hearsay — Regardless of Whether the Declarant Is Available as a Witness [Judgments Involving Personal, Family, or General History, or a Boundary]

The following are not excluded by the rule against hearsay, regardless of whether the declarant is available as a witness:

....

(23) *Judgments Involving Personal, Family, or General History, or a Boundary.* A judgment that is admitted to prove a matter of personal, family, or general history, or boundaries, if the matter:

(A) was essential to the judgment; and

(B) could be proved by evidence of reputation.

ADVISORY COMMITTEE'S NOTE

....

Exception (23). A hearsay exception in this area was originally justified on the ground that verdicts were evidence of reputation. As trial by jury graduated from the category of neighborhood inquests, this theory lost its validity. It was never valid as to chancery decrees. Nevertheless the rule persisted, though the judges and writers shifted ground and began saying that the judgment or decree was as good evidence as reputation. See City of London v. Clerke, Carth. 181, 90 Eng.Rep. 710 (K.B. 1691); Neill v. Duke of Devonshire, 8 App.Cas. 135 (1882). The shift appears to be correct, since the process of inquiry, sifting, and scrutiny which is relied upon to render reputation reliable is present in perhaps greater measure in the process of litigation. While this might suggest a broader area of application, the affinity to reputation is strong, and paragraph (23) goes no further, not even including character.

The leading case in the United States, Patterson v. Gaines, 47 U.S. (6 How.) 550, 599 (1847), follows in the pattern of the English decisions, mentioning as illustrative matters thus provable: manorial rights, public rights of way, immemorial custom, disputed boundary, and pedigree. More recent recognition of the principle is found in Grant Bros. Construction Co. v. United States, 232 U.S. 647 (1914), in action for penalties under Alien Contract Labor Law, decision of board of inquiry of Immigration Service admissible to prove alienage of laborers, as a matter of pedigree; United States v. Mid-Continent Petroleum Corp., 67 F.2d 37 (10th Cir. 1933), records of commission enrolling Indians admissible on pedigree; Jung Yen Loy v. Cahill, 81 F.2d 809 (9th Cir. 1936), board decisions as to citizenship of plaintiff 's father admissible in proceeding for declaration of citizenship. *Contra*, In re Estate of Cunha, 49 Haw. 273 (1966).

COMMENTARY ON FEDERAL AND FLORIDA RULE DIFFERENCES

Federal Rule 803(23) creates an exception to the hearsay rule for evidence of judgments as proof of matters of personal, family or general history, or boundaries, to the extent that such determinations were essential to the judgment and the same would be provable by evidence of reputation. The types of matters that are provable by evidence of reputation are examined in the Commentary to Federal Rules 803(19)-(21) and Florida Stat. § 90.803(19)-(21).

This very narrow exception to the hearsay rule is the only one that paves the way for admitting civil judgments over a hearsay objection. *See McKinney v. Galvin*, 701 F.2d 584, 586 n.5 (6th Cir. 1983); *see also U.S. v. Jones*, 29 F.3d 1549, 1554 (11th Cir. 1994) (holding that the provision for admitting certain types of judgments under this exception and Federal Rule 803(22) implicitly restricts expansively interpreting any other hearsay exception to admit other types of judgments).

The Florida Evidence Code has no comparable hearsay exception, and thus such judgments cannot overcome a hearsay objection in Florida state courts. *See Napoli v. State*, 596 So. 2d 782, 786 (Fla. 1st DCA 1992); *State v. Dubose*, 11 So. 2d 477, 481 (Fla. 1943) (en banc).

Florida Stat. § 90.803(22). Hearsay Exceptions; Availability of Declarant Immaterial [Former Testimony]

The provision of s. 90.802 to the contrary notwithstanding, the following are not inadmissible as evidence, even though the declarant is available as a witness:

....

(22) Former testimony. Former testimony given by the declarant which testimony was given as a witness at another hearing of the same or a different proceeding, or in a deposition taken in compliance with law in the course of the same or another proceeding, if the party against whom the testimony is now offered, or, in a civil action or proceeding, a predecessor in interest, or a person with a similar interest, had an opportunity and similar motive to develop the testimony by direct, cross, or redirect examination; provided, however, the court finds that the testimony is not inadmissible pursuant to s. 90.402 or s. 90.403.

....

SPONSORS' NOTE (1976 ENACTMENT)

This exception makes admissible testimony given by a witness at a civil trial when it is introduced at a subsequent civil trial which is a retrial of the same proceeding. Thus, in a retrial of a case it is unnecessary to call as a witness a person who testified during the first trial. This exception expands the use of evidence given at a former trial from that provided in existing Fla. Stat. § 92.22 which allowed the use of this evidence only when "a substantial reason...why the original witness or document is not produced" is shown. Under this exception, this evidence is admissible regardless of availability of the witness.

See § 90.804(2)(a) for a related exception.

COMMENTARY ON FEDERAL AND FLORIDA RULE DIFFERENCES

Florida Stat. § 90.803(22) creates an exception to the hearsay rule for former testimony given as a witness at another hearing of the same or a different proceeding, or in a deposition, provided that the party against whom it is offered—or in a civil proceeding, a predecessor in interest or a person with a similar interest—had an opportunity and similar motive to develop the testimony by direct, cross, or re-direct examination, subject to exclusion for lack of relevancy or pursuant to Florida Stat. § 90.403.

Prior to 1998, this exception applied only to "[f]ormer testimony given by the declarant at a civil trial, when used in a retrial of said trial involving identical parties and the same facts"; for other types of former testimony, resort had to be made to Florida Stat. § 90.804(2)(a), which requires a showing of unavailability. See *State v. Abreu*, 837 So. 2d 400, 400-02 (Fla. 2003). In 1998, the Florida legislature amended Florida Stat. § 90.803(22) so as to make it applicable in all situations in which Florida Stat. § 90.804(2)(a) applies, effectively eliminating the unavailability requirement for all uses of former testimony. See *id*. The Florida Supreme Court has held Florida Stat. § 90.803(22) unconstitutional under the Confrontation Clause to the extent that it permits the prosecution in a criminal case to use a witness's testimony from a previous proceeding without a showing of unavailability. See *id*. at 402-06. Moreover, the Florida Supreme Court refused to adopt Florida Stat. § 90.803(22) as amended by the legislature, and so it appears to be inapplicable even in civil cases, save for when the former testimony is in a retrial of a civil case involving the same parties and the same facts as provided for under the pre-1998 version of the rule. *See In re Amendments to the Fla. Evidence Code*, 782 So. 2d 339, 341-42 (Fla. 2000); *Grabau v. Department of Health, Bd. of Psychology*, 816 So. 2d 701, 706-09 (Fla. 1st DCA 2002).

No hearsay exception in the federal rules of evidence permits former testimony to be admitted absent a showing of unavailability. Federal Rule 804(b)(1) creates an exception to the hearsay rule for former testimony when the declarant is unavailable as a witness, and that provision, along with Florida Stat. § 90.804(2)(a), is examined later in this Article.

Florida Stat. § 90.803(23). Hearsay Exceptions; Availability of Declarant Immaterial [Statement of Child Victim]

The provision of s. 90.802 to the contrary notwithstanding, the following are not inadmissible as evidence, even though the declarant is available as a witness:

....

(23) Hearsay exception; statement of child victim.

(a) Unless the source of information or the method or circumstances by which the statement is reported indicates a lack of trustworthiness, an out-of-court statement made by a child victim with a physical, mental, emotional, or developmental age of 11 or less describing any act of child abuse or neglect, any act of sexual abuse against a child, the offense of child abuse, the offense of aggravated child abuse, or any offense involving an unlawful sexual act, contact, intrusion, or penetration performed in the presence of, with, by, or on the declarant child, not otherwise admissible, is admissible in evidence in any civil or criminal proceeding if:

1. The court finds in a hearing conducted outside the presence of the jury that the time, content, and circumstances of the statement provide sufficient safeguards of reliability. In making its determination, the court may consider the mental and physical age and maturity of the child, the nature and duration of the abuse or offense, the relationship of the child to the offender, the reliability of the assertion, the reliability of the child victim, and any other factor deemed appropriate; and

2. The child either:

a. Testifies; or

b. Is unavailable as a witness, provided that there is other corroborative evidence of the abuse or offense. Unavailability shall include a finding by the court that the child's participation in the trial or proceeding would result in a substantial likelihood of severe emotional or mental harm, in addition to findings pursuant to s. 90.804(1).

(b) In a criminal action, the defendant shall be notified no later than 10 days before trial that a statement which qualifies as a hearsay exception pursuant to this subsection will be offered as evidence at trial. The notice shall include a written statement of the content of the child's statement, the time at which the statement was made, the circumstances surrounding the statement which indicate its reliability, and such other particulars as necessary to provide full disclosure of the statement.

(c) The court shall make specific findings of fact, on the record, as to the basis for its ruling under this subsection.

....

COMMENTARY ON FEDERAL AND FLORIDA RULE DIFFERENCES

Florida Stat. § 90.803(23) creates an exception to the hearsay rule, applicable in civil and criminal proceedings, for statements by children who are victims of physical or sexual abuse or neglect. The exception applies only if the child has a mental, emotional, or developmental age of 11 or less and the statement describes the act of abuse. See FLA. STAT. § 90.803(23)(a). The relevant date for determining the child's age for purposes of this hearsay exception is the date when the statement was *made*, not the date of *trial*. See *State v. Contreras*, 979 So. 2d 896, 908 (Fla. 2008). For a statement to be admitted under this exception, the trial court must find—in a hearing held outside the jury's presence—that the statement was made under circumstances that provide sufficient indicia that the statement is reliable. See FLA. STAT. § 90.803(23)(a)(1). Moreover, for the statement to be admitted, the child must either testify or the trial court must find him to be unavailable as a witness, with the term defined to include a finding that the child's participation in the trial would result in a substantial likelihood of severe emotional or mental harm. See FLA. STAT. § 90.803(23)(a)(2). If the child does not testify, however, there must be other corroborative evidence of the abuse or offense. See *id.; State v. Townsend*, 635 So. 2d 949, 957 (Fla. 1994). Furthermore, in criminal cases, the defendant must be given notice at least ten days in advance of trial that the government intends to offer a statement under this exception, which notice shall include the content of the statement, the time it was made, and the circumstances that indicate its reliability. See FLA. STAT. § 90.803(23)(b). The trial court's findings with respect to these various foundational requirements must be specific and on the record. See FLA. STAT. § 90.803(23)(c); See *Hopkins v. State*, 632 So. 2d 1372, 1376 (Fla. 1994). Even if all of these requirements are satisfied, the trial court retains discretion to exclude the child's hearsay statements under Florida Stat. § 90.403. See *Pardo v. State*, 596 So. 2d 665, 667-68 (Fla. 1992).

To the extent that a statement is testimonial within the meaning of *Crawford v. Washington*, 541 U.S. 36 (2004), it violates the Confrontation Clause to offer a statement under this exception against a defendant in a criminal case unless the child testifies at trial, or he is shown to be unavailable *and* the defendant had a prior opportunity to cross-examine the child concerning the statement. See *Contreras*, 979 So. 2d at 901-08.

There is no comparable exception to the federal hearsay rule. Statements by child victims are admissible if they fit within one of the other exceptions to the hearsay rule and—when offered against the defendant in a criminal case—satisfy the requirements of the Confrontation Clause.

Florida Stat. § 90.803(24). Hearsay Exceptions; Availability of Declarant Immaterial [Statement of Elderly Person or Disabled Adult]

The provision of s. 90.802 to the contrary notwithstanding, the following are not inadmissible as evidence, even though the declarant is available as a witness:

....

(24) Hearsay exception; statement of elderly person or disabled adult.

(a) Unless the source of information or the method or circumstances by which the statement is reported indicates a lack of trustworthiness, an out-of-court statement made by an elderly person or disabled adult, as defined in s. 825.101, describing any act of abuse or neglect, any act of exploitation, the offense of battery or aggravated battery or assault or aggravated assault or sexual battery, or any other violent act on the declarant elderly person or disabled adult, not otherwise admissible, is admissible in evidence in any civil or criminal proceeding if:

1. The court finds in a hearing conducted outside the presence of the jury that the time, content, and circumstances of the statement provide sufficient safeguards of reliability. In making its

determination, the court may consider the mental and physical age and maturity of the elderly person or disabled adult, the nature and duration of the abuse or offense, the relationship of the victim to the offender, the reliability of the assertion, the reliability of the elderly person or disabled adult, and any other factor deemed appropriate; and

2. The elderly person or disabled adult either:

a. Testifies; or

b. Is unavailable as a witness, provided that there is corroborative evidence of the abuse or offense. Unavailability shall include a finding by the court that the elderly person's or disabled adult's participation in the trial or proceeding would result in a substantial likelihood of severe emotional, mental, or physical harm, in addition to findings pursuant to s. 90.804(1).

(b) In a criminal action, the defendant shall be notified no later than 10 days before the trial that a statement which qualifies as a hearsay exception pursuant to this subsection will be offered as evidence at trial. The notice shall include a written statement of the content of the elderly person's or disabled adult's statement, the time at which the statement was made, the circumstances surrounding the statement which indicate its reliability, and such other particulars as necessary to provide full disclosure of the statement.

(c) The court shall make specific findings of fact, on the record, as to the basis for its ruling under this subsection.

COMMENTARY ON FEDERAL AND FLORIDA RULE DIFFERENCES

Florida Stat. § 90.803(24) creates an exception to the hearsay rule, applicable in civil and criminal proceedings, for statements by elderly persons or disabled adults who are victims of physical or sexual abuse or neglect. The exception applies to people 60 years of age or older who are suffering from the infirmities of aging or those 18 years or older who suffer from a condition of physical or mental incapacitation. See FLA. STAT. § 825.101(4)-(5).

For a statement to be admitted under this exception, the trial court must find—in a hearing held outside the jury's presence—that the statement was made under circumstances that provide sufficient indicia that the statement is reliable. See FLA. STAT. § 90.803(24)(a)(1). Moreover, for the statement to be admitted, the person must either testify or the trial court must find him to be unavailable as a witness, with the term defined to include a finding that the person's participation in the trial would result in a substantial likelihood of severe emotional, mental, or physical harm. See FLA. STAT. § 90.803(24)(a)(2). If the person does not testify, however, there must be other corroborative evidence of the abuse or offense. See id. Furthermore, in criminal cases, the defendant must be given notice at least ten days in advance of trial that the government intends to offer a statement under this exception, which notice shall include the content of the statement, the time it was made, and the circumstances that indicate its reliability. See FLA. STAT. § 90.803(24)(b). The trial court's findings with respect to these various foundational requirements must be specific and on the record. See FLA. STAT. § 90.803(24)(c).

The Florida Supreme Court has held that this statute is facially unconstitutional under the Confrontation Clause when applied to statements made by elderly adults in criminal cases. *Conner v. State*, 748 So. 2d 950, 960 (Fla. 1999). However, the Court has upheld the statute's constitutionality as applied to statements by a mentally disabled adult that are non-testimonial within the meaning of *Crawford v. Washington*, 541 U.S. 36 (2004). *See State v. Hosty*, 944 So. 2d 255, 261-63 (Fla. 2006). The Court has left open the questions whether the statute is constitutional as applied to physically disabled adults who have no mental impairment or as it applies generally in civil cases. *See Hosty*, 944 So. 2d at 263; *Conner*, 748 So. 2d at 960 n.11.

There is no comparable exception to the federal hearsay rule. Statements by child victims are admissible if they fit within one of the other exceptions to the hearsay rule and—when offered against the defendant in a criminal case—satisfy the requirements of the Confrontation Clause.

Federal Rule 804(a). Exceptions to the Rule Against Hearsay — When the Declarant Is Unavailable as a Witness [Criteria for Being Unavailable]

(a) **Criteria for Being Unavailable.** A declarant is considered to be unavailable as a witness if the declarant:

(1) is exempted from testifying about the subject matter of the declarant's statement because the court rules that a privilege applies;

(2) refuses to testify about the subject matter despite a court order to do so;

(3) testifies to not remembering the subject matter;

(4) cannot be present or testify at the trial or hearing because of death or a then-existing infirmity, physical illness, or mental illness; or

(5) is absent from the trial or hearing and the statement's proponent has not been able, by process or other reasonable means, to procure:

(A) the declarant's attendance, in the case of a hearsay exception under Rule 804(b)(1) or (6); or

(B) the declarant's attendance or testimony, in the case of a hearsay exception under Rule 804(b)(2), (3), or (4).

But this subdivision (a) does not apply if the statement's proponent procured or wrongfully caused the declarant's unavailability as a witness in order to prevent the declarant from attending or testifying.

....

ADVISORY COMMITTEE'S NOTE

As to firsthand knowledge on the part of hearsay declarants, see the introductory portion of the Advisory Committee's Note to Rule 803.

Subdivision (a). The definition of unavailability implements the division of hearsay exceptions into two categories by Rules 803 and 804(b).

At common law the unavailability requirement was evolved in connection with particular hearsay exceptions rather than along general lines. For example, see the separate explications of unavailability in relation to former testimony, declarations against interest, and statements of pedigree, separately developed in McCormick §§ 234, 257, and 297. However, no reason is apparent for making distinctions as to what satisfies unavailability for the different exceptions. The treatment in the rule is therefore uniform although differences in the range of process for witnesses between civil and criminal cases will lead to a less exacting requirement under item (5). See Rule 45(e) of the Federal Rules of Civil Procedure and Rule 17(e) of the Federal Rules of Criminal Procedure.

Five instances of unavailability are specified:

(1) Substantial authority supports the position that exercise of a claim of privilege by the declarant satisfies the requirement of unavailability (usually in connection with former testimony). Wyatt v. State, 35 Ala.App. 147 (1950); State v. Stewart, 85 Kan. 404 (1911); Annot., 45 A.L.R.2d 1354; Uniform Rule 62(7)(a); California Evidence Code § 240(a)(1); Kansas Code of Civil Procedure § 60-459(g)(1). A ruling by the judge is required, which clearly implies that an actual claim of privilege must be made.

(2) A witness is rendered unavailable if he simply refuses to testify concerning the subject matter of his statement despite judicial pressures to do so, a position supported by similar considerations of practicality. Johnson v. People, 152 Colo. 586 (1963); People v. Pickett, 339 Mich. 294, 45 A.L.R.2d 1341 (1954). *Contra*, Pleau v. State, 255 Wis. 362 (1949).

(3) The position that a claimed lack of memory by the witness of the subject matter of his statement constitutes unavailability likewise finds support in the cases, though not without dissent. McCormick § 234, p. 494. If the claim is successful, the practical effect is to put the testimony beyond reach, as in the other instances. In this instance, however, it will be noted that the lack of memory must be established by the testimony of the witness himself, which clearly contemplates his production and subjection to cross-examination.

(4) Death and infirmity find general recognition as grounds. McCormick §§ 234, 257, 297; Uniform Rule 62(7)(c); California Evidence Code § 240(a)(3); Kansas Code of Civil Procedure § 60-459(g)(3); New Jersey Evidence Rule 62(6)(c). See also the provisions on use of depositions in Rule 32(a)(3) of the Federal Rules of Civil Procedure and Rule 15(e) of the Federal Rules of Criminal Procedure.

(5) Absence from the hearing coupled with inability to compel attendance by process or other reasonable means also satisfies the requirement. McCormick § 234; Uniform Rule 62(7)(d) and (e); California Evidence Code § 240(a)(4) and (5); Kansas Code of Civil Procedure § 60-459(g)(4) and (5); New Jersey Rule 62(6)(b) and (d). See the discussion of procuring attendance of witnesses who are nonresidents or in custody in Barber v. Page, 390 U.S. 719 (1968).

If the conditions otherwise constituting unavailability result from the procurement or wrongdoing of the proponent of the statement, the requirement is not satisfied. The rule contains no requirement that an attempt be made to take the deposition of a declarant.

....

REPORT OF HOUSE COMMITTEE ON THE JUDICIARY

Rule 804(a)(3). Rule 804(a)(3) was approved in the form submitted by the Court. However, the Committee intends no change in existing federal law under which the court may choose to disbelieve the declarant's testimony as to his lack of memory. See *United States v. Insana*, 423 F.2d 1165, 1169–1170 (2nd Cir.), cert. denied, 400 U.S. 841 (1970).

Rule 804(a)(5). Rule 804(a)(5) as submitted to the Congress provided, as one type of situation in which a declarant would be deemed "unavailable", that he be "absent from the hearing and the proponent of his statement has been unable to procure his attendance by process or other reasonable means." The Committee amended the Rule to insert after the word "attendance" the parenthetical expression "(or, in the case of a hearsay exception under subdivision (b)(2), (3), or (4), his attendance or testimony)". The amendment is designed primarily to require that an attempt be made to depose a witness (as well as to seek his attendance) as a precondition to the witness being deemed unavailable. The Committee, however, recognized the propriety of an exception to this additional requirement when it is the declarant's former testimony that is sought to be admitted under subdivision (b)(1).

....

REPORT OF SENATE COMMITTEE ON THE JUDICIARY

Rule 804(a)(5). Subdivision (a) of rule 804 as submitted by the Supreme Court defined the conditions under which a witness was considered to be unavailable. It was amended in the House.

The purpose of the amendment, according to the report of the House Committee on the Judiciary, is "primarily to require that an attempt be made to depose a witness (as well as to seek his attendance) as a precondition to the witness being unavailable."[36]

Under the House amendment, before a witness is declared unavailable, a party must try to depose a witness (declarant) with respect to dying declarations, declarations against interest, and declarations of pedigree. None of these situations would seem to warrant this needless, impractical and highly restrictive complication. A good case can be made for eliminating the unavailability requirement entirely for declarations against interest cases.[37]

In dying declaration cases, the declarant will usually, though not necessarily, be deceased at the time of trial. Pedigree statements which are admittedly and necessarily based largely on word of mouth are not greatly fortified by a deposition requirement.

Depositions are expensive and time-consuming. In any event, deposition procedures are available to those who wish to resort to them. Moreover, the deposition procedures of the Civil Rules and Criminal Rules are only imperfectly adapted to implementing the amendment. No purpose is served unless the deposition, if taken, may be used in evidence. Under Civil Rule (a)(3) and Criminal Rule 15(e), a deposition, though taken, may not be admissible, and under Criminal Rule 15(a) substantial obstacles exist in the way of even taking a deposition.

For these reasons, the committee deleted the House amendment.

The committee understands that the rule as to unavailability, as explained by the Advisory Committee "contains no requirement that an attempt be made to take the deposition of a declarant." In reflecting the committee's judgment, the statement is accurate insofar as it goes. Where, however, the proponent of the statement, with knowledge of the existence of the statement, fails to confront the declarant with the statement at the taking of the deposition, then the proponent should not, in fairness, be permitted to treat the declarant as "unavailable" simply because the declarant was not amenable to process compelling his attendance at trial. The committee does not consider it necessary to amend the rule to this effect because such a situation abuses, not conforms to, the rule. Fairness would preclude a person from introducing a hearsay statement on a particular issue if the person taking the deposition was aware of the issue at the time of the deposition but failed to depose the unavailable witness on that issue.

....

CONFERENCE REPORT

Rule 804 defines what hearsay statements are admissible in evidence if the declarant is unavailable as a witness. The Senate amendments make four changes in the rule.

---

[36] H.Rept. 93-650, at p. 15.
[37] Uniform rule 63(10); Kan.Stat.Anno. 60-460(j); 2A N.J.Stats.Anno. 84-63(10).

Rule 804(a)(5). Subsection (a) defines the term "unavailability as a witness". The House bill provides in subsection (a)(5) that the party who desires to use the statement must be unable to procure the declarant's attendance by process or other reasonable means. In the case of dying declarations, statements against interest and statements of personal or family history, the House bill requires that the proponent must also be unable to procure the declarant's *testimony* (such as by deposition or interrogatories) by process or other reasonable means. The Senate amendment eliminates this latter provision.

The Conference adopts the provision contained in the House bill.

....

ADVISORY COMMITTEE'S NOTE (2011 AMENDMENT)

The language of Rule 804 has been amended as part of the general restyling of the Evidence Rules to make them more easily understood and to make style and terminology consistent throughout the rules. These changes are intended to be stylistic only. There is no intent to change any result in any ruling on evidence admissibility.

No style changes were made to Rule 804(b)(3), because it was already restyled in conjunction with a substantive amendment, effective December 1, 2010.

Florida Stat. § 90.804(1). Hearsay Exceptions; Declarant Unavailable [Definition of unavailability]

(1) Definition of unavailability. "Unavailability as a witness" means that the declarant:

(a) Is exempted by a ruling of a court on the ground of privilege from testifying concerning the subject matter of the declarant's statement;

(b) Persists in refusing to testify concerning the subject matter of the declarant's statement despite an order of the court to do so;

(c) Has suffered a lack of memory of the subject matter of his or her statement so as to destroy the declarant's effectiveness as a witness during the trial;

(d) Is unable to be present or to testify at the hearing because of death or because of then-existing physical or mental illness or infirmity; or

(e) Is absent from the hearing, and the proponent of a statement has been unable to procure the declarant's attendance or testimony by process or other reasonable means.

However, a declarant is not unavailable as a witness if such exemption, refusal, claim of lack of memory, inability to be present, or absence is due to the procurement or wrongdoing of the party who is the proponent of his or her statement in preventing the witness from attending or testifying.

....

SPONSORS' NOTE (1976 ENACTMENT)

Subsection (1) The common-law hearsay exceptions developed different requirements of unavailability for different hearsay exceptions. The unavailability requirements for the exceptions of former testimony, declarations, and statement of pedigree, as they evolved at common law, are discussed in McCormick,

Evidence §§ 255, 280, and 322 (2nd ed. 1972). In this section, the treatment of unavailability is uniform since there is no apparent reason for making distinctions between different types of unavailability in the different exceptions.

Unavailability is defined in Uniform Rule 62(7), Calif. Evid. Code § 240, Kansas Code of Civ. Pro. § 60-459, and New Jersey Evid.Rule 62(6) to include the circumstances described in paragraphs (a), (d), and (e). Wisc. Rule Evid. 908.04(a) and Prop. Fed. Rule Evid. 804 are similar to this section. The testimony of the witness, when he refuses to testify despite an order by the judge and when he has suffered a lack of memory on the subject matter, is equally unavailable. In Anderson v. Gaither, 120 Fla. 263, 268, 162 So. 877, 879 (1935) the Court recognized that:

> The admission in evidence of Stuart's deposition taken in 1929, although Stuart was personally in court and called as a witness at the last trial held in 1933, was (at least) within the sound discretion of the court, when it appeared from the circumstances that witness's memory at time of giving the earlier deposition was obviously clearer as to details than his personal testimony given from the witness stand four years later.

A witness is also considered unavailable if he simply refuses to testify concerning the subject matter of his statement despite judicial pressures to do so, a position supported by considerations of practicality. See McCormick, Evidence § 253 (2nd ed. 1972) (citing cases); Annot., 45 A.L.R.2d 1341.

Florida courts have recognized death, James v. State, 254 So.2d 838 (Fla. 1st Dist. 1971); whereabouts unknown, Putnal v. State, 56 Fla. 86, 47 So. 864 (1908); disqualification by insanity, bodily infirmity which renders attendance at court dangerous and unduly burdensome, sickness with inability to attend court, Habig v. Bastian, 117 Fla. 864, 158 So. 508 (1935); and diminished memory, Anderson v. Gaither, 120 Fla. 263, 162 So. 877 (1935), as reasons for justifying the admission of former testimony.

....

COMMENTARY ON FEDERAL AND FLORIDA RULE DIFFERENCES

Florida Stat. § 90.804 and its federal counterpart, Federal Rule 804, set forth a series of restricted exceptions to the hearsay rule, so denominated because they can only be invoked if a showing is first made that the declarant is "unavailable as a witness." The reason for this prerequisite to admissibility is a belief that, unlike evidence falling within the scope of the unrestricted exceptions, evidence falling within the scope of these exceptions are not equal in quality to testimony by the declarant on the stand; thus, such evidence should be admitted only if the declarant is "unavailable" to testify on the stand. See Advisory Committee's Note to FED. R. EVID. 804(b). Because these rules contains multiple provisions, the rules, their legislative history, and the commentary to the rules are broken down by exception.

Florida Stat. § 90.804(1) and its federal counterpart, Federal Rules 804(a), define the circumstances under which a witness will be deemed to be "unavailable." The federal and Florida provisions set forth a set of five nearly identical circumstances in which a witness is deemed unavailable so as to permit their hearsay statements to be admitted under one of the restricted hearsay exceptions.

First, both the Florida and federal rules provide that a declarant is deemed unavailable if he is exempted by court ruling from testifying concerning the subject matter of his statement on the grounds of privilege. See FLA. STAT. § 90.804(1)(a); FED. R. EVID. 804(a)(1). There are no substantive differences between these two provisions.

Second, both the Florida and federal rules define as unavailable a declarant who refuses to testify concerning the subject matter of his statement despite a court order to do so. *See* FLA. STAT. § 90.804(1)(b); FED. R. EVID. 804(a)(2). Some federal case law views a court *order* as an essential prerequisite to invoking this exception, *see U.S. v. Zappola*, 646 F.2d 48, 54 (2d Cir. 1981), but Eleventh Circuit precedent appears to hold that judicial pressure to testify that falls short of an actual order satisfies this requirement. *See U.S. v. Bizzard*, 674 F.2d 1382, 1387 (11th Cir. 1982). The Florida courts do not appear to view an actual court order as an essential prerequisite to invoking this exception. *See Peterson v. State*, 810 So. 2d 1095, 1099 (Fla. 5th DCA 2002) (judge urging witness to testify suffices, and in any event an order not required when it would serve no purpose); *Happ v. Moore*, 784 So. 2d 1091, 1101 (Fla. 2001) (court order not required when it would be futile, such as when witness makes clear that he will not testify even if the court imprisoned him).

A third situation under both the Florida and federal rules in which a witness will be deemed unavailable is due to his lack of memory of the subject matter of his statement. *See* FLA. STAT. § 90.804(1)(c); FED. R. EVID. 804(a)(3). The provisions are worded somewhat differently, with the federal rule applying if the witness "testifies to not remembering the subject matter" and the Florida rule applying if the witness "[h]as suffered a lack of memory," but under the latter rule the witness's testimony that he does not remember can serve as the basis for making a finding that he has suffered a lack of memory, *see Penalver v. State*, 926 So. 2d 1118, 1134-35 (Fla. 2006).

Fourth, both the federal and Florida rules define as unavailable a witness who is unable to appear and testify because she is dead or because of a then-existing physical or mental illness or infirmity. *See* FLA. STAT. § 90.804(1)(d); FED. R. EVID. 804(a)(4). There are no substantive differences between these two provisions.

The final circumstance under both the Florida and federal rules that will render a witness "unavailable" is his absence from the hearing coupled with the proponent's inability to procure his attendance (whether through formal process or through less formal means). *See* FLA. STAT. § 90.804(1)(e); FED. R. EVID. 804(a)(5); *U.S. v. Samaniego*, 345 F.3d 1280, 1283-84 (11th Cir. 2003). The key difference between the two provisions is that under the federal rule, when seeking to invoke the restricted exceptions for statements under belief of impending death, statements against interest, or statements of personal or family history, the inability to procure the declarant's *attendance*, standing alone, does not render him unavailable as a witness; an effort must also be made to get the declarant's *testimony* (such as by deposition or interrogatories) and to offer that testimony, and only if that effort also fails will the witness be deemed unavailable. *See* FED. R. EVID. 804(a)(5); Conference Report to FED. R. EVID. 804(a)(5).

At the end of both the federal and Florida rules is a caveat: a declarant will not be deemed unavailable as a witness if her exemption, refusal, claim of lack of memory, inability to be present, or absence results from the procurement or wrongdoing of the party who seeks to offer her statement into evidence. *See* FLA. STAT. § 90.804(1); FED. R. EVID. 804(a). There are no substantive differences between these two provisions.

Federal Rule 804(b)(1). Exceptions to the Rule Against Hearsay — When the Declarant Is Unavailable as a Witness [Former Testimony]

....

(b) The Exceptions. The following are not excluded by the rule against hearsay if the declarant is unavailable as a witness:

(1) *Former Testimony.* Testimony that:

(A) was given as a witness at a trial, hearing, or lawful deposition, whether given during the current proceeding or a different one; and

(B) is now offered against a party who had — or, in a civil case, whose predecessor in interest had — an opportunity and similar motive to develop it by direct, cross-, or redirect examination.

....

ADVISORY COMMITTEE'S NOTE

....

Subdivision (b). Rule 803, *supra*, is based upon the assumption that a hearsay statement falling within one of its exceptions possesses qualities which justify the conclusion that whether the declarant is available or unavailable is not a relevant factor in determining admissibility. The instant rule proceeds upon a different theory: hearsay which admittedly is not equal in quality to testimony of the declarant on the stand may nevertheless be admitted if the declarant is unavailable and if his statement meets a specified standard. The rule expresses preferences: testimony given on the stand in person is preferred over hearsay, and hearsay, if of the specified quality, is preferred over complete loss of the evidence of the declarant. The exceptions evolved at common law with respect to declarations of unavailable declarants furnish the basis for the exceptions enumerated in the proposal. The term "unavailable" is defined in subdivision (a).

Exception (1). Former testimony does not rely upon some set of circumstances to substitute for oath and cross-examination, since both oath and opportunity to cross-examine were present in fact. The only missing one of the ideal conditions for the giving of testimony is the presence of trier and opponent ("demeanor evidence"). This is lacking with all hearsay exceptions. Hence it may be argued that former testimony is the strongest hearsay and should be included under Rule 803, *supra*. However, opportunity to observe demeanor is what in a large measure confers depth and meaning upon oath and cross-examination. Thus in cases under Rule 803 demeanor lacks the significance which it possesses with respect to testimony. In any event, the tradition, founded in experience, uniformly favors production of the witness if he is available. The exception indicates continuation of the policy. This preference for the presence of the witness is apparent also in rules and statutes on the use of depositions, which deal with substantially the same problem.

Under the exception, the testimony may be offered (1) against the party *against* whom it was previously offered or (2) against the party *by* whom it was previously offered. In each instance the question resolves itself into whether fairness allows imposing, upon the party against whom now offered, the handling of the witness of the earlier occasion. (1) If the party against whom now offered is the one against whom the testimony was offered previously, no unfairness is apparent in requiring him to accept his own prior conduct of cross-examination or decision not to cross-examine. Only demeanor has been lost, and that is inherent in the situation. (2) If the party against whom now offered is the one *by* whom the testimony was offered previously, a satisfactory answer becomes somewhat more difficult. One possibility is to proceed somewhat along the line of an adoptive admission, i.e. by offering the testimony proponent in effect adopts it. However, this theory savors of discarded concepts of witnesses' belonging to a party, of litigants' ability to pick and choose witnesses, and of vouching for one's own witnesses. Cf. McCormick § 246, pp. 526–527; 4 Wigmore § 1075. A more direct and acceptable approach is simply to recognize direct and redirect examination of one's own witness as the equivalent of cross-examining an opponent's witness. Falknor, Former Testimony and the Uniform Rules: A Comment, 38 N.Y.U.L.Rev. 651, n. 1 (1963); McCormick § 231, p. 483. See also 5 Wigmore § 1389. Allowable techniques for dealing with hostile, double-crossing, forgetful, and mentally deficient witnesses leave no substance to a claim that one could not adequately develop his own witness at the former hearing. An even less appealing argument is presented when failure to develop fully was the result of a deliberate choice.

The common law did not limit the admissibility of former testimony to that given in an earlier trial of the same case, although it did require identity of issues as a means of insuring that the former handling of the witness was the equivalent of what would now be done if the opportunity were presented. Modern decisions reduce the requirement to "substantial" identity. McCormick § 233. Since identity of issues is significant only in that it bears on motive and interest in developing fully the testimony of the witness, expressing the matter in the latter terms is preferable. *Id.* Testimony given at a preliminary hearing was held in California v. Green, 399 U.S. 149 (1970), to satisfy confrontation requirements in this respect.

As a further assurance of fairness in thrusting upon a party the prior handling of the witness, the common law also insisted upon identity of parties, deviating only to the extent of allowing substitution of successors in a narrowly construed privity. Mutuality as an aspect of identity is now generally discredited, and the requirement of identity of the offering party disappears except as it might affect motive to develop the testimony. Falknor, *supra*, at 652; McCormick § 232, pp. 487–488. The question remains whether strict identity, or privity, should continue as a requirement with respect to the party against whom offered. The rule departs to the extent of allowing substitution of one with the right and opportunity to develop the testimony with similar motive and interest. This position is supported by modern decisions. McCormick § 232, pp. 489–490; 5 Wigmore § 1388.

Provisions of the same tenor will be found in Uniform Rule 63(3)(b); California Evidence Code §§ 1290–1292; Kansas Code of Civil Procedure § 60-460(c)(2); New Jersey Evidence Rule 63(3). Unlike the rule, the latter three provide either that former testimony is not admissible if the right of confrontation is denied or that it is not admissible if the accused was not a party to the prior hearing. The genesis of these limitations is a caveat in Uniform Rule 63(3) Comment that use of former testimony against an accused may violate his right of confrontation. Mattox v. United States, 156 U.S. 237 (1895), held that the right was not violated by the Government's use, on a retrial of the same case, of testimony given at the first trial by two witnesses since deceased. The decision leaves open the questions (1) whether direct and redirect are equivalent to cross-examination for purposes of confrontation, (2) whether testimony given in a different proceeding is acceptable, and (3) whether the accused must himself have been a party to the earlier proceeding or whether a similarly situated person will serve the purpose. Professor Falknor concluded that, if a dying declaration untested by cross-examination is constitutionally admissible, former testimony tested by the cross-examination of one similarly situated does not offend against confrontation. Falknor, *supra*, at 659–660. The constitutional acceptability of dying declarations has often been conceded. Mattox v. United States, 156 U.S. 237, 243 (1895); Kirby v. United States, 174 U.S. 47, 61 (1899); Pointer v. Texas, 380 U.S. 400, 407 (1965).

....

REPORT OF HOUSE COMMITTEE ON THE JUDICIARY

....

Rule 804(b)(1). Rule 804(b)(1) as submitted by the Court allowed prior testimony of an unavailable witness to be admissible if the party against whom it is offered or a person "with motive and interest similar" to his had an opportunity to examine the witness. The Committee considered that it is generally unfair to impose upon the party against whom the hearsay evidence is being offered responsibility for the manner in which the witness was previously handled by another party. The sole exception to this, in the Committee's view, is when a party's predecessor in interest in a civil action or proceeding had an opportunity and similar motive to examine the witness. The Committee amended the Rule to reflect these policy determinations.

....

REPORT OF SENATE COMMITTEE ON THE JUDICIARY

....

Rule 804(b)(1). *Former testimony.* Rule 804(b)(1) as submitted by the Court allowed prior testimony of an unavailable witness to be admissible if the party against whom it is offered or a person "with motive and interest similar" to his had an opportunity to examine the witness.

The House amended the rule to apply only to a party's predecessor in interest. Although the committee recognizes considerable merit to the rule submitted by the Supreme Court, a position which has been advocated by many scholars and judges, we have concluded that the difference between the two versions is not great and we accept the House amendment.

....

Florida Stat. § 90.804(2)(a). Hearsay Exceptions; Declarant Unavailable [Former Testimony]

....

(2) Hearsay exceptions. The following are not excluded under s. 90.802, provided that the declarant is unavailable as a witness:

(a) Former testimony. Testimony given as a witness at another hearing of the same or a different proceeding, or in a deposition taken in compliance with law in the course of the same or another proceeding, if the party against whom the testimony is now offered, or, in a civil action or proceeding, a predecessor in interest, had an opportunity and similar motive to develop the testimony by direct, cross, or redirect examination.

....

SPONSORS' NOTE (1976 ENACTMENT)

....

<u>Subsection (2)(a)</u> The former testimony exception makes admissible under specified circumstances testimony that has previously been given under oath and subject to cross-examination. Ideal conditions are lacking only in that the jury is unable to judge the demeanor of the witness.

Under this exception, the former testimony of a witness may be offered against a party who was a party to the previous action or proceeding. If the testimony is offered against the same party that it was offered against in the previous proceeding, no unfairness is apparent in requiring him to accept his own prior conduct on cross-examination or decision not to cross examine. If the testimony was originally offered by the party it is now being offered against, the party should not be heard to object to evidence that he once offered in his own behalf. If the testimony is offered in a criminal trial, the party against whom it is now offered must have been a party to the prior trial. In a civil action, a predecessor-in-interest of a party must have been a party to the prior proceeding.

The common law did not limit the admissibility of former testimony to the testimony given in an earlier trial of the same case, but it did require identity of issues. Identity of issues is significant only in that it bears on motive and interest in fully developing the testimony of the witness, and modern decisions have reduced this requirement to "substantial" identity. McCormick, Evidence § 257 (2nd ed. 1972); McDougald v. Imler, 153 Fla. 619, 15 So.2d 418 (1943) (testimony at former trial was admissible on issue of gross negligence, even though former trial was on issue of simple negligence).

The common law also insisted upon identity of parties, deviating only to the extent of allowing substitution of successors who were in a narrowly construed privity. The requirement of identity of the offering party has disappeared except as it might affect motive to develop the testimony, and only the presence in the prior suit of the party against whom the former testimony is now offered is significant. Falknor, Former Testimony and the Uniform Rules: A Comment, 38 N.Y.U. L. Rev. 651, no. 1 (1963); McCormick, Evidence § 256 (2nd ed. 1972). For example, existing Fla. Stat. § 92.22 requires only "That the party against whom the evidence is offered, or his privy, was a party on the former trial." The question remains whether strict identity or privity should continue as a requirement with respect to the party against whom the testimony is offered. McCormick reasons that "identity of parties" is "a convenient phrase to indicate a situation where the underlying requirement of adequacy of the present opponent's opportunity to cross-examine would usually be satisfied." McCormick, Evidence § 256 (2nd ed. 1972). Wigmore felt that:

> It ought, then, to be sufficient to inquire whether the former testimony was given upon such an issue that the party opponent in that case had the same interest and motive in his cross-examination that the present opponent has; and the determination of this ought to be left entirely to the trial judge....

5 Wigmore, Evidence § 1388 (3rd ed. 1940) (emphasis in original).

In Florida the admissibility of former testimony has been governed by Fla. Stat. § 92.22, which reads:

92.22 Use of former bills of exceptions as evidence; use of evidence given on former trial. In the event it be made to appear to the satisfaction of the court that any evidence used at a trial of a civil case, whether oral or written, and incorporated in a bill of exceptions, or incorporated in the record proper can not be had, then the bill of exceptions taken at the trial, or the evidence incorporated in the record of the trial, may be used as evidence upon any subsequent trial or hearing of the case, or in any other civil cause or civil proceeding, as to any matter in issue at a previous trial or hearing; and, further, in the event that such evidence is not so preserved as before stated, then the same may be used at a subsequent trial or hearing, or in any other civil cause or civil proceeding involving substantially the same issue; if:

(1) Such evidence has at such former trial been reported stenographically or reduced to writing in the presence of the court;

(2) That the party against whom the evidence is offered, or his privy, was a party on the former trial;

(3) That the issue is substantially the same in both cases;

(4) That a substantial reason is shown why the original witness or document is not produced; and

(5) That the court is satisfied that the report of such evidence taken at such former trial is a correct report.

In Osburn v. Stickel, 187 So.2d 89 (Fla. 3rd Dist. 1966), the court rejected a contention that the "former testimony was admissible in evidence because it was given upon such an issue that the party opponent in that case had the same interest and motive in cross-examination that the present opponent has," and ruled that it was error to have admitted the testimony because of the lack of privity between the parties.

The court apparently concluded that the five provisions at the end of the statute applied to the entire statute.

A literal interpretation of Fla. Stat. § 92.22 also might suggest that the former testimony must have been given at a "trial," but the statute in one instance also refers to a "previous trial or hearing." The statute also provides for admissibility of such evidence at a subsequent "trial," "hearing," or any other "civil cause or civil proceeding." It is unclear whether any distinction was intended. The common-law approach as stated in Putnal v. State, 56 Fla. 86, 47 So. 864 (1908) was:

> In order that former testimony may be provable, it must have been taken in the course of a judicial proceeding in a competent tribunal. The particular character of the tribunal or proceeding, however, is immaterial, so long as it is judicial in nature.

Fla. Rules of Civ. Proc. 1.330 and 1.290(a)(4), which permit testimony taken by deposition to be admissible in certain cases, are not affected by this section.

The former testimony exception applies in criminal cases only when the party against whom the testimony is offered had previously offered it in his own behalf or if the party offering the testimony was a party to the action in which the testimony was given and had the right to cross-examine the declarant with an interest and motive similar to that which he has at the hearing. The use of testimony during a trial which was given during the accused's preliminary hearing is not violative of his right to confrontation. California v. Green, 399 U.S. 149, 90 S.Ct. 1930, 26 L.Ed.2d 489 (1970). The Supreme Court of Florida recognized the former testimony exception in criminal cases in Richardson v. State, 247 So.2d 296 (Fla. 1971) where it commented:

> A time-honored and universally recognized exception to the hearsay rule is the so-called "former testimony" exception. Under this rule, evidence of third parties as to the testimony of a deceased witness given under oath in a preliminary hearing or other judicial proceeding where the defendant was represented by counsel, had opportunity to confront and cross-examine the witness, is admissible in a subsequent trial.

> ...One of the recognized methods of proof is by testimony of any first-hand observer of the giving of the former testimony....

> ...The Blackwell decision, citing many authorities, holds: "It has long been a settled rule of evidence, as one of the exceptions to the general rule excluding hearsay, that the testimony of a witness given in a former action, or at a former stage of the same action, is competent in a subsequent action, or in a subsequent proceeding of the same action, where it is shown that such witness is dead, has become insane or disqualified, is beyond the jurisdiction of the court...cannot conveniently be found or has been kept away by the opposite party, where it is also shown that the former giving of such testimony was under oath and that opposing party cross-examined, or was afforded an opportunity to cross-examine such witness."

Richardson v. State, 247 So.2d at 300-01.

Provisions of the same tenor will be found in Uniform Rule 63(3)(b); Calif. Evid. Code §§ 1290-92; Kansas Code of Civ. Pro. § 60-460(c)(2); New Jersey Evid. Rule 63(3); Fed. Rule Evid. 804(b)(1).

....

COMMENTARY ON FEDERAL AND FLORIDA RULE DIFFERENCES

Florida Stat. § 90.804(2)(a) and its federal counterpart, Federal Rule 804(b)(1), create an exception to the hearsay rule—when the declarant is "unavailable as a witness" as defined in

Florida Stat. § 90.804(1) or Federal Rule of Evidence 804(a)—for former testimony given as a witness at another hearing of the same or a different proceeding, or in a deposition. Under the Florida rule, a distinction is drawn in criminal cases between discovery depositions and regular depositions, and only the latter, not the former, fall within the scope of the phrase "deposition" as used in the Florida rule. *See State v. Green*, 667 So. 2d 756, 759-60 (Fla. 1995) (collecting cases).

A prerequisite to invoking either provision is a showing that the party against whom the testimony is now offered (or in a civil case, a predecessor in interest), had both an opportunity and similar motive to develop the testimony by direct, cross, or redirect examination. *See* FLA. STAT. § 90.804(2)(a); FED. R. EVID. 804(b)(1)(B). The most likely situation in which former testimony will not be admissible on the grounds of a lack of an "opportunity" to develop the testimony is when an effort is made to offer a declarant's grand jury testimony against the defendant indicted by that grand jury, as a criminal defendant is not entitled to examine witnesses at all in grand jury proceedings. *See U.S. v. Clarke*, 2 F.3d 81, 83 (4th Cir. 1993); *U.S. v. Fernandez*, 892 F.2d 976, 981 (11th Cir. 1989). The only other circumstance in which an opportunity is likely to be deemed lacking is when cross-examination in the earlier proceeding was so limited by the trial judge as not to be adequate or meaningful. *See U.S. v. King*, 713 F.2d 627, 630 & n.5 (11th Cir. 1983). With respect to the motive requirement, under both the federal and Florida rules the motive need only be similar, not identical, and this determination involves a highly fact-specific inquiry. *See U.S. v. Miles*, 290 F.3d 1341, 1352-53 (11th Cir. 2002); *Garcia v. State*, 816 So. 2d 554, 564-65 (Fla. 2002).

In civil cases, both the Florida and federal rules leave open the possibility that the party against whom former testimony is offered was not herself a party to the earlier proceeding, but rather that her "predecessor in interest" was, a phrase the scope of which few decisions have examined. *See Lloyd v. American Export Lines, Inc.*, 580 F.2d 1179 (3d Cir. 1978). What is clear, however, is that in a criminal case, it does not suffice that some *other* party with similar interests had the opportunity and similar motive (such as a co-defendant in a separate trial); the exception can be invoked only if the party against whom the former testimony is now offered was party to the earlier proceedings. *See U.S. v. Deeb*, 13 F.3d 1532, 1535 (11th Cir. 1994).

A separate hearsay exception under Florida law permits certain types of former testimony to be admitted in the absence of a showing of unavailability. *See* FLA. STAT. § 90.803(22) and Commentary to FLA. STAT. § 90.803(22). There is no comparable federal provision.

Federal Rule 804(b)(2). Exceptions to the Rule Against Hearsay — When the Declarant Is Unavailable as a Witness [Statement Under the Belief of Imminent Death]

....

(b) The Exceptions. The following are not excluded by the rule against hearsay if the declarant is unavailable as a witness:

....

    (2) *Statement Under the Belief of Imminent Death.* In a prosecution for homicide or in a civil case, a statement that the declarant, while believing the declarant's death to be imminent, made about its cause or circumstances.

....

ADVISORY COMMITTEE'S NOTE

....

Exception (2). The exception is the familiar dying declaration of the common law, expanded somewhat beyond its traditionally narrow limits. While the original religious justification for the exception may have lost its conviction for some persons over the years, it can scarcely be doubted that powerful psychological pressures are present. See 5 Wigmore § 1443 and the classic statement of Chief Baron Eyre in Rex v. Woodcock, 1 Leach 500, 502, 168 Eng.Rep. 352, 353 (K.B. 1789).

The common law required that the statement be that of the victim, offered in a prosecution for criminal homicide. Thus declarations by victims in prosecutions for other crimes, e.g. a declaration by a rape victim who dies in childbirth, and all declarations in civil cases were outside the scope of the exception. An occasional statute has removed these restrictions, as in Colo.R.S. § 52-1-20, or has expanded the area of offenses to include abortions, 5 Wigmore § 1432, p. 224, n. 4. Kansas by decision extended the exception to civil cases. Thurston v. Fritz, 91 Kan. 468 (1914). While the common law exception no doubt originated as a result of the exceptional need for the evidence in homicide cases, the theory of admissibility applies equally in civil cases and in prosecutions for crimes other than homicide. The same considerations suggest abandonment of the limitation to circumstances attending the event in question, yet when the statement deals with matters other than the supposed death, its influence is believed to be sufficiently attenuated to justify the limitation. Unavailability is not limited to death. See subdivision (a) of this rule. Any problem as to declarations phrased in terms of opinion is laid at rest by Rule 701, and continuation of a requirement of first-hand knowledge is assured by Rule 602.

Comparable provisions are found in Uniform Rule 63(5); California Evidence Code § 1242; Kansas Code of Civil Procedure § 60-460(e); New Jersey Evidence Rule 63(5).

....

REPORT OF HOUSE COMMITTEE ON THE JUDICIARY

....

Rule 804(b)(2). Rule 804(b)(3) as submitted by the Court (now Rule 804(b)(2) in the bill) proposed to expand the traditional scope of the dying declaration exception (i.e. a statement of the victim in a homicide case as to the cause or circumstances of his believed imminent death) to allow such statements in all criminal and civil cases. The Committee did not consider dying declarations as among the most reliable forms of hearsay. Consequently, it amended the provision to limit their admissibility in criminal cases to homicide prosecutions, where exceptional need for the evidence is present. This is existing law. At the same time, the Committee approved the expansion to civil actions and proceedings where the stakes do not involve possible imprisonment, although noting that this could lead to forum shopping in some instances.

....

Florida Stat. § 90.804(2)(b). Hearsay Exceptions; Declarant Unavailable [Statement Under Belief of Impending Death]

....

(2) Hearsay exceptions. The following are not excluded under s. 90.802, provided that the declarant is unavailable as a witness:

....

(b) Statement under belief of impending death. In a civil or criminal trial, a statement made by a declarant while reasonably believing that his or her death was imminent, concerning the physical cause or instrumentalities of what the declarant believed to be impending death or the circumstances surrounding impending death.

....

SPONSORS' NOTE (1976 ENACTMENT)

....

<u>Subsection (2)(b)</u> This exception renders admissible the statements of an unavailable declarant made by the declarant while believing that his death was imminent. Only statements which concern the cause or circumstances of what he believed to be his impending death are admissible.

The common-law rule made dying declarations admissible when the victim had given up all hope of recovery, and the victim, in fact, had died. McCormick, <u>Evidence</u> § 282 (2nd ed. 1972). Existing Florida law allows the admission of a dying declaration only in prosecutions for the death of the declarant. <u>Johnson v. State</u>, 63 Fla. 16, 58 So. 540 (1912). The admission of the hearsay testimony is justified on the grounds of necessity and the sense of impending death making a false decision by the deceased improbable. In <u>Coatney v. State</u>, 61 Fla. 19, 55 So. 285 (1911) the court said:

> In a prosecution for homicide evidence of declarations made by the deceased before his death as to the facts that actually caused his subsequent death or as to circumstances that actually resulted in his subsequent death, is admissible either for or against the deceased, upon proper predicate being laid, where such declarations were made at a time when the deceased was <u>in</u> extremis and really believed he could not recover, and where the deceased would have been competent to testify as to such facts or circumstances had he lived. The declaration of the deceased need not have been made in the presence of the accused, and the making of it under circumstances stated may be testified to by any competent witness, such evidence being admissible on the ground of necessity and the sense of impending death making a false declaration by the deceased improbable. Whether a proper predicate has been laid for the introduction of evidence of a dying declaration is to be determined primarily by the court, and when the evidence is admitted its weight and credibility are for the jury to determine.

Declarations by victims in prosecutions for other crimes than homicide and statements offered in civil cases have not been admissible. While the common law recognized the exceptional need for the evidence in homicide cases, it is not logical to limit it to those cases. The rationale of admissibility applies equally in civil cases and in prosecutions for crimes other than homicide. While the religious justification for the common-law exception may have lost its conviction for some persons, it can scarcely be doubted that there are still powerful psychological pressures to be truthful when death is imminent. See 5 Wigmore, <u>Evidence</u> § 1443 (3rd ed. 1940). McCormick, <u>Evidence</u> § 283 (2nd ed. 1970) reasons:

> The requirement of consciousness of impending death arguably tends to guarantee a sufficient degree of special reliability, and the requirement that declarant be dead and thus unavailable as a witness is an ample showing of the necessity for the use of hearsay. This simple rationale of dying declarations sufficed the courts up to the beginning of the eighteen hundreds, and these declarations were admitted in civil and criminal cases without distinction and seemingly without untoward results.

Florida, in limiting admissibility of dying declarations to homicide prosecutions, has recognized death merely as a type of unavailability which permits the admission of such evidence. Under this subsection, it is no longer necessary that the declarant actually die in order for the declaration to be admissible. However, the declarant must believe his death is imminent, and he must be unavailable as defined in Section 90.804(1).

As under existing law, when a proper predicate has been laid, the declaration is admissible if declarant would have been competent to so testify had he lived. Questions as to declarations phrased in terms of opinions are governed by Section 90.701. Section 90.604 requires the declarant have first-hand knowledge of the facts recounted.

Similar provisions are found in Uniform Rule 63(5); Calif. Evid. Code § 1242; Kansas Code of Civ. Pro. § 60-469(e); Wisc. Rule Evid. 908.04(b)(3). New Jersey Evid. Rule 63(5) is limited to criminal cases. Fed. Rule Evid. 804(b)(3) applies to homicide prosecutions and civil actions.

....

COMMENTARY ON FEDERAL AND FLORIDA RULE DIFFERENCES

Florida Stat. § 90.804(2)(b) and its federal counterpart, Federal Rule 804(b)(2), create an exception to the hearsay rule—when the declarant is "unavailable as a witness" as defined in Florida Stat. § 90.804(1) or Federal Rule of Evidence 804(a)—for so-called statements under belief of impending (or imminent) death, also known as "dying declarations."

Under both the federal and Florida rules, the exception applies only if, when the declarant made the statement, he believed his death to be imminent. The standard for making this factual determination is similar under both rules. *Compare Henry v. State*, 613 So. 2d 429, 431 (Fla. 1992) ("[T]he court should satisfy itself, on the totality of the circumstances, 'that the deceased knew and appreciated his condition as being that of an approach to certain and immediate death.'") *and Williams v. State*, 967 So. 2d 735, 749 (Fla. 2007) ("the declarant must believe death is imminent and inevitable with no hope of recovery"), *with U.S. v. Angleton*, 269 F. Supp. 2d 878, 883 (S.D. Tex. 2003) (holding that court must determine, from facts and circumstances surrounding the statement, that declarant had a "settled hopeless expectation that death is near at hand"). Moreover, under both the federal and Florida rules, only statements concerning the cause of what the declarant believed to be impending death or the circumstances surrounding it are admissible under these provisions. *See Labon v. State*, 868 So. 2d 1222, 1223 (Fla. 3d DCA 2004); *U.S. v. Fernandez*, 892 F.2d 976, 983 n.5 (11th Cir. 1989). However, neither provision requires that the declarant *actually* die; any form of unavailability is sufficient to invoke either exception. *See* Advisory Committee's Note to FED. R. EVID. 804(b)(2); Sponsors' Note to FLA. STAT. § 90.804(2)(b).

A key difference between the federal and Florida rules is that the latter applies to a broader number of types of proceedings than does the former. The federal rule can be invoked *only* "[i]n a prosecution for homicide or in a civil case." *See* FED. R. EVID. 804(b)(2). By contrast, the Florida rule can be invoked in any type of case. *See* FLA. STAT. § 90.804(2)(a) (specifying that it can be invoked "[i]n a civil or criminal trial"); Sponsors' Note to FLA. STAT. § 90.804(2)(b).

Federal Rule 804(b)(3). Exceptions to the Rule Against Hearsay — When the Declarant Is Unavailable as a Witness [Statement Against Interest]

....

(b) The Exceptions. The following are not excluded by the rule against hearsay if the declarant is unavailable as a witness:

....

(3) *Statement Against Interest.* A statement that:

    (A) a reasonable person in the declarant's position would have made only if the person believed it to be true because, when made, it was so contrary to the declarant's proprietary or pecuniary interest or had so great a tendency to invalidate the declarant's claim against someone else or to expose the declarant to civil or criminal liability; and

    (B) is supported by corroborating circumstances that clearly indicate its trustworthiness, if it is offered in a criminal case as one that tends to expose the declarant to criminal liability.

....

ADVISORY COMMITTEE'S NOTE

....

Exception (3). The circumstantial guaranty of reliability for declarations against interest is the assumption that persons do not make statements which are damaging to themselves unless satisfied for good reason that they are true. Hileman v. Northwest Engineering Co., 346 F.2d 668 (6th Cir. 1965). If the statement is that of a party, offered by his opponent, it comes in as an admission, Rule [801(d)(2)], and there is no occasion to inquire whether it is against interest, this not being a condition precedent to admissibility of admissions by opponents.

The common law required that the interest declared against be pecuniary or proprietary but within this limitation demonstrated striking ingenuity in discovering an against-interest aspect. Higham v. Ridgway, 10 East 109, 103 Eng.Rep. 717 (K.B. 1808); Reg. v. Overseers of Birmingham, 1 B. & S. 763, 121 Eng.Rep. 897 (Q.B. 1861); McCormick, § 256, p. 551, nn. 2 and 3.

The exception discards the common law limitation and expands to the full logical limit. One result is to remove doubt as to the admissibility of declarations tending to establish a tort liability against the declarant or to extinguish one which might be asserted by him, in accordance with the trend of the decisions in this country. McCormick § 254, pp. 548–549. Another is to allow statements tending to expose declarant to hatred, ridicule, or disgrace, the motivation here being considered to be as strong as when financial interests are at stake. McCormick § 255, p. 551. And finally, exposure to criminal liability satisfies the against-interest requirement. The refusal of the common law to concede the adequacy of a penal interest was no doubt indefensible in logic, see the dissent of Mr. Justice Holmes in Donnelly v. United States, 228 U.S. 243 (1913), but one senses in the decisions a distrust of evidence of confessions by third persons offered to exculpate the accused arising from suspicions of fabrication either of the fact of the making of the confession or in its contents, enhanced in either instance by the required unavailability of the declarant. Nevertheless, an increasing amount of decisional law recognizes exposure to punishment for crime as a sufficient stake. People v. Spriggs, 60 Cal.2d 868 (1964); Sutter v. Easterly, 354 Mo. 282 (1945); Band's Refuse Removal, Inc. v. Fairlawn Borough, 62 N.J.Super. 522 (1960); Newberry v. Commonwealth, 191 Va. 445 (1950); Annot., 162 A.L.R. 446. The requirement of corroboration is included in the rule in order to effect an accommodation between these competing considerations. When the statement is offered by the accused by way of exculpation, the resulting situation is not adapted to control by rulings as to the weight of the evidence, and hence the provision is cast in terms of a requirement preliminary to admissibility. Cf. Rule 406(a). The requirement of corroboration should be construed in such a manner as to effectuate its purpose of circumventing fabrication.

Ordinarily the third-party confession is thought of in terms of exculpating the accused, but this is by no means always or necessarily the case: it may include statements implicating him, and under the general theory of declarations against interest they would be admissible as related statements. Douglas v. Alabama, 380 U.S. 415 (1965), and Bruton v. United States, 389 U.S. 818 (1968), both involved confessions by codefendants which implicated the accused. While the confession was not actually offered in evidence in *Douglas*, the procedure followed effectively put it before the jury, which the Court ruled to be error. Whether the confession might have been admissible as a declaration against penal interest was not considered or discussed. *Bruton* assumed the inadmissibility, as against the accused, of the implicating confession of his codefendant, and centered upon the question of the effectiveness of a limiting instruction. These decisions, however, by no means require that all statements implicating another person be excluded from the category of declarations against interest. Whether a statement is in fact against interest must be determined from the circumstances of each case. Thus a statement admitting guilt and implicating another person, made while in custody, may well be motivated by a desire to curry favor with the authorities and hence fail to qualify as against interest. See the dissenting opinion of Mr. Justice White in *Bruton*. On the other hand, the same words spoken under different circumstances, *e.g.*, to an acquaintance, would have no difficulty in qualifying. The rule does not purport to deal with questions of the right of confrontation.

The balancing of self-serving against dissenting aspects of a declaration is discussed in McCormick § 256.

For comparable provisions, see Uniform Rule 63(10); California Evidence Code § 1230; Kansas Code of Civil Procedure § 60-460(j); New Jersey Evidence Rule 63(10).

....

REPORT OF HOUSE COMMITTEE ON THE JUDICIARY

....

Rule 804(b)(3). Rule 804(b)(4) as submitted by the Court (now Rule 804(b)(3) in the bill) provided as follows:

> *Statement against interest.* A statement which was at the time of its making so far contrary to the declarant's pecuniary or proprietary interest or so far tended to subject him to civil or criminal liability or to render invalid a claim by him against another or to make him an object of hatred, ridicule, or disgrace, that a reasonable man in his position would not have made the statement unless he believed it to be true. A statement tending to exculpate the accused is not admissible unless corroborated.

The Committee determined to retain the traditional hearsay exception for statements against pecuniary or proprietary interest. However, it deemed the Court's additional references to statements tending to subject a declarant to civil liability or to render invalid a claim by him against another to be redundant as included within the scope of the reference to statements against pecuniary or proprietary interest. See *Gichner* v. *Antonio Triano Tile and Marble Co.*, 410 F.2d 238 (D.C.Cir. 1968). Those additional references were accordingly deleted.

The Court's Rule also proposed to expand the hearsay limitation from its present federal limitation to include statements subjecting the declarant to criminal liability and statements tending to make him an object of hatred, ridicule, or disgrace. The Committee eliminated the latter category from the subdivision as lacking sufficient guarantees of reliability. See *United States* v. *Dovico*, 380 F.2d 325, 327 nn. 2, 4 (2nd Cir.), cert. denied, 389 U.S. 944 (1967). As for statements against penal interest, the Committee shared the view of the Court that some such statements do possess adequate assurances of reliability and should be admissible. It believed, however, as did the Court, that statements of this type tending to exculpate the accused are more suspect and so should have their admissibility conditioned upon some further provision insuring trustworthiness. The proposal in the Court Rule to add a requirement of simple corroboration was, however, deemed ineffective to accomplish this purpose since the accused's own testimony might suffice while not necessarily increasing the reliability of the hearsay statement. The Committee settled upon the language "unless corroborating circumstances clearly indicate the trustworthiness of the statement" as affording a proper standard and degree of discretion. It was contemplated that the result in such cases as *Donnelly* v. *United States*, 228 U.S. 243 (1912), where the circumstances plainly indicated reliability, would be changed. The Committee also added to the Rule the final sentence from the 1971 Advisory Committee draft, designed to codify the doctrine of *Bruton* v. *United States*, 391 U.S. 123 (1968). The Committee does not intend to affect the existing exception to the *Bruton* principle where the codefendant takes the stand and is subject to cross-examination, but believed there was no need to make specific provision for this situation in the Rule, since in that event the declarant would not be "unavailable".

....

REPORT OF SENATE COMMITTEE ON THE JUDICIARY

....

Rule 804(b)(3). The rule defines those statements which are considered to be against interest and thus of sufficient trustworthiness to be admissible even though hearsay. With regard to the type of interest declared against, the version submitted by the Supreme Court included inter alia, statements tending to subject a declarant to civil liability or to invalidate a claim by him against another. The House struck these provisions as redundant. In view of the conflicting case law construing pecuniary or proprietary interests narrowly so as to exclude, e.g., tort cases, this deletion could be misconstrued.

Three States which have recently codified their rules of evidence have followed the Supreme Court's version of this rule, i.e., that a statement is against interest if it tends to subject a declarant to civil liability.[38]

The committee believes that the reference to statements tending to subject a person to civil liability constitutes a desirable clarification of the scope of the rule. Therefore, we have reinstated the Supreme Court language on this matter.

The Court rule also proposed to expand the hearsay limitation from its present federal limitation to include statements subjecting the declarant to statements tending to make him an object of hatred, ridicule, or disgrace. The House eliminated the latter category from the subdivision as lacking sufficient guarantees of reliability. Although there is considerable support for the admissibility of such statements (all three of the State rules referred to supra, would admit such statements), we accept the deletion by the House.

The House amended this exception to add a sentence making inadmissible a statement or confession offered against the accused in a criminal case, made by a codefendant or other person implicating both himself and the accused. The sentence was added to codify the constitutional principle announced in *Bruton* v. *United States*, 391 U.S. 123 (1968). *Bruton* held that the admission of the extrajudicial hearsay statement of one codefendant inculpating a second codefendant violated the confrontation clause of the sixth amendment.

---

[38] Nev.Rev.Stats. § 51.345; N.Mex.Stats. (1973 Supp.) § 20-4-804(4); West's Wis.Stats.Anno. (1973 Supp.) § 908.045(4).

The committee decided to delete this provision because the basic approach of the rules is to avoid codifying, or attempting to codify, constitutional evidentiary principles, such as the fifth amendment's right against self-incrimination and, here, the sixth amendment's right of confrontation. Codification of a constitutional principle is unnecessary and, where the principle is under development, often unwise. Furthermore, the House provision does not appear to recognize the exceptions to the *Bruton* rule, e.g. where the codefendant takes the stand and is subject to cross examination; where the accused confessed, see *United States* v. *Mancusi*, 404 F.2d 296 (2d Cir. 1968), cert. denied 397 U.S. 942 (1907); where the accused was placed at the scene of the crime, see *United States* v. *Zelker*, 452 F.2d 1009 (2d Cir. 1971). For these reasons, the committee decided to delete this provision.

....

CONFERENCE REPORT

....

Rule 804(b)(3). The Senate amendment to subsection (b)(3) provides that a statement is against interest and not excluded by the hearsay rule when the declarant is unavailable as a witness, if the statement tends to subject a person to civil or criminal liability or renders invalid a claim by him against another. The House bill did not refer specifically to civil liability and to rendering invalid a claim against another. The Senate amendment also deletes from the House bill the provision that subsection (b)(3) does not apply to a statement or confession, made by a codefendant or another, which implicates the accused and the person who made the statement, when that statement or confession is offered against the accused in a criminal case.

The Conference adopts the Senate amendment. The Conferees intend to include within the purview of this rule, statements subjecting a person to civil liability and statements rendering claims invalid. The Conferees agree to delete the provision regarding statements by a codefendant, thereby reflecting the general approach in the Rules of Evidence to avoid attempting to codify constitutional evidentiary principles.

....

ADVISORY COMMITTEE'S NOTE (2010 AMENDMENT)

Subdivision (b)(3). Rule 804(b)(3) has been amended to provide that the corroborating circumstances requirement applies to all declarations against penal interest offered in criminal cases. A number of courts have applied the corroborating circumstances requirement to declarations against penal interest offered by the prosecution, even though the text of the Rule did not so provide. *See, e.g., United States* v. *Alvarez*, 584 F.2d 694, 701 (5th Cir. 1978) ("by transplanting the language governing exculpatory statements onto the analysis for admitting inculpatory hearsay, a unitary standard is derived which offers the most workable basis for applying Rule 804(b)(3)"); *United States* v. *Shukri*, 207 F.3d 412 (7th Cir. 2000) (requiring corroborating circumstances for against-penal-interest statements offered by the government). A unitary approach to declarations against penal interest assures both the prosecution and the accused that the Rule will not be abused and that only reliable hearsay statements will be admitted under the exception.

All other changes to the structure and wording of the Rule are intended to be stylistic only. There is no intent to change any other result in any ruling on evidence admissibility.

The amendment does not address the use of the corroborating circumstances for declarations against penal interest offered in civil cases.

In assessing whether corroborating circumstances exist, some courts have focused on the credibility of the witness who relates the hearsay statement in court. But the credibility of the witness who relates the statement is not a proper factor for the court to consider in assessing corroborating circumstances. To base admission or exclusion of a hearsay statement on the witness's credibility would usurp the jury's role of determining the credibility of testifying witnesses.

ADVISORY COMMITTEE'S NOTE (2011 AMENDMENT)

The language of Rule 804 has been amended as part of the general restyling of the Evidence Rules to make them more easily understood and to make style and terminology consistent throughout the rules. These changes are intended to be stylistic only. There is no intent to change any result in any ruling on evidence admissibility.

No style changes were made to Rule 804(b)(3), because it was already restyled in conjunction with a substantive amendment, effective December 1, 2010.

Florida Stat. § 90.804(2)(c). Hearsay Exceptions; Declarant Unavailable [Statement Against Interest]

....

(2) Hearsay exceptions. The following are not excluded under s. 90.802, provided that the declarant is unavailable as a witness:

....

(c) Statement against interest. A statement which, at the time of its making, was so far contrary to the declarant's pecuniary or proprietary interest or tended to subject the declarant to liability or to render invalid a claim by the declarant against another, so that a person in the declarant's position would not have made the statement unless he or she believed it to be true. A statement tending to expose the declarant to criminal liability and offered to exculpate the accused is inadmissible, unless corroborating circumstances show the trustworthiness of the statement.

....

SPONSORS' NOTE (1976 ENACTMENT)

....

Subsection (2)(c) This exception makes admissible statements against interest by an unavailable declarant which are against his pecuniary or proprietary interest or tend to subject him to civil or criminal liability so that a reasonable man in his position would not have made the statement unless he believed it to be true.

This subsection substantially restates the common-law exception of "declarations against interest." The circumstantial probability of trustworthiness is that the fact stated, being against the declarant's interest, is not likely to have been stated untruthfully. The common law required that the interest declared against be pecuniary or proprietary. McCormick, Evidence § 277 (2nd ed. 1972). However,

> assurance of the veracity of his statement made against that interest. Moreover, since the conviction of a crime ordinarily entails economic loss, the traditional concept of a "pecuniary interest" could logically include one's "penal interest." (Compare the theory that admits a third

person's confession of a crime on the ground that the crime was also a tort, thus subjecting the declarant to civil liability for damages, a pecuniary interest.) (citations omitted).

The recent decision by the United States Supreme Court in Chambers v. Mississippi, 410 U.S. 284, 93 S.Ct. 1038, 35 L.Ed. 2d 297 (1973) compels the admission of declarations against penal interest in at least some cases despite a contrary state evidentiary rule which does not recognize the exception to the hearsay rule. In an opinion by Justice Powell, the Court held that the combination of the Mississippi rules denying an exception to the hearsay rule for declarations against a penal interest and prohibiting impeaching one's own witness was a violation of due process rights:

> Among the most prevalent of those exceptions [to the hearsay rule] is the one applicable to declarations against interest—an exception founded on the assumption that a person is unlikely to fabricate a statement against his own interest at the time it is made. Mississippi....recognizes no...exception for declarations...against the penal interest of the declarant.

> ...Exclusion, where the limitation prevails, is usually premised on the view that admission would lead to the frequent presentation of perjured testimony to the jury....

> The hearsay statements involved in this case were originally made and subsequently offered at trial under circumstances that provided considerable assurance of their reliability. First, each of McDonald's [the witness-declarant] confessions was made spontaneously to a close acquaintance shortly after the murder had occurred. Second, each one was corroborated by some other evidence in the case....Third, whatever may be the parameters of the penal interest rationale, each confession here was in a very real sense self-incriminatory and unquestionably against interest....Finally, if there was any question about the truthfulness of the extra-judicial statements, McDonald was present in the courtroom and had been under oath. He could have been cross-examined by the State, and his demeanor and responses weighed by the jury....

> ...The testimony rejected by the trial court here bore persuasive assurances of trustworthiness and thus was well within the basic rationale of the exception for declarations against interest.....In these circumstances, where constitutional rights directly affecting the ascertainment of guilt are implicated, the hearsay rule may not be applied mechanistically to defeat the ends of justice. 410 U.S. at 299-302, 93 S.Ct. at 1047-49, 35 L.Ed. 2d at 311-13 (citations omitted).

This subsection could not make admissible against a criminal defendant statements which violated his right of confrontation. See Bruton v. United States, 391 U.S. 123, 88 S.Ct. 1620, 20 L.Ed.2d 476 (1968). If that issue is not determinative, third-party confessions which implicate the accused as well as those that are exculpating, would be admissible if they are, in fact, declarations against the interest of the declarant when made.

It has been noticed previously in Gard, Florida Evidence Rule 161, that "There is a remarkable lack of Florida case law on this subject." Florida courts have tended to blur the distinction between admissions of a party opponent and declarations against interest, frequently using the term "admissions against interest." In one case Wise v. Western Union Tel. Co., 177 So.2d 765 (Fla. 1st Dist. 1965) the court applied the "declaration against interest" designation to a statement, although it was not shown that the statement was against the interest of the declarant himself, nor was his unavailability demonstrated. It would appear, however, that the statement was admissible as an admission of a party opponent as one made by a party's agent.

....

COMMENTARY ON FEDERAL AND FLORIDA RULE DIFFERENCES

Florida Stat. § 90.804(2)(c) and its federal counterpart, Federal Rule 804(b)(3), create an exception to the hearsay rule—when the declarant is "unavailable as a witness" as defined in Florida Stat. § 90.804(1) or Federal Rule of Evidence 804(a)—for so-called statements against interest.

Both rules define the "against interest" concept broadly to include not only statements against the declarant's pecuniary or proprietary interest, but also those against the declarant's penal interest, in other words, those statements that may subject him to criminal liability. *See Jones v. State*, 678 So. 2d 309, 314 n.3 (Fla. 1996); *Williamson v. U.S.*, 512 U.S. 594, 598-99 (1994). However, neither rule covers statements against "social" interest. *See generally* Reports of House, Senate Committees on the Judiciary to FED. R. EVID. 804(b)(3). The inquiry under both rules is an objective one, asking whether, at the time the statement was made, it was so contrary to the declarant's interests that a reasonable person in his position would not have made the statement unless he believed it to be true. *See Smith v. State*, 746 So. 2d 1162, 1167 (Fla. 1st DCA 1999); *U.S. v. Turner*, 475 F. Supp. 194, 198 (E.D. Mich. 1978).

In *Williamson*, 512 U.S. at 600-01, the U.S. Supreme Court held that the against interest hearsay exception encompasses only those specific portions of a statement that are self-inculpatory, and that it does not encompass non-self-inculpatory statements contained within a broader narrative that is generally self-inculpatory. The Florida courts have adopted a similar reading of the Florida provision. *See Antunes-Salgado v. State*, 987 So. 2d 222, 226 (2d DCA 2008); *Perez v. State*, 980 So. 2d 1126, 1133 (Fla. 3d DCA 2008); *Smith*, 746 So. 2d at 1168.

The Florida exception has a proviso indicating that when a statement tending to expose the declarant to criminal liability is offered to *exculpate* the accused, it cannot be admitted unless corroborating circumstances show the trustworthiness of the statement. *See* FLA. STAT. § 90.804(2)(c). The federal exception has a similar proviso, but it was broadened in 2010 to require such a showing *whenever* it is offered in a criminal case, whether to inculpate or exculpate the accused. *See* FED. R. EVID. 804(b)(3)(B). Under both the Florida and Federal rules, this trustworthiness determination is limited to an assessment of the *declarant's* trustworthiness, *not* the trustworthiness of the witness who is testifying to what the declarant allegedly said. *See Carpenter v. State*, 785 So. 2d 1182, 1203 (Fla. 2001); Advisory Committee Note to 2010 Amendment to Federal Rule 804(b)(3).

Federal Rule 804(b)(4). Exceptions to the Rule Against Hearsay — When the Declarant Is Unavailable as a Witness [Statement of Personal or Family History]

....

(b) The Exceptions. The following are not excluded by the rule against hearsay if the declarant is unavailable as a witness:

....

    (4) *Statement of Personal or Family History.* A statement about:

        (A) the declarant's own birth, adoption, legitimacy, ancestry, marriage, divorce, relationship by blood, adoption, or marriage, or similar facts of personal or family history, even though the declarant had no way of acquiring personal knowledge about that fact; or

(B) another person concerning any of these facts, as well as death, if the declarant was related to the person by blood, adoption, or marriage or was so intimately associated with the person's family that the declarant's information is likely to be accurate.

....

ADVISORY COMMITTEE'S NOTE

....

Exception (4). The general common law requirement that a declaration in this area must have been made ante litem motam has been dropped, as bearing more appropriately on weight than admissibility. See 5 Wigmore § 1483. Item [(A)] specifically disclaims any need of firsthand knowledge respecting declarant's own personal history. In some instances it is self-evident (marriage) and in others impossible and traditionally not required (date of birth). Item [(B)] deals with declarations concerning the history of another person. As at common law, declarant is qualified if related by blood or marriage. 5 Wigmore § 1489. In addition, and contrary to the common law, declarant qualifies by virtue of intimate association with the family. *Id.*, § 1487. The requirement sometimes encountered that when the subject of the statement is the relationship between two other persons the declarant must qualify as to both is omitted. Relationship is reciprocal. *Id.*, § 1491.

For comparable provisions, see Uniform Rule 63(23), (24), (25); California Evidence Code §§ 1310, 1311; Kansas Code of Civil Procedure § 60-460(u), (v), (w); New Jersey Evidence Rules 63(23), 63(24), 63(25).

....

Florida Stat. § 90.804(2)(d). Hearsay Exceptions; Declarant Unavailable [Statement of Personal or Family History]

....

(2) Hearsay exceptions. The following are not excluded under s. 90.802, provided that the declarant is unavailable as a witness:

....

(d) Statement of personal or family history. A statement concerning the declarant's own birth, adoption, marriage, divorce, parentage, ancestry, or other similar fact of personal or family history, including relationship by blood, adoption, or marriage, even though the declarant had no means of acquiring personal knowledge of the matter stated.

....

SPONSORS' NOTE (1976 ENACTMENT)

....

Subsection (2)(d) This exception provides a hearsay exception for a statement concerning an unavailable declarant's own family history. As stated in Cone v. Benjamin, 157 Fla. 800, 821-22, 27 So.2d 90, 101 (1946):

Generally speaking, the theory underlying the acceptance of the declarations as to pedigree made by deceased persons who were members of or intimately connected with the family is based upon the theory that such persons were familiar with those matters of family history, tradition and repute with which the members of most families are most familiar, although based upon hearsay within the family, and that, having been made before any controversy had arisen, there was no motive to speak other than the truth.

The common-law requirement that the statements must have been made prior to the controversy (ante litem motam) has been eliminated since it bears more appropriately on weight than admissibility. See 5 Wigmore, Evidence § 1483 (3rd ed. 1940). The need for firsthand knowledge of declarant's own personal history is not necessary. In some instances the knowledge is self-evident (marriage) and in others impossible and traditionally not required (date of birth).

For comparable provisions, see Uniform Rule 63(23), (24), (25); Calif. Evid. Code §§ 1310, 1311; Kansas Code of Civ. Pro. § 60-460(u), (v), (w); New Jersey Evid. Rules 63(23), 63(24), 63(25); Wisc. Rule Evid. 908.04(b)(5); Fed. Rule Evid. 804(b)(5).

COMMENTARY ON FEDERAL AND FLORIDA RULE DIFFERENCES

Florida Stat. § 90.804(2)(d) and its federal counterpart, Federal Rule 804(b)(4), create an exception to the hearsay rule—when the declarant is "unavailable as a witness" as defined in Florida Stat. § 90.804(1) or Federal Rule of Evidence 804(a)—for statements regarding personal or family history.

Under both the federal and Florida rules, a statement by an unavailable declarant concerning his *own* personal or family history, including birth, adoption, marriage, divorce, parentage (or legitimacy), ancestry, or relationship by blood, adoption, or marriage is admissible under this exception even if the declarant had no means of acquiring personal knowledge of the matter stated. *See* FED. R. EVID. 804(b)(4)(A); FLA. STAT. § 90.804(2)(d). These provisions are broader than Federal Rule 803(19) and its Florida counterpart, Florida Stat. § 90.803(19) in that they excuse *two* layers of hearsay: the external layer, the statement by a declarant about his own personal or family history, and the internal layer, the fact that the declarant obtained that information from other sources.

The federal rule is, however, broader than the Florida rule in that it also provides for the admission of statements by an unavailable declarant concerning these same facts of personal or family history, including the death of, someone *other than* the declarant, so long as the declarant was related to that person by blood, adoption, or marriage or was "so intimately associated with" that person's family as to be likely to have accurate information concerning the matter. *See* FED. R. EVID. 804(b)(4)(B).

Federal Rule 804(b)(5). Exceptions to the Rule Against Hearsay — When the Declarant Is Unavailable as a Witness [Transferred to Rule 807]

....

(b) The Exceptions. The following are not excluded by the rule against hearsay if the declarant is unavailable as a witness:

....

(5) [Transferred to Rule 807]

....

COMMENTARY ON FEDERAL AND FLORIDA RULE DIFFERENCES

Federal Rule 804(b)(5) was deleted in 1997 and its contents transferred to Federal Rule 807.

Federal Rule 804(b)(6). Exceptions to the Rule Against Hearsay — When the Declarant Is Unavailable as a Witness [Statement Offered Against a Party That Wrongfully Caused the Declarant's Unavailability]

....

(b) The Exceptions. The following are not excluded by the rule against hearsay if the declarant is unavailable as a witness:

....

(6) *Statement Offered Against a Party That Wrongfully Caused the Declarant's Unavailability.* A statement offered against a party that wrongfully caused — or acquiesced in wrongfully causing — the declarant's unavailability as a witness, and did so intending that result.

ADVISORY COMMITTEE'S NOTE (1997 AMENDMENT)

Exception (b)(6). Rule 804(b)(6) has been added to provide that a party forfeits the right to object on hearsay grounds to the admission of a declarant's prior statement when the party's deliberate wrongdoing or acquiescence therein procured the unavailability of the declarant as a witness. This recognizes the need for a prophylactic rule to deal with abhorrent behavior "which strikes at the heart of the system of justice itself." *United States v. Mastrangelo*, 693 F.2d 269, 273 (2d Cir. 1982), *cert. denied*, 467 U.S. 1204 (1984). The wrongdoing need not consist of a criminal act. The rule applies to all parties, including the government.

Every circuit that has resolved the question has recognized the principle of forfeiture by misconduct, although the tests for determining whether there is a forfeiture have varied. *See, e.g., United States v. Aguiar*, 975 F.2d 45, 47 (2d Cir. 1992); *United States v. Potamitis*, 739 F.2d 784, 789 (2d Cir.), *cert. denied*, 469 U.S. 918 (1984); *Steele v. Taylor*, 684 F.2d 1193, 1199 (6th Cir. 1982), *cert. denied*, 460 U.S. 1053 (1983); *United States v. Balano*, 618 F.2d 624, 629 (10th Cir. 1979), *cert. denied*, 449 U.S. 840 (1980); *United States v. Carlson*, 547 F.2d 1346, 1358–59 (8th Cir.), *cert. denied*, 431 U.S. 914 (1977). The foregoing cases apply a preponderance of the evidence standard. *Contra United States v. Thevis*, 665 F.2d 616, 631 (5th Cir.) (clear and convincing standard), *cert. denied*, 459 U.S. 825 (1982). The usual Rule 104(a) preponderance of the evidence standard has been adopted in light of the behavior the new Rule 804(b)(6) seeks to discourage.

COMMENTARY ON FEDERAL AND FLORIDA RULE DIFFERENCES

Federal Rule 804(b)(6) creates an exception to the hearsay rule for a statement offered against a party that has engaged or acquiesced in wrongdoing that was intended to, and did, procure the unavailability of the declarant as a witness. In effect, the rule provides that a party who engages in misconduct calculated to make a witness unavailable to testify waives his right to object on hearsay grounds to statements made by that declarant and offered against the defendant. See *U.S. v. Zlatogur*, 271 F.3d 1025, 1028 (11th Cir. 2001).

The sort of wrongful conduct encompassed by Federal Rule 804(b)(6) includes killing, assaulting or bribing the declarant, as well as threats of harm, suggestions of future retribution, and the like. *See U.S. v. Scott*, 284 F.3d 758, 763-64 (7th Cir. 2002). To invoke the exception, it need only be shown by a preponderance of the evidence—even in a criminal case—that the party against whom the evidence is offered engaged or acquiesced in wrongdoing. *See Zlatogur*, 271 F.3d at 1028.

The Florida Evidence Code contains no provision analogous to Federal Rule 804(b)(6). *See Chavez v. State*, 25 So. 3d 49, 52-54 (Fla. 1st DCA 2009).

Florida Stat. § 90.804(2)(e). Hearsay Exceptions; Declarant Unavailable [Statement by Deceased or Ill Declarant Similar to One Previously Admitted]

....

(2) Hearsay exceptions. The following are not excluded under s. 90.802, provided that the declarant is unavailable as a witness:

....

(e) Statement by deceased or ill declarant similar to one previously admitted. In an action or proceeding brought against the personal representative, heir at law, assignee, legatee, devisee, or survivor of a deceased person, or against a trustee of a trust created by a deceased person, or against the assignee, committee, or guardian of a mentally incompetent person, when a declarant is unavailable as provided in paragraph (1)(d), a written or oral statement made regarding the same subject matter as another statement made by the declarant that has previously been offered by an adverse party and admitted in evidence.

COMMENTARY ON FEDERAL AND FLORIDA RULE DIFFERENCES

Florida Stat. § 90.804(2)(e) creates an exception to the hearsay rule for certain types of statements by a deceased or ill declarant. The exception applies in actions or proceedings brought against the personal representative, heir, assignee, legatee, devisee, or survivor of a deceased person; those brought against a trustee of a trust created by a deceased person; and those brought against the assignee, committee, or guardian of a mentally incompetent person. *See* FLA. STAT. § 90.804(2)(e). The exception can be invoked only if the declarant is "unavailable as a witness" as defined in Florida Stat. § 90.804(1)(d), meaning that the declarant must be dead or suffering from a physical or mental illness or infirmity. Moreover, the exception applies only to a statement made by the declarant regarding the *same* subject matter as another statement made by the declarant that had previously been offered by an adverse party and admitted in evidence. *See id.*

This exception was added by the legislature in 2005 in conjunction with the repeal of Florida Stat. § 90.602, the Florida "Dead Man's Statute," which prohibited an interested person in the types of actions enumerated in Florida Stat. § 90.804(2)(e) from testifying as to an oral communication with the deceased or a mentally incompetent person. *See* FLA. STAT. § 90.602 (2004); Fla. H., CS for HB 523 (2005), Staff Analysis (Apr. 1, 2005). *See also In re Amendments to the Fla. Evidence Code*, 960 So. 2d 762, 762-64 (Fla. 2007) (order by Florida Supreme Court adopting amendment to § 90.804(2)(e) to the extent that it is procedural). The purpose of creating the hearsay exception was to allow the estate of a deceased or mentally incompetent person to more easily present rebuttal evidence to counteract testimony by a person bringing a claim against an estate that is permitted as a result of the repeal of the Dead Man's Statute, the ultimate result of the two changes being that more evidence overall is admitted, with the trier of fact weighing the credibility of the various witnesses. *See* Fla. H., CS for HB 523 (2005), Staff Analysis (Apr. 1, 2005).

The Federal Rules of Evidence contain no provision analogous to Florida Stat. § 90.804(2)(e).

Federal Rule 805. Hearsay Within Hearsay

Hearsay within hearsay is not excluded by the rule against hearsay if each part of the combined statements conforms with an exception to the rule.

ADVISORY COMMITTEE'S NOTE

On principle it scarcely seems open to doubt that the hearsay rule should not call for exclusion of a hearsay statement which includes a further hearsay statement when both conform to the requirements of a hearsay exception. Thus a hospital record might contain an entry of the patient's age based on information furnished by his wife. The hospital record would qualify as a regular entry except that the person who furnished the information was not acting in the routine of the business. However, her statement independently qualifies as a statement of pedigree (if she is unavailable) or as a statement made for purposes of diagnosis or treatment, and hence each link in the chain falls under sufficient assurances. Or, further to illustrate, a dying declaration may incorporate a declaration against interest by another declarant. See McCormick § 290, p. 611.

ADVISORY COMMITTEE'S NOTE (2011 AMENDMENT)

The language of Rule 805 has been amended as part of the restyling of the Evidence Rules to make them more easily understood and to make style and terminology consistent throughout the rules. These changes are intended to be stylistic only. There is no intent to change any result in any ruling on evidence admissibility.

Florida Stat. § 90.805. Hearsay Within Hearsay

Hearsay within hearsay is not excluded under s. 90.802, provided each part of the combined statements conforms with an exception to the hearsay rule as provided in s. 90.803 or s. 90.804.

SPONSORS' NOTE (1976 ENACTMENT)

The Advisory Committee's Note to Proposed Federal Rule of Evidence 805 explains the need for this section:

> On principle it scarcely seems open to doubt that the hearsay rule should not call for exclusion of a hearsay statement which includes a further hearsay statement when both conform to the requirements of a hearsay exception. Thus a hospital record might contain an entry of a patient's age based on information furnished by his wife. The hospital record would qualify as a regular entry except that the person who furnished the information was not acting in the routine of the business. However, her statement independently qualifies as a statement of pedigree (if she is unavailable) or as a statement made for purposes of diagnosis or treatment, and hence each link in the chain falls under sufficient assurances. Or, further to illustrate, a dying declaration may incorporate a declaration against interest by another declarant. See McCormick, Evidence § 290 (2nd ed. 1972).

For similar provisions, see Uniform Rule 66, Calif. Evid. Code § 1201; Kansas Code of Civ. Pro. § 60-466; New Jersey Evid. Rule 66. See McCormick, Evidence § 313 (2nd ed. 1972).

No Florida cases were found in this area.

COMMENTARY ON FEDERAL AND FLORIDA RULE DIFFERENCES

Florida Stat. § 90.805 and its federal counterpart, Federal Rule 805, set forth the rule governing the admissibility of hearsay within hearsay. The rules are identical to one another, and provide that hearsay within hearsay can be admitted into evidence so long as each layer of hearsay falls within an exception to the hearsay rule. The term hearsay as used in these provisions is defined in Florida Stat. § 90.801 and its federal counterpart, Federal Rule 801, and the exceptions thereto are set forth in Florida Stat. §§ 90.803-90.804 and Federal Rules 803-804 and 807.

Federal Rule 806. Attacking and Supporting the Declarant's Credibility

When a hearsay statement — or a statement described in Rule 801(d)(2)(C), (D), or (E) — has been admitted in evidence, the declarant's credibility may be attacked, and then supported, by any evidence that would be admissible for those purposes if the declarant had testified as a witness. The court may admit evidence of the declarant's inconsistent statement or conduct, regardless of when it occurred or whether the declarant had an opportunity to explain or deny it. If the party against whom the statement was admitted calls the declarant as a witness, the party may examine the declarant on the statement as if on cross-examination.

ADVISORY COMMITTEE'S NOTE

The declarant of a hearsay statement which is admitted in evidence is in effect a witness. His credibility should in fairness be subject to impeachment and support as though he had in fact testified. See Rules 608 and 609. There are however, some special aspects of the impeaching of a hearsay declarant which require consideration. These special aspects center upon impeachment by inconsistent statement, arise from factual differences which exist between the use of hearsay and an actual witness and also between various kinds of hearsay, and involve the question of applying to declarants the general rule disallowing evidence of an inconsistent statement to impeach a witness unless he is afforded an opportunity to deny or explain. See Rule 613(b).

The principal difference between using hearsay and an actual witness is that the inconsistent statement will in the case of the witness almost inevitably of necessity in the nature of things be a *prior* statement, which it is entirely possible and feasible to call to his attention, while in the case of hearsay the inconsistent statement may well be a *subsequent* one, which practically precludes calling it to the attention of the declarant. The result of insisting upon observation of this impossible requirement in the hearsay situation is to deny the opponent, already barred from cross-examination, any benefit of this important technique of impeachment. The writers favor allowing the subsequent statement. McCormick § 37, p. 69; 3 Wigmore § 1033. The cases, however, are divided. Cases allowing the impeachment include People v. Collup, 27 Cal.2d 829 (1946); People v. Rosoto, 58 Cal.2d 304 (1962); Carver v. United States, 164 U.S. 694 (1897). *Contra*, Mattox v. United States, 156 U.S. 237 (1895); People v. Hines, 284 N.Y. 93 (1940). The force of *Mattox*, where the hearsay was the former testimony of a deceased witness and the denial of use of a subsequent inconsistent statement was upheld, is much diminished by *Carver*, where the hearsay was a dying declaration and denial of use of a *subsequent* inconsistent statement resulted in reversal. The difference in the particular brand of hearsay seems unimportant when the inconsistent statement is a subsequent one. True, the opponent is not totally deprived of cross-examination when the hearsay is former testimony or a deposition but he is deprived of cross-examining on the statement or along lines suggested by it. Mr. Justice Shiras, with two justices joining him, dissented vigorously in *Mattox*.

When the impeaching statement was made *prior* to the hearsay statement, differences in the kinds of hearsay appear which arguably may justify differences in treatment. If the hearsay consisted of a simple statement by the witness, e.g. a dying declaration or a declaration against interest, the feasibility of affording him an opportunity to deny or explain encounters the same practical impossibility as where the statement is a subsequent one, just discussed, although here the impossibility arises from the total absence of anything resembling a hearing at which the matter could be put to him. The courts by a large majority have ruled in favor of allowing the statement to be used under these circumstances. McCormick § 37, p. 69; 3 Wigmore § 1033. If, however, the hearsay consists of former testimony or a deposition, the possibility of calling the prior statement to the attention of the witness or deponent is not ruled out, since the opportunity to cross-examine was available. It might thus be concluded that with former testimony or depositions the conventional foundation should be insisted upon. Most of the cases involve depositions, and Wigmore describes them as divided. 3 Wigmore § 1031. Deposition procedures at best are cumbersome and expensive, and to require the laying of the foundation may impose an undue burden. Under the federal practice, there is no way of knowing with certainty at the time of taking a deposition whether it is merely for discovery or will ultimately end up in evidence. With respect to both former testimony and depositions the possibility exists that knowledge of the statement might not be acquired until after the time of the cross-examination. Moreover, the expanded admissibility of former testimony and depositions under Rule 804(b)(1) calls for a correspondingly expanded approach to impeachment. The rule dispenses with the requirement in all hearsay situations, which is readily administered and best calculated to lead to fair results.

Notice should be taken that Rule 26(f) of the Federal Rules of Civil Procedure, as originally submitted by the Advisory Committee, ended with the following:

" . . . and, without having first called them to the deponent's attention, may show statements contradictory thereto made at any time by the deponent."

This language did not appear in the rule as promulgated in December, 1937. See 4 Moore's Federal Practice ¶¶ 26.01[9], 26.35 (2d ed.1967). In 1951, Nebraska adopted a provision strongly resembling the one stricken from the federal rule:

"Any party may impeach any adverse deponent by self-contradiction without having laid foundation for such impeachment at the time such deposition was taken." R.S.Neb. § 25-1267.07.

For similar provisions, see Uniform Rule 65; California Evidence Code § 1202; Kansas Code of Civil Procedure § 60-462; New Jersey Evidence Rule 65.

The provision for cross-examination of a declarant upon his hearsay statement is a corollary of general principles of cross-examination. A similar provision is found in California Evidence Code § 1203.

REPORT OF SENATE COMMITTEE ON THE JUDICIARY

Rule [806], as passed by the House and as proposed by the Supreme Court provides that whenever a hearsay statement is admitted, the credibility of the declarant of the statement may be attacked, and if attacked may be supported, by any evidence which would be admissible for those purposes if the declarant had testified as a witness. Rule 801 defines what is a hearsay statement. While statements by a person authorized by a party-opponent to make a statement concerning the subject, by the party-opponent's agent or by a coconspirator of a party—see rule 801(d)(2)(c), (d) and (e)—are traditionally defined as exceptions to the hearsay rule, rule 801 defines such admission by a party-opponent as statements which are not hearsay. Consequently, rule 806 by referring exclusively to the admission of hearsay statements, does not appear to allow the credibility of the declarant to be attacked when the declarant is a coconspirator, agent or authorized spokesman. The committee is of the view that such statements should open the declarant to attacks on his credibility. Indeed, the reason such statements are excluded from the operation of rule 806 is likely attributable to the drafting technique used to codify the hearsay rule, viz. some statements, instead of being referred to as exceptions to the hearsay rule, are defined as statements which are not hearsay. The phrase "or a statement defined in rule 801(d)(2)(c), (d) and (e)" is added to the rule in order to subject the declarant of such statements, like the declarant of hearsay statements, to attacks on his credibility.[39]

CONFERENCE REPORT

The Senate amendment permits an attack upon the credibility of the declarant of a statement if the statement is one by a person authorized by a party-opponent to make a statement concerning the subject, only by an agent of a party-opponent, or one by a coconspirator of the party-opponent, as these statements are defined in Rules 801(d)(2)(C), (D) and (E).The House bill has no such provision.

The Conference adopts the Senate amendment. The Senate amendment conforms the rule to present practice.

ADVISORY COMMITTEE'S NOTE (2011 AMENDMENT)

The language of Rule 806 has been amended as part of the restyling of the Evidence Rules to make them more easily understood and to make style and terminology consistent throughout the rules. These changes are intended to be stylistic only. There is no intent to change any result in any ruling on evidence admissibility.

Florida Stat. § 90.806. Attacking and Supporting Credibility of Declarant

(1) When a hearsay statement has been admitted in evidence, credibility of the declarant may be attacked and, if attacked, may be supported by any evidence that would be admissible for those purposes if the declarant had testified as a witness. Evidence of a statement or conduct by the declarant at any time inconsistent with the declarant's hearsay statement is admissible, regardless of whether or not the declarant has been afforded an opportunity to deny or explain it.

(2) If the party against whom a hearsay statement has been admitted calls the declarant as a witness, the party is entitled to examine the declarant on the statement as if under cross-examination.

SPONSORS' NOTE (1976 ENACTMENT)

This section deals with the impeachment of a declarant whose hearsay statement is in evidence as distinguished from the impeachment of a witness who has testified. Evidence used to impeach a hearsay declarant is not inadmissible because it is collateral. Section 90.614(2) requiring that a witness may be provided an opportunity to deny or explain a prior inconsistent statement before he may be impeached, does not apply to a hearsay declarant.

The declarant of a hearsay statement which is admitted in evidence is in effect a witness. His credibility should in fairness be subject to impeachment and support as though he had in fact testified. See Sections 90.609 and 90.610. However, the difference between hearsay testimony and that of an actual witness makes it difficult to follow the same rule as when impeaching a witness who testifies.

A principal difference between using hearsay and the testimony of an actual witness is that an inconsistent statement of a witness almost inevitably will be a prior statement, while in the case of

---

[39] The committee considered it unnecessary to include statements contained in Rule 801(d)(2)(A) and (B)—the statement by the party-opponent himself or the statement of which he has manifested his adoption—because the credibility of the party-opponent is always subject to an attack on his credibility.

hearsay the inconsistent statement may well be a <u>subsequent</u> one, which practically precludes calling it to the attention of the declarant, as Section 90.614(2) requires. The result of insisting that a hearsay declarant be given an opportunity to explain or deny an inconsistent statement prior to introducing extrinsic evidence of the inconsistent statement would be to deny the opponent, already barred from cross-examination, any benefit of this important technique of impeachment. The writers favor allowing the subsequent statement despite an inability to call it to the attention of the declarant, McCormick, <u>Evidence</u> § 32 (2nd ed. 1972); 3 Wigmore, <u>Evidence</u> § 1033 (3d ed. 1940). The cases, however, are divided. See cases noted in 3 Wigmore, <u>Evidence</u> §§ 1030-33 (3rd ed. 1940).

The difference in the particular type of hearsay seems unimportant when the inconsistent statement is a <u>subsequent</u> one. When the hearsay is former testimony or a deposition, the opponent is not totally deprived of cross-examination, but he is deprived of cross-examining on the inconsistent statement or along lines suggested by it. The few cases in this area from other jurisdictions generally hold that a party may not dispense with the requirement of asking the witness whether he made the contradictory statement. See 3 Wigmore, <u>Evidence</u> § 1032 (3rd ed. 1940).

Except for depositions and former testimony, the feasibility of affording the hearsay declarant an opportunity to deny or explain <u>prior</u> inconsistent statements encounters the same practical impossibilities that are encountered with <u>subsequent</u> inconsistent statements. There is a total absence of a hearing at which the matter could be put to the declarant. In the case of dying declarations, the courts by a large majority have ruled in favor of allowing the statement to be used without requiring the preliminary question to be asked. 3 Wigmore, <u>Evidence</u> § 1033 (3rd ed. 1940).

When the hearsay consists of former testimony or a deposition, it is possible to call the prior statement to the attention of the witness or deponent since the opportunity to cross-examine was available. It might thus be concluded that with former testimony or depositions the conventional foundation should be insisted upon. Wigmore describes the cases as divided, 3 Wigmore, <u>Evidence</u> § 1030 (3rd ed. 1940). However, deposition procedures are cumbersome and expensive, and to require the laying of the foundation may impose an undue burden. There is no way of knowing with certainty at the time of taking a deposition whether it is merely for discovery or will ultimately be used as evidence. The possibility also exists that knowledge of the statement might not be acquired until after the time of cross-examination. Therefore, this section dispenses with the requirement that the witness be first offered the opportunity to explain or deny an inconsistent statement in all hearsay situations, which is easily administered and best calculated to lead to fair results.

In <u>Seaboard Coast Line R.R. v. Hunt</u>, 299 So.2d 84 (Fla. 1st Dist. 1974) it was error to admit evidence of statements inconsistent with a hearsay declaration of a witness who did testify, because the hearsay declarant had not been asked the necessary foundation questions that were required by Fla. Stat. § 90.10.

For similar provisions, see Uniform Rule 65; Calif. Evid. Code §§ 1202-03; Kansas Code of Civ. Pro. § 60-462; New Jersey Evid. Rule 65; Prop. Fed. Rule Evid. 806; Wisc. Rule Evid. 908.06.

COMMENTARY ON FEDERAL AND FLORIDA RULE DIFFERENCES

Florida Stat. § 90.806 and its federal counterpart, Federal Rule 806, govern the impeachment and rehabilitation of hearsay declarants. Under these rules, when a hearsay statement has been admitted under an exception to the hearsay rule, the credibility of the declarant may be attacked, and if attacked, may be rehabilitated, by any evidence that could have been used to impeach or rehabilitate the declarant had he testified at trial as a witness. Thus, as a general rule, one is subject to the *same* requirements for impeaching a hearsay declarant as would be the case had the person appeared live and testified. However, with respect to one form of impeachment, the standard requirements are relaxed; the rules dispense with the requirement that an opportunity to deny or explain be given before extrinsic evidence of an inconsistent statement (whether made before or after the hearsay statement was made) is introduced. *See State v. Hill*, 504 So. 2d 407, 410 (Fla. 2d DCA 1987); Advisory Committee's Note to FED. R. EVID. 806. Yet with respect to other forms of impeachment, the rules are the same as they would be had the witness appeared at trial, even if the circumstances would make it impossible to invoke that method of impeachment. *See U.S. v. Saada*, 212 F.3d 210, 219-22 (3d Cir. 2000) (holding that Rule 608(b)'s ban on extrinsic evidence of prior bad acts applies, even if that makes resort to that method of impeachment impossible, since the declarant was dead and thus could not be called as a witness and asked about his prior bad acts, although noting contrary authority). Both rules, however, permit the party against whom the hearsay statement was admitted to call the declarant as a witness, and if he does, allows him to examine the declarant on the statement as if on cross-examination. *See* FED. R. EVID. 806; FLA. STAT. § 90.806(2). Thus, for example, if a hearsay statement is admitted against a party, that party can call the declarant as a witness and inquire about his prior bad acts. *See Saada*, 212 F.3d at 222.

The rules only apply if a declarant's statement has been admitted as hearsay, in other words, as proof of the truth of the matter asserted therein; if the statement is admitted for a non-hearsay purpose, then these rules are not triggered. *See U.S. v. Price*, 792 F.2d 994, 996-97 (11th Cir. 1986).

One important difference between the federal and Florida rules is that the latter rule applies to all statements of an opposing party set forth in FLA. STAT. § 90.803(18) while the federal rule only applies to authorized statements, vicarious statements, and co-conspirator statements, but *not* to individual or adopted statements. *Compare* FLA. STAT. § 90.806(1) (stating that it applies whenever a "hearsay statement" is admitted, with statements of an opposing party under Florida law viewed as hearsay falling within a hearsay exception), *with* FED. R. EVID. 806 (stating that it applies whenever "a hearsay statement—or a statement defined in Rule 801(d)(2)(C), (D), or (E)" is admitted, with federal law deeming statements of an opposing party to fall outside the scope of the term "hearsay"). This means that under Florida law, the government can introduce a criminal defendant's individual or adopted statements and then try to impeach his credibility with respect to the self-serving portions of the statements by, for example, introducing evidence of his prior convictions, a result that cannot be achieved under the federal rule. *See Kelly v. State*, 857 So. 2d 949, 949-50 (Fla. 4th DCA 2003). *See also* Margaret Meriwether Cordray, *Evidence Rule 806 and the Problem of Impeaching the Nontestifying Declarant,* 56 OHIO ST. L.J. 495, 533 (1995).

Federal Rule 807. Residual Exception

(a) In General. Under the following circumstances, a hearsay statement is not excluded by the rule against hearsay even if the statement is not specifically covered by a hearsay exception in Rule 803 or 804:

(1) the statement has equivalent circumstantial guarantees of trustworthiness;

(2) it is offered as evidence of a material fact;

(3) it is more probative on the point for which it is offered than any other evidence that the proponent can obtain through reasonable efforts; and

(4) admitting it will best serve the purposes of these rules and the interests of justice.

(b) Notice. The statement is admissible only if, before the trial or hearing, the proponent gives an adverse party reasonable notice of the intent to offer the statement and its particulars, including the declarant's name and address, so that the party has a fair opportunity to meet it.

ADVISORY COMMITTEE'S NOTE (1997 AMENDMENT)

The contents of Rule 803(24) and Rule 804(b)(5) have been combined and transferred to a new Rule 807. This was done to facilitate additions to Rules 803 and 804. No change in meaning is intended.

ADVISORY COMMITTEE'S NOTE (RULE 803(24))

The preceding 23 exceptions of Rule 803 and the first five exceptions of Rule 804(b), infra, are designed to take full advantage of the accumulated wisdom and experience of the past in dealing with hearsay. It would, however, be presumptuous to assume that all possible desirable exceptions to the hearsay rule have been catalogued and to pass the hearsay rule to oncoming generations as a closed system. Exception (24) and its companion provision in rule [804(b)(5)] are accordingly included. They do not contemplate an unfettered exercise of judicial discretion, but they do provide for treating new and presently unanticipated situations which demonstrate a trustworthiness within the spirit of the specifically stated exceptions. Within this framework, room is left for growth and development of the law of evidence in the hearsay area, consistently with the broad purposes expressed in Rule 102. See Dallas County v. Commercial Union Assur. Co., 286 F.2d 388 (5th Cir. 1961).

REPORT OF HOUSE COMMITTEE ON THE JUDICIARY (RULE 803(24))

The proposed Rules of Evidence as submitted to Congress contained identical provisions in Rules 803 and 804 (which set forth the various hearsay exceptions), to the effect that the federal courts could admit any hearsay statement not specifically covered by any of the stated exceptions, if the hearsay statement was found to have "comparable circumstantial guarantees of trustworthiness."

The Committee deleted these provisions (proposed Rule 803(24) and [804(b)(5)]) as injecting too much uncertainty into the law of evidence and impairing the ability of practitioners to prepare for trial. It was noted that Rule 102 directs the courts to construe the Rules of Evidence so as to promote "growth and development." The Committee believed that if additional hearsay exceptions are to be created, they should be by amendments to the Rules, not on a case-by-case basis.

REPORT OF SENATE COMMITTEE ON THE JUDICIARY (RULE 803(24))

The proposed Rules of Evidence submitted to Congress contained identical provisions in rules 803 and 804 (which set forth the various hearsay exceptions), admitting any hearsay statement not specifically covered by any of the stated exceptions, if the hearsay statement was found to have "comparable circumstantial guarantees of trustworthiness." The House deleted these provisions (proposed rules 803(24) and [804(b)(5)]) as injecting "too much uncertainty" into the law of evidence and impairing the ability of practitioners to prepare for trial. The House felt that rule 102, which directs the courts to construe the Rules of Evidence so as to promote growth and development, would permit sufficient flexibility to admit hearsay evidence in appropriate cases under various factual situations that might arise.

We disagree with the total rejection of a residual hearsay exception. While we view rule 102 as being intended to provide for a broader construction and interpretation of these rules, we feel that, without a separate residual provision, the specifically enumerated exceptions could become tortured beyond any reasonable circumstances which they were intended to include (even if broadly construed). Moreover, these exceptions, while they reflect the most typical and well recognized exceptions to the hearsay rule, may not encompass every situation in which the reliability and appropriateness of a particular piece of hearsay evidence make clear that it should be heard and considered by the trier of fact.

The committee believes that there are certain exceptional circumstances where evidence which is found by a court to have guarantees of trustworthiness equivalent to or exceeding the guarantees reflected by the presently listed exceptions, and to have a high degree of [probativeness] and necessity could properly be admissible.

The case of *Dallas County* v. *Commercial Union Assoc. Co., Ltd.*, 286 F.2d 388 (5th Cir. 1961) illustrates the point. The issue in that case was whether the tower of the county courthouse collapsed because it was struck by lightning (covered by insurance) or because of structural weakness and deterioration of the structure (not covered). Investigation of the structure revealed the presence of charcoal and charred timbers. In order to show that lightning may not have been the cause of the charring, the insurer offered a copy of a local newspaper published over 50 years earlier containing an unsigned article describing a fire in the courthouse while it was under construction. The Court found that the newspaper did not qualify for admission as a business record or an ancient document and did not fit within any other recognized hearsay exception. The court concluded, however, that the article was trustworthy because it was inconceivable that a newspaper reporter in a small town would report a fire in the courthouse if none had occurred. See also *United States* v. *Barbati*, 284 F.Supp. 409 (E.D.N.Y. 1968).

Because exceptional cases like the Dallas County case may arise in the future, the committee has decided to reinstate a residual exception for rules 803 and 804(b).

The committee, however, also agrees with those supporters of the House version who felt that an overly broad residual hearsay exception could emasculate the hearsay rule and the recognized exceptions or vitiate the rationale behind codification of the rules.

Therefore, the committee has adopted a residual exception for rules 803 and 804(b) of much narrower scope and applicability than the Supreme Court version. In order to qualify for admission, a hearsay statement not falling within one of the recognized exceptions would have to satisfy at least four conditions. First, it must have "equivalent circumstantial guarantees of trustworthiness." Second, it must be offered as evidence of a material fact. Third, the court must determine that the statement "is more probative on the point for which it is offered than any other evidence which the proponent can procure through reasonable efforts." This requirement is intended to insure that only statements which have high probative value and necessity may qualify for admission under the residual exceptions. Fourth, the court must determine that "the general purposes of these rules and the interests of justice will best be served by admission of the statement into evidence."

It is intended that the residual hearsay exceptions will be used very rarely, and only in exceptional circumstances. The committee does not intend to establish a broad license for trial judges to admit hearsay statements that do not fall within one of the other exceptions contained in rules 803 and 804(b). The residual exceptions are not meant to authorize major judicial revisions of the hearsay rule, including its present exceptions. Such major revisions are best accomplished by legislative action. It is intended that in any case in which evidence is sought to be admitted under these subsections, the trial judge will exercise no less care, reflection and caution than the courts did under the common law in establishing the now-recognized exceptions to the hearsay rule.

In order to establish a well-defined jurisprudence, the special facts and circumstances which, in the court's judgment, indicates that the statement has a sufficiently high degree of trustworthiness and necessity to justify its admission should be stated on the record. It is expected that the court will give the opposing party a full and adequate opportunity to contest the admission of any statement sought to be introduced under these subsections.

CONFERENCE REPORT (RULE 803(24))

The Senate amendment adds a new subsection, (24), which makes admissible a hearsay statement not specifically covered by any of the previous twenty-three subsections, if the statement has equivalent circumstantial guarantees of trustworthiness and if the court determines that (A) the statement is offered as evidence of a material fact; (B) the statement is more probative on the point for which it is offered than any other evidence the proponent can procure through reasonable efforts; and (C) the general purposes of these rules and the interests of justice will best be served by admission of the statement into evidence.

The House bill eliminated a similar, but broader, provision because of the conviction that such a provision injected too much uncertainty into the law of evidence regarding hearsay and impaired the ability of a litigant to prepare adequately for trial.

The Conference adopts the Senate amendment with an amendment that provides that a party intending to request the court to use a statement under this provision must notify any adverse party of this intention as well as of the particulars of the statement, including the name and address of the declarant. This notice must be given sufficiently in advance of the trial or hearing to provide any adverse party with a fair opportunity to prepare to contest the use of the statement.

ADVISORY COMMITTEE'S NOTE (2011 AMENDMENT)

The language of Rule 807 has been amended as part of the restyling of the Evidence Rules to make them more easily understood and to make style and terminology consistent throughout the rules. These changes are intended to be stylistic only. There is no intent to change any result in any ruling on evidence admissibility.

COMMENTARY ON FEDERAL AND FLORIDA RULE DIFFERENCES

Federal Rule 807 is a residual exception to the hearsay rule, which gives a federal court the ability to admit a hearsay statement, even if it doesn't fall within one of the exceptions set forth in Federal Rules 803 and 804, if the court finds, *inter alia* that it has equivalent circumstantial guarantees of trustworthiness to hearsay admitted under those rules. Other requirements for invoking the rule include that the statement bears on a material fact, that it is the most probative evidence addressing that fact, that its admission is consistent with the rules of evidence and advances the interests of justice, and that adequate notice has been given to the adverse party. *See U.S. v. Rodriguez*, 218 F.3d 1243, 1246 (11th Cir. 2000). Because of the notice requirement, appellate courts will not entertain for the first time on appeal arguments that evidence might have been admissible under this provision. *See Rowland v. American Gen. Fin., Inc.*, 340 F.3d 187, 195 (4th Cir. 2003).

By contrast, Florida has not adopted a residual exception to the hearsay rule; if a statement does not fit within one of the exceptions to the hearsay rule set forth in Florida Stat. §§ 90.803-90.804, Florida courts lack any authority to admit them for a hearsay purpose. *See Fitzpatrick v. State*, 900 So. 2d 495, 515 n.7 (Fla. 2005); *State v. Smith*, 573 So. 2d 306, 315 n.7 (Fla. 1990).

ARTICLE IX. AUTHENTICATION AND IDENTIFICATION

Federal Rule	Florida Stat. §	Description
901	90.901	Authenticating or Identifying Evidence
902	90.902	Evidence That Is Self-Authenticating
903	90.903	Subscribing Witness's Testimony
—	90.91	Photographs of Property Wrongfully Taken; Use in Prosecution, Procedure; Return of Property to Owner

Federal Rule 901. Authenticating or Identifying Evidence

(a) In General. To satisfy the requirement of authenticating or identifying an item of evidence, the proponent must produce evidence sufficient to support a finding that the item is what the proponent claims it is.

(b) Examples. The following are examples only — not a complete list — of evidence that satisfies the requirement:

(1) *Testimony of a Witness with Knowledge.* Testimony that an item is what it is claimed to be.

(2) *Nonexpert Opinion About Handwriting.* A nonexpert's opinion that handwriting is genuine, based on a familiarity with it that was not acquired for the current litigation.

(3) *Comparison by an Expert Witness or the Trier of Fact.* A comparison with an authenticated specimen by an expert witness or the trier of fact.

(4) *Distinctive Characteristics and the Like.* The appearance, contents, substance, internal patterns, or other distinctive characteristics of the item, taken together with all the circumstances.

(5) *Opinion About a Voice.* An opinion identifying a person's voice — whether heard firsthand or through mechanical or electronic transmission or recording — based on hearing the voice at any time under circumstances that connect it with the alleged speaker.

(6) *Evidence About a Telephone Conversation.* For a telephone conversation, evidence that a call was made to the number assigned at the time to:

(A) a particular person, if circumstances, including self-identification, show that the person answering was the one called; or

(B) a particular business, if the call was made to a business and the call related to business reasonably transacted over the telephone.

(7) *Evidence About Public Records.* Evidence that:

(A) a document was recorded or filed in a public office as authorized by law; or

(B) a purported public record or statement is from the office where items of this kind are kept.

(8) *Evidence About Ancient Documents or Data Compilations.* For a document or data compilation, evidence that it:

(A) is in a condition that creates no suspicion about its authenticity;

(B) was in a place where, if authentic, it would likely be; and

(C) is at least 20 years old when offered.

(9) *Evidence About a Process or System.* Evidence describing a process or system and showing that it produces an accurate result.

(10) *Methods Provided by a Statute or Rule.* Any method of authentication or identification allowed by a federal statute or a rule prescribed by the Supreme Court.

ADVISORY COMMITTEE'S NOTE

Subdivision (a). Authentication and identification represent a special aspect of relevancy. Michael and Adler, Real Proof, 5 Vand.L.Rev. 344, 362 (1952); McCormick §§ 179, 185; Morgan, Basic Problems of Evidence 378 (1962). Thus a telephone conversation may be irrelevant because on an unrelated topic or because the speaker is not identified. The latter aspect is the one here involved. Wigmore describes the need for authentication as "an inherent logical necessity." 7 Wigmore § 2129, p. 564.

This requirement of showing authenticity or identity falls in the category of relevancy dependent upon fulfillment of a condition of fact and is governed by the procedure set forth in Rule 104(b).

The common law approach to authentication of documents has been criticized as an "attitude of agnosticism," McCormick, Cases on Evidence 388, n. 4 (3rd ed. 1956), as one which "departs sharply from men's customs in ordinary affairs," and as presenting only a slight obstacle to the introduction of forgeries in comparison to the time and expense devoted to proving genuine writings which correctly show their origin on their face, McCormick § 185, pp. 395, 396. Today, such available procedures as requests to admit and pretrial conference afford the means of eliminating much of the need for authentication or identification. Also, significant inroads upon the traditional insistence on authentication and identification have been made by accepting as at least prima facie genuine items of the kind treated in Rule 902, *infra*. However, the need for suitable methods of proof still remains, since criminal cases pose their own obstacles to the use of preliminary procedures, unforeseen contingencies may arise, and cases of genuine controversy will still occur.

Subdivision (b). The treatment of authentication and identification draws largely upon the experience embodied in the common law and in statutes to furnish illustrative applications of the general principle set forth in subdivision (a). The examples are not intended as an exclusive enumeration of allowable methods but are meant to guide and suggest, leaving room for growth and development in this area of the law.

The examples relate for the most part to documents, with some attention given to voice communications and computer print-outs. As Wigmore noted, no special rules have been developed for authenticating chattels. Wigmore, Code of Evidence § 2086 (3rd ed. 1942).

It should be observed that compliance with requirements of authentication or identification by no means assures admission of an item into evidence, as other bars, hearsay for example, may remain.

Example (1) contemplates a broad spectrum ranging from testimony of a witness who was present at the signing of a document to testimony establishing narcotics as taken from an accused and accounting for custody through the period until trial, including laboratory analysis. See California Evidence Code § 1413, eyewitness to signing.

Example (2) states conventional doctrine as to lay identification of handwriting, which recognizes that a sufficient familiarity with the handwriting of another person may be acquired by seeing him write, by exchanging correspondence, or by other means, to afford a basis for identifying it on subsequent occasions. McCormick § 189. See also California Evidence Code § 1416. Testimony based upon familiarity acquired for purposes of the litigation is reserved to the expert under the example which follows.

Example (3). The history of common law restrictions upon the technique of proving or disproving the genuineness of a disputed specimen of handwriting through comparison with a genuine specimen, by either the testimony of expert witnesses or direct viewing by the triers themselves, is detailed in 7 Wigmore §§ 1991–1994. In breaking away, the English Common Law Procedure Act of 1854, 17 and 18 Vict., c. 125, § 27, cautiously allowed expert or trier to use exemplars "proved to the satisfaction of the judge to be genuine" for purposes of comparison. The language found its way into numerous statutes in this country, e.g., California Evidence Code §§ 1417, 1418. While explainable as a measure of prudence in the process of breaking with precedent in the handwriting situation, the reservation to the judge of the question of the genuineness of exemplars and the imposition of an unusually high standard of persuasion are at variance with the general treatment of relevancy which depends upon fulfillment of a condition of fact. Rule 104(b). No similar attitude is found in other comparison situations, e.g., ballistics comparison by jury, as in Evans v. Commonwealth, 230 Ky. 411 (1929), or by experts, Annot., 26 A.L.R.2d 892, and no reason appears for its continued existence in handwriting cases. Consequently Example (3) sets no higher standard for handwriting specimens and treats all comparison situations alike, to be governed by Rule 104(b). This approach is consistent with 28 U.S.C. § 1731: "The admitted or proved handwriting of any person shall be admissible, for purposes of comparison, to determine genuineness of other handwriting attributed to such person."

Precedent supports the acceptance of visual comparison as sufficiently satisfying preliminary authentication requirements for admission in evidence. Brandon v. Collins, 267 F.2d 731 (2d Cir. 1959); Wausau Sulphate Fibre Co. v. Commissioner of Internal Revenue, 61 F.2d 879 (7th Cir. 1932); Desimone v. United States, 227 F.2d 864 (9th Cir. 1955).

Example (4). The characteristics of the offered item itself, considered in the light of circumstances, afford authentication techniques in great variety. Thus a document or telephone conversation may be shown to have emanated from a particular person by virtue of its disclosing knowledge of facts known peculiarly to him; Globe Automatic Sprinkler Co. v. Braniff, 89 Okl. 105 (1923); California Evidence Code § 1421; similarly, a letter may be authenticated by content and circumstances indicating it was in reply to a duly authenticated one. McCormick § 192; California Evidence Code § 1420. Language patterns may indicate authenticity or its opposite. Magnuson v. State, 187 Wis. 122 (1925); Arens and Meadow, Psycholinguistics and the Confession Dilemma, 56 Colum.L.Rev. 19 (1956).

Example (5). Since aural voice identification is not a subject of expert testimony, the requisite familiarity may be acquired either before or after the particular speaking which is the subject of the identification, in this respect resembling visual identification of a person rather than identification of handwriting. Cf. Example (2), *supra*, People v. Nichols, 378 Ill. 487 (1942); McGuire v. State, 200 Md. 601 (1952); State v. McGee, 336 Mo. 1082 (1935).

Example (6). The cases are in agreement that a mere assertion of his identity by a person talking on the telephone is not sufficient evidence of the authenticity of the conversation and that additional evidence of his identity is required. The additional evidence need not fall in any set pattern. Thus the content of his statements or the reply technique, under Example (4), *supra*, or voice identification under Example (5), may furnish the necessary foundation. Outgoing calls made by the witness involve additional factors bearing upon authenticity. The calling of a number assigned by the telephone company reasonably supports the assumption that the listing is correct and that the number is the one reached. If the number is that of a place of business, the mass of authority allows an ensuing conversation if it relates to business reasonably transacted over the telephone, on the theory that the maintenance of the telephone connection is an invitation to do business without further identification. Matton v. Hoover Co., 350 Mo. 506 (1942); City of Pawhuska v. Crutchfield, 147 Okl. 4 (1930); Zurich General Acc. & Liability Ins. Co. v. Baum, 159 Va. 404 (1932). Otherwise, some additional circumstance of identification of the speaker is required. The authorities divide on the question whether the self-identifying statement of the person answering suffices. Example (6) answers in the affirmative on the assumption that usual conduct respecting telephone calls furnish adequate assurances of regularity, bearing in mind that the entire matter is open to exploration before the trier of fact. In general, see McCormick § 193; 7 Wigmore § 2155; Annot., 71 A.L.R. 5, 105 id. 326.

Example (7). Public records are regularly authenticated by proof of custody, without more. McCormick § 191; 7 Wigmore §§ 2158, 2159. The example extends the principle to include data stored in computers and similar methods, of which increasing use in the public records area may be expected. See California Evidence Code §§ 1532, 1600.

Example (8). The familiar ancient document rule of the common law is extended to include data stored electronically or by other similar means. Since the importance of appearance diminishes in this situation, the importance of custody or place where found increases correspondingly. This expansion is necessary in view of the widespread use of methods of storing data in forms other than conventional written records.

Any time period selected is bound to be arbitrary. The common law period of 30 years is here reduced to 20 years, with some shift of emphasis from the probable unavailability of witnesses to the unlikeliness of a still viable fraud after the lapse of time. The shorter period is specified in the English Evidence Act of 1938, 1 & 2 Geo. 6, c. 28, and in Oregon R.S.1963, § 41.360(34). See also the numerous statutes prescribing periods of less than 30 years in the case of recorded documents. 7 Wigmore § 2143.

The application of Example (8) is not subject to any limitation to title documents or to any requirement that possession, in the case of a title document, has been consistent with the document. See McCormick § 190.

Example (9) is designed for situations in which the accuracy of a result is dependent upon a process or system which produces it. X rays afford a familiar instance. Among more recent developments is the computer, as to which see Transport Indemnity Co. v. Seib, 178 Neb. 253 (1965); State v. Veres, 7 Ariz.App. 117 (1968); Merrick v. United States Rubber Co., 7 Ariz.App. 433 (1968); Freed, Computer Print-Outs as Evidence, 16 Am.Jur.Proof of Facts 273; Symposium, Law and Computers in the Mid-Sixties, ALI-ABA (1966); 37 Albany L.Rev. 61 (1967). Example (9) does not, of course, foreclose taking judicial notice of the accuracy of the process or system.

Example (10). The example makes clear that methods of authentication provided by Act of Congress and by the Rules of Civil and Criminal Procedure or by Bankruptcy Rules are not intended to be superseded. Illustrative are the provisions for authentication of official records in Civil Procedure Rule 44 and Criminal Procedure Rule 27, for authentication of records of proceedings by court reporters in 28 U.S.C. § 753(b) and Civil Procedure Rule 80(c), and for authentication of depositions in Civil Procedure Rule 30(f).

ADVISORY COMMITTEE'S NOTE (2011 AMENDMENT)

The language of Rule 901 has been amended as part of the restyling of the Evidence Rules to make them more easily understood and to make style and terminology consistent throughout the rules. These changes are intended to be stylistic only. There is no intent to change any result in any ruling on evidence admissibility.

Florida Stat. § 90.901. Requirement of Authentication or Identification

Authentication or identification of evidence is required as a condition precedent to its admissibility. The requirements of this section are satisfied by evidence sufficient to support a finding that the matter in question is what its proponent claims.

SPONSORS' NOTE (1976 ENACTMENT)

Authentication and identification are implicit in the concept of relevancy. McCormick, Evidence § 218 (2nd ed. 1972); Weinstein & Berger, Basic Rules of Relevancy in the Proposed Federal Rules of Evidence, 4 Ga. L. Rev. 43 (1969). For example, a telephone conversation may be irrelevant because it is on an unrelated topic or because the speaker is not identified. The latter aspect is involved in authentication and identification.

This section recognizes the long-established principle that evidence is inadmissible unless accompanied by some showing of its genuineness. See, e.g., DeLong v. Williams, 232 So.2d 246 (Fla. 4th Dist. 1970) (unauthenticated transcript of prior hearing not admissible). This preliminary requirement falls within the category of conditional relevancy and is governed by the procedure set forth in Section 90.105(2) granting the court the power to admit evidence subject to the introduction of evidence sufficient to support a finding of relevancy. Once a prima facie showing of authenticity is made, the evidence comes in, and the ultimate question of authenticity is for the jury. McCormick, Evidence § 227 (2nd ed. 1972). The admission into evidence of a matter merely indicates initial sufficiency for presentation to the trier of fact. Once the matter is in evidence the opposing party is free to challenge its genuineness. The court or the jury may find it to be not genuine. 7 Wigmore, Evidence § 2128, p. 564 (3rd ed. 1940). Authentication and identification do not assure admission into evidence, since other bars, hearsay for example, may still remain. Brown, Authentication and the Contents of Writings, 1969 Law & Social Order 611. The requirement of authentication is not limited to writings, but requires identification whenever any personal connection with a corporeal object is assumed in the offer. 7 Wigmore, Evidence § 2129 (3rd ed. 1940).

In recent years, numerous writers have seriously questioned the rigid traditional standards by which otherwise relevant evidence has been tested for authenticity. See Strong, Liberalizing the Authentication of Private Writings, 52 Cornell L.Q. 284 (1967); Brown, Authentication and the Contents of Writings, 1969 Law & Social Order 611. McCormick suggested that the principal common-law justification for the requirement of authentication, as a check on the perpetration of fraud, is no longer valid. The common-law skepticism is contrary to the assumptions of genuineness encountered in everyday experience and genuineness may be correctly assumed in 99 of 100 cases. In addition, the slight obstacles to fraud which are posed by rigid requirements are generally outweighed by the "time, expense, and occasional untoward results entailed by the traditional negative attitude toward authenticity." McCormick, Evidence § 218, p. 545 (2nd ed. 1972).

The need for authentication and identification has been reduced by modern pre-trial practice, including requests for admission of genuineness, and the pre-trial conference. See Fla. R. Civ. Pro. 1.200, 1.370. However, a need for suitable means of proof still exists since criminal cases pose their own obstacles to the use of preliminary procedures and involve a higher standard of proof, unforeseen contingencies may arise, and cases of genuine controversy will still occur.

For similar provisions, see Calif. Evid. Code §§ 1400, 1401; New Jersey Evid. Rule 67; Kansas Code of Civ. Pro. § 60-464; Fed. Rule Evid. 901(a).

The following are examples of when courts have found evidence to be properly authenticated:

(a) Testimony of a witness with knowledge that a matter is what it is claimed to be. This means of establishing the genuineness of offered evidence was recognized in Florida in Leighton v. Harmon, 111 So.2d 697, 701-02 (Fla. 2nd Dist. 1959):

> The authenticity of the instrument...may be proved by anyone who has knowledge of the facts. The source of knowledge of the witness is subject to the test of cross-examination by the opposition.

See Harwell v. Blake, 180 So.2d 173, 175 (Fla. 2nd Dist. 1965) which suggests that for certain records to be admissible "someone should have testified with knowledge of the record."

The scope of this means of authentication encompasses a wide range of situations, such as testimony of a witness who was present at the signing of a document, see Calif. Evid. Code § 1413 (eyewitness to signing), or testimony tracing the custody of bullets from the time they were taken from the victim up to the time of their introduction into evidence at the trial. Calloway v. State, 189 So.2d 617 (Fla. 1966). See Fed. Rule Evid. 901(b)(1).

(b) Non-expert opinion testimony as to the genuineness of handwriting based upon sufficient familiarity not acquired for the purposes of the litigation. See Clark v. Grimsley, 270 So.2d 53 (Fla. 1st Dist. 1972) (authentication of deceased's handwritten letters by testimony of frequent visitor familiar with handwriting). Familiarity may be established in any number of ways, such as when the witness has seen the person write on different occasions, Pittman v. State, 51 Fla. 94, 41 So. 385 (1906), or has seen writings purporting to be those of the person in question under circumstances indicating their genuineness. Familiarity with the writing obtained for the purposes of litigation is only admissible as expert testimony and is not admissible under this subsection.

Whether a lay witness is sufficiently familiar with the supposed writer's handwriting is a preliminary question of fact, governed by Section 90.105(2). In a close case where proof of handwriting will determine an essential element in a criminal prosecution, the court may exercise its discretion in determining whether sufficient familiarity exists and demand expert testimonial proof. See Note, Authentication and the Best Evidence Rule under the Federal Rules of Evidence, 16 Wayne L. Rev. 195, 200 (1969).

See Fed. Rule Evid. 901(b)(2); Calif. Evid. Code § 1416. (Fla. Stat. § 92.03 provides for jury consideration of disputed writings.)

(c) The appearance, contents, substance, internal patterns or other distinctive characteristics in conjunction with other circumstances may be sufficient to authenticate the evidence. For example, the "reply letter" doctrine is recognized as a method of authenticating a letter received in reply to one mailed by the sender in Boykin v. State, 40 Fla. 484, 488, 24 So. 141, 143 (1898):

> The rule is that where a letter is addressed to a party at his post office address, and is sent by mail, and a reply thereto, purporting to be from the party to whom it is sent, is received by the sender of the letter in due course of mail, the letter thus received in reply is admissible in evidence without proof that it is in the handwriting of, or signed by, the party purporting to have sent it.

See Atlas Subsidiaries of Florida, Inc. v. O. & O. Inc., 166 So.2d 458 (Fla. 1st Dist. 1964) (letter apparently in reply held admissible); Calif. Evid. Code § 1420 (authentication by evidence of reply).

The Florida rule is quite broad. For example, in Silva v. Exchange Nat. Bank, 56 So.2d 332 (Fla. 1951) the Supreme Court upheld the authenticity of a typewritten, unsigned letter, where the envelope containing the letter was addressed in the purported writer's handwriting and bore his return address. In general, authentication by circumstances is based on the assumption that a communication or document, which discloses knowledge that only the purported sender would be likely to have, was made by the person with such knowledge. McCormick, Evidence § 225 (2nd ed. 1972). See Calif. Evid. Code § 1421 (authentication by content).

Authentication occurs in any situation where the offered item, considered in light of the circumstances, logically indicates the personal connection sought to be proved. For example, see Worley v. State, 263 So.2d 613 (Fla. 4th Dist. 1972) (distinct characteristics of voiceprint justifies admission to corroborate identification of telephone bomb-threat caller).

(d) Authentication of aural identifications made under circumstances connecting them with the speaker. As noted by the court in Weinshenker v. State, 223 So.2d 561, 563 (Fla. 3rd Dist. 1969): "It is well settled in Florida that a person may be identified...solely by means of voice recognition." See Cason v. State, 211 So.2d 604 (Fla. 2nd Dist. 1968). This rule has been applied to electronic means of voice reproduction. See Worley v. State, 263 So.2d 613 (Fla. 4th Dist. 1972) (telephone).

Since identification by hearing a voice is not the subject of expert testimony, the requisite familiarity may be acquired either before or after the particular speaking which is the subject of the identification, in this respect, resembling visual identification of a person. See <u>Simon v. State</u>, 209 So.2d 682 (Fla. 3rd Dist. 1968) (robbery victim identified defendant upon apparently later recognition of his voice).

See Fed. Rule Evid. 901(b)(5).

(e) Generally in most jurisdictions a statement of identity by a person talking on a telephone is not in itself sufficient proof of such identity, in the absence of corroborating circumstances. See Annot., 105 A.L.R. 326 (1936), 71 A.L.R. 5 (1931) (admissibility of telephone conversations in evidence). Corroboration could be shown by voice identification, see example (d), or by a disclosure of information known only to the person calling or called, see example (c). Another simple means exists to identify the person called, based on evidence of a call which is made to the number assigned by the telephone company, together with the person answering identifying himself as the party called. When considered in light of the accuracy of the telephone system and the absence of motive or opportunity for premeditated fraud, this evidence justifies the conclusion that the party called was the one intended to be reached. McCormick, <u>Evidence</u> § 226 (2nd ed. 1972).

In the case of a call to a business office, the constant use of telephones as a means of conducting business dictates admission of such calls. Where a conversation with someone who assumed to have the requisite authority is within the normal scope of transactions carried out over the telephone, no further proof of identification is required.

See Fed. Rule Evid. 901(b)(6).

(f) Public documents held in public offices have long been exempt from the ordinary requirements of authenticity. In <u>Bell v. Kendrick</u>, 25 Fla. 778, 785, 6 So. 868, 869 (1889), the Florida Supreme Court recognized that:

> Official registers or books kept by persons in public office, in which they are required, whether by statute or by the nature of the office, to write down particular transactions occurring in the course of their public duties...are generally admissible in evidence, notwithstanding their authenticity is not confirmed by the ordinary test of truth....

It is well established that public records may be authenticated by proof of proper custody alone. McCormick, <u>Evidence</u> § 224 (2nd ed. 1972). Generally, Florida courts have justified dispensing with the requirement of further proof of public documents on the theory of judicial notice. See, e.g., <u>Florida Accountants Ass'n v. Dandelake</u>, 98 So.2d 323, 327 (Fla. 1957) ("This court takes judicial notice of the public records of this state."). Indeed, a wide range of public documents has been judicially noticed. See <u>State ex rel. Douglas v. Cone</u>, 133 Fla. 17, 182 So. 449 (1938) (reports from Treasurer's Office); <u>State ex rel. Glynn v. McNayr</u>, 133 So.2d 312 (Fla. 1961) (election results in office of Secretary of State). As Wigmore has noted, such judicial notice amounts to a ruling that custody is sufficient evidence of genuineness. 7 Wigmore, <u>Evidence</u> § 2158, p. 627 (3rd ed. 1940).

While existing Florida law does not explicitly provide for the authentication of public records stored in computers or by other modern storage methods, reasoning similar to that in the previously discussed rule would be applicable. Cf., Fla.Stat. § 92.36(2) (records kept by means of electronic data processing admissible under Business Records Act).

See Fed. Rule Evid. 901(b)(7); Calif. Evid. Code §§ 1532, 1600.

(g) Ancient documents may be authenticated by application of the ancient document rule which has long been a part of Florida law. In <u>Clark v. Cochran</u>, 79 Fla. 788, 794, 85 So. 250, 253 (1920) the Supreme Court found certain old documents to be admissible:

> These documents bore dates from 1857 to 1880...they came from a place where they would naturally be found if genuine...and there is no evidence of fraud or suspicious

circumstances....[W]e think the documents offered in this case were admissible as ancient documents.

The ancient document exception to the requirement of extrinsic proof of authenticity has been justified on at least two grounds: difficulty of proof after so long a period of time and the unlikelihood of a still viable fraud. McCormick, Evidence § 223 (2nd ed. 1972). Although the common law provided for a period of thirty years, the Florida courts have not established a time period. The trend in recent years toward statutory reduction, 7 Wigmore, Evidence § 2143 (3rd ed. 1940), and a shorter period is justified by the same principles which justified the common-law period. See Fla. Stat. § 92.08 (deeds and powers of attorney of record for 20 years as evidence of the truth of the facts therein).

This rule should be expanded to include data stored in computer banks or by other modern storage techniques. Since appearance in such cases becomes meaningless, the importance of custody or place where found will increase correspondingly.

The application of this method is not limited to title documents, see Drake v. Fort Lauderdale, 227 So.2d 709 (Fla. 4th Dist.1969) (ancient map), or to recorded instruments, Sullivan v. Richardson, 33 Fla. 1, 14 So. 692 (1894) (documents found in an old trunk), but extends to any document which meets the criteria.

See Oregon Rev. Stat.1963, § 41.360(34); Fed. Rule Evid. 901(b)(9).

(h) A writing is authenticated when it is offered against a party who had admitted its authenticity or acted upon it as authentic. A writing which is admitted to be genuine by the person against whom it is offered or which he has acted upon as authentic in the ordinary course of his affairs possesses trustworthiness. Wigmore found such a rule inferred from daily experience and further, to be justified by placing the burden of disproving genuineness on the person to whom evidence was most readily available. 7 Wigmore, Evidence § 2160 (3rd ed. 1940); see Calif. Evid. Code § 1414; Note, Authentication and the Best Evidence Rule under the Proposed Federal Rules of Evidence, 16 Wayne L. Rev. 195 (1969); Cone v. Benjamin, 27 So.2d 90 (Fla. 1946) (volume containing family tree authenticated by evidence that family members regarded it as genuine).

(i) Methods of authentication may be provided by the legislature or rules of court. For example Fla. R. Civ. Pro. 1.310(f) provides for authentication of depositions and Fla. Stat. § 656.23 provides for authentication of copies of certain bank records.

See Fed. Rule Evid. 901(b)(10).

COMMENTARY ON FEDERAL AND FLORIDA RULE DIFFERENCES

Florida Stat. § 90.901 and its federal counterpart, Federal Rule 901, set forth the standard for authenticating or identifying evidence. Under both Florida and federal law, the requirement of authentication or identification is a condition precedent to admissibility, and is satisfied under both federal and Florida practice by evidence sufficient to support a finding that the matter in question is what its proponent claims. Under this standard, the trial court does not make a determination that the evidence is or is not in fact authentic, but rather admits it so long as it finds that sufficient evidence of its authenticity has been introduced such that a reasonable trier of fact could find it to be authentic. See State v. Hampton, 44 So. 3d 661, 664 (Fla. 2d DCA 2010); Van Den Borre v. State, 596 So. 2d 687, 691 (Fla. 4th DCA 1992); Ricketts v. City of Hartford, 74 F.3d 1397, 1409-11 (2d Cir. 1996); U.S. v. Caldwell, 776 F.2d 989, 1001-02 (11th Cir. 1985). Once that determination is made by the trial court, it admits the evidence (assuming it is not subject to exclusion under some other rule of evidence), with the opposing party free to challenge its authenticity before the trier of fact, who is ultimately free to determine its authenticity. See Caldwell, 776 F.2d at 1001-02; State v. Love, 691 So. 2d 620, 622 (Fla. 5th DCA 1997); Sponsors' Note to FLA. STAT. § 90.901.

Federal Rule 901(b) sets forth a list of ten illustrative methods for complying with the standard for authenticating or identifying evidence, which the rule stresses are "examples only — not a complete list — of evidence that satisfies the requirement." No examples appear in the text of the Florida rule, although a list nearly identical to that set forth in Federal Rule 901(b) is set forth in the Sponsors' Note to Florida Stat. § 90.901.

Both the Florida and federal rules recognize testimony by a witness with first-hand knowledge that a matter is what it is claimed to be as a valid method of authentication. This includes such things as authenticating a document by the testimony of a witness who was present when it was signed to testimony tracing the chain of custody of an item of evidence from seizure to trial. *See* FED. R. EVID. 901(b)(1); Advisory Committee's Note to FED. R. EVID. 901(b)(1); Sponsors' Note to FLA. STAT. § 90.901 (paragraph (a)).

Testimony in the form of nonexpert opinion as to the genuineness of handwriting is a recognized method of authentication under both Florida and federal law, provided that the opinion is based on familiarity not acquired for purposes of the litigation. *See* FED. R. EVID. 901(b)(2); Advisory Committee's Note to FED. R. EVID. 901(b)(2); Sponsors' Note to FLA. STAT. § 90.901 (paragraph (b)).

Under the federal rule, handwriting may also be authenticated through comparison of a disputed specimen with a genuine specimen, either through the testimony of an expert or by direct comparison by the trier of fact without the aid of an expert. *See* FED. R. EVID. 901(b)(3); Advisory Committee's Note to FED. R. EVID. 901(b)(3). These examples are not among those set forth in the Sponsors' Note to the Florida rule, and although the Florida case law recognizes expert testimony as a method of authenticating handwriting, *see, e.g., Redmond v. State,* 731 So. 2d 77, 78 (Fla. 2d DCA 1999), it provides that a specimen cannot be authenticated through comparison by the trier of fact without the aid of expert testimony. *See Redmond,* 731 So. 2d at 79; *Huff v. State,* 437 So. 2d 1087, 1090 (Fla. 1983).

Both Florida and federal law provide that evidence may be authenticated based on appearance, contents, substance, internal patterns, or other distinctive characteristics, taken in conjunction with circumstances, including through such techniques as the reply letter doctrine or by the fact that a writing discloses knowledge of facts known to a particular person. *See* FED. R. EVID. 901(b)(4); Advisory Committee's Note to FED. R. EVID. 901(b)(4); Sponsors' Note to FLA. STAT. § 90.901 (paragraph (c)).

Both Florida and federal law recognize voice identification by a lay witness as a method of identifying a particular person as the one whose voice the witness heard, so long as the witness has heard the person's voice at any time under circumstances connecting it with the alleged speaker. *See* FED. R. EVID. 901(b)(5); Advisory Committee's Note to FED. R. EVID. 901(b)(5); Sponsors' Note to FLA. STAT. § 90.901 (paragraph (d)).

Under both Florida and federal law, mere self-identification by the caller in an *incoming* telephone call is insufficient, standing alone, to identify that person as the caller; something more, such as voice identification, is required. However, both Florida and federal law recognize that in the case of an *outgoing* telephone call, dialing the number assigned to a particular person or business—when coupled with self-identification by the recipient—satisfies the requirement of identification with respect to the recipient. *See* FED. R. EVID. 901(b)(6); Advisory Committee's Note to FED. R. EVID. 901(b)(6); Sponsors' Note to FLA. STAT. § 90.901 (paragraph (e)).

Proof of custody by a public office or agency, without more, is sufficient to authenticate public records or reports under both Federal and Florida law. *See* FED. R. EVID. 901(b)(7); Advisory Committee's Note to FED. R. EVID. 901(b)(7); Sponsors' Note to FLA. STAT. § 90.901 (paragraph (f)).

The federal rule recognizes the ancient document rule, under which a document can be authenticated by showing that it is in such condition as to create no suspicion concerning its authenticity, it was in a place where it, if authentic, would likely be, and it has been in existence 20 years or more at the time it is offered. *See* FED. R. EVID. 901(b)(8); Advisory Committee's Note to FED. R. EVID. 901(b)(8). A document so authenticated automatically overcomes a hearsay objection as well. *See* FED. R. EVID. 803(16). Florida law likewise recognizes the ancient document rule as a method of authentication, and while the Sponsors' Note to Florida Stat. § 90.901 does not specify 20 years, it notes that the trend is in that direction. *See* Sponsors' Note to FLA. STAT. § 90.901 (paragraph (g)). Nonetheless, the related hearsay exception under Florida law specifies a period of 20 years, strongly implying that the required period is the same for authenticating a document as an ancient one. *See* FLA. STAT. § 90.803(16).

The federal rule recognizes that authentication can be accomplished with evidence describing a process or system used to produce a result and showing that the process or system produces an accurate result. *See* FED. R. EVID. 901(b)(9); Advisory Committee's Note to FED. R. EVID. 901(b)(9). Thus, for example, a photograph taken by an automatic camera in a bank can be authenticated through testimony establishing the reliability of the process that creates the photograph. *See, e.g., U.S. v. Rembert*, 863 F.2d 1023, 1026 (D.C. Cir. 1988). While this method is not discussed in the Sponsors' Note to the Florida rule, the Florida Supreme Court has recognized this as a valid method of satisfying the requirement of authentication. *See Hannewacker v. City of Jacksonville Beach*, 419 So. 2d 308, 310-12 (Fla. 1982).

The Florida rule recognizes that a writing is authenticated when offered against a party who has admitted its authenticity or acted upon it as authentic. *See* Sponsors' Note to FLA. STAT. § 90.901 (paragraph (h)). While not set forth in the federal rule, federal law likewise recognizes that evidence can be authenticated through a party's admission. *See* FED. R. CIV. P. 36.

Finally, both the Florida and federal rules recognize that any method of authentication provided for by statute or rule is likewise valid to satisfy the requirement of authentication. *See* FED. R. EVID. 901(b)(10); Advisory Committee's Note to FED. R. EVID. 901(b)(10); Sponsors' Note to FLA. STAT. § 90.901 (paragraph (i)).

Federal Rule 902. Evidence That Is Self-Authenticating

The following items of evidence are self-authenticating; they require no extrinsic evidence of authenticity in order to be admitted:

(1) *Domestic Public Documents That Are Sealed and Signed.* A document that bears:

    (A) a seal purporting to be that of the United States; any state, district, common-wealth, territory, or insular possession of the United States; the former Panama Canal Zone; the Trust Territory of the Pacific Islands; a political subdivision of any of these entities; or a department, agency, or officer of any entity named above; and

    (B) a signature purporting to be an execution or attestation.

(2) *Domestic Public Documents That Are Not Sealed but Are Signed and Certified.* A document that bears no seal if:

    (A) it bears the signature of an officer or employee of an entity named in Rule 902(1)(A); and

    (B) another public officer who has a seal and official duties within that same entity certifies under seal — or its equivalent — that the signer has the official capacity and that the signature is genuine.

(3) *Foreign Public Documents.* A document that purports to be signed or attested by a person who is authorized by a foreign country's law to do so. The document must be accompanied by a

final certification that certifies the genuineness of the signature and official position of the signer or attester — or of any foreign official whose certificate of genuineness relates to the signature or attestation or is in a chain of certificates of genuineness relating to the signature or attestation. The certification may be made by a secretary of a United States embassy or legation; by a consul general, vice consul, or consular agent of the United States; or by a diplomatic or consular official of the foreign country assigned or accredited to the United States. If all parties have been given a reasonable opportunity to investigate the document's authenticity and accuracy, the court may, for good cause, either:

(A) order that it be treated as presumptively authentic without final certification; or

(B) allow it to be evidenced by an attested summary with or without final certification.

(4) *Certified Copies of Public Records.* A copy of an official record — or a copy of a document that was recorded or filed in a public office as authorized by law — if the copy is certified as correct by:

(A) the custodian or another person authorized to make the certification; or

(B) a certificate that complies with Rule 902(1), (2), or (3), a federal statute, or a rule prescribed by the Supreme Court.

(5) *Official Publications.* A book, pamphlet, or other publication purporting to be issued by a public authority.

(6) *Newspapers and Periodicals.* Printed material purporting to be a newspaper or periodical.

(7) *Trade Inscriptions and the Like.* An inscription, sign, tag, or label purporting to have been affixed in the course of business and indicating origin, ownership, or control.

(8) *Acknowledged Documents.* A document accompanied by a certificate of acknowledgment that is lawfully executed by a notary public or another officer who is authorized to take acknowledgments.

(9) *Commercial Paper and Related Documents.* Commercial paper, a signature on it, and related documents, to the extent allowed by general commercial law.

(10) *Presumptions Under a Federal Statute.* A signature, document, or anything else that a federal statute declares to be presumptively or prima facie genuine or authentic.

(11) *Certified Domestic Records of a Regularly Conducted Activity.* The original or a copy of a domestic record that meets the requirements of Rule 803(6)(A)-(C), as shown by a certification of the custodian or another qualified person that complies with a federal statute or a rule prescribed by the Supreme Court. Before the trial or hearing, the proponent must give an adverse party reasonable written notice of the intent to offer the record — and must make the record and certification available for inspection — so that the party has a fair opportunity to challenge them.

(12) *Certified Foreign Records of a Regularly Conducted Activity.* In a civil case, the original or a copy of a foreign record that meets the requirements of Rule 902(11), modified as follows: the certification, rather than complying with a federal statute or Supreme Court rule, must be signed in a manner that, if falsely made, would subject the maker to a criminal penalty in the country where the certification is signed. The proponent must also meet the notice requirements of Rule 902(11).

ADVISORY COMMITTEE'S NOTE

Case law and statutes have, over the years, developed a substantial body of instances in which authenticity is taken as sufficiently established for purposes of admissibility without extrinsic evidence to that effect, sometimes for reasons of policy but perhaps more often because practical considerations reduce the possibility of unauthenticity to a very small dimension. The present rule collects and incorporates these situations, in some instances expanding them to occupy a larger area which their underlying considerations justify. In no instance is the opposite party foreclosed from disputing authenticity.

Paragraph (1). The acceptance of documents bearing a public seal and signature, most often encountered in practice in the form of acknowledgments or certificates authenticating copies of public records, is actually of broad application. Whether theoretically based in whole or in part upon judicial notice, the practical underlying considerations are that forgery is a crime and detection is fairly easy and certain. 7 Wigmore § 2161, p. 638; California Evidence Code § 1452. More than 50 provisions for judicial notice of official seals are contained in the United States Code.

Paragraph (2). While statutes are found which raise a presumption of genuineness of purported official signatures in the absence of an official seal, 7 Wigmore § 2167; California Evidence Code § 1453, the greater ease of effecting a forgery under these circumstances is apparent. Hence this paragraph of the rule calls for authentication by an officer who has a seal. Notarial acts by members of the armed forces and other special situations are covered in paragraph (10).

Paragraph (3) provides a method for extending the presumption of authenticity to foreign official documents by a procedure of certification. It is derived from Rule 44(a)(2) of the Rules of Civil Procedure but is broader in applying to public documents rather than being limited to public records.

Paragraph (4). The common law and innumerable statutes have recognized the procedure of authenticating copies of public records by certificate. The certificate qualifies as a public document, receivable as authentic when in conformity with paragraph (1), (2), or (3). Rule 44(a) of the Rules of Civil Procedure and Rule 27 of the Rules of Criminal Procedure have provided authentication procedures of this nature for both domestic and foreign public records. It will be observed that the certification procedure here provided extends only to public records, reports, and recorded documents, all including data compilations, and does not apply to public documents generally. Hence documents provable when presented in original form under paragraphs (1), (2), or (3) may not be provable by certified copy under paragraph (4).

Paragraph (5). Dispensing with preliminary proof of the genuineness of purportedly official publications, most commonly encountered in connection with statutes, court reports, rules, and regulations, has been greatly enlarged by statutes and decisions. 5 Wigmore § 1684. Paragraph (5), it will be noted, does not confer admissibility upon all official publications; it merely provides a means whereby their authenticity may be taken as established for purposes of admissibility. Rule 44(a) of the Rules of Civil Procedure has been to the same effect.

Paragraph (6). The likelihood of forgery of newspapers or periodicals is slight indeed. Hence no danger is apparent in receiving them. Establishing the authenticity of the publication may, of course, leave still open questions of authority and responsibility for items therein contained. See 7 Wigmore § 2150. Cf. 39 U.S.C. § 4005(b), public advertisement prima facie evidence of agency of person named, in postal fraud order proceeding; Canadian Uniform Evidence Act, Draft of 1936, printed copy of newspaper prima facie evidence that notices or advertisements were authorized.

Paragraph (7). Several factors justify dispensing with preliminary proof of genuineness of commercial and mercantile labels and the like. The risk of forgery is minimal. Trademark infringement involves serious penalties. Great efforts are devoted to inducing the public to buy in reliance on brand names, and substantial protection is given them. Hence the fairness of this treatment finds recognition in the cases. Curtiss Candy Co. v. Johnson, 163 Miss. 426 (1932), Baby Ruth candy bar; Doyle v. Continental Baking Co., 262 Mass. 516 (1928), loaf of bread; Weiner v. Mager & Throne, Inc., 3 N.Y.S.2d 918 (1938), same. And see W.Va.Code 1966, § 47-3-5, trade-mark on bottle prima facie evidence of ownership. *Contra*, Keegan v. Green Giant Co., 150 Me. 283 (1954); Murphy v. Campbell Soup Co., 62 F.2d 564 (1st Cir. 1933). Cattle brands have received similar acceptance in the western states. Rev.Code Mont.1947, § 46-606, State v. Wolfley, 75 Kan. 406 (1907); Annot., 11 L.R.A.(N.S.) 87. Inscriptions on trains and vehicles are held to be prima facie evidence of ownership or control. Pittsburgh, Ft. W. & C. Ry. v. Callaghan, 157 Ill. 406 (1895); 9 Wigmore § 2510a. See also the provision of 19 U.S.C. § 1615(2) that marks, labels, brands, or stamps indicating foreign origin are prima facie evidence of foreign origin of merchandise.

Paragraph (8). In virtually every state, acknowledged title documents are receivable in evidence without further proof. Statutes are collected in 5 Wigmore § 1676. If this authentication suffices for documents of the importance of those affecting titles, logic scarcely permits denying this method when other kinds of documents are involved. Instances of broadly inclusive statutes are California Evidence Code § 1451 and N.Y.CPLR 4538, McKinney's Consol.Laws 1963.

Paragraph (9). Issues of the authenticity of commercial paper in federal courts will usually arise in diversity cases, will involve an element of a cause of action or defense, and with respect to presumptions and burden of proof will be controlled by Erie Railroad Co. v. Tompkins, 304 U.S. 64 (1938). Rule 302, *supra*. There may, however, be questions of authenticity involving lesser segments of a case or the case may be one governed by federal common law. Clearfield Trust Co. v. United States, 318 U.S. 363 (1943). Cf. United States v. Yazell, 382 U.S. 341 (1966). In these situations, resort to the useful authentication provisions of the Uniform Commercial Code is provided for. While the phrasing is in terms of "general commercial law," in order to avoid the potential complications inherent in borrowing local statutes, today one would have difficulty in determining the general commercial law without referring to the Code. See Williams v. Walker-Thomas Furniture Co., 350 F.2d 445 (1965). Pertinent Code provisions are sections 1-202, 3-307, and 3-510, dealing with third-party documents, signatures on negotiable instruments, protests, and statements of dishonor.

Paragraph (10). The paragraph continues in effect dispensations with preliminary proof of genuineness provided in various Acts of Congress. See, for example, 10 U.S.C. § 936, signature, without seal, together with title, prima facie evidence of authenticity of acts of certain military personnel who are given notarial powers; 15 U.S.C. § 77f(a), signature on SEC registration presumed genuine; 26 U.S.C. § 6064, signature to tax return prima facie genuine.

REPORT OF HOUSE COMMITTEE ON THE JUDICIARY

Rule 902(8). Rule 902(8) as submitted by the Court referred to certificates of acknowledgment "under the hand and seal of" a notary public or other officer authorized by law to take acknowledgments. The Committee amended the Rule to eliminate the requirement, believed to be inconsistent with the law in some States, that a notary public must affix a seal to a document acknowledged before him. As amended the Rule merely requires that the document be executed in the manner prescribed by State law.

Rule 902(9). The Committee approved Rule 902(9) as submitted by the Court. With respect to the meaning of the phrase "general commercial law", the Committee intends that the Uniform Commercial Code, which has been adopted in virtually every State, will be followed generally, but that federal commercial law will apply where federal commercial paper is involved. See *Clearfield Trust Co. v. United States*, 318 U.S. 363 (1943). Further, in those instances in which the issues are governed by *Erie R. Co. v.*

Tompkins, 304 U.S. 64 (1938), State law will apply irrespective of whether it is the Uniform Commercial Code.

ADVISORY COMMITTEE'S NOTE (2000 AMENDMENT)

The amendment adds two new paragraphs to the rule on self-authentication. It sets forth a procedure by which parties can authenticate certain records of regularly conducted activity, other than through the testimony of a foundation witness. See the amendment to Rule 803(6). 18 U.S.C. § 3505 currently provides a means for certifying foreign records of regularly conducted activity in criminal cases, and this amendment is intended to establish a similar procedure for domestic records, and for foreign records offered in civil cases.

A declaration that satisfies 28 U.S.C. § 1746 would satisfy the declaration requirement of Rule 902(11), as would any comparable certification under oath.

The notice requirement in Rules 902(11) and (12) is intended to give the opponent of the evidence a full opportunity to test the adequacy of the foundation set forth in the declaration.

ADVISORY COMMITTEE'S NOTE (2011 AMENDMENT)

The language of Rule 902 has been amended as part of the restyling of the Evidence Rules to make them more easily understood and to make style and terminology consistent throughout the rules. These changes are intended to be stylistic only. There is no intent to change any result in any ruling on evidence admissibility.

Florida Stat. § 90.902. Self-Authentication

Extrinsic evidence of authenticity as a condition precedent to admissibility is not required for:

(1) A document bearing:

(a) A seal purporting to be that of the United States or any state, district, commonwealth, territory, or insular possession thereof; the Panama Canal Zone; the Trust Territory of the Pacific Islands; or a court, political subdivision, department, officer, or agency of any of them; and

(b) A signature by the custodian of the document attesting to the authenticity of the seal.

(2) A document not bearing a seal but purporting to bear a signature of an officer or employee of any entity listed in subsection (1), affixed in the officer's or employee's official capacity.

(3) An official foreign document, record, or entry that is:

(a) Executed or attested to by a person in the person's official capacity authorized by the laws of a foreign country to make the execution or attestation; and

(b) Accompanied by a final certification, as provided herein, of the genuineness of the signature and official position of:

1. The executing person; or

2. Any foreign official whose certificate of genuineness of signature and official position relates to the execution or attestation or is in a chain of certificates of genuineness of signature and official position relating to the execution or attestation.

The final certification may be made by a secretary of an embassy or legation, consul general, consul, vice consul, or consular agent of the United States or a diplomatic or consular official of the foreign country assigned or accredited to the United States. When the parties receive reasonable opportunity to investigate the authenticity and accuracy of official foreign documents, the court may order that they be treated as presumptively authentic without final certification or permit them in evidence by an attested summary with or without final certification.

(4) A copy of an official public record, report, or entry, or of a document authorized by law to be recorded or filed and actually recorded or filed in a public office, including data compilations in any form, certified as correct by the custodian or other person authorized to make the certification by certificate complying with subsection (1), subsection (2), or subsection (3) or complying with any act of the Legislature or rule adopted by the Supreme Court.

(5) Books, pamphlets, or other publications purporting to be issued by a governmental authority.

(6) Printed materials purporting to be newspapers or periodicals.

(7) Inscriptions, signs, tags, or labels purporting to have been affixed in the course of business and indicating ownership, control, or origin.

(8) Commercial papers and signatures thereon and documents relating to them, to the extent provided in the Uniform Commercial Code.

(9) Any signature, document, or other matter declared by the Legislature to be presumptively or prima facie genuine or authentic.

(10) Any document properly certified under the law of the jurisdiction where the certification is made.

(11) An original or a duplicate of evidence that would be admissible under s. 90.803(6), which is maintained in a foreign country or domestic location and is accompanied by a certification or declaration from the custodian of the records or another qualified person certifying or declaring that the record:

(a) Was made at or near the time of the occurrence of the matters set forth by, or from information transmitted by, a person having knowledge of those matters;

(b) Was kept in the course of the regularly conducted activity; and

(c) Was made as a regular practice in the course of the regularly conducted activity,

provided that falsely making such a certification or declaration would subject the maker to criminal penalty under the laws of the foreign or domestic location in which the certification or declaration was signed.

SPONSORS' NOTE (1976 ENACTMENT)

A number of exceptions to the requirement of authentication have been recognized in statutes and case law over the years. Based on experience, policy considerations and the unlikelihood of forgery, the law has come to recognize that the genuineness of certain writings could be safely presumed, at least for the purposes of admission into evidence. Under this section, the documents described, if otherwise admissible, will be admitted without proof of genuineness beyond what is purported on the face of the document itself. However, the opposing party is not foreclosed from challenging the authenticity of the document once it is admitted in evidence. This procedure dispenses with the necessity of proof of authenticity when there is no real dispute as to such authenticity, while assuring the parties the right to contest the authenticity when there is a real dispute.

<u>Subsection (1)</u> This subsection assumes, for the purposes of admissibility, the genuineness of a public document bearing an official seal and a signature. At common law, the genuineness of a document bearing an official seal was established simply by production of the document for inspection. Note, <u>Authentication and the Best Evidence Rule Under the Federal Rules of Evidence</u>, 16 Wayne L. Rev. 195, 210 (1969). In <u>Groover v. Coffee</u>, 19 Fla. 61, 71 (1882), in sustaining the authenticity of certain land grants bearing the Georgia Governor's seal, the Supreme Court noted that: "Courts recognize, without other proof than inspection, the seals of other states and nations." Such a rule finds justification in the inconvenience of furnishing further proof, and the fact that forgery is a crime and detection is fairly easy and certain. 7 Wigmore, <u>Evidence</u> § 2161, p. 638 (3rd ed. 1940).

The theory of judicial notice alone may satisfy the requirement of authentication of documents bearing seals of this state. See § 90.202(13). However, this subsection provides for the authentication of documents bearing the seal of a court, political subdivision, department, office, or agency of this state when accompanied by a signature purporting to be an attestation of the seal. The design of seals of foreign jurisdictions would frequently be unfamiliar to the judge, and the justification for the presumption of genuineness lies in the additional requirement of a signature. In this situation, the impression of the seal is sufficient to satisfy the first general requirement of authenticity, that the document was genuinely executed by the purported signer in his official capacity. Judicial notice that the signed holds the office that he claims completes the authentication. 7 Wigmore, <u>Evidence</u> § 2161, p. 639 (3rd ed. 1940).

While the rule is most often recognized with respect to certified copies, see Fla. Stat. § 92.12 (copies of records of public officers), it is broadly applied. See, e.g., Fla.Stat. § 92.18 (certificate of official acts by state officers); Fla.Stat. § 92.20 (certificates relating to agricultural products issued under seal of United States governmental departments).

For similar rules, see Calif. Evid. Code § 1452 (official seals presumed genuine); Fed. Rule Evid. 902(1).

<u>Subsection (2)</u> This subsection raises a presumption of genuineness of purported official signatures in the absence of an official seal. This rule conflicts with several older Florida cases which held that the genuineness of a document bearing only an official signature must be proved by extrinsic evidence. For example, in <u>Cobb v. State</u>, 82 Fla. 233, 89 So. 417 (1921) the court ruled inadmissible a marriage certificate purportedly from a New York public official, signed in his official capacity:

> We think the trial court erred in admitting this paper because of a total lack of proof of its authenticity. It is not even dignified by an official seal....[T]here is nothing outside the assertions of the paper itself...to identify the authenticity or even the genuineness of the paper as being bona fide what it purports to be on its face.

See <u>Yellow River R.R. v. Harris</u>, 35 Fla. 385, 17 So. 568 (1895) (signed receipt from United States Land Office not self-verifying).

More recently exceptions to this requirement of proof have been created by statute. See Fla. Stat. § 92.32 (official records signed by United States officer or employee presumed genuine).

Justification for the older rule was expressed in <u>Yellow River R.R.</u>, <u>supra</u> at 569, "were the rule otherwise, a forged receipt in proper form might be fraudulently made to answer the same purpose as the genuine article." See also 7 Wigmore, <u>Evidence</u> § 2167 (3rd ed. 1940). While fear of fraud remains a valid concern of the law of authentication, see comment to Section 90.901, the diminished importance of the seal and the improved methods of detecting forgeries seem to justify the more permissive rule. See Calif. Evid. Code § 1453 (domestic official signature presumed genuine and authorized). Prop. Fed. Rule Evid. 902(2) provides for authentication of a public document not under seal only when a public officer, who has a seal and official duties in the same district as the person who signed the document, certifies under seal that the signer has the official capacity and that the signature is genuine.

Subsection (3) This subsection restates, with some expansion, existing § 92.032 of the Florida Statutes, the existing procedure for authentication of foreign documents. An official foreign document is self-authenticating when it is attested by a person in his official capacity who is authorized by the laws of the foreign country to make the attestation and is accompanied by a "final certification" of the authority of the attesting foreign official by a United States foreign service officer or an official of the foreign country who is assigned to the United States. Although a United States foreign service officer can certify the genuineness of signature and official position of the executing or attesting person, this subsection recognizes that he may not be able to certify to the official position and signature of the particular foreign official. Accordingly, the original signature of that foreign official is permitted to be certified by a higher foreign official, whose signature can in turn be certified by a still higher official, and such certification can be continued until a foreign official is reached as to whom the United States foreign service officer has adequate information upon which to base his final certification.

The § 92.032 requirement of a seal by the certifying officer has been eliminated, for the reasons stated in Section 90.902(2). Under this subsection, a certificate of genuineness may be made by a diplomatic officer of the foreign nation, if he is assigned to the United States, as well as by a U.S. foreign service officer. The signature of such an official would be as easily verifiable as the signature of a United States official.

Finally, the judge may order that uncertified documents be treated as presumptively genuine, where all parties have had a chance to investigate their authenticity. Cf. Fla. R. Civ. Pro. 1.200 (pre-trial evidentiary arguments). This provision, as well as the provision for summaries, in the event of voluminous records, see 4 Wigmore, Evidence § 1230 (Chadbourn rev. 1972), is a matter of convenience.

For similar provisions, see Calif. Evid. Code § 1454; Fed. Rule Evid. 902(3).

Subsection (4) This subsection provides for self-authentication of copies of public records, including data compilations, when the document is authorized by law to be recorded or filed and is actually filed or recorded in a public office and is certified by the custodian or authorized person as a true and correct copy. The copy itself becomes, upon certification, a public document and to be authenticated the certificate must comply with either subsection (1), (2) or (3).

The presumption of genuineness under this subsection applies only to copies of public records, reports and recorded documents authorized by law to be recorded and filed and actually recorded and filed in a public office and does not apply to copies of public documents in general. Consequently, some public documents, for example, a register of deeds, may not be authenticated under this subsection but when presented in original form may be authenticated under subsection (1), (2) or (3). Also, certified copies of most corporate records are not covered by this subsection since they are not required by law to be filed. Since certification of a copy eliminates the need for proof of the genuineness of the original, 5 Wigmore, Evidence § 1677, p. 745 (3rd ed. 1940), the applicability of this subsection is limited to those public documents which contain safeguards as to their authenticity, such as recorded documents which have been proved or acknowledged. Copies of public documents not included in subsection must be authenticated by other means. See, e.g., Section 90.901.

This provision is similar to existing Fla. Stat. § 92.32, which presumes the authenticity of a certified copy of official reports and records signed by an authorized official or employee of the United States government. That statute is extended by this subsection to recorded documents, and includes all political subdivisions within the United States.

See Fed. Rule Evid. 902(4).

Subsection (5) Publications purporting to be made under authority of government have long been self-authenticating and exempt from the requirement of preliminary proof of authenticity. For example, in Thiesen v. Gulf, F. & A.R.R., 75 Fla. 28, 68, 78 So. 491, 503 (1917) (on rehearing), the Florida Supreme Court stated:

> The American State Papers...is a publication under the authority of the Senate of the United States...these documents are received in evidence without other proof of their authenticity than the published volume.

While the rule has been applied by statute to published volumes of statutes and reports of court decisions, see Fla. Stat. §§ 92.01-92.03, several cases have extended the principle to a variety of government publications. See, e.g., State ex rel. Board of Commissioners v. Helseth, 104 Fla. 208, 140 So. 655 (1932) (legislative journals); Freimuth v. State, 249 So.2d 754 (Fla. 1st Dist. 1971) (Federal Register). See Fed. Rule Evid. 902(5).

Subsection (6) This subsection provides that printed materials purporting to be newspapers or periodicals shall be presumed authentic. The unlikelihood of forgery and the relative ease with which forged publications could be refuted by the publisher serve to justify the admission of printed matter in evidence without further proof. The presumption involved here is actually quite narrow, i.e., a purported copy of a newspaper or periodical is presumed genuine for purposes of admission into evidence. However, the question of authorship and responsibility for the items contained in the publication may remain. Cf. Fla. Stat. § 817.41 (presumption that the person receiving benefits of false advertising is responsible therefor). See Brown, Authentication and the Contents of Writings, 1969 Law & Social Order 611, 632. See Fed. Rule Evid. 902(6).

Subsection (7) This subsection extends the presumption to trade inscriptions and the like. A number of justifications exist for this provision: the risk of forgery is minimal, trademark infringement is a crime, great efforts are devoted to inducing the public to buy in reliance on brand names and substantial protection is given them.

Generally, the question has arisen in products liability cases. In view of modern mass-marketing techniques, the better rule seems to place the burden on the registrant of the trademark or label to disprove his connections with the product. Such a rule not only draws the conclusion from everyday experience, but often places the burden of proof on the party best able to refute the presumption. See Brown, Authentication and the Contents of Writings, 1969 Law & Social Order 611, 629.

See Fed. Rule Evid. 902(7).

Subsection (8) Florida's Uniform Commercial Code, Fla. Stat. ch. 671-87, provides in several instances for self-authentication of certain commercial papers. See, e.g., Fla. Stat. § 671.202 (authorized third-party document is prima facie evidence of its own authenticity).

This subsection makes clear that established commercial practices for authentication are not foreclosed by this code of evidence as an appropriate means of proof of genuineness.

See Fed. Rule Evid. 902(9).

Subsection (9) This subsection continues in effect existing statutory provisions relating to self-authentication. See, e.g., Fla. Stat. § 90.01 (acknowledgment authenticated by seal and signature of certain persons); Fla. Stat. § 372.051 (copies of certain records of the Game and Fresh Water Fish Commission certified by the director under his seal are admissible without further authentication).

COMMENTARY ON FEDERAL AND FLORIDA RULE DIFFERENCES

FLORIDA AND FEDERAL EVIDENCE RULES

Florida Stat. § 90.902 and its federal counterpart, Federal Rule 902, provide that certain types of evidence are deemed to be "self-authenticating," meaning that extrinsic evidence of authenticity is not required as a condition precedent to admissibility. Nonetheless, as with evidence that is not self-authenticating, the opposing party is free to challenge authenticity before the trier of fact, who ultimately determines authenticity. *See* Advisory Committee's Note to FED. R. EVID. 902; Sponsors' Note to FLA. STAT. § 90.902.

Both the federal and Florida rules deem to be self-authenticating domestic public documents under seal of the United States or any state, district, commonwealth, territory, or insular possession of the United States (as well as the Panama Canal Zone and the Trust Territory of the Pacific Islands), including any political subdivision, department, officer, or agency thereof. *See* FED. R. EVID. 902(1); FLA. STAT. § 90.902(1). Unlike the federal rule, the Florida rule specifies that it covers documents from any "court" of any of those entities, but the federal rule has been interpreted to extend to such documents as well. *See AMFAC Distribution Corp. v. Harrelson*, 842 F.2d 304, 306-07 & n.5 (11th Cir. 1988). There thus appear to be no substantive differences between the two rules.

Both the federal and Florida rules provide that under certain circumstances, domestic public documents of the entities set forth in the previous paragraph can be self-authenticating even if not under seal. The Florida rule provides that such documents are self-authenticating if they purport to bear a signature of an officer or employee of the entity affixed in his official capacity. *See* FLA. STAT. § 90.902(2). The federal rule, by contrast, is less permissive, deeming such documents to be self-authenticating only if a public officer having a seal and official duties in the district or political subdivision certifies under seal that the signer has official capacity and that the signature is genuine. *See* FED. R. EVID. 902(2); Sponsors' Note to FLA. STAT. § 90.902(2).

Both the federal and Florida rules provide for foreign public documents to be self-authenticating under certain circumstances. Under both rules, a document purporting to be executed or attested in an official capacity by a person authorized by the laws of a foreign country to make the execution or attestation is self-authenticating if accompanied by a final certification—made by certain enumerated diplomatic officials—of the genuineness of the signature and official position of the executing or attesting person or of any foreign official whose certificate of genuineness of signature and official position relates to the execution or attestation or is in a chain of certificates of genuineness of signature and official position relating to the execution or attestation. *See* FED. R. EVID. 902(3); FLA. STAT. § 90.902(3). *See also U.S. v. Deverso*, 518 F.3d 1250, 1256 (11th Cir. 2008) (describing Federal Rule 902(3) as containing two requirements: there must be some indication that the *document* is what it purports to be, and there must be some indication that the *official* vouching for the document is who he purports to be). Both rules give the trial court discretion to treat such a document as self-authenticating even in the absence of a final certification if reasonable opportunity has been given to all parties to investigate the authenticity and accuracy of the document. *See* FED. R. EVID. 902(3); FLA. STAT. § 90.902(3). There are no substantive differences between the two rules.

Both the federal and Florida rules provide that a copy of an official public record, report, or entry, or of a document authorized by law to be recorded or filed and actually recorded or filed in a public office, is self-authenticating if certified as correct by the custodian or other person authorized to make the certification by a certificate that complies with the requirements of one of the above-enumerated subsections or with an applicable statute or court rule. *See* FED. R. EVID. 902(4); FLA. STAT. § 90.902(4). There are no substantive differences between the two rules.

Both the federal and Florida rules deem to be self-authenticating books, pamphlets, or other publications purporting to be issued by a governmental authority; printed materials purporting to be newspapers or periodicals; and inscriptions, signs, tags, or labels purporting to have been affixed in the course of business and indicating ownership, control, or origin. *See* FED. R. EVID. 902(5)-(7); FLA. STAT. § 90.902(5)-(7). There are no substantive differences between the two rules for these types of evidence.

The federal rule provides that a document accompanied by a certificate of acknowledgement executed in the manner provided by law by a notary public or other officer authorized by law to take acknowledgments is self-authenticating. *See* FED. R. EVID. 902(8). An analogous, albeit somewhat more broadly worded provision under Florida law deems such documents to be self-authenticating. *See* FLA. STAT. § 90.902(10) (deeming self-authenticating "[a]ny document properly certified under the law of the jurisdiction where the certification is made.").

Both the Florida and federal rules deem self-authenticating commercial paper, signatures thereon, and documents relating thereto to the extent provided by law. *See* FED. R. EVID. 902(9); FLA. STAT. § 90.902(8). The Florida rule refers to the Uniform Commercial Code while the federal rule refers to "general commercial law," but the latter phrase is understood to be a reference to the Uniform Commercial Code. *See U.S. v. Varner*, 13 F.3d 1503, 1507 (11th Cir. 1994). There are no substantive differences between the two rules for these types of evidence.

Both the Florida and federal rules deem self-authenticating any signature, document, or other matter declared by Congress (or in the case of the Florida rule, the Legislature) to be presumptively or prima facie genuine or authentic. *See* FED. R. EVID. 902(10); FLA. STAT. § 90.902(9). There are no substantive differences between the two rules for these types of evidence, save for differences in the legislative acts incorporated by reference.

Both the Florida and federal rules provide that the original or duplicate of business records admissible under the exceptions to the hearsay rule set forth in Federal Rule 803(6) and Florida Stat. § 90.803(6) are self-authenticating if accompanied by a certification by the custodian of records or other qualified witness of a business setting forth the foundational requirements for admitting such documents as business records. *See* FED. R. EVID. 902(11)-(12); FLA. STAT. § 90.902(11). The federal rule treats domestic and foreign business records differently, requiring that the former by certified in any manner complying with a federal statute or rule prescribed by the Supreme Court (which would include a declaration that satisfies 28 U.S.C. § 1746, *see* Advisory Committee's Note to 2000 Amendment to FED. R. EVID. 902), while the latter must be signed in a manner that, if falsely made, would subject the maker to criminal penalty under the laws of the country where signed. *Compare* FED. R. EVID. 902(11), *with* FED. R. EVID. 902(12). The Florida rule, by contrast, addresses both domestic and foreign documents in a single provision, requiring that falsely making the certification or declaration would subject the maker to criminal penalty under the laws of the foreign or domestic location where signed. *See* FLA. STAT. § 90.902(11). Although the federal rules do not cover foreign records offered in criminal cases, those are covered by a separate statutory provision. *See* Advisory Committee's Note to 2000 Amendment to FED. R. EVID. 902 (citing 18 U.S.C. § 3505). The federal provisions require that a party intending to invoke them provide written notice to all adverse parties and make the record and declaration available for inspection sufficiently in advance of their offer into evidence to provide the adverse parties a fair opportunity to challenge them. *See* FED. R. EVID. 902(11)-(12). The notice requirement under the Florida rule is contained in Florida Stat. § 90.803(6)(c), which provides a similar notice requirement for domestic records but for foreign records requires notice as soon after arraignment as possible or, in a civil case, 60 days before trial. *See* FLA. STAT. § 90.803(6)(c). Moreover, the Florida rule requires that a party opposing admission so move pre-trial. *See id.*

Federal Rule 903. Subscribing Witness's Testimony

A subscribing witness's testimony is necessary to authenticate a writing only if required by the law of the jurisdiction that governs its validity.

ADVISORY COMMITTEE'S NOTE

The common law required that attesting witnesses be produced or accounted for. Today the requirement has generally been abolished except with respect to documents which must be attested to be valid, e.g.

wills in some states. McCormick § 188. Uniform Rule 71; California Evidence Code § 1411; Kansas Code of Civil Procedure § 60-468; New Jersey Evidence Rule 71; New York CPLR Rule 4537.

ADVISORY COMMITTEE'S NOTE (2011 AMENDMENT)

The language of Rule 903 has been amended as part of the restyling of the Evidence Rules to make them more easily understood and to make style and terminology consistent throughout the rules. These changes are intended to be stylistic only. There is no intent to change any result in any ruling on evidence admissibility.

Florida Stat. § 90.903. Testimony of Subscribing Witness Unnecessary

The testimony of a subscribing witness is not necessary to authenticate a writing unless the statute requiring attestation requires it.

SPONSORS' NOTE (1976 ENACTMENT)

This section provides that the testimony of attesting witnesses is not necessary unless specifically provided by statute. In Windle v. Sibold, 241 So.2d 165 (Fla. 4th Dist. 1970), the court said:

> Appellees contend that there is still in effect in this state the common law principle that when a written instrument attested by a subscribing witness is offered as evidence, its execution must be proved by such subscribing witness if he is available as a witness and is competent to testify....[I]t is our view that this common law rule was long ago abolished as part of the adjective law of this state.

While the common law required that attesting witnesses be produced or accounted for, McCormick, Evidence § 220, p. 545 (2nd ed. 1972), the requirement has generally been abolished. See Calif. Evid. Code § 1411; Kansas Code of Civ. Pro. § 60-468; Uniform Rule of Evid. 71; Fed. Rule Evid. 903.

This section does not eliminate the requirement of the testimony of a subscribing witness when a statute specifically requires it. See, e.g., Fla. Stat. § 732.24 (proof of wills).

COMMENTARY ON FEDERAL AND FLORIDA RULE DIFFERENCES

Florida Stat. § 90.903 and its federal counterpart, Federal Rule 903, provide that when an attested writing (such as a will) is offered into evidence, it is not necessary to call the subscribing witnesses (or account for their absence) to authenticate the document unless specifically required by the substantive law that governs the dispute. In this regard, both the federal and Florida rules represent a break from the common law. See Advisory Committee's Note to FED. R. EVID. 903; Sponsors' Note to FLA. STAT. § 90.903.

Florida Stat. § 90.91. Photographs of Property Wrongfully Taken; Use in Prosecution, Procedure; Return of Property to Owner

In any prosecution for a crime involving the wrongful taking of property, a photograph of the property alleged to have been wrongfully taken may be deemed competent evidence of such property and may be admissible in the prosecution to the same extent as if such property were introduced as evidence. Such photograph shall bear a written description of the property alleged to have been wrongfully taken, the name of the owner of the property, the location where the alleged wrongful taking occurred, the name of the investigating law enforcement officer, the date the photograph was taken, and the name of the photographer. Such writing shall be made under oath by the investigating law enforcement officer, and the photograph shall be identified by the signature of the photographer. Upon the filing of such photograph and writing with the law enforcement authority or court holding such property as evidence, the property may be returned to the owner from whom the property was taken.

COMMENTARY ON FEDERAL AND FLORIDA RULE DIFFERENCES

Florida Stat. § 90.91 provides that, in a prosecution for a crime involving the wrongful taking of property, a photograph of the property alleged to have been wrongfully taken is competent evidence of the property and is admissible to the same extent as if the property itself were introduced in evidence. To be admissible under this section, the photograph must bear a written description of the property allegedly taken, the location where it occurred, the name of the investigating law enforcement officer, the date the photograph was taken, and the name of the photographer. *See* FLA. STAT. § 90.91. The writing must be made under oath by the investigating officer, and the photograph must be signed by the photographer. *Id.* The purpose of the provision is to make it possible to return stolen property to its rightful owner as quickly as possible, rather than requiring that she wait until the end of trial and appellate proceedings to get her property back. *See Thomas v. State*, 568 So. 2d 92, 93 (Fla. 2d DCA 1990).

Under Florida law, photographs can usually be authenticated merely by calling *any* witness who has knowledge that the photograph is a fair and accurate representation of what it depicts; there is no requirement as a general rule that the photographer herself attest to its accuracy. *See Bryant v. State*, 810 So. 2d 532, 536 (Fla. 1st DCA 2002). Thus, photographs admitted in criminal prosecutions for the wrongful taking of property in accordance with this provision are subject to much more stringent authentication requirements than are photographs generally. *See State v. Hyatt*, 690 So. 2d 677, 678 n.2 (Fla. 3d DCA 1997).

There is no analogous provision in the federal rules of evidence. Under the federal rules, in a prosecution for the wrongful taking of property, a photograph of stolen property can, like photographs generally, be authenticated by calling *any* witness who has knowledge that the photograph is a fair and accurate representation of what it depicts. *See People of Terr. of Guam v. Ojeda*, 758 F.2d 403, 407-08 (9th Cir. 1985). Moreover, the best evidence rule does not compel production of the stolen property itself, as that rule applies only to writings, recordings, and photographs, not to chattels. *See id.* at 407.

ARTICLE X. CONTENTS OF WRITINGS, RECORDINGS, AND PHOTOGRAPHS

Federal Rule	Florida Stat. §	Description
1001	90.951	Definitions That Apply to This Article
1002	90.952	Requirement of the Original
1003	90.953	Admissibility of Duplicates
1004	90.954	Admissibility of Other Evidence of Content
1005	90.955	Copies of Public Records to Prove Content
1006	90.956	Summaries to Prove Content
1007	90.957	Testimony or Statement of a Party to Prove Content
1008	90.958	Functions of the Court and Jury

Federal Rule 1001. Definitions That Apply to This Article

In this article:

(a) A "writing" consists of letters, words, numbers, or their equivalent set down in any form.

(b) A "recording" consists of letters, words, numbers, or their equivalent recorded in any manner.

(c) A "photograph" means a photographic image or its equivalent stored in any form.

(d) An "original" of a writing or recording means the writing or recording itself or any counterpart intended to have the same effect by the person who executed or issued it. For electronically stored information, "original" means any printout — or other output readable by sight — if it accurately reflects the information. An "original" of a photograph includes the negative or a print from it.

(e) A "duplicate" means a counterpart produced by a mechanical, photographic, chemical, electronic, or other equivalent process or technique that accurately reproduces the original.

ADVISORY COMMITTEE'S NOTE

In an earlier day, when discovery and other related procedures were strictly limited, the misleading named "best evidence rule" afforded substantial guarantees against inaccuracies and fraud by its insistence upon production of original documents. The great enlargement of the scope of discovery and related procedures in recent times has measurably reduced the need for the rule. Nevertheless important areas of usefulness persist: discovery of documents outside the jurisdiction may require substantial outlay of time and money; the unanticipated document may not practically be discoverable; criminal cases have built-in limitations on discovery. Cleary and Strong, The Best Evidence Rule: An Evaluation in Context, 51 Iowa L.Rev. 825 (1966).

Paragraph[s (a) and (b)]. Traditionally the rule requiring the original centered upon accumulations of data and expressions affecting legal relations set forth in words and figures. This meant that the rule was one essentially related to writings. Present day techniques have expanded methods of storing data, yet the essential form which the information ultimately assumes for usable purposes is words and figures. Hence the considerations underlying the rule dictate its expansion to include computers, photographic systems, and other modern developments.

Paragraph ([d]). In most instances, what is an original will be self-evident and further refinement will be unnecessary. However, in some instances particularized definition is required. A carbon copy of a contract executed in duplicate becomes an original, as does a sales ticket carbon copy given to a customer. While strictly speaking the original of a photograph might be thought to be only the negative, practicality and common usage require that any print from the negative be regarded as an original. Similarly, practicality and usage confer the status of original upon any computer printout. Transport Indemnity Co. v. Seib, 178 Neb. 253 (1965).

Paragraph ([e]). The definition describes "copies" produced by methods possessing an accuracy which virtually eliminates the possibility of error. Copies thus produced are given the status of originals in large measure by Rule 1003, *infra*. Copies subsequently produced manually, whether handwritten or typed, are not within the definition. It should be noted that what is an original for some purposes may be a duplicate for others. Thus a bank's microfilm record of checks cleared is the original as a record. However, a print offered as a copy of a check whose contents are in controversy is a duplicate. This result is substantially consistent with 28 U.S.C. § 1732(b). Compare 26 U.S.C. § 7513(c), giving full status as originals to photographic reproductions of tax returns and other documents, made by authority of the Secretary of the Treasury, and 44 U.S.C. § 399(a), giving original status to photographic copies in the National Archives.

REPORT OF HOUSE COMMITTEE ON THE JUDICIARY

Rule 1001([c]). The Committee amended this Rule expressly to include "video tapes" in the definition of "photographs."

ADVISORY COMMITTEE'S NOTE (2011 AMENDMENT)

The language of Rule 1001 has been amended as part of the restyling of the Evidence Rules to make them more easily understood and to make style and terminology consistent throughout the rules. These changes are intended to be stylistic only. There is no intent to change any result in any ruling on evidence admissibility.

Florida Stat. § 90.951. Definitions

For purposes of this chapter:

(1) "Writings" and "recordings" include letters, words, or numbers, or their equivalent, set down by handwriting, typewriting, printing, photostating, photography, magnetic impulse, mechanical or electronic recording, or other form of data compilation, upon paper, wood, stone, recording tape, or other materials.

(2) "Photographs" include still photographs, X-ray films, videotapes, and motion pictures.

(3) An "original" of a writing or recording means the writing or recording itself, or any counterpart intended to have the same effect by a person executing or issuing it. An "original" of a photograph includes the negative or any print made from it. If data are stored in a computer or similar device, any printout or other output readable by sight and shown to reflect the data accurately is an "original."

(4) "Duplicate" includes:

(a) A counterpart produced by the same impression as the original, from the same matrix; by means of photography, including enlargements and miniatures; by mechanical or electronic rerecording; by chemical reproduction; or by other equivalent technique that accurately reproduces the original; or

(b) An executed carbon copy not intended by the parties to be an original.

SPONSORS' NOTE (1976 ENACTMENT)

This section sets forth the definitions to be used in the application of the "best evidence" rule, Sections 90.[952]-90.[958].

Although early Florida cases interpreted the concept of the "best evidence" or original document rule to mean that the highest degree of accessible proof must be produced, Orman v. Barnard, Adams & Co., 5 Fla. 528 (1854), that broad principle has been discredited and today the "best evidence" doctrine applies only to those cases when, in attempting to prove the contents of a writing, a party is required to produce the original writing. In re Mobilift Equipment, Inc., 415 F.2d 841 (5th Cir. 1969); Firestone Service Stores, Inc. v. Wynn, 131 Fla. 94, 179 So. 175 (1938). While the general expansion of discovery procedures and technical advances in the field of document processing and reproduction reduce the need for rigid adherence to the rule, some areas remain where the rule is useful and important, e.g., the document is not practically discoverable, the document is outside the jurisdiction resulting in the significant expenditure of time and money, and the document is unavailable due to the limited scope of discovery in criminal cases.

<u>Subsection (1)</u> Traditionally, the "best evidence" rule requirement of the production of the original concerned collections of materials expressing legal relations set forth in words and figures. This interpretation essentially confined the rule to matters related to writings. Although modern techniques utilize various methods to store data, the basic usable form remains one of words and figures. The definition of "writings" and "recordings," which is expanded in this subsection to reflect the increased use of computers, photographic systems and other modern techniques, is similar to and compatible with the general Florida definition of "writings," Fla.Stat. § 1.01 (1971) and the Florida definition of "writings" for use in the Uniform Commercial Code. Fla. Stat. § 671.201(46) (1971).

See Fed. Rule Evid. 1001(1).

<u>Subsection (2)</u> This definition of photographs attempts to include those items which permit the greatest and most flexible use of modern techniques. See Fed. Rule Evid. 1001(2).

<u>Subsection (3)</u> This subsection defines the term "original." In most cases, what is an original is either self-evident or easily determinable and usually does not require further elaboration. When a maker of a writing executes one or more copies at the same time with the intent to impart equal status to each, each of the copies so executed is an "original" both by this subsection and existing Florida law. <u>Lockwood v. L. & L. Freight Lines, Inc.</u>, 126 Fla. 474, 171 So. 236 (1936). While it is possible to consider the negative as the only original of a photograph, practicality and common usage require that any print from the negative be regarded as an original. Similarly, common usage requires that any computer printout be given status as an original. See Fed. Rule Evid. 1001(3).

<u>Subsection (4)</u> This subsection defines the term "duplicate" as being a copy which is so accurately reproduced as to eliminate almost every possibility of error. Manually reproduced copies, as by typing or handwriting, are excluded from the definition. Copies with such inherent accuracy to be included as duplicates are in large measure given the status of originals under the rule as set forth in Section 90.[953]. Florida has approved the use of the modern technology of making copies that are described in this subsection in the Uniform Photographic Copies of Business and Public Records as Evidence Act, Fla. Stat. § 92.35. This practice is consistent with federal procedures giving full status as originals to photographic reproductions of tax returns, 26 U.S.C. § 7513(c), and status as originals to photographic copies in the National Archives, 44 U.S.C. § 399(a). See Fed. Rule Evid. 1001(4).

COMMENTARY ON FEDERAL AND FLORIDA RULE DIFFERENCES

Florida Stat. § 90.951 and its federal counterpart, Federal Rule 1001, set forth the definitions of the terms used in the provisions of the best evidence rule.

Florida Stat. § 90.951(1) and Federal Rule 1001(a), (b) provide broad definitions of the words "writing" and "recording." Under both the Florida and federal rules, for example, information on a computer screen qualifies as a writing. Arguably, however, the Florida definition, through the addition of the phrase "upon paper, wood, stone, recording tape, or other materials," is broader than the federal rule. This is because under the federal rule, when one is dealing with a so-called inscribed chattel—an object with words on it, such as a tombstone, t-shirt, bottle, or the like—the trial court has discretion to decide whether to treat it as a "writing" (in which case it is subject to the best evidence rule) or a "chattel" (in which case it is not). *See U.S. v. Duffy*, 454 F.2d 809, 812 (5th Cir. 1972) (indicating that factors guiding discretion include the complexity of the writing and its centrality to the case). Because the Florida rule specifies that writings include things that appear upon "wood, stone...or other materials," it appears to clearly encompass inscribed chattels within the scope of the best evidence rule.

Florida Stat. § 90.951(2) and Federal Rule 1001(c) provide broad definitions of the word "photograph," defined to include a photographic image or its equivalent stored in any form, such as still photographs, X-ray films, videotapes, and motion pictures.

The definition of "original" is set forth in Florida Stat. § 90.951(3) and Federal Rule 1001(d). Both rules contemplate that there can be multiple originals of a document, defining the phrase to include not only a writing or recording itself, but also any counterpart intended to have the same effect, such as when a contract is executed in duplicate, triplicate, or quadruplicate. *See, e.g., Greater Kansas City Laborers Pension Fund v. Thummel*, 738 F.2d 926, 928 (8th Cir. 1984). Moreover, under both rules, an original of a photograph includes not just the negative but also any print made therefrom, and an original of data stored on a computer includes not just the data itself, but also any printout or other output visible by sight shown to accurately reflect the data.

The definition of "duplicate" is set forth in Florida Stat. § 90.951(4) and Federal Rule 1001(e). Under both rules, a reproduction made by mechanical or electronic means, such as by using a photocopier, is defined as a "duplicate." By contrast, a reproduction made manually—where, for example, a person looks at the original and types or writes out a copy of the same—is *not* considered a duplicate. *See O'Neal v. Bolling*, 409 So. 2d 1171, 1172 n.1 (Fla. 3d DCA 1982); Advisory Committee's Note to FED. R. EVID. 1001(e). Moreover, under both rules, a duplicate of a duplicate is a duplicate, such as a photocopy of a photocopy or a photocopy of a carbon copy. *See Fredericks v. Howell*, 426 So. 2d 1200, 1203 (Fla. 4th DCA 1983); *Lowery v. State*, 402 So. 2d 1287, 1289 (Fla. 5th DCA 1981); *U.S. v. Carroll*, 860 F.2d 500, 507 (1st Cir. 1988). And under both rules, a videotape or audiotape which is enhanced—such as through enlargement of selected images or adjustment of contrast, brightness, or volume—is deemed to be a duplicate. *See Bryant v. State*, 810 So.2d 532, 536-38 (Fla. 1st DCA 2002); *U.S. v. Seifert*, 351 F. Supp. 2d 926, 926-29 (D. Minn. 2005); *U.S. v. Johnson*, 362 F. Supp. 2d 1043, 1067 (N.D. Iowa 2005).

Federal Rule 1002. Requirement of the Original

An original writing, recording, or photograph is required in order to prove its content unless these rules or a federal statute provides otherwise.

ADVISORY COMMITTEE'S NOTE

The rule is the familiar one requiring production of the original of a document to prove its contents, expanded to include writings, recordings, and photographs, as defined in Rule [1001(a)-(c)], *supra*.

Application of the rule requires a resolution of the question whether contents are sought to be proved. Thus an event may be proved by nondocumentary evidence, even though a written record of it was made. If, however, the event is sought to be proved by the written record, the rule applies. For example, payment may be proved without producing the written receipt which was given. Earnings may be proved without producing books of account in which they are entered. McCormick § 198; 4 Wigmore § 1245. Nor does the rule apply to testimony that books or records have been examined and found not to contain any reference to a designated matter.

The assumption should not be made that the rule will come into operation on every occasion when use is made of a photograph in evidence. On the contrary, the rule will seldom apply to ordinary photographs. In most instances a party *wishes* to introduce the item and the question raised is the propriety of receiving it in evidence. Cases in which an offer is made of the testimony of a witness as to what he saw in a photograph or motion picture, without producing the same, are most unusual. The usual course is for a witness on the stand to identify the photograph or motion picture as a correct representation of events which he saw or of a scene with which he is familiar. In fact he adopts the picture as his testimony, or, in common parlance, uses the picture to illustrate his testimony. Under these circumstances, no effort is made to prove the contents of the picture, and the rule is inapplicable. Paradis, The Celluloid Witness, 37 U.Colo.L.Rev. 235, 249–251 (1965).

On occasion, however, situations arise in which contents are sought to be proved. Copyright, defamation, and invasion of privacy by photograph or motion picture falls in this category. Similarly as to situations in which the picture is offered as having independent probative value, e.g. automatic photograph of bank robber. See People v. Doggett, 83 Cal.App.2d 405 (1948), photograph of defendants engaged in indecent act; Mouser and Philbin, Photographic Evidence — Is There a Recognized Basis for Admissibility? 8 Hastings L.J. 310 (1957). The most commonly encountered of this latter group is of course, the X ray, with substantial authority calling for production of the original. Daniels v. Iowa City, 191 Iowa 811 (1921); Cellamare v. Third Acc. Transit Corp., 77 N.Y.S.2d 91 (1948); Patrick & Tilman v. Matkin, 154 Okl. 232 (1932); Mendoza v. Rivera, 78 P.R.R. 569 (1955).

It should be noted, however, that Rule 703, *supra*, allows an expert to give an opinion based on matters not in evidence, and the present rule must be read as being limited accordingly in its application. Hospital records which may be admitted as business records under Rule 803(6) commonly contain reports interpreting X rays by the staff radiologist, who qualifies as an expert, and these reports need not be excluded from the records by the instant rule.

The reference to Acts of Congress is made in view of such statutory provisions as 26 U.S.C. § 7513, photographic reproductions of tax returns and documents, made by authority of the Secretary of the Treasury, treated as originals, and 44 U.S.C. § 399(a), photographic copies in National Archives treated as originals.

ADVISORY COMMITTEE'S NOTE (2011 AMENDMENT)

The language of Rule 1002 has been amended as part of the restyling of the Evidence Rules to make them more easily understood and to make style and terminology consistent throughout the rules. These changes are intended to be stylistic only. There is no intent to change any result in any ruling on evidence admissibility.

Florida Stat. § 90.952. Requirement of Originals

Except as otherwise provided by statute, an original writing, recording, or photograph is required in order to prove the contents of the writing, recording, or photograph.

SPONSORS' NOTE (1976 ENACTMENT)

This section, which is a restatement of the "best evidence" rule requiring the production of the original document to prove its contents, expands the rule to include the originals of writings, recordings, and photographs as defined in Sections 90.[951](1) and (2). Apparently, this section restates the rule followed in Florida cases. In re Mobilift Equipment, Inc., 415 F.2d 841 (5th Cir. 1969); Firestone Service Stores v. Wynn, 131 Fla. 94, 179 So. 175 (1938). Similar provisions are contained in the Model Code of Evid. Rule 602 (1942) and the Calif. Evid. Code § 1500.

This section is not applicable on each occasion that a photograph is introduced as evidence. If it were, only the original photograph would be admissible and oral testimony of the witness could be excluded. In most cases a photograph is used to illustrate the testimony of a witness. Normally, the witness identifies a photograph, videotape, or motion picture as being a correct representation of that which he observed or a scene with which he is familiar and adopts it as his own testimony. Since no effort is made to prove the contents, the rule is inapplicable. An original is required rather than permitting a witness to testify to what he saw or heard, in those few cases when the contents are sought to be proved, e.g., a copyright infringement action based on a movie film or a defamation action.

Although the admissibility of X-rays under the "best evidence" rule has apparently never been ruled on directly by Florida courts, the implication is that such materials would be admissible and an expert would be permitted to testify as to what they show, etc. State ex rel. Carter v. Call, 64 Fla. 144, 59 So. 789 (1912); Williamson Candy Co. v. Lewis, 144 So.2d 522 (Fla. 3rd Dist. 1962). Presumably, Florida follows the weight of authority in other jurisdictions requiring production of the original X-ray, if an expert is going to testify as to what the X-ray disclosed. Daniels v. Iowa City, 191 Iowa 811, 183 N.W. 415 (1921); Patrick & Tillman v. Matkin[], 7 P.2d 414 (Okla. 1932). However, it should be noted that under Section 90.704 the basis of an expert's testimony does not have to be admissible.

The reference in this section to the statutory exception for the production of the original refers to the numerous statutory provisions providing for the admissibility of photographic or microphotographic copies without regard to the status of the original. This reference alerts the user that the documentary evidence he is seeking to introduce may not require production of the original. Examples of this exception include Fla. Stat. § 92.35 (Uniform Photographic Copies of Business and Public Records as Evidence Act), Fla. Stat. § 230.331(2) (district school records), and Fla. Stat. § 658.11(3) (banking and trust company records). A certificate of the secretary-treasurer of the Board of Dentistry as to the contents of certain records is made admissible by Fla. Stat. § 466.28. Additional statutory provisions are included in the comment to Section 90.[953].

See Fed. Rule Evid. 1002; Calif. Evid. Code § 1550. For a general discussion of the application of this section, see Brown, Authentication and Contents of Writings, 1969 Law & Soc.Order 611; Note, Authentication and the Best Evidence Rule Under the Federal Rules of Evidence, 16 Wayne L. Rev. 195 (1969).

COMMENTARY ON FEDERAL AND FLORIDA RULE DIFFERENCES

Florida Stat. § 90.952 and its federal counterpart, Federal Rule 1002, set forth the best evidence rule. Both the Florida and federal versions provide that when a party *seeks to prove the contents* of a writing, recording, or photograph, the original writing, recording, or photograph must be used, unless otherwise provided.

There are two different circumstances in which one is said to be seeking to prove the contents of a writing, and thus two circumstances in which the best evidence rule requires production of the original. First, when proof of the content of a writing, recording, or photograph is an element of the underlying substantive claim or defense. And second, when practical circumstances make it necessary to prove the content of a writing, recording, or photograph.

Both the Florida and federal versions of the best evidence rule require production of the original when proof of the content of a writing, recording, or photograph is an *element* of the underlying substantive claim or defense. Libel suits are an example of this: the underlying substantive law requires that the plaintiff be defamed in writing, and thus an element of the underlying offense requires proving that a writing was published by the defendant that contains defamatory matter about the plaintiff. *See* Advisory Committee's Note to FED. R. EVID. 1002; Sponsors' Note to FLA. STAT. § 90.952; *Harris v. State*, 755 So. 2d 766, 767 (Fla. 4th DCA 2000).

A best evidence rule objection also applies under Florida and federal law when a witness is called to testify about an event—such as a bank robbery—that he did not actually witness but learned about only by observing a videotape or audiotape of the same. Under those circumstances, an effort is being made to prove the contents of a recording, and thus the best evidence rule requires production of the recording itself. *See Russell v. State*, 844 So. 2d 725, 727-28 (Fla. 5th DCA 2003); *McKeehan v. State*, 838 So. 2d 1257, 1258-60 (Fla. 5th DCA 2003); *U.S. v. Bennett*, 363 F.3d 947, 953 (9th Cir. 2004). *See also Williams v. State*, 386 So. 2d 538, 540 (Fla. 1980) (testimony by a person as to what the victim of an attempted murder had written on a piece of paper barred by the best evidence rule). However, even if a videotape, audiotape, or other documentary evidence of an event exists, so long as a person witnessed the events firsthand, the best evidence rule does not prefer the documentary evidence of the event over the firsthand testimony of the witness. *Wimbledon Townhouse Condominium I, Ass'n, Inc. v. Wolfson*, 510 So. 2d 1106, 1107-08 (Fla. 4th DCA 1987); *U.S. v. Holland*, 223 Fed. Appx. 891, 898 (11th Cir. 2007); *U.S. v. Gonzales-Benitez*, 537 F.2d 1051, 1053-54 (9th Cir. 1976). Similarly, the best evidence rule is not implicated where a witness adopts a photograph or videotape when they are used to explain the testimony of the witness, such as when an eyewitness to an event testifies that a photograph or a videotape is a correct representation of the scene that he saw. *See Darling v. State*, 966 So. 2d 366, 383 (Fla. 2007); *Reid v. State*, 799 So. 2d 394, 398-99 (Fla. 4th DCA 2001); *Harris v. State*, 755 So. 2d 766, 767 (Fla. 4th DCA 2000); *Bennett*, 363 F.3d at 953.

One potential difference between the Florida and federal rules *may* be in the situation in which a person testifies that books or records have been examined and found *not* to contain any reference to a designated matter. While strictly speaking, one is *arguably* in that situation attempting to prove the contents of writings, the federal rule—based on language contained in the Advisory Committee's Note—is deemed inapplicable in that situation. *See U.S. v. Madera*, 574 F.2d 1320, 1323 n.3 (5th Cir. 1978); Advisory Committee's Note to FED. R. EVID. 1002. Neither the text of the Florida rule nor the Sponsors' Note to the same discusses this issue, nor is there any precedent on point.

Federal Rule 1003. Admissibility of Duplicates

A duplicate is admissible to the same extent as the original unless a genuine question is raised about the original's authenticity or the circumstances make it unfair to admit the duplicate.

ADVISORY COMMITTEE'S NOTE

When the only concern is with getting the words or other contents before the court with accuracy and precision, then a counterpart serves equally as well as the original, if the counterpart is the product of a method which insures accuracy and genuineness. By definition in Rule 1001([e]), *supra*, a "duplicate" possesses this character.

Therefore, if no genuine issue exists as to authenticity and no other reason exists for requiring the original, a duplicate is admissible under the rule. This position finds support in the decisions, Myrick v. United States, 332 F.2d 279 (5th Cir. 1964), no error in admitting photostatic copies of checks instead of original microfilm in absence of suggestion to trial judge that photostats were incorrect; Johns v. United States, 323 F.2d 421 (5th Cir. 1963), not error to admit concededly accurate tape recording made from original wire recording; Sauget v. Johnston, 315 F.2d 816 (9th Cir. 1963), not error to admit copy of agreement when opponent had original and did not on appeal claim any discrepancy. Other reasons for acquiring the original may be present when only a part of the original is reproduced and the remainder is needed for cross-examination or may disclose matters qualifying the part offered or otherwise useful to the opposing party. United States v. Alexander, 326 F.2d 736 (4th Cir. 1964). And see Toho Bussan Kaisha, Ltd. v. American President Lines, Ltd., 265 F.2d 418, 76 A.L.R.2d 1344 (2d Cir. 1959).

REPORT OF HOUSE COMMITTEE ON THE JUDICIARY

The Committee approved this Rule in the form submitted by the Court, with the expectation that the courts would be liberal in deciding that a "genuine question is raised as to the authenticity of the original."

ADVISORY COMMITTEE'S NOTE (2011 AMENDMENT)

The language of Rule 1003 has been amended as part of the restyling of the Evidence Rules to make them more easily understood and to make style and terminology consistent throughout the rules. These changes are intended to be stylistic only. There is no intent to change any result in any ruling on evidence admissibility.

Florida Stat. § 90.953. Admissibility of Duplicates

A duplicate is admissible to the same extent as an original, unless:

(1) The document or writing is a negotiable instrument as defined in s. 673.1041, a security as defined in s. 678.1021, or any other writing that evidences a right to the payment of money, is not itself a security agreement or lease, and is of a type that is transferred by delivery in the ordinary course of business with any necessary endorsement or assignment.

(2) A genuine question is raised about the authenticity of the original or any other document or writing.

(3) It is unfair, under the circumstance, to admit the duplicate in lieu of the original.

SPONSORS' NOTE (1976 ENACTMENT)

This section recognizes that when the primary goal of the party offering a duplicate is to place the words or other contents before the court, the duplicate serves his purpose as well as does the original. Apparently, existing Florida case law is in conflict with this section and allows the introduction of photographic copies only when the original is unavailable. Wicker v. Board of Public Instruction, 31 So.2d 635 (Fla. 1947). However, various existing statutory provisions provide photographs or microphotographs of records shall be treated as originals. See Fla. Stat. § 15.16 (records of Department of State); Fla. Stat. § 18.20(4) (records of State Treasurer); Fla. Stat. § 28.30 (certain vouchers and cancelled warrants of clerk of circuit court); Fla. Stat. § 229.781 (Department of Education records); Fla. Stat. §§ 320.833, 321.23 (records of Department of Highway Safety and Motor Vehicles).

The effect of this section, which is applicable only if the duplicate is produced by a method which insures accuracy and genuineness, see Section 90.[951](4), is to save time and expense previously wasted on producing the original when an equally reliable counterpart is at hand. Sufficient protections exist to insure that the interests of the adverse party are not compromised. The duplicates are not treated as originals when (1) a negotiable instrument, security, or generally any other writing which evidences a right to the payment of money and is of a type which in the ordinary course of business is transferred by delivery with any necessary endorsement or assignment, (2) there is a genuine question as to the authenticity of the original, or (3) when, under the circumstances, the admission of the duplicate would be unfair. See Fed. Rule Evid. 1003.

COMMENTARY ON FEDERAL AND FLORIDA RULE DIFFERENCES

Florida Stat. § 90.953 and its federal counterpart, Federal Rule 1003, delineate the circumstances in which a duplicate is admissible to the same extent as an original. Both provisions state as a general principle that a duplicate (as defined in Florida Stat. § 90.951(4) and Federal Rule 1001(e)) *is* admissible to the same extent as an original. However, the federal rule contains two exceptions to this general principle while the Florida rule contains three exceptions.

The first exception in the federal rule is when a genuine question is raised about the authenticity of the original. When questions are raised about the authenticity of the original, the original itself must be produced unless production is excused by Federal Rule 1004. See *Pro Bono*

Invs., Inc. v. Gerry, 2005 WL 2429777, at *5 (S.D.N.Y. Sept. 30, 2005). The Florida rule contains a similar provision, although that provision on its face seems broader in that it applies to situations in which "[a] genuine question is raised about the authenticity of the original *or any other document or writing*." FLA. STAT. § 90.953(2) (emphasis added). Arguably, this language is designed to encompass the possibility that a question is raised not about the authenticity of the *original* but instead a question about the authenticity of the *duplicate*, such as a claim that it was altered after photocopying the original. *See, e.g., Hutchinson v. State*, 580 So. 2d 257, 262-63 (Fla. 1st DCA 1991); *Fredericks v. Howell*, 426 So. 2d 1200, 1201 (Fla. 4th DCA 1983). Under the federal rule, a challenge to the authenticity of the duplicate is a separate issue not covered by Rule 1003, and where the challenge is to the authenticity of the duplicate, the trial court should not exclude the duplicate unless no reasonable jury could conclude that it was authentic. *See* 31 CHARLES ALAN WRIGHT & VICTOR JAMES GOLD, FEDERAL PRACTICE AND PROCEDURE: EVIDENCE § 8004 (2000).

The second exception in the federal rule is when it would be "unfair" to admit the duplicate in lieu of the original. Unfairness would exist where, for example, the duplicates are incomplete or illegible. *See Amoco Prod. Co. v. United States*, 619 F.2d 1383, 1391 (10th Cir. 1980). The Florida rule contains a similarly worded provision. *See* FLA. STAT. § 90.953(3).

The most significant difference between the Florida and Federal rules is that the Florida rule contains a third exception for situations in which "[t]he document or writing is a negotiable instrument as defined in § 673.1041, a security as defined in § 678.1021, or any other writing that evidences a right to the payment of money, is not itself a security agreement or lease, and is of a type that is transferred by delivery in the ordinary course of business with any necessary endorsement or assignment." FLA. STAT. § 90.953(1). The exception is intended to apply in situations in which an action is brought on a negotiable instrument, such as a promissory note, or similar document, and the rationale for requiring the original to be produced is to preclude the possibility that the instrument has already been negotiated and to prevent its further negotiation. *See Perry v. Fairbanks Capital Corp.*, 888 So. 2d 725, 727 (Fla. 5th DCA 2004); *Pennsylvania Blue Shield v. Wolfe*, 575 So. 2d 1361, 1363 (Fla. 3d DCA 1991); *Lowery v. State*, 402 So. 2d 1287, 1288-89 (Fla. 5th DCA 1981). However, the exception does not apply to documents that merely evidence a right to receive payment of money, but only to those instruments that are thought to embody the right itself. *See Perry*, 888 So. 2d at 726-27 (does not apply to a mortgage); *Tillman v. Smith*, 472 So. 2d 1353, 1354 (Fla. 5th DCA 1985) (does not apply to an antenuptial agreement). Moreover, because the purpose of the exception is to preclude the possibility that the original instrument has already been negotiated and to prevent its further negotiation when an action is brought on a negotiable instrument, it does not apply when a duplicate of a negotiable instrument or similar document is introduced in other types of proceedings. *See Pennsylvania Blue Shield*, 575 So. 2d at 1363 (does not apply in suit by doctor against insurance company seeking payment for services rendered when photocopy of canceled check is offered to prove defendant had already paid part of doctor's claim); *Lowery*, 402 So. 2d at 1288-89 (does not apply in criminal prosecution for uttering a forged check when photocopy of check is offered into evidence).

Federal Rule 1004. Admissibility of Other Evidence of Content

An original is not required and other evidence of the content of a writing, recording, or photograph is admissible if:

(a) all the originals are lost or destroyed, and not by the proponent acting in bad faith;

(b) an original cannot be obtained by any available judicial process;

(c) the party against whom the original would be offered had control of the original; was at that time put on notice, by pleadings or otherwise, that the original would be a subject of proof at the trial or hearing; and fails to produce it at the trial or hearing; or

(d) the writing, recording, or photograph is not closely related to a controlling issue.

ADVISORY COMMITTEE'S NOTE

Basically the rule requiring the production of the original as proof of contents has developed as a rule of preference: if failure to produce the original is satisfactorily explained, secondary evidence is admissible. The instant rule specifies the circumstances under which production of the original is excused.

The rule recognizes no "degrees" of secondary evidence. While strict logic might call for extending the principle of preference beyond simply preferring the original, the formulation of a hierarchy of preferences and a procedure for making it effective is believed to involve unwarranted complexities. Most, if not all, that would be accomplished by an extended scheme of preferences will, in any event, be achieved through the normal motivation of a party to present the most convincing evidence possible and the arguments and procedures available to his opponent if he does not. Compare McCormick § 207.

Paragraph ([a]). Loss or destruction of the original, unless due to bad faith of the proponent, is a satisfactory explanation of nonproduction. McCormick § 201.

Paragraph ([b]). When the original is in the possession of a third person, inability to procure it from him by resort to process or other judicial procedure is a sufficient explanation of nonproduction. Judicial procedure includes subpoena duces tecum as an incident to the taking of a deposition in another jurisdiction. No further showing is required. See McCormick § 202.

Paragraph ([c]). A party who has an original in his control has no need for the protection of the rule if put on notice that proof of contents will be made. He can ward off secondary evidence by offering the original. The notice procedure here provided is not to be confused with orders to produce or other discovery procedures, as the purpose of the procedure under this rule is to afford the opposite party an opportunity to produce the original, not to compel him to do so. McCormick § 203.

Paragraph ([d]). While difficult to define with precision, situations arise in which no good purpose is served by production of the original. Examples are the newspaper in an action for the price of publishing defendant's advertisement, Foster-Holcomb Investment Co. v. Little Rock Publishing Co., 151 Ark. 449 (1922), and the streetcar transfer of plaintiff claiming status as a passenger, Chicago City Ry. Co. v. Carroll, 206 Ill. 318 (1903). Numerous cases are collected in McCormick § 200, p. 412, n. 1.

REPORT OF HOUSE COMMITTEE ON THE JUDICIARY

Rule 1004([a]). The Committee approved Rule 1004([a]) in the form submitted to Congress. However, the Committee intends that loss or destruction of an original by another person at the instigation of the proponent should be considered as tantamount to loss or destruction in bad faith by the proponent himself.

ADVISORY COMMITTEE'S NOTE (2011 AMENDMENT)

The language of Rule 1004 has been amended as part of the restyling of the Evidence Rules to make them more easily understood and to make style and terminology consistent throughout the rules. These changes are intended to be stylistic only. There is no intent to change any result in any ruling on evidence admissibility.

Florida Stat. § 90.954. Admissibility of Other Evidence of Contents

FLORIDA AND FEDERAL EVIDENCE RULES

The original of a writing, recording, or photograph is not required, except as provided in s. 90.953, and other evidence of its contents is admissible when:

(1) All originals are lost or destroyed, unless the proponent lost or destroyed them in bad faith.

(2) An original cannot be obtained in this state by any judicial process or procedure.

(3) An original was under the control of the party against whom offered at a time when that party was put on notice by the pleadings or by written notice from the adverse party that the contents of such original would be subject to proof at the hearing, and such original is not produced at the hearing.

(4) The writing, recording, or photograph is not related to a controlling issue.

SPONSORS' NOTE (1976 ENACTMENT)

The "best evidence" rule has often been explained as a rule of preference, that of admitting evidence of the highest possible quality. Where failure to produce the original is satisfactorily explained, secondary evidence is admissible. This section prescribes the circumstances under which production of the original is excused.

"Degrees" of secondary evidence have been established by existing Florida cases, i.e., secondary evidence must be the best available evidence under the circumstances. This results in the establishment of a hierarchy of preferences and a complex procedure for implementing them. Wicker v. Board of Public Instruction, 31 So.2d 635 (Fla. 1947); Continental Aviation Corp. v. Southern Bell Tel. & Tel. Co., 173 So.2d 750 (Fla. 3rd Dist. 1965), aff'd, 183 So.2d 200 (1966).

What is felt to be the better view, reflected in this section, is to make no discrimination between "degrees" of secondary evidence. The wide range of discovery devices presently available to counsel insures that any pertinent documents will be known by counsel and can be used if there is contradictory oral testimony. The consequences of the failure to produce the "best evidence" are an adequate safeguard to meet the ends of justice. McCormick, Evidence § 241 (2nd ed. 1972).

This approach has been adopted in several modern evidence codes. Fed. Rule Evid. 1004; Model Code of Evid. Rule 602; Uniform Rule of Evid. 70.

Subsection (1) When the original is lost or destroyed and there is no bad faith shown by the proponent, including his authorization or causation of loss or destruction by a third party, such loss or destruction is a satisfactory explanation for the nonproduction. If the destruction was not fraudulent, other evidence is admissible. Since there often will not be direct evidence of the destruction, circumstantial evidence of an appropriate search will suffice. In re McCollom's Estate, 88 So.2d 537 (Fla. 1956).

Chapter 71 of the Florida Statutes codifies the inherent power of courts of general jurisdiction to reestablish lost or destroyed records. See Pearce v. Thacker[a]y, 13 Fla. 574 (1871). The chapter offers any interested person, including a litigant, a judicial procedure to reestablish, as an "original," any lost private or public writing or record.

This subsection, in addition to codifying a portion of the common-law "best evidence" rule, provides a litigant the choice of accounting for the loss of the original and introducing secondary evidence or of utilizing the procedure of Chapter 71 to reestablish the secondary evidence as an original through the equity proceeding.

Similar provisions to this subsection are contained in Calif. Evid. Code § 1501; New Jersey Evid. Rule 70.

<u>Subsection (2)</u> When an original is in control of a third person, and the document cannot be obtained by resort to judicial process, it is an adequate explanation of nonproduction. No additional showing is required. McCormick, <u>Evidence</u> § 238 (2nd ed. 1972); Calif. Evid. Code § 1502; New Jersey Evid. Rule 70.

<u>Subsection (3)</u> A party in possession of an original may prevent the admission of secondary evidence against him by producing the original when put on notice that proof of its contents will be offered. While the opposing party must receive proper and adequate notice, see Calif. Evid. Code § 1503; New Jersey Evid. Rule 70; Prop. Fed. Rule Evid. 1004(3); this subsection does not require that the party be served with said notice as does existing Florida law. <u>Hanover Fire Ins. Co. v. Lewis</u>, 1 So. 863 (Fla. 1887); <u>Green v. Hood</u>, 120 So.2d 223 (Fla. 2nd Dist. 1960). This notice to produce should not be confused with discovery devices, Fla. R. Civ. Pro. 1.310, 1.350, since under this section the party is offered the opportunity to produce the original but is not compelled to do so. McCormick, <u>Evidence</u> § 239 (2nd ed. 1972).

<u>Subsection (4)</u> Where the contents of a writing, recording or photograph are collateral matters not directly in issue, no good purpose is served by requiring production of the original. <u>Firestone Service Stores, Inc. v. Wynn</u>, 179 So. 175 (Fla. 1938); McCormick, <u>Evidence</u> § 234 (2nd ed. 1972). See Calif. Evid. Code § 1504; New Jersey Evid. Rule 70; Fed. Rule Evid. 1004(4).

COMMENTARY ON FEDERAL AND FLORIDA RULE DIFFERENCES

Florida Stat. § 90.954 and its federal counterpart, Federal Rule 1004, delineate the circumstances in which production of the original of a writing, recording, or photograph is excused and "other evidence" is permitted to prove its contents. The Florida and federal rules set forth four similar circumstances in which production of the original will be excused.

First, under both rules, production of the original is excused if all originals are lost or destroyed, unless the proponent lost or destroyed them in bad faith. *See* FLA. STAT. § 90.954(1); FED. R. EVID. 1004(a). Under both rules, the mere fact that the proponent was responsible for the original's loss or destruction does not necessarily imply bad faith. *See England v. State*, 940 So. 2d 389, 401 (Fla. 2006); *Insurance Co. of State of Pennsylvania v. Genova Express Lines, Inc.*, 605 So. 2d 941, 942-43 (Fla. 3d DCA 1992); *Estate of Gryder v. Commissioner*, 705 F.2d 336, 338 (8th Cir. 1983).

Second, under both rules, production of the original is excused if it is in the possession of a third person and cannot be obtained by judicial procedure, such as a subpoena. *See* FLA. STAT. § 90.954(2); FED. R. EVID. 1004(b). The one significant difference is that the Florida provision can be invoked upon a showing that the original "cannot be obtained *in this state* by any judicial process or procedure," FLA. STAT. § 90.954(2) (emphasis added), while the federal rule contemplates resort to extraterritorial discovery techniques before excusing production of the original, *see* Advisory Committee's Note to FED. R. EVID. 1004(b) ("Judicial procedure includes subpoena duces tecum as an incident to the taking of a deposition in another jurisdiction.").

Third, under both rules, production of the original is excused if the original was under the control of the party against whom offered at a time when that party was put on notice that the contents of the original would be the subject of proof at the hearing, and the original is not produced by that party at the hearing. *See* FLA. STAT. § 90.954(3); FED. R. EVID. 1004(c). A potential difference between the two provisions is that the federal rule requires only that the party be put on notice "by pleadings *or otherwise*," while the Florida rule requires that the notice be given "by the pleadings or by *written* notice." Thus, while oral notice would potentially be permissible under the federal rule, written notice appears to be required under the Florida rule.

Fourth, under both rules, production of the original is excused if it involves a collateral matter. *See* FLA. STAT. § 90.954(4); FED. R. EVID. 1004(d).

Once production of the original is excused under Federal Rule 1004 or Fla. Stat § 90.954, no distinctions are made between degrees of secondary evidence. In other words, once production of an original is excused, a party is free to resort to secondary evidence of her choosing, with no sub-preference for, say, a duplicate before resort to oral testimony. *See U.S. v. Lanzon*, 639 F.3d 1293, 1301-02 (11th Cir. 2011); *U.S. v. Dadamuratov*, 340 Fed. Appx. 540, 546-47 (11th Cir. 2009); *Fredericks v. Howell*, 426 So. 2d 1200, 1201 (Fla. 4th DCA 1983); *Lowery v. State*, 402 So. 2d 1287, 1289 (Fla. 5th DCA 1981).

Federal Rule 1005. Copies of Public Records to Prove Content

The proponent may use a copy to prove the content of an official record — or of a document that was recorded or filed in a public office as authorized by law — if these conditions are met: the record or document is otherwise admissible; and the copy is certified as correct in accordance with Rule 902(4) or is testified to be correct by a witness who has compared it with the original. If no such copy can be obtained by reasonable diligence, then the proponent may use other evidence to prove the content.

ADVISORY COMMITTEE'S NOTE

Public records call for somewhat different treatment. Removing them from their usual place of keeping would be attended by serious inconvenience to the public and to the custodian. As a consequence judicial decisions and statutes commonly hold that no explanation need be given for failure to produce the original of a public record. McCormick § 204; 4 Wigmore §§ 1215–1228. This blanket dispensation from producing or accounting for the original would open the door to the introduction of every kind of secondary evidence of contents of public records were it not for the preference given certified or compared copies. Recognition of degrees of secondary evidence in this situation is an appropriate *quid pro quo* for not applying the requirement of producing the original.

The provisions of 28 U.S.C. § 1733(b) apply only to departments or agencies of the United States. The rule, however, applies to public records generally and is comparable in scope in this respect to Rule 44(a) of the Rules of Civil Procedure.

ADVISORY COMMITTEE'S NOTE (2011 AMENDMENT)

The language of Rule 1005 has been amended as part of the restyling of the Evidence Rules to make them more easily understood and to make style and terminology consistent throughout the rules. These changes are intended to be stylistic only. There is no intent to change any result in any ruling on evidence admissibility.

Florida Stat. § 90.955. Public Records

(1) The contents of an official record or of a document authorized to be recorded or filed, and actually recorded or filed, with a governmental agency, either federal, state, county, or municipal, in a place where official records or documents are ordinarily filed, including data compilations in any form, may be proved by a copy authenticated as provided in s. 90.902, if otherwise admissible.

(2) If a party cannot obtain, by the exercise of reasonable diligence, a copy that complies with subsection (1), other evidence of the contents is admissible.

SPONSORS' NOTE (1976 ENACTMENT)

ARTICLE X. CONTENTS OF WRITINGS, RECORDINGS, AND PHOTOGRAPHS

Section 119.011 of the Florida statutes defines a "public record" as any tangible thing made or received pursuant to law in the transaction of official business. This section does not govern personal or business records or records which are not required to be filed or recorded with a governmental agency. Such materials are covered under Sections 90.[952]-90.[954]. In view of the inconvenience to the public and custodian involved in the removal of public records from the custodial office, existing Florida law follows the long-accepted position of allowing certified copies of public records to be utilized in evidence in lieu of the original. One early case followed the common-law rule and allowed such certified copies to be used irrespective of the presence of a statutory provision. Simmons v. Spratt, 20 Fla. 495 (1884).

Existing § 92.29, which presently provides for the admissibility of photocopies of certain records, would be narrowed. It provides that a photographic reproduction of a writing, whether or not certified, made by a governmental agency in the regular course of business, which is or may be filed and recorded, may be admitted as an original whether or not the original is in existence. Section 90.[955] requires a certified copy of a document which was actually filed and recorded. This section does not overrule various existing statutory provisions which provide that photocopies of certain government records should be treated as originals. See Fla. Stat. § 339.32 (certain records of Department of Transportation); Fla. Stat. § 382.50 (certain records of state registrar of vital statistics); Fla. Stat. § 402.19 (certain records of Department of Health & Rehabilitative Services); Fla. Stat. § 409.385 (certain records of Department of Family Services).

Subsection (2) This subsection provides for degrees of secondary evidence, i.e., reasonable diligence to procure a certified or compared copy must be demonstrated before other evidence of the contents may be admitted.

Under the Uniform Photographic Copies of Business and Public Records as Evidence Act, Fla. Stat. § 92.35, a business may destroy certain records and photographic copies thereof are admissible as originals. A party may use a certified copy of a § 92.35 photocopy under this section. For example, the microfilm records of a bank or the "Xeroxed" copies of deeds in a courthouse would both be treated as originals, and certified copies of them would be admissible if the prerequisites of this section are met.

Similar provisions are contained in Calif. Evid. Code § 1506 (admitting writings in custody of officer as well as public records); Fed. Rule Evid. 1005; Model Code of Evid.Rule 517; New Jersey Evid. Rule 70 (document in possession of public officer); Kansas Code Civ. Pro. § 60-465.

COMMENTARY ON FEDERAL AND FLORIDA RULE DIFFERENCES

Florida Stat. § 90.955 and its federal counterpart, Federal Rule 1005, modify the best evidence rule for public records. Both rules apply to official records as well as to documents authorized to be recorded or filed and actually recorded or filed, with the former referring to documents produced by government officials and the latter to documents produced by private persons but recorded or filed with the government, such as deeds and mortgages.

Florida Stat. § 90.955(1) provides that when one seeks to prove the contents of such documents, they are automatically excused from producing the original and may instead offer "a copy authenticated as provided in § 90.902." Federal Rule 1005 likewise excuses production of the original, permitting resort to a "copy [that] is certified as correct in accordance with Rule 902(4) or is *testified to be correct by a witness who has compared it with the original*." (emphasis added) While the federal rule thus permits the use of a certified or a compared copy, it is unclear whether the Florida rule permits both types of copies or only a certified copy. On the one hand, the Sponsors' Note to Florida Stat. § 90.955(2) appears to assume that § 90.955(1) permits both types of copies. *See* Sponsors' Note to FLA. STAT. § 90.955(2) ("This subsection provides for degrees of secondary evidence, i.e., reasonable diligence to procure a *certified or compared copy* must be demonstrated before other evidence of the contents may be admitted."). On the other hand, § 90.955(1) only sanctions "a copy authenticated as provided in § 90.902," and the latter provision does not list testimony by a person who has compared it with the original as a permissible method of authenticating a public record. *See* FLA. STAT. § 90.902. No precedents have addressed the issue.

In any event, Federal Rule 1005 and Florida Stat. § 90.955 are in two respects more permissive than are the rules governing non-public records. First, the term "copy" as used in these two provisions is broader than the term "duplicate" as used in Federal Rule 1003 and Florida Stat. § 90.953: a "copy," unlike a "duplicate," need not be reproduced by mechanical means, and indeed can even be a hand-written copy. Second, Federal Rule 1005 and Florida Stat. § 90.955 permit resort to a copy *without exception*, while resort to a duplicate when non-public records are involved is subject to the exceptions set forth in Federal Rule 1003 and Florida Stat. § 90.953.

However, in another respect, Federal Rule 1005 and Florida Stat. § 90.955 are more restrictive than are the rules governing non-public records. Unlike Federal Rule 1004 and Florida Stat. § 90.954, which do not recognize degrees of secondary evidence, Federal Rule 1005 and Florida Stat. § 90.955 *do* recognize degrees of secondary evidence, permitting resort to other types of evidence only if a copy cannot be obtained with reasonable diligence. *See* FED. R. EVID. 1005; Advisory Committee's Note to Federal Rule 1005; FLA. STAT. § 90.955(2); Sponsors' Note to FLA. STAT. § 90.955(2).

Federal Rule 1006. Summaries to Prove Content

The proponent may use a summary, chart, or calculation to prove the content of voluminous writings, recordings, or photographs that cannot be conveniently examined in court. The proponent must make the originals or duplicates available for examination or copying, or both, by other parties at a reasonable time and place. And the court may order the proponent to produce them in court.

ADVISORY COMMITTEE'S NOTE

The admission of summaries of voluminous books, records, or documents offers the only practicable means of making their contents available to judge and jury. The rule recognizes this practice, with appropriate safeguards. 4 Wigmore § 1230.

ADVISORY COMMITTEE'S NOTE (2011 AMENDMENT)

The language of Rule 1006 has been amended as part of the restyling of the Evidence Rules to make them more easily understood and to make style and terminology consistent throughout the rules. These changes are intended to be stylistic only. There is no intent to change any result in any ruling on evidence admissibility.

Florida Stat. § 90.956. Summaries

When it is not convenient to examine in court the contents of voluminous writings, recordings, or photographs, a party may present them in the form of a chart, summary, or calculation by calling a qualified witness. The party intending to use such a summary must give timely written notice of his or her intention to use the summary, proof of which shall be filed with the court, and shall make the summary and the originals or duplicates of the data from which the summary is compiled available for examination or copying, or both, by other parties at a reasonable time and place. A judge may order that they be produced in court.

SPONSORS' NOTE (1976 ENACTMENT)

In cases where the only practical method of presenting the contents of voluminous books, records or reports to the court and jury is by the use of summaries presented by a competent witness, they should be admitted into evidence. For example, in Scott v. Caldwell, 37 So.2d 85 (Fla. 1948) the Supreme Court stated:

> When pertinent and essential facts can be ascertained only by an examination of a large number of entries in books of account, an expert accountant, who has made examination and analysis of the books and figures, may testify as a witness and give summarized statements of what the books show as a result of his investigation, provided the books themselves are accessible to the court and parties.

See Perma Spray Mfg. Co. v. La France Indus., Inc., 161 So.2d 13 (Fla. 3rd Dist. 1964). The opportunity to examine and copy the materials upon which the summary is based is preserved, and, when appropriate, production before the court may be required. See Prop. Fed. Rule Evid. 1006; Calif. Evid. Code § 1509; New Jersey Evid. Code 70(1)(g); Kansas Code Civ. Pro. § 60-467.

COMMENTARY ON FEDERAL AND FLORIDA RULE DIFFERENCES

Florida Stat. § 90.956 and its federal counterpart, Federal Rule 1006, delineate the circumstances in which a party will be permitted to present the contents of voluminous writings, recordings, or photographs in the form of a chart, summary, or calculation. Absent this provision, offering such a chart, summary, or calculation would violate the best evidence rule when offered to prove the contents of the underlying writings, recordings, or photographs. The term "summary" includes not only a written summary, but also a summary presented in oral form through the testimony of a witness. *See Bowmar Instrument Corp. v. Fidelity Electronics, Ltd.*, 466 So. 2d 344, 345 (Fla. 3d DCA 1985); *Nichols v. Upjohn Co.*, 610 F.2d 293, 294 (5th Cir. 1980).

Both the federal and Florida rules apply only if the underlying documents are so "voluminous" that they cannot be conveniently examined in court by the trier of fact. While neither rule defines the requisite quantum with greater specificity, case law suggests that it need not be literally impossible for the trier of fact to examine the underlying documents, but rather that it would be difficult and inconvenient to comprehend them. *See U.S v. Bray*, 139 F.3d 1104, 1109 (6th Cir. 1998).

The Florida rule requires that a party who intends to use a summary give "timely written notice of his or her intention to use the summary, proof of which shall be filed with the court," a requirement described as "strict." *Tallahassee Hous. Auth. v. Florida Unemployment Appeals Comm'n*, 483 So. 2d 413, 415 (Fla. 1986). The rule does not define the term "timely," although the case law indicates that the question whether notice is timely turns on whether it provides the opposing party with sufficient time to investigate and analyze the underlying records to determine whether the summary is accurate. *See T/F Systems, Inc. v. Malt*, 814 So. 2d 511, 512-13 (Fla. 4th DCA 2002). While no similar requirement exists in the text of the federal rule, the requirement that the proponent make the documents available to the opposing party (discussed in the next paragraph) has been construed as containing an implicit notice requirement. *See Air Safety, Inc. v. Roman Catholic Archbishop of Boston*, 94 F.3d 1, 8 (1st Cir. 1996).

Both the federal and Florida rules require that the proponent of the summary make the underlying documents available to the opposing party for examination, or copying, or both at a reasonable time and place. However, the Florida rule *also* requires that the *summary* document be made available to the other parties, while the federal rule requires only that the underlying source materials be made available. *See Bowmar Instrument Corp.*, 466 So. 2d at 345; *U.S. v. Foley*, 598 F.2d 1323, 1338 (4th Cir. 1979).

Federal case law holds that even though the underlying documents are not themselves offered into evidence, the proponent of the summary must establish that they would be admissible into evidence; thus, if the underlying documents are hearsay not within any hearsay exception, the summary is likewise inadmissible. *See Bray*, 139 F.3d at 1109-10. Florida authority implicitly applies the Florida rule in a similar manner. *See Tallahassee Housing Authority*, 483 So. 2d at 414.

Finally, both the Florida and federal rules require that the foundation for admitting the summary be laid through the testimony of a qualified witness, who includes either the person who prepared the summary or another person who is familiar with the underlying documents and the summary. *See Bray*, 139 F.3d at 1110; *See T/F Systems, Inc.*, 814 So. 2d at 513.

Federal Rule 1007. Testimony or Statement of a Party to Prove Content

The proponent may prove the content of a writing, recording, or photograph by the testimony, deposition, or written statement of the party against whom the evidence is offered. The proponent need not account for the original.

ADVISORY COMMITTEE'S NOTE

While the parent case, Slatterie v. Pooley, 6 M. & W. 664, 151 Eng.Rep. 579 (Exch.1840), allows proof of contents by evidence of an oral admission by the party against whom offered, without accounting for nonproduction of the original, the risk of inaccuracy is substantial and the decision is at odds with the purpose of the rule giving preference to the original. See 4 Wigmore § 1255. The instant rule follows Professor McCormick's suggestion of limiting this use of admissions to those made in the course of giving testimony or in writing. McCormick § 208, p. 424. The limitation, of course, does not call for excluding evidence of an oral admission when nonproduction of the original has been accounted for and secondary evidence generally has become admissible. Rule 1004, *supra*.

A similar provision is contained in New Jersey Evidence Rule 70(1)(h).

ADVISORY COMMITTEE'S NOTE (2011 AMENDMENT)

The language of Rule 1007 has been amended as part of the restyling of the Evidence Rules to make them more easily understood and to make style and terminology consistent throughout the rules. These changes are intended to be stylistic only. There is no intent to change any result in any ruling on evidence admissibility.

Florida Stat. § 90.957. Testimony or Written Admissions of a Party

A party may prove the contents of writings, recordings, or photographs by the testimony or deposition of the party against whom they are offered or by that party's written admission, without accounting for the nonproduction of the original.

SPONSORS' NOTE (1976 ENACTMENT)

The parent case of this section, Slatterie v. Pooley, 6 M. & W. 664, 151 Eng. Rep. 579 (Exch. 1840), allowed the terms of a writing to be proved by the testimony of a third party who heard the defendant orally admit its authenticity. It was assumed that a party would not make false declarations favorable to his opponent. This decision has been objected to because of the ease with which oral admissions can be fabricated. For this reason, the only reported Florida case, Bellamy v. Hawkins, 17 Fla. 750 (1880), refused to admit admissions of a party to prove the content of a writing. However, desirable simplification of proof is obtained and accuracy is preserved when the admissions of a party, which are admissible to prove the contents of a writing, are limited to those made during the giving of testimony or in writing. See McCormick, Evidence § 242 (2nd ed. 1972).

Oral out-of-court admissions of the contents of writings, recordings or photographs are freely admissible as secondary evidence under Section 90.[954] where the nonproduction of the original has been explained. Similar provisions are contained in Fed. Rule Evid. 1007; New Jersey Evid. Rule 70; and Model Code of Evid. Rule 602 (1942).

COMMENTARY ON FEDERAL AND FLORIDA RULE DIFFERENCES

Florida Stat. § 90.957 and its federal counterpart, Federal Rule 1007, create an exception to the best evidence rule that allows evidence of certain admissions of the party against whom the evidence is offered to be used to prove the contents of a writing, recording, or photograph without the need to account for nonproduction of the original.

Under both the federal and Florida rules, only written admissions by the opposing party and oral testimony (at trial or in a deposition) by an opposing party can be used; the rule does not allow the use of oral admissions (such as verbal statements made other than when testifying). The rationale for so limiting the scope of the rules is a concern that it is too easy for a party to falsely allege that an opposing party made an oral admission, which—unlike a written admission or one made while testifying—cannot be readily verified. See Advisory Committee's Note to FED. R. EVID. 1007; Sponsors' Note to FLA. STAT. § 90.957.

Federal Rule 1008. Functions of the Court and Jury

Ordinarily, the court determines whether the proponent has fulfilled the factual conditions for admitting other evidence of the content of a writing, recording, or photograph under Rule 1004 or 1005. But in a jury trial, the jury determines — in accordance with Rule 104(b) — any issue about whether:

(a) an asserted writing, recording, or photograph ever existed;

(b) another one produced at the trial or hearing is the original; or

(c) other evidence of content accurately reflects the content.

ADVISORY COMMITTEE'S NOTE

Most preliminary questions of fact in connection with applying the rule preferring the original as evidence of contents are for the judge, under the general principles announced in Rule 104, *supra*. Thus, the question whether the loss of the originals has been established, or of the fulfillment of other conditions specified in Rule 1004, *supra*, is for the judge. However, questions may arise which go beyond the mere administration of the rule preferring the original and into the merits of the controversy. For example, plaintiff offers secondary evidence of the contents of an alleged contract, after first introducing evidence of loss of the original, and defendant counters with evidence that no such contract was ever executed. If the judge decides that the contract was never executed and excludes the secondary evidence, the case is at an end without ever going to the jury on a central issue. Levin, Authentication and Content of Writings, 10 Rutgers L.Rev. 632, 644 (1956). The latter portion of the instant rule is designed to insure treatment of these situations as raising jury questions. The decision is not one for uncontrolled discretion of the jury but is subject to the control exercised generally by the judge over jury determinations. See Rule 104(b), *supra*.

For similar provisions, see Uniform Rule 70(2); Kansas Code of Civil Procedure § 60-467(b); New Jersey Evidence Rule 70(2), (3).

ADVISORY COMMITTEE'S NOTE (2011 AMENDMENT)

The language of Rule 1008 has been amended as part of the restyling of the Evidence Rules to make them more easily understood and to make style and terminology consistent throughout the rules. These changes are intended to be stylistic only. There is no intent to change any result in any ruling on evidence admissibility.

Florida Stat. § 90.958. Functions of Court and Jury

(1) Except as provided in subsection (2), when the admissibility under this chapter of other evidence of the contents of writings, recordings, or photographs depends upon the existence of a preliminary fact, the question as to whether the preliminary fact exists is for the court to determine.

(2) The trier of fact shall determine whether:

(a) The asserted writing ever existed.

(b) Another writing, recording, or photograph produced at the trial is the original.

(c) Other evidence of the contents correctly reflects the contents.

SPONSORS' NOTE (1976 ENACTMENT)

Subsection (1) As indicated in Section 90.105, preliminary questions of fact in applying the rule preferring the original as evidence of contents are for the judge. Similarly, the satisfactory explanation of nonproduction of the conditions set forth in Section 90.[954] is for determination by the judge. Existing Florida cases indicate that the judge has denied admission of secondary evidence when the proper predicate as codified in Section 90.[954] has not been laid. Firestone Service Stores v. Wynn, 179 So. 175 (Fla. 1938); Green v. Hood, 120 So.2d 223 (Fla. 2nd Dist. 1960).

Subsection (2) This subsection insures that the issues enumerated therein will raise a jury question, since a ruling by the judge would foreclose consideration by trier of fact. For example, without this subsection, if one party introduces secondary evidence of a contract and the other denies its execution, the judge could take from the jury the decision on the ultimate issue of the existence of the contract by making a preliminary ruling that the writing never existed and excluding the secondary evidence. Therefore, once the proper foundation has been laid for the introduction of secondary evidence, the resolution of the conflict over the existence of a writing, or whether other evidence correctly reflects the contents is for the jury to determine.

Similar provisions are contained in Fed. Evid. Rule 1008; New Jersey Evid. Rule 70; Kansas Code of Civ. Pro. § 60-467(b); Model Code of Evid. Rule 602 (1942), and Uniform Rule of Evid. 70(3). See McCormick, Evidence § 54 (2nd ed. 1972); Calif. Evid. Code §§ 400, 402.

COMMENTARY ON FEDERAL AND FLORIDA RULE DIFFERENCES

Florida Stat. § 90.958 and its federal counterpart, Federal Rule 1008, delineate the role of the judge in deciding preliminary questions when applying the best evidence rule. The rules are thus a specific application of the principles set forth in Florida Stat. § 90.105(1)-(2) and Federal Rule 104(a)-(b).

Under both the Florida and federal rules, most preliminary questions in connection with applying the best evidence rule are for the judge alone to decide. Thus, it is the judge who decides such preliminary questions of fact as whether the originals have been lost or destroyed, and if so, whether it was in bad faith, under Federal Rule 1004(a) or Florida Stat. § 90.954(1), or whether the originals are not obtainable under Federal Rule 1004(b) or Florida Stat. § 90.954(2). Similarly, the judge alone would decide whether "reasonable diligence" has been exercised under Federal Rule 1005 or Florida Stat. § 90.955(2).

However, both Florida Stat. § 90.958(2) and the second sentence of Federal Rule 1008 limit the role of the judge for certain questions that arise involving the application of the best evidence rule. Under these provisions, the following issues, when raised, are deemed jury questions: (a) whether the asserted writing ever existed; (b) whether another writing, recording, or photograph produced at the trial is the original; (c) whether other evidence of contents correctly reflects the contents. When such issues are raised in the application of the best evidence rule, the judge plays only a screening role in accordance with the principles set forth in Florida Stat. § 90.105(2) and Federal Rule 104(b).

Federal Rule 1008(a) and Florida Stat. § 90.958(2)(a) refer to the situation in which the plaintiff seeks to invoke Rule 1004, claiming, say, that the original of a writing, such as a contract, has been lost, and the defendant counters that there was nothing to lose because no such contract ever existed. In this circumstance, the rules instruct that the court is to decide only whether there is sufficient evidence that the trier of fact reasonably could find that such a contract existed. Having done so, the court is then to decide only whether, given that a reasonable jury could find that the contract existed, the plaintiff has satisfied the court that all such originals are lost or destroyed.

Federal Rule 1008(b) and Florida Stat. § 90.958(2)(b) refer to the situation in which both parties introduce what they purport to be originals of the contract. So long as a reasonable jury could believe each one to be the authentic original, the question is one for the jury to decide, and both are to be admitted.

Finally, Federal Rule 1008(c) and Florida Stat. § 90.958(2)(c) provide that once the court has decided to permit the introduction of secondary evidence, it is up to the jury to evaluate the secondary evidence offered. Thus, if the court holds that secondary evidence of contents is permitted because the original is lost or destroyed, and the parties each testify to their own version of the contents of the original, it is for the jury to decide whom to believe.

ARTICLE XI. MISCELLANEOUS RULES

Federal Rule	Florida Stat. §	Description
1101	90.103	Applicability of the Rules
1102	—	Amendments
1103	90.101	Title

Federal Rule 1101. Applicability of the Rules

(a) To Courts and Judges. These rules apply to proceedings before:

- United States district courts;

- United States bankruptcy and magistrate judges;

- United States courts of appeals;

- the United States Court of Federal Claims; and

- the district courts of Guam, the Virgin Islands, and the Northern Mariana Islands.

(b) To Cases and Proceedings. These rules apply in:

- civil cases and proceedings, including bankruptcy, admiralty, and maritime cases;

- criminal cases and proceedings; and

- contempt proceedings, except those in which the court may act summarily.

(c) Rules on Privilege. The rules on privilege apply to all stages of a case or proceeding.

(d) Exceptions. These rules — except for those on privilege — do not apply to the following:

(1) the court's determination, under Rule 104(a), on a preliminary question of fact governing admissibility;

(2) grand-jury proceedings; and

(3) miscellaneous proceedings such as:

- extradition or rendition;

- issuing an arrest warrant, criminal summons, or search warrant;

- a preliminary examination in a criminal case;

- sentencing;

- granting or revoking probation or supervised release; and

- considering whether to release on bail or otherwise.

(e) Other Statutes and Rules. A federal statute or a rule prescribed by the Supreme Court may provide for admitting or excluding evidence independently from these rules.

ADVISORY COMMITTEE'S NOTE

Subdivision (a). The various enabling acts contain differences in phraseology in their descriptions of the courts over which the Supreme Court's power to make rules of practice and procedure extends. The act concerning civil actions, as amended in 1966, refers to "the district courts...of the United States in civil actions, including admiralty and maritime cases...." 28 U.S.C. § 2072, Pub.L. 89-773, § 1, 80 Stat. 1323. The bankruptcy authorization is for rules of practice and procedure "under the Bankruptcy Act." 28 U.S.C. § 2075, Pub.L. 88-623, § 1, 78 Stat. 1001. The Bankruptcy Act in turn creates bankruptcy courts of "the United States district courts and the district courts of the Territories and possessions to which this title is or may hereafter be applicable." 11 U.S.C. §§ 1(10), 11(a). The provision as to criminal rules up to and including verdicts applies to "criminal cases and proceedings to punish for criminal contempt of court in the United States district courts, in the district courts for the districts of the Canal Zone and Virgin Islands, in the Supreme Court of Puerto Rico, and in proceedings before United States magistrates." 18 U.S.C. § 3771.

These various provisions do not in terms describe the same courts. In congressional usage the phrase "district courts of the United States," without further qualification, traditionally has included the district courts established by Congress in the states under Article III of the Constitution, which are "constitutional" courts, and has not included the territorial courts created under Article IV, Section 3, clause 2, which are "legislative" courts. Hornbuckle v. Toombs, 85 U.S. 648 (1873). However, any doubt as to the inclusion of the District Court for the District of Columbia in the phrase is laid at rest by the provisions of the Judicial Code constituting the judicial districts, 28 U.S.C. § 81 et seq., creating district courts therein, id. § 132, and specifically providing that the term "district court of the United States" means the court so constituted. Id. § 451. The District of Columbia is included. Id. § 88. Moreover, when these provisions were enacted, reference to the District of Columbia was deleted from the original civil rules enabling act. 28 U.S.C. § 2072. Likewise Puerto Rico is made a district, with a district court, and included in the term. Id. § 119. The question is simply one of the extent of the authority conferred by Congress. With respect to civil rules it seems clearly to include the district courts in the states, the District Court for the District of Columbia, and the District Court for the District of Puerto Rico.

The bankruptcy coverage is broader. The bankruptcy courts include "the United States district courts," which includes those enumerated above. Bankruptcy courts also include "the district courts of the Territories and possessions to which this title is or may hereafter be applicable." 11 U.S.C. §§ 1(10), 11(a). These courts include the district courts of Guam and the Virgin Islands. 48 U.S.C. §§ 1424(b), 1615. Professor Moore points out that whether the District Court for the District of the Canal Zone is a court of bankruptcy "is not free from doubt in view of the fact that no other statute expressly or inferentially provides for the applicability of the Bankruptcy Act in the Zone." He further observes that while there seems to be little doubt that the Zone is a territory or possession within the meaning of the Bankruptcy Act, 11 U.S.C. § 1(10), it must be noted that the appendix to the Canal Zone Code of 1934 did not list the Act among the laws of the United States applicable to the Zone. 1 Moore's Collier on Bankruptcy ¶ 1.10, pp. 67, 72, n. 25 (14th ed. 1967). The Code of 1962 confers on the district court jurisdiction of:

"(4) actions and proceedings involving laws of the United States applicable to the Canal Zone; and

"(5) other matters and proceedings wherein jurisdiction is conferred by this Code or any other law." Canal Zone Code, 1962, Title 3, § 141.

Admiralty jurisdiction is expressly conferred. Id. § 142. General powers are conferred on the district court, "if the course of proceeding is not specifically prescribed by this Code, by the statute, or by applicable rule of the Supreme Court of the United States..." Id. § 279. Neither these provisions nor § 1(10) of the Bankruptcy Act ("district courts of the Territories and possessions to which this title is or may hereafter be applicable") furnishes a satisfactory answer as to the status of the District Court for the District of the Canal Zone as a court of bankruptcy. However, the fact is that this court exercises no bankruptcy jurisdiction in practice.

The criminal rules enabling act specified United States district courts, district courts for the districts of the Canal Zone and the Virgin Islands, the Supreme Court of the Commonwealth of Puerto Rico, and proceedings before United States commissioners. Aside from the addition of commissioners, now magistrates, this scheme differs from the bankruptcy pattern in that it makes no mention of the District Court of Guam but by specific mention removes the Canal Zone from the doubtful list.

The further difference in including the Supreme Court of the Commonwealth of Puerto Rico seems not to be significant for present purposes, since the Supreme Court of the Commonwealth of Puerto Rico is an appellate court. The Rules of Criminal Procedure have not been made applicable to it, as being unneeded and inappropriate, Rule 54(a) of the Federal Rules of Criminal Procedure, and the same approach is indicated with respect to rules of evidence.

If one were to stop at this point and frame a rule governing the applicability of the proposed rules of evidence in terms of the authority conferred by the three enabling acts, an irregular pattern would emerge as follows:

Civil actions, including admiralty and maritime cases — district courts in the states, District of Columbia, and Puerto Rico.

Bankruptcy — same as civil actions, plus Guam and Virgin Islands.

Criminal cases — same as civil actions, plus Canal Zone and Virgin Islands (but not Guam).

This irregular pattern need not, however, be accepted. Originally the Advisory Committee on the Rules of Civil Procedure took the position that, although the phrase "district courts of the United States" did not include territorial courts, provisions in the organic laws of Puerto Rico and Hawaii would make the rules applicable to the district courts thereof, though this would not be so as to Alaska, the Virgin Islands, or the Canal Zone, whose organic acts contained no corresponding provisions. At the suggestion of the Court, however, the Advisory Committee struck from its notes a statement to the above effect. 2 Moore's Federal Practice ¶ 1.07 (2nd ed. 1967); 1 Barron and Holtzoff, Federal Practice and Procedure § 121 (Wright ed. 1960). Congress thereafter by various enactments provided that the rules and future amendments thereto should apply to the district courts of Hawaii, 53 Stat. 841 (1939), Puerto Rico, 54 Stat. 22 (1940), Alaska, 63 Stat. 445 (1949), Guam, 64 Stat. 384–390 (1950), and the Virgin Islands, 68 Stat. 497, 507 (1954). The original enabling act for rules of criminal procedure specifically mentioned the district courts of the Canal Zone and the Virgin Islands. The Commonwealth of Puerto Rico was blanketed in by creating its court a "district court of the United States" as previously described. Although Guam is not mentioned in either the enabling act or in the expanded definition of "district court of the United States," the Supreme Court in 1956 amended Rule 54(a) to state that the Rules of Criminal Procedure are applicable in Guam. The Court took this step following the enactment of legislation by Congress in 1950 that rules theretofore or thereafter promulgated by the Court in civil cases, admiralty, criminal cases and bankruptcy should apply to the District Court of Guam, 48 U.S.C. § 1424(b), and two Ninth Circuit decisions upholding the applicability of the Rules of Criminal Procedure to Guam. Pugh v. United States, 212 F.2d 761 (9th Cir. 1954); Hatchett v. Guam, 212 F.2d 767 (9th Cir. 1954); Orfield, The Scope of the Federal Rules of Criminal Procedure, 38 U. of Det.L.J. 173, 187 (1960).

From this history, the reasonable conclusion is that Congressional enactment of a provision that rules and future amendments shall apply in the courts of a territory or possession is the equivalent of mention in an enabling act and that a rule on scope and applicability may properly be drafted accordingly. Therefore the pattern set by Rule 54 of the Federal Rules of Criminal Procedure is here followed.

The substitution of magistrates in lieu of commissioners is made in pursuance of the Federal Magistrates Act, P.L. 90-578, approved October 17, 1968, 82 Stat. 1107.

Subdivision (b) is a combination of the language of the enabling acts, *supra*, with respect to the kinds of proceedings in which the making of rules is authorized. It is subject to the qualifications expressed in the subdivisions which follow.

Subdivision (c), singling out the rules of privilege for special treatment, is made necessary by the limited applicability of the remaining rules.

Subdivision (d). The rule is not intended as an expression as to when due process or other constitutional provisions may require an evidentiary hearing. Paragraph (1) restates, for convenience, the provisions of the second sentence of Rule 104(a), supra. See Advisory Committee's Note to that rule.

(2) While some states have statutory requirements that indictments be based on "legal evidence," and there is some case law to the effect that the rules of evidence apply to grand jury proceedings, 1 Wigmore § 4(5), the Supreme Court has not accepted this view. In Costello v. United States, 350 U.S. 359 (1965), the Court refused to allow an indictment to be attacked, for either constitutional or policy reasons, on the ground that only hearsay evidence was presented.

"It would run counter to the whole history of the grand jury institution, in which laymen conduct their inquiries unfettered by technical rules. Neither justice nor the concept of a fair trial requires such a change." *Id.* at 364.

The rule as drafted does not deal with the evidence required to support an indictment.

(3) The rule exempts preliminary examinations in criminal cases. Authority as to the applicability of the rules of evidence to preliminary examinations has been meag[er] and conflicting. Goldstein, The State and the Accused: Balance of Advantage in Criminal Procedure, 69 Yale L.J. 1149, 1168, n. 53 (1960); Comment, Preliminary Hearings on Indictable Offenses in Philadelphia, 106 U. of Pa.L.Rev. 589, 592–593 (1958). Hearsay testimony is, however, customarily received in such examinations. Thus in a Dyer Act case, for example, an affidavit may properly be used in a preliminary examination to prove ownership of the stolen vehicle, thus saving the victim of the crime the hardship of having to travel twice to a distant district for the sole purpose of testifying as to ownership. It is believed that the extent of the applicability of the Rules of Evidence to preliminary examinations should be appropriately dealt with by the Federal Rules of Criminal Procedure which regulate those proceedings.

Extradition and rendition proceedings are governed in detail by statute. 18 U.S.C. §§ 3181–3195. They are essentially administrative in character. Traditionally the rules of evidence have not applied. 1 Wigmore § 4(6). Extradition proceedings are accepted from the operation of the Rules of Criminal Procedure. Rule 54(b)(5) of Federal Rules of Criminal Procedure.

The rules of evidence have not been regarded as applicable to sentencing or probation proceedings, where great reliance is placed upon the presentence investigation and report. Rule 32(c) of the Federal Rules of Criminal Procedure requires a presentence investigation and report in every case unless the court otherwise directs. In Williams v. New York, 337 U.S. 241 (1949), in which the judge overruled a jury recommendation of life imprisonment and imposed a death sentence, the Court said that due process does not require confrontation or cross-examination in sentencing or passing on probation, and that the judge has broad discretion as to the sources and types of information relied upon. Compare the recommendation that the substance of all derogatory information be disclosed to the defendant, in A.B.A. Project on Minimum Standards for Criminal Justice, Sentencing Alternatives and Procedures § 4.4, Tentative Draft (1967, Sobeloff, Chm.). Williams was adhered to in Specht v. Patterson, 386 U.S. 605 (1967), but not extended to a proceeding under the Colorado Sex Offenders Act, which was said to be a new charge leading in effect to punishment, more like the recidivist statutes where opportunity must be given to be heard on the habitual criminal issue.

Warrants for arrest, criminal summonses, and search warrants are issued upon complaint or affidavit showing probable cause. Rules 4(a) and 41(c) of the Federal Rules of Criminal Procedure. The nature of the proceedings makes application of the formal rules of evidence inappropriate and impracticable.

Criminal contempts are punishable summarily if the judge certifies that he saw or heard the contempt and that it was committed in the presence of the court. Rule 42(a) of the Federal Rules of Criminal

Procedure. The circumstances which preclude application of the rules of evidence in this situation are not present, however, in other cases of criminal contempt.

Proceedings with respect to release on bail or otherwise do not call for application of the rules of evidence. The governing statute specifically provides:

"Information stated in, or offered in connection with, any order entered pursuant to this section need not conform to the rules pertaining to the admissibility of evidence in a court of law." 18 U.S.C.A. § 3146(f).

This provision is consistent with the type of inquiry contemplated in A.B.A. Project on Minimum Standards for Criminal Justice, Standards Relating to Pretrial Release, § 4.5(b), (c), p. 16 (1968). The references to the weight of the evidence against the accused, in Rule 46(a)(1), (c) of the Federal Rules of Criminal Procedure and in 18 U.S.C.A. § 3146(b), as a factor to be considered, clearly do not have in view evidence introduced at a hearing under the rules of evidence.

The rule does not exempt habeas corpus proceedings. The Supreme Court held in Walker v. Johnston, 312 U.S. 275 (1941), that the practice of disposing of matters of fact on affidavit, which prevailed in some circuits, did not "satisfy the command of the statute that the judge shall proceed 'to determine the facts of the case, by hearing the testimony and arguments.'" This view accords with the emphasis in Townsend v. Sain, 372 U.S. 293 (1963), upon trial-type proceedings, id. 311, with demeanor evidence as a significant factor, id. 322, in applications by state prisoners aggrieved by unconstitutional detentions. Hence subdivision (e) applies the rules to habeas corpus proceedings to the extent not inconsistent with the statute.

Subdivision (e). In a substantial number of special proceedings, *ad hoc* evaluation has resulted in the promulgation of particularized evidentiary provisions, by Act of Congress or by rule adopted by the Supreme Court. Well adapted to the particular proceedings, though not apt candidates for inclusion in a set of general rules, they are left undisturbed. Otherwise, however, the rules of evidence are applicable to the proceedings enumerated in the subdivision.

REPORT OF HOUSE COMMITTEE ON THE JUDICIARY

Subdivision (a) as submitted to the Congress, in stating the courts and judges to which the Rules of Evidence apply, omitted the Court of Claims and commissioners of that Court. At the request of the Court of Claims, the Committee amended the Rule to include the Court and its commissioners within the purview of the Rules.

Subdivision [(e)] was amended merely to substitute positive law citations for those which were not.

ADVISORY COMMITTEE'S NOTE (2011 AMENDMENT)

The language of Rule 1101 has been amended as part of the restyling of the Evidence Rules to make them more easily understood and to make style and terminology consistent throughout the rules. These changes are intended to be stylistic only. There is no intent to change any result in any ruling on evidence admissibility.

Florida Stat. § 90.103. Scope; Applicability

(1) Unless otherwise provided by statute, this code applies to the same proceedings that the general law of evidence applied to before the effective date of this code.

....

COMMENTARY ON FEDERAL AND FLORIDA RULE DIFFERENCES

Florida Stat. § 90.103 and its federal counterpart, Federal Rule 1101 (which is cross-referenced by Federal Rule 101), delineate the types of proceedings to which the Florida Evidence Code and the Federal Rules of Evidence, respectively, are applicable.

Federal Rule 1101(a) specifies in detail the various specialized federal courts to which the federal rules of evidence apply. Federal Rule 1101(b) specifies that the rules apply generally to civil and criminal proceedings, admiralty and maritime cases, non-summary contempt proceedings, and proceedings under Title 11 of the U.S. Code. Federal Rule 1101(c) provides that the rules of privilege are always applicable. Federal Rule 1101(d) provides that the rules of evidence (other than those governing privileges) are inapplicable in grand jury proceedings, when the trial court is determining preliminary questions of fact under Federal Rule 104, and to various miscellaneous proceedings. Finally, Federal Rule 1101(e) indicates that federal statutes or other federal rules may set forth modified rules of evidence for specialized proceedings.

The types of proceedings in which the Florida Evidence Code applies are discussed in the Commentary to Federal Rule 101 and Florida Stat. § 90.103. The Florida Evidence Code, unlike the Federal Rules of Evidence, are applicable when the trial court is determining preliminary questions of fact. *See* Commentary to FED. R. EVID. 104 and FLA. STAT. § 90.105.

Federal Rule 1102. Amendments

These rules may be amended as provided in 28 U.S.C. § 2072.

ADVISORY COMMITTEE'S NOTE (2011 AMENDMENT)

The language of Rule 1102 has been amended as part of the restyling of the Evidence Rules to make them more easily understood and to make style and terminology consistent throughout the rules. These changes are intended to be stylistic only. There is no intent to change any result in any ruling on evidence admissibility.

COMMENTARY ON FEDERAL AND FLORIDA RULE DIFFERENCES

Federal Rule 1102 provides that the Federal Rules of Evidence may be amended as provided for in 28 U.S.C. § 2072. That statute gives the U.S. Supreme Court power to prescribe rules of evidence for the federal courts, subject to a requirement that those rules not abridge, enlarge, or modify substantive rights. *See* 28 U.S.C. § 2072. The Supreme Court does not typically propose or modify rules of evidence on its own, but instead relies on recommendations from the Judicial Conference, which in turn relies on recommendations from the Standing Committee on Rules of Practice and Procedure, which in turn relies on recommendations from the Advisory Committee on Federal Rules. *See generally* 28 U.S.C. § 2073. For a change to the rules to take effect, the Supreme Court must transmit the proposed change to Congress by May 1 of the year in which it is to take effect, and it shall take effect no earlier than December 1 of the year in which it was transmitted to Congress. *See* 28 U.S.C. § 2074(a). Action is not necessary on Congress's part for a rule prescribed by the Supreme Court to take effect, except for rules involving evidentiary privileges, which have no effect until approved by Act of Congress. *See* 28 U.S.C. § 2074(b). In addition, Congress can amend or create new rules of evidence on its own. *See, e.g.*, FED. R. EVID. 413-15.

The Florida Evidence Code was enacted by the Florida legislature. Technically, however, the Florida constitution gives the Florida Supreme Court the authority to adopt rules of practice and procedure for the Florida courts, and gives the legislature the power to repeal such rules by a two-thirds vote of each house. *See* FLA. CONST. art. V, § 2(a). To avoid declaring those portions of the rules that are deemed procedural (and thus within the power of the Supreme Court to prescribe) unconstitutional for that reason, the Florida Supreme Court adopted the Florida Evidence Code subsequent to its promulgation by the Florida legislature. *See In re Florida Evidence Code*, 372 So. 2d 1369 (Fla. 1979). On subsequent occasions, when the legislature has adopted new rules or amended earlier rules, the Supreme Court has typically, but not always, officially adopted those changes as well. *See, e.g., In re Amendments to the Florida Evidence Code*, 782 So. 2d 339 (Fla. 2000).

Federal Rule 1103. Title

These rules may be cited as the Federal Rules of Evidence.

ADVISORY COMMITTEE'S NOTE (2011 AMENDMENT)

The language of Rule 1103 has been amended as part of the restyling of the Evidence Rules to make them more easily understood and to make style and terminology consistent throughout the rules. These changes are intended to be stylistic only. There is no intent to change any result in any ruling on evidence admissibility.

Florida Stat. § 90.101. Short Title

This chapter shall be known and may be cited as the "Florida Evidence Code."

COMMENTARY ON FEDERAL AND FLORIDA RULE DIFFERENCES

Florida Stat. § 90.101 and its federal counterpart, Federal Rule 1103, set forth the official titles of the rules of evidence in the Florida and federal courts, respectively.

CPSIA information can be obtained
at www.ICGtesting.com
Printed in the USA
LVOW06s0906110717

540918LV00004BA/51/P

540918LV00